DEPARTMENT OF
WISCONSIN

THOMAS J. McCRORY

Trails Books
Black Earth, Wisconsin

Library of Congress Control Number: 2004098951
ISBN: 1-931599-28-9

Editor: Eva Šolcová
Photos: Thomas J. McCrory's personal collection, unless otherwise noted
Design: Colin Harrington
Cover Photo: From Thomas J. McCrory's personal collection

This project has been funded in part by the Wisconsin Veterans Museum Foundation.

Printed in the United States of America by Sheridan Books
10 09 08 07 06 05   6 5 4 3 2 1

Trails Books, a division of Trails Media Group, Inc.
P.O. Box 317 • Black Earth, WI 53515
(800) 236-8088 • e-mail: books@wistrails.com
www.trailsbooks.com

DEDICATION

This book is dedicated to the generation of "boys in blue" who saved the country from disunion during the Civil War. Off to war as young men, some were killed, many more were sickened or injured, and most came home forever changed. Eventually, they banded together in the Grand Army of the Republic and similar organizations, and traveled through their life's course continuing to represent the cause that they had served. Their legacy is the patriotism we share today.

TABLE OF CONTENTS

INTRODUCTION

The Grand Army of the Republic served the needs of its members in a variety of ways. The G.A.R. was, at once, a fraternal society, charitable group, special interest lobby, patriotic organization, and political club. Under a banner that proclaimed their mission as one of "Fraternity, Charity, Loyalty," the G.A.R. secured massive pensions for Union Army veterans and helped to elect five United States presidents along with thousands of state and local officials around the nation. There is some truth to the old saying that the G.A.R. controlled all of the offices in the land "from president to dog catcher."

In addition, the G.A.R. played an important role in the social and civic life of numerous communities in Wisconsin as well as other states. For this reason, among others, Thomas J. McCrory's *Grand Army of the Republic: Department of Wisconsin* is a useful local history. And, since the G.A.R. left a trail of monuments, badges, publications, and ephemera wherever it became established, county historical societies, libraries, and municipal museums often retained collections of the organization's historical materials. Tom McCrory's book will certainly be of assistance in identifying these objects as well as placing the background of the G.A.R. into a particular community context.

As travelers enjoy Wisconsin's historical or cultural sites, they may become interested in the Civil War and seek informa-tion regarding the state's role in the conflict. McCrory's book offers a window through which the experiences of the Civil War veterans' generation can be viewed as well as a tour guide of local communities where G.A.R. activities took place.

Geneologists are undoubtedly going to find the work of interest because of the number of people identified as participating in the G.A.R. and its programs. Antique collectors will at last be able to classify the various G.A.R. badges. Dealers can arrange and price the badges based on rarity. In other words, the book should appeal to various publics.

McCrory's book is a uniquely appropriate project for the Wisconsin Veterans Museum. The Veterans Museum and the agency that operates it trace their lineage to the G.A.R. The museum, for example, was established in 1901 by legislative enactment and named the G.A.R. Memorial Hall. It occupied space in the state capitol for some ninety years. The Department of Veterans Affairs eventually took over for the G.A.R. when the Civil War veterans could no longer operate the Grand Army Home for Veterans, a retirement center situated at King, Wisconsin. It is with the highest level of satisfaction, therefore, that the Wisconsin Veterans Museum participated in the publication process by sponsoring the book.

—*Richard Zeitlin, Director, Wisconsin Veterans Museum*

ACKNOWLEDGMENTS

A number of people and organizations have contributed to the completion of this book. The staff of the Wisconsin Veterans Museum assisted with the selection of materials to be included in the photographic sections of the publication, as well as guided me through the museum's archives. I specifically want to acknowledge the help of Bill Brewster and Richard Harrison. The research collections of the Wisconsin Veterans Museum are a treasure trove of material relating to the work of the G.A.R., as well as other veteran's organizations, both in terms of artifacts as well as historical documents. The research for the book could not have been completed without the hospitality, accessibility, and genuine interest extended to me by the museum as an institution.

The Wisconsin Department of Veterans Affairs oversees the Wisconsin Veterans Museum and to that agency goes the credit of providing the necessary support to operate the facility at such a qualitatively high level of public service. The agency's executives, including Secretary Raymond G. Boland and his successor, John A. Scocos, are hereby recognized. The history of Wisconsin veterans is rich and their many contributions are sometimes underappreciated. The production of additional historical works will hopefully improve the situation.

The Wisconsin Veterans Museum Foundation granted the financial resources to publish this work. Contributions to the foundation enable the Wisconsin Veterans Museum to fulfill its important educational mission. The Foundation is controlled by a volunteer board of directors. The entire board is to be thanked, along with Foundation President William Hustad and Executive Director Richard Zeitlin. Of course, the generosity of donors is sincerely acknowledged.

Additionally I'd like to thank James I. Metz, a retired Oshkosh newspaper editor and author of several books on history, for the close collaboration with me in fashioning a format to present my years of research in a manner and mode that I hope the reader finds interesting, coherent and importantly, useful. His devotion to this project was essential to its completion.

Other individuals who have greatly aided me with information and access to many fine collections are: James Schmidt; Marc and Beth Storch; George Kane; James Peterson; Dan Freimark; Craig Johnson; Melvin Riley; John Groat; Mike Wertel; Randy Novak; Rich Beggs; Twilah DeBoer; Kim Heltemes; Stephen A. Michaels; Jerry Carlton; Brad Larson; Scott Cross; Patricia Schroeder; Ron Zarling; Rod Dary; Fran Sprain; Sue Eddy; Peter Schrake; Kathy Waddell; and Mrs. Warren Moede.

And of course to my wife, Gail, and my children Kim and David, for their understanding and patience over the years of my travels throughout the great state of Wisconsin.

—Thomas J. McCrory

CHAPTER ONE

IN BILLY'S OWN IMAGE

A part of Civil War mythology is that it was fought by two types of men—Billy Yank and Johnny Reb (and, no doubt, by a huge number of clones of each)—with singularity of purpose, heroic dedication, and God-like perseverance. And when it was over Billy and Johnny shook hands and bade each other farewell, Godspeed and we'll meet again some day across the stone wall on Cemetery Ridge.

A great deal of serious Civil War history written since then has attempted to confront and to deal with this mythology.

The armies at the time were as multifaceted as any the United States has ever seen. And Johnny Reb and Billy Yank were as diverse, except for their drawls.

This volume examines the postwar experience, lived by some (but not all) the Billy Yanks, nor even by all the Billy Yanks who made their homes in Wisconsin. It examines the experiences of those who sought to extend the adventure of their lives, for whatever reason, through association with other veterans in the Grand Army of the Republic.

"Grand Army of the Republic."

The very name evoked images of grandeur, of Olympian effort, of mighty victory. Grand Army. A superlative body of men. Men who were, in every sense of the word, crusaders, to protect and preserve God's gift to this continent: the Republic.

Historians of the Grand Army of the Republic tell us that the G.A.R. was born in Illinois, far from the scenes of the war's actions, but the conclusion is inescapable that the seed was sown in Washington, D.C.

The mighty armies of the victorious Republic—the Army of the Potomac, the Army of the Tennessee, and the Army of Georgia from the West—gathered around Washington in May of 1865, and in a most remarkable pageant marched for two days before the public. Roman legions two thousand years before had so marched, and civil governments quaked with fear, for often as not the Romans were determined to install their military commander to rule the state.

No such motive was in the hearts of those veterans parading down Pennsylvania Avenue before President Andrew Johnson and his cabinet officials that May 23 and 24. Instead, they basked in a sense of great accomplishment. The troops were going home.

Without a doubt, the experience of marching in this Grand Review was not only a climax to their war experience, it was something they—or at least a good many of them in future times—would cherish. It was a collective celebration of triumph

even as they had shared so much tribulation. Tribulations sometimes tend to fade in memory. But the sense of triumph remains crisp, unceasingly vibrant; it can be savored forever.

At no time did the G.A.R., the Goliath of Civil War veterans' organizations, approach having the allegiance of anything near half the eligible men, although the membership numbers were statistically significant. One authority believed that the number of Billy Yanks enrolled in the G.A.R. did not ever exceed 20 percent of the pool.[1]

This may not have held true for the Department of Wisconsin. In 1889, the peak membership year for the G.A.R. in Wisconsin, department membership totaled 13,978. In its 1885 Wisconsin census, the state government had counted 29,000 veterans, and through additions made by the secretary of state for the next two years raised it to 34,000, the well-rounded figures suggest approximately one-third of Wisconsin veterans were in the G.A.R.—a far cry from saturation.[2] In 1896, data reveal that the Department of Wisconsin had 44 percent of eligible men at that time. Overall, however, approximately one in three Wisconsin Civil War veterans became G.A.R. members. Not until about the 1940s, when the eligible pool had dwindled to a few handfuls of veterans, was Civil War service tantamount to G.A.R. membership.

Still, for many of the men who had established that unique bond that comes from sharing hardships and danger with others, the postwar years seemed to cry out for some vehicle, some means to extend, prolong, and duplicate the camaraderie that had been so much of their lives during their time of coming to manhood. Some sort of veterans' organization seemed inevitable. In fact, an array of organizations had begun even while the war was still going on. This sometimes took place within a specific command—for instance, the Third Army Corps Union was formed September 2, 1863.[3] The Society of the Army of the Tennessee followed, organized in the captured state capitol building in Raleigh, North Carolina, just days before Confederate General Joseph E. Johnston surrendered. Soon after, the Society of the Army of the Cumberland formed, which was itself soon followed by a half dozen other societies based on

1. Robert C. Nesbit, *History of Wisconsin*, ed. by William Fletcher Thompson (Madison: State Historical Society of Wisconsin, 1985), 3:542.
2. *Proceedings of Twenty-first Annual Encampment of the Department of Wisconsin, Grand Army of the Republic*, (Baraboo: Republic Print, 1887), 37.
3. Francis A. Lord, *They Fought for the Union*, (New York: Bonanza Books, 1960), 334.

membership in particular Union fighting forces: the Army of the James, the Army of the Potomac, the Army of West Virginia. Soon, too, some more generic organizations rose such as the Military Order of the Loyal Legion of the United States, open to all officers honorably discharged from Union service.[4]

And immediately after discharge, while memories of that Grand Review were still fresh, groups formed almost spontaneously and throughout the North. These might be considered to have been somewhat disjointed efforts, with little in common with each other in terms of format, goals, and ambitions. Except that the organizing veterans seemed to be motivated by a perceived need to perpetuate the unique adventures they had undergone during the war and to extend the close unity with comrades who had served with them during the war. These organizations were often called "soldiers and sailors leagues," serving the enlisted men as the Loyal Legion did the officers. These leagues were not exclusively for enlisted men, however. Enlisted men and officers came together as veterans in their home communities, most often with men from their units in the war—again united their efforts to keep alive their memories. However, the leagues lacked cohesiveness, and their objectives were not well articulated. They were self-governing and were under no supervision from any higher authority.

Even so, veterans had many reasons for banding together. To some, the patriotic motives that drove them to war—such as love of Union, defense of the nation's institutions, and upholding the flag—did not dissipate with the war's end. Also many of the thoughtful young men were concerned that comrades who were victims of war in body or in spirit might not be properly cared for on their return home. Means of caring for significant numbers of disabled men were insufficient. The mechanics of doing so were unfamiliar, the responsibility for doing so uncertain. Others saw on their return that those who had not left home had progressed economically while veterans had to start from scratch. They felt it was their duty to help close the gap. Such feelings led to association with others of like mind and eventually to political involvements. But without question, comradeship was one of the principal reasons veterans came together.[5]

Illinois was far from unique in spawning such groups; it happened throughout the North. But the concept of the Grand Army of the Republic arose in Illinois, and it was in Illinois that

the mix of men was such that the complexion of the G.A.R.—warts and all—was first fashioned.

Dr. Benjamin Franklin Stephenson was one of the countless individuals who had mused during interludes in warfare about what might happen after the conflict. Stephenson followed through on his musings by forming an association of veterans. He crafted his template for a veterans' organization very carefully and completely, and other veterans in central Illinois followed his model. It had a discernable form that could be readily understood—and easily exported.

DR. BENJAMIN F. STEPHENSON

Stephenson was a surgeon of the Fourteenth Illinois Infantry, and he often discussed a postwar future with his tent mate, Chaplain William J. Rutledge. They agreed soldiers who had shared the fortunes of war would surely want to form some sort of association to preserve the memories of their common experiences. They also agreed that if they both survived, they would work together to form such an organization.[6]

Within months of mustering out, Dr. Stephenson had developed a substantial body of notes about rituals for a proposed organization. He circulated some of his ideas among friends in late 1865. He and Rutledge corresponded about their ideas and got together in Springfield, Illinois, in March of 1866 to put substance into their early formulations.

W.J. RUTLEDGE

Dr. Stephenson also collaborated with others in those early months of 1866, getting ideas from a number of different groups then organizing. The name of his new organization itself was borrowed in part from other assemblages. One, out of Missouri, was styled "The Grand Army of Progress."[7] The moment when the title "Grand Army of the Republic" was attached to Stephenson's new order is part of the misty and uncertain lore of those formative months.

It is clear that Stephenson and his cohorts had their rituals and formulations in order and ready to be printed by April of 1866, and the underpinnings of the G.A.R. were to be kept secret, just as was the case with scores of other societies and fraternal organizations of the era. Rituals, revealed only to the initiated, were a very common practice among fraternal groups in the mid-1800s and beyond.

To assure strict secrecy, and at the suggestion of Illinois Republican Governor Richard Oglesby, an early enthusiast for the new order, it was decided to send the material to the

4. Robert B. Beath, *History of the Grand Army of the Republic*, (New York: Bryan, Taylor & Co., 1889), 18.

5. It can be seen, then, that the G.A.R.'s watchwords of "Fraternity," "Charity," and "Loyalty" were essentially rooted in the very nature of the Civil War veteran, motivating them well before the actual formation of the organization itself.

6. This is the standard history of the order as formally presented in Beath's *History*. Discovery in the 1990s of papers (Roger Heiple Collection) of Dr. Stephenson written during 1866 (not known when Beath was writing) suggest that the role given Dr. Rutledge may be inaccurate, corroborating a claim by Stephenson's daughter in her biography of her father that Stephenson was sole originator. This is also the view of G.A.R. historian Roger Heiple of Illinois. In either scenario, Dr. Stephenson was certainly the primary progenitor of the Grand Army of the Republic.

7. Beath, *History*, 35.

Decatur Tribune, where the editor and the printers were all veterans who could be trusted to uphold the character of the new group's foundations.

While this project was under way, a number of veterans in Decatur (the matter was "secret," but not "top secret," obviously) developed interest in organizing a local body under the forms Stephenson and his co-workers developed, ideas being set into type by the *Tribune* compositors. Perhaps these veterans were the printers themselves, but it seems unlikely that the printers were the only veterans behind the movement.

Thus, while the Grand Army of the Republic was born in the workings of Stephenson and others in Springfield that early spring of 1866, the first Post of the G.A.R. was chartered on April 6, 1866, at Decatur. Stephenson signed the charter as commander of the Department of Illinois,[8] with Robert M. Woods, one of the Springfield organizers, attesting as adjutant general.

While the G.A.R. was just one of many efforts to organize veterans, it enjoyed certain advantages over most of the other embryonic groups. The organization had a discernable form well ahead of other groups. Rather than develop the ideas behind the G.A.R. from scratch, Dr. Stephenson and company had borrowed ideas from a number of sources and had incorporated elements popular among fraternal organizations at the time.

For example, secret rituals were a common practice among fraternal organizations. (During the late 1880s and early 1890s—the order's most active years—the matter of secrecy was a stumbling block with the Catholic Church. But the problem was overcome when General William S. Rosecrans, a convert to Catholicism during his West Point years,[9] secured a finding from the hierarchy favorable to the order. However, some Lutheran synods, particularly in Minnesota, adamantly opposed membership in the G.A.R. for their communicants.)[10] Then too, the order was already speaking to some of the issues that were of concern to veterans, in addition to addressing the need among veterans to perpetuate camaraderie.

Above all, the Grand Army of the Republic had, with its name, struck a chord with men who had come out of war with a sense of having been part of something glorious and inspiring on an unprecedented scale. If they took to heart the words of Julia Ward Howe—and many of them did—they had been engaged in nothing less than a Holy Cause. The G.A.R. gained rapid preeminence among veterans' organizations because it most nearly embodied the exalted image that Billy Yank, now a veteran, held about himself.

8. This is a chicken-or-egg situation. The Department of Illinois was not formally organized until July 12, 1866, but somebody had to authorize the first post. Certainly Stephenson was entitled to sign that charter since he was the indisputable founder of the Grand Army of the Republic.
9. Paige Smith, *Trial by Fire*, (New York: McGraw-Hill, 1982), 236.
10. Frank H. Heck, *The Civil War Veteran*, (Oxford, Ohio: Mississippi Valley Press, 1941), 6–7.

CHAPTER TWO

A START TOO FAST

Throughout Wisconsin in the twelve months following the end of the Civil War, veterans gathered, casting about for a formula to direct their organizational aspirations. Various soldiers and sailors leagues seemed to point the way to national or regional associational structure for veterans in some of the larger cities. Deficiencies existed.

Veterans in Madison formed such a league. Just weeks before the group was founded, its secretary, George F. Rowell, heard of the establishment of the Decatur post of the new Grand Army of the Republic. He and James K. Proudfit, president of the Madison league and a Republican legislator, contacted the Springfield group for information on their new organization and received copies of the G.A.R.'s constitution and an enthusiastic letter urging that the inquirers establish the order in Wisconsin.[1]

Proudfit sent out a call to the 13 other Soldiers and Sailors Leagues in Wisconsin, as well as to individual veterans, to convene in Madison to consider the information the Springfield people had sent. The convention was held in Madison on June 7, 1866. Robert W. Woods, the department adjutant general of the Decatur charter, came up from Springfield to explain the rituals and the work of the new G.A.R.

JAMES PROUDFIT

Wisconsin veterans responded enthusiastically. The assembly resolved to urge all Soldiers and Sailors Leagues of Wisconsin to become posts under the new Grand Army of the Republic. The convention itself further resolved to institute itself as the Department of Wisconsin. Woods installed the officers the convention elected, and thus, on that June date in 1866, the Wisconsin Department of the Grand Army of the Republic came into being. As it happened, it was the first department in the nation. Illinois, which was by

this time spawning posts in addition to Decatur—at Springfield, for instance—did not make the Department of Illinois official until the department held a convention on July 12, 1866.[2]

In the Wisconsin order, Proudfit became the first department commander. And Rowell, who initially learned of the new order in Illinois, was chosen adjutant general.

A "Council of Administration," an executive committee charged with advising the officers between conventions (or encampments as they soon were to be called) was established. The first council for the Department of Wisconsin consisted of Thomas S. Allen, Jeremiah Rusk, A. J. Bartlett, and E. A. Calkins. Allen was the new secretary of state, and Rusk was state bank comptroller. Rusk would later serve in Congress and as governor of Wisconsin for seven years.[3] Prestigious individuals joined the Department of Wisconsin right from the start.

Allen headed the resolutions committee at the founding meeting, and one of the resolutions it submitted revealed the motivation of veterans. Since Woods, the apostle from Springfield, assisted the resolutions committee that day, it is significant not only as an expression of the Wisconsin veterans, but in revealing at least some of the contemporary thinking of the founders of the Department of Wisconsin.

"Resolved," it said, "that we tender our grateful acknowledgment of the just and kindly spirit manifested by Congress in the passage of resolutions in favor of giving the preference in appointment to positions of honor and profit within the gift of the National Government, other things being equal, to those who faithfully served in the Union army during the war of the rebellion, and the recent circular of the President of the United States of the same import . . ."

The propriety of doing this, especially for those disabled in service, seemed beyond question, they averred. But then they added a disclaimer:

At the same time we disclaim any disposition on the part of the brave and patriotic men whom we represent, the volunteer soldiers of Wisconsin, to claim office as the reward of their services, or to place themselves in the position of clamorous office seekers. They regard, as every true American should, the independence of private life and the prizes that wait upon individual enterprises in the industrial and business pursuits open to all in this free land as offering incentives to a worthy ambi-

1. Hosea W. Rood, "The Grand Army of the Republic and the Wisconsin Department," in *Wisconsin, Its History and Its People*, ed. by Milo Quaife (Chicago: The S. J. Clarke Publishing Company, 1924.), 549.
2. Ibid., 550.
3. Henry C. Campbell, ed., *Wisconsin in Three Centuries*, 1634–1905 (New York: Century History, 1906), 4:264.
4. Robert B. Beath, *History of the Grand Army of the Republic*, (New York: Bryan, Taylor & Co., 1889), 538.

tion preferable to those offered by a greedy scramble for place and favor of politicians.[4]

Don't even try to tempt us, said the convention. "The fulsome flatteries and unsolicited promises of demagogues of whatever political party" bring feelings of "profound disgust and indignation" because such demagogues assume that "the soldiers who risked their lives in defense of their country are a horde of greedy office seekers capable of being lured by promises of official patronage into the service of the political tricksters . . . "[5]

ROBERT M. WOODS

The founders of the Department of Wisconsin were, of course, familiar with the words in the constitution of the G.A.R. That document had been circulated before the convention. And at the convention, Adjutant General Woods reiterated those principles.

By affiliating with the Grand Army, the leaders of Wisconsin's Civil War veterans subscribed to the following principles:

1. To preserve those kind and fraternal feelings which have bound together, with the strong cords of love and affection, the comrades in arms of many battles, sieges, and marches.

2. To make these ties available in works and results of kindness of favor and material aid to those in need of assistance.

3. To make provision, where it is not already done, for the support, care, and education of soldiers' orphans, and for the maintenance of the widows of deceased soldiers.

4. To protect and assist disabled soldiers, whether because of wounds, sickness, old age, or misfortune.

5. To establish and defend the late soldiery of the United States morally, socially, and politically, with a view of inculcating a proper appreciation of their services to the country, and to a recognition of such services and claims by the American people.

6. To maintain true allegiance to the United States of America based upon paramount respect for, and fidelity to, the national constitution and laws, manifested by the discountenance of whatever may tend to weaken loyalty, incite to insurrection, treason, rebellion, or in any manner impairs the efficiency and permanency of our free institutions, together with a defense of universal liberty, equal rights, and justice to all men.[6]

Here were the elements that forever marked the order: Fraternity, Charity, Loyalty. But the history of the Grand Army

of the Republic demonstrates that upholding all of the ideals the order stood for in the abstract occasionally fell short in reality. The order's disdain for public office, for instance, was not always manifested nor respected, and this had serious consequences. Feelings of fraternal affection did not forestall the practice, typical of fraternal orders of the time, of blackballing prospective members for unspecified reasons. Another practice picked up from other fraternal sources, a multitiered system of membership, had disastrous consequences for the G.A.R.

Members of the new Department of Wisconsin threw themselves immediately into the work of bringing the G.A.R. message to the veterans of Wisconsin. Two days after the convention established the department, a meeting of the Madison Soldiers and Sailors League was held and the members debated the proposition of converting their organization into a Post of the G.A.R.

The veterans discussed the matter and when voted on, it carried, although not unanimously. The league thereupon adjourned, and the majority remained behind and constituted itself as a G.A.R. post, electing Joshua W. Tolford as commander and Henry Sandford as adjutant. Thus Post 1 was born. The following day, June 10, 1866, the post received its charter from the Department of Wisconsin.

Among the seventeen charter members of Post 1, in addition to department officers Proudfit and Rowell, was Lucius Fairchild, a veteran of the Second Wisconsin Infantry who had lost an arm at Gettysburg. The previous November, Fairchild had been elected governor of Wisconsin. He would be a power in the G.A.R. for many years, including serving as national commander in 1886, and in Republican politics, a proud waver of the "Bloody Shirt."

While Wisconsin was first to embrace the G.A.R., there were other states not far behind. The evangelical zeal of the Springfield founders was by no means limited to Adjutant General Woods. The Illinois founders gladly assisted those in Iowa, Minnesota, Indiana, Missouri, and other state groups who wanted to enter the fold. Iowa was chartered July 12, Minnesota on August 1. The Indiana Department was organized August 20, 1866. General Carl Schurz, a prewar Wisconsinite, organized the Missouri Department in May 1867, although individual posts in that state were chartered in the latter half of 1866. The movement spread quickly throughout the North through 1866 and into 1867.

In October 1866, Dr. Stephenson issued a call for a national convention at Indianapolis, and when it convened on November 20, representatives were present from Illinois, Wisconsin, Missouri, Iowa, Ohio, Indiana, Kansas, New York, Pennsylvania, Kentucky, and the District of Columbia.[7]

5. Beath, *History*, 538.
6. Ibid., 45.
7. *Grand Army Blue Book* (Philadelphia: J. B. Lippincott, 1891), 5.

Within each of these developing departments, creation and acceptance of local posts moved ahead rapidly. Nowhere did the process develop more rapidly than in Wisconsin. Department Commander Proudfit traveled around the state to establish local posts. Soldiers and Sailors Leagues from around the state represented veterans at the June 7 convention, and Proudfit likely believed that they could become candidates for G.A.R. posts. It was a matter of getting them to fall into the formation.

Some came rapidly: Ripon became Post No. 2, chartered June 16. Post 3 was Mazomanie. Fond du Lac followed as the fourth local G.A.R. organization. Nearby Greenbush was No. 5. Then came Ahnepee, Edgerton, Green Bay, and, No. 9, Milwaukee. By August 16, 1866, the milestone of Post No. 10 was conferred on Oshkosh, maintaining a pace of one new post per week.

Then the pace quickened. Within three weeks of the chartering of Post No. 10, Racine, Mifflin, Sun Prairie, Menomonee, Butte des Morts, Watertown, Sturgeon Bay, Waterloo, Boscobel, Rome, and New London all came into the department, in that order.

It all came so fast, so very fast—in reality, entirely too fast.

Still, on September 8, 1866, the twenty-second post in the Wisconsin Department of the Grand Army of the Republic was chartered in the tiny community of Berlin, and this chartering was to become a benchmark for the department. Over the next decade, the Berlin post became quite prominent not only in the Department of Wisconsin but in the Grand Army itself as well.

Through 1866, the department continued to swell, but throughout 1867 the pace slowed somewhat. Black Earth followed Berlin, then Richland Center, Mineral Point, Waukau, Martinsville, Jefferson, Lodi, Aztalan, Lake Mills, Stockbridge, Platteville, Hebron, Albion, Eau Claire, Boscobel, Manitowoc, Chilton, Columbus, Dodgeville, Argyle, Princeton, Prescott, Wautoma, Markesan, Durand, and Cazenovia.

By the end of 1867 the Department of Wisconsin recorded 56 posts, including the unnamed Posts No. 49 through 53, plus posts at River Falls, Brodhead, and, No. 56, Milwaukee's second post.[8]

The unnamed posts 49 through 53 seems peculiar. Although the department set the posts aside for whatever reason, no post was ever assigned those numbers.[9] Growth had been so rapid that even rudimentary record keeping became confused. In the next few years most of the fifty-odd posts

failed. Among those that survived, a general reshuffling of post numbers took place. Some of the steadfast ones moved up in the pecking order, so to speak. Thus the Berlin Post eventually became nationally famous as "Post 4, Department of Wisconsin, Grand Army of the Republic" holding undisputed title as "the oldest G.A.R. post in the world."[10]

What had produced the killing frost of the young posts? Many, no doubt, were drawn into the department by the novelty of the new order, and novelty inevitably wears thin. Department of Wisconsin historian Hosea W. Rood considers this one factor in the demise of the posts. He notes, "Young men are apt, when a movement is popular, to go into it with enthusiasm; and then by-and-by, when it loses its novelty, to become indifferent. Many of the soldier boys just home from the war were barely out of their teens. As a sort of plaything the Grand Army was at first interesting—afterward not so much so."[11]

Another factor, according to Rood, was the growing pains of the organization. Although the G.A.R. appeared to be the most highly organized of available vehicles for veterans to engage, in fact the record keeping was sloppy, and many posts were reluctant to send up dues to higher authority. In addition, the rapid growth of the organization caused problems. While the lines of communication, from local post to state department to national organization, were specified, there had not been time for the tradition of orderly reporting to take hold. Department officers had little time to try to enforce reporting requirements. Some tried, and they found themselves dedicating a large portion of their time to the effort—with little success. "This lack of accurate business methods," said Rood, "tended toward demoralization . . ."

Department of Wisconsin Commander Proudfit, at the first Encampment in June of 1867, lamented "the neglect of many of the Posts . . . in not reporting to Department headquarters . . ." Of the nearly 50 posts on the books, only 16 sent men to the Encampment. Something obviously was wrong.

In addition, the recent soldier boys were of an age at which they had far more demands on their time than they would face later. Starting and raising families, working to support the growing numbers in those families, a myriad of other interests to pursue—all worked to curtail interest in being an active G.A.R. member. Life as a civilian seemed full enough.

Lastly, some of the reasons for the precipitous decline in the Grand Army of the Republic came from within the order itself.

8. *The Soldier's Friend*, January 1868. This was a monthly newspaper serving the early Grand Army of the Republic. This issue is the primary source for this listing of early Department of Wisconsin posts, since most of the department records between 1867 and 1882 have disappeared.

9. Department of Wisconsin General Order No. 6, *Berlin Courant*, December 14, 1871.

10. Rood, *The Grand Army*, 550. See Epilogue.

11. Ibid., 553.

CHAPTER THREE

A CASE OF NEARLY TERMINAL POLITICS

Union veterans generally voted Republican in 1864. For all the generalizations about the Union veteran—his religious fervor, or lack thereof; his addiction or aversion to gambling, whiskey, or any other vices; and just about any other aspect of his being that could make a fitting topic for a doctoral dissertation—his electoral inclination that year can be pretty firmly documented. Maybe not down the entire party line, but certainly in the run between Abraham Lincoln and George B. McClellan. Yankee soldiers decidedly favored the commander in chief.

A very good illustration here: in General William T. Sherman's Western armies, there were 11 infantry regiments from Wisconsin in the run-up to the 1864 election. Ten of them cast ballots overwhelmingly for Lincoln. The Seventeenth Wisconsin, largely Irish, many of them immigrants to Milwaukee, voted 206 to 52 for McClellan, and it was the *only one* of 52 regiments or batteries with Sherman from states allowing their soldiers to vote that did not support Lincoln.[1] Billy Yank left no doubt where he stood on prosecuting the war.[2]

Politics was an inevitable part of life during the Civil War, either as a soldier or as a civilian. It is hardly shocking that politics somehow carried over into the later lives of those who lived through those tumultuous times.

But between 1864 and 1866, the political world was turned upside down. Lincoln was dead, and the emotions his assassination caused reverberated throughout the reuniting nation. Some former soldiers feared that their victory on the battlefield could be lost by congressional leniency towards the late enemy.

Republican politics took a turn toward the radical, and some politicians saw a great opportunity to mobilize soldier sentiment toward harsh Reconstruction of the South. These politicians sought a new campaign to complete the victory, and many politicians with these sympathies were centered in Illinois.

There is some reason to believe that the foundation of the Grand Army of the Republic was intertwined with the radical Republican party ferment following Lincoln's assassination. A major study of the Springfield, Illinois, origins of this political movement suggests that Dr. Benjamin Stephenson himself may have had a political agenda, along with his publicly proclaimed fraternal/charitable motive, in formulating the order. Radical

Republicans played an important role in the rise of the G.A.R. from the start.[3]

Illinois Governor Richard Oglesby, a well-known radical and an early advocate of the new order, suggested the publication in Decatur of the order's secret manuals. There was nothing sinister, nothing evil, about political motivations; It was a very political era. During this period, the nation's political parties operated through clubs, enlisting support from various segments of the public. In the first postwar presidential campaign, in 1868, political clubs were widespread, and politics was a part of many veterans' groups.

G.A.R. leaders clearly had political agendas. At the first national convention at Indianapolis in November of 1866, delegates elected Illinois Republican General Stephen A. Hurlbut the first national commander. But the person who perhaps best personified the G.A.R.'s political focus was the order's second national commander, General John A. Logan.

Among the legion of politicians-made-generals in the Civil War, John A. Logan became preeminent. The combination of reasonably effective battlefield leadership and well-regarded political skill made for a powerful postwar career. Logan employed the two skills even during the war. He served in Congress while wearing two stars on his shoulder. Afterwards, he honed his Radical credentials as a comanager of the House's impeachment case against

GENERAL STEPHEN A. HURLBUT

---

1. Joseph T. Glaatthaar, *The March to the Sea and Beyond* (New York: New York University Press, 1985), 202. The tallies were: Third Wis., 305-21; Twelfth Wis., 338-57; Sixteenth Wis., 223-98; Eighteenth Wis., 103-33; Twenty-first Wis., 253-68; Twenty-second Wis., 332-10; Twenty-fifth Wis., 315-6; Twenty-sixth Wis., 110-88; Thirty-first Wis., 356-44; and Thirty-second Wis., 498-73. With three Wisconsin artillery batteries included, the Wisconsin vote for Lincoln among Sherman's men was 3,074 to 752, or 80.3 percent.

2. Mary Dearing, *Veterans in Politics: The Story of the GAR* (Baton Rouge: Louisiana State University Press, 1952), 45. The percentage of support for Lincoln was somewhat lower in the Army of the Potomac where McClellan had been a popular commander, but overall, the soldier vote was estimated to have gone 78 percent to Lincoln and 22 percent to McClellan.

3. Ibid., 84. Dearing makes a strong, nearly compelling case for the theory that the G.A.R. was seen by its founders primarily as a means of furthering Radical objectives in the political ferment of the times.

President Andrew Johnson before the Senate.[4]

The leaders of the Grand Army joined in the political fervor that characterized the campaign of 1868. But it is inaccurate to think of the G.A.R. as being solely political.

Both parties courted veterans, in or out of the G.A.R. Both were enthusiastic participants in the campaign that took on a quasi-military appearance through the parties' political clubs. In Wisconsin, the election year took on a particularly colorful flavor as the Republican "Tanners" Clubs and the Democratic "White Boys in Blue" marched, countermarched, vocalized, criticized, and on rare occasion came to blows on behalf of their party.

Torchlight parades, sometimes several miles long, lit up the nights in dozens of Wisconsin cities and towns during the summer and autumn of 1868. In almost every place, "companies" of Tanners—the name represented Grant's humble origins helping at his father's tannery—were organized along military lines. Milwaukee's Tanners formed an entire torchlight soldier brigade commanded by Col. George B. Goodwin. Janesville, La Crosse, Ripon, Fort Atkinson, and a dozen other cities and towns had clubs that could turn out two hundred or more "Tanner" torchbearers to show their enthusiasm before the hometown voters and to swell the ranks of paraders in nearby cities. The village of Hudson in the St. Croix River valley, as small as it was, still boasted a company of two hundred mounted Tanners plus a band and glee club.

The Democrats were not to be outdone. In Oshkosh they organized eight companies of White Boys in Blue with every company led by veterans. It wasn't a requirement to be a veteran in order to join the clubs, but the overwhelming majority of members were former soldiers. In the clubs, they were recreating what they had done in the army, and they put on an impressive performance.[5] "The parade and review of the 'White Boys in Blue' . . . was a brilliant affair," enthused Oshkosh's Democratic newspaper editor. "They were out in full companies, and marched in their usual good order, under command of Colonel [Gabe] Bouck, presenting a splendid appearance. The long columns of neatly uniformed men, as they appeared in line with torches, stepping off to the music, under command of able and experience[d] officers, presented a magnificent appearance, receiving the compliments of the people who looked admiringly upon them as they filed through the streets."[6]

They numbered more than five hundred torchbearers, winding "through some of the principal streets of the city," before finishing at party headquarters where Judge William Vilas of Madison addressed the throng.

The Democratic "White Boys in Blue" were not to be confused with Republican "Boys in Blue" Clubs in other states. These were men who "had to first emphasize their loyalty to the nation and its flag before indicating their political differences with Republican Reconstruction policies."[7] The "White" part of the name particularly signified dissent from the Radicals' policies regarding political equality for the freed slaves. Democrats campaigned heatedly against "Negro suffrage."

The White Boys in Blue were colorfully attired with blue shirts, blouses, or jackets trimmed with white, including a white rosette on the left chest and fastened with U.S. Army buttons. Each of the Democratic marchers wore a red belt and red cap or an army forage cap. Their officers wore the uniforms they wore on active duty.

The Tanners were a tad less colorful. They wore oilcloth caps and oilcloth capes, usually of red or white, and there were "local options" as to color combinations of the attire. On one matter, however, the

GABE BOUCK

Tanners were unified; they all had the distinguishing mark, a sheepskin leather apron, signifying the tanner's trade.[8]

Once, late in the campaign, a handful of Tanners showed up at a White Boys in Blue rally in Oshkosh, to the dismay of the latter who threatened to "clean up those damned Tanners!" It took only one rude remark from an intruder to set off a melee. "Some six or eight White Boys immediately attacked the 'Tanners' with lamps and torches. One was struck on the head with a torch, cutting a severe gash and causing partial insensibility for some time. The row was ended by the retreat of the 'Tanners' . . ."[9] The Democratic veterans may have had the edge in that encounter, but the Republicans had it all their own way in the election. Grant and his vice-presidential candidate, Schuyler Colfax, carried Wisconsin and the nation.

The Grand Army of the Republic was quite aware that the public perceived it as a secret political society, and in early 1868 declared—after heated argument during the National Encampment where some of the comrades made no bones about being politically motivated—that it would remain above the political fray. The encampment delegates adopted the wording "this association does not design to make nominations for office or to use its influence as a secret organization for partisan purposes."[10] But in fact, G.A.R. emblems were in abundant evidence in political circles that summer, worn by those actively seeking, first, to nominate Grant, and then, to ensure his election.

4. Stuart McConnell, *Glorious Contentment, the Grand Army of the Republic, 1865–1900* (Chapel Hill: University of North Carolina Press, 1992), 25.

5 . Charles D. Goff, "Torchlight Soldiers: A Wisconsin View of the Torchlight Parades of the Republican Party "Tanners" and the Democratic Party "White Boys in Blue" in the Presidential Election of U.S. Grant in 1868," (Paper prepared for reading before the Wisconsin Academy of Sciences, Arts and Letters, May 7, 1977).

6. *Oshkosh City Times*, September 29, 1868.

7. Goff, "Torchlight Soldiers," 2.

8. Ibid., 7.

9. *Oshkosh Northwestern*, November 5, 1868.

10. Robert B. Beath, *History of the Grand Army of the Republic*, (New York: Bryan, Taylor, & Co., 1889), 81.

The order paid a price for this. Not everyone, and not even every veteran, had a view of postwar America and the proper course of reconfiguring the nation that coincided with the program of the Radical Republicans. There were thousands upon thousands of men who had willingly gone to war because they believed in the government and the Union. But they had also been Democrats before the war, and they were unwilling to give up their affiliations regardless of circumstances and certainly not in order to follow the Radicals of the Republican Party. The Grand Army of the Republic was not going to tell them how to vote or whom to follow.

The fact that many Democratic sympathizers made up their ranks was not lost upon the G.A.R. leadership. The order continued to emphasize to the public that the Grand Army of the Republic was apolitical, and that its emblems and accouterments were not to be put to political use. The National Encampment of 1869 went further. It adopted Article 11 of Chapter 5 of its rules, which said that "No officer or comrade of the Grand Army of the Republic shall in any manner use this organization for partisan purposes, and no discussion of partisan questions shall be permitted at any of its meetings, nor shall any nomination for political office be made."[11]

This resolve was sort of *ex post barn door*, however. The membership rolls had already shrunk markedly. Hundreds of posts, once chartered, fell into disuse. The political operatives in the G.A.R. had won their battle when Grant was elected, but they now appeared to be losing the war to stay alive.

Someone said that "G.A.R." stood for "Generally All Republicans." But as noted, there were exceptions. But it would be decades before the public perception of the Grand Army was something other than as a political adjunct to the Republican Party.

If the problem with languishing membership for the Grand Army following the 1868 election had anything to do with the perception that it was a secret political society, then a recasting of its image to just another secret fraternal organization was written into the order's manual at the 1869 National Encampment in Cincinnati. They established a three-tiered system of membership. "It was thought that the Ritual could be made more attractive, thereby increasing the interest in Post meetings and adding to the strength and influence of the organization," was the way the *G.A.R. Blue Book* in later years officially described the effort. These "graded ranks" of membership were the work of several Eastern G.A.R. officials, particularly James Shaw of Rhode Island and J. Waldo Denny of Boston.

It was patterned after the forms used by the Masonic Order. One entered at the lowest degree, was promoted after due time to the next level, and finally, again after a minimum specified interval, advanced to the highest level. Each step was to be accompanied by ritual proceedings and instructions on understanding the meaning of the Grand Army of the Republic. Thus the post meetings would be more instructional and more interesting as men moved up through the ranks. It was not an unusual formula for fraternal organizations of the time.

JAMES SHAW

The first grade was that of "Recruit," the second was "Soldier," and the third was "Veteran." Members of the first grade were not eligible to hold office nor were they allowed to speak or vote at post meetings. And these "Recruits" could not advance to the next grade for at least two months.

Those who became "Soldiers" could vote and speak at meetings, but they were not eligible to hold post offices and could not be present at post meetings when some of their number were advanced to "Veteran" if they themselves were not eligible for the advancement. They were not eligible to move up until they had been a "Soldier" for six months.

Thus it would take approximately eight months for a newcomer to the order to achieve full membership rights, after which he could serve the post in any manner and even move up into department and national positions.

It apparently was a conscious effort on the part of Eastern G.A.R. leaders to shift the public's perception of the order from a political society into one with the simple innocence of a fraternal society.

But the Civil War veteran was not like every other fellow who wanted to affiliate with some congenial group of men for the novelty of the experience. He was a man who had earned his eligibility to associate with fellow veterans on a more or less equal footing by sharing the fatigues of the march, the dangers of battle, and the privations of war that had nothing to do with rank. And all this was long before the rituals committee of 1869 pieced together their three-tiered plan for revitalizing the order. In the words of the *G.A.R. Blue Books* in their primly concise telling of the order's history, "The system was in force two years, and during that time hundreds of Posts and thousands of members were lost to the Order because of their refusal to submit to the requirements of this reorganization."

In point of fact, what the politicizing Western G.A.R. leaders had failed to do to the order in spite of themselves, the Eastern G.A.R. fraternizers nearly managed to do in their own way. The Grand Army of the Republic, as the 1870s began, seemed to be on the road to extinction.

11. *Grand Army Blue Book*, (Philadelphia: J. B. Lippincott, 1891), 207.
12. McConnell, *Glorious Contentment*, 30.
13. *Grand Army Blue Book*, 8.

CHAPTER FOUR

BARELY SURVIVING

The three-tiered membership system ushered in the bleakest period of the Grand Army of the Republic's history. Whole departments disappeared. But the membership system was by no means the sole cause of decline. The G.A.R.'s reputation as a vehicle for partisan politicking had a long-term adverse effect and the whole range of other factors previously discussed were concurrently working against the order's strength. But the "Recruit/Soldier/Veteran" concept seemed to be the proverbial last straw, especially in Western states like Wisconsin.

In subsequent years, the period would be known to G.A.R. stalwarts as the "Great Falling Away." This was spoken in tones one might use to rue the "Great Locust Plague of Ought-Six" or "The Summer That Had No Rain," or some other memorable calamity from which survival seemed a miracle.

But the G.A.R. did survive. And the order's survival was, in some small sense, a miracle. The "Falling Away" had its greatest impact among the Western G.A.R. departments, although the Eastern G.A.R. ones were also heavily burdened. The Grand Army, in fact, was all but moribund in the very places from which it had risen. Illinois and its early posts—Decatur, Springfield and the rest—were, by 1871, essentially nonfunctioning.[1] The Department of Wisconsin, the oldest of the state organizations, was well along the same path with a few notable exceptions.

It may be instructive to examine more closely the origins and the stick-to-itiveness of the Wisconsin post, which eventually boasted that it was the oldest G.A.R. post in the world, a title that became acknowledged, with a fair degree of appreciation, within the Grand Army.[2] John H. Williams Post, Berlin, Wisconsin, was, in many ways, the archetypical early post of the Grand Army of the Republic. Berlin was just one of those many posts, called together by some small knot of enterprising veterans, inviting other men of the late war to share the new experience. Oscar F. Silver

and William A. Bugh, partners in law practice in Berlin, issued the call in August 1866 urging all soldiers and sailors of the Berlin area to meet at their office to form a local chapter of the new G.A.R. The reaction was favorable, and a formal chartering meeting was held a month later. The Berlin unit became Post 22.

Listed as charter members besides Silver and Bugh were D. D. La Bar, William Kees, Edward G. Waring, Thomas J. Davis, James A. Biggert, George W. Graves, Thomas C. Ryan, Chauncey Vedder, and Wiley B. Arnold. Bugh had been the first man from Berlin to enter the war, being commissioned a captain of Company G (Berlin Light Guards) in the Fifth Wisconsin just weeks after Fort Sumter. He was wounded at Williamsburg and then returned to Wisconsin, where he was commissioned lieutenant colonel of the Thirty-second Wisconsin Volunteer Infantry being assembled in the fall of 1862 at Oshkosh. The wound incapacitated him for field duty, however, and he later resigned. Silver was a first lieutenant in the Sixteenth Wisconsin Volunteer Infantry, beginning in 1861 at the age of 37. Kees also rose to captain in the Fifth Wisconsin. Waring became a second lieutenant in the Sixteenth Wisconsin. Davis served in the Twenty-second Wisconsin and ended the war with a commission.[3]

Among the charter members, then, were a fair percentage of former officers, but some of the others who answered the call spent the war as privates. A mix of officers and enlisted men was quite typical of G.A.R. units; this was, in fact, a distinguishing feature that perhaps was a cause for the order's immediate popularity among veterans. After all, even during the war there was usually no great chasm between the officers and men. The former were often elected by the latter; Bugh became the first post commander.

It was not so much the charter members who gave the post its distinctive character, however, as some of the veterans who joined the post soon after the post's founding became the driving force that carried the post into such prominence some years later. Griffith J. Thomas is a leading example. He would, in fact, become state G.A.R. commander for an unprecedented three years.[4] But even before that, his work with the Berlin post is cred-

GRIFF J. THOMAS
AS PRIVATE

ited as an important force in sustaining the post during the "Great Falling Away" period when so many posts faltered.[5]

1. Mary Dearing, *Veterans in Politics: The Story of the GAR*,(Baton Rouge: Louisiana State University Press, 1952), 189–190; Robert B. Beath, *History of the Grand Army of the Republic*,(New York: Bryan, Taylor & Co., 1889), 524. Only one Illinois post, Rockford, maintained its organization and continuity through the period. It was chartered October 3, 1866.
2. Beath, *History*, 539. Robert Beath was a former national commander of the G.A.R. and he asserts that Berlin "undoubtedly is the oldest Post in the Order with an unbroken record."
3. Joyce Bennett Stemler, *They Went South, Biographical Sketches of the Civil War Veterans from Berlin, Wisconsin* (Berlin, Wisc.: Berlin Historical Society, 1966).
4. Not until the 1940s—when there were practically no choices left and Lansing A. Wilcox, Wisconsin's last surviving Civil War veteran, served a succession of terms as state commander—was Thomas's three-year stint, 1879–1881, exceeded.
5. Stemler, *They Went South*, 114.

Justus P. Luther was another early leader. The man who brought the hallmark industry to town and gave rise to Berlin's sobriquet as the "Fur and Leather City," Luther would serve not only the post, but the Wisconsin Department (Council of Administration, 1875; Senior Vice Commander, 1878), and the national G.A.R. (Council of Administration, 1877) during the troubled 1870s. An extraordinary number of members of the Berlin Post served the Wisconsin Department in the 1870s; in fact, Berlin's G.A.R. members provided more leaders than any other post in the state, despite the larger numbers on the rolls from Milwaukee and Madison.

This lends credence to the belief that the steady men of the Williams Post—it was named after John Henry Williams who was killed at Shiloh, Berlin's first victim in the Civil War— were an important factor not only in sustaining their own post but in keeping the Department of Wisconsin functioning during a difficult period. And Berlin's G.A.R. activists served the order into the renaissance period, which in Wisconsin began about 1880.

William Bugh was the first from Berlin to serve at the department level. He became senior vice commander in 1867. Griff Thomas was state inspector in 1871. A. L. Tucker served as junior vice commander in 1873. Serving on the state Council of Administration were Luther in 1874, Z. C. Hamilton in 1875 and 1876, and Thomas in 1877. A. G. Dinsmore was junior vice commander that same year and T. B. Russell began a five-year stint as medical director. In 1878 Luther became senior vice commander and William Zickerick the state chaplain. That same year, S. J. Ellis served the first of two consecutive terms on the Council of Administration. In his second year, 1879, he was joined by Charles T. Swan as state chaplain, John D. Galloway as assistant adjutant general, and Nathaniel Pierce as assistant quartermaster general. Also in 1879, Griff Thomas became state commander for the first of three terms.

Thomas's term as state commander in the late 1870s and early 1880s coincided with the rejuvenation of the Wisconsin Department of the Grand Army of the Republic. L. T. Nichols of Berlin joined Thomas on the Council of Administration in 1880 and 1881, and they were joined by Hamilton as assistant quartermaster general the same years, and by Swan as state chaplain again in 1881.[6] And when Thomas's time as state commander was over, he took over Hamilton's position as assistant quartermaster general for the next two years. In the meantime, Thomas was named to the national History Commission during the national encampment in 1881.[7] Overall, the Williams Post maintained an outstanding record of serving higher office.

But just as important was the fact that the Berlin Post remained active and that, despite the laxity of other G.A.R. units in Wisconsin, it regularly reported to state headquarters and forwarded its dues. As if the follies of the Grand Army itself in those days were not enough to imperil its existence, the demon

of economic hard times appeared. By 1873 the nation was in an economic trough that would later be termed a "depression." Posts hanging on by slim threads had to let go entirely. Their members could not afford the dues. Some posts found it impossible to send their prescribed share to the state, and they simply did not report.

The precipitous nature of the "Falling Away" was described by S. W. Martin's veteran's newspaper *Soldier's Record*. Originally portrayed as a voice of the Grand Army of the Republic in Wisconsin, in its early publication years, 1868–69, the *Soldier's Record* became a source for the listing of early posts. But Martin carried little news of G.A.R. events, and within a matter of a few years— by 1870–71—the content of Martin's weekly, then semimonthly, paper was practically devoid of references to the order. It carried considerable news about regimental histories, unit reunions, and the aspirations of some for land grants for veterans as well as other concerns of the former boys in blue, but the G.A.R. itself apparently had become irrelevant to Martin's readers.

Department officers felt frustrated. They felt keenly the pressures that caused the "Great Falling Away," but did not know quite how to cope with the situation. They continued department functions, including the required encampments, but they were sorely tried when it came to keeping the spark going at the post level. In fact, it was all but impossible to get a dialogue going between state headquarters and the majority of posts.

THOMAS S. ALLEN

Commanders could not even be sure which posts still existed because so few sent up the necessary reports and dues. About the only sure way of knowing which posts were active was to count which ones were represented at the state encampment.

Department commanders in the early years came from either Madison or Milwaukee. The first Commander, James Proudfit was succeeded in 1867 by Henry A. Starr of Milwaukee. Jeremiah Rusk of Madison took command in 1868, followed by Thomas S. Allen, at that time of Madison, for the years 1869–70. Edward Ferguson of Milwaukee was commander in 1871 and 1872. Thus, with the order declining steeply, the top leadership came primarily from just two cities.

The annual encampment sites also stressed the two cities. From 1866 to 1871, all were held at Madison, and when it at last went to a new city, in 1872, it was to Milwaukee. Finally, in 1873, the annual encampment went elsewhere—to Berlin.

This does not mean that other posts were overlooked or excluded from top roles. The lists of other department officers in

6. Beath, *History*, 539–544.
7. Ibid., 244.

those years had representatives from a number of other posts around the state, and as previously explained, no post had greater representation in the department than the Williams Post of Berlin.

But for whatever reason, department headquarters seemed to have been treated as distant and somewhat irrelevant by some of the posts throughout the state as they struggled to cope with the declining interest and shrinking membership at the local level.

In 1871 State Commander Ferguson made a wholesale cleansing of the roster of posts. After giving notice in October of that year of his housecleaning intention, the commander ordered, on November 20, that "the charters of all posts in this department which are one year in arrears for reports or dues are annulled and cease from and after this date . . ."[8]

Ferguson included most of the fifty-odd posts chartered by 1867,[9] plus a number chartered between 1868 and 1870, namely, Bloomington, Sheboygan Falls, Monroe, Prairie du Sac, Mt. Hope, Salem, Lancaster, Cascade, Jamestown, Oregon, Waupaca, Beloit, Black River Falls, Patch Grove, Kenosha, Pensaukee, Alma, Appleton, Geneva, Waukesha, Wausau, and Mukwonago. In addition, four posts voluntarily surrendered their charters including Brodhead and Milwaukee Post 56, of which Ferguson had been commander. It presumably consolidated with one of the Milwaukee posts that did survive.

"The Grand Commander and his staff will, as heretofore, take pleasure in rendering the comrades of posts whose charters are annulled, any assistance in their power to organize new posts," intoned Commander Ferguson in General Order No. 6. Or they could transfer to one of the less than a dozen surviving posts, but a transferee "shall first place himself in good standing by the payment of his dues to date of dissolution of his post."[10]

The Department of Wisconsin dropped to 11 posts, and they were given numbers reflecting this new beginning. Madison retained No. 1 and Ripon stayed No. 2. Milwaukee's old No. 9 became Post 3, and Berlin swept up to Post 4 from Post 22. Then followed Cazenovia at No. 5, Beaver Dam at No. 6, Embarrass at No. 7, Milwaukee Veterans Home at No. 8, Winneconne at No. 9, Oshkosh at No. 10, and Racine at No. 11.[11]

"The Posts now belonging to the Department are congratulated by the Grand Commander upon their promotion, and he trusts that they will extend to him the same hearty cooperation in the future as they have in the past," concluded the fateful General Order No. 6.

ED FERGUSON

It might be symbolic of the low estate of the Department of Wisconsin that the *Soldier's Record* carried no reference to Ferguson nor to his wholesale housecleaning of the department. The Grand Army of the Republic had all but ceased to matter to the newspaper.

Ferguson had no illusions about the future, even though General Order No. 6 was aimed at streamlining the department. In his report for 1872 to Inspector General M. B. Goodrich at National Headquarters, the Wisconsin commander was brutally frank as prospects for the future of the department were discouraging. "The Department has never recovered from the blow inflicted by the adoption of the three-grade system, when many members of the Order were dropped, and the frequent changes subsequently made in the Ritual, and Rules and Regulations, by the National Encampment, have tended to prevent suspended comrades in the Department from renewing their faith in the Order."[12]

It was a somber valedictory for the outgoing state commander. He would be succeeded within the month by Andrew J. McCoy of Beaver Dam. If the 11 hard-core posts were willing to give "hearty cooperation" to the department, some of them were unable to do so. At the start of McCoy's term, five of the 11 posts were "suspended or disorganized."[13]

Senior Vice Commander George A. Hanaford of Milwaukee followed McCoy in command of the Department of Wisconsin, and in his first year as commander, 1874, Hanaford displayed a good deal of energy in attacking some of the problems besetting the department. He was instrumental in creating an official publication, the *Grand Army Sentinel*, a newspaper that would, unlike the *Soldier's Record*, be attuned to the order's needs. He even arranged for Griff Thomas to serve as editor. Even in the face of diminishing state membership, he aspired to national status for the *Sentinel*, and indeed it was heavy on news from departments around the country.[14]

Hanaford was acutely aware of the deficiencies he faced in his own department. He began by instituting another cleansing of the rolls of posts to remove those that were obviously not in communion, or at least not in communication, with the department. The attitude of the state's No. 1 G.A.R. Post, i.e., Madison's Cassius Fairchild Post 1, particularly vexed Hanaford. In his report to the semiannual encampment, Hanaford wrote:

Failing to obtain the reports of Post No. 1, Madison, by the usual methods . . . I notified the Commander on

8. For the full text of Commander Ferguson's Order No. 6, see Appendix A.

9. These were, in the order of their chartering, Mazomanie, Fond du Lac, Green Bush, Ahnapee, Edgerton. Green Bay, Mifflin, Sun Prairie, Menominee, Butte des Morts, Watertown, Sturgeon Bay, Waterloo, Boscobel, Rome, New London, Black Earth, Richland Center, Mineral Point, Waukau, Martinsville, Jefferson, Lodi, Aztalan, Lake Mills, Stockbridge, Platteville, Hebron, Albion, Eau Claire, Boscobel (a second charter), Manitowoc, Chilton, Columbus, Dodgeville, Argyle, Princeton, Prescott, Wautoma, Markesan, Durand, and River Falls.

10. General Order No. 6.

11. Inexplicably, Ferguson's Order No. 6 revoked the Oshkosh charter as No. 10 and Racine as Post 11, but in the same order reinstated them at their old numbers. Racine was dropped a few years later, but Oshkosh continued to operate under its original charter, suggesting that including Oshkosh and Racine in the revocation list was possibly in error.

12. *Seventh Annual Meeting of the National Encampment, Grand Army of the Republic*, the journal of 1873, 35.

13. Ibid.

14. *Grand Army Sentinel*, September, 1874.

May 2 [1874] that unless their reports were forwarded, and dues paid for the time in arrears—last two quarters of 1873 included—I should demand their charter. This had the effect to bring in reports for quarters in arrears for 1873, with amount of per capita tax due thereon. Threats and coaxing have failed to obtain reports or dues for quarters ending March 31st and June 30th [1874]. I have repeatedly called on the Commander to forward them and now recommend that its charter be suspended.

Another of the recalcitrant posts under Commander Hanaford's skin was Post 6 at Beaver Dam, the home post of his immediate predecessor, Commander McCoy. Post 6 had not filed reports since mid-1873 and "I have not been able to establish communication since I entered upon the duties of Commander. I cannot even learn their names," lamented Hanaford. He appointed McCoy a special aide-de-camp and directed him to take command of the post. But he subsequently did not hear from McCoy, either. Therefore, Hanaford ordered the charter suspended.[15] At the encampment at Oshkosh in July 1874, the attendees ratified the commander's orders to suspend the Beaver Dam charter, as well as Madison's.

Two weeks later Hanaford annulled the Madison and Beaver Dam charters along with posts in Ripon, Cazenovia, Embarrass, Winneconne, Racine, and Prairie du Chien. There was even a bit of irony in the location of the encampment that swept out the Madison and Beaver Dam posts. Oshkosh, just the year before, had been among the slumbering posts after its flourishing start as Post 10 in 1866.

Although the Oshkosh men would later claim that they never really were inactive (challenging the right of Berlin to the title as oldest post in the nation), the evidence is ample that rejuvenation of Post 10 began by 1873.

Leather merchant and Comrade Justus Luther recalled that he and several others from Berlin went to Oshkosh early in 1874 at the request of Commander Hanaford "and reinstated Phil Sheridan Post No. 10 and obligated the members and instated the officers, Gabe Bouck being installed as Commander."[16] The Oshkosh Post hosted the summer state encampment a few months after its revival, and Bouck went on to serve that year on the national Council of Administration. One of the star founders of the Department of Wisconsin, Thomas S. Allen, after finishing his term as secretary of state, bought a half interest in the *Oshkosh Northwestern* and became active within Post 10.

Rejuvenation of the Oshkosh Post was not really the beginning of a new dawn for the Department of Wisconsin, however. When the department encampment was held in Milwaukee in January of 1875, the posts in communication with Department Headquarters consisted of Phil Sheridan Post 3, Milwaukee; John Williams Post 4, Berlin; Edward Saxe Post 5, Wautoma; Veteran Post 8, the Soldier's Home in Milwaukee;

Oshkosh Post 10; and Charles Ford Post 13, Trempealeau. There were delegate slots for 31 men from the six posts, and, ominously, only 13 men registered, and two posts, Post 5 and Post 13, sent no representatives.[18]

Commander Hanaford was reelected at that encampment, but in his second term, the only post instituted was Post 2, Milwaukee, on June 9. That was Ripon's number, but the comrades in Ripon were unsuccessful in their attempts to resuscitate their post after Hanaford had revoked their charter.[19]

John Hancock of Oshkosh became the new state commander in 1876. Following him were Milwaukeeans Henry G. Rogers in 1877 and S. F. Hammond in 1878. The Milwaukee posts continued to show some strength in the state leadership. But during the terms of two Milwaukeeans, no posts were chartered or reinstituted. The Department of Wisconsin was indeed in the doldrums.

The nation itself was in anything but doldrums, however. Before Hancock turned the reigns over to Rogers, he alluded in his department valedictory to the national turmoil of the 1876 Samuel Tilden–Rutherford B. Hayes presidential campaign, a controversial campaign with a controversial outcome. He told the annual encampment that his year had been a "panorama of important events and not among the least has been the events attendant upon the great political struggle that we have just passed through, and I am happy to say to you that so far as I know, and I think I speak advisedly for this Department, no taint of a political nature has tarnished the escutcheon of the Grand Army of the Republic."[20]

The G.A.R. was still under a cloud of suspicion regarding the order's political leanings, and it was significant that, in that highly charged political year in which veterans were deeply involved, the Department of Wisconsin felt that it had met the Grand Army's self-proclaimed obligation to stand back from the fray.

A more telling detail of the encampment was that of the dozen men named to department positions, all were from Milwaukee, Oshkosh, or Berlin.[21]

By then, Saxe Post 5 of Wautoma had taken the unusual step of moving its meetings out of Wautoma where small-town politics had created opposition to it[22] and gathering instead at Willow Creek (Auroraville), some 20 miles away, before eventually

15. George A. Hanaford, *Commander's Report*, July 28, 1874, *in Statement and Proofs in Reference to John H. Williams Post No. 4 of Berlin, Wis. to the Right of Seniority of Posts in the Department of Wisconsin* (Berlin, Wisc., 1892), 5–6.
16. J. P. Luther affidavit, sworn October 13, 1891, in *Statement and Proofs* (Berlin, Wisc.), 8.
17 . The *Oshkosh Post's* early 1870s hiatus was officially recognized, and its earlier chartering did not overcome Berlin's title as the earliest continuously operating post in Wisconsin and therefore in the nation.
18. *Grand Army Sentinel*, February 1875.
19. Ibid.
20. *Weekly Northwestern*, Oshkosh, February 1, 1876.
21. Ibid.
22. *Grand Army Sentinel*, June 1875.

folding.[23] Similarly, Ford Post 13 quietly ceased its meetings on the banks of the Mississippi at Trempealeau.

Sadly, the records of the terms of administration for Department of Wisconsin officers serving during these lean years have been lost to history. Department records were kept faithfully during this entire period, but, around 1883, they were somehow lost. The missing records covered activities from 1867 to 1882.[24] It is difficult to give due credit to the efforts of these commanders and their cohorts during this period because of that gap, but the fact that the Grand Army of the Republic was at a low ebb in the early and mid 1870s is clear from all available evidence.

Moreover, because the G.A.R. was a secret society, newspaper accounts of their activities are scant. The state encampment, for instance, was held in Oshkosh on January 27, 1877, but Thomas S. Allen's newspaper gave little space to reporting the business of the gathering. The newspaper noted that the veterans were in town and were handsomely feted by the townspeople. But as to encampment business it merely said that reports were received and that "the reports referred to matters pertaining to the business of the order which would be of no special interest to the public."[25]

Doldrums they were, indeed, even into the later years of the 1870s. But there were glimmers of hope for the G.A.R., if one knew where to look—and looked carefully.

23. *Grand Army Sentinel*, September 1875.
24. Hosea W. Rood, "The Grand Army of the Republic and the Wisconsin Department," in *Wisconsin, Its History and Its People*, ed. By Milo Quaife, (Chicago: S. J. Clarke Publishing Company, 1924), 555. Thus there remain some mysteries about the existence and numbers of early posts. Brodhead, Hingham (Sheboygan County), and Milwaukee No. 56 were three posts surrendering their charters to Edward Ferguson in 1871, but the identity of Post 80, which also voluntarily turned in its charter, is unrecorded and therefore unknown. Additionally, the highest known number in use among those early posts was 87, Winneconne. Numbers 80, 82, and 83 are known to have been issued. If numbers 81, 84, 85, and 86 were issued, and there is no reason to think they were not, those posts are even more of a mystery than Post 80.
25. "G.A.R., Annual Encampment of the State Department," *Oshkosh Daily Northwestern*, January 26, 1877.

CHAPTER FIVE

MEMORIAL IMMORTALITY

"The 30th day of May, 1868, is designated for the purpose of strewing with flowers, or otherwise decorating, the graves of Comrades who died in defense of their country during the late rebellion, and those whose bodies now lie in almost every city, village and hamlet churchyard in the land."

So decreed John A. Logan, second national commander of the Grand Army of the Republic, and his words most assuredly lifted the G.A.R.

General Order No. 11, issued May 5 that year, in many ways became the salvation of the order. It called forth noble sentiments and gave G.A.R. members and, as it came to be, their successors and heirs-at-arms, an exalted mission to remember the underpinning principles that motivated the establishment of G.A.R. in the first place.

JOHN A. LOGAN

The Grand Army had its problems in its formative years, very many of which were self-generated. But it had, from its earliest moments, a sense of having been party to greatness and of having a debt to those whose sharing in that greatness was cut tragically short. Fraternity, Charity, Loyalty were all focused on doing proper homage to those men, and this was quite above the fractious issues that threatened the health, well-being, and even the existence of the G.A.R. during the lean years. As Logan said:

In this observance, no form of ceremony is prescribed, but Posts and Comrades will in their own way arrange such fitting services and testimonials of respect as circumstances may permit.

We are organized, Comrades, as our Regulations tell us, for the purpose, among other things 'of preserving and strengthening those kind and fraternal feelings which have bound together the soldiers, sailors and marines who united to suppress the late rebellion.' What can aid more to assure this result than by cherishing tenderly the memory of our heroic dead, who made their breasts a barricade between our country and its foes? Their soldier lives were the reveille of freedom to a race in chains, and their deaths a tattoo of rebellious tyranny in arms. We should guard their graves with sa-

cred vigilance. All that the consecrated wealth and taste of the nation can add to their adornment and security is but a fitting tribute to the memory of her slain defenders. Let no wanton foot tread rudely on such hallowed grounds. Let pleasant paths invite the coming and going of reverent visitors and fond mourners. Let no vandalism of avarice or neglect, no ravages of time, testify to the present or to the coming generations that we have forgotten as a people the cost of a free and undivided republic.

If other eyes grow dull and other hands slack, and other hearts cold in the solemn trust, ours shall keep it well as long as the light and warmth of life remain in us.

Let us, then, at the time appointed, gather around their sacred remains and garland the passionless mounds above them with the choicest flowers of springtime; let us raise above them the dear old flag they saved from dishonor; let us in this solemn presence renew our pledges to aid and assist those whom they have left among us, a sacred charge upon the nation's gratitude—the soldier's and the sailor's widow and orphan."

It was his purpose, wrote Logan, "to inaugurate this observance with the hope that it will be kept up from year to year, while a survivor of the war remains to honor the memory of his departed Comrades."

Logan extolled the press to call attention to General Order No. 11 and to do what it could to assure that there be ceremonies in accordance with it. Was Logan's famous General Order No. 11 really the genesis of Memorial Day? The standard history of the G.A.R., that is, the official story,[1] gives a fairly concise, and not entirely believable, narration.

As the story goes, in the spring of 1868, under the reign of General Logan, his adjutant general, N. P. Chipman, received a letter from a former private in the Union army. The private was an immigrant who wrote to recall that in his native Germany "it

N.P. CHIPMAN

---

1. Hosea W. Rood, "The Grand Army of the Republic and the Wisconsin Department," in *Wisconsin, Its History and Its People*, ed. by Milo Quaife, (Chicago: S. J. Clarke Publishing Company, 1924), 559–562.

was the custom of the people to assemble in the springtime and scatter flowers upon the graves of the dead" and suggested that the Grand Army do the same in memory of the Union dead.

"Good idea!" said Chipman, who wrote a draft order and showed it to Logan. "Great idea!" said Logan, polishing Chipman's draft and issuing the order.

Unfortunately, the name of the German soldier is not known. Such are the vagaries of history.

The story does have a certain plausibility to it. It would not be far-fetched for an old-world custom to be adapted to the New World.

As a matter of fact, it did not take until 1868 for the flower-strewing custom to reach America. In Waterloo, New York, for example, townspeople spread flowers over the graves of Civil War soldiers on May 5, 1866. The people of Waterloo not only decorated soldiers' graves that day, but the town closed down all business and flags flew at half-staff. It was a full-fledged day of memorial.[2]

An even earlier embryonic ceremony was described as having occurred May 1, 1865, just days after war's end, over Union graves in, of all places, Charleston, South Carolina.[3]

What is really anathema to the men of the Grand Army is the possibility, even the likelihood, that the custom arose first with the late enemy! But the evidence is irrefutable that some sort of custom was under way in the Confederacy to honor the men who fell for the southern cause. A tantalizing story is that Mrs. John A. Logan, the vivacious and attractive wife of the G.A.R. national commander, visited battlefields in Virginia in March of 1868 and was touched by the display of faded flags and wreaths that southern women had put on Confederate graves. Mary Logan claimed later that she described the scene to her husband, who was moved to order the Grand Army to do similarly.[4]

Southern women, from as early as 1865 and perhaps earlier, decorated Confederate graves in many places in the South. However, it seems unlikely that there was a standardized practice. Indeed, to this day there are annual days decreed in many southern states for honoring the graves of Confederates.

If full credit for introducing memorial ceremonies honoring the fallen men of the Civil War does not reside with the Grand Army of the Republic, there is enough evidence to credit the order with playing a key role in the creation of the tradition.

The Grand Army of the Republic exhibited two contrary, yet complementary, trends in the 1880s. In one sense the order

had a death wish. That is, it chose to remain a body for Civil War veterans exclusively, even after later wars produced new crops of young veterans having some of the needs that are common to war veterans. In 1898, when the G.A.R. was showing definite signs of shrinking via attrition and thereby losing its clout in national counsels, the Spanish-American War produced another group of men who had answered the call of their country. The G.A.R., without malice, chose not to expand its outlook.

Those new veterans formed their own organizations, principally the United Spanish War Veterans, which took the G.A.R. route, which is to say, choosing a finite future, and the Veterans of Foreign Wars, which has accepted veterans of subsequent conflicts and has now observed the centennial of its formation.

At the same time that the G.A.R. held to its decision not to extend the organization's life beyond the natural lives of its Civil War veterans, the comrades desired to perpetuate their ideals beyond the life expectancy of its members. The G.A.R. placed a high premium on teaching patriotism to the young, and it promoted Memorial Day.

Memorial Day was an immediate success, and its observance thereafter was a strong force in promoting the order. Although General Logan had declared in his General Order No. 11 that no specific ceremony was being prescribed, the holiday was very quickly swathed in tradition.

In Washington, D.C., where the Grand Army was headquartered, the order made elaborate preparations, and on the day itself, May 30, 1868, aided by delightful spring weather, a crowd of some 5,000 people visited Arlington, Virginia, the site of a cemetery containing the graves of 15,000 Union soldiers. The G.A.R. had seen to it that each of those graves had a small American flag marking it.

General and Mrs. Ulysses S. Grant were among the honored guests watching the proceedings, which included an address by General James A. Garfield, followed by a procession of children from the Soldier's and Sailor's Orphan Home plus a contingent of Grand Army men. To the booming of cannon, the children scattered the contents of flowers from baskets they carried over the graves.[5]

The press did, indeed, spread the word of General Logan's order throughout the country. In Madison, where the governor was also a G.A.R. luminary, the day was fully and faithfully observed. Cannons were heard in a dirge of firings at half-hour intervals, "waking the echoes in memory of our brave soldiers who went down to death," recalled Governor Lucius Fairchild. The morning was bright and clear, and flowers blossomed profusely. The day had been set at the right time of year, so far as having abundant flowers was concerned. It was, felt the governor, "just the fitting time to go to the home of the dead."

To that home they did go, some two thousand Madisonians walked in a procession more than a mile long and composed of

2. *World Book Encyclopedia* (Chicago: World Books, 1887), 392. Congress, in fact, has recognized Waterloo as the site of the original Memorial Day.

3. Charles F. Horner, *Life of James Redpath* (New York: 1926), 113–115, quoted in Dearing, *Veterans in Politics*, 177.

4. Mary Dearing, *Veterans in Politics: The Story of the GAR*, (Baton Rouge: Louisiana State University Press, 1952), 177.

5. Dearing, *Veterans in Politics*, 178.

"returned soldiers," municipal dignitaries, faculty and students of the University of Wisconsin, and regular citizens, and "all were provided with flowers, besides a whole wagon load."[6]

Memorial Day succeeded, although there were a few doubters who questioned its significance. The *New York Times* felt that the services would only rekindle the "smoldering flames that are almost extinguished in the breasts of the people of the two sections."[7]

The Grand Army of the Republic perceived Memorial Day as a crowning accomplishment. Whatever faults the public attributed to the G.A.R., Americans came to feel that the honoring of the dead was noble and necessary. The holiday had a very positive effect on the reputation of the fraternity. Afterwards, General Logan often declared that the issuance of General Order No. 11 was "the proudest achievement of my life."[8]

The commander expanded on what he hoped for with his famous order at an oration at Du Quoin, Illinois, the following Memorial (or Decoration) Day:

> The great and glorious objects for which these men poured out their blood and forfeited their lives should be kept alive in each heart. This is the grand idea we have in view.... Believing that they were right, and that their cause was a holy one, we have gathered around these sacred mounds today for the purpose of solemnly pledging ourselves that this noble purpose shall be carried out by us while we live; and that we will teach it to our children, so that when we too are numbered with the dead, those who remain may catch up the refrain of liberty and inspire every bosom with zeal to emulate the deeds of those who sleep before us.[9]

Such orations soon became central to the services that the order performed throughout the North. Unprescribed though they were, the ceremonies soon fell into a familiar pattern. The program at Chippewa Falls, Wisconsin, by G.A.R. Post 68, as recorded in 1887, was considered by one authority to be typical of "any of the thousands of such ceremonies performed across the North before 1900." It consisted of prayers and patriotic oratory and four "typically doleful musical numbers: 'Strew Blossoms on Their Graves,' 'Cover Them Over with Beautiful Flowers,' 'Cheers and Tears,' and 'God Save Our Union.'"[10]

The terms "Memorial Day" and "Decoration Day" were for a time interchangeable, but the "decoration" aspect, although always a significant part of the day, seemed to allow for more than the solemnities the G.A.R. desired. It soon became standard for the order to emphasize the "memorial" and to decry anything that smacked of fun. The men of the Chippewa Falls post, as late as 1894, denounced "any citizen or society taking part in or placing before the public any games of Base Ball or any other games that will entice the public and thereby detract from the proper observance of the day."[11]

Post 68 members, in fact, practiced drilling for its Memorial Day ceremonies, the only "drill" the old soldiers undertook in any regular fashion in their postwar years. Throughout Wisconsin, men of the G.A.R. spent weeks and months preparing for the event since it was becoming central to the life of their posts. They carefully planned so that no new graves of any comrades-at-arms, whether members of the Grand Army or not, would by chance be missed.

A touching concern for their comrades after the war, even unto death, was inherent in G.A.R. ideology. As early as 1867, little more than a year after their chartering, members of Berlin Post 22 procured a cemetery lot for, as the *Berlin Courant* phrased it, "the burial of friendless and indigent soldiers." One William Hays, a destitute veteran, had died in the winter of 1865 and was temporarily buried in the yard of the residence where he died. When the place was sold in 1867, the body had to be moved, and the city refused a lot in the municipal cemetery. G.A.R. members were upset by the refusal and procured a plot for Hays' reinterment, as well as for any others in that situation regardless of whether they had ever been affiliated with the order.[12]

Though John A. Logan had issued General Order No. 11 in the spring of the G.A.R.'s existence, it grew in importance not only as the Grand Army matured, but as the veterans themselves grew past their innate sense of immortality—the sense that drives young men to go to war in the first place—into the dawning that they, too, were approaching the divide over which more and more of their comrades had passed. Some measure of the importance that "memorial" played in the thinking of Grand Army of the Republic members was in the appearance of the somber "memorial" post badges. They were primarily worn for funerals of comrades, and the badges first appeared in the early 1880s as funerals became more frequent. Memorial badges came to be worn by each member marching in a Memorial Day procession. Sometimes they were the obverse of the post's regular badge but in mourning shades of black. Other manufacturers designed them as separate badges. Which type the post used was often up to which manufacturer the post quartermaster chose. But the memorial badge became a major part of the accoutrements of the well-appointed Civil War veteran.

By the turn of the twentieth century, of course, members of the Grand Army were well aware that their numbers were diminishing, and they welcomed the arrival of a new crop of

6. Fairchild to his sister, May 30–31, 1868, quoted in Dearing, *Veterans in Politics*, 178–179.

7. Ibid., 179.

8. George Francis Dawson, *Life and Services of Gen. John A. Logan* (Chicago: Belford, Clarke, 1887), 123.

9. Ibid., 125.

10. Stuart McConnell, *Glorious Contentment, the Grand Army of the Republic, 1865–1900*, (Chapel Hill: University of North Carolina Press, 1992), 184–185.

11. Ibid., 183–184.

12. *Berlin Courant*, November 2, 1867.

veterans with anticipation that G.A.R. values would be borne by the younger men. Memorial Day and all it symbolized would be the G.A.R.'s legacy.

The depth of feeling that the Civil War veteran had for his comrades and for his successors as defenders of the country, its rights, and its freedoms is difficult to express. Yet there were indicators. Jim Watson, a member of Berlin's famous G.A.R. Post 4, saluted every soldier of whatever conflict he passed on the street, every day of his life, no matter how many times that day they passed.

Many years later, Miss Mollie Crimmings of Berlin recalled that members of Post 4 marched for the funeral of every Berlin *World War I veteran* who died. She remembered them, also, as they sat in uniform, in a body, a handful of old men, at the funeral of her father, a former commander of Williams Post, in the fifty-ninth year of the venerable post's history.[13]

---

13. *Oshkosh Northwestern*, September 16, 1966.

CHAPTER SIX

GRIFF THOMAS TAKES CHARGE

Griffith J. Thomas had a number of talents including great dedication to his work. The resuscitation of the Department of Wisconsin G.A.R. required such dedication, and Thomas was able to turn things around.

Among the names that historians associate with the early and active years of the Wisconsin Department of the G.A.R., Thomas was probably the man most lacking in personal and/or political ambition. James Proudfit, the first commander, was a legislator to whom a G.A.R. title was another aspect of his political qualifications. Jeremiah Rusk and Thomas S. Allen, both in on the ground floor in the Wisconsin Department, had high political office in hand or in clear sight. Lucius Fairchild was not only the governor of Wisconsin at the time, but had national political aspirations as well. He rose to commander of the Grand Army of the Republic. And each of these men had a legitimate claim to the title of "general."

By contrast, Griff Thomas's title was "private." His dedication, however, was apparent early in life. At the age of fourteen he went to Oshkosh to enlist as a drummer boy in Company C of the Thirty-second Wisconsin, which was assembling there in the autumn of 1862. But before the regiment left Oshkosh, he was let go because of his age. He bided his time, returning to Berlin to apprentice as a printer with the *Berlin Courant.* In July 1863, now fifteen, he enlisted at Milwaukee as a drummer, Company B, First Wisconsin Heavy Artillery. He was mustered out of service in August 1865 at the age of eighteen.

Thomas was not a charter member of the Berlin Post. He did not return to Berlin immediately after discharge, but when he did come home he joined the post. He always remembered his sign-up date, April 16, 1867, and he was soon active in the post's affairs. In addition, at the age of twenty, he was selected for the part-time job of Berlin city clerk, and he held that job for a decade. His full-time job was as a printer, and then editor and publisher of the *Courant* (with a year or so stint as a printer for General Allen's *Oshkosh Northwestern* between titles with the *Courant*). But his passion was the Grand Army of the Republic, the Williams Post particularly, but the Department of Wisconsin as well.[1]

Thomas even published, in 1874 and 1875, the *Grand Army Sentinel,* the department's official newspaper at the time.[2] Under Thomas, the newspaper tried to put the best possible face on events in the G.A.R., but it inescapably portrayed the relatively sad state of the order. The *Sentinel's* eager reporting of the occasional reinstitution of a once-lost post in, say, the Department of Michigan, bespoke of hard times. Still the reporting of events from afar and the editorial commentary throughout disclosed the editor's unquenchable optimism for the eventual success of the order, and he felt that it was eminently worth everything he expended to achieve the G.A.R.'s success. In short, it was his passion.

That passion was needed by both post and department in the early and mid 1870s, for such passion was obviously lacking in the Grand Army. Thomas and the others of Post 4 saw to it that there were regular meetings, but as importantly, that there were regular reports and payments to the Department of Wisconsin.

By 1877, the Department of Wisconsin consisted essentially of the Berlin and Oshkosh posts, and a couple of Milwaukee posts. Credit for keeping the breath of life within the G.A.R. in Wisconsin goes to the veterans of those posts. It is tempting to carry the analogy further, to speak of the order "gasping" for breath. But in fact, the Grand Army was not gasping for breath, and although some members became somewhat dispirited—the Oshkosh post had to be dissuaded from disbanding at one point[3]—the men struggled to rejuvenate the order elsewhere.

Thomas, above all, bore that motivation over the years. In November 1878 he issued a call for a "reunion" of all soldiers and sailors from the late rebellion, at Berlin on New Year's Day of 1879.

At G.A.R. state meetings "held during the five years past, at Milwaukee and Oshkosh, the question of calling a general reunion of the veterans of the late war for the Union . . . has received . . . considerable attention—thus far without result," Thomas wrote in his formal call for the event.

1. Joyce Bennett Stemler, *They Went South, Biographical Sketches of the Civil War Veterans* from Berlin, Wisconsin, (Berlin, Wisc.: Berlin Historical Society, 1966), 113–114.

2. Ada Griswold, *Catalogue of Newspaper Files in the Library of the State Historical Society of Wisconsin* (Madison: 1911), 305. The *Sentinel* was moved to Milwaukee in 1875, and Department Commander George Hanaford continued his promotion of it until it ceased in 1877.

3. *Milwaukee Sentinel,* August 28, 1889.

The matter had often been "cussed and discussed" by Post 4 in Berlin during that time and the post at last decided to act on its own; hence the call to gather in that city.

"We . . . cordially invite all old soldiers and sailors who served honorably in the army and navy of the Union, residing in the State of Wisconsin without regard to former rank to meet with us on this occasion."

The invitation closed with a plea meant to tug at the memories of the maturing veterans:

Come, boys, come, we'll rally once again,
   As we did upon the battle plain:
Now, as then, united let us be
   In the blessed cause of Liberty.
Hail the Stars and Stripes forever!
   Let our cheers with joy resound!
And we'll sing our songs together –
   Songs we sung on the Old Camp Ground!

Thomas issued the call as chairman of the reunion committee, with A. L. Tucker of Post 4 signing as secretary.[4]

There are a number of quite significant things here. First, Berlin, with Thomas at the helm, was leading the way, essentially because no one else was leading. Second, the invitation came from Grand Army of the Republic men, but it was addressed to "soldiers and sailors" generally, and it was simply a request to get together for a "reunion" without any mention of further organizing, promising only "a hearty and generous welcome at the hands of our citizens and a jolly good time all around." In short, there was no G.A.R. hard sell here.

Third, the invitation had a nostalgic air to it, a recognition that the "soldiers and sailors" of '61 to '65 had grown older by a decade and a half, more or less. They would have a different outlook than they had when they were fresh from war.

Reunion day came and members of Berlin Post 4 seemed quite pleased with the results of their many weeks of preparation. Although the turnout of veterans from other parts of the state was not so large as they had hoped—fewer than one hundred—the overall turnout of veterans from the Berlin area and from surrounding counties was large: some three hundred men, which was considerably more than the membership of Grand Army of the Republic posts in the area, showed up. In fact, the number of members in good standing for the entire Department of Wisconsin on this date was a mere 135

men. The turnout of non-G.A.R. men indicated that there was latent interest among veterans who were not otherwise active in the order.

The New Year's Day event witnessed the singing of army songs, endless reminiscing, listening to and delivering speeches and poetic recitations, and relaxing with comrades. It was decidedly low key. The evening banquet was spread with four hundred places, and every one of them was filled. After several hours of a program consisting of musical numbers, toasts, and appropriate responses, the space was cleared around 11 p.m. for dancing, which, according to one account, "kept up till the wee small hours."[5]

One large item of business preceded the dancing, however. A permanent organization was formed, called the "Wisconsin Soldiers' and Sailors' Reunion Association." The new association chose Colonel Colwert K. Pier, a prominent Fond du Lac attorney and banker, as president; Major H. S. Town of Ripon as vice president; and the ubiquitous Griffith J. Thomas of Berlin as secretary.[6]

The following day, January 2, the regular encampment of the Department of Wisconsin, Grand Army of the Republic, was held at Berlin's Grand Army Hall. The most important business to come before the encampment was the question of whether the Department of Wisconsin should surrender its charter and become part of the Department of Illinois.[7]

It is possible that the fact that the Department of Illinois was really in no better condition than that of Wisconsin at the time had something to do with the failure of that proposition. But more importantly, Justus P. Luther, department senior vice commander at the time, was presiding in the absence of the commander, S. F. Hammond.

Luther, an early leader of Berlin Post 4, "brought his fist down on the table and said, 'I will never put that motion!'"[8] What, asked the small group of comrades, would Luther do? "Elect a *man* for Department Commander," Luther urged. "Elect Griff J. Thomas!"[9]

The hosts from Berlin were fired up; they were anything but defeatist. They had just put on their reunion and they were satisfied with its success, particularly with its drawing many veterans not affiliated with the order. There was still hope for the future of the G.A.R. That hope was personified by Griff Thomas. In due course, the encampment chose Thomas to be the new state commander.

January 2, 1879, was the lowest point in Department of Wisconsin history and at the same time a defining moment of its existence, worthy, at least metaphorically, of heaven-rending lightning flashes as if on the road to Damascus. The Department of Wisconsin that day began its ascent, one could almost say its dramatic ascent, from the depths it had fallen to during the trying 1870s to the very pinnacle of its strength and power by the end of the 1880s. And Griff Thomas led the way.

4. *Berlin Journal*, November 27, 1878.

5. *Berlin Courant*, January 4, 1879.

6. *Berlin Journal*, January 8, 1879.

7. Jerome Watrous, ed., *Memoirs of Milwaukee County* (Madison, Wisc.: Western Historical Association, 1909), 602.

8. *Forty-fifth Annual Encampment of the Department of Wisconsin, Grand Army of the Republic, Journal of Proceedings*, (Madison, Wisc.: Democrat Printing, 1911), 115.

9. Ibid.

Nor was Thomas alone. The new creation, the "Wisconsin Soldiers' and Sailors' Reunion Association," had a major impact upon that future, and its president, Colwert K. Pier, not even a Grand Army functionary at the time, assumed a significant role in veterans' affairs for the next year and beyond.[10]

Pier was the nephew and namesake of the first settler in Fond du Lac County back in 1836. He had rushed to be the first Fond du Lac man to enlist when the Civil War began, serving as a private with the First Wisconsin three-month regiment. Discharged, he attended law school in Albany, New York, returned to open practice in Fond du Lac, and then received a commission as lieutenant colonel of the Thirty-eighth Wisconsin when it was recruited in 1864.[11] Colonel Pier had the distinction of being second in command of the Thirty-eighth when it stepped off at the head of the entire Army of the Potomac in the Grand Review before President Andrew Johnson on May 23, 1865.[12] Pier had credentials.

A little more than a week after the Berlin festivities, Pier issued a circular from his home in Fond du Lac calling attention to the Reunion Association and its desire to hold a reunion in Milwaukee on June 8, 1880, of as many veterans as possible.

COLWERT PIER

"Every surviving soldier or sailor who enlisted from Wisconsin and was honorably discharged from the United States Military or Naval service is earnestly requested to write upon a postal card, name, occupation, post-office address, letter of company or companies, number of regiment or regiments in which he served, and send it to Griff J. Thomas . . . who will arrange and compile a roster in alphabetical order, by company or regiment, for record and publication. Sailors will give name of boat or boats on which they served."[13] "Comrades!" urged Pier. "Attend to this at once, or we shall not know whether you are dead, proud, or gone to Texas."

It worked. The circular was distributed throughout Wisconsin and even appeared in many publications outside the state, especially those catering specifically to veterans. Responses began to pour in to Berlin and to Thomas, and they continued for more than a year. Thousands of comrades were alive, not too proud, and were shunning Texas—and they were writing to share their remembrances of war incidents and bits of history, in addition to providing the requested information about the units in which they served.

Before the reunion date in June, Thomas, Pier, and Jerome Watrous compiled the men's colorful anecdotes and snippets of war stories into a series of articles published in the *Milwaukee Sunday Telegraph*, of which Watrous was editor. The series served to herald the 1880 reunion and, by heightening interest, helped to build its success.[14]

"I was chosen to lead the boys out of the wilderness," said Griff Thomas a long time after his selection as Department of Wisconsin commander. The statement had more matter-of-factness about it than braggadocio. "The feeling at the encampment of 1879 (at Berlin) was that the Grand Army should be perpetuated; that it should be built up, and that those present should do everything in their power to enlarge the membership."

For his part, the new commander would send out plenty of printed matter and many individual appeals trying to overcome the G.A.R.'s albatross: its reputation as a political vehicle. "I . . . wrote many personal letters to show that the order was not political and recited the real objects to be attained by it. It was a long, hard struggle."[15]

The struggle manifestly paid off. Thomas enjoyed the cooperation of many of the men who attended the pivotal Berlin encampment; he could not have done it alone. The turnaround began in the first year of Thomas's term when three posts were chartered: Darien on August 26, 1879, Butternut on November 12, and Delavan on November 28. These new charters alone just about doubled the number of active posts in the department.

The next year, as preparations were in full swing to stage the great 1880 reunion in Milwaukee, the Department of Wisconsin under Thomas was able to add six more posts, doubling the numbers again, even before the eagerly anticipated reunion.

On February 14, two posts were added. One was in Milwaukee and received, for reasons to be recounted later, the prestige of being given the No. 1 designation. Omro Post 7 came the same day. Baraboo was chartered March 4, followed by Reedsburg on April 10, Portage on April 13, and Amherst on April 16.[16] A large turnaround seemed to be under way.

There were several factors working in favor of the rejuvenation of the order in Wisconsin and in the other departments of the G.A.R. around the same time. The matter easiest to portray as crucial to the resurgence was, of course, the soldiers' and sailors' reunion in Milwaukee in the middle of 1880. But the reunion was not simply a cause so much as it was a symptom. Veterans had matured and enjoyed a bit more leisure time than they had had in 1865 when they came home to disadvantages compared with those who had not gone to war.

10. Pier was not a charter member of the Fond du Lac G.A.R. Post 130, formed a few years after the 1880 reunion, but joined it shortly afterward its formation and was its second commander, according to A.T. Glaze, *Incidents and Anecdotes of Early Days and History of Business the City and County of Fond du Lac* (Fond du Lac, Wisc.: P. B. Haber Printing, 1905).

11. William D. Love, *Wisconsin in the War of the Rebellion* (Chicago: Church and Goodman, 1866), 1011–1013.

12. E. B. Quiner, *Military History of Wisconsin* (Chicago: Clark and Company, 1866), 845–853; and Robert W. Wells, *Wisconsin in the Civil War* (Milwaukee: Milwaukee Journal, 1961), 95.

13. Watrous, *Memoirs*, 602.

14. Ibid., 602–603.

15. Hosea W. Rood, "The Grand Army of the Republic and the Wisconsin Department," in *Wisconsin, Its History and Its People*, ed. By Milo Quaife, (Chicago: S. J. Clarke Publishing Company, 1924), 556.

16. *Proceedings of the Twenty-fourth Annual Encampment*, (Milwaukee, Wisc.: Ed. Keogh, 1890), 15.

This was an era of "joiners." Fraternal organizations of all sorts, literally hundreds of them, from the Odd Fellows to the Improved Order of Red Men, were being conceived, ritualized, and promoted in the second half of the nineteenth century. They arose because men wanted the social aspects of fraternalism. Yet there existed fierce competition among them as each sought to be distinctive. Most men of substance, as typical obituaries of the period attest, joined two, three, and sometimes even more fraternal orders. In addition to the attractiveness of having such social outlets, men probably joined for whatever advantage they could gain in their business affairs with their brother Masons or fellow Knights of Pythias or whatever.

The Grand Army of the Republic was one such fraternity but one with a big difference. Membership was restricted to those who had served honorably in the late war. A man could not buy his way in. The G.A.R pin on the lapel was a badge of honor. For anyone with even slight ambition, G.A.R. membership was very attractive.

To the individual of substance who also was a veteran, the order afforded a great opportunity to affiliate with like-minded, distinctive men and to gain whatever assistance these affiliations might bring to him in business, a benefit known as "reciprocal patronage." Members did business, as far as possible, with other members in preference to anyone else.

And even if the veteran was not a "man of substance" or even bordering on being one, there was another factor beginning to appear which piqued his interest: pension issues.

At the Berlin reunion in 1879, the veterans attending voted to urge their representatives in Washington to support a change in existing legislation that would make a disability pension applica-tion retroactive to discharge rather than effective upon approval.[17]

Such pensions were part of the landscape in veterans' circles from the beginning: a soldier disabled while performing his duty for his country was entitled to the government's assistance. But the criteria for saying who qualified for such assistance, and when, was frequently revisited and would undergo a considerable metamorphosis in the decade of the 1880s and beyond.

Guiding the reworking of pension laws became a key component of the G.A.R.'s national effort in those years. As veterans began to perceive that the order was working in their behalf on the pension issue, more former soldiers and sailors became members on the local level.

An important element of the rekindling of the G.A.R. spark, perhaps the most important, was the fact that a veteran's status began taking on new meaning. As his time of soldiering receded from sharp, and possibly painful, memory, the more pleasant aspects of a veteran's youthful experiences took on an allure. Liberating "secesh" chickens, playing pranks on some pompous lieutenant, swapping tales with messmates, sharing a tin of coffee or news from home, even straggling when there wasn't a spare ounce of energy to help one keep up, were easy to recall.

Billy Yank's beard is showing definite touches of gray. He is no longer young, but his thoughts turn to youth. Oh, to go back, to experience once again, the adventure of youth. To drink, once more, from the same canteen with his old comrades had an intoxicating appeal.

These motivating forces grew in importance as the 1870s crept into the 1880s. The next best thing to reliving the life of a Union soldier was sharing similar memories with other men in the Grand Army of the Republic.

---

17. *Berlin Courant*, January 4, 1879.

CHAPTER SEVEN

REUNION AND REJUVENATION

Griffith Thomas and Colwert Pier, in the year and a half after resolving to stage a gigantic reunion of soldiers and sailors in Milwaukee in the summer of 1880, devoted a prodigious amount of time and energy to making the reunion happen; they succeeded far beyond anything they could have reasonably expected. The reunion brought privates and corporals and sergeants by the tens of thousands to Milwaukee, and starred no less a personage than Lieutenant General (and former President) Ulysses S. Grant.

BADGE FROM 1880 REUNION

They set for themselves the ambitious project of assembling the name and unit of every Wisconsin man who participated in the war, plus the occupation and mailing address of every surviving state veteran. They encouraged all of these veterans to come to Milwaukee.

Pier, as president of the reunion association, headed the effort, with G.A.R. Commander Thomas serving as secretary. They enlisted hundreds of veterans in their organizing cause, many of them among the best-known leaders of Wisconsin troops during the war. They were also assisted by the Milwaukee Chamber of Commerce and Merchants Association, which readily appreciated the benefits the Cream City could reap from a week of entertaining tens of thousands of veterans.

"During the period [of the reunion, June 7 to June 12] a separate reunion of every regiment and company in the war, from this state, will also be held," Pier assured in his initial "prospectus" for the event. "Regimental and company officers who have not already done so are requested to issue a published call to the survivors of their respective commands for such a gathering . . ."

The Fond du Lac leader promised "a general encampment and parade of all the organized military companies of the state, together with the usual and appropriate exercises of a soldier's reunion such as "camp fires" "sham battles" etc., [which] cannot fail to make this occasion one of unparalleled interest and enjoyment."[1]

Most state newspapers published the association's public appeals, and veterans' publications throughout the nation also carried the invitations. The response was enthusiastic. Rufus Dawes of Marietta, Ohio, who led a Badger regiment (and

wrote one of the finest regimental histories to come out of the war), assured the committee by letter that he not only wished to be there but "will do all that I can to further its interests and secure its success."[2]

EDWARD S. BRAGG

General Edward S. Bragg, one-time commander of the Iron Brigade, also responded and called upon officers he knew from each of the five regiments of that famous brigade—including the Nineteenth Indiana and Twenty-fourth Michigan—to round up their men. The Iron Brigade Association evolved from this call, an association which thereafter held annual reunions for many years.[3]

Regimental and company commanders were also eager to bring it all about. General John Starkweather headed the First Regiment reunion efforts. General Thomas S. Allen worked to rally members from the Fifth Wisconsin. The Sixteenth's old commander, Thomas Reynolds, promised in his circular to his men that if permitted, he would take with him the "banners under which you so proudly marched to victory, that you may again have an opportunity of renewing your devotion to them." And this came to pass.[4]

The "Irish Brigade" of Sherman's Army, the Seventeenth Wisconsin, whose support of McClellan in the 1864 election was no indication of its being lukewarm for the cause, would be party to the reunion. General Harrison Hobart, famed participant in the breakout of federal officers from Libby Prison in Richmond during the war, urged the men of his Twenty-first Wisconsin to "rally once more to greet the living and revive the memories of the dead." Congressman Jeremiah Rusk rallied the Twenty-fifth. And so it went through regiment after regiment of infantry, plus the artillery batteries and cavalry units, that once looked longingly at Wisconsin as "home."

1. *Wisconsin Soldiers and Sailors Reunion Roster*, 1880 (Fond du Lac, Wisc.: Star Steam Job and Book Printers, 1880), 233.

2. Ibid., 30.

3. Richard H. Zeitlin, "In Peace and War: Union Veterans and Cultural Symbols—The Flags of the Iron Brigade," in *Giants in their Tall Black Hats: Essays on the Iron Brigade*, ed. by Alan T. Nolan and Sharon Eggleston Vipond (Bloomington: Indiana University Press, 1998), 169.

4. Ibid., 167.

Many of these gatherings of the various regiments to plan for this reunion resulted in more or less permanent regimental organizations holding their own reunions in future years. A call even went out for former prisoners of war, any "soldiers who were in the enemy's hands during their military service," to contact "General (J. A.) Kellogg of Wausau who has consented to take special charge of this interesting and impressive feature of the . . . reunion."[5]

If the officers responded with great enthusiasm, the rank and file matched their efforts. Members of the organizing committee noted with pleasure the press reports from around Wisconsin—and beyond. "A grand gathering of Wisconsin soldiers was held last evening at the Grand Pacific Hotel in Chicago for the purpose of making arrangements for attending the Reunion," read one clipping. "A county organization of survivors of the late 'onpleasantness'[sic] has been effected at Neillsville, and promised to show up strong at the June meeting," read another. Portage veterans also piped in. "It is said that every soldier in that county will attend, and one man up there has quit smoking long enough to save the necessary ducats."[6] Veterans in Fond du Lac came up with a novel way of gathering names and of urging participation in the reunion: they arranged with clerks at the polls in the April election of 1879 to have blanks upon which to record the names and addresses of veterans who voted. Old soldier poll watchers were recruited to assure that the lists were compiled. One newspaper opined that the reunion would be "as far removed from everything of a party character as it is possible for any gathering to be. Such Democrats as Bragg, Hancock, Robinson, Hobart, Vilas and a host of others who will take an active part in the demonstration, would not be apt to do so if the reunion was in the interest of the Republican Party. Such Republicans as Allen, Hincks, Bintliff, Pier, Rusk and many others, would not be likely to engage in the enterprise if it was to be run in the interest of the Democratic Party."[7]

The Grand Reunion was not a Grand Army of the Republic function, although G.A.R. members made no attempt to conceal the fact that they were intimately involved in the event's planning and implementation. The hard-to-live-down reputation of political involvement notwithstanding, the G.A.R. would be entirely in accord with the spirit of the reunion, and it would be strictly for the purpose of giving "all soldiers in the State of Wisconsin" a once-in-a-lifetime opportunity to revisit the greatest experience of their lives.

The invitation to "all soldiers in the State of Wisconsin" enticed veterans of the Mexican War to write to ask to be included, and this brought assent from the planners for them and for War of 1812 veterans to be included in the Grand Parade on June 10.[8]

Then there was the *gemütlichkeit* factor. The citizens of Milwaukee looked forward to this event. So, too, did the merchants and manufacturers. An event of such scale could result in something really big for Milwaukee, and leading men of the city immersed themselves in the planning and, later, in the staging of the reunion.

A huge committee, mercifully broken down into about a dozen subgroups, representing the Board of Trade, banking and insurance interests, brewing interests—the names of Captain Fred Pabst, Val Blatz, August Uihlein, and Fred Miller were prominent in this grouping—distillers, hoteliers, and various sections of the city of Milwaukee government. In all, well in excess of one hundred men assured the host city's generous participation in accommodating the tens of thousands of people who would be there in June.

Plenty of details needed to be worked out, and during the first half of 1880, several hundred committees—both of veterans and of Milwaukeeans—met frequently to iron out every conceivable facet of the reunion, from overall planning to locating encampment facilities; arranging subsistence and transportation; issuing invitations; advertising the event; providing decorations, music, and security; and even to arranging special accommodations for soldiers from other states. It was a huge undertaking.

The planning paid off as the appointed week arrived. Soldiers by the thousands, plus thousands of regular citizens, streamed into Milwaukee. The latter were, probably, largely the wives and children of the veterans.

Countless others just wanted to absorb the pageantry of this once-in-a-lifetime event. And some, naturally, saw the assembling crowds as a way of making a modest to middling profit. All streamed into Milwaukee in the 24 to 48 hours preceding the awaited day, Monday, June 7, 1880.

Something else preceded the great day as well: rain. For 10 days before the event, "flood after flood has gathered in clouds and precipitated itself through space; the lightnings have been let loose and have blazed over the firmament from horizon to horizon till the black sky of night looked like an outer globe of fire," waxed one newspaper reporter. It had a predictable result: "There is mud enough already about Camp Reunion to remind the visitors of the winters of Virginia and Tennessee."[9]

Observers were confident that the weather had taken a favorable turn by opening day, and to an extent it had. "The cool northern breezes tempered the June sun," that day, said one report, making it "perfection for the purposes of the gathering." But perfection did not last the week, which was generally quite warm and muggy, with intermittent showers.[10] The less-than-ideal conditions, though, did not seem to make the event any less satisfying for the participants.

5. *Wisconsin Soldiers and Sailors*, 235–237.

6. Ibid., 239. Railroads of the state cooperated on the price of those ducats. Those attending the reunion were charged only a cent and a half per mile traveled to get there.

7. *Wisconsin Soldiers and Sailors*, 289.

8. Ibid., 239, 272.

9. *Milwaukee Journal Sentinel*, June 7, 1880.

10. Zeitlin, "In Peace and War," 168.

"Camp ways are prevailing among the old boys from the rural districts to a remarkable degree. Thousands of them appear to want to renew their army experiences as veritably as they can for a few days. They want to sleep in tents, and probably will desire to cook their 'grub' in halves of canteens if they can procure such perishable frying pans.... [W]oolen blankets in many instances appear to be the same articles that were brought home in 1865, and will doubtless help immensely towards the resuscitation of camp memories," observed one reporter.[11]

The tent camp was located at North Point on the lakeshore and accommodated between twenty and thirty thousand veterans, each bringing blanket, tin cup, plate, and other utensils, and paying fifty cents a day for the "grub."[12] Many of the generals, of course, found hotel accommodations. And those who were not veterans occupied every available room for hire in the city, as well as in outlying towns.

Just about the entire city of Milwaukee was decorated for the occasion. The *Milwaukee Sentinel* devoted several columns of space to describing some of the decorations. "Across East Water Street bridge . . . the whole street is gorgeously arrayed. Scarcely a foot of front but is covered with glory and flags," read one paragraph. And there were plenty of other paragraphs conveying the message that all Milwaukee was festooned with flags, bunting, evergreen stringers, green boughs—anything that would tell the world that the burghers were heartily joining the festivities of the week.

Without a doubt, the efforts were worthwhile. Reporters estimated that the number of visitors to the Cream City that week just about doubled Milwaukee's population of 150,000.[13] Visitors were everywhere. Whether it was William Koch's beer hall, Swetland's oyster house (both earning special mention as having particularly fine decorations), or any of the hundreds of additional saloons and eating places enjoying the bounty of catering to "the old boys from rural districts" and to their hungry and/or thirsty kin.

Still, the most important place in the city for veterans was the lakeshore. Here was, from the first day through the last—from the hearty greetings between long-ago comrades on Monday, June 7, to the sometimes heart-tugging farewells of departing companions, now growing old, of Saturday, June 12—the essence of the reunion, amid the hundreds of tents and the informalities of the thousands of old soldiers within the camp. They came to recapture something from their youthful past and succeeded in doing so. In groups of a half dozen or so they talked and remembered and sang and laughed.

Reporters made some effort to capture the storytelling mood. "Stories! Why there was no end to them, and all good ones. Bacon says that a story with a good point to it must not be tabooed just for the reason that it is a trifle tart, and if the ladies would all agree with Bacon's philosophy a number of stories with excellent points might be produced which otherwise must

go down to posterity unrecorded in print."[14] But what tart ones reached the reporter's ear went unrecorded in the *Sentinel*?

In addition to the stories, some of the veterans managed a trick or two among themselves and with others. One night, a young militiaman on guard duty about the camp patrolled in the vicinity of a cannon loaded with a blank cartridge to be used for a salute. A couple of wily and sleepless veterans decided to have some fun. While one distracted the young guard, the other managed to discharge the cannon. "It made the young militiaman think of home for a minute as the echoes resounded over the lake," the reporter chuckled.[15]

Some regiments held reunion festivities for their former members. The Fifth Wisconsin had its gathering at the West Side Turner Hall. Its leader, General Thomas S. Allen, greeted the members wearing the uniform he wore during the war, receiving the boys "in a most hospitable manner." One of the more unusual reunions was that of Wisconsin veterans of the Mexican War; roughly 30 of them gathered in Milwaukee for the week. Even as their younger compatriots of the Civil War reminisced, the elders of that earlier war did likewise.

"'Do you remember our meeting at Vera Cruz?' asked one old veteran of another as they conned over the battles of the Mexican campaign. 'Aye, well I do,' answered the old comrade, 'and well do I recall the hardtack we subsisted on the first day we viewed old Vera.'" Thus the Sentinel reporter recorded while eavesdropping on the old soldiers.[16] In the ensuing Grand Review, these old-timers rode in a beautifully decorated omnibus, surrounded by 15 10- to 12-year-old girls from the Sixth Ward school.

That Grand Review was the centerpiece of the week, a stirring spectacle and the main reason why tens of thousands of people, Milwaukeeans and out-of-towners, had come to the city. Before their eyes marched the gallant heroes reliving the triumph of their lives. Here were some thirty thousand men, veterans of the Civil War, most of them, plus current-day militia companies from throughout the state, marching in a procession measuring three miles long.

They marched proudly under the very flags they had followed into battle. These had been brought out from their repository in Madison, and the crowds sensed that they were privy to a very special sight. "When the flags torn by shot and shell were borne by, a quiver went through the vast assemblage and a moment after, the wildest excitement prevailed."[17]

Lieutenant General Ulysses S. Grant, along with one of Grant's favorite subordinates—and a favorite of the soldiers,

---

11. *Milwaukee Journal Sentinel*, June 7, 1880.
12. Zeitlin, "In Peace and War," 168; *Wisconsin Soldiers and Sailors*, 273.
13. Zeitlin, "In Peace and War," 168.
14. *Milwaukee Sentinel*, June 9, 1880.
15. Ibid.
16. Ibid.
17. Zeitlin, "In Peace and War," 168; *Milwaukee Sentinel*, June 11, 1880.

U. S. GRANT

too—Major General Philip H. Sheridan, reviewed them all. One of the most famous survivors of the Civil War was featured in that parade, and though no one knew it at the time, it would be his last public appearance in Wisconsin. Old Abe, mascot of the Eighth Wisconsin back when he was a young eagle and the men of the Eighth were eager young volunteers, had come through the war and lived in splendid retirement in the state Capitol in Madison, coming out for just such festive occasions as soldier reunions.

Old Abe occupied his accustomed place on a perch, as oblivious to the noisy drum corps marching nearby as he had been to the frightful sounds of war, while he received the plaudits of the crowds as he passed. "His magnificent eyes blazed with the inward excitement and pleasure [they] always manifested on military occasions," the Eighth's historian recounted.[18] Old Abe expired the following year, 1881, nearly 20 years after leaving the Wisconsin north woods for his youthful adventure into war.[19]

The celebration of their own youthful adventures by the thousands of veterans was originally scheduled for Wednesday, June 9, but was put off a day, partly because of the weather and partly because General Grant was tied up early in the week as the Republican convention in Chicago had him in the running for the presidential nomination again, opposing James G. Blaine. After a couple dozen ballots the nomination went instead to General James A. Garfield.

Grant not only reviewed the huge procession on June 10, but went down and marched along with the men for part of the way. It allowed more of the thousands of spectators to see the ex-president.

Afterwards, the general went to the campsite on the lakeshore to see for himself the huge assembly of his former soldiers. Word of his arrival spread through the place, and a crowd gathered and called for Grant to give a speech.

"I should be very happy to address you, but I am not in the habit of making speeches, and moreover not many of this vast assemblage would be able to hear my voice. It has been a great pleasure in this my third visit to Milwaukee to have had the op-

The great 1880 Soldiers and Sailors Reunion in Milwaukee not only was a huge success for Wisconsin veterans, but it had national ramifications as well. The front page of Harper's Weekly for July 3, 1880, featured the sketches shown here. The publication also carried an article about the event on an inside page. It seems unlikely that the huge reunion and the almost concurrent resurrection nationally of the Grand Army of the Republic was simply coincidence.

portunity of meeting so many of my old comrades in arms. I am very glad to see you all well . . ."[20]

Their one-time commander uttered a few more phrases in tribute to the men and their willingness to sacrifice for the preservation of their country, then retired. A few others in the party, including General Charles S. Hamilton, host to the Grants while they stayed in Milwaukee, and Wisconsin Governor William E. Smith, filled in with their own remarks for the occasion.

The following morning, Friday, June 11, a memorial service was held under the auspices of the Grand Army of the Republic. Colwert Pier, reunion chairman, and Department Commander Griff Thomas presided. Thomas told those attending that the first part of the week had been given, essentially, for entertainment, but now it was time to honor "the memory of those who left us on many a hard-fought field," the *Sentinel* reported.[21]

Colonel Samuel Fallows, late commander of the Forty-ninth Wisconsin and now a Methodist bishop in Chicago, preached the sermon. Besides recounting many of the agonies of the war, Bishop Fallows spoke of a new age. He had recently attended a general conference of his church where men, formerly leaders of secession, spoke movingly of peace and reconciliation.[22]

SAMUEL FALLOWS

The *Sentinel* provided a fitting summary for the week, observing, on June 1 that "While the reunion will serve to bring back old scenes and old companions to the veterans, it will also serve to remind us that nationality costs something. There will be empty sleeves and halting steps enough to add to the force of the suggestion. In every day life there is too much forgetfulness of the seasons of trial and sacrifice by which the blessings of good government are guaranteed. It does us good to be reminded of those things, and serves to enlarge the spirit of patriotism."

---

18. Anonymous, *The Eagle Regiment, Eighth Wisconsin Infantry Volunteers* (Belleville, WI.: Recorder Printers, 1890), 89.

19. Ibid., 90. Through the taxidermist's art, Old Abe continued to inspire veterans who came to see him in the state Capitol in Madison for another 23 years. In 1904 the Capitol burned, and the remains of the famous eagle were destroyed. Several of Old Abe's molted feathers, properly attested to, are on display in the Veterans' Museum on the Capitol Square in Madison.

20. *Milwaukee Sentinel*, June 1, 1880.

21. Ibid.

22. Ibid.

CHAPTER EIGHT

ON THE WAY TO THE HEIGHTS

The work of running the Grand Army of the Republic's Department of Wisconsin went on through the great Soldiers' Reunion of 1880. Commander Griffith J. Thomas gained a great deal of satisfaction—and a measure of vexation.

The matter of Madison Post No. 1, known as the Cassius Fairchild Post contributed to the latter. The post, in all probability, was a functioning organization, to at least some degree (it claimed to be such some years later). It had already suffered the fate of having its charter revoked by Commander George A. Hannaford in 1874. The post had sent along some, but not all, of the arrears to the department. The members of the Fairchild Post apparently responded to Hannaford's revocation by anteing up the arrears, and they coaxed Hannaford the following year into reinstating it under the original charter, with its prized original numeric designation.[1]

But the post promptly fell into arrears again. By the time Thomas took office at the beginning of 1879, he had just four posts reporting, and Post 1 was not one of them. "Repeated calls made upon No. 1 . . . which was supposed to be in operation, failed to bring any response and it was suspended from the roll of the Department for non-payment of per capita tax," Thomas later recalled. He acted quickly after taking office.

There was new interest in the Grand Army of the Republic after the Grand Reunion. Thomas found himself in the happy position of acting upon applications for new posts. "I determined upon the reorganization of the Department by giving new posts the numbers of posts that had become defunct. I had a little faith that old No. 1 would finally come to the front and reserved that number to the very last before assigning it to a new post."

The "very last" came on February 14, 1880. Thomas tried throughout 1879 to cajole reports from the Madison post, without success. On that date he gave the prized number to a new Milwaukee post, comprised of members of old Post No. 3 which had surrendered its charter the year before. The post became E. B. Wolcott Post No. 1.[2]

Madison howled and growled. They had to have their old charter, they argued, because they were beneficiaries of a bequest by a comrade and the bequest was to the post under its original charter. Thomas was adamant that they had lost their

No. 1 designation. Thomas issued a new charter to Madison as Post 11, but in order to safeguard the bequest, he gave them authority to work under the old charter granted June 10, 1866.[3]

The nature of the problem the Madison G.A.R. faced is difficult to discern. The records of the Department of Wisconsin have been missing since 1882. In addition, records of the Madison Post, according to one history of the organization, "were lost in the Capitol fire, February 27, 1904; and so we cannot with any degree of certainty tell much of its history up to that date."[4]

It is certain, however, that its membership had slipped somewhat in quality as well as quantity from its original chartering. Some of the founders had moved on. Former Secretary of State Thomas S. Allen was at Oshkosh. Jeremiah Rusk left state government and was elected to Congress from Viroqua. His seven-year gubernatorial stint was still ahead of him.[5]

Probably most importantly, though, Governor Lucius Fairchild, a thorough Madisonian, had capped his career in Wisconsin politics (as it was fading) by accepting a federal appointment to diplomatic service. He had sent out feelers in 1872 as to the possibility of his becoming commander in chief of the Grand Army of the Republic. Had he succeeded, of course, the Madison post would probably have done all it had to do to keep in communication with higher headquarters. But Ambrose E. Burnside, then the commander, wanted another term, and the powers of G.A.R. politics made it clear that Fairchild had no chance.[6]

In October 1872, then, Lucius Fairchild went to Liverpool, England, and the Fairchild Post, at the time named after his brother Cassius, went into arrears. Fairchild had a strong

1. Griffith J. Thomas to J. A. Biggert, Berlin, August 22, 1889. Reprinted from *Statement and Proofs*, 7.

2. Wolcott was a prominent Milwaukee physician, as well as Wisconsin surgeon general in the Civil War, who had died the month before the post was organized. Jerome Watrous, ed., *Memoirs of Milwaukee County* (Madison, WI: Western Historical Association, 1909), 479.

3. Thomas, 7. The original charter date was recognized, but the continuity of the post was not recognized, thus giving Berlin Post 4 precedence as the oldest continuous post.

4. *Roster of Lucius Fairchild Post No. 11, Department of Wisconsin, Grand Army of the Republic* (Madison, Wisc.: January 1, 1922).

5. Fred L. Holmes, ed., *Wisconsin: Stability, Progress, Beauty*, (Chicago: Lewis Publishing, 1946), 2:161.

6. Sam Ross, *The Empty Sleeve: A Biography of Lucius Fairchild*, (Madison: State Historical Society of Wisconsin, 1964), 157.

reputation in the G.A.R., and in veterans' circles generally, well beyond Wisconsin. He had converted from a prewar Democrat into a thorough, rabid, Radical Republican who brought waving the bloody shirt almost to an art form. His staunch support for U.S. Grant for president in 1868 and for a second term in 1872 was rewarded with his appointment to a foreign post. It was a step forward for the ambitious one-armed veteran, and he served in several diplomatic capacities for almost a decade—a decade in which his presence in Grand Army affairs, as well as in Republican councils, perceptibly dimmed.

The Madison Post, a short time after it lost its No. 1 designation decided to change its name from Cassius Fairchild to C. (for Cadwallader) C. Washburn Post No. 11.[7] The Madison veterans certainly had a viable post after Thomas re-chartered them, but they had little to say in department councils. From its first reinstitution by Commander George Hannaford in 1875 until 1886, when Lucius Fairchild, who had returned from abroad, was elected state commander, Post 11 had just one member serve in a department office.[8]

The lethargic performance of the Madison veterans in the early 1880s was anything but typical of the Department of Wisconsin itself. Griff Thomas's success in running the department and enlarging the size and scope of the order succeeded spectacularly. The huge impetus for expansion, which was unquestionably a result of the great reunion of 1880, was matched in his third year when another six posts were added to the rolls—a stunning turnaround in the fortunes of the Grand Army of the Republic in the short span of three years. Coming into command with just three or four posts in the entire state, Thomas could look at the roster at the end of his service showing more than twenty active, functioning—and reporting—posts, including Madison. And individual membership in the order had shown a commensurate growth as well. There had been just 135 enrolled members in the four posts at the beginning of his term. Membership totals for the Department of Wisconsin after his three years was approaching one thousand.

Thomas could be pardoned if, in his report to the department encampment at the close of his administration, he showed a tinge of pride that the Grand Army of the Republic had taken on a new lease on life in the State of Wisconsin. He felt encouraged. Thomas gave the comrades in his departing speech something of a testimonial to the spirit and meaning of the G.A.R. as he understood them:

> Our objects are spread wide before the world, and challenge the admiration and veneration of all. It is in no respect a political organization. In our ranks today are all the illustrious soldiers of the war representing every shade of political and religious opinion. In its highest civic relation it ennobles to a loftier citizenship, to a warmer patriotism, and to a high faith in American institutions . . .
>
> We have met with opposition, and to a certain extent we shall still meet it; but comrades, the edict has gone forth, and the Grand Army of the Republic is bound to become a power for good in this beloved state of ours . . .
>
> It rests with us to show to those about us that we are actuated by a spirit of true fraternity. . . . It rests with us to prove that ours is that charity which never turns its back upon a suffering soldier, or the widow or orphan of those who fell in our holy cause. It rests with us to show the people of Wisconsin that, having proven our loyalty to our country and our flag, we propose to continue [to be] loyal to every sacred trust committed to our keeping.[9]

Thomas set the Department of Wisconsin on its dramatic course of enlargement, and it met his expectation that it would, in future years, be a power in the state. The pattern of growth accelerated even more rapidly in the post-Thomas years. His successor was Herbert M. Enos of Post 19, Waukesha. Enos was an old West Pointer from New York, stationed in 1861 at Fort Union, New Mexico Territory. He watched several officers from Fort Union join the southerners; he stayed with the Union.[10] Enos, a bachelor, was talented in business and put that to use in the department which saw the number of posts triple in his single term.[11]

Not only were the number of posts up to sixty by the beginning of 1883, but Assistant Adjutant General R. L. Gove's report to the encampment at Portage that year showed almost as strong an increase in total members, up from somewhat under a thousand to almost 2,500.[12]

Some of this rapid growth was accompanied by the familiar growing pains of the previous decade. Assistant Adjutant General Gove of Waukesha alluded to it in his report. "The work at Department Headquarters is accumulating, and if there is not something done towards making a complete record, there must at some future period be experienced great confusion and trouble at arriving at any clear idea of its work."[13]

---

7. The change honored a cavalry major general in the war and later governor of Wisconsin, 1872–74. Cadwallader Washburn died May 14, 1882. The name change was approved the same year, according to the 1883 official *Proceedings*. The post received its third name in 1896, honoring Lucius Fairchild after his death on May 23 of that year.

8. Robert B. Beath, *History of the Grand Army of the Republic*, (New York: Bryan, Taylor & Co., 1889), 539–44. The single exception was W. H. Bennett, who was on the Council of Administration in 1884.

9. Hosea W. Rood, "The Grand Army of the Republic and the Wisconsin Department," in *Wisconsin, Its History and Its People*, ed. by Milo Quaife (Chicago: S. J. Clarke Publishing Company, 1924), 557–58.

10. *Forty-seventh Annual Encampment of the Department of Wisconsin, Grand Army of the Republic, Journal of Proceedings*, (Madison, Wisc.: Democrat Printing, 1913), 110.

11. *Proceedings, Seventeenth Encampment*, (Waukesha: WI: Freeman Book and Job Printing House, 1883), l0.

12. Ibid., 11.

13. Ibid., 12.

As a matter of fact, it was in 1883 that the earlier Department records disappeared. Griff Thomas reported that he forwarded all the records he had inherited from his predecessor as well as all the records generated during his three terms to Enos at Waukesha.[14]

What became of those records baffled the Department in later years. Some assume that the entire set of records was somehow inadvertently destroyed, but there is no hard evidence of that. However, they are not known to exist. Gove's plea to the 1883 encampment that "it would take a good, competent man three months to write up the records of the Department so that it would show a perfect history of all its works, and the standing of all its members"[15] suggests that he was worried about past as well as steadily mounting contemporary records that were growing apace with the Department of Wisconsin.

Commander Enos also warned the comrades that the workload on Gove and on his predecessor, Thomas, now assistant quartermaster general of the department, was becoming too much of a burden for part-time, uncompensated men. This was particularly true, Enos noted, in light of the fact that Thomas, who had been ill during the latter months of his tenure as commander, was having continued ill-health and that his work devolved upon the assistant adjutant general.[16]

Although the element of paperwork chaos was reminiscent of the early years of boom and bust, there was an important difference: there was no "bust." The old, reliable posts appeared perfectly robust—Enos reported eighteen of the twenty he inherited showed membership gains—and so were the new posts.

The 1883 Portage Encampment brought a second dynamic leader for this growth-filled decade to the top of the department: Philip Cheek Jr. of Post 9, Baraboo. While Cheek was department commander over the next two years, the Grand Army of the Republic in the State of Wisconsin experienced a growth in real numbers nothing short of phenomenal. Coming to the helm with sixty active posts, Cheek and a corps

PHILIP CHEEK

of more than 25 mustering officers added another 69 during the year, and members in good standing rose from just under 2,500 to almost six thousand by the encampment in Janesville in January 1884.

Cheek estimated he spent 143 days during his first year on department business, setting himself the task of visiting as many posts as possible—he attended more than 30 campfires and reunions during 1883—but it just was not possible any longer for the commander to visit every post of the department.

Cheek told the comrades at Janesville about the missing records. "We are satisfied that there is a record in large books . . .

and kept for some time, now in existence, but where they are we have been unable to ascertain." He still hoped they would show up, "as without them the full official record cannot be written."[17]

If 1883 was a good year for Cheek and the Department of Wisconsin, the following year proved to be no letdown. Cheek was named to a second term at the Janesville Encampment, which thereupon decreed one term to be the norm. The one-term criterion remained with the Department of Wisconsin, with one notable exception,[18] until well into the twentieth century when few members remained alive.[19]

That confidence was well placed. At the end of his term Cheek reflected that his second year had been almost as full as his first, measured by the number of new posts in 1884—60—and the increase in total membership for the state from just under six thousand to almost ten thousand. And of course the growth was accompanied by a matching increase in the amount of business to be transacted by the department. "We have had Department Headquarters open during business hours the entire year without cost to the Department where the A.A.G. [assistant adjutant general] or some other Department officer has been on duty."[20] The department, in other words, was being conducted on a professional basis and the troublesome times of headquarters being inundated with paperwork and overwhelmed by the sheer magnitude of the order seemed past.

In fact, under Cheek, the office of assistant adjutant general was essentially an executive secretary who received an annual salary. Following his term as department commander, Cheek was appointed assistant adjutant general and served the department for two years in that capacity. Cheek continued to be active in department affairs, usually appointed to an encampment committee. Moreover, the Iron Brigade veteran who took a disabling wound in that cornfield at Antietam, served several three-year terms as a trustee of the Department of Wisconsin, his service ending with his death in 1911.

The pace of adding posts at the rate of five per month or so, as occurred in the 24 months of Phil Cheek's tenure as commander, could not continue indefinitely. When his successor, James Davidson, Post 30, Sparta, was chosen in the 1885 en-

14. Rood, *The Grand Army*, 555-56.

15. *Proceedings, Seventeenth Encampment*, 12.

16. Thomas continued as assistant quartermaster general in 1884 in spite of health problems. According to Joyce Bennett Stemler, *They Went South, Biographical Sketches of the Civil War Veterans from Berlin, Wisconsin* (Berlin, WI: Berlin Historical Society, 1966), 114, Thomas moved from Berlin, Wisconsin, in 1886, to Harvard in Clay County, Nebraska, where he was editor and publisher of the *Harvard Courier* for 28 years. He was active in local politics in Nebraska and died in Harvard on February 28, 1926, at the age of 79.

17. *Proceedings of Eighteenth Annual Encampment of the Department of Wisconsin, Grand Army of the Republic*, (Baraboo, Wisc.: Republic Print, 1884), 11.

18. In February 1889, Augustus G. Weissert of Milwaukee was reelected department commander, but he resigned in his second term when he was elected national senior vice commander at the August 1889 National Encampment in Milwaukee. *Proceedings of Twenty-fourth Encampment*, 22.

19. Rood, *The Grand Army*, 567.

20. *Proceedings of Nineteenth Annual Encampment of the Department of Wisconsin, Grand Army of the Republic*, (Baraboo, Wisc.: Republic Print, 1885), 26.

campment at Madison, the health and well-being of the Department of Wisconsin, and indeed, of the Grand Army of the Republic itself (on the national level), was beyond doubt.

The 1885 encampment received a report from A. O. Wright, Post 61, New Lisbon, who was appointed the task the year before of finding out the number of soldiers in poorhouses in the state. He found that there were at least 50 in such county institutions, and that another 25 or so were receiving relief. He found also that several soldiers' widows were in poorhouses and seven on county relief. Additionally Wright found 61 former soldiers confined as insane.[21] The G.A.R. turned to providing charitable assistance for fellow veterans. At the same time, William Stanley, Post 1, Milwaukee, the department inspector, reported that 67 of the department's 190 posts had failed to establish relief funds. "While all posts are disposed to help needy comrades with a liberal hand, they can better perform this work by establishing a relief fund," Stanley admonished.[22]

Fraternity, Charity, Loyalty, were taken seriously, and charity was not the least of these. Relief funds at the post level allowed charity to be dispensed on a very personal, first-hand-knowledge basis, and hence it may not have been "liberal" by latter-day welfare-state standards. Welfare fraud would have been nigh unto impossible on the post level.

Those "relief funds" were, practically from the beginning, required of Grand Army posts; hence Department Inspector Stanley's dismay at finding so many posts without one. But the funds were acquired by various means. Chippewa Falls Post 68 was perhaps typical in that its fund was raised through dues and muster fees, and it was then dispensed as needed. Need was not usually considered long-term. Post 68 voted a one-time stipend of $20 to the widow of Comrade John H. Brown, for instance, but declined, as unable to do so, her requests for further assistance.[23]

Berlin Post 4 raised money regularly through staging theatricals such as "The Color Guard" and "The Daily Union Spy" and other entertainments. Their aid might take a practical form as when it bought a sewing machine—Weed's Family Favorite—for Comrade Charlie Barnes's widow.[24]

Still, the post relief system, which served well enough while the great majority of veterans were generally healthy and able to care for themselves, broke down. More of the old soldiers found themselves in hard times now and then, exacerbated by economic slowdowns—the slump of 1887 would duplicate that of 1873—and local efforts could not adequately provide relief. When times became hard, Commander Davidson spoke of the changing times to the 1886 encampment: "Although the winters have silently frosted our hair and we might make poor time at 'double quick,' yet our hearts are young . . ."[25] The Department of Wisconsin had added 26 more posts under the Sparta leader, but the era of tremendous expansion gave way to one of steady but unspectacular growth. Department membership amounted to now just over 11,000 in 1885–86.

Commander Davidson had put on 14,000 miles traveling on behalf of the department, including a trip to New York to represent the state G.A.R. at the funeral of General Grant. His administration was also professional. And it was another year in which more of their former leaders no longer answered to roll call.

One who did answer at that encampment in Milwaukee in February of 1886 was Lucius Fairchild. He had found that his decade in diplomatic service abroad left his political base in Wisconsin a bit rusty.[26] So he turned to the place where his popularity still held a bright shine, and his comrades of the Grand Army of the Republic did not let him down. They elected him department commander.

21. Ibid., 39-41.
22. Ibid, 32.
23. Stuart McConnell, *Glorious Contentment, the Grand Army of the Republic, 1865–1900* (Chapel Hill: University of North Carolina Press, 1992), 127.
24. *Berlin Journal*, September 3, 1872.
25. *Proceedings of Twentieth Encampment*, 26.
26. Sam Ross, *The Empty Sleeve: A Biography of Lucius Fairchild*, (Madison: State Historical Society of Wisconsin, 1964), 201.

CHAPTER NINE

COMMANDER FAIRCHILD TAKES CENTER STAGE

The remarkable return to good health of the Department of Wisconsin during the decade of the 1880s must be understood within the context of the resurrection of the entire Grand Army of the Republic. This was the order's finest hour.

Those factors that allowed the handful of faithful to march with Griffith Thomas from the depths of despair in 1879 to the heights they attained in just a decade were the same factors that roused Union veterans around the country. Pride was a big factor. They had now enough years behind them that they could look back with a degree of perspective. They had kept the Union from being torn apart.

There would be no better way of recognizing Union soldiers, most G.A.R. men agreed, than to acknowledge the debt the country owed its saviors. This germ of an idea—that a debt was owed the veterans—rose in stages, from a belief that the soldier who suffered loss of limb or other injury, or his widow and orphans, had a reasonable claim on the government for support, to the contention that the country owed all its soldier-saviors a debt which could never be adequately repaid. The least the nation could do would be to provide every one of them a pension in recognition of that debt of gratitude.

The Pension Bill of 1862 allowed soldiers suffering permanent injury or disability from their service to collect a monthly amount based upon rank and upon the seriousness of the disability. The law required the claim to be filed within a year of discharge in order to be paid from the discharge date. Otherwise, it would be paid beginning with the date the claim was allowed. Widows and minor children of soldiers who died were eligible to receive support as well.[1]

The first major change in the federal policy came in 1879, with the passage of the Arrears Act. All claims established before July 1, 1880, would be paid from discharge rather than from the date the claim was approved. This brought a deluge of claims for back pay, or "arrears," and put hefty sums of money into the pockets of some veterans. Moreover, it opened the doors, and the eyes, of those veterans to the potential for more.

At the same time the Arrears Act eased the burden of proof needed to establish the service-relatedness of the claimed disability.[2] A flood of new claims ensued, some of which ranged from vague to outright fraudulent.

At any rate, the decade of the 1880s saw the emergence of the disability pension for Union veterans as a compelling political issue. The Grand Army of the Republic, which had only mildly lobbied for veteran pensions in its earliest days, picked up the matter—and rapidly gained members as it did so. By 1884, the order had tripled its membership since 1880.[3]

Throughout the 1880s the pension question, manifested in literally hundreds of forms, kept the G.A.R. busy and kept it out front as the primary organization dedicated to looking after veterans' interests. G.A.R. rhetoric underwent change during these years as well. Whereas the veterans of 1865 saw pensions being for the war-disabled, by the 1880s some believed that they had earned a pension simply for their service. Some were "disabled" by time, and were not they entitled to pensions? It was pension or the poorhouse for many aging veterans, and their numbers were growing year after year.

The Grand Army of the Republic moved skillfully and cautiously back into politics. The political party balance of the 1880s was extremely thin, and the G.A.R. had learned not to appear to be "Generally All Republican," although its natural propensity was in that direction.[4] It learned to play both parties to its advantage. The "soldier vote" could swing any election to either party depending on how the candidates were seen on the soldiers' overriding concern: pensions.

Into the midst of the pension ferment, a Wisconsinite came to the fore. The National Encampment of the Grand Army of the Republic in San Francisco in August of 1886, chose Lucius Fairchild as the new national commander.[5] Of the several dozen men who led the G.A.R. over the decades of its influence there were some who were talented, a number whose devotion to the

1. Stuart McConnell, *Glorious Contentment, the Grand Army of the Republic, 1865–1900,* (Chapel Hill: University of North Carolina Press, 1992), 143.
2. Ibid., 145–146.
3. Ibid., 148.
4. *Proceedings of the Nineteenth Annual Encampment of the Department of Wisconsin, Grand Army of the Republic,* (Baraboo, Wisc.: Republic Print, 1885), 25. In 1885, Wisconsin Department Commander Phil Cheek commented, "I am proud to say that in a heated political canvass [in which Democrat Grover Cleveland was elected president] that it did not meddle with or take part in politics, and I congratulate the Comrades . . . that they kept the fair name and fame of the G.A.R. above criticism and . . . stopped the cavil of those who willfully misrepresent the aims and object or our Order. . . ."
5. Sam Ross, *The Empty Sleeve: A Biography of Lucius Fairchild,* (Madison: State Historical Society of Wisconsin, 1964), 202–203.

order was extremely valuable, and some who were just natural leaders. But only two could be readily characterized as charismatic. One was John A. Logan. The other was Lucius Fairchild.

Both were adept politicians. Both had the ability to inspire "the boys" with their oratory and to set the Grand Army of the Republic on a course they deemed fitting and necessary. The former governor of Wisconsin, who left his arm at Gettysburg and made an empty sleeve a positive trademark, had great political ambition. But the Machiavellian nature of Wisconsin politics frustrated him, and he eventually focused attention on the issue of veterans' affairs. Fairchild headed the Wisconsin Commandery of the Military Order of the Loyal Legion from 1884 to 1886, and during this time he made the rounds of G.A.R. posts around the state. The ensuing notoriety paid off when he was elected Department of Wisconsin commander at the February 1886 encampment.[6]

LUCIUS FAIRCHILD

Fairchild immediately set out to position himself for higher office and deftly used his political acumen to become the favored candidate as national commander that August. His maneuvering ensured his victory. Within a month of rising to national commander, Fairchild made national headlines with his response to a natural disaster, an earthquake that did tremendous damage to Charleston, South Carolina. Let the men of the Grand Army contribute relief money for the suffering souls in that former secession bastion, urged Fairchild. Then he himself traveled to the scene of devastation and offered the hand of reunion and reconciliation to his former enemies. It was an interesting, if peculiar, triumph for the man so adept at waving the bloody shirt.

"I have [no bitter animosities] in my breast I know, and today if I should meet the soldier whose aim made this armless sleeve, I would grasp his hand by the only hand he left me and have no hard feelings toward him," he told members of the Palmetto Guard, who responded by making him an honorary member of that Confederate veterans' organization.[7]

Fairchild's right hand of reconciliation went just so far, however. And it did not extend very far at all in the direction of Democratic President Grover Cleveland. The president had a habit of vetoing private pension bills on the grounds that they were essentially unjustified raids on the treasury. President Cleveland considered such bills fraudulent attempts

to put money in the hands of self interested people. And it was Cleveland's bluntness—political ineptitude, as some called it—that rankled so many of the pension-oriented men of the Grand Army.

The private pension bills were one thing, but the president then vetoed the pending Dependent Pension Bill, a bill that would have enlarged the concept of who should receive a pension. It would allow pensions for those veterans who were disabled for reasons other than their military service. Anything that might make a veteran unable to support himself and therefore "dependent" upon society for sustenance would be considered a pensionable disability.[8]

The G.A.R. lobbied hard for the Dependent Pension Bill. Fairchild recommended that local posts let the president know of their support for the bill. But he disavowed that request when he realized that to involve local G.A.R. posts in national lobbying would dilute the power of the national organization in Washington. Fairchild and the order—on a national level—contented themselves with making it clear that the G.A.R. supported the bill.

Fairchild pulled no punches when the president signed a rather innocuous order. Fairchild was attending a meeting of a local post in New York City on the night of June 15, 1887, when the post commander read a report of Cleveland's directive. It instructed the secretary of war to return all captured Confederate battle flags in his care to the southern

GROVER CLEVELAND

states where they originated. The comrades were outraged and called for their distinguished guest to respond. Commander Fairchild expressed his outrage in clear and unmistakable terms.

"May God palsy the hand that wrote that order! May God palsy the brain that conceived it! May God palsy the tongue that dictated it!"[9]

Fairchild fairly shouted the anathemas. He went on to elaborate on what he called a "sacrilege" in giving up the trophies of war bought with Union boys' blood. His audience went wild. He had struck a deep-felt vein of emotion. Captured flags were scarcely less symbolic of the cause than the flags under which they fought.

The national uproar that followed Fairchild's reaction was a surprise and something of an embarrassment to the G.A.R. "Fairchild of the three palsies" was a sobriquet that followed him to the grave. But it was also an immediate embarrassment to President Cleveland, and he quickly withdrew the flag order.

For the rest of his term as national commander (about three months), Fairchild continued his active leadership of the order, but he shied away from any new political confrontations, going so far as to avoiding a meeting with Cleveland at the next

6. Ibid., 202.

7. Ibid., 204.

8. McConnell, *Glorious Contentment*, 150–151.

9. Ross, *The Empty Sleeve*, 206–209. Ross gives a stimulating account of the "palsy" speech and its aftermath.

encampment at St. Louis. Cleveland withdrew his acceptance of an invitation to attend.

Although Lucius Fairchild's tenure as national commander featured a certain flamboyance not always associated with the national leadership, it was a factor in the period of growth for the Grand Army of the Republic, which had forged itself into a

JAMES TANNER

powerful and ongoing force for veterans' interests. When the one-armed Madisonian left office in 1887, membership topped 355,000.

During the next few years, until the National Encampment in Milwaukee in August of 1889 and then in Boston in 1890, the numbers continued upward. Some consider the Milwaukee meeting to have been the highest point in Grand Army history. It certainly was the finest hour for the Department of Wisconsin in staging that record-breaking event. It came right at the time the political might of the order was flourishing. When Benjamin Harrison defeated Grover Cleveland for the presidency, and he appointed the Grand Army's Apostle of Pensions, "Corporal"

James Tanner, as the new pension commissioner.

Tanner lost both legs in the war. He became a tireless champion of pensions for veterans and rose to high counsels within the G.A.R. on the strength of his pension campaigning.[10] The encampments included many generals, but the corporal commanded greater attention at Milwaukee than all of them except William T. Sherman. At the Plankenton House, where Tanner was staying, "there is a crowd of veterans anxious to get sight of the pension dispenser," reported one newspaper even before the encampment opened.[11]

The pension issue now revolved around whether to pension veterans on the basis of some disability however acquired, or to have a "service pension" given to every Union veteran who reached age 62. The G.A.R. in 1888 favored the service pension, and the order reaffirmed this in Milwaukee in 1889. In 1890, Congress enacted a new Dependent Pension Bill, but in practice, especially with Corporal Tanner doing the interpreting, every veteran was considered "dependent" based simply upon age.[12]

The Pension Act of 1890 became the largest social benefit program in American history until the New Deal. Hundreds of millions of dollars passed into the hands of Union veterans.

10. McConnell, *Glorious Contentment*, 37.
11. *Oshkosh Northwestern*, August 27, 1889.
12. Ibid., 2, 3.

CHAPTER TEN

GEMÜTLICHKEIT
AND THE G.A.R.

When the Twenty-third National Encampment of the Grand Army of the Republic took over the City of Milwaukee on August 28, 29, and 30, 1889, everything that could make it a memorable event was in place. The G.A.R.'s influence stood at its peak. Membership had con-

tinued to grow; the campaign for pensions was attracting more and more old soldiers, and the order's voice in Washington had never been stronger. Throughout the country the activities of local G.A.R. posts and state encampments brought attention from the press and an avid following among the public. The National Encampment amplified all of this.

Milwaukee was primed for its role as 1889 host to the veterans. The city had successfully welcomed the great reunion of Wisconsin veterans in 1880. It planned to outdo that smashing success for veterans from around the nation.

The Tuesday-morning opening session reflected the G.A.R.'s status as an organization enjoying great success. Commander-in-Chief William Warner's address, the traditional encampment-opening report of the order's leader on his year's stewardship, was unabashed: "The Grand Army of the Republic is the grandest civic organization the world has ever seen—its list of membership is the nation's roll of honor, containing the most illustrious names in history, the names of the

brave men who, in the darkest days of the rebellion, followed the Stars and Stripes . . . as the emblem of an indissoluble union of indestructible states."[1]

Warner noted that "enrolled under the banner of Fraternity, Charity and Loyalty," the G.A.R. had 410,686 members in 6,711 Posts and 42 Departments.[2] Only this month, "we scaled the walls of Fort Sumter, there organized a Grand Army Post and installed the officers on the ramparts of that historic fort."[3]

Trainload after trainload of veterans from all parts of the country had arrived earlier, and the auxiliary organizations, the Women's Relief Corps and the Sons of Veterans, began their own activities on Monday, August 26, 1889. The latter staged an evening campfire with Commander Warner attending.

The public highlight of an encampment is the parade staged at midday of the first day. The Milwaukee march drew crowds of more than one hundred thousand people. The parade included almost a third of the nation's Grand Army men marching as of yore to the military airs they had known a quarter century before.

As was traditional, the host department marched last, and the proud Wisconsin contingent was massive. Approximately seven thousand members of state G.A.R. posts had come to Milwaukee, about half the total of members enrolled. The parade started about an hour late, and by the time the Wisconsin veterans were to move out, a fair contingent of the host-department comrades, made weary by the heat, decided to mingle with the crowds rather than to march.

The Wisconsin delegation was the largest by far, and it took, from first Wisconsin man to last, almost an hour and fifteen minutes for the state attendees to pass. C. C. Washburn Post 11 of Madison was the lead contingent, based on its charter date,[4] with Lucius Fairchild in the fore, "his armless sleeve neatly pinned to the breast of his coat, his step as light and elastic as it was a quarter century ago, and his eye brightening at the cheers which his well-known form and features elicited along the line of march."[5] In all, veterans from 130 Wisconsin posts marched, and a number of the posts brought along bands. The Milwaukee Juvenile Band accompanied Post 2, Milwaukee. Post 10, Oshkosh, brought the town's finest band, the Arions, and Post 241, Oshkosh, not to be outdone, also brought a band. Woolcott Post 1 had the Fourth Infantry Band. And another

1. *Journal of the Twenty-third Annual Session of the National Encampment* (St. Louis: A. Wipple, 1889), 33.

2. Ibid., 33–36. The figure includes a considerable number of suspended comrades. Those "in good standing" at this time numbered 382,598.

3. *Journal of the Twenty-third Annual Session of the National Encampment, Grand Army of the Republic, August 28, 29, 30, 1889, Milwaukee,* (St. Louis, Missouri: Wipple, 1889), 35.

4. Perhaps it was according the Madison post this primacy which ranked Post 4 of Berlin, for it was in the years following the 1889 parade that the issue of which post was oldest—Madison, Oshkosh, or Berlin—was contested before Department of Wisconsin councils until the issue was resolved in Berlin's favor.

5. *Milwaukee Sentinel,* August 28, 1889.

Milwaukee post, from the Soldier's Home, brought a 17-piece band. The Waupaca post was accompanied by the Veterans Home band. The posts at Baraboo and Ashland brought drum corps, as did the Sparta and Janesville posts. Other bands represented the Racine, Waukesha, La Crosse, Fond du Lac, and Stoughton Posts. Wisconsin's men marched proudly and in step to some pretty fine music.

"Well, boys, we ain't so young as we were once, and marching don't come so easy as it did in the '60s, but we stuck it out; yes, sir, we stuck it out, anyhow, for we may never march together again." So said one of the gray-bearded Badgers as his unit disbanded at the end of the march. "He and his comrades skipped around the corner for a glass of ginger ale with alacrity if not agility," a *Milwaukee Sentinel* reporter who watched at the finish observed.[6]

There were plenty of dignitaries in Milwaukee that week. Clara Barton, president of the Red Cross and a national figure since her Civil War nursing experience, stood out. Military names of the past were legion on the streets of Milwaukee and in the reviewing stand for the parade.

None, however, caused quite the commotion stirred up by the appearance of William Tecumseh Sherman. The old soldier, more irascible than ever, arrived the day before the proceedings, via the Chicago & Northwestern, and was met by a delegation of

WILLIAM T. SHERMAN

comrades at the depot. The head of the delegation, an old navy captain, went aboard the train to introduce himself and tell the general that an escort was waiting on the platform. "All right," said the worn-out traveler, "I don't care who walks along as long as I get to the hotel."[7]

At the hotel, and just about everywhere the old commander of the West went in Milwaukee, people clamored around him wanting to shake his hand. After the parade as he left the reviewing stand, a woman—"she weighed a ton and had the grip of a grizzly," the *Sentinel* reporter explained[8]—rushed up, grabbed his hand and started pumping. "I tell you I won't shake hands, and when I say I won't, I won't," he exclaimed angrily and shoved his hands in his pockets.

Nonetheless, Sherman later went to the National Soldier's Home and spent considerable time bantering with the old soldiers living there, evidently enjoying the experience. He may have been short of patience with the dignitaries who necessarily surrounded him at an event such as the encampment, but with the old soldiers whose affection for him began on memorable marches through Georgia and other points South, he was the "Uncle Billy" they remembered. And he relished it.[9]

In the West Side Turner Hall precincts following the parade, the business of the Twenty-third National Encampment resumed in evening session, and the speculation of two days on the streets was confirmed when the comrades elected Russell A. Alger of Michigan to be the next commander in chief.[10]

Following adjournment that night, the hall became the scene of a campfire, presided over by Augie Weissert. Weissert, a one-time soldier in the Eighth Wisconsin, the famed Eagle Regiment, and now commander of the Department of Wisconsin, had just been elected senior vice commander in chief. Governor William D. Hoard welcomed the campfire attendees.

Outside those precincts, the night was also a busy one, with many of the bands that marched in the parade continuing the celebration on the streets with impromptu concerts. Some encampment attendees availed themselves of the opportunity Milwaukee visitors have often seized; they visited a brewery. The Pabst establishment was popular, according to one press account. There the firm was "giving away canes, little bottles of beer and books describing the encampment." The reporter was informed that 50,000 canes had been given out the first day of the encampment. Small wonder that "the general feeling among the veterans from all the states is that the encampment has been a grand success."[11]

6. Ibid.
7. Ibid.
8. *Milwaukee Sentinel*, August 29, 1889.
9. Ibid.
10. *Journal of the Twenty-third*, 137.
11. *Milwaukee Sentinel*, August 31, 1889.

One New York delegate said he had never enjoyed an encampment as much. "Why, I never saw such hospitable people in my life."[12]

Other encampment business proceedings went on in Turner Hall. Among the more than a dozen resolutions submitted by the various departments for national consideration was one from the Department of Wisconsin asking that the federal government "mark the battle lines of the Army of Northern Virginia in some plain, substantial manner (at Gettysburg) and thus show to the world that our brave boys met and repulsed a 'foe worthy of their steel.'"[13] Although the battlefield now had plenty of monuments, "not one rod of the twenty-three miles of (the Confederate) battle-lines has been marked."[14] The resolution was offered by Lucius Fairchild, whose military career had climaxed on that battlefield. The encampment adopted the resolution.[15]

Incoming Commander Alger admonished the comrades that while they were in Milwaukee to have a good time, they also were present for serious business. "We have questions that are coming before us every year, and that will increase in importance with the years perhaps, and we feel the responsibility for the care of our comrades who cannot care for themselves; and as you are here to formulate demands upon the Government for our comrades, it must be done wisely; consider well what we do; but when we have resolved what we will do, let us have no division, but stand together."[16]

The pension issue, in other words, was still a controversial one. While the usual conception of the Grand Army of the Republic is of an organization seemingly united in support of pensions for all, in reality, a significant minority of the comrades still held to the old belief that pensions were for the disabled and that the able-bodied should take care of themselves as they always had.[17] The issue now revolved around dependent pensions versus service pensions. Whichever gained the encampment's endorsement, Alger pleaded, let the G.A.R. back that action unequivocally.

The encampment resolved, as it had the year before, to ask for a pension based on service. After Tuesday's huge parade, Milwaukeeans and their thousands of guests eagerly awaited the climactic event of the entire week, a mock naval engagement.

"It was a gallant fight, and right gallantly did the local militiamen repulse an attempt . . . by a hostile fleet to bombard the city, land a force of marines in small boats and sack the town." A *Sentinel* reporter observed, "a magnificent sight and 300,000 men, women and children witnessed it" including all the old soldiers seated in a specially constructed amphitheater, their admissions all paid for by Captain Fred Pabst at a dollar a vet.[18]

The multitudes came early and watched as the boats sat at anchor, and as the batteries and militia companies formed on shore and moved into position. The old soldiers amused themselves by singing familiar songs—"'Marching Through Georgia' seemed to be the favorite," said the newspaper—while they waited for the "battle" to begin.

Four minutes after 7:30 p.m., the fight began with a trio of United States boats, playing the attacking force, "approaching" the shoreline, and "for half an hour there was an incessant roar of artillery, screaming and hissing of shells and bursting of rockets high in the air." One vet was taken up in the excitement. "Lay down, lay down," he yelled as he ducked his head until the laughter of the others reminded him that "this was but a paper shell and not one of those deadly missiles that so often hurtled through the air and make cripples or corpses of the men around him."[19]

Those "paper shells" continued to arch through the air for 30 minutes, the artillery on shore replying to the firing from the boats out in the harbor. Then the firing of the fleet slacked and the "marine" force presumably put out into the darkness in small boats heading for shore. No such force in fact headed in, but the mock battle included lines of infantrymen, seven companies of foot soldiers, laying down a deafening fire of 50,000 blank cartridges.

With the amphibious force driven off, the defending artillery resumed its barrage, and the brigantine *Holley* burned to the waterline, a seeming victim of the artillery. A short while later (after the incendiary boat had relocated for its second part in the script), the gunboat *Dexter* lit up the water. And here the flames reached the "magazine" and blew the boat to pieces in a huge fireball.

"The battle was over and the victory was Milwaukee's" gloated the reporter.[20] Bands began to play, and pyrotechnics continued the celebration. Two thousand men had played their roles. The cost of the battle was put at $10,000. The burning of the *Holley* alone cost $800.

The Twenty-third National Encampment thus ended.[21]

12. *Oshkosh Northwestern*, August 30, 1889.

13. *Proceedings of the Twenty-third Annual Encampment of the Department of Wisconsin, Grand Army of the Republic*, (Milwaukee, Wisc.: Ed. Keogh, 1889), 169.

14. Ibid.

15. *Journal*, 169.

16. Ibid., 139

17. Stuart McConnell, *Glorious Contentment, the Grand Army of the Republic, 1865–1900*, (Chapel Hill: University of North Carolina Press, 1992), 154.

18. *Milwaukee Sentinel*, August 31, 1889.

19. Ibid.

20. Ibid.

21. Milwaukee would host two more national encampments. In 1923, with membership down to just over 65,000, the G.A.R. held its 57th gathering in Cream City and it was a far cry from the 1889 affair. Frank A. Walsh of Wisconsin was elected senior vice commander that year, following a tradition of giving that office to a member of the host department. In 1926 Walsh was chosen as the third commander in chief from Wisconsin, and this was not a part of any traditional progression through offices to the top; the G.A.R. had no such tradition. In 1943, with the G.A.R. now down to under four hundred members, the order returned to Milwaukee. Again in accordance with tradition, the senior vice commander for that year was from Wisconsin: Lansing A. Wilcox who would become the state's last surviving Civil War veteran. Also attending that Milwaukee convention was Albert T. Woolson of Duluth, Minnesota, who would be the final living member of the Grand Army of the Republic.

CHAPTER ELEVEN

THE TEXTBOOK WARS

Senior Vice Commander Henry P. Fischer of Milwaukee inherited from Lucius Fairchild a Department of Wisconsin that was strong, healthy, and growing—almost in spite of itself. The 1887 encampment, in fact, ratified an order to stop chartering additional posts in the belief that existing ones were widespread enough to accommodate any new members. This followed Assistant Adjutant General Phil Cheek's final report in an executive capacity noting that the department had added 14 new posts and that total membership topped ten thousand.

Cheek also reported the department's response to National Commander Fairchild's plea for donations for victims of the Charleston, South Carolina, earthquake. The total taken in was $1,054.06, with posts contributing anywhere from a dollar, by several, to $460.63 by Madison's Post 11.[1]

The shortsightedness of the nonproliferation order was soon apparent to the department commander selected by the 1887 encampment, Michael Griffin of Eau Claire. It was, he said, "an embarrassment from the very outset."[2] He interpreted the order as an admonishment to use care in chartering, but he argued that the commander could not be deprived of the power to charter. He prudently exercised the power 14 times in his term.

Two of the largest achievements of the Department of Wisconsin in this latter half of the decade came under Griffin. The enduring one established a veterans' home under G.A.R. auspices near Waupaca in 1887. A second, and profoundly emotional, achievement with far-reaching consequences was an inquiry into the quality of the teaching of history in the nation's schools. It began quietly enough. In an evening session of the 1887 encampment in Milwaukee, in the midst of a flurry of resolutions on pensions, widows, poorhouses, the pension medical boards, and the deficiencies of the National Soldier's Home in Milwaukee, Comrade Phil Cheek offered a resolution on behalf of Post 14 of Portage.

Post 14 members, it said, had studied Barnes' *History of the United States*, a textbook used in Portage public schools, and "It is the opinion of this Department Encampment that said history (so far as it relates to the late Rebellion) is unreliable, and was written more with the purpose of finding a market for it in that portion of our country lately in rebellion against the Government, than with the purpose of recording the facts of history."[3] Comrade John Hancock of Madison moved that a

committee of three be appointed to study the matter and report to the next encampment.

The group came back to the encampment the following year with a report about school history books that horrified department leaders. Hancock's committee observed:

[We] find that they all alike signally fail to comprehend the cause that resulted in the war of the rebellion; [we] conclude that the histories at the present time used in our common school system were compiled for the purpose of a national system of education, South as well as North, and in doing this the efforts to be impartial and non-sectional, have in many instances gone beyond the bounds of reason; that that possibly might be overlooked if the Southern section of our country would accept them, or embody their substance in the histories compiled, published and there used; when in our histories every latitude is given to the South, even to the extent that a student after finishing the study is unable to comprehend the differences between the two sections that resulted in the war, and unable to comprehend which was right and which was wrong, indeed to comprehend that even there was a right or wrong side to that struggle for the preservation of the Union; after going to that extreme, evidently to secure their adoption and use in the South, and avoid the charges of being partisan or sectional, still they are spurned and refused a recognition there except to a limited extent.[4]

Northern history texts seemed inadequate, the committee believed. But when they looked at some southern texts, they made the northern texts pale by comparison "to what is deemed of so much importance . . . [that we] ask that it be recognized and given that consideration which the importance and magnitude of the subject demands."[5] The committee believed the southern textbooks revealed a lopsided view of history.

1. *Proceedings of the Twenty-first Annual Encampment of the Department of Wisconsin* (Baraboo, Wisc.: Republic Print, 1887), 41.
2. *Proceedings of the Twenty-second Annual Encampment of the Department of Wisconsin* (Eau Claire, Wisc.: Daily Free Press Print., 1888), 27.
3. *Proceedings of the Twenty-first Annual Encampment*, 85.
4. *Proceedings of the Twenty-second Annual Encampment of the Department of Wisconsin* (Eau Claire, WI: Daily Free Press, 1888), 58.
5. Ibid.

For example, the committee noted that *Davidson's School History of South Carolina* (1869) stated that "The cause of secession, which was the cause of the war, was very much the same thing that caused Nullification in 1832; Congress kept passing laws which it had no right to pass according to the Constitution."

The committee reported that textbook went on to state that "on the 20th of December, 1860, the ordinance of secession was passed. By this act South Carolina ceased to be a State in the Union, and became again a separate and sovereign State, as she was before the ratifying of the Constitution seventy-two years previous."[6]

The committee presented a sample of another text, J. S. Blackburn and W. N. McDonald's *Southern History*, 12th Edition, it said of secession, "In justification of this measure it was alleged that the property, lives, and liberty of the citizens were threatened by the aggressive aspect of the incoming administration."

The committee noted that the same book told how "to fill her armies the North had a better and more successful mode; she offered immense bounties and high pay; induced by these, thousands of European mercenaries enlisted; the South had nothing but her gallant Children to put in the field, and thus she was condemned to stake her most precious jewels against the trash of Europe."[7]

The committee specifically condemned Alexander Stephens, late vice president of the Confederacy and an unabashed apologist for its cause (he coined the euphemism "War Between the States"), who penned a text for use in southern schools to "indoctrinate them with this monstrous heresy" of states rights, "i.e., placing the sovereignty of the state above the Union."[8]

ALEXANDER STEPHENS

Committeemen Hancock, A. O. Wright of New Lisbon, and H. C. Curtis of Hartford averred in their report: "These Southern histories don't fail to make known their side of this question. They are full of it. No disguise on their part that what we deem Treason is there made respectable; while our histories on the same subject are comparatively silent, indeed are so lamentably deficient upon this question that it were far better to discard all history of our country during the epoch of 1860–65 than to admit them to our schools as now compiled."[9]

In a long and forceful conclusion the committee urged that a "broad, comprehensive, constitutional, Union loving patriotism should be taught in the schools; we have had one epoch of supineness and apathy upon this question, and the result was that Wisconsin had to send 90,000 of her best citizens to the field, of whom 12,000 never returned."

Then came a strong statement considered shocking to some of the old soldiers. The committee called upon "the ex-soldiers of the Confederacy, whose bravery on many a well fought field we can amply attest, that having honestly surrendered as they did and professing to love the Union as they now do, they use their influence against the doctrine of States Rights which was the chief cause of our sad fraternal strife, and which if continued to be taught may again be the cause of another Civil War."[10]

Shouts and calls of approval rang from the floor for the committee's views. "The report," said the minutes, "was unanimously adopted by a rising vote."

Chairman Hancock did not want it to rest there. He moved to send a copy of the committee's report to department headquarters around the country. Further, Hancock requested that a committee be appointed "to see to it that the said report is brought properly to the attention of the National Encampment . . ." And finally that copies be sent to teachers' associations around the country. Department Commander Griffin selected a high-powered committee to develop national support for the Wisconsin Department's position on the teaching of history: Lucius Fairchild, Phil Cheek, E. B. Gray of Milwaukee, E. A. Shores of Ashland, and John Meehan of Darlington.[11]

Former National Commander Fairchild and the committee presented their proposals for history textbook reform it to the next National Encampment, in Columbus, Ohio, in September of 1888.[12] The conclave endorsed the report from the Department of Wisconsin, and it became a G.A.R. cause, assuming national prominence in ensuing years.

In 1891 the order appointed a "Committee on a Systematic Plan of Teaching the Lessons of Loyalty to Our County and One Flag."[13] That group reported the next year—the year that Wisconsinite Augie Weissert was elected national commander—in terms a little less strident than the Wisconsin report put it, that there was need for "correction" of many of the history textbooks in use. The committee's report said such books tended to "omit, gloss over, and even to misinterpret the history of the war."[14]

Here was an issue that went to the heart of the order. What was loyalty if not to stand guard lest the fruits of the veterans' sacrifices be forgotten in the cause of giving offense to no one? And worse, that it might be lost by standing idle while one's late enemy reasserts the very principles for which it fought and lost nearly a quarter century before. If new generations would not

6. Ibid., 59.

7. Ibid., 60.

8. Ibid., 61.

9. Ibid., 63.

10. Ibid., 64.

11. Ibid., 65.

12. Robert B. Beath, *History of the Grand Army of the Republic*, (New York: Bryan, Taylor & Co., 1889), 371.

13. Stuart McConnell, *Glorious Contentment, the Grand Army of the Republic, 1865–1900* (Chapel Hill: University of North Carolina Press, 1992), 225.

14. *Journal of the Twenty-Sixth National Encampment, Grand Army of the Republic*, Washington D.C., September 21 & 22, (Albany, New York: S. H. Wentworth, 1892), 81.

learn the true causes that the veterans fought for, the fighting and losses would have been in vain.

The history textbook controversy spawned in Portage brought an enlarged emphasis on the Loyalty part of the G.A.R. triad. Thereafter, Loyalty evoked a real sense of mission in the minds of G.A.R. activists. Even after the furor diminished, the Grand Army of the Republic placed more attention on membership patriotism as part of its mission. During the G.A.R.'s later years, when membership numbers were shrink-ing, the inculcation of patriotism—the values and the motives that had sent them off to war—helped the understanding of new generations.

Posts in the 1890s put great emphasis on nationalism. America was changing in the new decade, and in many ways it was leaving the Civil War veteran behind. The nation's role on the world stage was unfamiliar to the Boys in Blue. But they understood patriotism, and they supported their government with expressions of loyalty.

CHAPTER TWELVE

CHARITY IS A HOME AT KING

Fraternity, Charity, Loyalty were the guiding principles of the Grand Army of the Republic from its inception But the latter two were emphasized differently by the order over time. Loyalty in the late 1880s took on the times' sensitive slant reflecting a need to instill the G.A.R.'s sense of patriotism to generations that knew not the tumult and the triumphs of the Civil War era. Charity likewise evolved into something large-scale after the young men of '65 began assisting comrades who suffered reverses.

While a post relief fund was a requirement for many years, the mandate was dropped in 1888, presumably because the need for relief seemed to be outstripping the ability of posts to maintain the funds.[1] It was clear that there was no diminution of the need. In fact, by this time and for some years afterward, discussion of the pension issue was predicated upon how to help the needy veteran, the one who was disabled by his service, and eventually, the one who was disabled, period.

The Grand Army's sense of charity reflected a desire to help the needy among the men who shared the burdens of battle. However, it was not focused exclusively upon convincing the government to provide pensions for them. During the 1880s, the order also focused on inaugurating soldiers' homes as its rolls began to expand. New York opened the first such home in 1879, followed by soldiers' homes in Massachusetts (1881), Vermont (1884), Illinois (1885), and Rhode Island and Pennsylvania (1886).[2]

During the 1880s, the Department of Wisconsin was unhappy with the National Soldiers' Home operated by the federal government in Milwaukee. "The present National Home for Disabled Volunteer Soldiers at Milwaukee being inadequate, for want of room, to accommodate all of our brave, unfortunate companions in arms who are knocking for admission. . . , something should and must be done to provide homes for our suffering, homeless Comrades," declared Commander Henry Fischer at the 1887 encampment. "I would also call your attention to the ad-

visability of calling upon the state to make provisions for a Veterans Home, thereby following the noble example of Illinois, Michigan, Iowa and other states."[3]

The encampment responded with a resolution to establish a home under G.A.R. auspices, with a committee being named to oversee the effort, headed by Dr. Frederick A. Marden of Milwaukee. Serving with him were Albert O. Wright of New Lisbon, Benjamin F. Bryant of La Crosse, James Cumberledge of Manitowoc, and Joseph H. Marston of Appleton. The five constituted the incorporators of the home.

F.A. MARDEN

Dr. Marden was the primary planner for the home, and he was a visionary. Up until this time, federal homes and state homes were established for ex-soldiers. But Marden believed that the Wisconsin home should accept not just old soldiers, but admit wives and widows of veterans as well, an unprecedented concept. Moreover, thought Marden, the home should be composed of cottages so as to accommodate the husbands and wives in a setting that did not disrupt the family structure. (The cottage concept had the added advantage of putting such buildings within the fiscal capabilities of individual posts to sponsor. It had much more appeal than having just one, big fund drive for a single, large institution.)

The committee of five had authority to proceed with raising funds, finding a suitable location, and receiving gifts of land or other contributions, and they proceeded rapidly with their project.

They also lobbied the legislature to pass a bill for a state subsidy for needy veterans at the home at $3 per week, and the legislation was enacted.

The G.A.R. was at the height of its prestige, and communities around the state vied to be the site of the institution. The committee narrowed the field to six towns: Waupaca, Sheboygan, Watertown, Evansville, Berlin, and New Lisbon. The five committee members visited each in that order. Waupaca received the honor, and, seeing the idyllic location today, it is not difficult to understand why. The home sat on 78 acres beside a scenic lake. In addition, a hotel stood on the site, as did several cottages. The City of Waupaca and town residents provided additional financial incentives. Waupaca it would be.[4]

Because the site already had buildings quite usable for the purposes envisioned, preparations went relatively quickly. One

1. Stuart McConnell, *Glorious Contentment, the Grand Army of the Republic, 1865–1900*, (Chapel Hill: University of North Carolina Press, 1992), 127.

2. Ibid., 143.

3. *Proceedings of the Twenty-first Annual Encampment of the Department of Wisconsin*, (Baraboo, Wisc.: Republic Print, 1887), 34.

4. Richard H. Zeitlin, "The Debt of Gratitude: The Wisconsin G.A.R.", in *Veterans Affairs in Wisconsin; King Centennial Issue*, (Madison, Wisc.: Wisconsin Department of Veterans Affairs, 1987), 5-6.

setback was the untimely death of the originator of the bold concept for the home, Dr. Marden, on September 24, 1887. Still, just a week later on October 1, 1887, the incorporators took possession of the property and admitted their first "inmates" at once.[5] By the first of the next year they had 10 residents—five men and five women.

That the incorporators were farseeing men may be concluded from the fact that when the deed for the property was first drawn, a deed that stipulated that if ever the property ceased to be a home for veterans of the Civil War, then it would revert to the City of Waupaca. The committee insisted on a change.

"In the course of nature," they told the 1888 encampment, "it must eventually cease to be used for a home for the veterans of the Civil War," so the deed, at their insistence, was amended so that the property would revert to the city only if it ceased to be used for some charitable purpose. "We believe that when the Grand Army of the Republic passes away, it will be easy to find some charitable purpose for which this property can be used, and that the state or some body of persons can be found ready to use it for such purposes."[6]

The Grand Army Home for Veterans at Waupaca was dedicated on August 29, 1888. Delegations arrived for the

COTTAGE AT KING

dedication in the days leading up to the event, and the visitors set up camp on the grounds, turning the property into a fair semblance of an encampment.

"They pitched their tents among the trees, along the banks of the lake until on dedication day there was a city of canvas," wrote Hosea W. Rood years later.[7] "Estimates placed the number of people . . . at fully six thousand. Most of the people carried dinner baskets and so made a great picnic of the occasion. The old comrades held in the forenoon an impromptu Campfire."

As head of the committee of incorporators, Joseph Marston presided over the dedication. The officials were especially proud that theirs was the first such home in the United States open to wives and widows, and they gave credit for the concept to the late Dr. Marden.

The Grand Army's home received generous support from the taxpayers of Wisconsin. It could not have been so had not the G.A.R. been willing to use the power of its sizeable membership to promote its agenda to the politicians in Madison. By this time, many of the politicians in Madison were veterans themselves, something that had not always been true after the war. In the dark days of the G.A.R. around 1877, not one of the six state constitutional officers was a veteran. Ten years later, when the Wisconsin Department was flexing its political muscle and was seeking financial support for the new home outside Waupaca, all but the

lieutenant-governor were veterans.[8]

In 1889 the legislature appropriated a handsome sum, $50,000, to use for permanent improvements for the home, on such things as a waterworks, a sewage-disposal system, fire protection, and a steam heating system. With its cottage concept, the home became a little community.[9]

In exchange for the financial support, the state wanted to hold the deed to the property. The department acceded to this provided that the Grand Army of the Republic could continue to have control over the operation. For the next 30 years, the G.A.R. operated the home, and incorporated some of the order's quasi-military forms at the institution. The superintendent, for instance, was titled "Commandant," a designation that continues to the present.

"Boys in Blue" muster on parade ground at Veterans Home, 1903.

It was not the state alone that had an eye on how veterans were cared for in such institutions. The federal government, too, kept watch. In 1917, Washington declared its opposition to the duality of the operation at the home, that is, to the state's ownership and the Grand Army's governance. So the G.A.R. bowed out—on paper—and the State of Wisconsin took official control of the operation of the home.[10]

In point of fact, however, the Department of Wisconsin kept effective control; all of the members of the Board of Managers were appointed from the ranks of the G.A.R. It was not until 1920, when Comrade Jerome A. Watrous (one of the prime promoters of that famous 1880 soldiers' and sailors' reunion in Milwaukee as editor of the *Milwaukee Sunday Telegraph*) retired as commandant on his eightieth birthday, that a non–Civil War

5. *Proceedings of the Twenty-second Annual Encampment of the Department of Wisconsin*, (Eau Claire, WI: Daily Free Press, 1888), 68.

6. *Proceedings of the Twenty-third Annual Encampment of the Department of Wisconsin, Grand Army of the Republic*, (Milwaukee, Wisc.: Ed. Keogh, 1889), 93–94.

7. Cliff Borden: "The Early Years", *Veterans Affairs in Wisconsin, King Centennial Issue*, (Madison, Wisc.: n.p., 1987), 8, quoting *Hosea W. Rood, History of Wisconsin Veterans' Home, 1886–1926*, (Madison, Wisc.: Democrat Printing, 1926), 27.

8. Robert C. Nesbit, *History of Wisconsin*, ed. by William Fletcher Thompson, (Madison, Wisc.: State Historical Society of Wisconsin, 1985), 543–544.

9. Borden, "The Early Years," 9.

10. Ibid., 9–10.

veteran was put in charge. Not until 1929, however, when the legislature decreed that the Home at Waupaca be under control of the state adjutant general, was the umbilical to the Grand Army of the Republic finally severed.[11]

By this time the political clout of the Department of Wisconsin had long been consigned to happy memory. Total department membership in 1929 diminished to under one thousand for the first time since Griff Thomas's era of resuscitation 48 years earlier.

In addition, the home's origin as a progeny of the City of Waupaca had evolved; there was now a "community" in the environs of the home quite apart from Waupaca, with employees' homes and shops outside the grounds of the facility itself. It had become a village, although unincorporated.

In 1941, the unincorporated, unnamed village acquired the name of "King," and by extension, the home would be popularly identified by the same name.[12] Prior to 1941, its postal designation was "Wisconsin Veterans Home."

"We believe that when the Grand Army of the Republic passes away," the incorporators of 1887 had prophesized, "it will be easy to find some charitable purpose for which this property can be used. . . ." And it came to pass.

The state decided in 1923 that the home would be opened to veterans of the Spanish-American War, the Philippine Insurrection, and of the China Relief Expedition. It was just shy of a quarter century after most of those veterans had served their country. These veterans were now beginning to show their age as their predecessors, the Civil War veterans, had when they had lived a quarter century beyond the time of serving their country.

Thanks to the men of the G.A.R, there already existed a home where aging veterans who had answered the country's call could be provided for in their declining years. Over the succeeding decades, the legacy of the G.A.R. would be there to serve the men and women who had responded to the call of their nation in the twentieth century.

11. Ibid., 11.

12. The name of "King" honors a Wisconsin soldier who had the unique distinction of serving in five wars: the Civil War, the Indian Wars, the Spanish-American War, the Philippine Insurrection, and World War I. He was Brigadier General Charles King. Richard Zeitlin provides a biographical sketch of King in "Charles King," *Veterans Affairs in Wisconsin, King Centennial Issue*, (Madison, Wisc.: Wisconsin Department of Veterans Affairs, 1987), 31-32. Charles King was the son of Rufus King, first commander of what became the Iron Brigade. The younger King became the architect of the Wisconsin National Guard and was on active duty until 1922, having a total of 70 years of active military service, longer than any American soldier.

CHAPTER THIRTEEN

BEGINNING TO SHOW ITS AGE

As the decade of the 1890s began, the typical Union veteran was well over halfway to the biblical three score years and ten. And in terms more worldly, he was approaching the point at which his age would be topping the life-expectancy tables of the time.[1] As the veterans aged, their concerns reflected a changed lifestyle. This became particularly evident as the veterans gathered for their encampments.

The Milwaukee National Encampment in August of 1889 had been a high point for the Grand Army of the Republic's Department of Wisconsin, and in some respects, for the G.A.R. itself. The G.A.R. had taken the department commander, Augie Weissert, from the Department of Wisconsin and when he was installed as national senior vice commander; Leander Ferguson of Milwaukee was elevated to the top of the department.

Ferguson reported to the 1890 state encampment at Milwaukee that the department was making good progress, boosted by hosting the national meeting the year before. However, the membership totals were not higher than the number in good standing the year before, although the department did charter 20 new posts.

Ferguson made special mention of Post 261, mustered on August 16, 1889, at Keshena by Assistant Adjutant General E. B. Gray of Elkhorn. The post's members, said the commander, were all Indians. "The only one of its kind," he boasted.[2]

Post 261 was made up of Menominees from their reservation, and it was an active G.A.R. post for a number of years. As such, it received a bit of notoriety, including a report published in a national Grand Army newspaper in 1892 telling of a visit made to the post on behalf of the national office from an aide-de-camp from Marinette, George Thorne.[3]

Keshena, Thorne said, consisted of "one long, straight street, and presents a very pleasant but quiet appearance, built up on either side with scattered cottages all painted white, the United States Agency buildings, an Indian hotel, a store, G.A.R. building, a Catholic church and two extensive and beautiful school buildings."

Thorne was met at the depot in Shawano by the commander and senior vice commander[4] who "kept [him] busy answering their various questions about G.A.R. work . . . and other matters relating to the Order, in which they were deeply interested." The trio stopped at the hotel and looked down the street "where the comrades were just starting from the Post room in a body, under command of the Adjutant, with their elegant flag in front and every member armed with his own rifle. They were marching up to salute and welcome (me) for this was a great day in Keshena."

Most of the members wore some aspect of the G.A.R. uniform. Thorne found that Post 261 had about 50 members, all with good war records, "mostly as sharpshooters or scouts." They conducted a post meeting, and "I was greatly surprised and pleased with their blunt but straightforward way of doing G.A.R. work. Many of them cannot speak English, therefore the business is mainly conducted in their own language, in a manner peculiarly Indian, without much regard to parliamentary practice. But I noticed they always reached a correct, practical result."

When the meeting ended, the commander of Post 261 told Thorne, "We thank you much for coming to see us. You tell the Commander-in-Chief that the Indians are good brothers, and we thank him for sending one of his officers here. We are glad you came, for you do us all much good, and learn us many new things. We hope you will come and see us again."[5]

The Department of Wisconsin embarked early in this decade on an effort to get more flags into the public schools so that, as Commander Ferguson put it, the children "shall come to know what it cost in blood and treasure to preserve the union of states, which is their heritage." Wisconsin showed leadership in a program that was picked up by other departments as part of their own ways to promote patriotism.

Benjamin F. Bryant of La Crosse succeeded Ferguson as the leader of Wisconsin Grand Army men, and he summarized his year when they met in Oshkosh on March 10, 1891, by declaring that "there are as yet no signs of decadence." It will come, he admitted. "Time must after a while, in the nature of things, make gaps in our ranks which we shall be unable to fill, but that time has not yet come."[6]

1. U.S. actuarial tables do not begin until 1900, but these indicate a man born that year could expect to live to age 47, according to modern Social Security Administration data. An earlier table, from the Central Bureau of Statistics, Sweden, indicates a Swedish man born about 1845—a likely birth date for Civil War veterans who by 1890 would be 45 years old—had a similar life expectancy of 47 years.
2. *Proceedings of the Twenty-fourth Annual Encampment of the Department of Wisconsin, Grand Army of the Republic*, Milwaukee, Wisc.: Ed. Keogh, 1890), 67.
3. *National Tribune*, January 14, 1892.
4. Although Thorne did not use their names, the *Proceedings of the Twenty-fourth Annual Encampment*, 66, lists Joseph Lamotte as commander and Louis Kaquette as senior vice commander of Post 261 for 1892.
5. *National Tribune*, January 14, 1892.
6. *Proceedings of the Twenty-fifth Annual Encampment, Department of Wisconsin, Grand Army of the Republic*, (Milwaukee, Wisc.: 1891), 67.

Figures for the year indicated slight slippage in total membership in good standing. "In good standing" was the key. The figures of members under suspension for failure to pay dues were creeping up. He urged post commanders to try harder to bring these members back. He also urged more efforts to recruit from among the veterans who had never joined.

The subject of death was not precisely the keynote of the encampment, but it was probably on the comrades' minds now more often than at past encampments. Just the month before, on July 14, General William T. Sherman had died. "Uncle Billy" had always been a great favorite with the "boys," who remembered his visit to Milwaukee just two years before.

Additionally, the ranks of former Department of Wisconsin commanders suffered their first loss through death. A. J. McCoy, who led the boys when they—and the department—were young, back in 1873, died the year of the 1891 encampment. The department lost a total of 195 comrades in the preceding 12 months, said Bryant, and it could expect "that until the taps are sounded for the last comrade who passes over the river of death, the roll of the departed will swell as the years go by."[7]

It is not accurate to say that the conclave in Oshkosh had a morbid air about it. It had the usual array of Grand Army business, including the presentation of reports and scrutinization of the operation of the Grand Army Home at King. The annual amenities of the concurrent meetings of the Women's Relief Corps and the Sons of Union Veterans were exchanged. The auxiliary groups began assuming a larger role in the encampments.

One noteworthy thing marked the Oshkosh encampment. For the first time in decades, the comrades elected a private to lead them. He was William H. Upham, who, two years after ending his term leading the Department of Wisconsin, was elected governor of Wisconsin.

The Grand Army in Wisconsin under Upham was still hovering five hundred or so men shy of 14,000 members, as it had since 1889. It was both an encouragement and a vexation: encouraging in that the order seemed to be maintaining its strength, and a vexation because it was clear that there was seepage in membership through nonpayment of dues. There were indications that interest in the order was beginning to slacken, and it can be said that the golden age of fraternalism was over. The hundreds of orders and fraternal organizations such as the Independent Order of Good Templars that competed for the loyalty of men in the latter half of the nineteenth century found that the old spark just was not enough to keep the men in the organizations.

By 1892, in the term of Chauncey B. Welton, who had succeeded Upham, the discerning could tell there was waning interest. Figures given to the 1893 convention at La Crosse were unambiguous. Suspensions rose. In one sense this year was another high point in Department of Wisconsin history because Augie Weissert of Milwaukee had been chosen national commander in chief, another feather in the cap of the oldest Grand Army department in the nation.[8]

Department of Wisconsin activists remained busy. They kept close tabs on everything within their areas of concern, including pensions, patriotism, and, in 1892, the future of the Wisconsin Agriculture Society fairgrounds, known intimately to many of them as "Camp Randall."

The grounds were up for sale, and the department was working to keep the property out of private hands, hands that might not grasp the sacredness of the property. Welton was able to assure the encampment of 1893 that the State of Wisconsin was poised to buy it with the intention to eventually use it for the nearby University of Wisconsin.[9]

When E. A. Shores became department commander in 1893, it was no longer possible to talk in terms of growth of the order. Membership was still strong enough so that the Grand Army of the Republic had political clout. But the totals were slipping somewhat, and the decline was not entirely attributable to the deaths of the older veterans.

It is possible that by this point the pension issue no longer fired up the boys. The passage of the federal Pension Act of 1890 meant generous benefits and wide eligibility. Though the movement for "service pensions," which is to say pensioning veterans on the basis of their having served without having to show a need, was practically preempted by the liberal interpretation of the Dependent Pension Act of 1890, there was still some agitation over the size of pensions in later years. But for all practical purposes, the Grand Army won the argument over the issue in 1890, and the need for presenting a united front of veterans could no longer be successfully argued. This rallying point for G.A.R. membership lost its punch.[10]

Shores and succeeding department commanders put great emphasis on promoting the display of the American flag in the public schools. Shores exhorted the comrades at the 1894 encampment to see that every school was provided with a flag, and he also proposed that posts hold a public campfire each year to give regular citizens—especially the schoolchildren—an object lesson in patriotism.

WILLIAM UPHAM

7. Ibid., 73.

8. There would not be another national commander from Wisconsin until Frank A. Walsh's election in 1926.

9. *Proceedings of the Twenty-seventh Annual Encampment of the Department of Wisconsin, Grand Army of the Republic,* (Madison, Wisc.: M. J. Cantwell, 1893), 57.

10. Mary Dearing, *Veterans in Politics: The Story of the GAR* (Baton Rouge: Louisiana State University Press, 1952), 445-46.

The 1894 encampment reached back into the past to name a new department commander, selecting Jerome Watrous of Milwaukee, whose credentials included helping to promote the 1880 Milwaukee reunion. He was likewise a champion of displaying the flag at schools and declared to the comrades that "it is no slight honor for Wisconsin that the agitation to place the flag on our public school began within its borders." Seventeen states now had laws requiring the flag to be displayed at schools, as Wisconsin had legislated.[11]

The 1895 encampment in Green Bay chose William D. Hoard, the state's governor in 1891, to head the Department of Wisconsin. Interestingly, former Department Commander William H. Upham took the governor's office that year.

It was Hoard who at last conceded that the times were changing, and so, too, the men. "We are all growing old, and many are becoming weary. Every year doubles the emphasis of our weakness. The Post room is too far away; the warm corner by the fireside was never so grateful to us as now, to hear nothing but the same old ritual has become tiresome; it is of more comfort to stay at home and read or converse; and, finally 'hard times' (it was another year of depressed economy) has sorely pinched very many."

He suggested holding more campfires at a county level. "There is nothing that quickens the blood and reinvigorates the flagging resolve of an old soldier like a good camp fire." But it was not just for the "old soldier;" they were to instruct the public on the themes of patriotism.[12]

Patriotism remained a recurring theme within the Grand Army of the Republic during this period. "Does any one suppose that had the Southern people been reared on the lessons of national loyalty, they would have followed their leaders into the swamps of disunion and destruction?" Hoard asked.

Patriotism. And death. At one time, in the youthful years of the G.A.R., the department medical director often provided medical attention to needy veterans—as did post medical officers routinely. Now the department's top doctor dealt with the statistics of death among the comrades, and at the thirtieth encampment at Racine in 1896, Dr. J. T. Reeve of Appleton reported 224 comrades died during the year, the largest number so far, yet a figure that came from incomplete reporting from the posts. The deceased ranged in age from 42 to 85.[13] The statistics of death gained more prominence each year in the encampment proceedings.

This was no less true the following year when D. Lloyd Jones of Stevens Point presided as department commander at the encampment in Eau Claire. Surgeon Reeve had 276 deaths to report—again from incomplete reports by posts—including one-time National Commander-in-Chief Lucius Fairchild. The age range of the late comrades was between 43 years and 93 years.[14]

The following year, 1898, the Department of Wisconsin met at Appleton, presided over by E. B. Gray, who had served the department in various subordinate roles for many years. The proceedings had a somewhat different flavor, more of an air of the present than any encampment had shown in the decade. The encampment was held at the outset of the Spanish-American War, and the old warriors were experiencing the same pumped-up feeling of patriotism that they had when they themselves went to war a third of a century before.

E.B. GRAY

When war preparations began, declared Commander Gray, the question arises in the minds of comrades as to "What is the duty of the Grand Army of the Republic? It did not seem proper for our great Order of half a million men . . ." (Commander Gray was on a roll, so overstating numbers by a mere two hundred thousand might be overlooked) " . . . to stand still and only look at the procession as it passed by. A large portion of the comrades desired to do something for the nation once more."

Enlisting was out of the question, but the national G.A.R. had an idea: posts could recruit enrollments of younger men. Gray was proud to report that the Department of Wisconsin enrolled two thousand names, to be ready in case the war would require another contingent from Wisconsin. To some members, the exercise seemed futile, but, said Gray, "it has served . . . to keep the Grand Army of the Republic in touch with the stirring events of the day." By actively recruiting, "each one of these veterans . . . knows . . . in case of necessity, he has a stalwart recruit in his place."[15]

The encampment was swept up in the fever of the new war so much that a resolution was offered calling upon the next national encampment to modify requirements for admission to the G.A.R. "in such manner that after the close of the present war, the honorably discharged soldiers and sailors who have served therein in aid of the cause of Cuban independence and to avenge the treacherous destruction of the battleship *Maine* and the murder of her brave crew, may be eligible for membership therein."[16]

This brought instant response from some of the most prominent figures attending the encampment, including leadoff respondent, past National Commander Augie Weissert of Milwaukee. "Had the comrade who prepared that resolution studied

11. *Proceedings of the Twenty-ninth Annual Encampment of the Department of Wisconsin, Grand Army of the Republic,* (Milwaukee, Wisc.: Swain and Tate Printers, 1895), 50.
12. *Proceedings of the Thirtieth Annual Encampment of the Department of Wisconsin, Grand Army of the Republic,* (Milwaukee, Wisc.: Ed. Keogh, 1896), 50–51.
13. Ibid., 84–96.
14. *Proceedings of the Twenty-first Annual Encampment of the Department of Wisconsin, Grand Army of the Republic,* (Baraboo, Wisc.: Republic Print, 1887), 70.
15. *Thirty-second Annual Encampment of the Department of Wisconsin, Grand Army of the Republic, Journal of Proceedings,* (n.p., 1897–98), 60–61.
16. Ibid., 117–18.

the principles of the Grand Army of the Republic, he would have found that there is no association, and there undoubtedly will never be another association, with the same principles binding its members together as binds us. The test of the Grand Army of the Republic membership is loyalty. . . ."

He was emphatic, animated, blunt: "The memory of those who died that the Union might live would not permit me for one instant to even think of assenting to the modification of our constitution . . . so as to admit to membership those who drew their swords or bore arms against the Union!"

AUGUSTUS WEISSERT

"The line must be drawn somewhere," he proclaimed, "and it is best to leave it where drawn by the founders of the Order—on loyalty, yes loyalty even unto death!"[17]

Past Department Commander Jerome Watrous made a somewhat different point. The volunteers now in the war against Spain went "with the same love in their hearts for the government and the flag; they are just as good men as we were; they deserve just as much praise as we did." They will be earning their own place. "Do not let us forestall them by turning over to them that which we are nearly through with. Let this society die with the Union veterans of the War of the Rebellion."

Immediate past Department Commander Jones was succinct. "There is but one Grand Army of the Republic," he said. "Let the other wars settle themselves."

The resolution was tabled.[18]

Weissert, even as he opposed opening the G.A.R. rolls to anyone who had ever served the Confederacy, felt constrained to say that he would always "do my utmost to teach my countrymen of the north to love those of the south, and to obliterate all sectionalism, all prejudices growing out of the war. . . ."

Watrous would "esteem it an honor to grasp the hand of a Joe Wheeler or a Fitzhugh Lee (one-time Confederate generals) or any one of a thousand men once against us," for their brave response to the nation's current call, "but let them make their society and give it a place in the hearts of the American people a third of a century from now, that is like the place that we hold in their hearts."[19]

17. Ibid., 118.
18. Ibid., 120.
19. Ibid., 119.

CHAPTER FOURTEEN

CAMPFIRES QUICKEN THE BLOOD

The Spanish-American War awakened the old soldiers of the Grand Army of the Republic to the fact that the world they had known was in fact quite dissimilar to the world they were then observing. Coming, as it did, on the threshold of a new century, it probably inspired some introspection on behalf of the comrades.

The 1899 encampment in Milwaukee heard Department Commander Charles H. Russell, talking in that vein. "The union which our service preserved is intact," observed this second department chief to come out of Post 4 of Berlin. It represents "a united people that knows no sectional lines, with a flag that now represents a power and a majesty second to no nation on earth." The nation's victory over Spain lifted the national spirit, the American vision of its place in the world, and the men of the G.A.R. felt as exalted as every other American about it.

But Commander Russell grew quickly pensive. Even amidst the "solid ranks of proud Americans" that day, "our thoughts go back to the thousands of graves beneath the pines of our now beloved sunny South, where sleep our comrades who gave their lives. . . ."

"Could an artist stand on this platform today and make a picture that would show the spirit forms of absent comrades around the living ones here, what an impressive picture that would be! Nothing in the eloquence of man's tongue, no word painting however gifted, could so impress this encampment with a sense of fraternity as would such a picture."[1]

Fraternity. That's the word: the soul of that Grand Army that rose from the restless days of 1866 when Billy Yank began yearning for the close comradeship that sustained him through the horrors of war. The three abiding principles were Fraternity, Charity, Loyalty. And the greatest of these was Fraternity.

Fraternity, in its numerous manifestations, was always an important part of the Grand Army of the Republic. It became even more important when there was nothing left for the old soldiers to do but wait for the final roll call. They waited with comrades, while sharing all those things that had been important in their past.

The campfire rose to be one of the most important aspects of Grand Army life. It "quickened the blood," in the words of the old dairyman and Department Commander William Hoard

back in 1895. He urged more and grander campfires because they had proven—over decades of use—to be a source of much satisfaction to the soldiers, and incidentally, were a great way to impress the public with the importance and value of the Grand Army, past and present.

Campfires were, of course, the aspect of army life that the veterans could most easily wax nostalgic about, and in some limited ways, duplicate. The campfires reminded the veterans of happy times, not when they were on the march or undergoing all the hardships of campaigning, but when they were spending time as dusk was setting in, talking, joking, and singing while the fires that had warmed their evening meal still flickered and still warded off the chill of the advancing evening.

In contrast with much of the rest of their military experience, the time around a campfire was one of the pleasant times. And what was pleasant is worth remembering, extending, and experiencing anew.

Eventually, the G.A.R. campfires took on a form and character that did not exactly mimic the original. The talks were a bit more formal, the whole a bit more structured, especially when the campfires were held to show the public what Grand Army men had gone through. It became a public-relations tool. Only the comrades had experienced the real thing, but the stay-at-homes and the new generation were allowed to stick their head under the tent flap, so to speak, and pretend that they, too, were a part of what the veterans were sharing with each other.

The true campfire of those earlier days when the order was flourishing might consist of an old-time army meal, that is, coffee, hardtack, and beans, and sitting around smoking clay pipes, drinking (the matter of sobriety at post functions was a continuing concern up the chain of command), and telling war stories.[2]

Stories, plus military calls with bugle or drum, and the singing of war songs were staples of the campfire. The stories might be the impromptu type typical of what was heard while sitting around during wartime, or they may have been more formal presentations, the veterans telling their personal

1. *Thirty-third Annual Encampment of the Department of Wisconsin, Grand Army of the Republic, Journal of Proceedings*, (n.p., 1898–99), 53–54.
2. Stuart McConnell, *Glorious Contentment, the Grand Army of the Republic, 1865–1900*, (Chapel Hill: University of North Carolina Press, 1992), 175.

remembrances of aspects of their campaigns after having reflected on them for a while, and probably committing it all to paper beforehand.

The campfire was an enduring aspect of G.A.R. life. And now, as the new century approached, the campfire was one of the last things that would endure. Comrades passed away. Issues that fired the imagination and filled the rolls also passed. Even the imperative of Charity diminished with the declining economic status of members of the G.A.R. and the availability of pensions. Higher powers in the organization were handling a lot of that.

The campfire at the 1907 encampment at Oshkosh was perhaps typical of the latter-day campfires, and it was on a large scale.

"It was raining after the manner of the deluge of old," went the account; "yet the old fellows marched out into the night very much as they used to go to picket—as if they were on duty and rain did not count."

The program lasted from 8:30 to 11 p.m., and, in addition to the G.A.R. men, the audience included Spanish-American War veterans and members of the allied G.A.R. organizations. The preliminaries included music and welcome addresses from the hosts, but the main attractions were speeches by prominent comrades.

Former Governor George Peck, known perhaps more as a humorist ("Peck's Bad Boy") than as a politician, was first up. "Proof of his ability to entertain was not lacking during his talk," the anonymous essayist declared. "Forget the sad things of the past, and remember the funny things," counseled Peck. "You will be young as long as you live and have a good time and talk it over."

Ex-governor Edward Scofield was more somber. "Though your days are numbered, you still have work to do in the creation of a new spirit of saneness and rugged honesty in the American people," he advised them.

General Arthur MacArthur—the father of future General Douglas MacArthur—was a Wisconsinite who went to the Civil War as a teenager and stayed in the service for forty-five years. He assured the comrades that "American guns were never fired in war without contributing materially to the happiness and welfare of mankind. The Grand Army has future. Let us impress this idea upon the coming men of America."

Last was Bishop Samuel Fallows of Chicago, who assured the graying men: "I predict that this nations will not falter or go down. And I feel no sadness for those of us members of the Grand Army who are crossing to the other side. We are going to a better battlefield, to a more glorious service."

The crowd joined in by singing patriotic songs and capped off the program with a verse of "Auld Lang Syne."[3]

Fraternity was unendingly comforting—comforting as exemplified in those campfires and comforting through the continuation of the Grand Army itself.

The Department of Wisconsin's 1900 encampment, in West Superior, had a note of sadness at the outset in that the commander elected the year before, Henry Harnden, died in office. It was the first such loss, but it would not be the last. His successor's address conveyed some of the pervading gloom. Sam Tallmadge lamented that membership losses, by now quite marked, "[are] attributed to a seeming lack of interest on the part of our Comrades."[4]

Not everything was regress. The department was occasionally signing on new people, and that year it chartered its second Indian Post, No. 278, on the Oneida Reservation.

G.A.R. Hall in Capitol c. 1901. 'Old Abe' is in glass case left of center.

A recurring theme in the early 1900s was that the department still had recruiting options since its membership rolls constituted only about a third of living Civil War veterans.

The annual adjutant reports noted that those outside the fold owed it to the Grand Army to join since it had gained so many benefits for them as veterans of the war. There was a bit of resentment oozing from between the lines.

The year 1901 saw something of real progress, and the end

3. Anonymous, "Something Besides Business at Grand Army Encampments," in *Forty-first Annual Encampment of the Department of Wisconsin, Grand Army of the Republic, Journal of Proceedings,* (Madison, Wisc.: Democrat Printing, 1907), 142–48.

4. *Thirty-fourth Annual Encampment of the Department of Wisconsin, Grand Army of the Republic, Journal of Proceedings,* (n.p., 1899–90), 53.

to a thorny internal department issue of long standing. Debate had gone on for years about whether to establish a permanent office for the department or to continue, as it had, moving the state headquarters to wherever the commander was located. It took a dispute with the State Historical Society of Wisconsin to accomplish resolution, though. The sacred battle flags were then in the custody of the society, and the G.A.R. was unhappy with how the society displayed them.[5] The veterans got the state legislature to give the G.A.R. quarters in the Capitol, and permanence was assured. It was to be a "Memorial Hall for Soldiers and Sailors of Wisconsin" as well as to serve as department headquarters.

Members were urged to donate relics and mementos for permanent display in the new hall.[6]

The comrades responded well, for Department Commander A. H. DeGroff was pleased to inform the 1902 encampment that "as a Memorial Hall the main room is the depository of a growing collection of interesting and instructive war relics, (and) a library of about 500 books. . . . This room is intended to preserve in a concrete form the materials out of which history is made, and to so arrange them for observation that the study of them may be both pleasant and profitable."[7]

It was pleasant and profitable far and wide. Commander James H. Agen proudly reported to the next year's encampment that not only were Wisconsinites finding it so, but the hall was "attracting much attention from visitors from all parts of the United States." As many as ten thousand visitors had come through the headquarters.

"Perhaps the most interesting and interested of these soldier visitors was our worthy comrade who signed his name 'Theodore Roosevelt, Oyster Bay, New York, Colonel First United States Volunteer Cavalry.'"

"He was much pleased with the room and what it contained of war relics. . . ." said Agen. "He was especially delighted to see 'Old Abe,' the Wisconsin war eagle."[8]

"Old Abe" was then the number one relic, clinging tenaciously to a perch and looking every bit the war bird as when he was alive a quarter century before. He was enclosed in a glass case in the G.A.R. Memorial Hall after the veterans had pressured the government to bring the bird over from the State Historical Society building in April of 1903.[9]

But everything soon changed. At 3:00 p.m. on February 27, 1904, the stately Capitol in Madison caught fire, apparently from a gas jet too close to the varnished ceiling near the Assembly chamber. By 6:00 that morning the building had been essentially reduced to ruins, a hollow shell, with many of the state offices burned. Thanks to the exertions of some, including Governor Robert M. LaFollette, university students, state employees, and plenty of passersby, certain invaluable state articles were removed.

"Included in the burned portion was Grand Army Hall. The battle flags and other army relics were saved," it was reported around the state by the Associated Press.[10]

The battle flags had indeed were saved. Jacob Baar, a Chicago salesmen and frequent Madison visitor, was awakened by the commotion and, along with Elmer Elver, the proprietor of the Elver House where he was staying, rushed to the Capitol rotunda, where the flags were on display. Baar told reporters that they quickly broke open the cases "and the sacred relics were carried out" by himself, Elver, "J. C. Boyd, Tom Nelson and others."[11]

Sparing these "sacred relics" made it possible for veterans to swallow hard and accept the loss of the G.A.R. Hall and most of its contents. They had lavished their energies on collecting and supplying the hall with books and artifacts of their time of trial and triumph. It was a major loss. Yet, thank God, the flags they followed in countless battles had been carried out to safety.

Stoic acceptance goes just so far, however, and it stopped short at the terrible loss of the G.A.R.'s most important relic.

"There is one loss that seems greater than any of the others—greater, some think, than all others," wrote Department Historian Hosea Rood the next day. His emotion welled up. "I can hardly get my pencil to say that Old Abe is gone."[12]

It would be several years before the Capitol was rebuilt, and the Department of Wisconsin had to use other quarters in Madison in the meantime. However, the fire had no impact upon the functioning of the department itself, and caused scarcely a ripple of comment at the next annual encampment.

What did cause a ripple, though, was the use to which Camp Randall was put on Memorial Day that year. The high schools of Wisconsin held an athletic competition that day, playing games on that sacred soil even as members of Fairchild Post 11 were passing by on their way to cemetery solemnities. Department Commander Agen was aghast. "If our university and high schools manifest an indifference concerning the sacred purpose of Memorial Day and unite in making it a great gala day of sports and games, the young people in these schools will come to care very little for anything the day is intended to commemorate," he lamented to the encampment.[13]

So long as the Grand Army of the Republic could draw a breath, the sacred character of Memorial Day would be attested to and defended. It was a trust that seemed to grow in intensity as the years wore on, as the rolls of deceased comrades grew, and as the number carrying on that trust diminished.

5. Howard Michael Madaus and Richard H. Zeitlin, *Flags of the Iron Brigade* (Madison: Wisconsin Veterans Museum, 1997), 104.

6. *Thirty-fifth Annual Encampment of the Department of Wisconsin, Grand Army of the Republic, Journal of Proceedings*, (Madison, Wisc.: Democrat Printing, 1901), 70.

7. *Thirty-sixth Annual Encampment of the Department of Wisconsin, Grand Army of the Republic, Journal of Proceedings*, (Madison, Wisc.: Democrat Printing, 1902), 62.

8. *Thirty-seventh Annual Encampment of the Department of Wisconsin, Grand Army of the Republic, Journal of Proceedings*, (Madison, Wisc.: Democrat Printing, 1903), 71.

9. Richard H. Zeitlin, *Old Abe: The War Eagle* (Madison: State Historical Society of Wisconsin, 1986), 92.

10. *Oshkosh Northwestern*, February 27, 1904.

11. *Wisconsin State Journal*, February 27, 1904.

12. Ibid.

13. *Thirty-seventh Annual Encampment*, 76.

Concern among G.A.R. men for "the young people" also intensified. The old soldiers wished that patriotism, the love of flag, country and Union—the whole set of values that were in the very souls of Grand Army men—would survive them.

At the 1905 encampment at La Crosse, Louis Sholes of Milwaukee offered a resolution asking creation of the posts of "patriotic instructor" at both the national and department levels. The idea carried at the department encampment and was accepted at the national encampment that year.[14] The duties were not new, but the focus of the effort was intensified by this change. In Wisconsin, it took on a decidedly increased emphasis, particularly when Comrade Rood of Madison's Lucius Fairchild Post 11 was named state patriotic instructor in 1906.

Rood put his whole being into the role. He started by sending each post a list of questions about how Memorial Day and patriotic programs were to be conducted in the town and the schools, and asked each post to appoint its own patriotic instructor to coordinate with him.

He also contacted as many schools in the state as he could in an attempt to ascertain how schools viewed their roles in the matter of patriotic holidays and of history in general. Those replying had some edifying responses. As Rood noted, "I find that nearly every school room has a flag. This is better than I expected." Still, from his surveying he felt that there was room for increasing patriotic instruction and urged the comrades to become involved, either as instructors or by supporting the G.A.R. Memorial Hall at Madison.[15]

Though Rood was generally disappointed in 1907 by the few posts that had appointed patriotic instructors, he was still pleased with the work of those who did create the position. He urged others to follow their examples.

"There should be a close relation of the Grand Army to the schools. If we saved the country a half a century ago, it is the children of today who must maintain it and its free institutions half a hundred years hence. The time is not far away when, with no little pride, men and women will tell that in their childhood they used to see soldiers who took part in the Civil War. . . ."[16]

Rood's exhortations took hold. More posts reported they had appointed patriotic instructors, and at the encampment at Eau Claire on June 15 and 16, 1909, men of the G.A.R. fanned out to all the schools in the vicinity of the encampment city and gave patriotic talks.

Part of the success the department had with its patriotic endeavors, Rood told the encampment, was because State Superintendent of Public Instruction Charles P. Cary was "in hearty sympathy with us" over patriotic instruction.[17]

Comrade Rood's reports to the annual encampments became major features of each year's program. In 1910 he was able to record that there were now 119 posts with patriotic instructors, although he conceded that "I expect a few of those 119 do not so much as know they have received so honorable an appointment."

He considered it honorable and more. "A commander has influence within the Order, but a patriotic instructor reaches out in every direction, especially into the schools, where our boys and girls are receiving their first ideas of, and training for, good citizenship; and this field is all but limitless."

This year, too, the drive catalyzed the construction of a memorial arch at Camp Randall. Rood foresaw that "when the gate and arch and park are in good order, the whole will stand in the years to come as a silent, yet effective, teacher of patriotism in connection with our great university." The drive was successful and the resulting massive arch still stands boldly at the site where most of the soldiers who left Wisconsin for the Civil War received their first taste of military life.

CAMP RANDALL MEMORIAL ARCH

The concept of marking and commemorating state sites branched out, in future years, into efforts to have other "places of rendezvous" about the state marked. "At Milwaukee there were Camps Scott, Washburn, Sigel and Holton; at Kenosha, Camp Harvey; at Racine, Camp Utley; at Fond du Lac, Camp Hamilton; at Oshkosh, Camp Bragg; at Ripon, Camp Fremont; at La Crosse, Camp Salomon; and at Janesville, Camps Tredway and Barstow," according to Rood.[18]

The efforts for commemorating these, over succeeding years, were spottily successful, since the matter was left to local posts rather than asking the legislature to provide funds to do for these what it had done for Camp Randall. Some of the camp

14. *Thirty-ninth Annual Encampment of the Department of Wisconsin, Grand Army of the Republic, Journal of Proceedings*, (Madison, Wisc.: Democrat Printing, 1905), 146.

15. *Forty-first Annual Encampment of the Department of Wisconsin, Grand Army of the Republic, Journal of Proceedings*, (Madison, Wisc.: Democrat Printing, 1907), 95–105.

16. Forty-second Annual Encampment of the Department of Wisconsin, Grand Army of the Republic, Journal of Proceedings, (Madison, Wisc.: Democrat Printing, 1908), 90–101.

17. Forty-third Annual Encampment of the Department of Wisconsin, Grand Army of the Republic, Journal of Proceedings, (Madison, Wisc.: Democrat Printing, 1909), 89–101.

18. Forty-fifth Annual Encampment of the Department of Wisconsin, Grand Army of the Republic, Journal of Proceedings, (Madison, Wisc.: Democrat Printing, 1911), 79–94.

sites, especially those in Milwaukee, were already in areas thoroughly urbanized.

Department encampments began to lose much of their drama, but once in a while there were moments of fire, even in the twentieth century.

The national commander in chief for 1906 came to the state gathering in Marinette that year, and it was none other than Corporal James Tanner, the well-remembered pension commissioner of more than a decade before, and the legless old champion of veterans' benefits had given up none of his feistiness.

Tanner had been to the Milwaukee National Encampment at the peak of his power. He was a favorite of many of the Wisconsin veterans, and the 1905 department encampment had instructed its delegation to support Tanner for commander in chief.

The issue now was on retaining veterans in government jobs, and he was campaigning again. "To have the veterans at 70 years of age kicked out of office into the street was not right," the legless corporal told his Wisconsin friends.

The movement toward a civil service was at root, and a Republican congressman, James Tawney of Minnesota, was behind it, but Tanner was unswayed. "It was the work of a man who was eight years old when the battle of Gettysburg was fought," he snarled.[19]

The corporal had put his finger on precisely what was happening. People coming into positions of power in Washington and elsewhere, for that matter, were people who were too young to have experienced the Civil War, or even to remember it. This was a hard fact for the surviving Corporal Tanners of the Grand Army of the Republic to accept.

There were some things that the old soldiers were coming to accept, however gradually, and with a bit of reluctance. A case in point was brought up by Department Commander Hiram Smith in his address to the 1912 encampment at Antigo.

"We commend to the attention of the comrades of this department the invitation of our Commander in Chief to the United Confederate Veterans to participate in the celebration of the semicentennial of the Battle of Gettysburg in July, 1913. We approve the spirit of this document, every line of which is characterized by good sense, patriotism and the spirit of Christian forgiveness.

"At the same time we protest against any act or utterance that shall obliterate in the hearts and minds of future generations the perfidy of the attempt to destroy the Union in order that human slavery might be perpetuated. We of the North join with the people of the South in saying that the heroes of this great battle wore both the blue and the gray."[20]

There were still those who drew distinctions, immutable and eternal distinctions, between the two causes, and let those causes, blue and gray, never become entwined.

But that the old soldiers of the Grand Army of the Republic would not now demur when their leaders asserted that "the heroes . . . wore both the blue and the gray" was a historic acknowledgement in itself.[21]

Could it be? Could Billy Yank and Johnny Reb be ready, at last, to clasp hands across the stone wall on Cemetery Ridge?

It seemed so.

Just leave your Confederate flags at home, Johnny.[22]

19. *Fortieth Annual Encampment of the Department of Wisconsin, Grand Army of the Republic, Journal of Proceedings,* (Madison, Wisc.: Democrat Printing, 1906), 74–5.

20. *Forty-sixth Annual Encampment of the Department of Wisconsin, Grand Army of the Republic, Journal of Proceedings,* (Madison, Wisc.: Democrat Printing, 1912), 61.

21. It was not an official delegation of the Wisconsin G.A.R., but 303 veterans from Wisconsin, survivors of the battle 50 years before, made the pilgrimage to Gettysburg, Pennsylvania, at the end of June and first three days of July for the 1913 anniversary of the great battle. Cf., *Fifty-first Annual Encampment of the Department of Wisconsin, Grand Army of the Republic, Journal of Proceedings,* (Madison, Wisc.: Democrat Printing, 1917), 68. Some Confederate flags were present— "offensively paraded"—according to one veteran years later. Cf., *Journal of the Seventy-first National Encampment of the Department of Wisconsin, Grand Army of the Republic,* (Washington, D.C.: U.S. Government Printing Office, 1938), 89.

22. As late as 1930 the matter of flags was a bone of national contention. A reunion between Union and Confederate veterans was in the negotiating stage. The latter proposed to march carrying their battle flags in the parade. National G.A.R. Commander Edwin J. Foster of Massachusetts, a former Badger (Fortieth Wisconsin Volunteer Infantry), declared: "There will be no reunion for we will never march behind the Stars and Bars." R. D. Sneed, his Confederate counterpart, answered that "We will never march without them." There was no such reunion. Cf., *Journal of the Sixty-fourth Annual Encampment of the Department of Wisconsin, Grand Army of the Republic* (n.p., 1930), 97. And when the seventy-fifth anniversary of the Battle of Gettysburg in 1938 approached, the 1937 national encampment, meeting in Madison, resolved to take part but "at such reunion to have in view only the flag of this United States of America." For some of the lively discussion on the issue at that encampment by these largely nonagenarians, see Appendix B, Page 348.

CHAPTER FIFTEEN

IT'S ALL ABOUT LOYALTY

Efforts to assure the permanence of the Grand Army of the Republic by opening it to the veterans' heirs—first to their sons and then to their successors as soldiers—were half-hearted at best and doomed from their inception. Most G.A.R. veterans did not want permanence.

An ongoing organization maintains its vibrancy by handing on leadership to those whose relative youth brings vitality.

The Grand Army of the Republic, by its considered choice, would have none of that. The Department of Wisconsin continued for as long as a veteran or two was physically able to come to an encampment.[1] The encampments became anachronistic. They retained the time-honored forms for conducting business, but there was no business to conduct.

In consequence, the annual encampments seemed to be permeated with a whiff of disheartenment. The tough leadership demanded of prior times, when real issues were involved and when the Grand Army of the Republic had a major impact upon the direction of the nation and of the state, receded.

The leaders now were survivors, primarily; men who had been journeymen for the order in their younger days, but now were at the front of the platform because the demands for dynamic leadership had passed, and the men who could give such leadership had passed as well.

This yearly procession of veterans to the top as department commander brought men who were past the fullness of their vigor by many years. The department, of course, was itself well past its prime in membership totals. The numbers told of death: death of the individuals who comprised the Grand Army of the Republic, death of posts once active and thriving and now reduced to few or no veterans able to maintain them. The death of the G.A.R. itself loomed.

In no way should fault be imputed to these latter-day leaders simply because none rose to the stature of a Phil Cheek or an Augustus Weissert. The men who led the Department of Wisconsin in the years from, roughly, the era of the Great War,

until the end of the department in the 1940s had been doomed by the nature of G.A.R. membership rules. They could not retire and let younger men take over, no matter how weary they became. Into their eighties and even nineties they made their annual trek to the encampment in spite of infirmities; they were doomed to march with slowing step toward that foreordained end, and doomed to carry on the old forms without the hope that something of the Grand Army's character could somehow survive.

These well-worn "forms" were the regular reports of commander, vice commanders, assistant adjutant, assistant quartermaster,[2] judge advocate, and so forth down the familiar list. Not everyone appeared depressed. Many speeches at the encampments during these years were predicated on the idea that the Grand Army of the Republic had maintained its lofty ideals, had set an example for others to follow, and that the comrades no longer answering roll call had achieved ultimate triumph.

Occasionally there were voices heard from the past, as in 1916 when Griff Thomas wrote from Nebraska on the occasion of the Fiftieth Department Encampment at Ripon. "Of those who were active in the work when it was my privilege to have an humble part, but few are left. . . . Those pioneer days . . . were strenuous days, requiring patience, sacrifice of time and money and oftentimes humiliation. It was very hard to bring the comrades to understand that there was something more than political advantage to come from membership . . . that its objects were higher and nobler. . . . We were having uphill work at even old Berlin in the early '70s."

Still, wrote the venerable commander, remembered by those at this historic fiftieth encampment more through department legend than in person, it has been "worthwhile to have served your country in the Grand Army of the Union . . . [which service] entitled you to serve your country and your comrades in the Grand Army of the Republic."[3]

There were still moments of some relevance in department encampments, when the Department of Wisconsin spoke on issues of the day. But the voice no longer thundered.

When the War to End All Wars raged in Europe, the comrades in encampment assembled at Ashland in June of 1918, listened as Commander William A. Wyse of Reedsburg exclaimed that "we meet under circumstances such as have never surrounded us before since the organization of the Grand Army, with our sons and brothers facing a foreign foe, and offering up

---

1. That last annual encampment was in 1949. In 1950, at Sheboygan, a "Memorial Encampment" was held, and Lansing Wilcox was the sole member of the department. *Official Program, Memorial Encampment of the Department of Wisconsin, Grand Army of the Republic, Sheboygan, June 11–14, 1950*, 7.

2. These officers were "assistants" to the national adjutant and national quartermaster, but were in full charge of their duties within the Department of Wisconsin.

3. *Fiftieth Annual Encampment of the Department of Wisconsin, Grand Army of the Republic, Journal of Proceedings*, (Madison, Wisc.: Cantwell Printing, 1916), 92.

their young lives if need be for democracy and the defense of their homes."

To show their solidarity, and acting on a rumor or two, the members voted unanimously that "if there are in our membership any [German-sympathizing] enemies of our Republic they should be found out and dishonorably discharged from the Grand Army of the Republic, interned during the war, and deprived of their pensions."

As always it was eminently relevant for the Department to examine its ongoing stewardship of the Grand Army Home at King. It was the remaining facet of the order's middle watchword, Charity. In fact, a greater share of the time of each encampment seems to have been consumed in receiving reports of the home. Committees of the department still made regular visits to Waupaca, still fussed and worried over the accommodations their comrades had there. Encampment journals even carried rosters of those resident at the home, men and women, and, of course, the annual necrology of the institution.

The giants of the Department of Wisconsin's past were disappearing. James Proudfit, whose distinction it was to have been the first man in the country elected to be a department commander[4] as Wisconsin's first leader in 1866, died in 1917.

Jerome Watrous, part of the small band that revived the department in 1880 and who held just about every office thereafter including commander, died in 1922 while serving as assistant adjutant general. The next year, former National Commander Augie Weissert died.

However, one giant lived on: Hosea W. Rood.

The one-time schoolteacher who had taken the job in 1906 as department patriotic instructor—against his better judgment—was continuing in that position, and not only filling it admirably, but providing a spark of meaningfulness to the proceedings. While much of what was put before the comrades reflected the declining state of the order, Rood's reports almost always carried a message of hope that the Grand Army of the Republic still had relevance for the future.

HOSEA ROOD

Youth was his primary concern. In his own youth Rood became a teacher, just home from the army. From 1866 to 1900, he was involved in education and was a school principal, over some three decades in Dakota, Coloma, Packwaukee, Hancock, Omro, Shawano, Sun Prairie, Palmyra, and Washburn. Years later, young pupils were still very much his mission.[5]

"Never before since the days when we were soldiers has American patriotism been more manifest than it is now," Rood reflected in 1917 as Doughboys were going to France. "Because of this we are naturally wrought up patriotically." This was

reflected, as he visited schools around the state—Rood was making as many as one hundred appearances a year before schools—where he found "both teachers and pupils interested in talks about the flag and upon other patriotic topics."

He concluded by urging his comrades to set an example. "We can by our lives, in a quiet way, lead our younger citizens to be anxious to do what they can to serve the country we served."[6]

It was much the same when in June of 1918 the patriotic instructor commented on the outpouring of patriotism the war had produced. Never before had so many responses from the local posts as to their programs for patriotism been received.

This was an especially important year because finally, after an absence since fire evicted them in 1904, the G.A.R. was back in the state Capitol, and its Memorial Hall, Fourth Floor, North Wing, was under Rood's superintendence. It was dedicated on Flag Day that year, and the precious flags of Wisconsin's Civil War regiments, plus those from the Spanish-American War, were housed there.[7] In addition, he had the added responsibility of national patriotic instructor in 1919.

As the 1920s began, the patriotic instructor saw some changes taking place. "The Americanism of our children and their children must depend upon the Americanism taught in these days of unrest—these day of transition after the great World War—a war of greater significance than the most of us can understand."

Nonetheless Rood was pleased that a new organization, the American Legion, had taken on Memorial Day as their own day. "We may be sure that in the years to come, as they think of their dead comrades asleep under the poppies of Flanders Field, they will not forget us."[8]

Rood's health began failing as the 1920s moved on, but his spirit remained strong. He produced booklets in those days for distribution in the schools, primarily on the flag, and he lobbied the legislature, successfully, to require "in all the schools instruction in citizenship, which really means Americanism."

Yet he found some things disquieting. In 1923, he told the encampment that there was a positive danger growing, and "it comes not from foreign nations, but from within—that is, a seeming growing disregard for law, for the sacredness of law." A pervasive disdain for Prohibition was widespread in the country, and "our boys and girls can see for themselves this general disregard for law."[9]

4. The Department of Illinois was credited with an earlier foundation date, but its first commander was the order's founder, Dr. Benjamin F. Stephenson, who was not elected.
5. *Wisconsin State Journal*, November 27, 1933.
6. *Fifty-first Annual Encampment of the Department of Wisconsin, Grand Army of the Republic, Journal of Proceedings*, (Madison, Wisc.: Democrat Printing, 1917), 60–4.
7. *Fifty-second Annual Encampment of the Department of Wisconsin, Grand Army of the Republic, Journal of Proceedings*, (Madison, Wisc.: Democrat Printing, 1918), 65–75.
8. *Fifty-fourth Annual Encampment of the Department of Wisconsin, Grand Army of the Republic, Journal of Proceedings*, (Madison, Wisc.: Democrat Printing, 1920), 53–9.
9. *Journal of the Fifty-seventh Annual Encampment of the Department of Wisconsin, Grand Army of the Republic, Journal of Proceedings*, (Madison, Wisc.: n.p., 1923), 41–2.

Rood became a virtual shut-in that year because of an improperly mended leg fracture sustained in a bicycle accident at age 78 as he rode to work at the G.A.R. Hall in the Capitol.

He moved to Milton and carried on with his duties as patriotic instructor as well as he could.

Rood had little empathy with comrades who shied away from duties as post patriotic instructors by claiming to be too old or too feeble. "A comrade in such a position should be as active as he can—*find something to do*, and do it," he exhorted.[10]

And this he practiced. He could not easily get around. But he could, and did, write. He wrote for the state superintendent of schools' Memorial Day Annual (as he had for 24 years) and corresponded on the duties of his office with both post officers and with national officers. And he wrote a history of the Grand Army Home at King that was published in 1925.[11]

New issues arose in the later years of that decade, and Hosea Rood noted and addressed them. "Some of our young men in these days are denouncing war under every circumstance telling us from the platform how horrible war is. But who of us that have stood in the battle line have need to be told all this, for we know from experience just how terrible it is. Had we in our young manhood been extreme pacifists what would now be the condition of our country?"[12]

Rood let go of the task of patriotic instructor at last in 1929. But the death of his successor in 1930 brought him out of retirement, and he again reported to the 1931 encampment at La Crosse on the activities of the office he first filled in 1906. There were fewer than a hundred comrades at the encampment.

It seems almost an anticlimax that Hosea Rood was nominated for department commander in 1932—and was defeated. The loss was probably not a disappointment to him since he had always contended that a commander influenced only the order while a patriotic instructor influenced generations to come.

He continued, through correspondence, to exert his influence on the future as department patriotic instructor until his death on November 26, 1933, at the age of 88.[13]

Rood's activities and his reports thereon were highlights of the encampment–of the Department of Wisconsin, itself. In fact, Rood perceived what few of the comrades may have really understood: the legacy of their beloved Grand Army had somehow to be passed to newer generations if their efforts and sacrifices were to abide. Rood, in fact, tended to give a rather brief

oral report from the floor, referring the comrades to his complete report to appear in the official proceedings later. He recognized the attention span of his audience of octogenarians.

Much of the floor time at the gatherings of the 1920s and 1930s was spent in formalities between the old soldiers and the allied organizations meeting concurrently: the Woman's Relief Corps, Sons of Union Veterans, Sons of Union Veterans Auxiliary, Ladies of the G.A.R., and Daughters of Union Veterans. Each had its own agenda for the year ahead, but put in much convention time doting on the old fellows.

The Daughters of Union Veterans sent an invitation to the floor during encampment proceedings at Appleton in 1934. It was to a father-daughter luncheon.

"We will be glad to accept the invitation, especially when there is something to eat," happily responded Department Commander Henry Held.

"We want you to have the nice things, and we know all of you will enjoy it. Thank you comrades, and our blessings go to all of you," replied the luncheon chairman, Dorothy Walsh.[14]

This was the quintessential business of Grand Army encampments through the 1930s and into the 1940s. Receive the bouquets and blessings of the young folks whether it be from sons and daughters, or from the veterans of other wars who, frankly, looked with undisguised admiration on the old fellows and what they had done for the country and for themselves.

HENRY HELD

The Boys of 1861 to 1865 had earned this, whether it was an invitation to lunch or dinner at an encampment or to a memorial service at home. They had earned respect. They had survived this long. But they had earned it many years before, as had, for that matter, the hundreds of thousands of their comrades who stood up with them against the storm of Rebellion.

As the Grand Army men became mere remnants, they were cherished precisely as that: remnants of an era, of a cause, of a particularly interesting aspect of American history. The last few decades of the Department of Wisconsin were in one sense golden ones. The issues that excited the veterans in earlier times were long forgotten. The order no longer was suspect as a political creature. By now, in fact, few begrudged them the fairly generous pensions they had achieved.

These men took all the pride they were entitled to take as the surviving link to a time of glorious deeds and stunning accomplishment. They had become icons of a defining point in the nation's being. They basked in the outpouring of respect.

They made appearances, as their lifetime commitment obligated them, at the Memorial Day observances in all the cities and towns of the state where a G.A.R. presence remained. The

10. *Journal of the Fifty-eighth Annual Encampment of the Department of Wisconsin, Grand Army of the Republic*, (n.p., 1924), 38–44.

11. *Journal of the Fifty-ninth Annual Encampment of the Department of Wisconsin, Grand Army of the Republic*, (n.p., 1925), 37–42.

12. *Journal of the Sixty-first Annual Encampment of the Department of Wisconsin, Grand Army of the Republic*, (n.p., 1927), 34–8.

13. *Journal of the Sixty-eighth Annual Encampment of the Department of Wisconsin, Grand Army of the Republic*, (n.p., 1934), 74.

14. *Journal of the Sixty-eighth Annual Encampment of the Department of Wisconsin, Grand Army of the Republic*, (n.p., 1934), 36.

solemn day had taken hold, and it would survive them, thanks to the younger men of the United Spanish War Veterans and of the American Legion.

Campfires no longer burned. Fraternity was now simply silent communing with comrades, many marked by government-issue headstones in the nearby cemetery, friends of a lifetime who one by one had slipped away. And others, marked or unmarked, were in the Wilderness, at Shiloh, Chattanooga, Andersonville, and in dozens of locales far away, both in distance and in time.

Loyalty was a life to be lived, but more: A lesson to be taught. The Grand Army's grand legacy.

It was, in truth, what their lives had been all about.

EPILOGUE

The Wisconsin Department of the Grand Army of the Republic, at the high point in its history, had 264 posts scattered throughout the state. A number of the larger cities had two posts, and Milwaukee, of course, had eight, from prestigious E. B. Wolcott Post 1 to Rank and File Post 240. Most of the posts were in small cities and small towns.

In 1889, for example, the roster of posts listed such places as New Centerville, Grand Rapids, Wyalusing, Evansville, La Valle, Kilbourn, Excelsior, Warren Mills, Eagle Corners, West Lima, Rock Elm, Merrillan, Forestville, De Soto, Colby, Cadott, Knapp, Lime Ridge, Bee Town, Sextonville, Briggsville, Argyle, Lynxville, Windoro, Cataract, Prairie Farm, Trimbelle, and Pedee.[1]

The presence of the G.A.R. permeated the society of late nineteenth and early twentieth-century Wisconsin. In many of those small communities, and for that matter, in most of the cities, post functions, particularly campfires, but a myriad of other activities such as dances, picnics, and music and drama programs, were major events in the life of the community. The G.A.R. was a part of the community ambiance that has come to be thought of as integral to "quality of life."

The loss of posts from the Department of Wisconsin was a matter the department stoically accepted. For a time department officials encouraged amalgamating members from posts having only one or two members into nearby larger posts, perhaps at the county seat.

But it was hard for many of the old soldiers to give up their post charters even when the only function left was the steady breathing of the lone survivor. And when that stopped, well … So, very often the post died right along with the last Civil War soldier in town.

Members of Post 4, the John H. Williams Post of Berlin, were acutely aware of their unique status as being in the oldest Grand Army of the Republic post in existence—aware and extraordinarily proud of the fact. They faced the prospect of its expiration with a certain élan. On September 9, 1931, four of the five surviving members—all now in or approaching their nineties—got into a car and were driven to Madison where they ceremoniously "loaned" their precious charter to the State Historical Society of Wisconsin.[2]

Thus assuring the preservation of their treasure without surrendering it, the frail old men returned home to await the final call.

The fifth final call came on April 18, 1937, to the person of Alexander Parsons. His funeral "will provide the last occasion for the display of the colors of the now non-existent John H. Williams Post," a Berlin editor ruefully noted.[3]

The post had survived the vicissitudes of Grand Army, and various other, fortunes and misfortunes for 70 years, four months, and 21 days.

The burial obsequies for Parsons, and in a sense for the John H. Williams Post, were provided by the Frank O'Connor Post of the American Legion and the Max Krause Post of the Veterans of Foreign Wars.[4]

Last five members of Post 4 of Berlin show their famous charter. Standing, from left, are William Eldred, George W. Morton and Frank D. Murdock. Seated, from left, are Alexander Parsons and Henry L. Marsh.

1. *Proceedings of the Twenty-fourth Annual Encampment of the Department of Wisconsin, Grand Army of the Republic*, (Milwaukee, Wisc.: Ed. Keogh, 1892), 32–65.
2. *Berlin Evening Journal*, September 10, 1931.
3. *Berlin Evening Journal*, April 19, 1937.
4. *Berlin Evening Journal*, April 22, 1937.

The Department of Wisconsin went on, of course, without the benefit of having Post 4 on the roster, or for that matter, almost any of its once numerous posts. It was now no longer a matter of enumerating posts, but of counting individual surviving veterans.

The department continued its yearly encampments until 1951. By then it had just one member, Lansing A. Wilcox of Cadott in Chippewa County who was, necessarily, department commander, the last in a line of 76 commanders that began with James Proudfit in 1866.

Wilcox was active in the Grand Army of the Republic for quite a few years. A Wisconsin native who joined the Fourth Wisconsin Cavalry at age 17 in 1864, he served in Louisiana and Texas, apparently not seeing any combat. He lived at Cadott for many years and became postmaster of the tiny community in the early 1900s. He moved to the state of Washington some time in the 1920s, and his G.A.R. activities there brought him to the position, in 1937, of department commander of the Department of Washington and Alaska.[5]

Wilcox moved back to Cadott about 1943 and was again involved in the Grand Army Department of Wisconsin. When the national encampment was held at Milwaukee in 1943, it was Wilcox who was honored from the host department with election as national senior vice commander.

Comrade Wilcox remained at Cadott, or rather, on his farm a few miles outside of the town until 1950, when his infirmities became too much. He moved, fittingly, to the Grand Army Home at King, near Waupaca, where he observed his 105th birthday on March 3, 1951.

In the autumn of that year, the old soldier died. He had said at the birthday fete that he was expecting the final call, and it came on September 30, a Saturday.

On Monday, Gil Stordock, commandant of the Home at King, conducted "the Grand Army ritual for the last time in Wisconsin."[6]

LANSING WILCOX

The following day, Tuesday, October 3, 1951, a typical early autumn afternoon in Chippewa County, Lansing Wilcox, the last of some 90,000 Wisconsin men who answered patriotism's call in the frightful 1860s, was committed to the ground of Cadott Cemetery, with impressive military pomp and the eulogies of the state's leaders.[7]

Wilcox, and all of those men, and the Grand Army of the Republic's Department of Wisconsin itself, now belonged to the ages.

5. *Appleton Post Crescent*, October 1, 1951.

6. *Cadott Sentinel*, October 6, 1951.

7. Ibid.

THE FIRST YEARS

FIRST RESPONSE 1866-1870

The Grand Army of the Republic quickly expanded after it was founded in 1866, and nowhere was it more successful than in Wisconsin. Just about as rapidly, the order went into a precipitous decline, none more precipitous than in the Department of Wisconsin. The map above shows the locations of those early posts, begun in 1866, 1867, and 1868. By 1874 only three of these early posts remained, and the active status of two of them—Madison and Oshkosh—was questionable.

Little is known of the posts founded in these years, except their location and, in a good number of cases, the name of the first commander. Historians know the original names the posts adopted for only a couple of the posts; most are designated only by their community. The scarcity of records from this era is keenly felt. Most records of the Department of Wisconsin were lost sometime around 1883. Their loss places these early posts into a sort of Arthurian mist. Nonetheless, some records survive, which though scarce, provide a window into what the history of these posts.

The posts that survived to at least 1874—Madison, Oshkosh, and Berlin—have their own histories, although the Madison and Oshkosh posts suffered the loss of some of their own records by fire. Madison housed its records in the Capitol building, but those records burned in the 1904 Capitol fire. Oshkosh's records succumbed to a fire that destroyed a major portion of the city in 1875. However, Berlin's records survived, and they show that the post regularly sent necessary reports, and payments, to the Wisconsin Department, unlike the Madison and Oshkosh posts, which had been lax in meeting their obligations to state headquarters during this era. All three posts had original charter dates that preceded almost all others in the country, with the exceptions of a handful of Illinois posts. All of those Illinois posts eventually lapsed, leaving the three early Wisconsin posts to battle it out for the title of the longest continuing post in the G.A.R.; Berlin's John H. Williams Post 4 was eventually declared the oldest.

At the time of chartering, Berlin was the twenty-second Wisconsin post constituted. We possess the names, primarily, because the national G.A.R. publication, *The Soldier's Friend*, printed a list of chartered Wisconsin posts in January 1868. The list included 56 posts, although the active status of six of them is questionable. Boscobel was given two numbers, 19 and 37, and

numbers 49, 50, 51 and 52 had no cities listed. Subsequent information indicates that some numbers, for whatever reason, were never assigned.

It was this publication of the Wisconsin roster that provides the only information we have on the names of the men who were commanders of the posts. It cannot be confirmed that these men were the first commanders of the posts, as the list was compiled as of the end of 1867, and some of the early posts may have changed commanders by then. However, having names of individuals attached to the G.A.R. units indicates, at least at the outset, that they were active, functioning units.

Ed Ferguson of Post 56 in Milwaukee is one name on the list. He later became state commander and performed the initial housecleaning that rid the roster of many of the early posts, which by then (1871) had ceased to function. Ferguson's order of November 20, 1871, a copy of which *The Berlin Journal* published at the time and thus is available to posterity despite the loss of department records of the period (and is printed here as Appendix A, page 347, not only disposed of the moribund posts on *The Soldier's Friend* roster but trimmed off a number which apparently were chartered from 1868 to 1870. Nothing is known of these posts except their post number and location.

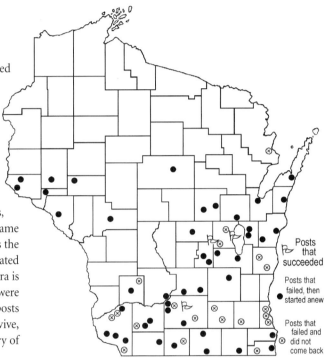

Posts that succeeded

Posts that failed, then started anew

Posts that failed and did not come back

Ferguson's housecleaning, under General Order No. 6 of 1871, notes that Posts 65 and 80 had previously surrendered their charters voluntarily, causing some additional confusion. Although Post 65 is known to have been at Hingham in Sheboygan County, there is no extant record of any name or location for Post 80. It is lost to posterity.

Not quite lost to posterity were some 20 posts that were founded in those early years but failed. What little is known of them is given on the table on the next page. It is worth noting, though, that almost all of them were in counties with at least one other G.A.R. post. What is perhaps more significant is what happened in all those communities where early posts failed and where new posts were later formed when the Grand Army of the Republic was on the rebound. More about these "second tries" follows immediately after the next two tables.

THE POSTS THAT NEVER CAME BACK

Town	No.	County	Commander	Chartered	Revoked
Greenbush	5	Sheboygan Co.	H. C. Stannard	1866	1871
Milwaukee	9	Milwaukee Co.	J. W. Fitch	1866	1871
Mifflin	12	Iowa Co	J. T. Jones	1866	1871
Butte des Morts	15	Winnebago Co.	John McCabe	1866	1871
Waukau	26	Winnebago Co.	H. Clark	1866	1871
Martinsville	27	Dane Co.	George R. Pyle	1866	1871
Aztalan	30	Jefferson Co.	Lewis Jones	1866	1871
Hebron	34	Jefferson Co.	S. H. Bailey	1866	1871
Albion	35	Dane Co.	J. H. Potter	1866-67	1871
Cazenovia	48	Richland Co.		1866-67	1874
Marquette	53	Marquette Co.	W. W. Dantz	1866-67	1870-71
Milwaukee	56	Milwaukee Co.	E. Ferguson	1867	1871
Mount Hope	61	Grant Co.	C. B. Falley	1868?	1871
Salem	62	Kenosha Co.	H. S. Philips	1868?	1871
Hingham	65	Sheboygan Co	H. Dashiell	1868?	1891
Jamestown	67	Grant Co.		1868?	1871
Patch Grove	72	Grant Co.		1868?	1871
Pensaukee	74	Oconto Co.		1868?	1871
Embarrass	74	Waupaca Co.	David L. Messer	1868?	1871
Mukwanago	82	Waukesha Co.		1868?	1871

FIRST RESPONSE 1866-1870

Among the failed posts in the early years in places where new posts were formed and eventually succeeded, those listed below give the names of their commanders serving in 1868. They may have been the first commander, but not necessarily so. In many instances this list is the only concrete evidence available, other than the post number, that these posts were at one time actually functioning units.

COMMANDERS OF EARLY POSTS

Town	Post	Commander	County	Chartered	Revoked
Ripon	2	H. S. Town	Fond du Lac Co.	1866	1874
Mazomanie	3	H. R. Learned	Dane Co.	1866	1871
Fond du Lac	4	L. H. Cary	Fond du Lac Co.	1866	1871
Algoma	6	Andrew Sloggy	Kewaunee Co.	1866	1871
Edgerton	7	S.L. Lord	Rock Co.	1866	1871
Green Bay	8	C. B. Wheelock	Brown Co.	1866	1871
Racine	11	J. O. Bartlett	Racine Co.	1869	1874
Sun Prairie	13	J. C. Spencer	Dane Co.	1866	1871
Menominee	14	Thomas Blair	Dunn Co	1866	1871
Watertown	16	Henry L. Aram	Jefferson Co.	1866	1871
Sturgeon Bay	17	J. Harris. Jr.	Door Co.	1866	1871
Waterloo	18	M. V. Hutchinson	Jefferson Co.	1866	1871
Rome	20	J. L. Ackley	Jefferson Co.	1866	1871
New London	21	E. P. Perry	Waupaca Co.	1866	1871
Black Earth	23	Wells R. High	Dane Co.	1866	1871
Mineral Point	25	J. H. Vivian	Iowa Co.	1866	1871
Jefferson	28	J. N. P. Bird	Jefferson Co.	1866	1871
Lodi	29	W. Schermerhorn	Columbia Co.	1866	1871
Stockbridge	32	C. W. Thurston	Calumet Co.	1866	1871
Platteville	33	George B. Carter	Grant Co.	1866	1871
Boscobel	37	W. W. Boskin	Grant Co.	1866	1871
Manitowoc	38	Henry E. Ziely	Manitowoc Co.	1866-67	1871
Columbus	40	Charles L. Dering	Columbia Co.	1866-67	1871
Dodgeville	41	George H. Otis	Iowa Co.	1866-67	1871
Argyle	42	T. A. Rossing	LaFayette Co.	1866-67	1871
Princeton	43	O. N. Russell	Green Lake Co.	1866-67	1871
Prescott	44	D. J. Dill	Pierce Co.	1866-67	1871
Wautoma	45	Alviah Nash	Waushara Co.	1866-67	1871
Markesan	46	L. S. Knox	Green Lake Co.	1866-67	1871
Durand	47	H. D. Dyer	Pepin Co.	1866-67	1871
Brodhead	55	T. A. Jackson	Green Co.	1867	1871

SECOND TRY

The total number of *posts* within the Department of Wisconsin was considerably more than the number of *communities* having posts at some time or another, because 71 of those communities gave the Grand Army a "second try."

The great majority of the towns in this category had posts in the first four years or so of the order's history. But many of these early posts failed, and they were trimmed from the roster of active posts in 1871 or 1874.

But 15 other towns that later established new posts were places where the initial post, in most cases begun in the bounteous membership years of the 1880s, failed for reasons not now easily explained. Among these 15, 13 made the second effort to establish a post within five years of the initial failure; the exceptions were Sharon in Walworth County and Spencer in Marathon County, which founded new posts eight years after the first failure. Seven were reestablished around a year after their demise. This suggests that the same men who comprised the post membership when it ceased functioning were probably the instigators of the new post.

In contrast, the communities that came back after the great housecleanings of 1871 and 1874 were, on average, begun 11 years after the cleansing, and it seems more likely that the newer posts had a significantly different membership than the earlier posts. Of the 55 communities in this category, only one, Wautoma in Waushara County, returned in only three years—only to be defunct again five years later. A third effort at establishing a post at Wautoma was made in 1884, and it was success-

ful, lasting until 1938.

This exercise in beginning anew illustrates the Department of Wisconsin's efforts to keep the numbering system within bounds. Of the 71 communities having a second try, only one, Amherst in Portage County, ended up with a post number the second time the same as its first one. Amherst, like all of the new posts in towns that had previously had a post, had a new charter and not a reissue of the old one, so getting the same post number may have been but a coincidence.

Old numbers were frequently issued to new posts when an old number became available again, and some second-try posts were assigned a lower number than the initial post in that community had.

Most of the second tries were made in the 1880s, the years of expansive growth in the state and national G.A.R. Only a handful were founded after 1890, and only three in 1900 or beyond, the last being Westfield in Marquette County in 1906. This recharter was the final charter issued by the Department of Wisconsin. Westfield was Number 63, and the town was granted its charter two months after the new post at Ladysmith, which received charter No. 280, the highest number given.

Significantly, as the chart on the following pages shows, these second-try posts were largely successful, whether they were the early years fallouts (highlighted), or posts dropped later. Only four second tries could be considered to have failed again. Most had long years of service to their communities and to their members. They averaged just over 42 years duration.

SECOND TRY								
Town	First No.	Chartered	Ended	Years served	New No.	Chartered	Ended	Years served
Algoma	6	1866	1871	5	242	1888	1912	24
Alma	75	1868?	1871	3	196	1885	1919	34
Amherst	16	1880	1883	3	16	1884	1932	48
Appleton	76	1868?	1871	3	133	1884	1938	54
Arcadia	75	1883	1888	5	255	1889	1922	33
Argyle	42	1866-67	1871	4	206	1885	1915	30
Beaver Dam	64	1868?	1874	6	117	1883	1938	55
Beloit	70	1868?	1871	3	54	1882	1939	57
Black Earth	23	1866	1871	5	184	1884	1920	36
Black River Falls	71	1868?	1871	3	92	1883	1935	52
Bloomington	58	1868?	1871	3	134	1884	1931	47
Bocobel	37	1866	1871	5	101	1883	1941	58
Boyd	224	1886	1888	2	273	1892	1892	0
Brodhead	55	1867	1871	4	90	1883	1937	54

Town	First No.	Chartered	Ended	Years served	New No.	Chartered	Ended	Years served
Cadott	139	1884	1889	5	183	1891	1934	43
Cascade	66	1868?	1871	3	192	1885	1921	36
Chilton	39	1866-67	1871	4	205	1885	1933	48
Columbus	40	1866-67	1871	4	146	1884	1938	54
Cumberland	115	1883	1885	2	225	1886	1937	51
Dodgeville	41	1866-67	1871	4	109	1883	1931	48
Durand	47	1866-67	1871	4	82	1883	1924	41
Eau Claire	36	1866-67	1871	4	52	1882	1942	60
Eau Claire					162	1884	1887	3
Edgerton	7	1866	1871	5	137	1884	1936	52
Fond du Lac	4	1866	1871	5	130	1884	1939	55
Geneva	77	1868?	1871	3	27	1882	1936	54
Glenwood	272	1891	1893	2	233	1898	1918	20
Grantsburg	203	1885	1889	4	49	1902	1910	8
Green Bay	8	1866	1871	5	15	1876	1879?	2
Green Bay		*Third try was successful:*			124	1883	1936	53
Hayward	227	1885-86	1888	3	260	1889	1938	49
Jefferson	28	1866	1871	5	26	1882	1937	55
Kenosha	73	1868?	1871	3	230	1887	1942	55
Lake Mills	31	1866	1871	5	253	1889	1923	34
Lancaster	63	1868?	1871	3	132	1885	1942	57
Lodi	29	1866	1871	5	25	1882	1936	54
Manitowoc	38	1866-67	1871	4	18	1881	1934	53
Markesan	46	1666-67	1871	4	15	1885	1889	4
Mazomanie	3	1866	1871	5	56	1882	1929	47
Menominee	14	1866	1871	5	58	1883	1938	55
Mineral Point	25	1866	1871	5	125	1883	1938	55
Monroe	59	1868?	1871	3	102	1883	1936	53
Muscoda	71	1883	1896	13	279	1900	1924	24
Necedah	105	1883	1888	5	245	1889	1931	42
New London	21	1866	1871	5	46	1882	1938	56
Oregon	68	1868?	1871	3	123	1883	1927	44
Plainfield	15	1880	1883	3	197	1885	1937	52
Platteville	33	1866	1871	5	66	1883	1941	58
Prairie du Chien	12	1874	1874	0	37	1881	1941	60
Prairie du Sac	60	1868?	1871	3	35	1882	1906	24
Prescott	44	1866-67	1871	4	189	1884	1929	45
Princeton	43	1866-67	1871	4	228	1886	1913	27
Racine	11	1869	1874	5	17	1881	1936	55
Rice Lake	126	1884	1893	9	166	1894	1934	40
Richland Center	24	1866	1871	5	33	1882	1941	59

Posts which failed in the early years and were stricken from rolls in 1871 or 1874.

TOWN IN BOLD: *Posts which failed (five years or less) on second try.*

Town	First No.	Chartered	Ended	Years served	New No.	Chartered	Ended	Years served
Ripon	2	1866	1874	8	199	1885	1938	53
River Falls	54	1868	1871	3	177	1884	1934	50
Rome	20	1866	1871	5	262	1889	1910	21
Sharon	12	1880	1883	3	270	1891	1919	28
Sheboygan Falls	57	1868?	1871	3	12	1883	1936	53
Spencer	93	1883	1887	4	276	1895	1921	26
Stockbridge	32	1866	1871	5	40	1882	1920	38
Sturgeon Bay	17	1866	1871	5	226	1886	1919	33
Sun Prairie	13	1866	1871	5	208	1885	1906	21
Waterloo	18	1866	1871	5	119	1883	1902	19
Watertown	16	1866	1871	5	94	1883	1937	54
Waukesha	79	1868?	1871	3	19	1881	1937	56
Waupaca	69	1868?	1871	3	21	1881	1941	60
Wausau	83	1868?	1871	3	55	1882	1931	49
Wautoma	45	1866-67	1871	4	5	1874	1875	1
Wautoma			*Third try*	*was successful:*	135	1884	1938	54
Westfield	65	1883	1905	22	63	1906	1924	18
Winneconne	85	After 1872	1874	2	227	1889	1935	46

Posts which failed in the early years and were stricken from rolls in 1871 or 1874.

TOWN IN BOLD: *Posts which failed (five years or less) on second try.*

FIRST RESPONSE 1866-1870

Town	No.	Commander	County	Charter	Revoked	New #	Charter	Expired
Madison	1	J. M. Bull	Dane Co.	Jun. 10, 1866		11	Feb. 14, 1880	1940
Ripon	2	H. S. Town	Fond du Lac Co.	1866	Jul. 16, 1874	199	Jun. 13, 1885	1938
Mazomanie	3	H. R. Learned	Dane Co.	1866	Nov. 20, 1871	56	Dec. 1, 1882	1929
Milwaukee	3		Milwaukee Co.	1872-75				1878-79
Fond du Lac	4	L. H. Cary	Fond du Lac Co.	1866	Nov. 20, 1871	130	Jan. 19, 1884	1939
Greenbush	5	H. C. Stannard	Sheboygan Co.	1866	Nov. 20, 1871			
Algoma	6	Andrew Sloggy	Kewaunee Co.	1866	Nov. 20, 1871	242	Jan. 11, 1888	1912
Edgerton	7	S.L. Lord	Rock Co.	1866	Nov. 20, 1871	137	Feb. 11, 1884	1936
Green Bay	8	C. B. Wheelock	Brown Co.	1866	Nov. 20, 1871	124	Dec. 29, 1883	1936
Milwaukee	9	J. W. Fitch	Milwaukee Co.	1866	Nov. 20, 1871			
Oshkosh	10	A. B. Smedley	Winnebago Co.	Aug. 16, 1866				1938
Racine	11	J. O. Bartlett	Racine Co.	1869	Jul. 16, 1874	17	Jan. 24, 1881	1936
Mifflin	12	J. T. Jones	Iowa Co.	1866	Nov. 20, 1871			
Sun Prairie	13	J. C. Spencer	Dane Co.	1866	Nov. 20, 1871	208	Sep. 18, 1885	1906
Menominee	14	Thomas Blair	Dunn Co.	1866	Nov. 20, 1871	58	Jan. 6, 1883	1938
Butte des Morts	15	John McCabe	Winnebago Co.	1866	Nov. 20, 1871			
Watertown	16	Henry L. Aram	Jefferson Co.	1866	Nov. 20, 1871	94	Jul. 7, 1883	1937
Sturgeon Bay	17	J. Harris. Jr.	Door Co.	1866	Nov. 20, 1871	226	Oct. 16, 1886	1919
Waterloo	18	M. V. Hutchinson	Jefferson Co.	1866	Nov. 20, 1871	119	Nov. 7, 1883	1902
Rome	20	James L. Ackley	Jefferson Co.	1866	Nov. 20, 1871	262	Aug. 24, 1889	1910
New London	21	E. P. Perry	Waupaca Co.	1866	Nov. 20, 1871	46	Sep. 26, 1882	1938
Berlin	22	A. L. Tucker	Green Lake Co.	Sep. 8, 1866		4	Nov. 29, 1871	1937
Black Earth	23	Wells R. High	Dane Co.	1866	Nov. 20, 1871	184	Oct. 18, 1884	1920
Richland Center	24		Richland Co.	1866	Nov. 20, 1871	33	May 1, 1882	1941
Mineral Point	25	J. H. Vivian	Iowa Co	1866	Nov. 20, 1871	125	Dec. 20, 1883	1938
Waukau	26	H. Clark	Winnebago Co.	1866	Nov. 20, 1871			
Martinsville	27	George R. Pyle	Dane Co.	1866	Nov. 20, 1871			
Jefferson	28	J. N. P. Bird	Jefferson Co.	1866	Nov. 20, 1871	26	Apr. 15, 1882	1937
Lodi	29	W. Schermerhorn	Columbia Co.	1866	Nov. 20, 1871	25	Mar. 19, 1892	1936
Aztalan	30	Lewis Jones	Jefferson Co.	1866	Nov. 20, 1871			
Lake Mills	31		Jefferson Co.	1866	Nov. 20, 1871	253	May 28, 1889	1923
Stockbridge	32	C. W. Thurston	Calumet Co.	1866	Nov. 20, 1871	40	Oct. 6, 1882	1920
Platteville	33	George B. Carter	Grant Co.	Oct. 19, 1866	Nov. 20, 1871	66	Feb. 6, 1883	1941
Hebron	34	S. H. Bailey	Jefferson Co.	1866	Nov. 20, 1871			
Albion	35	J. H. Potter	Dane Co.	1866-67	Nov. 20, 1871			
Eau Claire	36		Eau Claire Co.	1866-67	Nov. 20, 1871	52	Nov. 8, 1882	1942
Boscobel	37	W. W. Boskin	Grant Co.	1866	Nov. 20, 1871	101	Aug. 15, 1883	1941
Manitowoc	38	Henry E. Ziely	Manitowoc Co.	1866-67	Nov. 20, 1871	18	Apr. 28, 1881	1934
Chilton	39		Calumet Co.	1866-67	Nov. 20, 1871	205	Aug. 28, 1885	1933

Italic: Did Not Return; Roman: Later as New Post; **Bold:** Succeeded

Town	No.	Commander	County	Charter	Revoked	New #	Charter	Expired
Columbus	40	Charles L. Dering	Columbia Co.	1866-67	Nov. 20, 1871	146	Apr. 10, 1884	1938
Dodgeville	41	George H. Otis	Iowa Co	1866-67	Nov. 20, 1871	109	Sep. 18, 1883	1931
Argyle	42	T. A. Rossing	LaFayette Co	1866-67	Nov. 20, 1871	206	Dec. 2, 1885	1915
Princeton	43	O. N. Russell	Green Lake Co.	1866-67	Nov. 20, 1871	228	Oct. 8, 1886	1913
Prescott	44	D. J. Dill	Pierce Co.	1866-67	Nov. 20, 1871	189	Dec. 16, 1884	1929
Wautoma	45	Alviah Nash	Waushara Co.	1866-67	Nov. 20, 1871	5	Jul. 25, 1874	1879
Markesan	46	L. S. Knox	Green Lake Co.	1666-67	Nov. 20, 1871	15	Aug. 22, 1885	1889
Durand	47	H. D. Dyer	Pepin Co.	1866-67	Nov. 20, 1871	82	May 17, 1883	1924
Cazenovia	48		Richland Co.	1866-67	Jul. 24, 1874			
Marquette	53	W. W. Dantz	Marquette Co.	1866-67				
River Falls	54		Pierce Co.	1867	Nov. 20, 1871	177	Aug. 23, 1884	1934
Brodhead	55	T. A. Jackson	Green Co.	1867	pre 11-29-71			
Milwaukee	56	E. Ferguson	Milwaukee Co.	1867	pre 11-29-71			
Sheboygan Falls	57		Sheboygan Co.	1868?	Nov. 20, 1871			
Bloomington	58	J. S . Frederich	Grant Co.	Sep. 11, 1867	Nov. 20, 1871	134	Feb. 8, 1884	1931
Monroe	59		Green Co.	1868?	Nov. 20, 1871	102	Aug. 28, 1883	1936
Prairie du Sac	60		Sauk Co.	1868?	Nov. 20, 1871	35	Jul. 1, 1882	1906
Mount Hope	61		Grant Co.	1868?	Nov. 20, 1871			
Salem	62		Kenosha Co.	1868?	Nov. 20, 1871	6	Nov. 29, 1871	
Lancaster	63		Grant Co.	1868?	Nov. 20, 1871	132	May 17, 1885	1942
Beaver Dam	64		Dodge Co.	1868?	Jul. 23, 1874			
Hingham	65		Sheboygan Co.	1868?	Nov. 20, 1871			
Cascade	66		Sheboygan Co.	1868?	Nov. 20, 1871	192	Feb. 26, 1885	1921
Jamestown	67		Grant Co.	1868?	Nov. 20, 1871			
Oregon	68		Dane Co.	1868?	Nov. 20, 1871	123	Nov. 26, 1883	1927
Waupaca	69		Waupaca Co.	1868?	Nov. 20, 1871	21	Oct. 26, 1881	1941
Beloit	70		Rock Co.	1868?	Nov. 20, 1871	54	Nov. 21, 1882	1939
Black River Falls	71		Jackson Co.	1868?	Nov. 20, 1871	92	Jun. 11, 1883	1935
Patch Grove	72		Grant Co.	1868?	Nov. 20, 1871			
Kenosha	73		Kenosha Co.	1868?	Nov. 20, 1871	230	Apr. 11, 1887	1942
Pensaukee	74		Oconto Co.	1868?	Nov. 20, 1871			
Alma	75		Buffalo Co.	1868?	Nov. 20, 1871	196	May 25, 1885	1914
Appleton	76		Outagamie Co.	1868?	Nov. 20, 1871	133	Jan. 31, 1884	1938
Geneva	77		Walworth Co.	1868?	Nov. 20, 1871	27	Apr. 18, 1882	1836
Embarrass	78		Waupaca Co.	1868?	Nov. 20, 1871			
Waukesha	79		Waukesha Co.	1868?	Nov. 20, 1871	19	May 24, 1881	1937
Mukwonago	82		Waukesha Co.	1868?	Nov. 20, 1871			
Wausau	83		Marathon Co.	1868?	Nov. 20, 1871	55	Dec. 5, 1882	1931
Winneconne	87		Winnebago Co.	1866-67	Jul. 16, 1874	227	Jan. 5, 1889	1935

Italic: **Did Not Return;** Roman: Later as New Post; **Bold: Succeeded**

COMPLETE ROSTER OF POSTS
BY COMMUNITY

POSTS WERE EVERYWHERE!

About 320 cities and towns had G.A.R posts. Because some failed and others were later started in the same location, these communities, each represented by a dot on the map, actually had some 404 posts.

During its lifespan, the G.A.R. had a considerable presence throughout Wisconsin, as the map of locales having posts in the state, this page, shows. The department chartered the first posts in 1866, just a year after the end of the Civil War, and the last new post, at Ladysmith, received its charter in 1906. During those four decades, the G.A.R. established more than four hundred posts.

Many of these, especially those founded in the first few years, did not survive. But among the communities where posts failed initially, many later reestablished and thrived.

All told, almost 320 Wisconsin communities had Grand Army units at one time or another. A few, such as Milwaukee, La Crosse, Oshkosh, Superior, and Berlin, had more than one post at the same time. Milwaukee's 12 posts did not all exist at the same time, but there was a multiplicity of posts in that city almost from the start.

The G.A.R. was everywhere in Wisconsin. Forest County was the only county that did not have at least one post at some time in the G.A.R.'s first 40 years. The distribution of the others is a fair representation of the population density of the state in the late nineteenth century. That distribution meant that the Grand Army of the Republic, Department of Wisconsin, enjoyed considerable political power at its zenith, which occurred in the 1890s and continued at least through the first decade of the twentieth century. The order influenced the legislature on a variety of issues that interested the veterans, from maintaining and governing the Grand Army Home at King to promoting patriotic themes in the state's schools.

The fact that so many of the G.A.R. posts of Wisconsin were in small towns is probably illustrative of the nature of the men who answered their country's call in 1861–65. The majority were from small towns and rural areas, and they returned to their homes to resume the lives they had set aside to settle the "late unpleasantness."

It must be remembered that never were there even close to 300 G.A.R. Posts active at one time. It seems the highest number in good standing at one time was 264. The dots on the map might be viewed as points of light which, one by one, over the years, flickered out until none remained.

The tables on the following pages show the complete list of 404 posts, right down to the mystery post, Post 80, even the location of which was lost with the records. The other 403, however, are known to have existed in specific locations. Many of them have more identity than just a home town and post number. They have a history. They carried on a tradition. They influenced their communities and left an imprint. Sometimes the only tangible evidence of the existence of a post may be a statue in front of the courthouse or a G.A.R. plot in the cemetery. But they left intangible imprints as well: an attitude, perhaps, which, down to the present generation, encouraged their sons and their later heirs to their own patriotic endeavors.

The Civil War, along with all its other attributes, permeated the whole fabric of society. (Even the American Revolution, according to some historians, had no more than a third of the colonists enthusiastic for the cause.) That pervasiveness, that sense of its being central to history, gave participants in the Civil War a feeling of having an ongoing responsibility for the country. This gave the G.A.R. incentive for coming into being and, as importantly, incentive to remain active for as long as possible. The Wisconsin posts of the Grand Army of the

Republic served their communities for a considerable number of years. They served the needs of their members, the veterans of the Civil War, and they served the civic needs of their communities as well.

Statistically, the local G.A.R. unit was active in the community for an average of just over 29 years—more than 33 years if one excludes the slew of posts that blossomed, withered, and died in the order's first five years. That is a long record of service for any organization with no aspirations for perpetuation. However, that figure does not tell much of the real story of post longevity. Ninety-five of the posts were active in their communities for a half-century or longer.

When Berlin's John H. Williams Post 4 ceased to exist with the death of its last member, the unit had been in service for 71 years. Two others, Lucius Fairchild Post 11, Madison, and Phil Sheridan Post 10, Oshkosh, expired after 74 and 72 years, respectively, after their charter dates. These three posts had battled each other in earlier years over which post had the longest continuous service in the Grand Army of the Republic, and Berlin was declared the longest. The other two each had a period in the 1870s when they were out of touch with the department, Madison for probably a couple of years and Oshkosh for about a year. But both operated from their original charter dates: Madison from June 10, 1866, and Oshkosh from August 16, 1866. Berlin's charter date was September 8, 1866. At this point in time, the contested honor may have been Berlin's but the longevity of the two runners-up is every bit as impressive.

It also is impressive that eight posts had 60 or more years of existence, beginning with Albert Weatherbe Post 128, Chetek, with 64 years; neighbors H. A. Tator Post 13 of Reedsburg and Joe Hooker Post 9 of Baraboo, both with 62 years; Theodore Sutphen Post 41, Evansville, with 61 years, and George H. Bell Post 53 of Wonewoc, James A. Garfield Post 21 of Waupaca, Phil W. Plummer Post 37 of Prairie du Chien, and Eagle Post 52 of Eau Claire, all with 60 years. Thirty-five posts operated in their towns for 55 to 59 years, and another 48 served from 50 to 54 years. In all, more than 23 percent of the posts survived a half century or longer. Another 60, or nearly 15 percent more, operated for 40 to 49 years.

There were posts on the other end of longevity, naturally. The shortest record was Post 12 of Prairie du Chien, which existed for just over two weeks. And Post 273 of Boyd, one of the later chartered posts, was dead in less than three months. Twenty-six of the posts chartered after the cleansing of the rosters in 1871 and 1874—a mere 6 percent—survived less than a decade.

Studying the complete roster of posts on the following pages suggests that for the most part the local posts fulfilled their purpose for as long as they could. The G.A.R. was much more than a passing fancy.

The Boys in Blue had been ubiquitous enough to have left a mark upon the state as a whole, and certainly upon the communities where the local post and its men, its programs and its influence, were remembered considerably past the time the last of them answered the final roll call.

POSTS BY COMMUNITY

Town	Post No.	County	Chartered	Extinct	Years existed
Abrams	29	Oconto Co.	Nov. 22, 1896	1940	44
Albany	69	Green Co.	Mar. 26, 1883	1906	23
Albion	35	Dane Co.	1866-67	Nov. 20, 1871	4
Algoma	6	Kewaunee Co.	1866	Nov. 20, 1871	5
	Known as Ahnapee before 1897				
Algoma	242	Kewaunee Co.	Jan. 11, 1888	1912	24
Alma	75	Buffalo Co.	1868?	Nov. 20, 1871	3
Alma	196	Buffalo Co.	May 25, 1885	1919	34
Alma Center	87	Jackson Co.	Jun. 15, 1883	1942	59
Amery	263	Polk Co.	Oct. 25, 1889	1904	15
Amherst	16	Portage Co.	1884	1932	3
Amherst	16	Portage Co.	Apr. 18, 1880	1883	48
Ahnapee	*See Algoma, #4 and #5*				
Antigo	78	Langlade Co.	May 15, 1883	1936	53
Appleton	76	Outagamie Co.	1868?	Nov. 20, 1871	3
Appleton	133	Outagamie Co.	Jan. 31, 1884	1938	54
Arcadia	75	Trempealeau Co.	1883	1888	5
Arcadia	255	Trempealeau Co.	Jun 28, 1889	1922	33

Town	Post No.	County	Chartered	Extinct	Years existed
Arena	107	Iowa Co.	Sep. 7, 1883	1917	34
Argyle	42	LaFayette Co.	1866-67	Nov. 20, 1871	4
Argyle	206	LaFayette Co.	Dec. 2, 1885	1915	30
Arkansaw	127	Pepin Co.	Dec. 29. 1893	1903	10
Ashland	140	Ashland Co.	Feb. 19, 1884	1938	54
Auburn	269	Fond du Lac Co.	Aug. 24, 1894	1898	4
	Also known as New Cassel				
Augusta	98	Eau Claire Co.	Aug. 3, 1883	1941	58
Auroraville	28	Waushara Co.	Jun. 4, 1882	1885	3
Aztalan	30	Jefferson Co.	1866	Nov. 20, 1871	5
Bangor	234	La Crosse Co.	May 28, 1887	1936	49
Baraboo	9	Sauk Co.	Mar. 4, 1880	1942	62
Barron	172	Barron Co.	Aug. 6, 1884	1931	47
Basswood	63	Richland Co.	Jan. 26, 1883	1901	18
	Also known as Eagle Corners in 1884, 1900 Journals				
Bayfield	249	Bayfield Co.	Mar. 24, 1889	1927	38
Bear Creek	51	Outagamie Co.	Nov. 26, 1897	1913	16
	Also known as Welcome 1898 to 1915				
Beaver Dam	6	Dodge Co.	1868?	Jul. 23, 1874	6
Beaver Dam	117	Dodge Co.	Oct. 29, 1883	1938	55
Beetown	175	Grant Co.	Aug. 16, 1884	Apr. 1, 1893	9
Belmont	*See Blaine, #46*				
Bell Center	*See Gays Mills, #136*				
Bellville	121	Dane Co.	Nov. 8, 1883	1931	48
Beloit	54	Rock Co.	Nov. 21, 1882	1939	57
Beloit	70	Rock Co.	1868?	Nov. 20, 1871	3
Berlin	4 (22)	Green Lake Co.	Sep. 8, 1866	Apr. 18, 1937	71
Berlin	139	Green Lake Co.	Feb. 11, 1898	1908	10
Birnamwood	178	Shawano Co.	Dec. 18, 1888	1932	44
Black Creek	116	Outagamie Co.	Oct. 25, 1883	1911	28
Black Earth	23	Dane Co.	1866	Nov. 20, 1871	5
Black Earth	184	Dane Co.	Oct. 18, 1884	1920	36
Black River Falls	71	Jackson Co.	1868?	Nov. 20, 1871	3
Black River Falls	92	Jackson Co.	Jun . 11, 1883	1935	52
Blaine	115	Portage Co.	Jun. 18, 1888	1903	15
	Also known as Belmont. (Belmont is town in which Blaine was located)				
Blanchardville	224	LaFayette Co.	Dec. 27, 1888	1931	43
Bloomer	147	Chippewa Co.	Mar. 31, 1884	1928	44
Bloomington	58	Grant Co.	Sept.11, 1867	Nov. 20, 1871	3
Bloomington	134	Grant Co.	Feb. 8, 1884	1931	47
Boaz	62	Richland Co.	Jan. 21, 1883	Jan. 1, 1898	15
Boscobel	37	Grant Co.	1866	Nov. 20, 1871	5
Boscobel	101	Grant Co.	Aug. 15, 1883	1941	58

Town	Post No.	County	Chartered	Extinct	Years existed
Boyceville	84	Dunn Co.	May 12, 1883	1919	36
	Known as Granger from 1883 to 1895				
	Also listed at Downing in 1887, 1888, 1900, 1901, 1905				
Boyd	224	Chippewa Co.	Oct. 27, 1886	1888	2
Boyd	273	Chippewa Co.	July 1, 1892	Sep. 24, 1892	0
Bradtville	*See Wyalusing #403*				
Brandon	136	Fond du Lac Co.	Mar. 7, 1884	1926	42
Briggsville	188	Marquette Co.	Oct. 27, 1884	1930	46
Brillion	222	Calumet Co.	Sep. 18, 1886	1917	31
Brodhead	55	Green Co.	1867	pre 11-20-71	4
Brodhead	90	Green Co.	Jun. 4, 1883	1937	54
Bruce	62	Rusk Co.	Jan. 4, 1902	1917	15
Burlington	201	Racine Co.	Aug. 6, 1885	1920	35
Butte des Morts	15	Winnebago Co.	1866	Nov. 20, 1871	5
Butternut	5	Ashland Co.	Nov. 12, 1879	1913	34
Cadott	139	Chippewa Co.	Mar. 12, 1884	Sep. 14, 1896	12
Cadott	183	Chippewa Co.	Dec. 29, 1891	1934	55
Cambridge	229	Dane Co.	Jan. 5, 1887	1928	41
Campbellsport	246	Fond du Lac Co.	Feb. 7, 1889	1919	30
Camp Douglas	*See Oakdale, #261*				
Cascade	66	Sheboygan Co.	1868?	Nov. 20, 1871	3
Cascade	192	Sheboygan Co.	Feb. 26, 1885	1921	36
Cashton	214	Monroe Co.	Feb. 11, 1886	1900	14
Cassville	218	Grant Co.	Jun. 19, 1886	1901-02	16
Cataract	235	Monroe Co.	Jun. 4, 1887	1896	9
Cazenovia	48	Richland Co.	1866-67	Jul. 24, 1874	7
Cedar Grove	62	Sheboygan Co.	Mar. 25, 1898	1901	3
Cedarburg	244	Ozaukee Co.	Jan. 21, 1889	1920	31
Chelsea	178	Taylor Co.	Sep. 27, 1884	1888	4
Chetek	128	Barron Co.	Jan. 15, 1884	1948	64
Chilton	39	Calumet Co.	1866-67	Nov. 20, 1871	4
Chilton	205	Calumet Co.	Aug. 28, 1885	1933	48
Chippewa Falls	68	Chippewa Co.	Mar. 15, 1883	1942	59
Clear Lake	142	Polk Co.	Mar. 7, 1884	1932	48
Clinton	70	Rock Co.	Apr. 18, 1883	1926	73
Clintonville	32	Waupaca Co.	May 28, 1882	1913	31
Colby	112	Clark/Marathon Cos.	Dec. 18, 1883	1931	48
Colfax	183	Dunn Co.	Oct. 15, 1884	1891	7
Coloma	269	Waushara Co.	July 7, 1891	May 14, 1894	3
Columbus	40	Columbia Co.	1866-67	Nov. 20, 1871	4
Columbus	146	Columbia Co.	Apr. 10, 1884	1938	54
Cumberland	115	Barron Co.	1883	1885	2

Town	Post No.	County	Chartered	Extinct	Years existed
Cumberland	225	Barron Co.	Sep 20, 1886	1937	51
Dallas	144	Barron Co.	Mar. 13, 1884	1907	23
Darien	3	Walworth Co.	Aug. 26, 1879	1922	43
Darlington	45	Lafayette Co.	Oct. 10, 1882	1937	55
Dartford	202	Green Lake Co.	Sep. 5, 1885	1931	46
	Also known as Green Lake				
Delevan	6	Walworth Co.	Nov. 28, 1879	1935	56
Depere	91	Brown Co.	Jun. 18, 1883	1937	54
Desoto	106	Vernon Co.	Oct. 16, 1883	1913	30
Dodgeville	41	Iowa Co.	1866-67	Nov. 20, 1871	4
Dodgeville	109	Iowa Co.	Sep. 18, 1883	1931	48
Dorchester	168	Clark Co.	Jul. 9, 1884	1928	44
Downing	*See Boyceville, #54*				
Durand	47	Pepin Co.	1866-67	Nov. 20, 1871	4
Durand	82	Pepin Co.	May 17, 1883	1924	41
Eagle	167	Waukesha Co.	Feb. 21, 1884	1887	3
Eagle Corners	*See Basswood, #29*				
Eagle River	167	Vilas Co.	Jul. 21, 1888	1890	2
Easton	*See White Creek, #391*				
East Troy	171	Walworth Co.	Aug. 16, 1884	1929	45
	Known as Troy until 1906				
Eau Claire	36	Eau Claire Co.	1866-67	Nov. 20, 1871	4
Eau Claire	52	Eau Claire Co.	Nov.8, 1882	1942	60
Eau Claire	162	Eau Claire Co.	Jul. 21, 1884	1886-87	3
EauGalle	167	Dunn Co.	Feb. 27, 1890	1913	23
Edgerton	7	Rock Co.	1866	Nov. 20, 1871	5
Edgerton	137	Rock Co.	Feb. 11, 1884	1936	52
Eleva	71	Trempealeau Co.	Apr. 26, 1896	1928	34
Elkhorn	76	Walworth Co.	May 10, 1883	1941	58
Ellsworth	118	Pierce Co.	Nov. 23, 1883	1927	44
Elroy	47	Juneau Co.	Oct. 6, 1882	1936	54
Embarass	78	Waupaca Co.	1868?	1874	6
Eureka	251	Winnebago Co.	Apr, 19, 1889	1926	37
Evansville	41	Rock Co.	Sep. 24, 1882	1943	61
Excelsior	51	Richland Co.	Oct. 27, 1882	Dec. 1896	14
Fairchild	166	Eau Claire Co.	Jun. 19, 1884	Aug. 11, 1893	9
Fall River	271	Columbia Co.	Sep. 28, 1891	1936	45
Fennimore	173	Grant Co.	Aug. 12, 1884	1935	51
Fish Creek	211	Door Co.	Oct. 24, 1885	1896	11
Florence	268	Florence Co.	Jun. 30, 1891	1928	37
Fond du Lac	4	Fond du Lac Co.	1866	Nov. 20, 1871	5
Fond du Lac	130	Fond du Lac Co.	Jan. 19, 1884	1939	55

Town	Post No.	County	Chartered	Extinct	Years existed
Forestville	97	Door Co.	Aug. 11, 1883	1901-02	19
Fort Atkinson	159	Jefferson Co.	Apr. 24, 1884	1923	39
Fountain City	257	Buffalo Co.	Jul 15, 1889	1938	49
Fox Lake	100	Dodge Co.	Aug. 29, 1883	1912	29
Fremont	160	Waupaca Co.	Apr. 30, 1884	1931	47
Friendship	122	Adams Co.	Dec. 13, 1883	1935	52
Galesville	258	Trempealeau Co.	Jul 24, 1889	1933	44
Gays Mills	80	Crawford Co.	Apr 24, 1883	1912	29
	Known as Bell Center before 1892				
Geneva	77	Walworth Co.	1868?	Nov. 20, 1871	3
	Also known as Lake Geneva				
Glenwood	233	St. Croix Co.	Dec. 3, 1898	1918	20
Glenwood	272	St. Croix Co.	Nov. 12, 1891	Jul. 7, 1893	2
Grand Rapids	*See Wisconsin Rapids, #397*				
Granger	*See Boyceville, #54*				
Grantsburg	49	Burnett Co.	Nov. 10, 1902	1910	8
Grantsburg	203	Burnett Co.	Sep. 25, 1885	1889	4
Gratiot	176	Lafayette Co.	Aug. 8, 1884	1922	38
Green Bay	8	Brown Co.	1866	Nov. 20, 1871	5
Green Bay	15	Brown Co.	1876	1879?	3
Green Bay	124	Brown Co.	Dec. 29, 1883	1936	53
Greenbush	5	Sheboygan Co.	1866	Nov. 20, 1871	5
Green Lake	*See Dartford, #96*				
Greenwood	213	Clark Co.	Oct. 20, 1888	1919	31
Hammond	182	St. Croix Co.	Sep. 17, 1884	1901-02	18
Hancock	150	Waushara Co.	Mar. 26, 1884	1911	27
Hartford	165	Washington Co.	May 31, 1884	1938	54
Hayward	227	Sawyer Co.	Oct. 6, 1886	1888	3
Hayward	260	Sawyer Co.	Aug. 20, 1889	1938	49
Hazel Green	266	Grant Co.	Apr. 22, 1891	1922	31
Hebron	34	Jefferson Co.	1866	Nov. 20, 1871	5
Hersey	200	St. Croix Co.	Jan. 8, 1886	1911	25
Hillsboro	141	Vernon Co.	Mar. 12, 1884	1936	52
Hingham	65	Sheboygan Co.	1867	1871	
Horicon	220	Dodge Co.	Jun. 15, 1886	1938	52
Hortonville	210	Outagamie Co.	Sep. 29, 1885	1931	46
Hudson	151	St. Croix Co.	Mar. 24, 1884	1938	54
Hurley	259	Iron Co.	Jul 30, 1889	Jun. 30, 1896	7
Independence	275	Trempealeau Co.	Jan. 26, 1893	1898	5
Iola	99	Waupaca Co.	Apr. 21, 1888	1908	20
Jamestown	67	Grant Co.	1868?	Nov. 20, 1871	3
Janesville	20	Rock Co.	Oct. 21, 1881	Apr. 12, 1937	56

Town	Post No.	County	Chartered	Extinct	Years existed
Jefferson	26	Jefferson Co.	Apr. 15, 1882	1937	55
Jefferson	28	Jefferson Co.	1866	Nov. 20, 1871	5
Juneau	31	Dodge Co.	Jun. 1, 1882	1929	47
Kaukauna	247	Outagamie Co.	Feb. 15, 1889	1934	45
Kendall	88	Monroe Co.	May 21, 1883	1905	22
Kenosha	73	Kenosha Co.	1868?	Nov. 20, 1871	3
Kenosha	230	Kenosha Co.	Apr. 11, 1887	1942	55
Keshena	261	Menominee Co.	Aug. 16, 1889	Apr. 5, 1933	44
Kewaunee	155	Kewaunee Co.	May 6, 1884	1919	35
Kiel	190	Manitowoc Co.	Dec. 27, 1884	1926	42
Kilbourn City	*See Wisconsin Dells, #396*				
King	126	Waupaca Co.	Jun. 14, 1893	1937	44
	Wisconsin Veterans Home was name until 1941				
Kingston	28	Green Lake Co.	Mar. 17, 1888	1930	42
Knapp	148	Dunn Co.	Apr. 9, 1884	1902	18
La Crosse	15	La Crosse Co.	Nov. 29, 1901	1922	21
La Crosse	38	La Crosse Co.	Aug. 17, 1882	1941	59
La Crosse	77	La Crosse Co.	May 5, 1883	1936	53
	Known as North La Crosse until 1884				
Ladysmith	280	Rusk Co.	Aug. 7, 1906	July, 1940	34
La Farge	*See Star, #344*				
Lake Geneva	27	Walworth Co.	Apr. 18, 1882	1936	54
	See also Geneva, #137				
Lake Mills	31	Jefferson Co.	1866	Nov. 20, 1871	5
Lake Mills	253	Jefferson Co.	May 28, 1889	1923	34
Lancaster	63	Grant Co.	1868?	Nov. 20, 1871	3
Lancaster	132	Grant Co.	May 17, 1885	1942	57
Lavalle	49	Sauk Co.	Oct. 26, 1882	1901-02	20
Lime Ridge	174	Sauk Co.	Aug. 11, 1888	1908	20
Little Wolf	*See Manawa, #198*				
Lodi	25	Columbia Co.	Mar. 19, 1882	1936	44
Lodi	29	Columbia Co.	1866	Nov. 20, 1871	5
Lone Rock	24	Richland Co.	Feb. 23, 1882	1940	58
Lowell	203	Dodge Co.	May 25, 1889	1934	45
Loyal	236	Clark Co.	Aug. 5, 1887	1911	24
Loyd	108	Richland Co.	Sep. 10, 1883	Nov. 14, 1893	10
Madison	11 (1)	Dane Co.	Jun. 10, 1866	Jan. 30, 1940	74
Maiden Rock	204	Pierce Co.	Aug. 1, 1885	1905	20
Manawa	120	Waupaca Co.	Nov. 6, 1883	1909	26
	Listed as Little Wolf in 1888				
Manitowoc	18	Manitowoc Co.	Apr. 28, 1881	1934	53
Manitowoc	38	Manitowoc Co.	1866-67	Nov. 20, 1871	4

Town	Post No.	County	Chartered	Extinct	Years existed
Marcellon	267	Columbia Co.	May 23, 1891	1903	12
Marinette	207	Marinette Co.	Sep. 14, 1885	1942	57
Marion	79	Waupaca Co.	May 11, 1883	1896	13
Markesan	15	Green Lake Co.	Aug. 22, 1885	1889	4
Markesan	46	Green Lake Co.	1866-67	Nov. 20, 1871	4
Marquette	53	Green Lake Co.	1866-67	67	0
Marshfield	110	Wood Co.	Oct. 23, 1883	1935	52
Martinsville	27	Dane Co.	1866	Nov. 20, 1871	5
Mather	248	Juneau Co.	Nov. 11, 1893	1903	10
Mauston	59	Juneau Co.	Jan. 10, 1883	1936	53
Mayville	43	Dodge Co.	Aug. 23, 1882	1935	53
Mazomanie	3	Dane Co.	1866	Nov. 20, 1871	5
Mazomanie	56	Dane Co.	Dec. 1, 1882	1929	47
Medford	145	Taylor Co.	Mar. 25, 1884	1933	49
Melrose	161	Jackson Co.	May 1, 1884	1910	26
Menasha	44	Winnebago Co.	Sep. 8, 1882	May 1,1933	51
Menomonee	14	Dunn Co.	1866	Nov. 20, 1871	5
Menomonie	58	Dunn Co.	Jan. 6, 1883	1938	55
	Also spelled Menomonee until 1888				
Merrill	131	Lincoln Co.	Jan. 24, 1884	1941	57
Merrillan	86	Jackson Co.	May 15,1883	1920	37
Merrimack	195	Sauk Co.	Apr. 25, 1885	1923	38
Mifflin	12	Iowa Co.	1866	Nov. 20, 1871	5
Milton	60	Rock Co.	Ja. 10, 1883	1931	48
Milwaukee	1	Milwaukee Co.	Jan. 14, 1880	1939	59
Milwaukee	2	Milwaukee Co.	Jun. 9, 1875	1918	43
Milwaukee	3	Milwaukee Co.	1870-71	1878-79	7
Milwaukee	9	Milwaukee Co.	1866	pre 11-20-71	5
Milwaukee	12	Milwaukee Co.	Sep16, 1875	1875-76	1
Milwaukee	56	Milwaukee Co.	1867	pre 11-20-71	4
Milwaukee	8 (84)	Milwaukee Co.	Apr. 26, 1870	1917	47
Milwaukee	211	Milwaukee Co.	May 17, 1898	1906	8
Milwaukee	223	Milwaukee Co.	Aug. 18, 1886	1938	52
Milwaukee	240	Milwaukee Co.	Jun. 7, 1888	1919	31
Milwaukee	250	Milwaukee Co.	Apr. 8, 1889	1923	34
Milwaukee	274	Milwaukee Co.	Jul. 26, 1892	1909	17
Mindoro	233	La Crosse Co.	Jun. 3, 1887	Jan. 1, 1898	11
Mineral Point	25	Iowa Co.	1866	Nov. 20, 1871	5
Mineral Point	125	Iowa Co.	Dec. 20, 1883	1938	55
Mondovi	95	Buffalo Co.	Jul. 14, 1883	1922	39
Monroe	59	Green Co.	1868?	Nov. 20, 1871	3
Monroe	102	Green Co.	Aug. 28, 1883	1936	53

Town	Post No.	County	Chartered	Extinct	Years existed
Montello	64	Marquette Co.	Feb. 23, 1883	1927	44
Monticello	113	Green Co.	Oct. 6, 1883	1909	26
Mount Hope	61	Grant Co.	1868?	Nov. 20, 1871	3
Mount Horeb	191	Dane Co.	Mar. 25, 1885	1942	57
Mukwonago	82	Waukesha Co.	1868?	Nov. 20, 1871	4
Muscoda	71	Grant Co.	Mar. 28, 1883	Feb.21, 1896	13
Muscoda	279	Grant Co.	Mar. 1, 1900	1924	24
Necedah	105	Juneau Co.	May 3, 1883	1887-88	5
Necedah	245	Juneau Co.	Feb. 9, 1889	1931	42
Neenah	129	Winnebago Co.	Jan. 18, 1884	1939	55
Neillsville	48	Clark Co.	Nov. 24, 1882	1932	50
Nelson	252	Buffalo Co.	Apr. 23, 1889	1910	21
New Cassel	*See Auburn, #22*				
New Centerville	15	St. Croix Co.	Apr. 13, 1889	1899	10
	Spelled New Centreville until 1892				
New Lisbon	61	Juneau Co.	Jan. 17, 1883	1937	54
New London	21	Waupaca Co.	1866	Nov. 20, 1871	5
New London	46	Waupaca Co.	Sep. 26, 1882	1938	56
New Richmond	103	St. Croix Co.	Sep. 18, 1883	1942	59
North Freedom	83	Sauk Co.	May 2, 1883	1926	43
North La Crosse	*See La Crosse Post 77, #181*				
Norwalk	179	Monroe Co.	Sep. 5, 1884	1931	47
Oakdale	29	Monroe Co.	Apr. 13, 1882	Aug. 17, 1895	13
	Camp Douglas listed as site of Post 29 in 1887				
Oakley	*See Pedee, # 278*				
Oconomowoc	194	Waukesha Co.	Mar. 26, 1885	1921	36
Oconto	74	Oconto Co.	Oct. 10, 1883	1938	55
Ogdensburg	239	Waupaca Co.	Nov. 3, 1887	Jul. 16, 1896	9
Omro	7	Winnebago Co.	Feb. 14, 1880	1936	56
Oneida	278	Brown Co.	Sep. 21, 1899	1926	27
Ontario	158	Vernon Co.	Apr. 19, 1884	1917	33
Oregon	68	Dane Co.	1868?	Nov. 20, 1871	3
Oregon	123	Dane Co.	Nov. 26, 1883	1927	44
Osceola Mills	164	Polk Co.	May 22, 1884	1900	16
	Changed to Osceola in 1897				
Oshkosh	10	Winnebago Co.	Aug. 16, 1866	1938	70
Oshkosh	241	Winnebago Co.	Dec. 22, 1887	1924	37
Osseo	93	Trempealeau Co.	May 28, 1888	1900	12
Oxford	143	Marquette Co.	Mar. 15, 1884	1926	42
Palmyra	138	Jefferson Co.	Feb. 16, 1884	1923	39
Pardeeville	186	Columbia Co.	Oct. 6, 1884	1938	54
Patch Grove	72	Grant Co.	1868?	Nov. 20, 1871	3

Town	Post No.	County	Chartered	Extinct	Years existed
Pedee	264	Green Co.	Feb. 12, 1890	1906	16
Oakley succeeded Pedee as mail address in 1899					
Pensaukee	74	Oconto Co.	1868?	Nov. 20, 1871	3
Pepin	108	Pepin Co.	Jul. 7, 1894	1910	16
Peshtigo	248	Marinette Co.	Feb. 16, 1889	Apr. 12, 1893	4
Pewaukee	105	Waukesha Co.	May 14, 1888	1904	16
Phillips	181	Price Co.	Sep. 7, 1884	1938	54
Pittsville	73	Wood Co.	May 10, 1883	1905	22
Plainfield	15	Waushara Co.	1880	1883	3
Plainfield	197	Waushara Co.	Aug. 22, 1885	1937	52
Platteville	33	Grant Co.	Oct. 19, 1866	Nov. 20, 1871	5
Platteville	66	Grant Co.	Feb. 6, 1883	1941	58
Plover	149	Portage Co.	Mar. 21, 1884	1938	52
Plum City	209	Pierce Co.	1885	1888	3
Plymouth	212	Sheboygan Co.	Nov. 9, 1885	1938	53
Port Washington	254	Ozaukee Co.	Jun. 25, 1889	1894	5
Portage	14	Columbia Co.	Apr. 13, 1880	1931	51
Potosi	162	Grant Co.	1892	1923	31
Poy Sippi	231	Waushara Co.	Apr. 11, 1887	1929	42
Poynette	23	Columbia Co.	Pre-1887	1888	1
Prairie du Chien	12	Crawford Co.	Jun. 30, 1874	Jul. 16, 1874	0
Prairie du Chien	37	Crawford Co.	Jul. 18, 1882	1941	60
Prairie du Sac	35	Sauk Co.	Jul. 1, 1882	1906	24
Prairie du Sac	60	Sauk Co.	1868?	Nov. 20, 1871	3
Prairie Farm	237	Barron Co.	Jul 16, 1887	1923	36
Prescott	44	Pierce Co.	1866-67	Nov. 20, 1871	4
Prescott	189	Pierce Co.	Dec. 16, 1884	1929	45
Princeton	43	Green Lake Co.	1866-67	Nov. 20, 1871	4
Princeton	228	Green Lake Co.	Oct. 8, 1886	1913	27
Racine	11	Racine Co.	1869	Jul. 16, 1874	5
Racine	17	Racine Co.	Jan. 24, 1881	1936	55
Reedsburg	13	Sauk Co.	Apr. 13, 1880	1942	62
Rhinelander	232	Oneida Co.	May 5, 1887	1908	21
Rice Lake	126	Barron Co.	Jan.3, 1884	Mar. 3, 1893	9
Rice Lake	166	Barron Co.	Aug. 1, 1894	1934	40
Richland Center	24	Richland Co.	1866	Nov. 20, 1871	5
Richland Center	33	Richland Co.	May 1, 1882	1941	59
Ripon	2	Fond du Lac Co.	1866	Jul. 16, 1874	8
Ripon	199	Fond du Lac Co.	Jun. 13, 1885	1938	53
River Falls	54	Pierce Co.	1868	Nov. 20, 1871	3
River Falls	177	Pierce Co.	Aug. 23, 1884	1934	50
Rock Elm	72	Pierce Co.	Mar. 27, 1883	1919	36

Town	Post No.	County	Chartered	Extinct	Years existed
Rockbridge	221	Richland Co.	Aug. 27, 1886	1908	22
Rome	20	Jefferson Co.	1866	Nov. 20, 1871	5
Rome	262	Jefferson Co.	Aug. 24, 1889	1910	21
Royalton	265	Waupaca Co.	Feb. 16, 1891	1899	8
Salem	62	Kenosha Co.	1868?	Nov. 20, 1871	3
	Listed as West Salem in 1868				
Seneca	216	Crawford Co.	Mar. 27, 1886	1901	15
Sextonville	185	Richland Co.	Oct. 7, 1884	1918	34
Seymour	198	Outagamie Co.	May 25, 1885	1914	29
Sharon	12	Walworth Co.	1880	1883	3
Sharon	270	Walworth Co.	Jul. 9, 1891	1919	28
Sauk City	*See Prairie du Sac #300*				
Shawano	81	Shawano Co.	May 4, 1883	1917	34
Sheboygan	187	Sheboygan Co.	Nov. 28, 1884	1938	54
Sheboygan Falls	12	Sheboygan Co.	July 10, 1883	1936	53
Sheboygan Falls	57	Sheboygan Co.	1868?	Nov. 20, 1871	3
Shell Lake	243	Washburn Co.	Jan. 21, 1888	1917	29
Shullsburg	96	Lafayette Co.	Jul. 16, 1883	1927	44
Soldiers Grove	152	Crawford Co.	May 3, 1884	1920	36
South Milwaukee	175	Milwaukee Co.	Nov. 15, 1893	1922	29
Sparta	30	Monroe Co.	Apr. 24, 1882	1934	52
Spencer	93	Marathon Co.	1883	1887	4
Spencer	276	Marathon Co.	Jan. 19, 1895	1921	26
Spooner	65	Washburn Co.	1903	1930	27
Spring Green	39	Sauk Co.	Jul. 15, 1882	1941	59
Spring Valley	272	Pierce Co.	Jan. 21, 1895	1929	34
St. Croix Falls	111	Polk Co.	Sep. 24, 1883	1921	38
Star	154	Vernon Co.	Apr. 23, 1884	1938	54
	Changed to La Farge in 1902				
Stevens Point	156	Portage Co.	Apr. 9, 1884	1938	54
Stockbridge	32	Calumet Co.	1866	Nov. 20, 1871	5
Stockbridge	40	Calumet Co.	Oct. 6, 1882	1920	38
Stoughton	153	Dane Co.	Mar. 29, 1884	1934	50
Sturgeon Bay	17	Door Co.	1866	Nov. 20, 1871	5
Sturgeon Bay	226	Door Co.	Oct. 16, 1886	1919	33
Sun Prairie	13	Dane Co.	1866	Nov. 20, 1871	5
Sun Prairie	208	Dane Co.	Sep. 18, 1885	1906	21
Superior	170	Douglas Co.	Aug. 9, 1884	1942	58
	Changed from West Superior in 1889				
Superior	273	Douglas Co.	Jan. 25, 1893	1904	11
Sylvan Corners	99	Richland Co.	Apr. 21, 1883	1888	5
Theresa	169	Dodge Co.	Jul. 10, 1884	1901	17

Town	Post No.	County	Chartered	Extinct	Years existed
Thorpe	163	Clark Co.	May 12, 1884	1911	27
Tomah	42	Monroe Co.	Aug. 14, 1882	1936	54
Trempealeau	13	Trempealeau Co.	1873-74	1875	2
Trimbelle	238	Pierce Co.	Aug. 11, 1887	1908	21
Troy	*See East Troy, #107*				
Turtle Lake	157	Barron Co.	Apr. 23, 1884	1915	31
Two Rivers	219	Manitowoc Co.	Jun. 16, 1886	1918	32
Union Grove	215	Racine Co.	Jan. 26, 1886	1920	34
Unity	217	Marathon Co.	May 20, 1886	1896	10
Verona	75	Dane Co.	Feb. 22, 1888	1921	33
Viola	85	Richland Co.	May 24, 1883	1927	44
Viroqua	36	Vernon Co.	Jul. 17, 1882	1937	55
Warren	*See Warren Mills, #368*				
Warren Mills	57	Monroe Co.	Dec. 30, 1882	1929	47
	Also known as Warren, 1892 to present				
Washburn	254	Bayfield Co.	Dec. 20, 1895	1900	5
Waterloo	18	Jefferson Co.	1866	Nov. 20, 1871	5
Waterloo	119	Jefferson Co.	Nov. 7, 1883	1902	19
Watertown	16	Jefferson Co.	1866	Nov. 20, 1871	5
Watertown	94	Jefferson Co.	Jul. 7, 1883	1937	54
Waukau	26	Winnebago Co.	1866	Nov. 20, 1871	5
Waukesha	19	Waukesha Co.	May 24, 1881	1937	56
Waukesha	79	Waukesha Co.	1868?	Nov. 20, 1871	3
Waupaca	21	Waupaca Co.	Oct. 26, 1881	1941	60
Waupaca	69	Waupaca Co.	1868?	Nov. 20, 1871	3
Waupun	114	Dodge Co.	Oct. 16, 1883	1934	51
Wausau	55	Marathon Co.	Dec. 5, 1882	1931	49
Wausau	83	Marathon Co.	1868?	Nov. 20, 1871	3
Wausaukee	277	Marinette Co.	Aug. 12, 1899	1901/02	3
Wautoma	5	Waushara Co.	Jul. 25, 1874	1875	5
Wautoma	45	Waushara Co.	1866-67	Nov. 20, 1871	4
Wautoma	135	Waushara Co.	Feb. 23, 1884	1938	54
Welcome	*See Bear Creek, #31*				
West Bend	193	Washington Co.	Mar. 21, 1885	1927	42
West Lima	67	Richland Co.	Mar. 15, 1883	1900	17
Westfield	63	Marquette Co.	Oct. 9, 1906	Jan. 25, 1924	18
Westfield	65	Marquette Co.	Feb. 28, 1883	Jul, 1902	19
West Salem	*See Salem #323*				
West Superior	*See Superior, #354*				
Weyauwega	180	Waupaca Co.	Sep. 6, 1884	1920	36
White Creek	209	Adams Co.	Mar. 23, 1889	1936	47
	Post 209 was listed in 1900 Journal at Easton, a nearby town				

Town	Post No.	County	Chartered	Extinct	Years existed
Whitehall	104	Trempealeau Co.	Aug. 29, 1883	1922	39
Whitewater	34	Walworth Co.	Jun. 29, 1882	Dec. 21, 1938	56
Winneconne	9 (85)	Winnebago Co.	1866-67	Jul. 16, 1874	3
Winneconne	227	Winnebago Co.	Jan. 5, 1889	1935	46
Wisconsin Dells	50	Columbia Co.	Oct. 26, 1882	1932	50
	Also known as Kilbourn, until 1895, and Kilbourn City until 1931				
Wisconsin Rapids	22	Wood Co.	Dec. 9, 1881	1938	57
	Also known as Grand Rapids until 1921				
Wisconsin Veterans Home	*See King, #176*				
Wittenberg	256	Shawano Co.	Jun 29, 1889	1902	13
Wolf Creek	79	Polk Co.	Jan. 15, 1898	1910	15
Wonewoc	53	Juneau Co.	Nov. 18, 1882	1942	60
Woodstock	89	Richland Co.	May 25, 1883	1905	22
Wrightstown	213	Brown Co.	Oct. 20, 1885	1887-88	3
Wyalusing	23	Grant Co.	Mar. 27, 1888	1912	24
	Listed as Bradtville in 1902				
Unknown	80			Nov. 20, 1871	0

Average duration of all 404 posts: **29.1 years** • Average excluding posts dropped by 1874: **33.3 years**

POSTS

BY COUNTY

The initial table of organization for the Grand Army of the Republic envisioned an intermediate step between department headquarters at the state level and the individual posts on the local level, but this hierarchy never took hold.

After the growing pains of the first few years, it was clear that the posts, if they were going to get into the habit of reporting at all, would have to report directly to the state level. Even that habit was slow in developing, and many of the early posts fell into dissolution because they did not keep contact, for whatever reason, with the higher level. A chain of command looks good on paper, but the veterans who had seen enough of chains of command in their recent past were not buying into this kind of organization.

In later years, however, when attrition was taking a heavy toll of the old soldiers, the Department of Wisconsin made some gestures toward an intermediate step by encouraging activities on a county level where individual posts were too small to carry on as of old. This setup was not as formal as the intermediate level originally planned, but it was, at that stage in the Grand Army's history, an innovative idea, meant to give added dimension to the Grand Army experience at a time when that experience was becoming less available in many locales.

By this time, however, members were so accustomed to thinking in terms of the post and department levels that another level did not have an allure. Activities on the county level, where they were occurring, did not assume an "official" status. The G.A.R. encouraged informal activities, such as campfires, which could keep the men involved, keep the G.A.R. before the public, and extend the life of the order in places where it was its membership was dying off.

It would not be appropriate to infer from this that before it was proposed there was not interplay among neighboring posts even while the order was in its busy years. These were gregarious times.

Posts did not exist in a vacuum, of course, and men of a given post would hold social events from time to time with other posts in the area, perhaps not on a formal countywide basis, but on the basis of the neighborliness that characterized the period. At the same time, if G.A.R. membership was a sound

Numbers are total of all posts started within a county, regardless of duration.

business benefit, that benefit extended beyond the post room. It could help a man establish business relationships in neighboring communities.

The map on this page shows the total number of posts in each county throughout the history of the department. These represent all 403 posts for which locations are known. One other is known only by number, but not by location. It must be recalled that each county's total included posts that failed. Dane County's 16 posts, for instance, included six that were closed by 1871.

Nonetheless the map is useful for illustrating the areas of the state where the Grand Army of the Republic filled an important role. Even though they include posts that failed, the figures still accurately portray where interest in the order was abiding. A great majority of those early failed posts were followed by new posts in the same community, and these by and large succeeded.

The charts on the following pages also give the breakdown of posts by county and provide a good point of reference for understanding G.A.R. activities in various regions.

Though the various posts in each county did not have the formal ties that an intermediate tier between local post and state department might have fashioned, there was still some sense of community among them short of such formulations.

POSTS BY COUNTY

County	No.	Post Name	Town	Chartered	Extinct	Page
Adams	122	Badgero	Friendship	Dec. 13, 1883	1935	198
Adams	209	Ennis T. Reed	White Creek	Mar. 23, 1889	1936	248
Ashland	5	J. H. Knight	Butternut	Nov. 12, 1879	1913	120
Ashland	140	George A. Custer	Ashland	Feb. 19, 1884	1938	210
Barron	115	Cumberland	Cumberland	1883	1885	195
Barron	126	Martin W. Heller	Rice Lake	Jan.3, 1884	Mar.3, 1893	201
Barron	128	Albert Weatherbe	Chetek	Jan. 15, 1884	1948	202
Barron	144	William Pitts	Dallas	Mar. 13, 1884	1907	211
Barron	157	W. W. Olds	Turtle Lake	Apr. 23, 1884	1915	218
Barron	166	Martin W. Heller	Rice Lake	Aug. 1, 1894	1934	223
Barron	172	Martin Watson	Barron	Aug. 6, 1884	1931	227
Barron	225	Cumberland	Cumberland	Sep 20, 1886	1937	256
Barron	237	August Roemhild	Prairie Farm	Jul 16, 1887	1923	263
Bayfield	249	Ambrose E. Burnside	Bayfield	Mar. 24, 1889	1927	270
Bayfield	254	Moses H. Hull	Washburn	Dec. 20, 1895	1900	273
Brown	8		Green Bay	1866	Nov. 20,1871	N/A
Brown	15	Governor Harvey	Green Bay	1876	1879	129
Brown	91	Samuel Harrison	Depere	Jun. 18, 1883	1937	181
Brown	124	Timothy O. Howe	Green Bay	Dec. 29, 1883	1936	199
Brown	213	Joe Mower	Wrightstown	Oct. 20, 1885	1887-88	250
Brown	278	Oneida	Oneida	Sep. 21, 1899	1926	286
Buffalo	75		Alma	1868?	Nov. 20, 1871	N/A
Buffalo	95	John W. Christian	Mondovi	Jul. 14, 1883	1922	183
Buffalo	196	Christopher Fimian	Alma	May 25, 1885	1919	240
Buffalo	252	Gouverneur K. Warren	Nelson	Apr. 23, 1889	1910	271
Buffalo	257	Peter Weber	Fountain City	Jul 15, 1889	1938	274
Burnett	49	W. S. Rosecrans	Grantsburg	Nov. 10, 1902	1910	153
Burnett	203	Grantsburg	Grantsburg	Sep. 25, 1885	1889	244
Calumet	32		Stockbridge	1866	Nov. 20, 1871	N/A
Calumet	39		Chilton	1866-67	Nov. 20, 1871	N/A
Calumet	40	Stockbridge/Benjamin J. Sweet	Stockbridge	Oct. 6, 1882	1920	147
Calumet	205	Chilton/Joseph B. Reynolds	Chilton	Aug. 28, 1885	1933	245
Calumet	222	Hiram M. Gibbs	Brillion	Sep. 18, 1886	1917	254
Chippewa	273	George Willich	Boyd	July 1, 1892	Sep. 24, 1892	283
Chippewa	68	James Comerford	Chippewa Falls	Mar. 15, 1883	1942	167
Chippewa	139	George M. Potter	Cadott	Mar. 12, 1884	Sep. 14, 1896	208

County	No.	Post Name	Town	Chartered	Extinct	Page
Chippewa	147	Nathaniel P. Lyon	Bloomer	Mar. 31, 1884	1928	213
Chippewa	183	George C. Ginty	Cadott	Dec. 29, 1891	1934	234
Chippewa	224	G. L. Park	Boyd	Oct. 27, 1886	1888	255
Clark	48	Charles G. Bacon	Neillsville	Nov. 24, 1882	1932	152
Clark	112	Isaac N. Earl	Colby	Dec. 18, 1883	1931	193
Clark	163	Francis Asbra Wellcome	Thorpe	May 12, 1884	1911	221
Clark	168	Howard F. Pruyn	Dorchester	Jul. 9, 1884	1928	225
Clark	213	John A. Eaton	Greenwood	Oct. 20, 1888	1919	250
Clark	236	Charles R. Gill	Loyal	Aug. 5, 1887	1911	262
Columbia	14	Lovell H. Rousseau	Portage	Apr. 13, 1880	1931	129
Columbia	23	A. McFarland	Poynette	Pre-1887	1888	136
Columbia	25	George Irwin	Lodi	Mar. 19, 1882	1936	137
Columbia	29		Lodi	1866	Nov. 20, 1871	N/A
Columbia	40		Columbus	1866-67	Nov. 20, 1871	N/A
Columbia	50	John Gillespie	Wisconsin Dells	Oct. 26, 1882	1932	154
Columbia	146	Frank A. Haskell/Harvey M. Brown	Columbus	Apr. 10, 1884	1938	212
Columbia	186	William Payne	Pardeeville	Oct. 6, 1884	1938	235
Columbia	267	William Atkinson	Marcellon	May 23, 1891	1903	279
Columbia	271	George H. Brayton	Fall River	Sep. 28, 1891	1936	282
Crawford	12		Prairie du Chien	Jun. 30, 1874	Jul. 16, 1874	N/A
Crawford	37	Phil W. Plummer	Prairie du Chien	Jul. 18, 1882	1941	145
Crawford	80	Orrin D. Chapman	Gays Mills	Apr 24, 1883	1912	175
Crawford	152	Phil Davenport	Soldiers Grove	May 3, 1884	1920	216
Crawford	216	Charles Green	Seneca	Mar. 27, 1886	1901	252
Dane	3		Mazomanie	1866	Nov. 20, 1871	N/A
Dane	11(1)	C. Fairchild/C.C.Washburn/L. Fairchild	Madison	Jun. 10, 1866	Jan. 30, 1940	125
Dane	13		Sun Prairie	1866	Nov. 20, 1871	N/A
Dane	23		Black Earth	1866	Nov. 20, 1871	N/A
Dane	27		Martinsville	1866	Nov. 20, 1871	N/A
Dane	35		Albion	1866-67	Nov. 20, 1871	N/A
Dane	56	Angus R. McDonald	Mazomanie	Dec. 1, 1882	1929	158
Dane	68		Oregon	1868?	Nov. 20, 1871	N/A
Dane	75	Sylvester Wheeler	Verona	Feb. 22, 1888	1921	171
Dane	121	Joe Mower	Bellville	Nov. 8, 1883	1931	198
Dane	123	Orson E. Rice	Oregon	Nov. 26, 1883	1927	199
Dane	153	Philo C. Buckman	Stoughton	Mar. 29, 1884	1934	216
Dane	184	Luther T. Pack	Black Earth	Oct. 18, 1884	1920	234
Dane	191	Lorenzo A. Dixon	Mount Horeb	Mar. 25, 1885	1942	238
Dane	208	William H. Hamilton	Sun Prairie	Sep. 18, 1885	1906	247
Dane	229	Franklin H. Potter	Cambridge	Jan. 5, 1887	1928	259
Dodge	6	James F. Ordway	Beaver Dam	1868?	Jul. 23, 1874	121
Dodge	31	John H. Ely	Juneau	Jun. 1, 1882	1929	141
Dodge	43	Raymond	Mayville	Aug. 23, 1882	1935	149

County	No.	Post Name	Town	Chartered	Extinct	Page
Dodge	100	George H. Stevens	Fox Lake	Aug. 29, 1883	1912	186
Dodge	114	Hans C. Heg	Waupun	Oct. 16, 1883	1934	194
Dodge	117	George Hall	Beaver Dam	Oct. 29, 1883	1938	196
Dodge	169	John Echternoch	Theresa	Jul. 10, 1884	1901	226
Dodge	203	Charles A. Blair/Fred Richter	Lowell	May 25, 1889	1934	244
Dodge	220	John A. Hauff	Horicon	Jun. 15, 1886	1938	253
Door	17		Sturgeon Bay	1866	Nov. 20, 1871	N/A
Door	97	William A. Nelson	Forestville	Aug. 11, 1883	1901-02	184
Door	211	E. E. Ellsworth	Fish Creek	Oct. 24, 1885	1896	249
Door	226	H. Smith Schuyler	Sturgeon Bay	Oct. 16, 1886	1919	257
Douglas	170	Alonzo Palmer	Superior	Aug. 9, 1884	1942	226
Douglas	273	J. D. Robie	Superior	Jan. 25, 1893	1904	284
Dunn	14		Menominee	1866	Nov. 20, 1871	N/A
Dunn	58	William Evans	Menomonie	Jan. 6, 1883	1938	159
Dunn	84	A. S. Bennett	Boyceville	May 12, 1883	1919	177
Dunn	148	Joseph Shannon/A. K. Humphrey	Knapp	Apr. 9, 1884	1902	214
Dunn	167	John Green	Eau Galle	Feb. 27, 1890	1913	225
Dunn	183	John B. Doughty	Colfax	Oct. 15, 1884	1891	233
Eau Claire	36		Eau Claire	1866-67	Nov. 20, 1871	N/A
Eau Claire	52	Eagle	Eau Claire	Nov. 8, 1882	1942	155
Eau Claire	98	John E. Perkins	Augusta	Aug. 3, 1883	1941	185
Eau Claire	162	Arthur C. Ellis	Eau Claire	Jul. 21, 1884	1886-87	221
Eau Claire	166	Maj. Nathan Paine	Fairchild	Jun. 19, 1884	Aug. 11, 1893	223
Florence	268	Joseph Dupont	Florence	Jun. 30, 1891	1928	280
Fond du Lac	2		Ripon	1866	Jul. 16, 1874	N/A
Fond du Lac	4		Fond du Lac	1866	Nov. 20, 1871	N/A
Fond du Lac	130	Edwin A. Brown	Fond du Lac	Jan. 19, 1884	1939	203
Fond du Lac	136	Benjamin F. Sheldon	Brandon	Mar. 7, 1884	1926	207
Fond du Lac	199	H. S. Eggleston	Ripon	Jun. 13, 1885	1938	242
Fond du Lac	246	Isaac Hendricks	Campbellsport	Feb. 7, 1889	1919	268
Fond du Lac	269	Edward Winslow Hincks	New Cassel	Aug. 24, 1894	1898	281
Grant	23	W. K. Forshay	Wyalusing	Mar. 27, 1888	1912	136
Grant	33		Platteville	Oct. 19, 1866	Nov. 20, 1871	N/A
Grant	37		Bocobel	1866	Nov. 20, 1871	N/A
Grant	58		Bloomington	Sep. 11, 1867	Nov. 20, 1871	N/A
Grant	61		Mount Hope	1868?	Nov. 20, 1871	N/A
Grant	63		Lancaster	1868?	Nov. 20, 1871	N/A
Grant	66	Platteville/William T. Sherman	Platteville	Feb. 6, 1883	1941	165
Grant	67		Jamestown	1868?	Nov. 20, 1871	N/A
Grant	71	J. B. Moore	Muscoda	Mar. 28, 1883	Feb.21, 1896	168
Grant	72		Patch Grove	1868?	Nov. 20, 1871	N/A
Grant	101	John McDermott	Bocobel	Aug. 15, 1883	1941	187
Grant	132	Thomas D. Cox	Lancaster	May 17, 1885	1942	204

County	No.	Post Name	Town	Chartered	Extinct	Page
Grant	134	William Hickok	Bloomington	Feb. 8, 1884	1931	205
Grant	162	Belknap Fuqua	Potosi	1892	1923	221
Grant	173	Sam Monteith	Fennimore	Aug. 12, 1884	1935	228
Grant	175	George W. Holloway	Beetown	Aug. 16, 1884	Apr. 1, 1893	229
Grant	218	J. Mueller	Cassville	Jun. 19, 1886	1901-02	252
Grant	266	William O. Topping	Hazel Green	Apr. 22, 1891	1922	279
Grant	279	H. W. Lawton	Muscoda	Mar. 1, 1900	1924	287
Green	55		Brodhead	1867	pre 11-20-71	N/A
Green	59		Monroe	1868?	Nov. 20, 1871	N/A
Green	69	Erastus Hoyt	Albany	Mar. 26, 1883	1906	167
Green	90	Wesley W. Patton	Brodhead	Jun. 4, 1883	1937	180
Green	102	Oscar F. Pinney	Monroe	Aug. 28, 1883	1936	188
Green	113	John Ross	Monticello	Oct. 6, 1883	1909	194
Green	264	Benjamin S. Davis	Oakley /Peedee	Feb. 12, 1890	1906	278
Green Lake	4(22)	John H. Williams	Berlin	Sep. 8, 1866	Apr. 18, 1937	118
Green Lake	15	Jerome Chesebro	Markesan	Aug. 22, 1885	1889	130
Green Lake	28	Newton Wilson/George Brayton	Kingston	Mar. 17, 1888	1930	139
Green Lake	43		Princeton	1866-67	Nov. 20, 1871	N/A
Green Lake	46		Markesan	1666-67	Nov. 20, 1871	N/A
Green Lake	53		Marquette	1867	1871	N/A
Green Lake	139	Charles Graves	Berlin	Feb. 11, 1898	1908	209
Green Lake	202	Elisha Harrison Randall	Dartford	Sep. 5, 1885	1931	243
Green Lake	228	Wallace Dantz	Princeton	Oct. 8, 1886	1913	258
Iowa	12		Mifflin	1866	Nov. 20 1871	N/A
Iowa	25		Mineral Point	1866	Nov. 20, 1871	N/A
Iowa	41		Dodgeville	1866-67	Nov. 20, 1871	N/A
Iowa	107	Allatoona	Arena	Sep. 7, 1883	1917	190
Iowa	109	Williamson	Dodgeville	Sep. 18, 1883	1931	191
Iowa	125	George H. Legate	Mineral Point	Dec. 20, 1883	1938	200
Iron	259	James S. Alban	Hurley	Jul 30, 1889	Jun. 30, 1896	275
Jackson	71		Black River Falls	1868?	Nov. 20, 1871	N/A
Jackson	86	Colonel E.E. Ellsworth	Merrillan	May 15,1883	1920	178
Jackson	87	Perrin C. Judkins	Alma Center	Jun. 15, 1883	1942	179
Jackson	92	William Moore	Black River Falls	Jun . 11, 1883	1935	181
Jackson	161	Elijah H. Amidon	Melrose	May 1, 1884	1910	220
Jefferson	16		Watertown	1866	Nov. 20, 1871	N/A
Jefferson	18		Waterloo	1866	Nov. 20, 1871	N/A
Jefferson	20		Rome	1866	Nov. 20, 1871	N/A
Jefferson	26	John E. Holmes	Jefferson	Apr. 15, 1882	1937	138
Jefferson	28		Jefferson	1866?	Nov. 20, 1871	N/A
Jefferson	30		Aztalan	1866	Nov. 20, 1871	N/A
Jefferson	31		Lake Mills	1866	Nov. 20, 1871	N/A
Jefferson	34		Hebron	1866	Nov. 20 1871	N/A

County	No.	Post Name	Town	Chartered	Extinct	Page
Jefferson	94	Oliver D. Pease	Watertown	Jul. 7, 1883	1937	183
Jefferson	119	Oscar F. Mattice	Waterloo	Nov. 7, 1883	1902	197
Jefferson	138	Joseph Bailey	Palmyra	Feb. 16, 1884	1923	208
Jefferson	159	Fort Atkinson	Fort Atkinson	Apr. 24, 1884	1923	219
Jefferson	253	Gustavus H. Bryant	Lake Mills	May 28, 1889	1923	272
Jefferson	262	Nicholas Friddle	Rome	Aug. 24, 1889	1910	277
Juneau	47	Henry C. Miles/Frank Prevy	Elroy	Oct. 6, 1882	1936	151
Juneau	53	George W. Bell	Wonewoc	Nov. 18, 1882	1942	156
Juneau	59	Angus S. Northrop	Mauston	Jan. 10, 1883	1936	160
Juneau	61	William P. Mitchell	New Lisbon	Jan. 17, 1883	1937	161
Juneau	105	Major William F. Dawes	Necedah	May 3, 1883	1887-88	189
Juneau	245	W. F. Dawes	Necedah	Feb. 9, 1889	1931	267
Juneau	248	Estrick Burbank	Mather	Nov. 11, 1893	1903	269
Kenosha	62		Salem	1868?	Nov. 20, 1871	N/A
Kenosha	73		Kenosha	1868?	Nov. 20, 1871	N/A
Kenosha	230	Frederick S. Lovell	Kenosha	Apr. 11, 1887	1942	259
Kewaunee			Algoma	1866	Nov. 20, 1871	N/A
Kewaunee		John M. Read	Kewaunee	May 6, 1884	1919	217
Kewaunee		Joseph Anderegg	Algoma	Jan. 11, 1888	1912	266
La Crosse		William McKinley	La Crosse	Nov. 29, 1901	1922	131
La Crosse		Wilson Colwell	La Crosse	Aug. 17, 1882	1941	145
La Crosse		John Flynn	La Crosse	May 5, 1883	1936	172
La Crosse		Nelson Quiggle	Mindoro	Jun. 3, 1887	Jan. 1, 1898	261
La Crosse		Cyprian Downer	Bangor	May 28, 1887	1936	261
Lafayette			Argyle	1866-67	Nov. 20, 1871	N/A
Lafayette		Darlington/Louis P. Harvey	Darlington	Oct. 10, 1882	1937	150
Lafayette		Thomas H. Oates	Shullsburg	Jul. 16, 1883	1927	184
Lafayette		John & James Cullin/John Bragg	Gratiot	Aug. 8, 1884	1922	230
Lafayette		Colwert Pier	Argyle	Dec. 2, 1885	1915	246
Lafayette		John E. Gurley	Blanchardville	Dec. 27, 1888	1931	256
Langlade		John A. Kellogg	Antigo	May 15, 1883	1936	173
Lincoln		Lincoln County	Merrill	Jan. 24, 1884	1941	204
Manitowoc		H. M. Walker	Manitowoc	Apr. 28, 1881	1934	133
Manitowoc			Manitowoc	1866-67	Nov. 20, 1871	N/A
Manitowoc		General Lytle	Kiel	Dec. 27, 1884	1926	237
Manitowoc		Joe Rankin	Two Rivers	Jun. 16, 1886	1918	253
Marathon		Lysander Cutler	Wausau	Dec. 5, 1882	1931	157
Marathon			Wausau	1868?	Nov. 20, 1871	N/A
Marathon		Henry O. Watrous	Spencer	1883	1887	182
Marathon		Unity	Unity	May 20, 1886	1896	252
Marathon		Henry O. Watrous	Spencer	Jan. 19, 1895	1921	285
Marinette		Samuel H. Sizer	Marinette	Sep. 14, 1885	1942	246
Marinette	248	William Taylor	Peshtigo	Feb. 16, 1889	Apr. 12, 1893	269

County	No.	Post Name	Town	Chartered	Extinct	Page
Marinette	277	Wausaukee	Wausaukee	Aug. 12, 1899	1901/02	286
Marquette	63	Thomas B. Crawford	Westfield	Oct. 9, 1906	Jan. 25, 1924	163
Marquette	64	W. S. Walker	Montello	Feb. 23, 1883	1927	163
Marquette	65	Thomas B. Crawford	Westfield	Feb. 28, 1883	Jul, 1902	164
Marquette	143	Joseph C. Miller	Oxford	Mar. 15, 1884	1926	211
Marquette	188	William J. Kershaw	Briggsville	Oct. 27, 1884	1930	236
Menominee	261	Joseph A. Ledergerber	Keshena	Aug. 16, 1889	Apr. 5, 1933	276
Milwaukee	1	E. B. Wolcott	Milwaukee	Jan. 14, 1880	1939	115
Milwaukee	2	Robert Chivas	Milwaukee	Jun. 9, 1875	1918	116
Milwaukee	3(9)	Phil Sheridan	Milwaukee	July, 1866	1878-79	117
Milwaukee	8	Veterans	Milwaukee	Apr. 26, 1870	1917	122
Milwaukee	12	John Sedgwick	Milwaukee	Sep16, 1875	1875-76	126
Milwaukee	56		Milwaukee	1867	pre 11-20-71	N/A
Milwaukee	175	Rufus King	South Milwaukee	Nov. 15, 1893	1922	229
Milwaukee	211	Old Guard	Milwaukee	May 17, 1898	1906	249
Milwaukee	223	George C. Drake	Milwaukee	Aug. 18, 1886	1938	255
Milwaukee	240	Rank & File	Milwaukee	Jun. 7, 1888	1919	264
Milwaukee	250	Robert Mueller	Milwaukee	Apr. 8, 1889	1923	270
Milwaukee	274	William Steinmeyer	Milwaukee	Jul. 26, 1892	1909	284
Monroe	29	Judson Kilpatrick	Oakdale	Apr. 13, 1882	Aug. 17, 1895	140
Monroe	30	John W. Lynn	Sparta	Apr. 24, 1882	1934	141
Monroe	42	Henry W. Cressey	Tomah	Aug. 14, 1882	1936	148
Monroe	57	Chadrles Edgerton	Warren Mills	Dec. 30, 1882	1929	158
Monroe	88	William A. Barstow	Kendall	May 21, 1883	1905	179
Monroe	179	Horace T. Sanders	Norwalk	Sep. 5, 1884	1931	231
Monroe	214	John Hazen	Cashton	Feb. 11, 1886	1900	251
Monroe	235	George A. Fisk	Cataract	Jun. 4, 1887	1896	262
Oconto	29	D. D. Barker	Abrams	Nov. 22, 1896	1940	140
Oconto	74		Pensaukee	1868?	Nov. 20 1871	N/A
Oconto	74	Edward A. Ramsey	Oconto	Oct. 10, 1883	1938	170
Oneida	232	John A. Logan	Rhinelander	May 5, 1887	1908	260
Outagamie	51	Starkweather	Bear Creek	Nov. 26, 1897	1913	155
Outagamie	76		Appleton	1868?	Nov. 20, 1871	N/A
Outagamie	116	J. W. Appleton	Black Creek	Oct. 25, 1883	1911	195
Outagamie	133	George D. Eggleston	Appleton	Jan. 31, 1884	1938	205
Outagamie	198	John Granzo	Seymour	May 25, 1885	1914	241
Outagamie	210	Francis Steffen	Hortonville	Sep. 29, 1885	1931	248
Outagamie	247	Paul H. Beaulieu	Kaukauna	Feb. 15, 1889	1934	268
Ozaukee	244	Winfield Scott Hancock	Cedarburg	Jan. 21, 1889	1920	267
Ozaukee	254	Frank Ellenbecker	Port Washington	Jun. 25, 1889	1894	272
Pepin	47		Durand	1866-67	Nov. 20, 1871	N/A
Pepin	82	Charles Coleman	Durand	May 17, 1883	1924	176
Pepin	108	James Little	Pepin	Jul. 7, 1894	1910	191

County	No.	Post Name	Town	Chartered	Extinct	Page
Pepin	127	Benjamin F. Allen	Arkansaw	Dec. 29. 1893	1903	202
Pierce	44		Prescott	1866-67	Nov. 20, 1871	N/A
Pierce	54		River Falls	1868	Nov. 20, 1871	N/A
Pierce	72	A. M. Howard/Custer	Rock Elm	Mar. 27, 1883	1919	169
Pierce	118	Ellsworth	Ellsworth	Nov. 23, 1883	1927	196
Pierce	177	I. N. Nichols	River Falls	Aug. 23, 1884	1934	230
Pierce	189	Rollin P.Converse	Prescott	Dec. 16, 1884	1929	237
Pierce	204	U. S. Grant	Maiden Rock	Aug. 1, 1885	1905	245
Pierce	209	Plum City	Plum City	1885	1888	247
Pierce	238	John A. Otis	Trimbelle	Aug. 11, 1887	1908	263
Pierce	272	Jeremiah Rusk	Spring Valley	Jan. 21, 1895	1929	283
Polk	79	George M. Emery	Wolf Creek	Jan. 15, 1898	1910	174
Polk	111	C. McKenzie	St. Croix Falls	Sep. 24, 1883	1921	193
Polk	142	Emerson Opdyke	Clear Lake	Mar. 7, 1884	1932	211
Polk	164	Carmi P. Garlick	Osceola Mills	May 22, 1884	1900	222
Polk	263	Daniel Chaplin	Amery	Oct. 25, 1889	1904	277
Portage	16	Irvin Eckles	Amherst	1884	1932	132
Portage	16	Gov. Louis P. Harvey	Amherst	Apr. 18, 1880	1883	132
Portage	115	Belmont	Blaine	Jun. 18, 1888	1903	195
Portage	149	Plover	Plover	Mar. 21, 1884	1938	214
Portage	156	Stevens Point	Stevens Point	Apr. 9, 1884	1938	218
Price	181	Phillips/Allen Jackson	Phillips	Sep. 7, 1884	1938	232
Racine	11		Racine	1869	Jul. 16, 1874	N/A
Racine	17	Gov. Louis P. Harvey	Racine	Jan. 24, 1881	1936	133
Racine	201	Martin Luther Crane	Burlington	Aug. 6, 1885	1920	243
Racine	215	George B. Lincoln	Union Grove	Jan. 26, 1886	1920	251
Richland	24		Richland Center	1866	Nov. 20, 1871	N/A
Richland	24	Henry Dillon	Lone Rock	Feb. 23, 1882	1940	137
Richland	33	W.H. Bennett	Richland Center	May 1, 1882	1941	143
Richland	48	Lyon	Cazenovia	1866-67	Jul. 24, 1874	152
Richland	51	William Wright	Excelsior	Oct. 27, 1882	Dec. 1896	154
Richland	62	James C. McIntyre	Boaz	Jan. 21, 1883	Jan. 1, 1898	161
Richland	63	Enos B. Cornwell	Basswood	Jan. 26, 1883	1901	162
Richland	67	Samuel F. Curtis	West Lima	Mar. 15, 1883	1900	166
Richland	85	Jerry Turner	Viola	May 24, 1883	1927	178
Richland	89	Nathan Hoyt	Woodstock	May 25, 1883	1905	180
Richland	99	Edwin Austin	Sylvan Corners	Apr. 21, 1883	1888	185
Richland	108	Andrew J. McNurlin	Loyd	Sep. 10, 1883	Nov. 14, 1893	191
Richland	185	Morris E. Sexton	Sextonville	Oct. 7, 1884	1918	235
Richland	221	C. E. McCarthy	Rockbridge	Aug. 27, 1886	1908	254
Rock	7		Edgerton	1866	Nov. 20, 1871	N/A
Rock	20	W. H. Sargent	Janesville	Oct. 21, 1881	Apr. 12, 1937	134
Rock	41	Theodore L. Sutphen	Evansville	Sep. 24, 1882	1943	147

County	No.	Post Name	Town	Chartered	Extinct	Page
Rock	54	Louis H. D. Crane	Beloit	Nov. 21, 1882	1939	157
Rock	60	Arthur D. Hamilton	Milton	Jan. 10, 1883	1931	160
Rock	70		Beloit	1868?	Nov. 20, 1871	N/A
Rock	70	Alexis Tallman	Clinton	Apr. 18, 1883	1926	168
Rock	137	Henry S. Swift	Edgerton	Feb. 11, 1884	1936	207
Rusk	62	Eugene A. Colburn	Bruce	Jan. 4, 1902	1917	162
Rusk	280	John E. Tourtellotte/Rusk County	Ladysmith	Aug. 7, 1906	July, 1940	287
Sauk	9	Joe Hooker	Baraboo	Mar. 4, 1880	1942	123
Sauk	13	H. A.Tator	Reedsburg	Apr. 13, 1880	1942	128
Sauk	35	N. S. Frost	Prairie du Sac	Jul. 1, 1882	1906	144
Sauk	39	Thomas J. Hungerford	Spring Green	Jul. 15, 1882	1941	146
Sauk	49	A. A. Matthews	LaValle	Oct. 26, 1882	1901-02	153
Sauk	60		Prairie du Sac	1868?	Nov. 20, 1871	N/A
Sauk	83	John Faller	North Freedom	May 2, 1883	1926	176
Sauk	174	A. D. Thornburg	Lime Ridge	Aug. 11, 1888	1908	228
Sauk	195	George Parsons	Merrimac	Apr. 25, 1885	1923	240
Sawyer	227	Solomon Meredith	Hayward	1885-86	1888	257
Sawyer	260	Solomon Meredith	Hayward	Aug. 20, 1889	1938	275
Shawano	81	William H. Hawley	Shawano	May 4, 1883	1917	175
Shawano	178	Henry C. Isbell	Birnamwood	Dec. 18, 1888	1932	231
Shawano	256	Edmund W. Long	Wittenberg	Jun 29, 1889	1902	274
Sheboygan	5		Greenbush	1866	Nov. 20, 1871	N/A
Sheboygan	12	Jairius Richardson	Sheboygan Falls	July 10, 1883	1936	127
Sheboygan	57		Sheboygan Falls	1868?	Nov. 20, 1871	N/A
Sheboygan	62	John Shaver	Cedar Grove	Mar. 25, 1898	1901	161
Sheboygan	65		Hingman	1868?	1871	N/A
Sheboygan	66		Cascade	1868?	Nov. 20, 1871	N/A
Sheboygan	187	Gustave Wintermeyer	Sheboygan	Nov. 28, 1884	1938	236
Sheboygan	192	Abner O. Heald	Cascade	Feb. 26, 1885	1921	238
Sheboygan	212	Henry P. Davidson	Plymouth	Nov. 9, 1885	1938	249
St. Croix	15	John Follensbee	New Centerville	Apr. 13, 1889	1899	131
St. Croix	103	Benjamin I. Humphrey	New Richmond	Sep. 18, 1883	1942	188
St. Croix	151	Edwin A. Clapp	Hudson	Mar. 24, 1884	1938	215
St. Croix	182	Sidney A. Bean	Hammond	Sep. 17, 1884	1901-02	233
St. Croix	200	Alexander Ricky	Hersey	Jan. 8, 1886	1911	242
St. Croix	233	Oscar F. Brown	Glenwood	Dec. 3, 1898	1918	261
St. Croix	272	Otis Hoyt	Glenwood	Nov. 12, 1891	Jul. 7, 1893	282
Taylor	145	General James Shields	Medford	Mar. 25, 1884	1933	212
Taylor	178	Chelsea	Chelsea	Sep. 27, 1884	1888	231
Trempealeau	13	Charles Ford	Trempealeau	1874	1875	128
Trempealeau	71	O. B. Rice	Eleva	Apr. 26, 1896	1928	169
Trempealeau	75	Myron Gardner	Arcadia	1883	1888	171
Trempealeau	93	W. G. Wheeler	Osseo	May 28, 1888	1900	182

County	No.	Post Name	Town	Chartered	Extinct	Page
Trempealeau	104	Winfield Scott	Whitehall	Aug. 29, 1883	1922	189
Trempealeau	255	Myron Gardner	Arcadia	Jun 28, 1889	1922	273
Trempealeau	258	Charles H. Ford	Galesville	Jul 24, 1889	1933	274
Trempealeau	275	Oliver A. Hegg	Independence	Jan. 26, 1893	1898	285
Vernon	36	Alex Lowrie	Viroqua	Jul. 17, 1882	1937	144
Vernon	106	James Mason	Desoto	Oct. 16, 1883	1913	190
Vernon	141	Henry Didiot	Hillsboro	Mar. 12, 1884	1936	210
Vernon	154	Allen McVey	Star	Apr. 23, 1884	1938	217
Vernon	158	James Williams	Ontario	Apr. 19, 1884	1917	219
Vilas	167	Lucius H. Drury	Eagle River	Jul. 21, 1888	1890	224
Walworth	3	Abraham Lincoln	Darien	Aug. 26, 1879	1922	117
Walworth	6	George H. Thomas	Delevan	Nov. 28, 1879	1935	121
Walworth	12	J. B. McPherson	Sharon	1880	1883	127
Walworth	27	J. B. McPherson	Lake Geneva	Apr. 18, 1882	1936	138
Walworth	34	Charles E. Curtice	Whitewater	Jun. 29, 1882	Dec. 21, 1938	143
Walworth	76	Walworth County/Rutherford B. Hayes	Elkhorn	May 10, 1883	1941	172
Walworth	77		Geneva	1868?	Nov. 20, 1871	N/A
Walworth	171	Henry Concklin	East Troy	Aug. 16, 1884	1929	227
Walworth	270	Duane Patten	Sharon	Jul. 9, 1891	1919	281
Washburn	65	F. Jackel	Spooner	1903	1930	165
Washburn	243	Newton S. Green	Shell Lake	Jan. 21, 1888	1917	266
Washington	165	George M. West	Hartford	May 31, 1884	1938	222
Washington	193	Andrew J. Fullerton	West Bend	Mar. 21, 1885	1927	239
Waukesha	19	William B. Cushing	Waukesha	May 24, 1881	1937	134
Waukesha	79		Waukesha	1868?	Nov. 20, 1871	N/A
Waukesha	82		Mukwonago	1868?	Nov. 20, 1871	N/A
Waukesha	105	M. G. Townsend	Pewaukee	May 14, 1888	1904	189
Waukesha	167	Franklin Bigelow	Eagle	Feb. 21, 1884	1887	224
Waukesha	194	Henry Bertram	Oconomowoc	Mar. 26, 1885	1921	239
Waupaca	21		New London	1866	Nov. 20, 1871	N/A
Waupaca	21	James A. Garfield	Waupaca	Oct. 26, 1881	1941	135
Waupaca	32	J. B. Wyman	Clintonville	May 28, 1882	1913	142
Waupaca	46	Henry Turner	New London	Sep. 26, 1882	1938	151
Waupaca	69		Waupaca	1868?	Nov. 20, 1871	N/A
Waupaca	78	John Matteson	Embarass	1868?	1874	173
Waupaca	79	I. Ramsdell	Marion	May 11, 1883	1896	174
Waupaca	99	Iola	Iola	Apr. 21, 1888	1908	186
Waupaca	120	J. B. Steadman	Manawa	Nov. 6, 1883	1909	197
Waupaca	126	F. A. Marden	King	Jun. 14, 1893	1937	201
Waupaca	160	Hiram Russell	Fremont	Apr. 30, 1884	1931	220
Waupaca	180	Andrew Chambers	Weyauwega	Sep. 6, 1884	1920	232
Waupaca	239	Chester A .Arthur	Ogdensburg	Nov. 3, 1887	Jul. 16, 1896	263
Waupaca	265	Bradford Phillips	Royalton	Feb. 16, 1891	1899	278

County	No.	Post Name	Town	Chartered	Extinct	Page
Waushara	5	Edward Saxe	Wautoma	Jul. 25, 1874	1875	120
Waushara	15	J. H. Roberts	Plainfield	1880	1883	130
Waushara	28	General Canby	Auroraville	Jun. 4, 1882	1885	139
Waushara	45		Wautoma	1866-67	Nov. 20 1871	N/A
Waushara	135	Edward Saxe	Wautoma	Feb. 23, 1884	1938	206
Waushara	150	Thomas Eubank	Hancock	Mar. 26, 1884	1911	215
Waushara	197	Walter Waterman	Plainfield	Aug. 22, 1885	1937	241
Waushara	231	James S. Ewing	Poy Sippi	Apr. 11, 1887	1929	260
Waushara	269	Archibald Wheeler	Coloma	July 7, 1891	May 14, 1894	280
Winnebago	7	J. F. Sawyer	Omro	Feb. 14, 1880	1936	122
Winnebago	9	George H. Thomas	Winneconne	Nov. 20, 1871	Jul. 16, 1874	123
Winnebago	10	Oshkosh/P.H. Sheridan	Oshkosh	Aug. 16, 1866	1938	124
Winnebago	15		Butte des Morts	1866	Nov. 20, 1871	N/A
Winnebago	26		Waukau	1866	Nov. 20, 1871	N/A
Winnebago	44	Joseph P. Shepard	Menasha	Sep. 8, 1882	May 1,1933	149
Winnebago	129	Hiram J. Lewis	Neenah	Jan. 18, 1884	1939	203
Winnebago	227	Azro Young	Winneconne	Jan. 5, 1889	1935	258
Winnebago	241	John W. Scott	Oshkosh	Dec. 22, 1887	1923	264
Winnebago	251	Henry E. Hess	Eureka	Apr, 19, 1889	1926	271
Wood	22	Wood County	Wisconsin Rapids	Dec.9, 1881	1938	135
Wood	73	James S. Alban	Pittsville	May 10, 1883	1905	170
Wood	110	Marshfield/James G. Blaine	Marshfield	Oct. 23, 1883	1935	192

POSTS
BY NUMBER

The Wisconsin Department of the Grand Army of the Republic had approximately 404 Posts during its 85-year history, each with a numeric designation. Practicing frugality, the department frequently recycled the numbers, so the highest post designation was that given to a post begun at Ladysmith in 1906, number 280.

The accompanying charts give the number, the post name (where it is known), the post's town, and county in which the post was located.

The practice of reusing numbers was begun as far back as 1871 when Commander Edward Ferguson rid the department's roster of moribund posts and reissued many of those numbers. Some posts received lower numbers in the reorganization. For example, Berlin's John H. Williams Post moved up from 22 to 4 on that occasion. A number of others were also moved up at that time, and a few years later, Madison was moved down the ladder from 1 to 11.

But for the most part, the numbers were assigned to new posts on an ascending basis, and when numbers were vacated by posts, they were given to whatever new post was in line for designation. Old posts were no longer given different numbers once they were established.

The following chart does not attempt to chronicle the early changes of numbers such as Berlin's, Madison's, etc., for doing so would simply cause confusion. Those that did have changes are listed under their final numeric designation.

But the chart does show clearly the results of that numeric recycling. There are two Post 2s, three 3s, five 12s, six 15s, etc.

Another thing that the chart illustrates is that there are gaps in our knowledge of post names. That is because the early department records, before 1883, are lost, and those posts that lived and died during that time are, for the most part, known by number but not by name.

One exception is Phil Sheridan Post 3, Milwaukee. The name of the post appears in a few references to early G.A.R. activity in Milwaukee; otherwise it, too, would be among the anonymous.

Since so much of what is known of the posts from the 1866 inception of the order in Wisconsin to the cleansing five years

later has been gleaned from an array of sources that are unofficial, it is impossible to claim complete certainty about the accuracy of the list posts. Hence the figure of 404 posts itself may not be definitive.

It is also possible that a couple of posts were chartered and floundered before they were recorded. A block of numbers was apparently set aside at one point for reasons unknown, and nothing on record says they were ever used to designate posts. However, this may have occurred.

The G.A.R., it must be emphasized, was a secret fraternity, so a new branch of a new order in a new town did not necessarily merit even a mention in the local newspaper—if there was one. So a post could certainly escape notice, and especially if it floundered soon after its inception.

One post is known only by number. The post is referred to only once in a document noting that a post with a number (80) had previously surrendered its charter. (Because there is no location noted for the post, it has not been included in the following list of Posts by Number, but it is included in the complete roster of posts that account for the 404 known posts of the Department of Wisconsin.)

The following chart, however, does list those many posts where there is good, though unofficial, evidence that they existed and documentation of where they existed. For example, Post 2 was started in Ripon, within days of the establishment of the G.A.R. in Wisconsin at Madison in 1866, and posts were started thereafter at Mazomanie, Fond du Lac, Greenbush, and Algoma (then known as Ahnapee), in quite rapid order. Several sources exist for this, one a newspaper list and others giving corroboration as to specific posts.

Thus the list of Posts of the Grand Army of the Republic that existed in the Department of Wisconsin has been reconstructed as accurately as careful research has been able to determine.

The following list should give readers quick access to the material that is known about each post. But it may also give an incentive to some to make further effort to "fill in the blanks" about when and where Civil War veterans first affiliated with the Grand Army of the Republic, however briefly, in those posts of the misty early years.

POSTS BY NUMBER

No.	Post Name	Town	County	Page
1	E.B. Wolcott	Milwaukee	Milwaukee Co.	115
2		Ripon	Fond du Lac Co.	116
2	Robert Chivas	Milwaukee	Milwaukee Co.	116
3	Phil Sheridan	Milwaukee	Milwaukee Co.	117
3	Abraham Lincoln	Darien	Walworth Co.	117
3		Mazomanie	Dane Co.	N/A
4(22)	John H. Williams	Berlin	Green Lake Co.	118
4		Fond du Lac	Fond du Lac Co.	N/A
5		Greenbush	Sheboygan Co.	119
5	Edward Saxe	Wautoma	Waushara Co.	120
5	J.H. Knight	Butternut	Ashland Co.	120
6	James F. Ordway	Beaver Dam	Dodge Co.	121
6	George H. Thomas	Delevan	Walworth Co.	121
6		Algoma	Kewaunee Co.	N/A
7	J. F. Sawyer	Omro	Winnebago Co.	122
7		Edgerton	Rock Co.	N/A
8	Veterans	Milwaukee	Milwaukee Co.	122
8		Green Bay	Brown Co.	N/A
9(85)	George H. Thomas	Winneconne	Winnebago Co.	177
9	Joe Hooker	Baraboo	Sauk Co.	123
9		Milwaukee	Milwaukee Co.	N/A
10	Oshkosh/Philip H. Sheridan	Oshkosh	Winnebago Co.	124
11(1)	Cassius Fairchild/C.C.Washburn/Lucius Fairchild	Madison	Dane Co.	125
11		Racine	Racine Co.	N/A
12	John Sedgwick	Milwaukee	Milwaukee Co.	126
12	James B. McPherson	Sharon	Walworth Co.	127
12	Jairus Richardson	Sheboygan Falls	Sheboygan Co.	127
12		Mifflin	Iowa Co.	N/A
12		Prairie du Chien	Crawford Co.	N/A
13	Charles Ford	Trempealeau	Trempealeau Co.	128
13	H. A.Tator	Reedsburg	Sauk Co.	128
13		Sun Prairie	Dane Co.	N/A
14	Lovell H. Rousseau	Portage	Columbia Co.	129
14		Menominee	Dunn Co.	N/A
15	Governor Harvey	Green Bay	Brown Co.	129
15	J .H. Roberts	Plainfield	Waushara Co.	130
15	Jerome Chesebro	Markesan	Green Lake Co.	130
15	John Follensbee	New Centerville	St. Croix Co.	131
15	William McKinley	La Crosse	La Crosse Co.	131
15		Butte des Morts	Winnebago Co.	N/A
16	Gov. Louis P. Harvey	Amherst	Portage Co.	132

No.	Post Name	Town	County	Page
16	Irvin Eckles	Amherst	Portage Co.	132
16		Watertown	Jefferson Co.	N/A
17	Gov. Louis P. Harvey	Racine	Racine Co.	133
17		Sturgeon Bay	Door Co.	N/A
18	H. M. Walker	Manitowoc	Manitowoc Co.	133
18		Waterloo	Jefferson Co.	N/A
19	William B. Cushing	Waukesha	Waukesha Co.	134
20	W. H. Sargent	Janesville	Rock Co.	134
20		Rome	Jefferson Co.	N/A
21	James A. Garfield	Waupaca	Waupaca Co.	135
21		New London	Waupaca Co.	N/A
22	Wood County	Wisconsin Rapids	Wood Co.	135
23	A. McFarland	Poynette	Columbia Co.	136
23	W. K. Forshay	Wyalusing	Grant Co.	136
23		Black Earth	Dane Co.	N/A
24	Henry Dillon	Lone Rock	Richland Co.	137
24		Richland Center	Richland Co.	N/A
25	George Irwin	Lodi	Columbia Co.	137
25		Mineral Point	Iowa Co.	N/A
26	John E. Holmes	Jefferson	Jefferson Co.	138
26		Waukau	Winnebago Co.	N/A
27	James B. McPherson	Lake Geneva	Walworth Co.	138
27		Martinsville	Dane Co.	N/A
28	General Canby	Auroraville	Waushara Co.	139
28	Newton Wilson/George Brayton	Kingston	Green Lake Co.	139
28		Jefferson	Jefferson Co.	N/A
29	Judson Kilpatrick	Oakdale	Monroe Co.	140
29	D. D. Barker	Abrams	Oconto Co.	140
29		Lodi	Columbia Co.	N/A
30	John W. Lynn	Sparta	Monroe Co.	141
30		Aztalan	Jefferson Co.	N/A
31	John H.Ely	Juneau	Dodge Co.	141
31		Lake Mills	Jefferson Co.	N/A
32	J. B. Wyman	Clintonville	Waupaca Co.	142
32		Stockbridge	Calumet Co.	N/A
33		Platteville	Grant Co.	142
33	W. H. Bennett	Richland Center	Richland Co.	143
34	Charles E. Curtice	Whitewater	Walworth Co.	143
34		Hebron	Jefferson Co.	N/A
35	N. S. Frost	Prairie du Sac	Sauk Co.	144
35		Albion	Dane Co.	N/A
36	Alex Lowrie	Viroqua	Vernon Co.	144
36		Eau Claire	Eau Claire Co.	N/A

No.	Post Name	Town	County	Page
37	Phil W. Plummer	Prairie du Chien	Crawford Co.	145
37		Boscobel	Grant Co.	N/A
38	Wilson Colwell	La Crosse	La Crosse Co.	145
38		Manitowoc	Manitowoc Co.	N/A
39	Thomas J. Hungerford	Spring Green	Sauk Co.	146
39		Chilton	Calumet Co.	N/A
40	Stockbridge/Benjamin J. Sweet	Stockbridge	Calumet Co.	147
40		Columbus	Columbia Co.	N/A
41	Theodore L. Sutphen	Evansville	Rock Co.	147
41		Dodgeville	Iowa Co.	N/A
42	Henry W. Cressey	Tomah	Monroe Co.	148
42		Argyle	LaFayette Co.	N/A
43	Raymond	Mayville	Dodge Co.	149
43		Princeton	Green Lake Co.	N/A
44	Joseph P. Shepard	Menasha	Winnebago Co.	149
44		Prescott	Pierce Co.	N/A
45	Darlington/Louis P. Harvey	Darlington	Lafayette Co.	150
45		Wautoma	Waushara Co.	N/A
46	Henry Turner	New London	Waupaca Co.	151
46		Markesan	Green Lake Co.	N/A
47	Henry C. Miles/Frank Prevy	Elroy	Juneau Co.	151
47		Durand	Pepin Co.	N/A
48	Lyon	Cazenovia	Richland Co.	152
48	Charles G. Bacon	Neillsville	Clark Co.	152
49	A. A. Matthews	LaValle	Sauk Co.	153
49	William S. Rosecrans	Grantsburg	Burnett Co.	153
50	John Gillespie	Wisconsin Dells	Columbia Co.	154
51	William Wright	Excelsior	Richland Co.	154
51	Starkweather	Bear Creek	Outagamie Co.	155
52	Eagle	Eau Claire	Eau Claire Co.	155
53		Marquette	Green Lake Co.	N/A
53	George W. Bell	Wonewoc	Juneau Co.	156
54	Louis H. D. Crane	Beloit	Rock Co.	157
54		River Falls	Pierce Co.	N/A
55	Lysander Cutler	Wausau	Marathon Co.	157
55		Brodhead	Green Co.	N/A
56	Angus R. McDonald	Mazomanie	Dane Co.	158
56		Milwaukee	Milwaukee Co.	N/A
57	Charles Edgerton	Warren Mills	Monroe Co.	158
57		Sheboygan Falls	Sheboygan Co.	N/A
58		Bloomington	Grant Co.	159
58	William Evans	Menomonie	Dunn Co.	159
59	Angus S. Northrop	Mauston	Juneau Co.	160

No.	Post Name	Town	County	Page
59		Monroe	Green Co.	N/A
60	Arthur D. Hamilton	Milton	Rock Co.	160
60		Prairie du Sac	Sauk Co.	N/A
61	William P. Mitchell	New Lisbon	Juneau Co.	161
61		Mount Hope	Grant Co.	N/A
62	James C. McIntyre	Boaz	Richland Co.	161
62	John Shaver	Cedar Grove	Sheboygan Co.	161
62	Eugene A. Colburn	Bruce	Rusk Co.	162
62		Salem	Kenosha Co.	N/A
63	Enos B. Cornwell	Basswood	Richland Co.	162
63	Thomas B. Crawford	Westfield	Marquette Co.	163
63		Lancaster	Grant Co.	N/A
64	W. S. Walker	Montello	Marquette Co.	163
65	Thomas B. Crawford	Westfield	Marquette Co.	164
65		Hingman	Sheboygan Co.	N/A
65	F. Jackel	Spooner	Washburn Co.	165
66	Platteville/William T. Sherman	Platteville	Grant Co.	165
66		Cascade	Sheboygan Co.	N/A
67	Samuel F. Curtis	West Lima	Richland Co.	166
67		Jamestown	Grant Co.	N/A
68	James Comerford	Chippewa Falls	Chippewa Co.	167
68		Oregon	Dane Co.	N/A
69	Erastus Hoyt	Albany	Green Co.	167
69		Waupaca	Waupaca Co.	N/A
70	Alexis Tallman	Clinton	Rock Co.	168
70		Beloit	Rock Co.	N/A
71	J. B. Moore	Muscoda	Grant Co.	168
71	O. B. Rice	Eleva	Trempealeau Co.	169
71		Black River Falls	Jackson Co.	N/A
72	A. M. Howard/Custer	Rock Elm	Pierce Co.	169
72		Patch Grove	Grant Co.	N/A
73	James S. Alban	Pittsville	Wood Co.	170
73		Kenosha	Kenosha Co.	N/A
74	Edward A. Ramsey	Oconto	Oconto Co.	170
74		Pensaukee	Oconto Co.	N/A
75	Sylvester Wheeler	Verona	Dane Co.	171
75	Myron Gardner	Arcadia	Trempealeau Co.	171
75		Alma	Buffalo Co.	N/A
76	Walworth County/Rutherford B. Hayes	Elkhorn	Walworth Co.	172
76		Appleton	Outagamie Co.	N/A
77	John Flynn	La Crosse	La Crosse Co.	172
77		Geneva	Walworth Co.	N/A
78	John Matteson	Embarass	Waupaca Co.	173

No.	Post Name	Town	County	Page
78	John A. Kellogg	Antigo	Langlade Co.	173
79	George M. Emery	Wolf Creek	Polk Co.	174
79	I. Ramsdell	Marion	Waupaca Co.	174
79		Waukesha	Waukesha Co.	N/A
80	Orrin D. Chapman	Gays Mills	Crawford Co.	175
81	William H. Hawley	Shawano	Shawano Co.	175
82	Charles Coleman	Durand	Pepin Co.	176
82		Mukwonago	Waukesha Co.	N/A
83	John Faller	North Freedom	Sauk Co.	176
83		Wausau	Marathon Co.	N/A
84	A. S. Bennett	Boyceville	Dunn Co.	177
85	Jerry Turner	Viola	Richland Co.	178
86	Colonel E.E. Ellsworth	Merrillan	Jackson Co.	178
87	Perrin C. Judkins	Alma Center	Jackson Co.	179
88	William A. Barstow	Kendall	Monroe Co.	179
89	Nathan Hoyt	Woodstock	Richland Co.	180
90	Wesley W. Patton	Brodhead	Green Co.	180
91	Samuel Harrison	Depere	Brown Co.	181
92	William Moore	Black River Falls	Jackson Co.	181
93	Henry O. Watrous	Spencer	Marathon Co.	182
93	W. G. Wheeler	Osseo	Trempealeau Co.	182
94	Oliver D. Pease	Watertown	Jefferson Co.	183
95	John W. Christian	Mondovi	Buffalo Co.	183
96	Thomas H. Oates	Shullsburg	Lafayette Co.	184
97	William A. Nelson	Forestville	Door Co.	184
98	John E. Perkins	Augusta	Eau Claire Co.	185
99	Edwin Austin	Sylvan Corners	Richland Co.	185
99	Iola	Iola	Waupaca Co.	186
100	George H. Stevens	Fox Lake	Dodge Co.	186
101	John McDermott	Boscobel	Grant Co.	187
102	Oscar F. Pinney	Monroe	Green Co.	188
103	Benjamin I. Humphrey	New Richmond	St. Croix Co.	188
104	Winfield Scott	Whitehall	Trempealeau Co.	189
105	Major William F. Dawes	Necedah	Juneau Co.	189
105	M. G. Townsend	Pewaukee	Waukesha Co.	189
106	James Mason	Desoto	Vernon Co.	190
107	Allatoona	Arena	Iowa Co.	190
108	Andrew J. McNurlin	Loyd	Richland Co.	191
108	James Little	Pepin	Pepin Co.	191
109	Williamson	Dodgeville	Iowa Co.	191
110	Marshfield/James G. Blaine	Marshfield	Wood Co.	192
111	C. McKenzie	St. Croix Falls	Polk Co.	193
112	Isaac N. Earl	Colby	Clark Co.	193

No.	Post Name	Town	County	Page
113	John Ross	Monticello	Green Co.	194
114	Hans C. Heg	Waupun	Dodge Co.	194
115	Belmont	Blaine	Portage Co.	195
115	Cumberland	Cumberland	Barron Co.	195
116	J. W. Appleton	Black Creek	Outagamie Co.	195
117	George Hall	Beaver Dam	Dodge Co.	196
118	Ellsworth	Ellsworth	Pierce Co.	196
119	Oscar F. Mattice	Waterloo	Jefferson Co.	197
120	J.B. Steadman	Manawa	Waupaca Co.	197
121	Joe Mower	Bellville	Dane Co.	198
122	(William W.) Badgero	Friendship	Adams Co.	198
123	Orson E. Rice	Oregon	Dane Co.	199
124	Timothy O. Howe	Green Bay	Brown Co.	199
125	George H. Legate	Mineral Point	Iowa Co.	200
126	Martin W. Heller	Rice Lake	Barron Co.	201
126	F. A. Marden	King	Waupaca Co.	201
127	Benjamin F. Allen	Arkansaw	Pepin Co.	202
128	Albert Weatherbe	Chetek	Barron Co.	202
129	Hiram J. Lewis	Neenah	Winnebago Co.	203
130	Edwin A. Brown	Fond du Lac	Fond du Lac Co.	203
131	Lincoln County	Merrill	Lincoln Co.	204
132	Thomas D. Cox	Lancaster	Grant Co.	204
133	George D. Eggleston	Appleton	Outagamie Co.	205
134	William Hickok	Bloomington	Grant Co.	205
135	Edward Saxe	Wautoma	Waushara Co.	206
136	Benjamin F. Sheldon	Brandon	Fond du Lac Co.	207
137	Henry S. Swift	Edgerton	Rock Co.	207
138	Joseph Bailey	Palmyra	Jefferson Co.	208
139	George M. Potter	Cadott	Chippewa Co.	208
139	Charles Graves	Berlin	Green Lake Co.	209
140	George A. Custer	Ashland	Ashland Co.	210
141	Henry Didiot	Hillsboro	Vernon Co.	210
142	Emerson Opdyke	Clear Lake	Polk Co.	211
143	Joseph C. Miller	Oxford	Marquette Co.	211
144	William Pitts	Dallas	Barron Co.	211
145	General James Shields	Medford	Taylor Co.	212
146	Frank A. Haskell/Harvey M. Brown	Columbus	Columbia Co.	212
147	Nathaniel P. Lyon	Bloomer	Chippewa Co.	213
148	Joseph Shannon/A. K. Humphrey	Knapp	Dunn Co.	214
149	Plover	Plover	Portage Co.	214
150	Thomas Eubank	Hancock	Waushara Co.	215
151	Edwin A. Clapp	Hudson	St. Croix Co.	215
152	Phil Davenport	Soldiers Grove	Crawford Co.	216

No.	Post Name	Town	County	Page
153	Philo C. Buckman	Stoughton	Dane Co.	216
154	Allen McVey	Star	Vernon Co.	217
155	John M. Read	Kewaunee	Kewaunee Co.	217
156	Stevens Point	Stevens Point	Portage Co.	218
157	W. W. Olds	Turtle Lake	Barron Co.	218
158	James Williams	Ontario	Vernon Co.	219
159	Fort Atkinson	Fort Atkinson	Jefferson Co.	219
160	Hiram Russell	Fremont	Waupaca Co.	220
161	Elijah H. Amidon	Melrose	Jackson Co.	220
162	Arthur C. Ellis	Eau Claire	Eau Claire Co.	221
162	Belknap Fuqua	Potosi	Grant Co.	221
163	Francis Asbra Wellcome	Thorpe	Clark Co.	221
164	Carmi P. Garlick	Osceola Mills	Polk Co.	222
165	George M. West	Hartford	Washington Co.	222
166	Maj. Nathan Paine	Fairchild	Eau Claire Co.	223
166	Martin W. Heller	Rice Lake	Barron Co.	223
167	Franklin Bigelow	Eagle	Waukesha Co.	224
167	Lucius H. Drury	Eagle River	Vilas Co.	224
167	John Green	EauGalle	Dunn Co.	225
168	Howard F. Pruyn	Dorchester	Clark Co.	225
169	John Echternoch	Theresa	Dodge Co.	226
170	Alonzo Palmer	Superior	Douglas Co.	226
171	Henry Concklin	East Troy	Walworth Co.	227
172	Martin Watson	Barron	Barron Co.	227
173	Sam Montieth	Fennimore	Grant Co.	228
174	A. D. Thornburg	Lime Ridge	Sauk Co.	228
175	George W. Holloway	Beetown	Grant Co.	229
175	Rufus King	South Milwaukee	Milwaukee Co.	229
176	John & James Cullin/John Bragg	Gratiot	Lafayette Co.	230
177	I. N. Nichols	River Falls	Pierce Co.	230
178	Chelsea	Chelsea	Taylor Co.	231
178	Henry C. Isbell	Birnamwood	Shawano Co.	231
179	Horace T. Sanders	Norwalk	Monroe Co.	231
180	Andrew Chambers	Weyauwega	Waupaca Co.	232
181	Phillips/Allen Jackson	Phillips	Price Co.	232
182	Sidney A. Bean	Hammond	St. Croix Co.	233
183	John B. Doughty	Colfax	Dunn Co.	233
183	George C. Ginty	Cadott	Chippewa Co.	234
184	Luther T. Park	Black Earth	Dane Co.	234
185	Morris E. Sexton	Sextonville	Richland Co.	235
186	William Payne	Pardeeville	Columbia Co.	235
187	Gustave Wintermeyer	Sheboygan	Sheboygan Co.	236
188	William J. Kershaw	Briggsville	Marquette Co.	236

No.	Post Name	Town	County	Page
189	Rollin P. Converse	Prescott	Pierce Co.	237
190	General Lytle	Kiel	Manitowoc Co.	237
191	Lorenzo A. Dixon	Mount Horeb	Dane Co.	238
192	Abner O. Heald	Cascade	Sheboygan Co.	238
193	Andrew J. Fullerton	West Bend	Washington Co.	239
194	Henry Bertram	Oconomowoc	Waukesha Co.	239
195	George Parsons	Merrimack	Sauk Co.	240
196	Christopher Fimian	Alma	Buffalo Co.	240
197	Walter Waterman	Plainfield	Waushara Co.	241
198	John Granzo	Seymour	Outagamie Co.	241
199	H. S. Eggleston	Ripon	Fond du Lac Co.	242
200	Alexander Ricky	Hersey	St. Croix Co.	242
201	Martin Luther Crane	Burlington	Racine Co.	243
202	Elisha Harrison Randall	Dartford	Green Lake Co.	243
203	Grantsburg	Grantsburg	Burnett Co.	244
203	Charles A. Blair/Fred Richter	Lowell	Dodge Co.	244
204	U. S. Grant	Maiden Rock	Pierce Co.	245
205	Chilton/Joseph B. Reynolds	Chilton	Calumet Co.	245
206	Colwert Pier	Argyle	LaFayette Co.	246
207	Samuel H. Sizer	Marinette	Marinette Co.	246
208	William H. Hamilton	Sun Prairie	Dane Co.	247
209	Plum City	Plum City	Pierce Co.	247
209	Ennis T. Reed	White Creek	Adams Co.	248
210	Francis Steffen	Hortonville	Outagamie Co.	248
211	E.E. Ellsworth	Fish Creek	Door Co.	249
211	Old Guard	Milwaukee	Milwaukee Co.	249
212	Henry P. Davidson	Plymouth	Sheboygan Co.	249
213	Joe Mower	Wrightstown	Brown Co.	250
213	John A. Eaton	Greenwood	Clark Co.	250
214	John Hazen	Cashton	Monroe Co.	251
215	George B. Lincoln	Union Grove	Racine Co.	251
216	Charles Green	Seneca	Crawford Co.	252
217	Unity	Unity	Marathon Co.	252
218	J. Mueller	Cassville	Grant Co.	252
219	Joe Rankin	Two Rivers	Manitowoc Co.	253
220	John A. Hauff	Horicon	Dodge Co.	253
221	C. E. McCarthy	Rockbridge	Richland Co.	254
222	Hiram M. Gibbs	Brillion	Calumet Co.	254
223	George C. Drake	Milwaukee	Milwaukee Co.	255
224	G. L. Park	Boyd	Chippewa Co.	255
224	John E. Gurley	Blanchardville	LaFayette Co.	256
225	Cumberland	Cumberland	Barron Co.	256
226	H. Smith Schuyler	Sturgeon Bay	Door Co.	257

No.	Post Name	Town	County	Page
227	Solomon Meredith	Hayward	Sawyer Co.	257
227	Azro Young	Winneconne	Winnebago Co.	258
228	Wallace Dantz	Princeton	Green Lake Co.	258
229	Franklin H. Potter	Cambridge	Dane Co.	259
230	Frederick S. Lovell	Kenosha	Kenosha Co.	259
231	James S. Ewing	Poy Sippi	Waushara Co.	260
232	John A. Logan	Rhinelander	Oneida Co.	260
233	Nelson Quiggle	Mindoro	La Crosse Co.	261
233	Oscar F. Brown	Glenwood	St. Croix Co.	261
234	Cyprian Downer	Bangor	La Crosse Co.	261
235	George A. Fisk	Cataract	Monroe Co.	262
236	Charles R. Gill	Loyal	Clark Co.	262
237	August Roemhild	Prairie Farm	Barron Co.	263
238	John A. Otis	Trimbelle	Pierce Co.	263
239	Chester A .Arthur	Ogdensburg	Waupaca Co.	263
240	Rank & File	Milwaukee	Milwaukee Co.	264
241	John W. Scott	Oshkosh	Winnebago Co.	264
242	Joseph Anderegg	Algoma	Kewaunee Co.	266
243	Newton S. Green	Shell Lake	Washburn Co.	266
244	Winfield Scott Hancock	Cedarburg	Ozaukee Co.	267
245	W. F. Dawes	Necedah	Juneau Co.	267
246	Isaac Hendricks	Campbellsport	Fond du Lac Co.	268
247	Paul H. Beaulieu	Kaukauna	Outagamie Co.	268
248	William Taylor	Peshtigo	Marinette Co.	269
248	Estrick Burbank	Mather	Juneau Co.	269
249	Ambrose E. Burnside	Bayfield	Bayfield Co.	270
250	Robert Mueller	Milwaukee	Milwaukee Co.	270
251	Henry E. Hess	Eureka	Winnebago Co.	271
252	Gouverneur K. Warren	Nelson	Buffalo Co	271
253	Gustvus H. Bryant	Lake Mills	Jefferson Co.	272
254	Frank Ellenbecker	Port Washington	Ozaukee Co.	272
254	Moses H. Hull	Washburn	Bayfield Co.	273
255	Myron Gardner	Arcadia	Trempealeau Co.	273
256	Edmund W. Long	Wittenberg	Shawano Co.	274
257	Peter Weber	Fountain City	Buffalo Co	274
258	Charles H. Ford	Galesville	Trempealeau Co.	274
259	James S. Alban	Hurley	Iron Co.	275
260	Solomon Meredith	Hayward	Sawyer Co.	275
261	Joseph A. Ledergerber	Keshena	Menominee Co.	276
262	Nicholas Friddle	Rome	Jefferson Co.	277
263	Daniel Chaplin	Amery	Polk Co.	277
264	Benjamin S. Davis	Oakley /Peedee	Green Co.	278
265	Bradford Phillips	Royalton	Waupaca Co.	278

No.	Post Name	Town	County	Page
266	William O. Topping	Hazel Green	Grant Co.	279
267	William Atkinson	Marcellon	Columbia Co.	279
268	Joseph Dupont	Florence	Florence Co.	280
269	Archibald Wheeler	Coloma	Waushara Co.	280
269	Edward Winslow Hincks	Auburn/New Cassel	Fond du Lac Co.	281
270	Duane Patten	Sharon	Walworth Co	281
271	George H. Brayton	Fall River	Columbia Co.	282
272	Otis Hoyt	Glenwood	St. Croix Co.	282
272	Jeremiah Rusk	Spring Valley	Pierce Co.	283
273	George Willich	Boyd	Chippewa Co.	283
273	J. D. Robie	Superior	Douglas Co.	284
274	William Steinmeyer	Milwaukee	Milwaukee Co.	284
275	Oliver A. Hegg	Independence	Trempealeau Co.	285
276	Henry O. Watrous	Spencer	Marathon Co.	285
277	Wausaukee	Wausaukee	Marinette Co.	286
278	Oneida	Oneida Reservation	Brown Co.	286
279	H.W. Lawton	Muscoda	Grant Co.	287
280	John E. Tourtellotte/Rusk County	Ladysmith	Rusk Co.	287

POSTS

BY NAME

If a common thread is to be found in the array of names by which Wisconsin's Grand Army Posts were known, it would probably be what, several wars hence, would be called "the common GI."

Of more than 330 posts whose names can be recorded today, the preponderance have names hardly celebrated, even when they were in operation; some were located many miles away from the post city. But to the veterans in those communities, the memories of fallen comrades were worthy of honor for as long as a veteran could keep a post alive.

They were heroes by most estimations. They were men who answered the call of their nation and gave their lives in response, whether in fevered death in a Mississippi swamp, in a forlorn charge on enemy breastworks, or from a single sharpshooter or bushwhacker bullet. Some gave their lives after they returned to civilized society, as their lives were shortened by the cumulative effect of months and years of uncommonly arduous toil, hardship, and privation.

These were the GI's of the Civil War, to be sure. Or perhaps they should be called today by the term they themselves most certainly would recognize and appreciate: Billy Yanks.

Most of them were army men. Only one Department of Wisconsin post bore the name of a navy hero: William B. Cushing Post 19 of Waukesha, named for the Wisconsinite who almost single-handedly sank the Confederate ironclad Albemarle.

One post was named for a bird rather than a man. But Old Abe the War Eagle was the most famous mascot of the Civil War, and probably the most famous American mascot in any war. Veterans at Eau Claire, where Old Abe was "mustered in" in 1861, called their G.A.R. post the Eagle Post.

One post chose to commemorate neither man nor beast, but rather, a battle. Arena's Post 107 was named for the Battle of Allatoona where Wisconsin troops took part in a dramatic, heroic defense of a north Georgia Union supply point not long after the fall of Atlanta.

About a dozen posts were named for civilians, including four honoring Louis Harvey, the Wisconsin governor who fell victim to the war, drowning while visiting Wisconsin troops after the Battle of Shiloh in 1862. Naturally, an early choice for a post name was Abraham Lincoln, taken by veterans at Darien in Walworth County. Two later presidents who also fell to assassins' bullets were honored with Posts named after them: William McKinley Post 15 of La Crosse and James A. Garfield Post 21 of

Waupaca. The slain presidents had also served as soldiers in the war, as had President Rutherford B. Hayes, for whom Post 76, Elkhorn, was named. A fifth president honored was Chester A. Arthur by Post 239, Ogdensburg, although Arthur never served in the armed forces.

An interesting choice was to honor James G. Blaine whose only apparent service to the country for which a G.A.R. post might be impressed was running against Grover Cleveland for president. Post 110 in Marshfield honored the runner-up. President Cleveland was decidedly not beloved by most G.A.R. men.

Three Milwaukee posts chose to celebrate Billy Yank in a sort of generic way. An early post at the National Veterans Home called itself Veterans Post 8. Post 211 was known as Old Guard Post. Post 240 was Rank & File Post.

Standards for naming Grand Army posts evolved relatively early, quickly conforming to certain standards. Prior to 1869 there were no rules. At first, posts adopted the names of popular war figures. There were Phil Sheridan posts in several departments by then, including Post 3 in Milwaukee.

In 1879 the order adopted some restrictions, thus: "... any Post may prefix the name of a deceased soldier or sailor who died in the service of our country during the rebellion, or of some other person eminent during the war for loyalty and efficiency. . . ." The next year the loophole of "other person eminent" was changed to read "other deceased person."

Also in 1879 the rules were relaxed a bit to make it possible to name a post after something other than a person. There already were examples of non-person posts in Wisconsin, for example, Veterans, Eagle, and a whole slew of posts named for the town or county of their locations. Presumably, too, this relaxation of the rules made legal the practice of naming a post after a soldier who did not die in the war, as was originally required, but died afterward.

It is evident from the rules that the honor was supposed to be posthumously awarded. Still, it appears that in Wisconsin there may have been a breach or two of that standard. J. H. Knight Post 5 in Ashland County was named in 1879 for the county's most prominent citizen; Knight was a veteran, but he lived until 1903. Colwert Pier Post 206 at Argyle was named in 1885, some years before the famed leader of the 1880 Soldier's and Sailor's Reunion in Milwaukee died. These posts were apparently named without regard to the "deceased-person" rule.

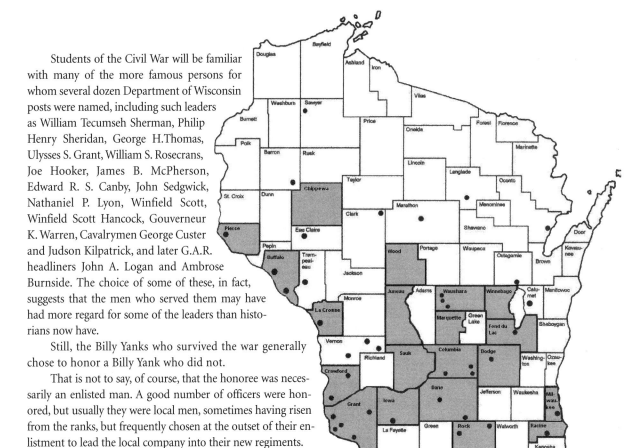

Students of the Civil War will be familiar with many of the more famous persons for whom several dozen Department of Wisconsin posts were named, including such leaders as William Tecumseh Sherman, Philip Henry Sheridan, George H. Thomas, Ulysses S. Grant, William S. Rosecrans, Joe Hooker, James B. McPherson, Edward R. S. Canby, John Sedgwick, Nathaniel P. Lyon, Winfield Scott, Winfield Scott Hancock, Gouverneur K. Warren, Cavalrymen George Custer and Judson Kilpatrick, and later G.A.R. headliners John A. Logan and Ambrose Burnside. The choice of some of these, in fact, suggests that the men who served them may have had more regard for some of the leaders than historians now have.

Still, the Billy Yanks who survived the war generally chose to honor a Billy Yank who did not.

That is not to say, of course, that the honoree was necessarily an enlisted man. A good number of officers were honored, but usually they were local men, sometimes having risen from the ranks, but frequently chosen at the outset of their enlistment to lead the local company into their new regiments.

And there were plenty of regiments represented. At least 43 of Wisconsin's 53 infantry regiments had at least one man whose name was inscribed on some G.A.R. post after the war. It is necessary to say "at least" in these situations because as many as a dozen names of honorees affixed to these posts cannot be identified.

All four Wisconsin cavalry regiments were represented on G.A.R. department rolls, as was the heavy artillery unit and at least four field artillery batteries. There were, incidentally, at least a dozen posts named for men whose service was with units from outside Wisconsin.

Not surprisingly, the earliest regiments recruited—First through Eighth—had the greatest number of men represented on post banners. These regiments served the longest and, in many respects, experienced some of the most vicious fighting.

In this regard it might be expected that the Iron Brigade would have large representation, and indeed it had. The Second Wisconsin had at least 13 posts; the Sixth Wisconsin had 18 posts and the Seventh Wisconsin had at least seven. This Wisconsin representation in the Army of the Potomac's early history saw especially desperate fighting and those who did return were especially prone to honor a comrade rather than some popular general.

The map here shows first where the three regiments were recruited over a wide swath of the state and then where posts were named for their fallen.

Non–Iron Brigade regiments had good postwar representation among G.A.R. post names: the Third Wisconsin had at least seven; the Fourth, in both its infantry and cavalry roles, had at least 14; and the Fifth had at least 13. The Eagle Regiment had at least a dozen, and at least half a dozen were named after each of the Eleventh, Twelfth, Fourteenth, and Sixteenth. And interestingly, the Thirty-sixth Wisconsin and Thirty-seventh Wisconsin, both late-recruited, also had at least half a dozen posts named after their men. These regiments had been in the thick of fighting in front of Petersburg and had major roles in the last year of the war.

Finally, among the later regiments, posts were named for at least one fallen comrade of the Forty-second, Forty-fourth, Forty-fifth, Forty-sixth, Forty-seventh, and Forty-ninth Wisconsin, reminders that memorable deeds and sacrifices were not the exclusive province of the Billy Yanks who went to war in 1861.

In a later chapter, "Posts in Detail," what is known about these men for whom Wisconsin veterans named their Grand Army Posts, will be told.

POSTS BY NAME

A	Post Name	No.	Town	County	Page
	Alban, James S.	259	Hurley	Iron Co.	275
	Alban, James S.	73	Pittsville	Wood Co.	170
	Allatoona	107	Arena	Iowa Co.	190
	Allen, Benjamin F.	127	Arkansaw	Pepin Co.	202
	Amidon, Elijah H.	161	Melrose	Jackson Co.	220
	Anderegg, Joseph	242	Algoma	Kewaunee Co.	266
	Appleton, J. W.	116	Black Creek	Outagamie Co.	195
	Arthur, Chester A.	239	Ogdensburg	Waupaca Co.	263
	Atkinson, William	267	Marcellon	Columbia Co.	279
	Austin, Edwin	99	Sylvan Corners	Richland Co.	185
B	**Post Name**	**No.**	**Town**	**County**	**Page**
	Bacon, Charles G.	48	Neillsville	Clark Co.	152
	Badgero, (William W.)	122	Friendship	Adams Co.	198
	Bailey, Joseph	138	Palmyra	Jefferson Co.	208
	Barker, D. D.	29	Abrams	Oconto Co.	140
	Barstow, William A.	88	Kendall	Monroe Co.	179
	Bean, Sidney A.	182	Hammond	St. Croix Co.	233
	Beaulieu, Paul H.	247	Kaukauna	Outagamie Co.	268
	Bell, George W.	53	Wonewoc	Juneau Co.	156
	Belmont	115	Blaine	Portage Co.	195
	Bennett, A. S.	84	Boyceville	Dunn Co.	177
	Bennett, W. H.	33	Richland Center	Richland Co.	143
	Bertram, Henry	194	Oconomowoc	Waukesha Co.	239
	Bigelow, Franklin	167	Eagle	Waukesha Co.	224
	Blaine, James G.	110	Marshfield	Wood Co.	192
	Blair, Charles A.	203	Lowell	Dodge Co.	244
	Bragg, John	176	Gratiot	Lafayette Co.	230
	Brayton, George	28	Kingston	Green Lake Co.	139
	Brayton, George H.	271	Fall River	Columbia Co.	282
	Brown, Edwin A.	130	Fond du Lac	Fond du Lac Co.	203
	Brown, Harvey M.	146	Columbus	Columbia Co.	212
	Brown, Oscar F.	233	Glenwood	St. Croix Co.	261
	Bryant, Gustavus H.	253	Lake Mills	Jefferson Co.	272
	Buckman, Philo C.	153	Stoughton	Dane Co.	216
	Burbank, Estrick	248	Mather	Juneau Co.	269
	Burnside, Ambrose E.	249	Bayfield	Bayfield Co.	270
C	**Post Name**	**No.**	**Town**	**County**	**Page**
	Canby, General Edward S.	28	Auroraville	Waushara Co.	139
	Chambers, Andrew	180	Weyauwega	Waupaca Co.	232
	Chaplin, Daniel	263	Amery	Polk Co.	277
	Chapman, Orrin D.	80	Gays Mills	Crawford Co.	175

	Post Name	No.	Town	County	Page
	Chelsea	178	Chelsea	Taylor Co.	231
	Chesebro, Jerome	15	Markesan	Green Lake Co.	130
	Chilton	205	Chilton	Calumet Co.	245
	Chivas, Robert	2	Milwaukee	Milwaukee Co.	116
	Christian, John W.	95	Mondovi	Buffalo Co.	183
	Clapp, Edwin A.	151	Hudson	St. Croix Co.	215
	Colburn, Eugene A.	62	Bruce	Rusk Co.	162
	Coleman, Charles	82	Durand	Pepin Co.	176
	Colwell, Wilson	38	La Crosse	La Crosse Co.	145
	Comerford, James	68	Chippewa Falls	Chippewa Co.	167
	Concklin, Henry	171	East Troy	Walworth Co.	227
	Converse, Rollin P.	189	Prescott	Pierce Co.	237
	Cornwell, Enos B.	63	Basswood	Richland Co.	162
	Cox, Thomas D.	132	Lancaster	Grant Co.	204
	Crane, Louis H. D.	54	Beloit	Rock Co.	157
	Crane, Martin Luther	201	Burlington	Racine Co.	243
	Crawford, Thomas B.	65	Westfield	Marquette Co.	164
	Crawford, Thomas B.	63	Westfield	Marquette Co.	163
	Cressey, Henry W.	42	Tomah	Monroe Co.	148
	Cullin, John & James	176	Gratiot	Lafayette Co.	230
	Cumberland	115	Cumberland	Barron Co.	195
	Cumberland	225	Cumberland	Barron Co.	256
	Curtice, Charles E.	34	Whitewater	Walworth Co.	143
	Curtis, Samuel F.	67	West Lima	Richland Co.	166
	Cushing, William B.	19	Waukesha	Waukesha Co.	134
	Custer, George A.	140	Ashland	Ashland Co.	210
	Custer, George A.	72	Rock Elm	Pierce Co.	169
	Cutler, Lysander	55	Wausau	Marathon Co.	157
D	**Post Name**	**No.**	**Town**	**County**	**Page**
	Dantz, Wallace	228	Princeton	Green Lake Co.	258
	Darlington	45	Darlington	Lafayette Co.	150
	Davenport, Phil	152	Soldiers Grove	Crawford Co.	216
	Davidson, Henry P.	212	Plymouth	Sheboygan Co.	249
	Davis, Benjamin S.	264	Oakley /Peedee	Green Co.	278
	Dawes, Maj. William F.	105	Necedah	Juneau Co.	189
	Dawes, W. F.	245	Necedah	Juneau Co.	267
	Didiot, Henry	141	Hillsboro	Vernon Co.	210
	Dillon, Henry	24	Lone Rock	Richland Co.	137
	Dixon, Lorenzo A.	191	Mount Horeb	Dane Co.	238
	Doughty, John B.	183	Colfax	Dunn Co.	233
	Downer, Cyprian	234	Bangor	La Crosse Co.	261
	Drake, George C.	223	Milwaukee	Milwaukee Co.	255
	Drury, Lucius H.	167	Eagle River	Vilas Co.	224
	Dupont, Joseph	268	Florence	Florence Co.	280

E	Post Name	No.	Town	County	Page
	Eagle	52	Eau Claire	Eau Claire Co.	155
	Earl, Isaac N.	112	Colby	Clark Co.	193
	Eaton, John A.	213	Greenwood	Clark Co.	250
	Echternoch, John	169	Theresa	Dodge Co.	226
	Eckles, Irvin	16	Amherst	Portage Co.	132
	Edgerton, Charles	57	Warren Mills	Monroe Co.	158
	Eggleston, George D.	133	Appleton	Outagamie Co.	205
	Eggleston, H. S.	199	Ripon	Fond du Lac Co.	242
	Ellenbecker, Frank	254	Port Washington	Ozaukee Co.	272
	Ellis, Arthur C.	162	Eau Claire	Eau Claire Co.	221
	Ellsworth	118	Ellsworth	Pierce Co.	196
	Ellsworth, Col. E. E.	86	Merrillan	Jackson Co.	178
	Ellsworth, E. E.	211	Fish Creek	Door Co.	249
	Ely, John H.	31	Juneau	Dodge Co.	141
	Emery, George M.	79	Wolf Creek	Polk Co.	174
	Eubank, Thomas	150	Hancock	Waushara Co.	215
	Evans, William	58	Menomonie	Dunn Co.	159
	Ewing, James S.	231	Poy Sippi	Waushara Co.	260
F	Post Name	No.	Town	County	Page
	Fairchild, Cassius	1	Madison	Dane Co.	115
	Fairchild, Lucius	11(1)	Madison	Dane Co.	125
	Faller, John	83	North Freedom	Sauk Co.	176
	Fimian, Christopher	196	Alma	Buffalo Co.	240
	Fisk, George A.	235	Cataract	Monroe Co.	262
	Flynn, John	77	La Crosse	La Crosse Co.	172
	Follensbee, John	15	New Centerville	St. Croix Co.	131
	Ford, Charles	13	Trempealeau	Trempealeau Co.	128
	Ford, Charles H.	258	Galesville	Trempealeau Co.	274
	Forshay, W. K.	23	Wyalusing	Grant Co.	136
	Fort Atkinson	159	Fort Atkinson	Jefferson Co.	219
	Friddle, Nicholas	262	Rome	Jefferson Co.	277
	Frost, N. S.	35	Prairie du Sac	Sauk Co.	144
	Fullerton, Andrew J.	193	West Bend	Washington Co.	239
	Fuqua, Belknap	162	Potosi	Grant Co.	221
G	Post Name	No.	Town	County	Page
	Gardner, Myron	75	Arcadia	Trempealeau Co.	171
	Gardner, Myron	255	Arcadia	Trempealeau Co.	273
	Garfield, James A.	21	Waupaca	Waupaca Co.	135
	Garlick, Carmi P.	164	Osceola Mills	Polk Co.	222
	Gibbs, Hiram M.	222	Brillion	Calumet Co.	254
	Gill, Charles R.	236	Loyal	Clark Co.	262
	Gillespie, John	50	Wisconsin Dells	Columbia Co.	154
	Ginty, George C.	183	Cadott	Chippewa Co.	234

	Post Name	No.	Town	County	Page
	Grant, U. S.	204	Maiden Rock	Pierce Co.	245
	Grantsburg	203	Grantsburg	Burnett Co.	244
	Granzo, John	198	Seymour	Outagamie Co.	241
	Graves, Charles	139	Berlin	Green Lake Co.	209
	Green, Charles	216	Seneca	Crawford Co.	252
	Green, John	167	EauGalle	Dunn Co.	225
	Green, Newton S.	243	Shell Lake	Washburn Co.	266
	Gurley, John E.	224	Blanchardville	LaFayette Co.	256
H	**Post Name**	**No.**	**Town**	**County**	**Page**
	Hall, George	117	Beaver Dam	Dodge Co.	196
	Hamilton, Arthur D.	60	Milton	Rock Co.	160
	Hamilton, William H.	208	Sun Prairie	Dane Co.	247
	Hancock, Winfield Scott	244	Cedarburg	Ozaukee Co.	267
	Harrison, Samuel	91	Depere	Brown Co.	181
	Harvey, Governor	15	Green Bay	Brown Co.	129
	Harvey, Gov. Louis P.	16	Amherst	Portage Co.	132
	Harvey, Gov. Louis P.	17	Racine	Racine Co.	133
	Harvey, Louis P.	45	Darlington	Lafayette Co.	150
	Haskell, Frank A.	146	Columbus	Columbia Co.	212
	Hauff, John A.	220	Horicon	Dodge Co.	253
	Hawley, William H.	81	Shawano	Shawano Co.	175
	Hayes, Rutherford B.	76	Elkhorn	Walworth Co.	172
	Hazen, John	214	Cashton	Monroe Co.	251
	Heald, Abner O.	192	Cascade	Sheboygan Co.	238
	Heg, Hans C.	114	Waupun	Dodge Co.	194
	Hegg, Oliver A.	275	Independence	Trempealeau Co.	285
	Heller, Martin W.	126	Rice Lake	Barron Co.	201
	Heller, Martin W.	166	Rice Lake	Barron Co.	223
	Hendricks, Isaac	246	Campbellsport	Fond du Lac Co.	268
	Hess, Henry E.	251	Eureka	Winnebago Co.	271
	Hickok, William	134	Bloomington	Grant Co.	205
	Hincks, Edward Winslow	269	Auburn	Fond du Lac Co.	281
	Holloway, George W.	175	Beetown	Grant Co.	229
	Holmes, John E.	26	Jefferson	Jefferson Co.	138
	Hooker, Joe	9	Baraboo	Sauk Co.	123
	Howard, A. M.	72	Rock Elm	Pierce Co.	169
	Howe, Timothy O.	124	Green Bay	Brown Co.	199
	Hoyt, Erastus	69	Albany	Green Co.	167
	Hoyt, Nathan	89	Woodstock	Richland Co.	180
	Hoyt, Otis	272	Glenwood	St. Croix Co.	282
	Hull, Moses H.	254	Washburn	Bayfield Co.	273
	Humphrey, A. K.	148	Knapp	Dunn Co.	214
	Humphrey, Benjamin I.	103	New Richmond	St. Croix Co.	188
	Hungerford, Thomas J.	39	Spring Green	Sauk Co.	146

I	Post Name	No.	Town	County	Page
	Iola	99	Iola	Waupaca Co.	186
	Irwin, George	25	Lodi	Columbia Co.	137
	Isbell, Henry C.	178	Birnamwood	Shawano Co.	231

J	Post Name	No.	Town	County	Page
	Jackel, F.	65	Spooner	Washburn Co.	165
	Jackson, Allen	181	Phillips	Price Co.	232
	Judkins, Perrin C.	87	Alma Center	Jackson Co.	179

K	Post Name	No.	Town	County	Page
	Kellogg, John A.	78	Antigo	Langlade Co.	173
	Kershaw, William J.	188	Briggsville	Marquette Co.	236
	Kilpatrick, Judson	29	Oakdale	Monroe Co.	140
	King, Rufus	175	South Milwaukee	Milwaukee Co.	229
	Knight, J. H.	5	Butternut	Ashland Co.	120

L	Post Name	No.	Town	County	Page
	Lawton, H. W.	279	Muscoda	Grant Co.	287
	Ledergerber, Joseph A.	261	Keshena	Menominee Co.	276
	Legate, George H.	125	Mineral Point	Iowa Co.	200
	Lewis, Hiram J.	129	Neenah	Winnebago Co.	203
	Lincoln County	131	Merrill	Lincoln Co.	204
	Lincoln, Abraham	3	Darien	Walworth Co.	117
	Lincoln, George B.	215	Union Grove	Racine Co.	251
	Little, James	108	Pepin	Pepin Co.	191
	Logan, John A.	232	Rhinelander	Oneida Co.	260
	Long, Edmund W.	256	Wittenberg	Shawano Co.	274
	Lovell, Frederick S.	230	Kenosha	Kenosha Co.	259
	Lowrie, Alex	36	Viroqua	Vernon Co.	144
	Lynn, John W.	30	Sparta	Monroe Co.	141
	Lyon	48	Cazenovia	Richland Co.	152
	Lyon, Nathaniel P.	147	Bloomer	Chippewa Co.	213
	Lytle, General	190	Kiel	Manitowoc Co.	237

M	Post Name	No.	Town	County	Page
	Marden, F. A.	126	King	Waupaca Co.	201
	Marshfield	110	Marshfield	Wood Co.	192
	Mason, James	106	Desoto	Vernon Co.	190
	Matteson, John	78	Embarass	Waupaca Co.	173
	Matthews, A. A.	49	LaValle	Sauk Co.	153
	Mattice, Oscar F.	119	Waterloo	Jefferson Co.	197
	McCarthy, C. E.	221	Rockbridge	Richland Co.	254
	McDermott, John	101	Bocobel	Grant Co.	187
	McDonald, Angus R.	56	Mazomanie	Dane Co.	158
	McFarland, A.	23	Poynette	Columbia Co.	136
	McIntyre, James C.	62	Boaz	Richland Co.	161
	McKenzie, C.	111	St. Croix Falls	Polk Co.	193

McKinley, William	15	La Crosse	La Crosse Co.	131
McNurlin, Andrew J.	108	Loyd	Richland Co.	191
McPherson, James B.	12	Sharon	Walworth Co.	127
McPherson, James B.	27	Lake Geneva	Walworth Co.	138
McVey, Allen	154	Star	Vernon Co.	217
Meredith, Solomon	227	Hayward	Sawyer Co.	257
Meredith, Solomon	260	Hayward	Sawyer Co.	275
Miles, Henry C.	47	Elroy	Juneau Co.	151
Miller, Joseph C.	143	Oxford	Marquette Co.	211
Mitchell, William P.	61	New Lisbon	Juneau Co.	161
Monteith, Sam	173	Fennimore	Grant Co.	228
Moore, J. B.	71	Muscoda	Grant Co.	168
Moore, William	92	Black River Falls	Jackson Co.	181
Mower, Joe	121	Bellville	Dane Co.	198
Mower, Joe	213	Wrightstown	Brown Co.	250
Mueller, J.	218	Cassville	Grant Co.	252
Mueller, Robert	250	Milwaukee	Milwaukee Co.	270
N Post Name	No.	Town	County	Page
Nelson, William A.	97	Forestville	Door Co.	184
Nichols, I. N.	177	River Falls	Pierce Co.	230
Northrop, Angus S.	59	Mauston	Juneau Co.	160
O Post Name	No.	Town	County	Page
Oates, Thomas H.	96	Shullsburg	Lafayette Co.	184
Old Guard	211	Milwaukee	Milwaukee Co.	249
Olds, W. W.	157	Turtle Lake	Barron Co.	218
Oneida	278	Oneida Reservation	Brown Co.	286
Opdyke, Emerson	142	Clear Lake	Polk Co.	211
Ordway, James F.	6	Beaver Dam	Dodge Co.	121
Oshkosh	10	Oshkosh	Winnebago Co.	124
Otis, John A.	238	Trimbelle	Pierce Co.	263
P Post Name	No.	Town	County	Page
Pack, Luther T.	184	Black Earth	Dane Co.	234
Paine, Maj. Nathan	166	Fairchild	Eau Claire Co.	223
Palmer, Alonzo	170	Superior	Douglas Co.	226
Park, G. L.	224	Boyd	Chippewa Co.	255
Parsons, George	195	Merrimack	Sauk Co.	240
Patten, Duane	270	Sharon	Walworth Co.	281
Patton, Wesley W.	90	Brodhead	Green Co.	180
Payne, William	186	Pardeeville	Columbia Co.	235
Pease, Oliver D.	94	Watertown	Jefferson Co.	183
Perkins, John E.	98	Augusta	Eau Claire Co.	185
Phillips	181	Phillips	Price Co.	232
Phillips, Bradford	265	Royalton	Waupaca Co.	278
Pier, Colwert	206	Argyle	LaFayette Co.	246

	Post Name	No.	Town	County	Page
	Pinney, Oscar F.	102	Monroe	Green Co.	188
	Pitts, William	144	Dallas	Barron Co.	211
	Platteville	66	Platteville	Grant Co.	165
	Plover	149	Plover	Portage Co.	214
	Plum City	209	Plum City	Pierce Co.	247
	Plummer, Phil W.	37	Prairie du Chien	Crawford Co.	145
	Potter, Franklin H.	229	Cambridge	Dane Co.	259
	Potter, George M.	139	Cadott	Chippewa Co.	208
	Prevy, Frank	47	Elroy	Juneau Co.	151
	Pruyn, Howard F.	168	Dorchester	Clark Co.	225
Q	**Post Name**	**No.**	**Town**	**County**	**Page**
	Quiggle, Nelson	233	Mindoro	La Crosse Co.	261
R	**Post Name**	**No.**	**Town**	**County**	**Page**
	Ramsdell, I.	79	Marion	Waupaca Co.	174
	Ramsey, Edward A.	74	Oconto	Oconto Co.	170
	Randall, Elisha Harrison	202	Dartford	Green Lake Co.	243
	Rank & File	240	Milwaukee	Milwaukee Co.	264
	Rankin, Joe	219	Two Rivers	Manitowoc Co.	253
	Raymond	43	Mayville	Dodge Co.	149
	Read, John M.	155	Kewaunee	Kewaunee Co.	217
	Reed, Ennis T.	209	White Creek	Adams Co.	248
	Reynolds, Joseph B.	205	Chilton	Calumet Co.	245
	Rice, O. B.	71	Eleva	Trempealeau Co.	169
	Rice, Orson E.	123	Oregon	Dane Co.	199
	Richardson, Jairus	12	Sheboygan Falls	Sheboygan Co.	127
	Richter, Fred	203	Lowell	Dodge Co.	244
	Ricky, Alexander	200	Hersey	St. Croix Co.	242
	Roberts, J. H.	15	Plainfield	Waushara Co.	130
	Robie, J. D.	273	Superior	Douglas Co.	284
	Roemhild, August	237	Prairie Farm	Barron Co.	263
	Rosecrans, William S.	49	Grantsburg	Burnett Co.	153
	Ross, John	113	Monticello	Green Co.	194
	Rousseau, Lovell H.	14	Portage	Columbia Co.	129
	Rusk County	280	Ladysmith	Rusk Co.	287
	Rusk, Jeremiah	272	Spring Valley	Pierce Co.	283
	Russell, Hiram	160	Fremont	Waupaca Co.	220
S	**Post Name**	**No.**	**Town**	**County**	**Page**
	Sanders, Horace T.	179	Norwalk	Monroe Co.	231
	Sargent, W. H.	20	Janesville	Rock Co.	134
	Sawyer, J. F.	7	Omro	Winnebago Co.	122
	Saxe, Edward	5	Wautoma	Waushara Co.	120
	Saxe, Edward	135	Wautoma	Waushara Co.	206
	Schuyler, H. Smith	226	Sturgeon Bay	Door Co.	257
	Scott, John W.	241	Oshkosh	Winnebago Co.	264

	Post Name	No.	Town	County	Page
	Scott, Winfield	104	Whitehall	Trempealeau Co.	189
	Sedgwick, John	12	Milwaukee	Milwaukee Co.	126
	Sexton, Morris E.	185	Sextonville	Richland Co.	235
	Shannon, Joseph	148	Knapp	Dunn Co.	214
	Shaver, John	62	Cedar Grove	Sheboygan Co.	161
	Sheldon, Benjamin F.	136	Brandon	Fond du Lac Co.	207
	Shepard, Joseph P.	44	Menasha	Winnebago Co.	149
	Sheridan, Philip H.	3	Milwaukee	Milwaukee Co.	117
	Sheridan, Philip H.	10	Oshkosh	Winnebago Co.	124
	Sherman, William T.	66	Platteville	Grant Co.	165
	Shields, General James	145	Medford	Taylor Co.	212
	Sizer, Samuel H.	207	Marinette	Marinette Co.	246
	Starkweather	51	Bear Creek	Outagamie Co.	155
	Steadman, J. B.	120	Manawa	Waupaca Co.	197
	Steffen, Francis	210	Hortonville	Outagamie Co.	248
	Steinmeyer, William	274	Milwaukee	Milwaukee Co.	284
	Stevens Point	156	Stevens Point	Portage Co.	218
	Stevens, George H.	100	Fox Lake	Dodge Co.	186
	Stockbridge	40	Stockbridge	Calumet Co.	147
	Sutphen, Theodore L.	41	Evansville	Rock Co.	147
	Sweet, Benjamin J.	40	Stockbridge	Calumet Co.	147
	Swift, Henry S.	137	Edgerton	Rock Co.	207
T	**Post Name**	**No.**	**Town**	**County**	**Page**
	Tallman, Alexis	70	Clinton	Rock Co.	168
	Tator, H. A.	13	Reedsburg	Sauk Co.	128
	Taylor, William	248	Peshtigo	Marinette Co.	269
	Thomas, George H.	6	Delevan	Walworth Co.	121
	Thomas, George H.	9 (85)	Winneconne	Winnebago Co.	177
	Thornburg, A. D.	174	Lime Ridge	Sauk Co.	228
	Topping, William O.	266	Hazel Green	Grant Co.	279
	Tourtellotte, John E.	280	Ladysmith	Rusk Co.	287
	Townsend, M. G.	105	Pewaukee	Waukesha Co.	189
	Turner, Henry	46	New London	Waupaca Co.	151
	Turner, Jerry	85	Viola	Richland Co.	178
U	**Post Name**	**No.**	**Town**	**County**	**Page**
	Unity	217	Unity	Marathon Co.	252
V	**Post Name**	**No.**	**Town**	**County**	**Page**
	Veterans	8	Milwaukee	Milwaukee Co.	122
W	**Post Name**	**No.**	**Town**	**County**	**Page**
	Walker, H. M.	18	Manitowoc	Manitowoc Co.	133
	Walker, W. S.	64	Montello	Marquette Co.	163
	Walworth County	76	Elkhorn	Walworth Co.	172
	Warren, Gouverneur K.	252	Nelson	Buffalo Co.	271
	Washburn, C. C.	11(1)	Madison	Dane Co.	125

	Post Name	No.	Town	County	Page
	Waterman, Walter	197	Plainfield	Waushara Co.	241
	Watrous, Henry O.	93	Spencer	Marathon Co.	182
	Watrous, Henry O.	276	Spencer	Marathon Co.	285
	Watson, Martin	172	Barron	Barron Co.	227
	Wausaukee	277	Wausaukee	Marinette Co.	286
	Weatherbe, Albert	128	Chetek	Barron Co.	202
	Weber, Peter	257	Fountain City	Buffalo Co.	274
	Wellcome, Francis Asbra	163	Thorpe	Clark Co.	221
	West, George M.	165	Hartford	Washington Co.	222
	Wheeler, Archibald	269	Coloma	Waushara Co.	280
	Wheeler, Sylvester	75	Verona	Dane Co.	171
	Wheeler, W. G.	93	Osseo	Trempealeau Co.	182
	Williams, James	158	Ontario	Vernon Co.	219
	Williams, John H.	4 (22)	Berlin	Green Lake Co.	118
	Williamson	109	Dodgeville	Iowa Co.	191
	Willich, George	273	Boyd	Chippewa Co.	283
	Wilson, Newton	28	Kingston	Green Lake Co.	139
	Wintermeyer, Gustave	187	Sheboygan	Sheboygan Co.	236
	Wolcott, E. B.	1	Milwaukee	Milwaukee Co.	115
	Wood County	22	Wisconsin Rapids	Wood Co.	135
	Wright, William	51	Excelsior	Richland Co.	154
	Wyman, J. B	32	Clintonville	Waupaca Co.	142
Y	**Post Name**	**No.**	**Town**	**County**	**Page**
	Yates	84	Milwaukee	Milwaukee Co.	N/A
	Young, Azro	227	Winneconne	Winnebago Co.	258

POSTS

IN DETAIL

The Post Room was the essence of the Grand Army of the Republic.

It was here that the veteran participated, as often as weekly but usually semimonthly or monthly, in the ritual and in the business of the G.A.R. It was here, in the flag-bedecked hall with ritual stations and all the trappings of the military life they knew so well, that the men of the order experienced the root meanings as well as the practicalities of Fraternity, Charity, and Loyalty.

Here they took comfort in the comradeship that permeated the hall. Here they discussed the misfortunes and acted to provide for the down-and-out veteran in their community—in an era when public programs of support for the destitute were virtually nonexistent—and their charity was extended whether the recipient was affiliated with the G.A.R. or not. Loyalty was an integral part of the scheme. It might be manifested in preparations for the sometimes ostentatious Memorial Day observance, or in more subtle, almost subliminal messages of patriotism, such as continually wearing the Grand Army pin, showing deference for the flag whenever possible, and by holding the country they had served in something like reverential awe.

All this occurred at the local, post level. But the department was also a vital constituent of the Grand Army scheme. The Department of Wisconsin during most of its years enjoyed the hearty participation of hundreds of veterans in the annual encampment. But many more hundreds did not leave their hometowns to march in the annual encampment parade, much less to be involved in the enactment of department business.

Nationally the Grand Army of the Republic gained renown for its programs, policies, and lobbying activities, which had a major impact on the nation and on the national treasury. The G.A.R. was the most successful organization ever to attempt such a powerful exertion on the political life of the country. Its critics[1] said the successful lobbying amounted to the largest raid ever perpetrated on the United States treasury. Its apologists said it came close to claiming just what was due to the men who saved the nation from destruction. But everyone agreed the G.A.R. was one powerhouse of an organization backed up by a huge number of members in thousands of posts nationwide.

In Wisconsin alone, there arose at least 404 posts. Not all of them were successful, but more than three quarters of these left behind enough documentation so that we can list in the following pages a post-by-post summary of available information.

It seems striking in looking at these posts in detail how essentially rural the Grand Army of the Republic was in Wisconsin. The vast array of communities having G.A.R. posts for a number of years probably is attributable to the fact that when Wisconsin responded to the Rebellion, the state's population was overwhelmingly rural. While Wisconsin was on the course of urbanization in the early twentieth century, the veterans, or at least a statistically significant number of them, retained their rural roots and maintained their small-town G.A.R. posts as long as they could.

As we look at the grassroots of the Wisconsin G.A.R., that rural flavor abides, even though there is good evidence of the importance of the urban posts, as well. The Milwaukee posts, for instance, had strong membership figures well into the twentieth century, and such urban posts provided much of the leadership at the department level.

But here we are studying the posts of Wisconsin as individual entities, whether urban or rural in origin. They all shared common characteristics, as this look at the details of each post reveals.

As often as possible, the names of charter members of each post are noted. The founding fathers, whether of the nation or of a post, are worthy of acknowledgment[1] here because they were investing their hopes and aspirations on a new and oft-times untried enterprise. Where charters are extant, all charter member names are listed. In many cases, contemporary accounts—often newspaper stories, but sometimes county histories compiled by outsiders, which were popular in the late nineteenth century—are the only sources for the listing of individual founders. Such sources, of course, are not infallible. Very often, the newspapers merely listed the names of the new post's officers, and this is sometimes the only available information about the post's members. In a good many other instances, the only name available from among the founders is that of the first commander, often given in the next state encampment journal.

Available annual enrollment figures for a post are presented in list form. It is agonizing that in the most active years of the order in Wisconsin, the department did not keep data on individual posts, as it did after 1903. But since statewide figures for

---

those years survive, it is possible to estimate, broadly, what individual post membership may have been in those years—bearing in mind that such extrapolation is fallible.

The final year of a post is not easy to ascertain. For the most part the final year on the chart is the last year for which department records indicate the post existed and had at least one member. Nonetheless the last year of existence noted may be off by a year or even more.

Some effort was made to ascertain who the final member was and to give, when possible, his date of death. Unfortunately, that information is not readily available in many communities. In the earlier posts, of course, that information is impossible to ascertain.

Another important piece of information about a post is the identity of the person for whom the post was named. Finding out this information turned out to be a major undertaking. Seldom did posts make an effort to preserve such identification. The honoree was so well known to the veterans that there seemed no need to give any information about him or it other than the name.

Unfortunately, in about a dozen instances, the name is all that is known today. All manner of sources were consulted, and, in some cases, assumptions had to be made. For instance, state records may give more than one soldier by the same name. It was then assumed that the one in a company raised in some proximity to the location of the post was the one for whom the post was named. It seems to be a valid assumption, but it is not quite as certain as having an affirmative statement on record telling for whom the post was named. One of the stumbling blocks to identifying honorees is that in some instances the honoree may not have been from Wisconsin. This is true of a few posts where identification could be made. However, the task of taking a search nationwide for positive identification of some the remaining names is impractical if not impossible.

For some of the many posts for which positive identification of the namesake could be made, we discovered pictures of the honoree, and we have included these in the following pages. The most unusual picture in that regard is a posthumous one of Jairus Richardson (Post 12, Sheboygan Falls).

Although in a few instances some information is given on the history of a post, this is done as an exception to the norm and for a specific purpose: to show the post's unique situation in relation to the overall story of the Department of Wisconsin. Post 4, Berlin, "the oldest G.A.R. post in the world," is a good example. Madison's fall from grace, from Post 1 to Post 11, is another. There are a few additional instances, e.g., where a post came into being through a schism within an older post. The circumstances as now known are given. It seemed of importance, too, in the case of the Department of Wisconsin's two Indian posts to discuss some of the history of their members' service, because the Department was proud it had the only all Indian posts in the nation.

But the norm was not to attempt to present a sketch of the history of the individual Post. Space limitations require this standard.

Sometimes previous local histories provided additional information on G.A.R. posts in their area. And there may be other sources locally for constructing at least a résumé-type look at the history of a post. The field, in other words, is a happy hunting ground for historians in each locality to give flesh and blood to the lives and actions of the men in blue who were such an important part of the history of their community.

We hope, in fact, that the details of individual posts as they appear on the following pages will serve as a starting point for history buffs throughout Wisconsin to build a much more complete accounting of the Grand Army of the Republic and its impact upon its grassroots members, whether the setting today is a hamlet or a metropolis-in-process.

E.B. WOLCOTT POST 1, Milwaukee

MILWAUKEE COUNTY • JANUARY 14, 1880–1942

CHARTER MEMBERS: Wm. L. Pavey, A. B. F. Way, S. F. Hammond, Frank W. Harwood, Florian J. Ries, W. E. Coates, J. P. Rundle, O. L. Rosenkrans, Henry A. Valentin, Henry G. Rogers, Henry C. Koch, C. P. Huntington, Edward Ferguson, I. M. Bean, Garth W. James, Chas. H. Boynton

| 1866 | 1871 | 1876 | 1881 | 1886 | 1891 | 1896 | 1901 | 1906 | 1911 | 1916 | 1921 | 1926 | 1931 | 1936 | 1941 | 1946 | 1951 |

MEMBERSHIP BY YEAR (ACCOUNTED FOR): 1880, 16; 1884, 89; 1887, 185; 1888, 234; 1889, 325; 1904, 281; 1905, 281; 1906, 270; 1907, 261; 1908, 252; 1909, 252; 1910, 242; 1911, 221; 1912, 205; 1913, 202; 1914, 195; 1915, 202; 1916, 189; 1917, 276; 1918, 206; 1919, 203; 1921, 161; 1922, 146; 1923, 143; 1924, 133; 1925, 118; 1926, 107; 1927, 101; 1928, 75; 1929, 63; 1930, 55; 1931, 48; 1932, 36; 1933, 31; 1934, 12; 1935, 14; 1936, 14; 1937, 12; 1938, 5; 1939, 5   **LAST MEMBER:** W.P. Bryant

ERASTUS B. WOLCOTT

The Wolcott Post succeeded Madison as the No. 1 post in the department. It was formed in 1880 by men who had been in previous Milwaukee posts that had surrendered their charters

The post was named for Erastus B. Wolcott, the surgeon general of Wisconsin during the war. He was never in service, but he took interest in soldiers and then in veterans. He was primarily responsible for the location of a National Soldiers Home in Milwaukee.

The post was mustered in by Department Commander Griff Thomas, assisted by members of the Robert Chivas and Veteran Posts of Milwaukee. For many years, Wolcott Post was the largest in the Department of Wisconsin. By its fiftieth anniversary in 1930, the post had mustered 712 men.

Wolcott was in many ways one of the more cosmopolitan posts in the state. Although members of the Twenty-fourth Wisconsin constituted the largest single unit represented, the roster included men from 21 states including West Virginia, Kentucky, Missouri, and Florida.

The post included veterans of the volunteer infantry, volunteer cavalry, volunteer artillery, the regular infantry, regular cavalry, regular artillery, U.S. Colored Troops, U.S. Sharpshooters, and the U.S. Navy.

Wolcott Post 1 had a significant distinction in that its membership provided two national commanders: August Weissert in 1892 and Frank Walsh in 1926. Both also served as senior vice commander, Weissert in 1889 and Walsh in 1923. Much earlier Walsh had been inspector general in 1902.

Members of Wolcott Post 1 gathered for this panoramic view on December 4, 1908, in their post hall. Photo provided by Milwaukee County Historical Society.

Prominent men of Post 1: Standing, from left: H. A. Vallentin, O. W. Carlson, J. P. Rundle, F. A. Walsh, and A. G. Weissert. Seated: J. B. Johnson, J. A. Watrous, S. H. Tallmadge, and G. L. Thomas. Weissert (1892) and Walsh (1926) served as national commanders. Watrous (1894), Rundle (1903), and Thomas (1932) were department Commanders. Photo provided by Milwaukee County Historical Society.

RIPON POST 2, Ripon

FOND DU LAC COUNTY • JUNE 16, 1866–AUGUST 1874

CHARTER MEMBERS: H. S. Town was the first commander.

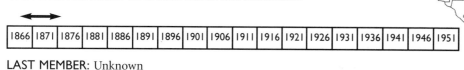

1866	1871	1876	1881	1886	1891	1896	1901	1906	1911	1916	1921	1926	1931	1936	1941	1946	1951

LAST MEMBER: Unknown

The second post chartered in Wisconsin, just nine days after the founding of the department, was at Ripon. The post was chartered on June 16, 1866, exactly one week after the post in Madison was organized.

Altogether, little is known about this endeavor.

At its birth, the local newspaper listed H. S. Town commander of the post, H. B. Williams adjutant, and A. Kinney as quartermaster. "The fact that our city was established as Post No. 2 (Madison being No. 1) speaks well for Ripon . . . [and of] success to the enterprise."

Ripon was a viable post when the first department cleansing took place in 1871. Ripon remained Post 2. There is a press report listing officers elected at a meeting of the post in June 1870. H. Bowerman was commander; W. T. Whiting, vice commander; W. R. Pearson, quartermaster; D. W. C. Root, adjutant; S. W. Stevens, quartermaster sergeant; W. R. Wyckoff, guard; and Thomas Harris, chaplain.

An historian of the successor post in Ripon, Eggleston Post 199, Leonard Mowers, writing in 1923, with information more or less hearsay, says of the demise of Ripon Post 2 (date unspecified) that "it was voted to throw up its charter and disband, and end up with a banquet. John Haas furnished the refreshments."

ROBERT CHIVAS POST 2, Milwaukee

MILWAUKEE COUNTY • JUNE 9, 1875–1918

CHARTER MEMBERS: C. O. Jennison, Andrew Wood, G. S. Staff, Theodore Springhuth, S. W. Rhode, B. F. Cook, Jno. Roach, John B. Abert, Wm. Shallock, Louis Holzhauser, J. W. Guysinger, Thomas Boland, Adam Schnurr, V. E. Wapple, J. M. Weichlein

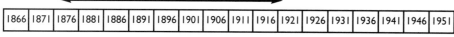

1866	1871	1876	1881	1886	1891	1896	1901	1906	1911	1916	1921	1926	1931	1936	1941	1946	1951

MEMBERSHIP BY YEAR (ACCOUNTED FOR): 1883, 252; 1884, 240; 1887, 311; 1888, 271; 1889, 298; 1904, 85; 1905, 77; 1906, 58; 1907, 56; 1908, 58; 1909, 46; 1910, 48; 1911, 46; 1912, 47; 1913, 40; 1914, 38; 1915, 38; 1916, 38; 1917, 33 **LAST MEMBER:** Unknown

The Robert Chivas Post was one of the early posts organized in Milwaukee. In those days a number of posts formed that for one reason or another disbanded relatively quickly, but the Chivas post survived for quite some time.

The Chivas post was formed by men who had been in the Phil Sheridan Post 3 of Milwaukee and who were still interested in maintaining a G.A.R. presence.

They chose the name of Robert Chivas to honor a young Milwaukeean killed in the war at Missionary Ridge. Chivas was first lieutenant of Company I of the Twenty-fourth Wisconsin, falling in his regiment's successful assault on that ridge on November 25, 1863.

The Chivas post was highly successful in the 1880s and maintained a fair membership into the twentieth century. In 1917 it still had 33 members, but by 1918 it was listed as extinct.

It quite possibly merged with some other Milwaukee post at that time.

PHIL SHERIDAN POST 3 (9), Milwaukee

MILWAUKEE COUNTY • 1871-1878 OR 1879

CHARTER MEMBERS: Unknown

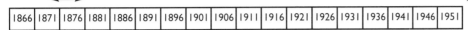

1866	1871	1876	1881	1886	1891	1896	1901	1906	1911	1916	1921	1926	1931	1936	1941	1946	1951

LAST MEMBER: Unknown

PHIL SHERIDAN

Philip Henry Sheridan was one of the soldiers' favorite generals, and it is not surprising that an early post of the G.A.R. in Wisconsin would bear his name .

It is difficult to verify how early Phil Sheridan Post 3 of Milwaukee was formed. The post received its designation as Post 3 in the 1871 cleansing of the roster of posts by Commander Edward Ferguson. It had been Post 9. Nor is its dissolution date firm, although the history of Wolcott Post 1 says that members of the Sheridan Post were among those chartering Post 1 in 1880.

"Little Phil" was the soldiers' name for the diminutive general who was born in Ohio (1831), graduated from West Point, and served typical antebellum humdrum assignments. But during the war he emerged as a pugnacious leader who caught U. S. Grant's attention, and late in the war, as a cavalry leader, then as independent commander, he gained renown.

Although post names were traditionally posthumous honors, the Sheridan Post was one of the exceptions. Sheridan died in 1888.

ABRAHAM LINCOLN POST 3, Darien

WALWORTH COUNTY • AUGUST 26, 1879–1922

CHARTER MEMBERS: J. B. Johnson, Rodney Seaver, J. P. Waite, Edwin E. Park, A. M. Cook, L. H. Stebbins, W. F. Enos, John McCannon, J. M. Vanderhoof, H. M. Fitzgerald, E. E. Hillman, Rosell S. Miner

1866	1871	1876	1881	1886	1891	1896	1901	1906	1911	1916	1921	1926	1931	1936	1941	1946	1951

MEMBERSHIP BY YEAR (ACCOUNTED FOR): 1879, 12; 1884, 17; 1887, 18; 1888, 22; 1889, 28; 1904, 17; 1905, 16; 1906, 16; 1907, 15; 1908, 15; 1909, 14; 1910, 13; 1911, 9; 1912, 8; 1913, 10; 1914, 10; 1915, 10; 1916, 10; 1917, 7; 1918, 7; 1919, 7; 1920, 7; 1921, 5   LAST MEMBER: Unknown

ABRAHAM LINCOLN

Members of this post chose the name of the president who was their commander in chief during the Civil War.

Abraham Lincoln, in addition to being the wartime president, also served as a militia officer in the Black Hawk War of 1832. His short time in the service was spent in Illinois and, briefly, in Wisconsin. In fact, as he was returning to Illinois, his horse was stolen near Whitewater, within 15 miles of Darien.

Lincoln was born February 12, 1809, and was assassinated on April 14, 1865, as the war was coming to a successful conclusion.

Soldiers overwhelmingly supported the president during the war. The assassination had a great impact upon them and was at least partially why so many veterans, at least in the G.A.R., were Republicans.

JOHN H. WILLIAMS POST 4, Berlin

GREEN LAKE COUNTY • SEPTEMBER 8, 1866– APRIL 18, 1937

CHARTER MEMBERS: Oscar F. Silver, William A. Bugh, D. D. La Bar, William Kees, Edward G. Waring, Thomas J. Davis, James A. Biggert, George W. Graves, Thomas C. Ryan, Chauncey Vedder, Wiley B. Arnold

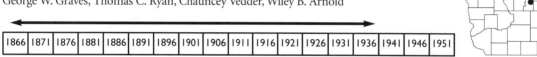

| 1866 | 1871 | 1876 | 1881 | 1886 | 1891 | 1896 | 1901 | 1906 | 1911 | 1916 | 1921 | 1926 | 1931 | 1936 | 1941 | 1946 | 1951 |

MEMBERSHIP BY YEAR (ACCOUNTED FOR): 1884, 47; 1887, 87; 1888, 70; 1889, 112; 1893, 123; 1907, 48; 1908, 58; 1909, 60; 1910, 60; 1911, 54; 1912, 53; 1913, 42; 1914, 38; 1915, 37; 1916, 34; 1917, 29; 1918, 26; 1919, 25; 1920, 25; 1921, 22; 1922, 19; 1923, 15; 1924, 14; 1925, 16; 1926, 15; 1927, 11; 1928, 11; 1929, 9; 1930, 6; 1931, 5; 1932, 5; 1933, 5; 1934, 4; 1935, 3; 1935, 3; 1937, 1   **LAST MEMBER:** Alexander Parsons

JOHN H. WILLIAMS

"The Oldest G.A.R. Post in the World" was named after the first soldier from Berlin to die in the Civil War.

John Henry Williams was born July 27, 1838, in Wales, and his parents brought him to this country as a baby, first to New York State, then to Waukesha, and finally to the town of Aurora outside of Berlin.

Williams became a printing apprentice and was engaged in printing in Berlin when the war began. He joined Company A of the Sixteenth Wisconsin and was chosen sergeant.

On the morning of April 6, 1862, at the opening of the Battle of Shiloh, he was killed in action. Williams was buried at Shiloh in an unmarked grave.

G.A.R. members on parade in Berlin, date unknown.

The prized charter given the Williams Post September 8, 1866, is proudly shown by these last surviving Post 4 members. Standing, from left: William Eldred, Commander George W. Morton, and Frank D. Murdock. Seated, from left: Alexander Parsons and Henry L. Marsh. The post ended upon Parsons' death April 18, 1937.

Members of John H. Williams Post 4, Berlin, hold a banner proclaiming the fiftieth anniversary of the post in 1916.

Williams Post marches in parade, with sign proclaiming Berlin's boast as "Oldest Post on Earth," date unknown.

POST 5, Greenbush

SHEBOYGAN COUNTY • JUNE 28, 1866–1871

CHARTER MEMBERS: Henry Stannard was the first commander.

←→

1866	1871	1876	1881	1886	1891	1896	1901	1906	1911	1916	1921	1926	1931	1936	1941	1946	1951

LAST MEMBER: Henry Stannard, died October 12, 1936.

Post 5 at Greenbush is one of those virtually unknown—and unknowable—posts of early Department of Wisconsin history with a small but significant exception: the post's first commander later became department commander.

But aside from that distinction, Post 5 was really typical of the half a hundred or so posts that blossomed into being with much enthusiasm and just as rapidly declined into nothing.

Just weeks after Post 1 was organized in 1866 at Madison, the veterans in the area of Sheboygan County around Greenbush were recruited into the fifth post in the state. Although there is no existing record of the event, its date—June 28, 1866—is known. It is reasonable to assume that the founding of the post occurred in the small community's primary meeting place, a carriage stop on the Sheboygan-to-Fond du Lac route operated for nearly 20 years by Sylvanus and Betsy Wade.

That carriage stop was the center of activities for Greenbush, which once was considered an up-and-coming community, but had received a severe blow to its civic pride and its hope for the future when the Sheboygan & Mississippi Railroad decided to go through Glenbeulah rather than Greenbush. It may have presaged the prospects of both the community as well as its Grand Army post.

Among the Greenbush veterans who in all probability joined Post 5 would have been two of the elder Wade's sons, Edward Sylvanus and Andrew Jackson Wade, both of whom had served in the Eighth or "Eagle" Regiment, in Company B, the Sheboygan County Independents. It is much more certain, though, that the Wade boys' soon-to-be brother-in-law was there. He was Henry Stannard, whose sister, Althea, was engaged to another Wade son, Hollis, or "H. C." That marriage was on Christmas Day of 1867.

H. C. and Althea soon took over active operation of the carriage stop from Sylvanus and Betsy. They would operate it as an inn until well into the twentieth century, hosting thousands of travelers, many of whom were on their way to new homes in interior Wisconsin. Today, it is a historic site operated by the Wisconsin Historical Society.

Henry Stannard (who also was known by the initials H. C.) had joined the Sheboygan County Independents along with the two Wade boys in 1861. He was one of the hundreds of Wisconsin men serving in the Mississippi Valley who were

stricken with illness severely enough so that they could no longer serve.

Henry Stannard was discharged in September of 1862, about the same time his father, Erastus W. Stannard, was recruiting a company, the Plymouth Union Rifles, which became Company B, Twenty-seventh Wisconsin Infantry. While his regiment was

ERASTUS
STANNARD

on a march in Mississippi in June of 1863, Captain Stannard was handing a rifle to a sick man riding in an ambulance when the piece went off and the bullet passed through Stannard's body. He died June 8, suffering for more than a day after the accident.

The Grand Army of the Republic was so new when Greenbush Post 5 was formed—it was probably one of the first two dozen posts in the country—that the practice of naming posts may not have begun. It is conceivable, however, that if the practice had begun before the demise of Post 5, it would have become Erastus W. Stannard Post after the town's most notable casualty of the war.

Unfortunately, almost everything about the Greenbush Post is speculation. Its date of formation, the fact that Henry Stannard was its commander, and that it was among the slew of such posts struck from the rolls in 1871 are all that are on record.

HENRY
STANNARD

It is difficult to tell whether the Greenbush veterans were disillusioned by their Grand Army experience. It appears that Stannard himself did not again get involved in the Order until a new post was organized in 1885 at Plymouth.

Interestingly, Stannard said in his application for membership in Henry P. Davidson Post 212 that he had not previously been a member of the G.A.R. This possibly suggests that the Greenbush experience had been fleeting. (That standard question was asked to prevent hopping from post to post in order to avoid paying dues.)

Stannard remained a resident, respected merchant, and, for some years, postmaster of Greenbush.

His Grand Army activities were thereafter with the Davidson Post, and he was quite active with the post. He enlarged his endeavors by joining the Sons of Union Veterans since his father's service made Henry eligible to join that organization. In 1926, as he was campaigning for the top job in the Wisconsin G.A.R., he was identified as the oldest member of the Wisconsin Sons organization.

Stannard's campaign was a success, and he was named commander of the Grand Army of the Republic, Department of Wisconsin, at the Racine encampment that year. He lived another 10 years, the "grand old man" of Greenbush.

EDWARD SAXE POST 5, Wautoma
WAUSHARA COUNTY • 1873–1875

CHARTER MEMBERS: J. N. P. Bird, commander; Hosea W. Rood, senior vice commander; August S. Rogers, junior vice commander; W. S. Munroe, adjutant; George Sexton, quartermaster; Ira L. Parker, officer of the day; Otis Call, officer of the guard

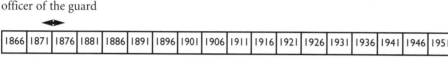

1866	1871	1876	1881	1886	1891	1896	1901	1906	1911	1916	1921	1926	1931	1936	1941	1946	1951

LAST MEMBER: Unknown

Veterans in and around the county seat of Waushara County had formed a G.A.R. post in the early, flush days of the Department of Wisconsin. It was numbered 45. Nothing is known of it except that it was stricken from the rolls in the 1871 wholesale cleansing of the department.

The men tried again, and by 1874 Wautoma was again on department records, this time as Edward Saxe Post 5. Its start was more auspicious, its members being installed by Department Commander George Hannaford, with Griff J. Thomas from nearby Berlin, editor of the Grand Army Sentinel, attending.

More significant, however, was the name of its senior vice commander: Hosea W. Rood. The young schoolteacher would become the dominant figure in the Grand Army's Department of Wisconsin during the early twentieth century.

This post survived barely into 1875 when disaffection for the order in Wautoma caused it to change its meeting place to Willow Springs, near Auroraville. It soon disbanded.

The Wautoma Post would be revived about nine years after Post 5 failed. The new Edward Saxe Post 135 served until 1938. See Post 135 for information on the Saxe Post.

J. H. KNIGHT POST 5, Butternut
ASHLAND COUNTY • NOVEMBER 12, 1879–1913

CHARTER MEMBERS: Unknown

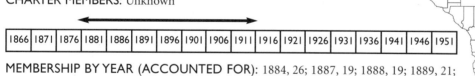

1866	1871	1876	1881	1886	1891	1896	1901	1906	1911	1916	1921	1926	1931	1936	1941	1946	1951

MEMBERSHIP BY YEAR (ACCOUNTED FOR): 1884, 26; 1887, 19; 1888, 19; 1889, 21; 1904, 11; 1905, 9; 1906, 9; 1907, 8; 1908, 8; 1909, 8; 1910, 5; 1911, 5; 1912, 5

LAST MEMBER: Unknown

JOHN H. KNIGHT

Post 5 of Butternut, the third G.A.R. post in the department to carry that number, was founded in 1879 in southern Ashland County.

It was renamed for John H. Knight, who came to northern Wisconsin in 1870 as an Indian Agent after an army career that began in 1861 as a volunteer with a Delaware regiment. (He was a native of Dover.) He received a Regular Army commission and fought throughout the Civil War. He remained in service after the war and served in the West. After resigning from the military in 1869, he was appointed to his post in Wisconsin. Knight became one of northern Wisconsin's leading speculators. He was elected the first mayor of Ashland when the city was founded in 1887. Knight died in 1903.

JAMES F. ORDWAY POST 6, Beaver Dam

DODGE COUNTY • 1868?–JULY 23, 1874

CHARTER MEMBERS: Unknown

←→

1866	1871	1876	1881	1886	1891	1896	1901	1906	1911	1916	1921	1926	1931	1936	1941	1946	1951

JAMES F. ORDWAY

LAST MEMBER: Unknown

James F. Ordway of Beaver Dam was a member of Company D, Fifth Wisconsin Infantry, which entered service in July of 1861 as the "Beaver Dam Rifles." Ordway rose to captain in the company and was killed in action November 7, 1863, at Rappahannock Station, Virginia.

Post 6 was one of the early posts chartered in the state that subsequently failed. And it is one of the few from that era for which a post name has survived. The charter of the Ordway Post was suspended July 23, 1874.

GEORGE H. THOMAS POST 6, Delevan

WALWORTH COUNTY • NOVEMBER 28, 1879–1935

CHARTER MEMBERS: Elias Dewey, Martin Mulville, Dr. H. D. Bullard, F. W. Hutchins, Rev. Joel Clark, E. B. Judson, W. A. Knilans, Dr. C. C. Blanchard, A. Corbin, W. P. Webster, Thomas Mosher, Evan Jones, W. B. Moffatt, Dr. D. B. Devendorf, I. C. Abbott, H. C. Clark, N. C. Williams, Charles Van Wagner, Peter Nelson, James Williams

←——————————————→

1866	1871	1876	1881	1886	1891	1896	1901	1906	1911	1916	1921	1926	1931	1936	1941	1946	1951

MEMBERSHIP BY YEAR (ACCOUNTED FOR): 1884, 56; 1887, 72; 1888, 69; 1889, 24; 1904, 28; 1905, 28; 1906, 24; 1907, 24; 1908, 26; 1909, 25; 1910, 24; 1911, 24; 1912, 21; 1913, 20; 1914, 20; 1915, 19; 1916, 19; 1917, 19; 1918, 14; 1919, 14; 1920, 14; 1921, 10; 1922, 9; 1923, 7; 1924, 7; 1925, 7; 1926, 7; 1927, 7; 1928, 5; 1929, 5; 1930, 4; 1931, 3; 1932, 3; 1933, 2; 1934, 1   **LAST MEMBER:** Unknown

GEORGE H. THOMAS

"The Rock of Chickamauga," General George H. Thomas, was the namesake of Delevan Post 6. He is one of the few "Southerners" to be so honored by a G.A.R. post.

Thomas was born in Virginia in 1816. He attended West Point and served in the Mexican War with distinction, and thereafter served primarily on frontier duty under Albert Sidney Johnston and Robert E. Lee. When the Civil War broke out he declined an offer of a position from the governor of Virginia and remained with the Union Army. Most of his subsequent service was with the Western Armies in which he distinguished himself not only at Chickamauga, but later in the decisive battle of Nashville where Thomas' army virtually destroyed the Confederate Army of Tennessee.

His troops greatly admired him; to many of them he was "Pap" Thomas. After the war he dodged the political intrigue swirling around President Andrew Johnson and the Radicals, asking to be assigned to the Department of the Pacific. He died in San Francisco in 1870.

Reunion of the Grand Army of the Republic, Post 6, Delevan, in front of the Methodist Church of Delevan, date unknown.

J.F. SAWYER POST 7, Omro

WINNEBAGO COUNTY • FEBRUARY 14, 1880–1936

CHARTER MEMBERS: E. D. Henry, C. B. Cope, B. Hamilton, W. D. Peterson, Geo. W. Bussey, Richard Reed Jr., A. P. Howard, S. A. Shufelt, W. W. Merrill, J. G. Pierce, C. B. Wilbur, S. W. Turner, L. W. Mattison, W. W. Wilcox, Joseph Alger, R. W. Reed, C. C. Morton, J. S. Johnson, J. M. Fowler, J. A. Stevens, E. T. Sheldon, C. R. Olin, J. C. Ford, J. W. Lamphier, E. Hammond, J. A. Farr, W. H. Reed, Willis Graves, Peter Lamphier, J. H. Shattuck, J. W. Rice, John Everts, A. E. Pierce, Francis Luscomb, R. D. Cook, O. D. Huie

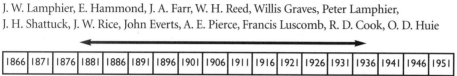

| 1866 | 1871 | 1876 | 1881 | 1886 | 1891 | 1896 | 1901 | 1906 | 1911 | 1916 | 1921 | 1926 | 1931 | 1936 | 1941 | 1946 | 1951 |

MEMBERSHIP BY YEAR (ACCOUNTED FOR): 1880, 36; 1884, 43; 1887, 46; 1888, 49; 1889, 60; 1904, 47; 1905, 47; 1906, 40; 1907, 38; 1908, 30; 1909, 28; 1910, 28; 1911, 18; 1912, 10; 1913, 10; 1914, 10; 1915, 16; 1916, 12; 1917, 15; 1918, 15; 1919, 15; 1920, 15; 1921, 15; 1922, 11; 1923, 11; 1924, 10; 1925, 10; 1926, 14; 1927, 12; 1928, 8; 1929, 7; 1930, 6; 1931, 6; 1932, 4; 1933, 3; 1934, 2; 1935, 2   **LAST MEMBER:** Aaron Barthomew Tice

James F. Sawyer Post 7, Omro, and its Women's Relief Corps pose in front of their hall, March 16, 1930

Ballot boxes used by the Sawyer Post. Members put a white or black ball down the cannon muzzle to vote on new members.

The G.A.R. post at Omro was named after one of its early members, James F. Sawyer of Door County. He enlisted in 1864 and was assigned to the Twenty-first Wisconsin, Company K. Sawyer took a bullet wound in the neck at Savannah, Georgia, and was subsequently assigned to the Third Wisconsin until the war ended. Sawyer was mustered out in July 1865 and settled in Omro. He became a G.A.R. member there, although he is not listed as a charter member. He died sometime before 1890.

J. F. Sawyer Post 7 was active in Omro until the 1930s. Its meeting hall was on North River Drive.

VETERANS POST 8, Milwaukee

MILWAUKEE COUNTY • APRIL 26, 1870–1917

CHARTER MEMBERS: Unknown

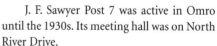

| 1866 | 1871 | 1876 | 1881 | 1886 | 1891 | 1896 | 1901 | 1906 | 1911 | 1916 | 1921 | 1926 | 1931 | 1936 | 1941 | 1946 | 1951 |

MEMBERSHIP BY YEAR (ACCOUNTED FOR): 1884, 50; 1887, 103; 1888, 116; 1889, 144; 1904, 66; 1905, 62; 1906, 47; 1907, 42; 1908, 53; 1909, 71; 1910, 66; 1911, 82; 1912, 121; 1913, 138; 1914, 142; 1915, 154; 1916, 174   **LAST MEMBER:** Unknown

One of the important posts in the Wisconsin Department of the Grand Army was the post in Milwaukee at the National Veterans Home. It was known simply as Veterans Post No. 8. This home was run by the federal government and served veterans beginning right after the war.

Originally it was Post 84, said by one account to have been chartered September 8, 1869; it was known as "Yates Post." The full name and identity of Yates is unknown.

The home in which Yates and then Veterans Post 8 got its members did not gain the G.A.R.'s full support, and thus there was incentive for the department to found its own home. In contrast to the Milwaukee institution, which did not accept wives or widows, the G.A.R.'s home near Waupaca did, the first such home in the nation to do so.

Nonetheless Veteran Posts No. 8 had a strong memberships roll right up until it was deactivated just before World War I.

JOE HOOKER POST 9, Baraboo

SAUK COUNTY • MARCH 4, 1880–1942

CHARTER MEMBERS: H. Albrecht, Phil Cheek, L. O. Holmes, T. C. Thomas, D. K. Noyes, Charles Bender, W. Palmer, George Bloom, J. C. Spencer, H. Stouthard, P. E. Longley, W. H. Staten, R. Delap, Volney Moore, Tom Scott, James Whitty, J. A. Pabodie

1866	1871	1876	1881	1886	1891	1896	1901	1906	1911	1916	1921	1926	1931	1936	1941	1946	1951

MEMBERSHIP BY YEAR (ACCOUNTED FOR): 1884, 144; 1887, 145; 1888, 140; 1889, 137; 1904, 132; 1905, 124; 1906, 121; 1907, 112; 1908, 111; 1909, 112; 1910, 116; 1911, 106; 1912, 104; 1913, 106; 1914, 98; 1915, 100; 1916, 94; 1917, 88; 1918, 86; 1919, 75; 1920, 70; 1921, 70; 1922, 68; 1923, 57; 1924, 52; 1925, 46; 1926, 37; 1927, 33; 1928, 23; 1929, 20; 1930, 20; 1931, 14; 1932, 10; 1933, 9; 1934, 7; 1935, 7; 1936, 5; 1937, 4; 1938, 2; 1939, 2 **LAST MEMBER:** Unknown

GENERAL JOSEPH HOOKER

Veterans often had a different perception of the generals they served under than later historians have had. A case in point is General Joseph Hooker. Historians have been less than kind to the general who was so completely out-generalled at Chancellorsville. But many of the soldiers were able to overlook that and to admire him for the qualities that he did show both before and after the bad time Stonewall Jackson gave him. The post at Baraboo chose to honor "Fighting Joe" Hooker.

Joe Hooker Post 9 was an important cog in the Grand Army of the Republic. It gave to the Department of Wisconsin one of its most important commanders, Phil Cheek, during the resuscitation of the order in the 1880s. Although not a charter member, Cheek joined immediately after the muster and was elected first commander of Post 9.

Joe Hooker Post 9 members posing, circa 1910. Note the man posing on a horse on the steps in back of the rest. This is probably symbolic of the Hooker Post since General Hooker, a man of small stature, was usually shown in wartime photos on horseback. Photo provided by the Sauk County Historical Society, Baraboo.

OSHKOSH POST 10, Oshkosh
WINNEBAGO COUNTY • AUGUST 16, 1866–1938

CHARTER MEMBERS: Abel B. Smedley, cheese box manufacturer;
Charles G. Finney Jr., proprietor, Oshkosh Northwestern; James Freeman, lawyer;
John W. Sprague, crockery; William R. Kennedy, lawyer; C. N. Paine, lumber mill;
Henry B. Harshaw, court clerk; Reuben Ash, clerk; Andrew Jackson, lawyer;
J. Copp Noyes, physician

| 1866 | 1871 | 1876 | 1881 | 1886 | 1891 | 1896 | 1901 | 1906 | 1911 | 1916 | 1921 | 1926 | 1931 | 1936 | 1941 | 1946 | 1951 |

MEMBERSHIP BY YEAR (ACCOUNTED FOR): 1867, 10; 1874, 66; 1876, 120; 1884, 50; 1887, 200; 1888, 108; 1889, 124; 1891, 66; 1904, 139; 1905, 118; 1906, 111; 1907, 107; 1908, 108; 1909, 108; 1910, 108; 1911, 95; 1912, 92; 1913, 86; 1914, 74; 1915, 70; 1916, 64; 1917, 61; 1918, 54; 1919, 53; 1920, 50; 1921, 46; 1922, 43; 1923, 37;1924, 40; 1925, 40; 1926, 41; 1927, 36;1928, 33; 1929, 29; 1930, 23; 1931, 16;1932, 13; 1933, 7;1934, 4; 1935, 4;1936, 3; 1937, 3   **LAST MEMBER:** Unknown

GENERAL P.H. SHERIDAN

In the first months of the existence of the Grand Army of the Republic in 1866, Wisconsin was quick to embrace the order and to organize posts. The tenth such, just weeks after the first had been organized in Madison, was at Oshkosh. It was chartered August 16, 1866, as simply "Oshkosh Post 10." In 1888 this veteran post chose a new name honoring General Philip H. Sheridan. It would be known as "P. H. Sheridan Post 10."

Sheridan was one of the top three Union generals in public esteem at the end of the war, ranking right after Grant and Sherman.

As a relatively young man (born 1831) and West Pointer, he had a good record as a cavalry commander and attracted U. S. Grant's attention. Grant put him in charge of the Army of the Shenandoah in 1864 with orders to make the area unusable by the Confederates. He did so. After the war he remained in the army and succeeded Sherman as general in chief. He died in 1888, just months after being promoted to to full general. The Oshkosh Post changed its name to honor him on September 28, 1888.

Oshkosh Civil War Veterans marching on Algoma Boulevard, Oshkosh, probably in a Memorial Day procession to the community cemetery, in the early 1900s

Post 10 of Oshkosh was one of the three Wisconsin posts contesting for the title as oldest in the order. While it was chartered before Berlin (and after Madison), it had a period of inactivity in about 1873 so its challenge to Berlin's claim was halfhearted at best, given that the fellows from the John W. Williams Post had come to Oshkosh to help resurrect the Oshkosh Post.

If P. H. Sheridan Post 10 had any claim to honor it was that it had maintained its original post number longer than the other two.

CASSIUS FAIRCHILD POST 1, Madison
C.C. WASHBURN POST 11, Madison
LUCIUS FAIRCHILD POST 11, Madison

DANE COUNTY • JANUARY 14, 1880–1939

CHARTER MEMBERS:[1] Charles H. Barton, John Betts, Ransom J. Chase, Francis Downs, Lucius Fairchild, Louis Gootman, Charles G. Mayers, George H. Meissner, Aaron A. Meredith, Henry C. Olney, Silas C. Pearson, James K. Proudfit, John Reynolds, Thomas Reynolds, George F. Rowell, Henry Sandford, Joshua W. Tolford

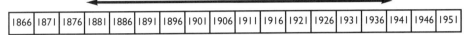

1866	1871	1876	1881	1886	1891	1896	1901	1906	1911	1916	1921	1926	1931	1936	1941	1946	1951

MEMBERSHIP BY YEAR (ACCOUNTED FOR): 1867, 17; 1884, 98; 1887, 180; 1888, 165; 1889, 168; 1904, 172; 1905, 174; 1906, 184; 1907, 188; 1908, 175; 1909, 173; 1910, 162; 1911, 157; 1912, 146; 1913, 145; 1914, 140; 1915, 145; 1916, 141; 1917, 135; 1918, 112; 1919, 113; 1920, 107; 1921, 103; 1922, 98; 1923, 90; 1924, 77; 1925, 74; 1926, 67; 1927, 52; 1928, 43; 1929, 36; 1930, 36; 1931, 30; 1932, 26; 1933, 21; 1934, 14; 1935, 14; 1936, 10; 1937, 9; 1938, 2; 1939, 1   **LAST MEMBER:** Charles F. Moulton, died January 30, 1940

The Wisconsin Department of the G.A.R. was organized in Madison on June 7, 1866, just weeks after the order was started in Illinois. Two days after the department was founded, veterans in Madison organized the first local G.A.R. post in the state, taking the designation Cassius Fairchild Post 1.

Cassius Fairchild had been colonel of the Sixteenth Wisconsin at the war's end and received a brevet brigadier generalship.

The post's early story is somewhat clouded by the fact that the post failed to keep up its contact with the department for a good number of years, and it was this failing which resulted in its original charter being revoked and a new charter and number, Post 11, being issued in 1880. (Because a brother's bequest stipulated that it was to go to Post 1, the post was allowed to function under the original charter, but its desire to retain the Post 1 designation was denied, and eventually its assertion of being the oldest continuing post was also denied by the department.)

CASSIUS FAIRCHILD

Post 11 changed its name in 1883 to C. C. Washburn Post to honor a former governor and important Civil War officer who had just died. Washburn had been colonel of the Second Wisconsin Cavalry and had a credible war record. But his primary service to the state was in politics, having served in Congress, along with two of his brothers, Israel from Maine and Elihu B. from Illinois, before the war. All three were noted Unionists. C. C. (for Cadwalader Coldoon) was reelected to Congress for two more terms after the war. In 1871 he was elected governor of Wisconsin. serving one term. He died in 1882.

The post continued as C. C. Washburn Post 11 for 13 years, or until after the post's most illustrious member, one-time national commander of the Grand Army of the Republic, Lucius Fairchild, died.

Lucius was the brother of the post's first namesake, Cassius Fairchild, and was a charter member of the post. He was governor of Wisconsin at the time, having returned from the war with one arm lost at Gettysburg and after compiling a superb record in combat with the Iron Brigade.

C.C. WASHBURN

Lucius Fairchild's political fortunes ran deep in Wisconsin politics and they culminated with his receiving a diplomatic appointment. He returned from abroad and became immersed in veterans' affairs, particularly with the G.A.R. He was elected Department of Wisconsin commander in February 1886 and national commander six months later. His flamboyant tenure as national commander was as the order was approaching the height of its influence. He and John Logan were the two most memorable top leaders of the Grand Army of the Republic.

LUCIUS FAIRCHILD

Fairchild lived in Madison for the rest of his years. He died May 23, 1896. Not long thereafter the post he helped to found changed its name to honor him.

---

1. These are the charter members under the Cassius Fairchild Post 1 charter of June 9, 1866. This charter was issued by Proudfit as Department Commander.

Members of Lucius Fairchild Post 11 pose in their Post Hall in 1907. This is an excellent view of a G.A.R. post room. Note the American flags used as curtains. This was considered perfectly acceptable at the time; the flags had been donated for that purpose. Within a decade or so, such use was no longer acceptable. Curtains were substituted. Photo provided by the Wisconsin Veterans Museum, Madison.

Officials of Lucius Fairchild Post 11 gathered for their portrait on January 1, 1924. Standing, from left: Inspector William Sauthoff, Officer of the Day K. L. Thompson, Adjutant John Liefield, and Sergeant Major G. W. Holt. Seated, from left: Surgeon G. R. Mitchell, Chaplain S. E. Lathrop, Senior Vice Commander R. C. Luther, Commander J. S. Meyers, Junior Vice Commander Martin Nelson, Quartermaster John Siggelko, and Quartermaster Sergeant C. H. Lang. The oldest in the group at the time was Sauthoff at age 89. Youngest, at 74, were Thompson and Holt. Photo provided by the Wisconsin Veterans Museum, Madison.

Members of the Fairchild Post sat for portrait on the fiftieth anniversary of original charter, June 9. 1916. The man in the front row with his hat on the ground is Hosea Rood, Department Patriotic Instructor for several decades. Photo provided by the Wisconsin Veterans Museum, Madison.

JOHN SEDGWICK POST 12, Milwaukee

MILWAUKEE COUNTY • SEPTEMBER 16, 1875–1875 OR 76

CHARTER MEMBERS: Unknown

1866	1871	1876	1881	1886	1891	1896	1901	1906	1911	1916	1921	1926	1931	1936	1941	1946	1951

LAST MEMBER: Unknown

JOHN SEDGWICK

One of the shorter-lived posts was the John Sedgwick Post 12, originated at the National Soldier's Home in Milwaukee late in 1875.

It is not the shortest, however; and ironically, that distinction goes to another Post 12, at Prairie du Chien. That Post 12, the name of which is not known, lasted a little more than two weeks, from June 30 to July 16, 1874. And that was the second Post 12. The first, at Mifflin, Iowa County, originated in 1866, but was among those annulled in 1871.

The Sedgwick Post lasted at least until the end of the year and possibly into 1876. It subsequently disbanded, and its members joined Veteran Post 8, also at the National Soldier's Home.

This third Post 12 was named for General John Sedgwick, commander of the VI Corps, Army of the Potomac, who was killed by a sharpshooter at Spotsylvania in 1864.

Sedgwick was one of the most loved senior officers in the army, called by his troops, with deep affection, "Uncle John." He was known as both a disciplinarian and as a general solicitous for the welfare of his men.

J.B. McPHERSON POST 12, Sharon

WALWORTH COUNTY • 1880-1883

CHARTER MEMBERS: Unknown

1866	1871	1876	1881	1886	1891	1896	1901	1906	1911	1916	1921	1926	1931	1936	1941	1946	1951

LAST MEMBER: Unknown

GENERAL J.B. McPHERSON

The J. B. McPherson Post 12 at Sharon in Walworth County was in operation for up to three years. But not much is known about it.

The post was named for General James Birdseye McPherson, one of the rising stars of Sheridan's western army in the latter half of the war, commanding the Army of the Tennessee in Sherman's Atlanta Campaign.

McPherson was an engineering officer before the war and did engineering duties early in the war, but was advanced to a combat role by late 1862; he advanced steadily. He was a favorite of General Sherman. By 1864, as the armies were advancing on Atlanta, McPherson was out ahead of his troops reconnoitering and was killed by Confederates as he hastened to try to escape capture. He was just 35 years old.

JARIUS RICHARDSON POST 12, Sheboygan Falls

SHEBOYGAN COUNTY • JULY 10, 1883–1936

CHARTER MEMBERS: J. M. Hunts, commander; T. C. Hawkins, senior vice commander; Joseph Osthelder, junior vice commander; E. P. Bryant, surgeon; George Spratt, chaplain; J. C. O'Brien, quartermaster; H. F. Wood, officer of the day; John Arnold, guard; A. T. Dean, sergeant major; and James Syma, second sergeant major

1866	1871	1876	1881	1886	1891	1896	1901	1906	1911	1916	1921	1926	1931	1936	1941	1946	1951

MEMBERSHIP BY YEAR (ACCOUNTED FOR): 1887, 67; 1888, 58; 1889, 64; 1900, 55; 1904, 46; 1905, 47; 1906, 46; 1907, 47; 1908, 46; 1909, 47; 1910, 39; 1911, 41; 1912, 40; 1913, 41; 1914, 38; 1915, 36; 1916, 33; 1917, 30; 1918, 26; 1919, 23; 1920, 21; 1921, 18; 1922, 15; 1923, 14; 1924, 13; 1925, 10; 1926, 10; 1927, 8; 1928, 5; 1929, 5; 1930, 5; 1931, 5; 1932, 4; 1933, 3; 1934, 2; 1935, 2 LAST MEMBER: W.P. Bryant, December 3, 1941, at Milwaukee.

JARIUS RICHARDSON

There was an earlier post at Sheboygan Falls, Post No. 57 organized in early 1868. W. H. Richardson was listed as commander, Quinn A. Danforth as quartermaster, and N. O. Adams as adjutant of Post 57. It may have had the name of Jairus Richardson as well. It gave up its charter in 1870.

A number of members from the defunct post tried again in 1883, and this became Post 12 at Sheboygan Falls, active until 1936.

The post was named for Jarius Richardson, a Sheboygan Falls native who was first lieutenant of Company H, First Wisconsin. Richardson was wounded at Chickamauga and died of his wounds at Chattanooga on October 5, 1863. His body was returned to Sheboygan Falls and the view at left supposedly is a postmortem picture taken before his funeral.

CHARLES FORD POST 13, Trempealeau

TREMPEALEAU COUNTY • AUGUST 26, 1879–1922

CHARTER MEMBERS: Unknown

1866	1871	1876	1881	1886	1891	1896	1901	1906	1911	1916	1921	1926	1931	1936	1941	1946	1951

LAST MEMBER: Unknown

CHARLES FORD

Charles Ford Post 13, Trempealeau, is listed in the *Grand Army Sentinel* of September 1874, as one of the six posts then existing in the Department of Wisconsin. (The others were Sheridan 3, Milwaukee; Williams 4, Berlin; Saxe 5, Wautoma; Veterans 8, Milwaukee; and Oshkosh 10.)

The *Sentinel* listed the officers of Ford Post that year as Henry A. Towner, commander; John H. Crossen, senior vice commander; H. C. Cobb, junior vice commander; George A. Corsely, adjutant; Charles C. Kribs, quartermaster; W. H. Burns, officer of the day; and T. W. Parkin, officer of the guard.

Ford Post had to have been organized after 1871 when a previous Post 13 at Sun Prairie was abolished. And it apparently was declining in 1875 when, although it was on department rolls, it was unrepresented at the state encampment.

Charles Ford was a soldier from Trempealeau, a town on the Mississippi River. In 1889 a new post, named for the same soldier but numbered 258, was organized at Galesville, which is located less than ten miles from Trempealeau. Ford was with the Forty-fifth Wisconsin.

H.A. TATOR POST 13, Darien

SAUK COUNTY • APRIL 13, 1880–1942

CHARTER MEMBERS: W. G. Hawley, W. I. Carver, O. W. Schonfeldt, W. A. Wyse, James Miles, C. F. Sheldon, H. P. Persons, A. S. Brooks, H. C. Hunt, W. O. Pietzsch, E. F. Bulow, R. E. Nichols, Peter Empser, B. Rathburn, Philo Lane, J. H. Fosnot, George Lawsha, S. L. Miller, M. H. Medberry, M. E. Seeley, D. G. Spicer, E. F. Seaver, David Sparks, H. B. Turney, George Swetland

1866	1871	1876	1881	1886	1891	1896	1901	1906	1911	1916	1921	1926	1931	1936	1941	1946	1951

MEMBERSHIP BY YEAR (ACCOUNTED FOR): 1884, 80; 1887, 80; 1888, 69; 1889, 76; 1904, 47; 1905, 49; 1906, 48; 1907, 44; 1908, 41; 1909, 41; 1910, 39; 1911, 37; 1912, 32; 1913, 31; 1914, 32; 1915, 32; 1916, 33; 1917, 30; 1918, 28; 1919, 25; 1920, 21; 1921, 19; 1922, 14; 1923, 12; 1924, 8; 1925, 8; 1926, 9; 1927, 8; 1928, 7; 1929, 7; 1930, 6; 1931, 6; 1932, 4; 1933, 3; 1934, 2; 1935, 2; 1936, 6; 1937, 2; 1938, 1; 1939, 1;   **LAST MEMBER:** James P. Poole

H.A. TATOR

H. A. Tator Post 13 was named after the man who led a company of men from Reedsburg into the Civil War, Company A, Nineteenth Wisconsin Infantry. Captain Henry A. Tator served throughout the war and was mustered out on April 29, 1865. He went west a few years after the war for his health, but it failed to improve, and he died September 24, 1869, in Brigham, Utah.

Tator Post had a long period of activity and was listed as a post as late as 1942.

LOVELL H. ROUSSEAU POST 14, Portage

COLUMBIA COUNTY • APRIL 13, 1880–1931

CHARTER MEMBERS: C. L. Dering, Sam. H. Reed, Peter Jameson, Wm. Meacher, Byron W. Pruyn, W. W. Bullard, Thomas Drew, M. D. Vaughan, E. M. Parsons, Geo. H. Chase, Ackerman W. Ducat, J. J. Guppey, Henry Neff, Geo. W. Marsh, Geo. Hartt, W. N. Barton, James Hume, Wm. Beattie, H. Sherman, Hugh J. Williams, J. P. Cawp, Ole W. Bendixon, W. D. Williams, Wm. F. Bailey, Wm. Edwards, Thomas Robinson, Daniel Jerome, J. Perkins, T. L. Kennon, James Price, J. D. Woruen, D. Culbert, Irving Bart, Wm. Edwards (the second of two members with this name)

1866	1871	1876	1881	1886	1891	1896	1901	1906	1911	1916	1921	1926	1931	1936	1941	1946	1951

MEMBERSHIP BY YEAR (ACCOUNTED FOR): 1884, 90; 1887, 49; 1888, 37; 1889, 59; 1904, 41; 1905, 39; 1906, 37; 1907, 44; 1908, 40; 1909, 40; 1910, 39; 1911, 37; 1912, 29; 1913, 27; 1914, 19; 1915, 21; 1916, 22; 1917, 20; 1918, 17; 1919, 17; 1920, 15; 1921, 12; 1922, 10; 1923, 11; 1924, 10; 1925, 10; 1926, 10; 1927, 6; 1928, 4; 1929, 3; 1930, 1

LAST MEMBER: Unknown

L.H. ROSSEAU

The Grand Army men at Portage chose to honor General Lovell Harrison Rousseau, a Kentuckian who was a staunch Unionist and rose to be a division commander in the Army of the Cumberland. Rousseau was a politician both before and after the war, but was commissioned in the Regular Army in 1867. He died in New Orleans as military governor in 1869.

The Portage Post gained a modicum of fame if not immortality by being first to raise, in 1887, the issue of textbook treatment of issues of the Civil War, which agitated the entire G.A.R. thereafter for some years.

HARVEY POST 15, Green Bay

BROWN COUNTY • MARCH 16, 1876–1879

CHARTER MEMBERS: T. B. Catlin, commander; L. J. Billings, senior vice commander; C. F. Wallwitz, junior vice commander; James Kerr, quartermaster; J. D. Lawe, officer of the day; George C, Sager, officer of the guard; John B. Eugene, adjutant

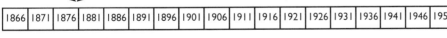

1866	1871	1876	1881	1886	1891	1896	1901	1906	1911	1916	1921	1926	1931	1936	1941	1946	1951

LAST MEMBER: Unknown

This is a second short-lived incarnation of the Grand Army of the Republic in Green Bay. (The first was Post 8, which existed briefly a decade earlier.) The existence of Post 15 is known only through a short paragraph in a book published in Green Bay in the year of its founding.

Its duration is unknown. The next post to bear the number 15 was chartered in 1880.

The selection of Harvey as the name of the post shows the high regard that many Civil War veterans had for Gov. Louis Harvey, who drowned on a visit to Wisconsin troops after the Battle of Shiloh. It was one of four posts to honor him. For further information about Harvey see Posts 16, 17, and 45.

J.H. ROBERTS POST 15, Plainfield

WAUSHARA COUNTY • 1880–1883

CHARTER MEMBERS: Unknown

1866	1871	1876	1881	1886	1891	1896	1901	1906	1911	1916	1921	1926	1931	1936	1941	1946	1951

LAST MEMBER: Unknown

Virtually nothing is known about this early post. Sadly, very little more is known about the man for whom this post in Plainfield was named. J. H. Roberts served in the Sixty-fourth New York Infantry and came to the Waushara County area after the war ended. He is buried in Belmont Cemetery, Town of Belmont in Portage County, across the line from Waushara County.

The post in Plainfield was the second of five posts numbered 15. It succeeded to that designation when the Department of Wisconsin decided to recycle the numbers it had used for the earliest posts begun in the first few years of the order's presence in the state.

The first Post 15, of which not a bit of evidence of its existence remains other than its notation on lists of the posts chartered in 1866 and revoked in 1871, was apparently begun in the village of Butte des Morts in Winnebago County.

JEROME CHESEBRO POST 15, Markesan

GREEN LAKE COUNTY • AUGUST 22, 1885–1889

CHARTER MEMBERS: M. Chesebro was the first commander.

1866	1871	1876	1881	1886	1891	1896	1901	1906	1911	1916	1921	1926	1931	1936	1941	1946	1951

MEMBERSHIP BY YEAR (ACCOUNTED FOR): 1888, 13 **LAST MEMBER:** Unknown

Of the early posts numbered 15, this third one, at Markesan in Green Lake County, has at least left behind some record of its namesake, Jerome Chesebro.

Chesebro (or Chesboro or Cheesebro as it is sometimes given) was second lieutenant of the "Fox River Zouaves" from Markesan, which became Company I of the Eleventh Wisconsin, mustered in October 1861.

The Eleventh took part in the campaign down the Mississippi. Chesebro was promoted to first lieutenant in March 1862. He died, as so many soldiers did in the Mississippi valley, of disease, at Grand Gulf on May 3, 1863.

JOHN FOLLENSBEE POST 15, New Centerville

ST. CROIX COUNTY • APRIL 13, 1889–1899

CHARTER MEMBERS: J.K. Hudson was the first commander.

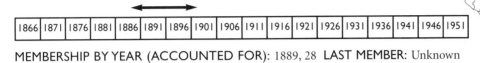

1866	1871	1876	1881	1886	1891	1896	1901	1906	1911	1916	1921	1926	1931	1936	1941	1946	1951

MEMBERSHIP BY YEAR (ACCOUNTED FOR): 1889, 28 **LAST MEMBER:** Unknown

The fourth post to bear the Number 15 was John Follensbee Post of New Centerville in St. Croix County.

While it existed for a decade, little record of the post has survived. Even the identity of Follensbee has not come to light, and the spelling of the name may be in question. There were at least two "John Follansbees" in Civil War service from Wisconsin. One, John W., was from Janesville, but another, John B. Follansbee, was listed from Rush River in St. Croix County.

WILLIAM McKINLEY POST 15, La Crosse

LA CROSSE COUNTY • NOVEMBER 29, 1901–1922

CHARTER MEMBERS: H. C. Morris, John C. Langdon, T. A. Lewis, Joseph Tucheck, T. C. Withrow, Henry Friese, J. W. Young, John S. Tillotson, M. H. Cram, R. R. Jones, Bernard Curley, John L. Sullivan, W. S. Holmes, T. J. Widvey, Asa Turner, Peter O'Rourke, Wm. Grover, Henry Gleason

1866	1871	1876	1881	1886	1891	1896	1901	1906	1911	1916	1921	1926	1931	1936	1941	1946	1951

MEMBERSHIP BY YEAR (ACCOUNTED FOR): 1901, 18; 1902, 19; 1906, 58; 1907, 47; 1908, 40; 1909, 37; 1910, 38; 1911, 36; 1912, 35; 1913, 17 **LAST MEMBER:** Unknown

WILLIAM McKINLEY

The fifth post to bear the Number 15 was the William McKinley Post of La Crosse. It was one of the later posts chartered by the Department of Wisconsin, notwithstanding its low number. It began in 1901, reached its membership zenith in 1906, and was listed as existing until 1922.

William McKinley was president of the United States, one of the many presidents who saw Civil War service. McKinley's service was relatively obscure. He rose from private to captain, and he was brevetted to major at the end of the war. His postwar career elevated him to president. Elected in 1897, he fell to an assassin's bullet in Buffalo, New York, dying September 14, 1901. The La Crosse Post was chartered two months after McKinley's death.

GOV. LOUIS P. HARVEY POST 16, Amherst

PORTAGE COUNTY • APRIL 18, 1880–1883

CHARTER MEMBERS: Unknown

1866	1871	1876	1881	1886	1891	1896	1901	1906	1911	1916	1921	1926	1931	1936	1941	1946	1951

LAST MEMBER: Unknown

GOV. LOUIS HARVEY

Louis Powell Harvey was Wisconsin's second governor during the Civil War and namesake of the first G.A.R. post in Amherst. While this Post 16 lasted only a few years, it is interesting that it chose to honor Harvey.

Louis Harvey succeeded Alexander Randall as governor in 1862 and continued the state's enthusiastic support of the war effort.

When news of the Battle of Shiloh reached Madison, Governor Harvey resolved to go down to the site and succor the many Wisconsin regiments that had been involved. While on this mission to the soldiers—a mission most appreciated by the hundreds of Wisconsin men who had fought and suffered there the governor lost his footing while transferring between two steamers and slipped into the water. He was swept away and drowned.

Harvey's widow, Cordella, became famous for her strong campaign to have hospitals established in the North so federal soldiers would be able to recover in the more healthful northern climate.

IRVIN ECKLES POST 16, Amherst

PORTAGE COUNTY • 1884–1931

CHARTER MEMBERS: A. J. Smith, T. W. Boss, H. H. Hoffman, W. Mason, F. Philips, I. Simcock, H. Evans, E. Hathaway, L. H. Hillstrom

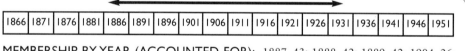

1866	1871	1876	1881	1886	1891	1896	1901	1906	1911	1916	1921	1926	1931	1936	1941	1946	1951

MEMBERSHIP BY YEAR (ACCOUNTED FOR): 1887, 43; 1888, 42; 1889, 42; 1904, 26; 1905, 31; 1906, 30; 1907, 29; 1908, 26; 1909, 26; 1910, 27; 1911, 25; 1912, 25; 1913, 24; 1914, 21; 1915, 19; 1916, 18; 1917, 18; 1918, 18; 1919, 18; 1920, 16; 1921, 13; 1922, 11; 1923, 10; 1924, 9; 1925, 8; 1926, 8; 1927, 5; 1928, 3; 1929, 1; 1930, 1; 1931, 1   **LAST MEMBER:** Herman H. Hoffman, April 1, 1931.

The Irvin Eckles Post 16 succeeded the Louis P. Harvey Post 16 in Amherst. They apparently were distinct posts. The latter was considered defunct by the Department of Wisconsin in 1883. By the following year, the Eckles Post was functioning, and it remained active into the 1930s.

The second Post 16 was named for Captain Irvin Eckles, a resident of nearby Plover who was captain of Company E, Thirty-second Wisconsin. The regiment was mustered in at Oshkosh in September 1862 and suffered its first battle casualties fighting with Sherman in Georgia and the Carolinas in 1864–65. Captain Eckles was one of the last soldiers of the company killed in action, on February 3, 1865, at Rivers Bridge or Salkahatchie, South Carolina. The records of Post 16 were destroyed in a fire that burned down their hall in April 1900.

GOV. (LOUIS P.) HARVEY POST 17, Racine
RACINE COUNTY • JANUARY 24, 1881–1936

CHARTER MEMBERS: L.C. Porter, J. C. Huggins, R. M. Boyd, F. Marshall, H. W. Wright, George E. Smith, A. N. Smith, Robert Augustine, E. B. Sage

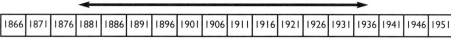

1866	1871	1876	1881	1886	1891	1896	1901	1906	1911	1916	1921	1926	1931	1936	1941	1946	1951

MEMBERSHIP BY YEAR (ACCOUNTED FOR): 1881, 9; 1887, 135; 1888, 178; 1889, 221; 1904, 149; 1905, 148; 1906, 132; 1907, 123; 1908, 121; 1909, 123; 1910, 125; 1911, 121; 1912, 116; 1913, 107; 1914, 102; 1915, 94; 1916, 86; 1917, 80; 1918, 76; 1919, 74; 1920, 70; 1921, 65; 1922, 53; 1923, 44; 1924, 41; 1925, 38; 1926, 32; 1927, 28; 1928, 21; 1929, 16; 1930, 14; 1931, 12; 1932, 12; 1933, 6; 1934, 2; 1935, 1   LAST MEMBER: David M. Oram

The fact that Racine soldiers chose the name of Governor Louis P. Harvey for their post tends to confirm that the governor, who became a casualty of the war effort, was much appreciated by the soldiers.

This Louis P. Harvey Post was a successful one right from its founding in 1881. It continued until the 1930s.

There is some record of an earlier Racine Post, probably formed in 1869, and presumably assigned number 11. One authority lists Henry Wright as its commander, with James O. Bartlett, Norton J. Field, Henry Sandford, and Charles Chipman as "prime movers." It failed after a few years. No name was recorded for it.

The Harvey Post was begun as the Department of Wisconsin was enjoying a resurgence. Commander Griff J. Thomas mustered the members of the post.

H. M. WALKER POST 18, Manitowoc
MANITOWOC COUNTY • APRIL 28, 1881–1934

CHARTER MEMBERS: J. S. Andersy, Fifth Wisconsin; W. J. Beasant, Twenty-ninth Wisconsin; F. C. Buerstatte, Twenty-sixth Wisconsin; H. C. Buhse, Ninth Wisconsin; J. H. Buhse, Ninth Wisconsin; C. W. Butler, Twenty-first Wisconsin; Ela Cone, Twenty-second Wisconsin; John Cone, Twenty-second Wisconsin; Jeremiah Cox, Twenty-seventh Wisconsin; James Cumberlidge, Oneida, New York, Cavalry; Charles Gastaveson, Fifteenth Wisconsin; Fred Heinemann, Ninth Wisconsin; Paul Leubner, Twenty-sixth Wisconsin; H. F. Liebenow, Twenty-fourth Wisconsin; John Mill, Fifth Wisconsin; Henry Noble, Twenty-first Wisconsin; James Noble, Twenty-first Wisconsin; Ferd. Ostenfeldt, Twenty-first Wisconsin; J. F. Reardon, Twenty-first Wisconsin; Henry Sanford, Second Wisconsin; G. G. Sedgwick, 105th Illinois; Frank Stirn, Fifth Wisconsin

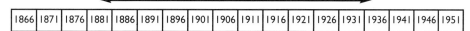

1866	1871	1876	1881	1886	1891	1896	1901	1906	1911	1916	1921	1926	1931	1936	1941	1946	1951

MARC AND BETH STORCH
HORACE M. WALKER

MEMBERSHIP BY YEAR (ACCOUNTED FOR): 1881, 22; 1884, 98; 1887, 127; 1888, 114; 1889, 128; 1904, 93; 1905, 84; 1906, 79; 1907, 74; 1908, 70; 1909, 66; 1910, 59; 1911, 57; 1912, 54; 1913, 32; 1914, 49; 1915, 50; 1916, 36; 1917, 30; 1918, 28; 1919, 22; 1920, 20; 1921, 18; 1922, 17; 1923, 14; 1924, 14; 1925, 10; 1926, 9; 1927, 8; 1929, 2; 1930, 2; 1931, 1   LAST MEMBER: Jacob A. Williams

Horace M. Walker Post Number 18 honors the captain who led the first volunteers from Manitowoc County into war. They became Company A, Fifth Wisconsin Infantry.

Walker was killed leading the company against Confederate forces at Rappahanock Station, Virginia, on November 7, 1863. Three of the charter members of Post 18 served under Walker in Company A.

WILLIAM B. CUSHING POST 19, Waukesha
WAUKESHA COUNTY • MAY 24, 1881-1937

CHARTER MEMBERS: H. Van Bugbee, Carl Busjaeger, M. L. Butterfield, G. J. Chamberlain, S. G. Curtis, E. Enos, H. M. Enos, J. J. Gibbs, R. L. Gove, T. W. Haight, J. G. Hart, D. Howell, Geo. Klock, Geo. Lindner, J. B. Lockney, John McGeen, Thomas McGeen, Andrew McKee, Hugo Philler, F. H. Putney, August Schley, B. Sears, B. C. Sears, Conrad Sehrt, Henry Sehrt, J. K. Smith, J. R. Spencer, E. B. Sweet, O. E. Tyler, Fred Wardrobe

1866	1871	1876	1881	1886	1891	1896	1901	1906	1911	1916	1921	1926	1931	1936	1941	1946	1951

MEMBERSHIP BY YEAR (ACCOUNTED FOR): 1884, 43; 1887, 96; 1888, 129; 1889, 143; 1904, 93; 1905, 91; 1906, 88; 1907, 95; 1908, 96; 1909, 93; 1910, 92; 1911, 93; 1912, 91; 1913, 86; 1914, 80; 1915, 73; 1916, 67; 1917, 57; 1918, 51; 1919, 47; 1920, 44; 1921, 41; 1922, 37; 1923, 34; 1924, 28; 1925, 24; 1926, 23; 1927, 22; 1928, 14; 1929, 14; 1930, 12; 1931, 10; 1932, 11; 1933, 10; 1934, 7; 1935, 5; 1936, 5   **LAST MEMBER:** Unknown

WILLIAM B. CUSHING

The Waukesha Grand Army Post 19 chose to honor one of Waukesha County's national heroes of the Civil War, William B. Cushing, the younger brother of Alonzo Cushing of Gettysburg fame. William, of course, won equal renown as a naval officer with a penchant for daring exploits with the blockade fleet. His crowning achievement was sinking the Confederate ram Albemarle off Plymouth, North Carolina, with a torpedo attack via a small boat in the dark of night. Cushing remained in service after the war. He died of exhaustion in 1874 at the age of 32. He is the only navy person for whom a G.A.R. post in Wisconsin is named.

WILLIAM H. SARGENT POST 20, Janesville
ROCK COUNTY • OCTOBER 21, 1881-APRIL 12, 1937

CHARTER MEMBERS: W. B. Britton, Wm. W. Berrell, T. T. Croft, E. G. Harlow, P. S. Fenton, E. P. Bly, E. Barry, S. H. Stone, Christian Yager, M. Griffin, Jas. A. Spencer, S. G. Sisson, John Lawler, G. W. Smith, A. C. Deming, Jerome Howland, John Andrews, D. Conger, Chas. Horn, H. A. Smith, Pliny Norcross, S. C. Cobb, W. T. Brayton, S. Putnam, H. M. Weaver, S. L. Lord, Henry Palmer, H. W. Perrigo, A. M. Pratt, A. Biutliff, J. D. Traueblie, A. F. Lee, Chas. N. Riker, M. Grall, J. C. Metcalf, John W. Belton, J. H. Bliss, C. J. Schottle, Ed. Murphy, R. W. King, Benj. R. Hilt, Clark Popple

1866	1871	1876	1881	1886	1891	1896	1901	1906	1911	1916	1921	1926	1931	1936	1941	1946	1951

MEMBERSHIP BY YEAR (ACCOUNTED FOR): 1881, 42; 1887, 168; 1888, 155; 1889, 139; 1904, 100; 1905, 104; 1906, 102; 1907, 99; 1908, 92; 1909, 94; 1910, 97; 1911, 80; 1912, 83; 1913, 80; 1914, 77; 1915, 73; 1916, 72; 1917, 68; 1918, 65; 1919, 61; 1920, 54; 1921, 43; 1922, 39; 1923, 33; 1924, 31; 1925, 30; 1926, 27; 1927, 23; 1928, 21; 1929, 18; 1930, 14; 1931, 10; 1932, 9; 1933, 7; 1934, 4; 1935, 2; 1936, 1   **LAST MEMBER:** Orion Sutherland, died April 12, 1937

In the exciting first days of the Civil War the Janesville Fire Zouaves headed to Camp Randall and became Company G in the regiment that would be known as the Eighth Wisconsin, soon to begin its legendary experience as the Eagle Regiment.

The regiment's last big engagement was at the Battle of Nashville, and the last officer killed in action was Lieutenant William H. Sargent of Janesville, now adjutant of the regiment, on December 16, 1864. His comrades from Janesville honored

Sargent when they formed their local post of the Grand Army of the Republic.

Members of the William H. Sargent Post of Janesville pose for their portrait in front of the Civil War monument after it was erected in front of the Rock County Courthouse in Janesville. This was probably not long after the monument was put in place in 1901.

JAMES A. GARFIELD POST 21, Waupaca

WAUPACA COUNTY • OCTOBER 26, 1881–1941

CHARTER MEMBERS: J. H. Woodnorth, commander; G. M. Chamberlain, senior vice commander; W. S. Bemis, junior vice commander; F. S. Woodnorth, officer of the day; A. D. Rice, quartermaster; E. B. Thompson, adjutant; D. L. Manchester, surgeon; F. D. Randall, chaplain; H. Ludington, officer of guard; O. H. Rowe, sergeant major

1866	1871	1876	1881	1886	1891	1896	1901	1906	1911	1916	1921	1926	1931	1936	1941	1946	1951

MEMBERSHIP BY YEAR (ACCOUNTED FOR): 1887, 66; 1888, 75; 1889, 87; 1904, 50; 1905, 51; 1906, 58; 1907, 57; 1908, 66; 1909, 66; 1910, 59; 1911, 58; 1912, 54; 1913, 44; 1914, 46; 1915, 44; 1916, 45; 1917, 44; 1918, 29; 1919, 28; 1920, 23; 1921, 19; 1922, 14; 1923, 15; 1924, 13; 1925, 12; 1926, 12; 1927, 8; 1928, 7; 1929, 8; 1930, 7; 1932, 6; 1933, 5; 1934, 5; 1935, 5; 1936, 3; 1937, 3; 1938, 2; 1939, 1   **LAST MEMBER:** Minor Rice

JAMES A. GARFIELD

James A. Garfield Post 21 was the Grand Army Post in Waupaca, predating the G.A.R.'s establishment of a home for old soldiers in a nearby area that came to be known as "King." Post 21 was named after the second president of the United States to be assassinated, James A. Garfield, who himself had a good military record with the Army of the Cumberland before resuming his political career.

Elected president in 1880, he was shot by a disappointed office seeker in July 1881, succumbing to the wound on September 19, 1881, just over a month before the Waupaca post was chartered.

WOOD COUNTY POST 22, Wisconsin Rapids

WOOD COUNTY • DECEMBER 9, 1881–1938

CHARTER MEMBERS: Elias H. Tickner, W. F. King, S. B. Huey, C. J. Carman, R. P. Bronson, F. W. Burt, William J. Cochran, Gilbert J. Jackson, Clarence S. Warren, Geo. W. Baker, M. S. Pratt, D. D. Demarais, D. C. Carey, E. A. Tenant, W. H. Cochran, Joseph L. Cotey, Thos. W. Pitts, Geo. R. Gardeier, William E. Simons, J. Q. Severance, M. J. McRaith, W. H. Brown, W. A. Keyes, F. B. Case, S. S. Burr, C. M. Atwood, John T. Miller

1866	1871	1876	1881	1886	1891	1896	1901	1906	1911	1916	1921	1926	1931	1936	1941	1946	1951

MEMBERSHIP BY YEAR (ACCOUNTED FOR): 1881, 27; 1884, 76; 1887, 75; 1888, 68; 1889, 82; 1904, 70; 1905, 68; 1906, 68; 1907, 62; 1908, 56; 1909, 53; 1910, 58; 1911, 57; 1912, 49; 1913, 56; 1914, 45; 1915, 42; 1916, 36; 1917, 34; 1918, 30; 1919, 22; 1920, 21; 1921, 19; 1922, 18; 1923, 17; 1924, 13; 1925, 12; 1926, 9; 1927, 9; 1928, 7; 1929, 6; 1930, 5; 1931, 4; 1932, 4; 1933, 3; 1934, 3; 1935, 2; 1936, 2; 1937, 2   **LAST MEMBER:** Unknown

Veterans in Wood County chose their charter location as name for their post. In 1881 the area was far from anything metropolitan. Originally the city was Grand Rapids, but in 1921 the locale was renamed Wisconsin Rapids. The picture on the left is of an unidentified Post 22 member from the time when they were meeting in "Grand Rapids." The flags are 45-star flags.

A. McFARLAND POST 23, Poynette

COLUMBIA COUNTY • 1884–1888

CHARTER MEMBERS: Unknown

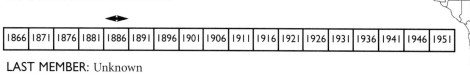

| 1866 | 1871 | 1876 | 1881 | 1886 | 1891 | 1896 | 1901 | 1906 | 1911 | 1916 | 1921 | 1926 | 1931 | 1936 | 1941 | 1946 | 1951 |

LAST MEMBER: Unknown

The short-lived post at Poynette in Columbia County bears the name of a soldier of the Twenty-third Wisconsin, a native of Arlington, just a few miles from Poynette. A. J. McFarland, a member of a prominent Columbia County family, rose in the ranks of the Twenty-third, being sergeant major at the time of his promotion to first lieutenant of Company K. In the campaign against Vicksburg, the Twenty-third was involved in heavy fighting on May 20, 1863, during which McFarland was wounded. He was returned to Wisconsin, but he died of his wounds at Portage, ironically, on July 4, the day Vicksburg surrendered to the besieging Union army. He is buried in Silver Lake Cemetery, Portage.

Nothing else is known about the effort of Poynette veterans to have their own Grand Army post.

W. K. FORSHAY POST 23, Wyalusing

GRANT COUNTY • MARCH 27, 1888–1912

CHARTER MEMBERS: Moses Dunn, commander; Milton Jacobs, senior vice commander; J. A. Bradley, junior vice commander; Jacob Shrade, adjutant; Edwin Glenn, quartermaster; T. F. Hart, surgeon; H. C. Jackson, chaplain; William Patterson, officer of the day; J. A. Bossi, officer of the guard.

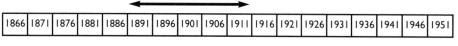

| 1866 | 1871 | 1876 | 1881 | 1886 | 1891 | 1896 | 1901 | 1906 | 1911 | 1916 | 1921 | 1926 | 1931 | 1936 | 1941 | 1946 | 1951 |

MEMBERSHIP BY YEAR (ACCOUNTED FOR): 1888, 24; 1889, 22; 1904, 9; 1905, 10; 1906, 11; 1907, 11; 1908, 11; 1909, 14; 1910, 9; 1911, 9   **LAST MEMBER:** Unknown

The G.A.R. Post at Wyalusing—later Brantville and then Bagley—was named after Wellington K. Forshay. Forshay was a member of Company F, Eighth Wisconsin, recruited mainly in Grant County. While serving with the Eagle Regiment he was taken prisoner at Bear Creek, and he was subsequently sent to Andersonville Prison in Georgia where he died August 8, 1864. Forshay is listed as among the hundreds of Andersonville victims buried in the National Cemetery there.

HENRY DILLON POST 24, Lone Rock

RICHLAND COUNTY • FEBRUARY 23, 1882–1940

CHARTER MEMBERS: N. B. Hood, commander; A. Wolf, senior vice commander; J. M. Bowers, junior vice commander; W. A. Garrison, adjutant; J. W. Reyma, officer of the day; A. J. Harrison, surgeon; Wm. Knapp, chaplain; E. J. Burdick, officer of the guard; C. H. Pierce, quartermaster

1866	1871	1876	1881	1886	1891	1896	1901	1906	1911	1916	1921	1926	1931	1936	1941	1946	1951

MEMBERSHIP BY YEAR (ACCOUNTED FOR): 1884, 55; 1887, 17; 1888, 14; 1889, 14; 1917, 7; 1918, 12; 1919, 10; 1920, 9; 1921, 8; 1922, 5; 1923, 4; 1924, 7; 1925, 6; 1926, 6; 1927, 5; 1928, 5; 1930, 3; 1931, 3; 1933, 1; 1934, 2; 1935, 2; 1936, 1; 1937, 1; 1938, 1; 1939, 1

LAST MEMBER: R. A. Hammond or J. H. Bettey

CAPT. HENRY DILLON

Post 24 took the name of Captain Henry Dillon of Lone Rock, commander of the Sixth Wisconsin Light Artillery. He was mustered out October 10, 1864.

In its early years the Dillon Post had more than 50 members, but the numbers dropped radically, and there may have been periods in which it was not functioning. It was listed as extinct in the 1903 state encampment journal. Nonetheless it was operating from about World War I until the late 1930s.

GEORGE IRWIN POST 25, Lodi

COLUMBIA COUNTY • MARCH 19, 1882–1936

CHARTER MEMBERS: J. R. Collins was first commander.

1866	1871	1876	1881	1886	1891	1896	1901	1906	1911	1916	1921	1926	1931	1936	1941	1946	1951

MEMBERSHIP BY YEAR (ACCOUNTED FOR): 1884, 47; 1887, 33; 1888, 43; 1889, 25; 1904, 27; 1905, 25; 1906, 23; 1907, 25; 1908, 20; 1909, 19; 1910, 15; 1911, 15; 1912, 11; 1913, 8; 1914, 9; 1915, 9; 1916, 9; 1917, 10; 918, 8; 1919, 9; 1920, 8; 1921, 7; 1922, 6; 1923, 6; 1924, 6; 1925, 5; 1926, 4; 1927, 4; 1928, 4; 1929, 3; 1930, 3; 1931, 3; 1932, 2; 1933, 2; 1934, 2; 1935, 2   **LAST MEMBER:** Unknown

At the first call for volunteers in the Civil War, Dr. George H. Irwin left his medical practice and joined the army as a private in Company G, "the Portage Guards," Second Wisconsin. Because of his training, he was made an assistant surgeon.

At the first battle of Bull Run, Dr. Irwin was wounded, and as a result of that, he left service and returned to Lodi.

His example made an impression in Lodi, which saw four companies recruited from the area during the war, including one led by his son, Dr. E. Howard Irwin, captain of Company H, Twenty-third Wisconsin.

GEORGE H. IRWIN

When the men of Lodi formed a Grand Army Post, they chose to honor Dr. George Irwin by naming the post after him.

Members of the George Irwin Post of Lodi, date unknown

JOHN E. HOLMES POST 26, Jefferson

JEFFERSON COUNTY • APRIL 15, 1882–1937

CHARTER MEMBERS: George W. Bird was the first commander.

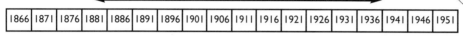

1866	1871	1876	1881	1886	1891	1896	1901	1906	1911	1916	1921	1926	1931	1936	1941	1946	1951

MEMBERSHIP BY YEAR (ACCOUNTED FOR): 1887, 34; 1888, 31; 1889, 28; 1904, 12; 1905, 11; 1906, 11; 1907, 10; 1908, 10; 1909, 10; 1910, 10; 1911, 10; 1912, 9; 1913, 10; 1914, 8; 1915, 10; 1916, 8; 1917, 7; 1918, 6; 1921, 4; 1922, 4; 1923, 33; 1924, 32; 1925, 28; 1926, 24; 1927, 23; 1928, 23; 1929, 19; 1930, 15; 1931, 13; 1932, 12; 1933, 10; 1934, 4; 1935, 3; 1936, 3   LAST MEMBER: Unknown

JEFFERSON HISTORICAL SOCIETY
JOHN E. HOLMES

The John E. Holmes Post of Jefferson was a post resuscitated in its later years.

The post was named for a Jefferson man who had a significant career before the war. John Edwin Holmes was the first lieutenant governor of Wisconsin from 1848 to 1850. He was 53 years old when he was appointed quartermaster of the Twenty-second Wisconsin, mustered in at Camp Utley, Racine, in August 1862.

Holmes was one of a large number of men in the regiment captured in March 1863 at Brentwood, Tennessee, by Confederate Buford Forest. They were held at Richmond for a few months until they were exchanged. Holmes had become ill during captivity, and he died June 8, 1863, at Annapolis, Maryland.

The G.A.R. Post in Jefferson bearing his name was declining after World War I until it received a transfusion of members from other Jefferson County posts, namely Fort Atkinson, Palmyra, and Lake Mills, which all closed in 1923. Holmes Post continued into the mid-1930s.

JAMES B. McPHERSON POST 27, Lake Geneva

WALWORTH COUNTY • APRIL 18, 1882–1936

CHARTER MEMBERS: Thomas H. Price was the first commander.

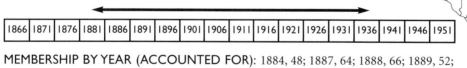

1866	1871	1876	1881	1886	1891	1896	1901	1906	1911	1916	1921	1926	1931	1936	1941	1946	1951

MEMBERSHIP BY YEAR (ACCOUNTED FOR): 1884, 48; 1887, 64; 1888, 66; 1889, 52; 1904, 48; 1905, 49; 1906, 49; 1907, 49; 1908, 39; 1909, 37; 1910, 37; 1911, 39; 1912, 38; 1913, 34; 1914, 34; 1915, 31; 1916, 21; 1917, 18; 1918, 16; 1919, 15; 1920, 13; 1921, 10; 1922, 7; 1923, 5; 1924, 4; 1925, 4; 1926, 3; 1927, 3; 1928, 3; 929, 3; 1930, 3; 1931, 3; 1932, 3; 1933, 3; 1934, 1; 1935, 15   LAST MEMBER: Henry DeLap

J. B. McPHERSON

The soldiers of Walworth County chose to honor General James B. McPherson not once but twice. Post 12 at Sharon was the original one by that name, but it disappeared after a few years. Twelve miles away, at Lake Geneva, another post was formed, and it likewise was named for the star corps commander in the West whose death was mourned by the whole Army of the West. It is possible that the two posts were somehow linked since the Sharon one disappeared with little trace about the same time as the Lake Geneva Post was organized. McPherson Post 27 did not so summarily disappear. It remained on the department roster until the middle 1930s.

GENERAL EDWARD CANBY POST 28, Auroraville

WAUSHARA COUNTY • JUNE 4, 1882–1885

CHARTER MEMBERS: Unknown

1866	1871	1876	1881	1886	1891	1896	1901	1906	1911	1916	1921	1926	1931	1936	1941	1946	1951

LAST MEMBER: Unknown

GENERAL E.R.S. CANBY

Although it lasted only a brief time, the post at Auroraville in Waushara County honored one of the lesser known but quite competent Union generals, Edward R. S. Canby. He had command in the Far West in the early part of the war and won a decisive victory over forces seeking to extend the Confederacy into New Mexico Territory. His victory at Glorieta Pass was called the "Gettysburg of the West" because it utterly destroyed the dream of the Confederacy for westward expansion.

It also was General Canby who, as commander in the deep South, accepted the surrender of the last Confederate army in the field, E. Kirby Smith's, more than a month after Appomattox.

Canby remained in the army and was slain by Indians while he was leading a peace mission in California in 1873.

NEWTON WILSON POST 28, Kingston
GEORGE BRAYTON POST 28, Kingston

GREEN LAKE COUNTY • MARCH 17, 1888–1930

CHARTER MEMBERS: E.C. Brayton, J. M. Chapel, G. A. Joslen, William W. Hunter, Thomas Gunderson, John Milligan, Fred Koh, C. P. Hewitt, William Gardner, Frank Knight, H. R. Price, August Gelanman, George Brayton

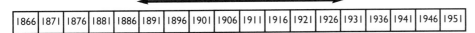

1866	1871	1876	1881	1886	1891	1896	1901	1906	1911	1916	1921	1926	1931	1936	1941	1946	1951

MEMBERSHIP BY YEAR (ACCOUNTED FOR): 1887, 13; 1888, 24; 1889, 25; 1904, 15; 1905, 15; 1906, 13; 1907, 13; 1908, 13; 1909, 10; 1910, 9; 1911, 8; 1912, 8; 1913, 8; 1914, 8; 1915, 8; 1916, 8;1917, 8; 1918, 8; 1919, 7; 1920, 7; 1921, 6; 1922, 6; 1923, 6; 1924, 6; 1925, 4; 1927, 3; 1928, 3; 1929, 2; 1930, 2   **LAST MEMBER:** Unknown

The G.A.R. post at Kingston was originally named for Newton D. Wilson, a private in Company C, Twenty-third Wisconsin. Like so many Civil War regiments, the Twenty-third suffered many more deaths from disease than from fighting. Thirty-eight were combat casualties. Newton Wilson was one of the 249 men of the regiment succumbing to disease. He died at Milliken's Bend on April 5, 1863.

The name of the post was changed on December 26, 1891, to the George F. Brayton Post, named after a charter member of Post 28 and its first junior vice commander.

JUDSON KILPATRICK POST 29, Oakdale

MONROE COUNTY • APRIL 13, 1882– AUGUST 17, 1895

CHARTER MEMBERS: Unknown

1866	1871	1876	1881	1886	1891	1896	1901	1906	1911	1916	1921	1926	1931	1936	1941	1946	1951

MEMBERSHIP BY YEAR (ACCOUNTED FOR): 1884, 19; 1887, 27; 1888, 21; 1889, 22   **LAST MEMBER:** Unknown

Hugh Judson "Kilcavalry" Kilpatrick was one of the dashing cavalry commanders of the war and a favorite with soldiers.

The G.A.R. Post 29 at Oakdale in Monroe County chose his name when it was chartered in 1882.

JUDSON KILPATRICK

A West Pointer, Kilpatrick was the first Regular Army officer wounded in the war, received in the skirmish called Big Bethel in Virginia.

Kilpatrick commanded with dash and aggressiveness, but his record did not rank him among the top cavalry men. He left the army after the war, turning to service as a diplomat. He was minister to Chile and died there in December 1881, about five months before the post at Oakdale chose to be known by his name.

The Kilpatrick Post surrendered its charter on August 17, 1895.

The men of the Judson Kilpatrick Post 29 have their picture taken with an Oakdale storefront as the backdrop, date unknown. Photo provided by the Wisconsin Veterans Museum, Madison.

D. D. BARKER POST 29, Abrams

OCONTO COUNTY • APRIL 22, 1896–1940

CHARTER MEMBERS: Jesse Birmingham was the first commander.

1866	1871	1876	1881	1886	1891	1896	1901	1906	1911	1916	1921	1926	1931	1936	1941	1946	1951

MEMBERSHIP BY YEAR (ACCOUNTED FOR): 1896, 30; 1904, 35; 1905, 35; 1906, 29; 1907, 32; 1908, 23; 1909, 27; 1910, 25; 1911, 22; 1912, 20; 1913, 20; 1914, 16; 1915, 20; 1916, 15; 1917, 17; 1918, 12; 1919, 12; 1920, 12; 1921, 12; 1922, 11; 1923, 10; 1924, 9; 1925, 8; 1926, 7; 1927, 5; 1928, 3; 1929, 3; 1930, 3; 1931, 2; 1932, 2; 1933, 2; 1934, 1; 1935, 3; 1936, 2; 1937, 2; 1938, 2; 1939, 2
LAST MEMBER: George Lince

The Civil War veterans of Abrams in Oconto County received designation as Post 29 the year after the men of Kilpatrick Post surrendered their charter. The new post chose to honor with the post's name Darius D. Barker, an Oconto County soldier who served with Company D, Third Cavalry, Reorganized. Barker was from Pensaukee. He survived the war and was mustered out July 29, 1865.

The Barker Post, after a relatively late beginning—by 1896 G.A.R. membership numbers were declining—has a long history. It was one of the rather few posts surviving until the 1940s.

JOHN W. LYNN POST 30, Sparta

MONROE COUNTY • APRIL 24, 1882–1934

CHARTER MEMBERS: James Davidson, Samuel Hoyt, Edwin W. Olin, L. C. Herrick, William H. Blyton, Alonzo E. Howard, Hugh T. Hogue, Alfred Dunbar, William Waste, William Kerrigan, Charles A. Hunt, James E. Perry, George A. Fisk, George Graham, George W. Shepherd, Sylvanus Holmes, William Summerfield, De Witt C. Beebe, Ira A. Hill, E. W. Robie, M. J. McOmber, Lucian A. McWithy, John Burk, John Winters, William Shepherd, James O'Connor, Joseph Jones, Franklin Campbell, Michael McPeak, Chauncy Bunce, Charles Slaver, Nathan B. Aldrich, Joseph W. Potter, Edward J. Hodgkin, William J. Jordan, Adelbert E. Bleekman, Bruce E. McCoy, Rufus S. Dodge, Ulrich Wettstein, Charles A. Bunce, Lucius M. Stevens, John W. Carter, William A. DeLong, Chauncy K. Kennedy, John Jarrett, Jeremiah Van Kirk, E. Crocker, Henry T. Bell, Robert Rathbun, W. H. Washburn, Walter A. Wodd, Byron M. Dunham, William N. Wilcox, S. F. Ketcham, Abraham Heath, Edward Busby, James P. Larry

1866	1871	1876	1881	1886	1891	1896	1901	1906	1911	1916	1921	1926	1931	1936	1941	1946	1951

MEMBERSHIP BY YEAR (ACCOUNTED FOR): 1882, 57; 1884, 102; 1887, 112; 1888, 124; 1889, 120; 1904, 61; 1905, 62; 1906, 51; 1907, 52; 1908, 49; 1909, 49; 1910, 62; 1911, 58; 1912, 55; 1913, 57; 1914, 56; 1915, 51; 1916, 52; 1917, 50; 1918, 45; 1919, 44; 1920, 39; 1921, 33; 1922, 33; 1923, 30; 1924, 25; 1925, 25; 1926, 16; 1927, 16; 1928, 11; 1929, 7; 1930, 6; 1931, 2; 1932, 2; 1933, 1   **LAST MEMBER:** William H. Blyton, a charter member.

Post 30, Sparta, was named for Captain John W. Lynn, a Sparta cavalry officer who died on the gunboat *Tyler* commanding a group of sharpshooters on the Yazoo River.

Lynn, captain of Company I, Fourth Wisconsin Cavalry, was detailed to the *Tyler* on July 14, 1862, when it encountered the rebel ram *Arkansas*, and a running fight onto the Mississippi ensued. A shell from the *Arkansas* killed Lynn and five of his sharpshooters.

Post 30 had more than one hundred members at its peak and continued to exist until the 1930s.

(Parenthetically, the last Civil War veteran in Monroe County was *not* a G.A.R. member. Charles Schlaver of Sparta died May 14, 1940, and was buried with military rites by Spanish War veterans.)

JOHN H. ELY POST 31, Juneau

DODGE COUNTY • JUNE 1, 1882–1929

CHARTER MEMBERS: H. C. Curtis, commander; F. W. Lueck, senior vice commander; P. H. Lewis, junior vice commander; C. A. Pettibone, quartermaster; W. E. Hallock, surgeon; Albert Schmidt, chaplain; O. F. Haner, officer of the day; A. J. Howe, officer of the guard; W. T. Ramsbusch, adjutant; E. J. Tyler, quartermaster sergeant; L. E. Haughton, sergeant major

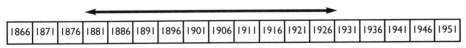

1866	1871	1876	1881	1886	1891	1896	1901	1906	1911	1916	1921	1926	1931	1936	1941	1946	1951

MEMBERSHIP BY YEAR (ACCOUNTED FOR): 1884, 24; 1887, 17; 1888, 19; 1889, 20; 1904, 12; 1905, 12; 1906, 12; 1907, 12; 1908, 12; 1909, 11; 1910, 12; 1911, 12; 1912, 12; 1913, 10; 1914, 7; 1915, 7; 1916, 7; 1917, 7; 1918, 7; 1919, 6; 1920, 6; 1921, 6; 1922, 5; 1923, 4; 1924, 4; 1925, 4; 1926, 3; 1927, 3; 1928, 3   **LAST MEMBER:** Unknown

MARC AND BETH STORCH
JOHN H. ELY

Veterans forming the G.A.R. post at Juneau in Dodge County chose to honor John H. Ely from that town by naming Post 31 after him.

Ely, lieutenant colonel of the Tenth Wisconsin Infantry, was wounded and taken prisoner at Chickamauga, Georgia, in 1863. He was taken to Libby Prison in Richmond, Virginia, and died there from the effects of his wounds. He entered the Tenth as captain of Company E from the Juneau area, and rose to second in command of the regiment. He was in charge of the regiment at Chickamauga, and he was shot several times while he tried to rally the Tenth as it was being overwhelmed. Ely was the highest ranking officer of the Tenth to die from combat.

J. B. WYMAN POST 32, Clintonville

WAUPACA COUNTY • MAY 28, 1882–1913

CHARTER MEMBERS: G. W. Sutherland, F. M. Guernsey, Frank Young, S. H. Brady, C. M. Glugmin, Irwin Gregory, James Webmone, H. S. Pickard, N. B. Carter, B. B. Hart, E. Ganes, H. Hartman, Henry Giebel, Wm. Shaw, H. H. Thorn, Wm. Cravin, E. Ewer, Geo. Waite, James McNeil, Gilroy Smith, W. H. Chavers, Wm. Paschen, Leroy Mark, Geo. McCorism, A. W. Willmarth

| 1866 | 1871 | 1876 | 1881 | 1886 | 1891 | 1896 | 1901 | 1906 | 1911 | 1916 | 1921 | 1926 | 1931 | 1936 | 1941 | 1946 | 1951 |

MEMBERSHIP BY YEAR (ACCOUNTED FOR): 1882, 25; 1884, 54; 1887, 42; 1888, 52; 1889, 60; 1904, 18; 1905, 16; 1906, 16; 1907, 14; 1908, 12; 1909, 9; 1910, 8; 1911, 10; 1912, 7

LAST MEMBER: Alanson James Huff, died May 30, 1928.

RICHARD K. BEGGS

The Clintonville Post had many years of activity, but very little information about the post survives. It was named for John B. Wyman. Wyman was from Amboy, Illinois, and enlisted as a private in the Thirteenth Illinois. He was appointed colonel on the strength of his having earlier led a crack militia company, the Chicago Light Guards. Wyman was killed in the assault at Chickasaw Bayou on December 28, 1862.

Here is a picture of members of Post 32, taken sometime before 1900 in front of their meeting place, the Ward House.

PLATTEVILLE POST 33, Platteville

GRANT COUNTY • OCTOBER 18, 1866–NOVEMBER 20, 1871

CHARTER MEMBERS: A. J. McCarwin, E. J. Bentley, R. Carter, Geo. B. Carter, C. C. Cheever, F. O. Grinfealt, E. F. Mears, B. J. Pugdale, Geo. W. Eastman, A. W. Bell, Herman Buchner, W. Homer Beebe

| 1866 | 1871 | 1876 | 1881 | 1886 | 1891 | 1896 | 1901 | 1906 | 1911 | 1916 | 1921 | 1926 | 1931 | 1936 | 1941 | 1946 | 1951 |

MEMBERSHIP BY YEAR (ACCOUNTED FOR): 1867, 12   **LAST MEMBER:** Unknown

The charter for Post 33 of Platteville is unique in that it is the only known charter to survive among those posts that began in the earliest days of the Wisconsin Department and were annulled by Commander Edward Ferguson in 1871.

Thus these charter members are the only men identified among the founders of all those dozens of early posts that existed so briefly.

The charter was issued to Post 33 of Platteville; whether the post adopted any other name is not known.

The post's charter is among those held by the Veterans Museum in Madison. It is unknown how such an early charter, which is about half the size of the usual charters issued to posts in later years, came to be preserved. No others from those failed posts are known to exist.

W. H. BENNETT POST 33, Richland Center
RICHLAND COUNTY • MAY 1, 1882–1941

CHARTER MEMBERS: D. G. James, Irvin Gribble, B. C. Hallin, George Jarvis, Christian Berger, A. J. Kinney, H. J. Wall, John Walworth, J. G. Bunnell, M. L. Sherman, Lewis Henry, Thomas B. Adams, Frank Hapgood, N. L. James, A. Lillybridge, J. W. Leik, Ira Monroe, O. H. Northrup, G. W. Putnam, A. S. Ripley, D. L. Downs, A. Hyatt

1866	1871	1876	1881	1886	1891	1896	1901	1906	1911	1916	1921	1926	1931	1936	1941	1946	1951

MEMBERSHIP BY YEAR (ACCOUNTED FOR): 1884, 46; 1887, 95; 1888, 107; 1889, 119; 1904, 64; 1905, 68; 1906, 74; 1907, 71; 1908, 75; 1909, 73; 1910, 66; 1911, 65; 1912, 62; 1913, 58; 1914, 58; 1915, 65; 1916, 61; 1917, 59; 1918, 55; 1919, 50; 1920, 49; 1921, 47; 1922, 32; 1923, 30; 1924, 28; 1925, 24; 1926, 20; 1927, 12; 1928, 10; 1929, 8; 1930, 8; 1931, 1; 1932, 1; 1933, 1; 1934, 1; 1935, 1; 1936, 1; 1937, 1; 1938, 1; 1939, 1   **LAST MEMBER:** Joseph Miller

W. H. Bennett, known as Henry Bennett, was from Richland County and joined Company H, Fifth Wisconsin Infantry, as a private at the opening of hostilities. Bennett distinguished himself with the Fifth and was chosen to be captain of Company B, Twenty-fifth Wisconsin Infantry. He was wounded and taken prisoner in July 1864, succumbing to his wounds at Macon, Georgia, on August 10, 1864.

CHARLES E. CURTICE POST 34, Whitewater
WALWORTH COUNTY • JUNE 29, 1882–1938

CHARTER MEMBERS: E. S. Redington; C. W. Steele; E. G. Horton, MD; E. D. Coe; E. D. Geer; J. J. Criger; G. L. Smith; John Brewin; Frank Rinney; Chas. Cadman; U. W. Hatch; J. Atherton; E. F. Donnelly; A. W. Bollard; J. O. Knowlton; Jno. Reichel; Oscar Smith; Ole Olson; Myron E. Hollis; Jacob Phillips; A. Ammon; G. Millis; Lewis Carpenter; S. S. Hayford; H. Pattee; D. N. Fowler; Sam Barfoot; A. J. Porden; W. J. McIntyre; A. H. Marskin; Jol. Kershaw; E. W. Rogers; Joseph Green, MD; J. A. Chamberlain; C. T. Higgins; C. W. Rockwell; Alex W. Griffin; Wm. Olds; Wm. Truman; Albert Stillman

1866	1871	1876	1881	1886	1891	1896	1901	1906	1911	1916	1921	1926	1931	1936	1941	1946	1951

MEMBERSHIP BY YEAR (ACCOUNTED FOR): 1882, 40; 1884, 79; 1887, 60; 1888, 65; 1889, 92; 1904, 39; 1905, 40; 1906, 44; 1907, 47; 1908, 49; 1909, 51; 1910, 47; 1911, 42; 1912, 39; 1913, 34; 1914, 34; 1915, 34; 1916, 25; 1917, 20; 1918, 17; 1919, 14; 1920, 13; 1921, 13; 1922, 12; 1923, 12; 1924, 11; 1925, 12; 1926, 12; 1927, 11; 1928, 9; 1929, 7; 1930, 7; 1931, 6; 1932, 6; 1933, 3; 1934, 3; 1935, 3; 1936, 3; 1937, 3; 1938, 2
LAST MEMBER: Augustus S. Anderson, died December 21, 1938, at age 90

Curtice Post 34—so it was chartered—was named for Charles E. Curtice from Whitewater who left his position as principal of the Whitewater Public Schools to lead the "Whitewater Light Infantry." He was captain of Company A, Fourth Wisconsin. The Fourth, of course, began as infantry and switched to cavalry midway through the war. Curtice served from April 1861 until he resigned February 15, 1865.

Members of C. E. Curtice Post 34, Whitewater, line up in the early 1900s. The flags around the posts bear 42 stars. Photo provided by the Walworth County Historical Society.

N. S. FROST POST 35, Prairie du Sac

SAUK COUNTY • JULY 1, 1882–1906

CHARTER MEMBERS: Philip Hoefer, Alex. McGinnis, Albert Mossback, J. W. Fancher, Jacob Bohn, Otto Stoddehman, Edward Oertel, L. Jergen, W. H. Waffle, G. Pheil, J. C. Pry, John Bleinlein, Alex. Ferber, J. A. Moore, W. A. Blackman, C. Cuind, Geo. Ferber, Wm. Logan, Josh McCoy, Frank Zimmerman, Stev. St. John, F. Clement, John Keller, John Wire, F. Groff

1866	1871	1876	1881	1886	1891	1896	1901	1906	1911	1916	1921	1926	1931	1936	1941	1946	1951

MEMBERSHIP BY YEAR (ACCOUNTED FOR): 1882, 25; 1884, 43; 1887, 35; 1888, 36; 1889, 40; 1900, 28; 1904, 20; 1905, 20   LAST MEMBER: Unknown

Captain Nathaniel S. Frost, a Prairie du Sac man, was captain of Company K of the Twenty-third Wisconsin Infantry when it entered service in August 1862. The regiment was first sent to Kentucky, and then to Tennessee in October and November. Captain Frost became ill in Memphis and died December 12, 1862, the first officer of the regiment to die. While the regiment saw combat in 1863 and 1864, its main losses were to illness. In all, 249 soldiers died of various illnesses. Post 35 was active until 1906. Its remaining members may have gone to other Sauk County posts that were nearby.

ALEX LOWRIE POST 36, Viroqua

VERNON COUNTY • JULY 17, 1882-1937

CHARTER MEMBERS: E. M. Rogers, J. H. Tate, H. A. Chase, T. G. Orr, H. C. Gosling, P. M. Peterson, L. Cobs, E. A. Wallar, Eugene Goman, R. S. McMichael, J. N. Curry, W. O. S. Whipple, Reuben May, S. Toney, M. C. Nichols, J. R. Casson, S. R. Pollard, William Clawater, D. W. C. Wilson, Ed Everitt, E. Kable, J. E. Newell, J. M. Vance, C. J. Cherrington, I. W. Blake, C. A. Roberts, Milton Southwick, Jos. Lamb, G. K. Hazen, H. P. Proctor, A. L. Russell, S. W. Clark

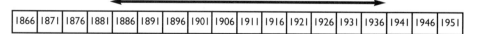

1866	1871	1876	1881	1886	1891	1896	1901	1906	1911	1916	1921	1926	1931	1936	1941	1946	1951

MEMBERSHIP BY YEAR (ACCOUNTED FOR): 1882, 32; 1884, 71; 1887, 98; 1888, 117; 1889, 128; 1904, 39; 1905, 30; 1906, 30; 1907, 28; 1908, 30; 1909, 30; 1910, 25; 1911, 25; 1912, 25; 1913, 27; 1914, 20; 1915, 20; 1916, 20; 1917, 15; 1918, 15; 1919, 14; 1920, 14; 1921, 14; 1922, 8; 1923, 7; 1924, 6; 1925, 9; 1926, 9; 1927, 5; 1928, 6; 1929, 6; 1930, 5; 1931, 5; 1932, 2; 1933, 2; 1934, 2; 1935, 1; 1936, 1   LAST MEMBER: Hugh Porter

The Alex Lowrie Post 36, Viroqua, bore the name of Alexander Lowrie from Jefferson, who was wounded at the Second Battle of Bull Run but continued in service until July 1865.

Lowrie joined Company I of the Sixth Wisconsin in 1861, one among some 15 new soldiers from Viroqua. Lowrie rose from the ranks to become an officer of that Iron Brigade company in 1864. He was appointed its captain on February 25, 1865, and finished his service at that rank. He died at Viroqua about two years before the post was organized. E. M. Rogers was the first commander.

Post 36 at its high point had well over one hundred members. Its decline was typical in many respects although its rolls were in single digits for 15 years, which was somewhat atypical.

PHIL W. PLUMMER POST 37, Prairie du Chien
CRAWFORD COUNTY • JULY 18, 1882–1941

CHARTER MEMBERS: Edward A. Whalen, commander; T. G. Bronson, senior vice commander; Amory Denis, junior vice commander; E. S. Eddy, adjutant; A. O. Wallin, quartermaster; S. E. Farnheim, chaplain; John Connant, surgeon; Daniel Webster, officer of the day; E. Van Vickle, guard; George Oswald, sergeant major; James Davidson, quartermaster sergeant

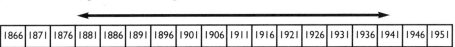

1866	1871	1876	1881	1886	1891	1896	1901	1906	1911	1916	1921	1926	1931	1936	1941	1946	1951

MEMBERSHIP BY YEAR (ACCOUNTED FOR): 1884, 42; 1887, 47; 1888, 49; 1889, 53; 1904, 39; 1905, 24; 1906, 21; 1907, 20; 1908, 20; 1909, 19; 1910, 19; 1911, 19; 1912, 19; 1913, 18; 1914, 18; 1915, 18; 1916, 15; 1917, 14; 1918, 12; 1919, 9; 1920, 10; 1921, 10; 1922, 8; 1923, 8; 1924, 8; 1925, 6; 1926, 6; 1927, 5; 1928, 4; 1929, 3; 1930, 3; 1931, 2; 1932, 2; 1933, 1; 1934, 2; 1935, 1; 1936, 1; 1937, 1; 1938, 1; 1939, 1   **LAST MEMBER:** William Huard

Phillip W. Plummer was the highest ranking of the 234 men of the Sixth Wisconsin to die from combat.

He left Prairie du Chien in June of 1861 as first lieutenant of Company C, the "Prairie du Chien Volunteers." He was major of the regiment in the famous Iron Brigade when he was killed at the Battle of the Wilderness on May 5, 1864.

Although it was never a large unit, the G.A.R. Post at Prairie du Chien maintained a core of dedicated members and bore the Plummer name for close to 70 years.

About a decade later, members of Plummer Post 37 again gather for a group picture. Photo provided by the Wisconsin Veterans Museum, Madison.

Decoration Day, 1908, Plummer Post at Prairie du Chien cemetery. Photo provided by the Wisconsin Veterans Museum, Madison.

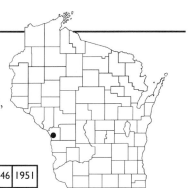

WILSON COLWELL POST 38, La Crosse
LA CROSSE COUNTY • AUGUST 17, 1882–1941

CHARTER MEMBERS: Edward Cronon, Milo Pitkin, Patrick Hallonan, B. F. Bryant, H. K. Vincent, E. Koops, T. J. Widney, G. M. Woodward, Charles S. Hildreth, Bernard Dunn, Charles A. Chatfield, Charles Otille, William Miller

1866	1871	1876	1881	1886	1891	1896	1901	1906	1911	1916	1921	1926	1931	1936	1941	1946	1951

MEMBERSHIP BY YEAR (ACCOUNTED FOR): 1884, 71; 1887, 124; 1888, 110; 1889, 145; 1904, 100; 1905, 99; 1906, 122; 1907, 122; 1908, 131; 1909, 125; 1910, 120; 1911, 116; 1912, 88; 1913, 87; 1914, 96; 1915, 91; 1916, 79; 1917, 66; 1918, 59; 1919, 52; 1920, 52; 1921, 54; 1922, 41; 1923, 41; 1924, 40; 1925, 30; 1926, 24; 1927, 20; 1928, 17; 1929, 17; 1930, 15; 1931, 17; 1932, 12; 1933, 11; 1934, 7; 1935, 6; 1936, 5; 1937, 2; 1938, 1; 1939, 1 **LAST MEMBER:** John A. Hart

WILSON COLWELL

When companies from across Wisconsin mustered in 1861 on President Lincoln's call for volunteers, Company B of La Crosse was one of the earliest to respond, and it was the first to arrive at Camp Randall in Madison in 1861 and joining the Second Wisconsin.

These La Crosse men were under the command of Captain Wilson Colwell, a native Pennsylvanian who had come to La Crosse in 1856. The story of Company B and of Colwell was the story of the Second Wisconsin—First Bull Run, Brawner's Farm, etc. The story for Colwell ended, however, September 14, 1862, when he was killed at South Mountain, Maryland, in the battle which gave to the Second and their comrades of the Sixth Wisconsin, Seventh Wisconsin, and Nineteenth Indiana the name of "Iron Brigade."

Wilson Colwell was the name selected when La Crosse veterans formed a G.A.R. Post in 1882. G. M. Woodward was the first commander. The post was one of western Wisconsin's largest ones and was an important contributor to the department for many years. It had almost one hundred members as late as World War I; it was one of the few posts to have more than a dozen members into the 1930s.

This picture of Wilson Colwell was taken at the Brady Studio in Washington, presumably in 1861 when the Second Wisconsin was stationed near there and still had their state-issue gray uniforms. Note the shoulder holster. This type of pose was frequently used to illustrate the tough nature of the westerners comprising the Iron Brigade. Photo provided by the Wisconsin Veterans Museum, Madison.

THOMAS HUNGERFORD POST 39, Spring Green

SAUK COUNTY • JULY 15, 1882–1941

CHARTER MEMBERS: D. D. Davies, commander; G. G. Reely, senior vice commander; W. H. Harris, junior vice commander; A. M. Hungerford, adjutant; Joseph Randal, quartermaster; J. G. Pelton, surgeon; W. M. Hathaway, chaplain; J. C. Hutson, officer of the day; Christ Aron, officer of the guard; J. D. Davies, sergeant major; L. Flinn, quartermaster sergeant

1866	1871	1876	1881	1886	1891	1896	1901	1906	1911	1916	1921	1926	1931	1936	1941	1946	1951

MEMBERSHIP BY YEAR (ACCOUNTED FOR): 1882, 21; 1884, 45; 1887, 49; 1888, 49; 1889, 52; 1904, 24; 1905, 20; 1906, 22; 1907, 23; 1908, 23; 1909, 23; 1910, 25; 1911, 23; 1912, 20; 1913, 19; 1914, 18; 1915, 16; 1916, 13; 1917, 13; 1918, 12; 1919, 11; 1920, 10; 1921, 10; 1922, 10; 1923, 10; 1924, 8; 1925, 5; 1926, 5; 1927, 5; 1928, 5; 1929, 3; 1930, 3; 1931, 3; 1932, 3; 1933, 2; 1934, 2; 1935, 1; 1936, 1; 1937, 1; 1938, 1; 1939, 1 **LAST MEMBER:** Fred Radel

Post 39 at Spring Green was named for one of the soldiers who left that Sauk County community in 1861, Thomas J. Hungerford. He was one of thirty-five Town of Spring Green boys who enlisted in the Sixth Wisconsin Battery. They fought in the armies in the West, and saw their heaviest fighting in the Battle of Corinth, sustaining twenty-seven casualties out of

ninety-seven engaged. Hungerford served his full three-year term, being mustered out on October 10, 1864.

The Hungerford Post, along with posts at Reedsburg and Baraboo, served Sauk County until the 1940s. The county had considerable impact upon the affairs of the department.

STOCKBRIDGE POST 40
BENJAMIN J. SWEET POST 40, Stockbridge

CALUMET COUNTY • OCTOBER 6, 1882–1920

CHARTER MEMBERS: Henry O. Dudley, Alfred J. Woosley, Christian Heller, Friedrich Pingel, Geo. W. Howe, Abr'm F. Hunter, Ozias C. Smith, Sam'l Aebischer, Warren Holt, W. H. Cook, Wm. Leander Eastman, Royal O. Bigford, Alfred C. Nugent, John M. Merrill, Napoleon Ebert, Michael Mayer, Geo. A. Johnson, Phineas Drake, J. H. Greely

1866	1871	1876	1881	1886	1891	1896	1901	1906	1911	1916	1921	1926	1931	1936	1941	1946	1951

MEMBERSHIP BY YEAR (ACCOUNTED FOR): 1882, 19; 1884, 46; 1887, 40; 1888, 43; 1889, 63; 1904, 14; 1905, 16; 1906, 16; 1907, 13; 1908, 12; 1909, 12; 1910, 10; 1911, 10; 1912, 8; 1913, 8; 1914, 8; 1915, 7; 1916, 9; 1917, 9; 1918, 7; 1919, 6   LAST MEMBER: Unknown

BENJAMIN
SWEET

The G.A.R. post at Stockbridge was known simply as Stockbridge Post 40 for its first two years, then chose to commemorate one of Calumet County's honored soldiers, Colonel Benjamin J. Sweet.

Sweet was the major of the Sixth Wisconsin when it left in 1861, and he served with that regiment until, in August 1862, he was appointed colonel of the Twenty-first Wisconsin. That regiment was organized at Camp Bragg, Oshkosh, and less than a month after deploying was heavily engaged in the battle at Perryville, Kentucky, where Colonel Sweet was seriously wounded. He was never able to rejoin the regiment.

THEODORE L. SUTPHEN POST 41, Evansville

ROCK COUNTY • SEPTEMBER 24, 1882–1943

CHARTER MEMBERS: James R. West, Henry W. Hamilton, William F. Williams, S. J. Baker, A. C. Thorpe, A. C. Gray, J. M. Evans, C. M. Smith, C. B. Morse, Josiah W. Blake, E. B. Mifflin, W. W. Eastman, James N. Patterson, D. H. Johnson, H. V. Jones, James R. Brown, Morris E. Waite, Joe H. West, George W. Hayward, Harrison Thompson, William H. Wainwright, C. A. Libby, George W. Dibble, George M. Bidwell, Martin B. Crary, William W. Wiggins, Patrick McGlenn, Wendell Powers, William Burk, William Wilcox, J. E. Gleave, E. S. Casler

1866	1871	1876	1881	1886	1891	1896	1901	1906	1911	1916	1921	1926	1931	1936	1941	1946	1951

MEMBERSHIP BY YEAR (ACCOUNTED FOR): 1884, 78; 1887, 57; 1888, 52; 1889, 50; 1904, 37; 1905, 38; 1906, 38; 1907, 35; 1908, 36; 1909, 36; 1910, 35; 1911, 34; 1912, 35; 1913, 27; 1914, 25; 1915, 24; 1916, 23; 1917, 16; 1918, 17; 1919, 15; 1920, 14; 1921, 12; 1922, 12; 1923, 12; 1924, 9; 1925, 9; 1926, 9; 1927, 9; 1929, 2; 1930, 5; 1931, 3; 1932, 2; 1933, 2; 1934, 2; 1935, 1; 1936, 1; 1937, 1; 1938, 1; 1939, 1   LAST MEMBER: J. Gardner Babcock

Theodore L. Sutphen, an Evansville soldier, was a member of Company H, Second Wisconsin Infantry, enlisting at the outset of the Civil War.

After the Second was brigaded with the Sixth and Seventh Wisconsin and the Nineteenth Indiana, they waited months for their first action. They were part of the Army of Virginia, General Pope's Army, seeking to locate Stonewall Jackson near Manassas. Jackson's army came out of hiding as a brigade, Gibbons', was marching past on the evening of August 28, 1862, and the Confederates hit the unsuspecting Federals hard. The Second suffered the worst casualties, and among those killed at Brawner's Farm that evening was Private Sutphen in this baptism of fire for the Iron Brigade.

Post 41 of Evansville was never one of the large ones, but it played a prominent role in Evansville life and continued in existence into the 1940s.

HENRY W. CRESSEY POST 42, Tomah

MONROE COUNTY • AUGUST 14, 1882–1936

CHARTER MEMBERS: J. B. Adams, C. A. Adams, William Alexander, W. N. Alverson, E. L. Bolton, H. S. Beardsley, A. D. Benjamin, W. T. Bristol, J. H. Beardsley, D. F. Crandall, E. L. Craig, W. H. Calkins, C. A. Crawford, C. K. Erwin, Charles Gilson, George Braham, H. D. Hollenbeck, Fred Johnson, S. Armstrong, A. W. Alderman, John Burnham

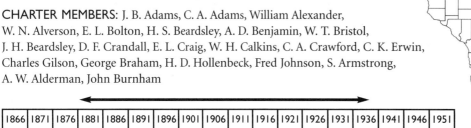

| 1866 | 1871 | 1876 | 1881 | 1886 | 1891 | 1896 | 1901 | 1906 | 1911 | 1916 | 1921 | 1926 | 1931 | 1936 | 1941 | 1946 | 1951 |

MEMBERSHIP BY YEAR (ACCOUNTED FOR): 1887, 52; 1888, 52; 1889, 57; 1904, 61; 1905, 55; 1906, 57; 1907, 55; 1908, 48; 1909, 45; 1910, 44; 1911, 43; 1912, 40; 1913, 33; 1914, 34; 1915, 27; 1916, 24; 1917, 19; 1918, 20; 1919, 17; 1920, 15; 1921, 14; 1922, 10; 1923, 8; 1924, 7; 1925, 7; 1926, 3; 1929, 3; 1930, 3; 1932, 2; 1933, 2; 1934, 1; 1935, 1

LAST MEMBER: A. E. Hollister

The Twenty-fifth Wisconsin was recruited in the western part of the state in 1862. One of its principal officers was future Governor Jeremiah Rusk.

The regiment was active in the Mississippi River valley but saw little combat until the Twenty-fifth joined Sherman's army in 1864. One of its major engagements was at Decatur, Georgia,

where the regiment suffered 18 killed or mortally wounded, its largest single battle loss. One of these was Private Henry W. Cressey of Company D, from Tomah.

It was to honor Cressey that the G.A.R. Post 42 in his home town chose his name. Cressey Post remained on the books until about 1935.

More often than not, group pictures of G.A.R. posts that have been preserved fail to identify all the men pictured on it. Not so this photo of Cressey Post 42 of Tomah. (It does, however, lack the other very common failing: a date.) Photo provided by the Monroe County Local History Room & Library, Sparta.

Seated, front row, from left: F. Weiss, Tom Reeke, Joe McGinis, H. O. Bigelow, Robert King, Joe Alton, N. Dinsmore, H. Fanning, Joe Organ, H. Leffingwell, B. Armstrong, W. Sherwood

Middle row, from left: H. S. Beardsley, E. Branan, J. H. Kellogg, J. Burnham, L. D. Wyatt, D. P. Rockwood, E. B. Marvin, D. Thompson, John Brecker, G. H. Dobbins, G. Waltenberger, N. R. Richardson

Top row, from left: E. G. Kinney, E. W. Cowles, J. Perry, A. Getman, C. W. Kenyon, J. Vandervort, Nathan Corey, I. Vandervort, W. B. Cassels, M. Flint, C. Vandervort, W. McLean, D. Spooner, H. C. Spaulding

RAYMOND POST 43, Mayville

DODGE COUNTY • AUGUST 23, 1882–1935

CHARTER MEMBERS: P. B. Lamoreaux, G. J. Clark, S. W. Lamoreaux, Pierre Peruot, C. R. Henderson, Lewis R. Baker, Chas. Rassow, Julius Nary, David Baum, Valentine Schwartz, August Clummer, Chris. Heckert, J. Zimmermann, Chas. Krueger, N. C. Lawrence, Fred Neiman, Eugene Barrott (as listed on reissued charter February 13, 1893)

1866	1871	1876	1881	1886	1891	1896	1901	1906	1911	1916	1921	1926	1931	1936	1941	1946	1951

MEMBERSHIP BY YEAR (ACCOUNTED FOR): 1882, 66; 1884, 26; 1887, 26; 1888, 27; 1889, 27; 1904, 23; 1905, 23; 1906, 22; 1907, 20; 1908, 21; 1909, 20; 1910, 20; 1911, 21; 1912, 22; 1913, 19; 1914, 17; 1915, 15; 1916, 11; 1917, 11; 1918, 11; 1919, 11; 1920, 10; 1921, 10; 1922, 9; 1923, 8; 1924, 8; 1925, 5; 1926, 4; 1927, 4; 1928, 3; 1929, 2; 1930, 1; 1932, 2; 1933, 1; 1934, 1   **LAST MEMBER:** Dr. D. J. Clark

An unidentified Post 43 member and his wife

The Grand Army Post at Mayville was always referred to simply as "Raymond Post 43." In fact, the post was named for Charles Raymond from Mayville, who had enlisted at the outset of the war in the Williamstown Union Rifles, which became Company E, Third Wisconsin. Raymond rose to corporal and served through the regiment's varied experiences until Chancellorsville, where he was killed May 3, 1863.

Raymond Post was one of eight Dodge County posts active from before the turn of the twentieth century; the county was a fertile G.A.R. area. Raymond Post was apparently never large. But its membership stayed relatively level well into the 1900s.

Courtesy, Mayville American Legion and Kevin Dier-Zimmel. Members of Raymond Post 43 pose for a picture in 1900. Front row, from left: Mike Lehner, Eugene Barrott, August Kluenner, Leonard Kehrmeyer, Frank Youngbeck; Second row, from left: Gottfried Bonack, Val. Schwartz, John Wild, Louis Lehner, Matt Haertle, Charles Rossow, Charles R. Henderson, William Borngraeber; Third row, from left: Herman Neitzel Sr., Charles Greget, George Holland, Charles Herker; Top row, from left: Gustav Rost, Charles Marquardt, Adolph Dowie

JOSEPH P. SHEPARD POST 44, Menasha

WINNEBAGO COUNTY • SEPTEMBER 8, 1882–MAY 1, 1933

CHARTER MEMBERS: Joseph Hinson, Norman Thatcher, J. C. Mossop, R. W. Northam, H. A. Eldredge, J. H. Dewolf, E. A. Eldredge, L. A. Phetteplace, A. W. Frances, C. C. Washburn, C. H. Van Cott, T. D. Phillips, J. J. Marshall, C. F. Augustin, W. E. Wheeler, P. Fileatreau, J. McCandless, George M. Payne, C. C. Bixby, C. A. Robinson, George W. Bradley, J. C. Goldsburough, G. H. Keyes, C. V. Donaldson, Fred Hercher, George W. Fay

1866	1871	1876	1881	1886	1891	1896	1901	1906	1911	1916	1921	1926	1931	1936	1941	1946	1951

MEMBERSHIP BY YEAR (ACCOUNTED FOR): 1882, 23; 1887, 42; 1888, 51; 1889, 54; 1904, 23; 1905, 24; 1906, 34; 1907, 25; 1908, 31; 1909, 31; 1910, 28; 1911, 30; 1912, 31; 1913, 30; 1914, 27; 1915, 26; 1916, 27; 1917, 24; 1918, 22; 1919, 17; 1920, 14; 1921, 9; 1922, 8; 1923, 8; 1924, 8; 1925, 7; 1926, 5; 1927, 5; 1928, 4; 1929, 3; 1930, 3; 1931, 1; 1932, 1; 1933, 1   LAST MEMBER: C. S. Lloyd, died May 1, 1933, at age 91

Menasha veterans of the Civil War named their G.A.R. Post 44 after Joseph Preston Shepard, a Menasha man who was a victim of the war.

Shepard went to war with Company G, Third Wisconsin, at the outset and was commissioned a second lieutenant by the end of 1861. His leg was shattered at Antietam in the famous fight for the cornfield—the Iron Brigade was not the only unit in that cornfield—and he died from the effect of this wound several weeks later, on November 10, 1861, at Frederick, Maryland. He is buried at Westfield, Massachusetts.

Although the men are not identified, they are probably the nine remaining members of Shepard Post 44 in 1921. Photo provided by the Menasha Historical Society.

DARLINGTON POST 45, (LOUIS P.) HARVEY POST 45, Darlington
LAFAYETTE COUNTY • OCTOBER 19, 1882–1937

CHARTER MEMBERS: R. H. Williams, J. F. McGinley, S. F. Stewart, L. A. Bigler, J. G. Knight, D. B. Dipple, J. B. Driver, Frank Walsh, C. Vickars, E. R. Campbell, John Haurahan, Geo. F. West, H. Southwick, James Dunbar, Silas Hill, J. Mullen, A. Baker, J. M. Dain

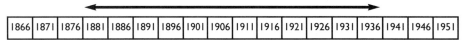

1866	1871	1876	1881	1886	1891	1896	1901	1906	1911	1916	1921	1926	1931	1936	1941	1946	1951

MEMBERSHIP BY YEAR (ACCOUNTED FOR): 1882, 18; 1887, 62; 1888, 61; 1889, 72; 1904, 42; 1905, 42; 1906, 42; 1907, 41; 1908, 40; 1909, 36; 1910, 31; 1911, 31; 1912, 30; 1913, 26; 1914, 22; 1915, 19; 1916, 19; 1917, 17; 1918, 13; 1919, 15; 1920, 15; 1921, 16; 1922, 15; 1923, 11; 1924, 11; 1925, 10; 1926, 9; 1927, 8; 1928, 8; 1929, 4; 1930, 4; 1931, 3; 1932, 3; 1933, 3; 1934, 1; 1935, 1; 1936, 1   LAST MEMBER: D. C. McCauley or Ed Stott

L. P. HARVEY

Four Grand Army posts in Wisconsin were named after the state's war-victim governor, Louis P. Harvey.

A brief post at Green Bay, from 1876 to about 1879, was first. Post 16, Amherst, was second, lasting from 1880 to 1883. Racine Post 17 in 1881 chose to honor Harvey, going by "Governor Harvey Post 17." Three years later, Post 45, after being known as "Darlington Post" for two years, also wished to honor Harvey. They were known simply as "Harvey Post 45." (Harvey's biographical information is given at Post 17 and at Post 16, Amherst.)

Harvey Post 45 continued until 1937.

HENRY TURNER POST 46, New London

WAUPACA COUNTY • SEPTEMBER 26, 1882–1938

CHARTER MEMBERS: S. D. Woodworth, Anthony Trayser, James C. Turney, Ira J. J. Turney, Aaron P. Ritter, Josiah Blackwood, Gabriel W. Cornish, Chas. F. Waterman, Henry Libby, J. F. Jacobus, M. B. Patchin, H. S. Pickard, H. P. Briggs, A. P. Masher, Wm. C. Kroll, E. W. Dexter, John C. Kroll, Thos. Logan, J. W. Dean

1866	1871	1876	1881	1886	1891	1896	1901	1906	1911	1916	1921	1926	1931	1936	1941	1946	1951

MEMBERSHIP BY YEAR (ACCOUNTED FOR): 1882, 19; 1884, 43; 1887, 57; 1888, 62; 1889, 75; 1904, 22; 1905, 21; 1906, 24; 1907, 24; 1908, 21; 1909, 20; 1910, 21; 1911, 29; 1912, 37; 1913, 39; 1914, 36; 1915, 40; 1916, 40; 1917, 36; 1918, 30; 1919, 24; 1920, 22; 1921, 20; 1922, 19; 1923, 13; 1924, 10; 1925, 11; 1926, 9; 1927, 7; 1928, 7; 1929, 4; 1930, 4; 1931, 4; 1932, 4; 1933, 4; 1934, 2; 1935, 2; 1936, 1; 1937, 1   **LAST MEMBER:** James Harland Heath, died May, 1937

MARC AND BETH STORCH
HENRY TURNER

G.A.R. Post 46, formed in New London in 1882, was named after Henry Turner.

Turner entered the service as first lieutenant of Company D, Twenty-first Wisconsin, which was organized in the fall of 1862. The company was recruited from Waupaca County. He was appointed captain of the company when its original captain died in November 1862, and Turner served as such until March 1865. Turner was grievously wounded in the neck during the Atlanta campaign, the ball going between the jugular and windpipe. He survived the war and died in Menasha not long before the New London Post was formed.

Post 46's minutes mention him on March 13, 1883, telling of receiving a portrait of Turner from a former surgeon of the Twenty-first to "honor the name and memory of our gallant comrade." Its present location is not known.

Post 46 met in the upper rooms of this building (entrance on right), sharing quarters there with the Odd Fellows.

James Harland (Harley) Heath, the last surviving member of Post 46.

Henry Turner Post 46 firing squad at a Decoration Day gathering, date unknown. Photo provided by the New London Public Museum.

HENRY C. MILES POST 47
FRANK PREVY POST 47, Elroy

JUNEAU COUNTY • OCTOBER 6, 1882–1936

CHARTER MEMBERS: James McClure, Henry Jones, Charles Beale, Starr (first name unknown), A. B. Doolittle, L. Johnson, E. W. Lake, Eliet Wyman, W. W. Millard, A. A. Starr, H. W. Nash, A. W. Alderman, C. E. Booth, C. H. Sherman, I. N. DuBois, William Stiedy, Tom Lindley, James Farra, Luman Pearsall, B. Harmon, C. Haas, Nelson Squire, Norris Philps, Philip Weber, William H. VanHoozen, R. W. Fowler, George Sweetland, Maffet (first name unknown)

1866	1871	1876	1881	1886	1891	1896	1901	1906	1911	1916	1921	1926	1931	1936	1941	1946	1951

MEMBERSHIP BY YEAR (ACCOUNTED FOR): 1882, 28; 1884, 13; 1887, 29; 1888, 24; 1889, 23; 1904, 23; 1905, 23; 1906, 18; 1907, 18; 1908, 15; 1909, 10; 1910, 20; 1911, 20; 1912, 20; 1913, 15; 1914, 10; 1915, 10; 1916, 10; 1917, 7; 1918, 7; 1919, 12; 1920, 11; 1921, 10; 1922, 10; 1923, 10; 1924, 7; 1925, 7; 1926, 6; 1927, 7; 1928, 7; 1929, 4; 1930, 3; 1931, 3; 1932, 3; 1933, 3; 1934, 2; 1935, 2; 1936, 2   **LAST MEMBER:** Unknown

The first name adopted by Post 47 of Elroy at its origin in 1882 was that of Henry C. Miles from Janesville, who was captain of Company F of the Thirty-fifth Wisconsin. Miles was dismissed from service in November 1864.

The post changed its name to Frank Prevy Post about 1888. Prevy was a soldier in Company F, Sixteenth Wisconsin,

and was among the 40 soldiers of that regiment killed on April 6, 1862, at Shiloh.

The first commander of the Elroy Post was Tom Lindley. The post was never large, having less than 30 members in all the years reports exist save one, yet the post continued into the 1930s.

LYON POST 48, Cazenovia
RICHLAND COUNTY • 1866 OR 1867–JULY 24, 1874

CHARTER MEMBERS: Unknown

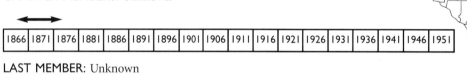

LAST MEMBER: Unknown

NATHANIEL LYON

Lyon Post 48, of Cazenovia was one of those very early posts that survived the November 1871 wholesale culling of the Department of Wisconsin, moving up, in fact to Post 5 at the same time the Berlin Post moved up from 22 to 4. Thereafter, however, nothing else is known of the post, and it was dropped from the G.A.R.'s rolls on the de-

partment's second cleansing of inactive posts in 1874.

The name Lyon presumably was chosen to honor General Nathaniel Lyon, who commanded Union forces in Missouri in the first year of the war. His forcefulness possibly kept that state in the Union. In leading his forces against Confederates at Wilson's Creek in August 1861, Lyon was killed leading a charge, making him the first Union general killed in the war. He was thus posthumously acclaimed a hero.

CHARLES G. BACON POST 48, Neillsville
CLARK COUNTY • NOVEMBER 24, 1882–1932

CHARTER MEMBERS: J. H. Kimball, commander; J. W. Tolford, senior vice commander; E. H. Markey, junior vice commander; Fred Reitz, adjutant; J. W. Ferguson, officer of the day; Henry Fuller, officer of the guard; E. L. Hoffman, quartermaster; James A. Barkhurst, quartermaster sergeant; Tom B. Philpott, surgeon; T. V. Carlton, chaplain

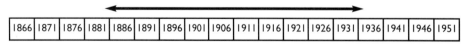

MEMBERSHIP BY YEAR (ACCOUNTED FOR): 1887, 71; 1888, 55; 1889, 55; 1904, 44; 1905, 32; 1906, 30; 1907, 32; 1908, 35; 1909, 34; 1910, 31; 1911, 34; 1912, 36; 1913, 27; 1914, 25; 1915, 25; 1916, 25; 1917, 19; 1918, 14; 1919, 12; 1920, 12; 1921, 12; 1922, 12; 1930, 3; 1931, 2; 1932, 2   **LAST MEMBER:** Unknown

The Grand Army post at Neillsville, Post 48, chartered in 1882, elected to honor a young Neillsville soldier, son of Orson Bacon, one of the early settlers in that part of Clark County.

The son was Charles G. Bacon, a soldier in Company I, Fourteenth Wisconsin, who was among those wounded at Shiloh on April 6, 1862. The younger Bacon died of his wounds at St. Louis a month later.

Post 48 had a fairly large membership in its early years, given the community's size, and a dozen veterans remained

members as late as 1922. There were no more reports from then until 1930, and the post was extinct after 1932.

A. A. MATTHEWS POST 49, La Valle

SAUK COUNTY • OCTOBER 26, 1882–1901

CHARTER MEMBERS: Unknown

1866	1871	1876	1881	1886	1891	1896	1901	1906	1911	1916	1921	1926	1931	1936	1941	1946	1951

MEMBERSHIP BY YEAR (ACCOUNTED FOR): 1884, 35; 1887, 20; 1888, 25; 1889, 41
LAST MEMBER: Unknown

The La Valle Post was named for Alfred A. Matthews, a private in Company G, Twenty-ninth Wisconsin Volunteer Infantry. Matthews enlisted from La Valle. He was wounded on May 16, 1863 at the Battle of Champions Hill during the Vicksburg Campaign. He died from his wounds on June 12, 1863.

The town where Matthews Post was active was, at that time, spelled "Lavalle." Its present spelling was adopted in 1924.

Matthews Post joined Gillespie Post of Wisconsin Dells in sponsoring the department's first "picket post" (see chapter regarding Picket Posts) at Delton in 1893.

The Matthews post surrendered its charter during 1901, or possibly early 1902, according to the 1902 state encampment journal.

W. S. ROSECRANS POST 49, Grantsburg

BURNETT COUNTY • NOVEMBER 10, 1902–1910

CHARTER MEMBERS: D. W. Fox (Co. A, 55th Penn.), John H. DeGrow (Co. I, 50th Penn.), Wm H. Palmer (Co. A, 3rd Wis. Cav.), Hans Jenson (Co. E, 2nd Minn. Inf.), Joel A. Hickerson (Co. C, 7th Minn. Inf.), P. D. Hickerson (Co. C, 7th Minn. Inf.), Ole C. Branstad (Co. A, 15th Wis. Inf.), E. P. Buck (Co. E, 1st Minn. Inf.), Erick Erickson (Co. E, 13th Ill. Inf.), Lorenzo D. Morris (Co. D, 2nd Colorado Inf.), D. E. Means (1st Minn. Batt. Light Art.), Newton Hickerson (Co. D, 21st Ohio Inf.) S. D. Rice (1st Batt. Yates Sharpshooters), Noble Wilson

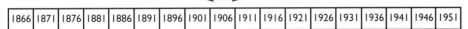

1866	1871	1876	1881	1886	1891	1896	1901	1906	1911	1916	1921	1926	1931	1936	1941	1946	1951

MEMBERSHIP BY YEAR (ACCOUNTED FOR): 1902, 14; 1905, 15; 1906, 15; 1907, 14; 1908, 14; 1909, 13
LAST MEMBER: Unknown

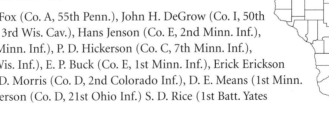

W.S. ROSECRANS

Rosecrans Post 49 was one of the last posts chartered (1902) and its charter portrays the changing times. It lists the units with which the members served. By then, many veterans had pulled up roots and made a life elsewhere. Most of Post 49's original members served with units from other states.

They chose to name the post after General William S. Rosecrans, who had a good record as commander of the Army of the Cumberland until he blundered at Chickamauga. Rosecrans was known for working well with volunteer troops. After the war he was active in the G.A.R. He died in 1898, just four years before the post at Grantsburg was organized.

Post membership essentially remained within a member or two of its original 14, and the post lasted only until 1910.

JOHN GILLESPIE POST 50,
Wisconsin Dells (Kilbourn City)

COLUMBIA COUNTY • OCTOBER 26, 1882–1932

CHARTER MEMBERS: Unknown

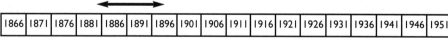

1866	1871	1876	1881	1886	1891	1896	1901	1906	1911	1916	1921	1926	1931	1936	1941	1946	1951

MEMBERSHIP BY YEAR (ACCOUNTED FOR): 1879, 12; 1884, 17; 1887, 18; 1888, 22; 1889, 28; 1904, 17; 1905, 16; 1906, 16; 1907, 15; 1908, 15; 1909, 14; 1910, 13; 1911, 9; 1912, 8; 1913, 10; 1914, 10; 1915, 10; 1916, 10; 1917, 7; 1918, 7; 1919, 7; 1920, 7; 1921, 5   **LAST MEMBER:** Unknown

MARC AND BETH STORCH
JOHN GILLESPIE

Post 50 was named after John Gillespie, who enlisted immedately after Fort Sumter on April 17, 1861, in Company E of the three-month First Wisconsin. He was released August 21, then joined Company E of the Twelfth Wisconsin on September 7, 1861. Gillespie was named first lieutenant on October 3, then captain on May 11 of the following year. In the Atlanta campaign he was wounded on July 21, 1864, and taken prisoner. The wound necessitated amputating his arm. Gillespie was mustered out June 7, 1865. He was elected to the state assembly for one term in 1868. He died January 21, 1871.

In its first decade the post membership exceeded one hundred, but it was less than half that in the early twentieth century. Gillespie Post joined with Matthews Post of La Valle in sponsoring the "picket post" at Delton, the first such adjunct group in the Department of Wisconsin.

WILLIAM WRIGHT POST 51, Excelsior

RICHLAND COUNTY • OCTOBER 27, 1882–DECEMBER 1896

CHARTER MEMBERS: B. F. Washburn; A. M. Stratton; C. J. Moore, commander; Samuel Yeager; William E. Morgan; D. G. Watters; H. S. Brown; Edward Smith, junior vice commander; David Clark; A. B. Shannon; Lewis Craigo, senior vice commander; William Guilliford; Edward Dosch, adjutant; and Alonzo Packer

1866	1871	1876	1881	1886	1891	1896	1901	1906	1911	1916	1921	1926	1931	1936	1941	1946	1951

MEMBERSHIP BY YEAR (ACCOUNTED FOR): 1883, 53; 1887, 20; 1888, 23; 1889, 21   **LAST MEMBER:** Unknown

Post 51 of Excelsior was named for William Wright, a veteran of Company B, Twenty-fifth Wisconsin, who served his term and returned to Excelsior to resume farming. He died at a relatively young age, a popular figure in his community. A childhood friend of Wright, Edward Dosch, the first adjutant, suggested that the post be named in his honor. William Wright Post began with a big surge of membership, more than tripling the enrollment in its first 12 months. But thereafter it gradually declined and was defunct by 1896.

STARKWEATHER POST 51, Bear Creek
OUTAGAMIE COUNTY • NOVEMBER 26, 1897–1913

CHARTER MEMBERS: Anderson Conner, Clark Smith, Geo. Richardson, Chas. Thielke, John Raisler, Gotlieb Raisler, Isaac Thorn, Richard Thorn, Eben Pusher, Solomon Bean, James Davis, Geo. Phillippi, Henry Calkins, Nelson Leanna, Robt. Grindle, Warren Jepsen, Washington Holt, E. Culbertson, Chas. Shoepke, Samuel Plumb, Reuben Sweet, David McGlin, Oliver Besaw, M. Sweeney

1866	1871	1876	1881	1886	1891	1896	1901	1906	1911	1916	1921	1926	1931	1936	1941	1946	1951

MEMBERSHIP BY YEAR (ACCOUNTED FOR): 1898, 24; 1904, 70; 1905, 16; 1906, 16; 1907, 15; 1908, 9; 1909, 8; 1910, 7; 1911, 5; 1912, 5   **LAST MEMBER:** Unknown

CRAIG JOHNSON
J. C. STARKWEATHER

When President Lincoln called for 75,000 militiamen after Fort Sumter, Wisconsin's quota was one regiment. This, the First Wisconsin, was led off to the seat of war in Virginia by Colonel John C. Starkweather. This was a three-months regiment, and it saw action at the fight called Falling Waters before its term expired and it returned to Wisconsin. Immediately thereafter Starkweather organized the new First Wisconsin, a three-year regiment, and it fought in the western theater the remainder of its term. Starkweather rose to brigade command and was promoted to brigadier general. When old soldiers in the Bear Creek area organized Post 51 in 1897, they chose to honor the man who led Wisconsin's first citizen soldiers to war 36 years before.

Men of Starkweather Post 51 pose at a memorial to assassinated President William McKinley in 1901. Note the somber setting, with its black-draped ribbons. The site was apparently a Catholic church, with pews, communion rail, and picture of the Sacred Heart in the background.

EAGLE POST 52, Eau Claire
EAU CLAIRE COUNTY • AUGUST 26, 1879–1942

CHARTER MEMBERS: E. M. Bartelt, Geo. A. Barry, J. L. Johnson, A. W. Munger, Myron Briggs, Thomas J. Hill, Victor Wolf, E. W. Allen, H. R. Curtiss, G. W. Britton, J. B. Demarest, M. E. O'Connell, Ira Shoemaker, J. F. Ellis, Geo. Lenz, D. C. Hope, Geo. W. Churchill, E. J. Farr, L. P. Hotchkiss, L. G. Delano, Jere Murphy, N. B. Rundle, Truman H. Hurlburt

1866	1871	1876	1881	1886	1891	1896	1901	1906	1911	1916	1921	1926	1931	1936	1941	1946	1951

MEMBERSHIP BY YEAR (ACCOUNTED FOR): 1882, 23; 1887, 179; 1888, 188; 1889, 210; 1904, 106; 1905, 110; 1906, 97; 1907, 109; 1908, 117; 1909, 113; 1910, 129; 1911, 123; 1912, 119; 1913, 112; 1914, 104; 1915, 103; 1916, 95; 1917, 80; 1918, 72; 1919, 66; 1920, 63; 1921, 60; 1922, 48; 1923, 46; 1924, 46; 1925, 47; 1926, 41; 1927, 41; 1928, 33; 1929, 31; 1930, 26; 1931, 21; 1932, 19; 1933, 16; 1934, 13; 1935, 12; 1936, 11; 1937, 9; 1938, 7; 1939, 6
LAST MEMBER: Unknown

OLD ABE

The most famous military mascot of the Civil War—some say in any war, since he's symbolized into the twenty-first century by the 101st Airborne's Screaming Eagle emblem—was "Old Abe," born in the Wisconsin wilds and carried off to war by a company of young Eau Claire volunteers. Old Abe became legendary, and it seems almost automatic that some of those young men, when they got together and formed a G.A.R. post, would name it for that mascot.

Eagle Post 52 of Eau Claire was distinguished among its peers, even as the Eighth Wisconsin was by the presence of Old Abe, and was a significant force in the Department of Wisconsin, providing it with two department commanders, Michael Griffin (1887) and Charles Henry (1913) and several other leaders.

The post was also a particularly strong one insofar as numbers was concerned. In 1912 it still had an enrollment of more

than one hundred members. Parenthetically, just four of the post's veterans were former members of Company C, Eighth Wisconsin, which brought Old Able along with them to Camp Randall in 1861: J. B. Demarest, Thomas J. Hill, John A. Jones and Charles Strasburg.

Another noteworthy characteristic of the men of Eagle Post 52: they were above the ordinarily hale and hearty. As late as the state encampment of 1934, the Eagle delegation numbered seven, and that was better than half the men on the roster of Post 52 that year.

The Eagle Post delegation poses at the 1934 Appleton Encampment. Photo provided by the Wisconsin Veterans Museum, Madison.

GEORGE W. BELL POST 53, Wonewoc

JUNEAU COUNTY • NOVEMBER 18, 1882–1942

CHARTER MEMBERS: Unknown

1866	1871	1876	1881	1886	1891	1896	1901	1906	1911	1916	1921	1926	1931	1936	1941	1946	1951

MEMBERSHIP BY YEAR (ACCOUNTED FOR): 1882, 66; 1887, 19; 1888, 14; 1889, 21; 1904, 23; 1905, 27; 1906, 24; 1907, 21; 1908, 25; 1909, 26; 1910, 23; 1911, 27; 1912, 25; 1913, 20; 1914, 21; 1915, 22; 1916, 20; 1917, 17; 1918, 16; 1919, 13; 1920, 12; 1921, 12; 1922, 10; 1923, 8; 1924, 7; 1925, 7; 1926, 6; 1927, 5; 1928, 4; 1929, 4; 1930, 3; 1931, 3; 1932, 3; 1933, 3; 1934, 3; 1935, 3; 1936, 2; 1937, 2; 1938, 1; 1939, 2   **LAST MEMBER:** Lawrence Snyder

Post 53 of Wonewoc was named after a Wonewoc boy, George W. Bell, who enlisted in Company B, Twelfth Wisconsin, in 1861, subsequently extended his enlistment, and was wounded before Atlanta in 1864. He died on August 4, 1864, at Marietta, Georgia, of his wounds.

The post maintained a strong membership for many years and remained on department rolls until 1941.

Members of Post 53 in the early 1900s. Back, from left: Joseph Snyder, Walt Drake, Lawrence Snyder, Isaac Huff, Hamburg (first name unknown), Henry W. Brown, an unknown man, John Segebrecht, JMV 'Joe' Sloniker. Middle, from left: Martin Hanzlik, Bill Church, _____, Phillip Dolen. Front: Eugene Dake, Rufus Griffa. Photo provided by Jim and Cindy Visgar.

LOUIS H. D. CRANE POST 54, Beloit
ROCK COUNTY • NOVEMBER 21, 1882–1939

CHARTER MEMBERS: S. Sherman, A. W. Bullock, J. W. Field, H. S. Hendee, John H. Lyle, Henry O. Mahar, W. H. Gilbert, R. J. Butler, J. M. Hoyt, W. H. Grinnell, Oscar Graves, Frank S. Walker, Chauncey H. Parmely, Chalmers Ingersoll, C. C. Wells, Geo. W. West, Edwin F. Hollister, Simon Smith, Luther C. Irish, W. H. Wheeler, Hugh Rilley, Chas. A. Rathbun, A. Malone, H. B. Haskell, S. L. Bibbins, Charles Newburgh

1866	1871	1876	1881	1886	1891	1896	1901	1906	1911	1916	1921	1926	1931	1936	1941	1946	1951

MEMBERSHIP BY YEAR (ACCOUNTED FOR): 1882, 26; 1884, 72; 1887, 82; 1888, 87; 1889, 106; 1904, 88; 1905, 82; 1906, 82; 1907, 75; 1908, 77; 1909, 77; 1910, 62; 1911, 62; 1912, 65; 1913, 60; 1914, 61; 1915, 56; 1916, 45; 1917, 53; 1918, 56; 1919, 44; 1920, 44; 1921, 48; 1922, 43; 1923, 36; 1924, 31; 1925, 26; 1926, 23; 1927, 22; 1928, 21; 1929, 17; 1930, 13; 1931, 10; 1932, 10; 1933, 10; 1934, 11; 1935, 10; 1936, 9; 1937, 9; 1938, 2 **LAST MEMBER:** James A. Perry

L. H. D. CRANE

The memory of a prominent Beloit man at the start of the Civil War, Louis H. D. Crane, was perpetuated by the veterans who chose that name for their G.A.R. post in 1882. Crane was clerk of the Wisconsin Assembly from 1858 to 1861, when he enlisted in the Third Wisconsin, being chosen second lieutenant of Company A. Crane advanced rapidly in the Third, becoming a major in June of 1862 and, not long after, lieutenant colonel of the regiment. He was killed at the Battle of Cedar Mountain in Virginia on August 9, 1862. He is buried in Oakwood Cemetery, Beloit.

Crane Post 54 was organized in 1882 with the assistance of members of Sargent Post of Janesville. The first commander was Chalmers Ingersoll. The post soon grew to more than a hundred members and was quite active over the course of the next decades. In 1909, one of its members, W. H. Grinnell, was department commander. Post 54 hosted the state encampment in 1929 in the post's forty-eighth year.

Crane Post members in 1925: (Front, from left) A. H. Trogner, A. C. Stevens, S. D. Ross, H. E. Mahar, George Lewis. (Middle) C. E. Gregg, J. A. Howe, W. H. Chesbrough, W. H. Wheeler, P. Crave, A. H. Livingston. (Back) O. J. Stiles, A. Schellenger, L. B. Witter, S. A. Skinner. Photo provided by the Beloit Historical Society.

Members of Crane Post 54 at Memorial Day, 1903, observance in Beloit. Photo provided by the Wisconsin Veterans Museum, Madison.

LYSANDER CUTLER POST 55, Wausau
MARATHON COUNTY • DECEMBER 5, 1882–1931

CHARTER MEMBERS: J. A. Kellogg, Ely Wright, W. B. Philbreek, W. W. De Voe, J. B. Vaughn, J. D. Womer, J. P. Briggs, S. M. Quaw, Miles Swope, Chili Averill

1866	1871	1876	1881	1886	1891	1896	1901	1906	1911	1916	1921	1926	1931	1936	1941	1946	1951

MEMBERSHIP BY YEAR (ACCOUNTED FOR): 1887, 84; 1888, 63; 1889, 83; 1904, 66; 1905, 57; 1906, 57; 1907, 57; 1908, 52; 1909, 51; 1910, 41; 1911, 38; 1912, 31; 1913, 31; 1914, 27; 1915, 27; 1916, 28; 1917, 20; 1918, 13; 1919, 16; 1920, 14; 1921, 10; 1922, 14; 1923, 10; 1924, 9; 1925, 6; 1927, 5; 1928, 5; 1930, 3   **LAST MEMBER:** Leander Swope, died 1933

CRAIG JOHNSON
LYSANDER CUTLER

Lysander Cutler, for whom Post 55 at Wausau was named was the commander of the Sixth Wisconsin Infantry of Iron Brigade fame. As colonel of the Sixth he was wounded in the famed brigade's first battle at Brawner's farm. He went on to command the brigade for a time and rose further to division command. His health failed before the end of the war and he survived the war for little more than a year. Cutler was well regarded by the men who served under him.

Cutler Post 55 was commanded initially by General J. A. Kellogg, who had an active part in the 1880 veterans' reunion which led to the expansion of the Department of Wisconsin in the succeeding years. The post at Antigo was later named for Kellogg. The Cutler Post was never one the large posts of the Department but it was an important one in central Wisconsin.

ANGUS R. MCDONALD POST 56, Mazomanie

DANE COUNTY • DECEMBER 1, 1882–1929

CHARTER MEMBERS: George G. Rowell was the first commander.

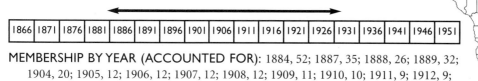

1866	1871	1876	1881	1886	1891	1896	1901	1906	1911	1916	1921	1926	1931	1936	1941	1946	1951

MEMBERSHIP BY YEAR (ACCOUNTED FOR): 1884, 52; 1887, 35; 1888, 26; 1889, 32; 1904, 20; 1905, 12; 1906, 12; 1907, 12; 1908, 12; 1909, 11; 1910, 10; 1911, 9; 1912, 9; 1913, 8; 1914, 8; 1915, 9; 1916, 10; 1917, 10; 1918, 9; 1919, 9; 1920, 8; 1921, 7; 1922, 7; 1923, 7; 1924, 6; 1925, 6; 1926, 5   **LAST MEMBER:** Unknown

ANGUS R.
McDONALD

Mazomanie had one of the early posts in the department, but it was one of those that did not take root. The second attempt in 1882 resulted in a successful, though never large, post.

It was named for Angus R. McDonald, a Mazomanie man who entered the army as first lieutenant of Company A, Eleventh Wisconsin. McDonald was wounded at Blakely, Alabama, late in the war and was mustered out May 15, 1865, as a captain. It was his postwar career, however, that brought McDonald his greatest notoriety. He was appointed state armorer by Governor Lucius Fairchild, and in that position he became custodian of Old Abe, the eagle mascot of the Eighth Wisconsin, which was kept in the Capitol after the war. McDonald became Old Abe's favorite keeper, in fact. The two had what was termed "an affectionate relationship."

CHARLES EDGERTON POST 57, Warren Mills

MONROE COUNTY • DECEMBER 30, 1882–1929

CHARTER MEMBERS: Unknown

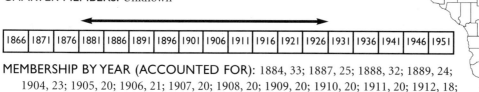

1866	1871	1876	1881	1886	1891	1896	1901	1906	1911	1916	1921	1926	1931	1936	1941	1946	1951

MEMBERSHIP BY YEAR (ACCOUNTED FOR): 1884, 33; 1887, 25; 1888, 32; 1889, 24; 1904, 23; 1905, 20; 1906, 21; 1907, 20; 1908, 20; 1909, 20; 1910, 20; 1911, 20; 1912, 18; 1913, 15; 1914, 13; 1915, 12; 1916, 9; 1917, 10; 1918, 9; 1919, 9; 1920, 8; 1921, 7; 1922, 6; 1923, 5; 1924, 5; 1925, 5; 1926, 3; 1927, 3; 1928, 3   **LAST MEMBER:** Unknown

The Warren Mills Post of the G.A.R. was, in its earliest years, the focal point of community life in the town. Charles Edgerton Post 57 had its own post hall, which was used for entertainment of all types and for meetings of most of the town's fraternal organizations. The post's heyday continued past the turn of the twentieth century, although the hall as community center was replaced by a newer one.

Post 57 was named for Charles Edgerton, a young man from the area who joined Company D of the Twenty-fifth Wisconsin and died from disease on August 19, 1863, at Helena, Arkansas.

POST 58, Bloomington

GRANT COUNTY • SEPTEMBER 11, 1867–NOVEMBER 20, 1871

CHARTER MEMBERS: J. S. Frederich, commander; John E. Connell, senior vice commander; George H. Smith, adjutant; J. M. Roberts, quartermaster; B. W. Breed, officer of the guard; R. J. Allen, guard

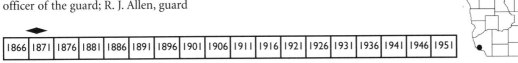

1866	1871	1876	1881	1886	1891	1896	1901	1906	1911	1916	1921	1926	1931	1936	1941	1946	1951

MEMBERSHIP BY YEAR (ACCOUNTED FOR): 1879, 12; 1884, 17; 1887, 18; 1888, 22; 1889, 28; 1904, 17; 1905, 16; 1906, 16; 1907, 15; 1908, 15; 1909, 14; 1910, 13; 1911, 9; 1912, 8; 1913, 10; 1914, 10; 1915, 10; 1916, 10; 1917, 7; 1918, 7; 1919, 7; 1920, 7; 1921, 5   **LAST MEMBER:** Unknown

Except for the organization date and the officers, nothing is known about the earliest post begun in Bloomington, Grant County, Post 58. It is not even certain what the post name was. It is certain, however, that it was among those posts that had become dormant by 1871 and was on the list of posts whose charter was revoked on November 20, 1871.

WILLIAM EVANS POST 58, Menonomie

DUNN COUNTY • JANUARY 6, 1883–1938

CHARTER MEMBERS: S. J. Bailey, Frank Kelley, J. A. Hill, J. G. Ingalls, T. J. George, E. H. Weber, John Lyle, W. W. Blair, Robert Cassidy, John Willard, F. Diedrich, S. R. Palmer, J. H. Snively, David McLain, E. L. Everts, N. P. Vanderhoof, D. W. Gilmore, Rockwell J. Flint, E. L. Doolittle, Charles Isted, John Scanlan, J. J. Myrick, A. A. Curtis, D. K. Hill, W. D. Young, John Knoble, George Manchester, Newell Burch

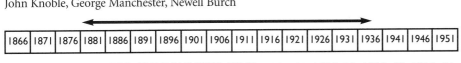

1866	1871	1876	1881	1886	1891	1896	1901	1906	1911	1916	1921	1926	1931	1936	1941	1946	1951

MEMBERSHIP BY YEAR (ACCOUNTED FOR): 1887, 81; 1888, 85; 1889, 90; 1904, 44; 1905, 31; 1906, 31; 1907, 36; 1908, 30; 1909, 39; 1910, 39; 1911, 32; 1912, 40; 1913, 41; 1914, 39; 1915, 36; 1916, 34; 1917, 32; 1918, 28; 1919, 29; 1920, 26; 1921, 22; 1922, 22; 1923, 21; 1924, 20; 1925, 16; 1926, 13; 1927, 8; 1928, 7; 1929, 6; 1930, 5; 1931, 5; 1932, 5; 1933, 4; 1934, 4; 1935, 2; 1936, 1; 1937, 1   **LAST MEMBER:** Rockwell J. Flint

Menomonie Post 58, named for William Evans, who led a company off to the war and was killed in battle, had a unique situation. Rockwell J. Flint, its first commander and a charter member, was also its last surviving member.

Evans was captain of Company K, Fifth Wisconsin, when it, mainly boys from Dunn County, left in May of 1861. Evans was wounded at Gold's Farm, Virginia, and died in the hospital at Philadelphia on July 28, 1862. Eight of his Company K "boys" became Evans Post members.

Evans Post 58 was successful in its first two decades and had, according to one source, a peak membership of 270 during that time. In the early years, the post was very active in community events as well as department affairs. Its active participation dwindled, of course, as its membership declined, but it was able to hold post meetings until well into the 1930s.

ANGUS S. NORTHROP POST 59, Mauston

JUNEAU COUNTY • JANUARY 10, 1883–1936

CHARTER MEMBERS: Orson Wright, John W. Bradley, W. H. Van Wie, Erastus Smith, J. C. Wetherby, P. R. Briggs, J. B. Swetland, W. B. Patterson, C. N. Holden, James L. Barney, D. W. Russell, R. R. Coombs, E. F. Aikens, John Organ, Amos Sumner, J. J. Herrick, Henry Schall, H. S. Spaulding, J. W. Hall, F. S. Veeder, Ralph Bowes, A. G. Lowe, Hiram Edwards, Salem Twist, J. T. Patterson, E. B. Robinson, Benj. Kimberly, John H. Allison, B. F. Parker

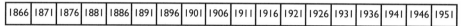

| 1866 | 1871 | 1876 | 1881 | 1886 | 1891 | 1896 | 1901 | 1906 | 1911 | 1916 | 1921 | 1926 | 1931 | 1936 | 1941 | 1946 | 1951 |

MEMBERSHIP BY YEAR (ACCOUNTED FOR): 1883, 29; 1884, 60; 1887, 59; 1888, 56; 1889, 77; 1904, 29; 1905, 25; 1906, 23; 1907, 33; 1908, 24; 1909, 21; 1910, 21; 1911, 17; 1912, 19; 1913, 40; 1914, 19; 1915, 21; 1916, 22; 1917, 22; 1918, 21; 1919, 19; 1920, 19; 1921, 19; 1922, 18; 1923, 17; 1924, 16; 1925, 15; 1926, 14; 1927, 11; 1928, 9; 1929, 8; 1930, 3; 1931, 4; 1932, 3; 1933, 2; 1934, 1; 1935, 1   **LAST MEMBER:** Burnett (first name unknown)

Angus S. Northrop, for whom Post 59 at Mauston was named, was first lieutenant of Company F, Sixteenth Wisconsin. He was killed in action at Corinth, Mississippi, on October 3, 1862, the second of only two officers of the Sixteenth Wisconsin to die in battle.

Members of Northrup Post 59, Mauston.

ARTHUR D. HAMILTON POST 60, Milton

ROCK COUNTY • JANUARY 10, 1883–1931

CHARTER MEMBERS: Alf. D. Burdick, Wm. Cole, Geo. W. Lanphear, Frank M. Wilbur, A. Delos Burdick, Clark A. Stillman, Jos. Davis, Kirk W. Tanner, E. F. Wiglief, W. H. Webb, A. W. Crane, J. E. Davidson, A. Judson Wells, W. H. Fross

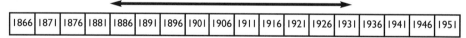

| 1866 | 1871 | 1876 | 1881 | 1886 | 1891 | 1896 | 1901 | 1906 | 1911 | 1916 | 1921 | 1926 | 1931 | 1936 | 1941 | 1946 | 1951 |

MEMBERSHIP BY YEAR (ACCOUNTED FOR): 1883, 14; 1887, 30; 1888, 31; 1889, 37; 1904, 32; 1905, 30; 1906, 30; 1907, 36; 1908, 35; 1909, 36; 1910, 32; 1911, 29; 1912, 24; 1913, 25; 1914, 24; 1915, 28; 1916, 25; 1917, 22; 1918, 22; 1919, 23; 1920, 20; 1921, 17; 1922, 17; 1923, 17; 1924, 14; 1925, 9; 1926, 9; 1927, 5; 1928, 3; 1929, 2; 1930, 1
LAST MEMBER: Peter Elphick

A Milton soldier who volunteered at the first call and joined Company H, Second Wisconsin, was honored by members of the G.A.R. in his home town by naming their post the Arthur D. Hamilton Post 60.

Hamilton was wounded in the Iron Brigade attack in the cornfield at the Battle of Antietam and died September 26, 1862, at Keedysville, Maryland, of his wounds.

The post enjoyed a steady membership beyond World War I, but the decline was rapid in the 1920s. It gave its furnishings to the Milton WRC (Womens Relief Corp) in 1925, and the post was extinct by 1931.

Members of Hamilton Post 60 in 1922.

WILLIAM P. MITCHELL POST 61, New Lisbon

JUNEAU COUNTY • JANUARY 17, 1883–1937

CHARTER MEMBERS: O. B. Chester, commander, H. P. Holmes, senior vice commander; L. Weed, junior vice commander; William McKay, quartermaster; Milo McWhorter, adjutant; N. M. Hess, officer of the day; Alfred Cook, officer of the guard; F. E. Boynton, surgeon; Alexander Adams, chaplain; F. E. Hurt, sergeant major; H. Norton, quartermaster sergeant; C. D. Curtis, Charles Smith, and C. E. Newman, trustees

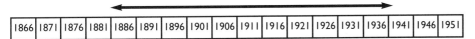

MEMBERSHIP BY YEAR (ACCOUNTED FOR): 1887, 33; 1888, 32; 1889, 37; 1904, 23; 1905, 23; 1906, 22; 1907, 22; 1908, 21; 1909, 21; 1910, 18; 1911, 18; 1912, 17; 1913, 16; 1914, 16; 1915, 13; 1916, 12; 1917, 9; 1918, 9; 1919, 9; 1920, 9; 1921, 10; 1922, 9; 1923, 8; 1924, 11; 1925, 12; 1926, 11; 1927, 8; 1928, 6; 1929, 5; 1930, 5; 1931, 5; 1932, 4; 1933, 2; 1934, 1; 1935, 1; 1936, 1   **LAST MEMBER:** H. B. Norton

New Lisbon's G.A.R. post, numbered 61, was named for William P. Mitchell, who was sergeant of Company H, the "Juneau County Rifles," in the Tenth Wisconsin, which left the state in November 1861.

Mitchell was killed in action on October 8, 1862, at the Battle of Perryville, Kentucky.

The post was never large but maintained an active and relatively constant membership, and it actually grew a bit in the 1920s when the post received some members from other Juneau County posts, which had become inactive.

JAMES C. MCINTYRE POST 62, Boaz

RICHLAND COUNTY • JANUARY 21, 1883–1898

CHARTER MEMBERS: Unknown

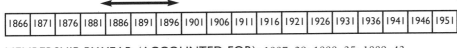

MEMBERSHIP BY YEAR (ACCOUNTED FOR): 1887, 29; 1888, 35; 1889, 43
LAST MEMBER: Unknown

James C. McIntyre, for whom the G.A.R. post at Boaz in Richland County was named, was a native of Spring Green and was killed in action at North Anna, Virginia, on May 27, 1864.

The James C. McIntyre Post 61 was active through the peak years of the Wisconsin Department but was extinct by 1898.

JOHN SHAVER POST 62, Cedar Grove

SHEBOYGAN COUNTY • MARCH 25, 1898–1901

CHARTER MEMBERS: Unknown

LAST MEMBER: Unknown

The short-lived post at Cedar Grove in Sheboygan County, of which very little is known, was named for John Shaver, who served in Company C, Fourth Wisconsin Cavalry. Shaver joined the unit in December 1864, and he was discharged the following July. A native of Cedar Grove, he returned there and was a prominent citizen after the war. He died January 8, 1896, a little less than two years before the post was organized.

Cedar Grove Civil War vets pose behind civic band, date unknown. Photo provided by the Sheboygan County Historical Research Center.

EUGENE A. COLBURN POST 62, Bruce

RUSK COUNTY • JANUARY 4, 1902–1917

CHARTER MEMBERS: E. E. Snyder, commander; G. W. Heaverin, senior vice commander; B. F. Brainerd, junior vice commander; Joel Burrington, surgeon; Eli Miller, chaplain; R. G. Walter Collins, officer of the day; Charles O. Thompson, officer of the guard; John Guttridge, quartermaster; Gust Nater, adjutant; John Rand, quartermaster sergeant

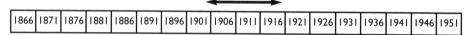

| 1866 | 1871 | 1876 | 1881 | 1886 | 1891 | 1896 | 1901 | 1906 | 1911 | 1916 | 1921 | 1926 | 1931 | 1936 | 1941 | 1946 | 1951 |

MEMBERSHIP BY YEAR (ACCOUNTED FOR): 1902, 12; 1904, 18; 1905, 18; 1906, 18; 1907, 18; 1908, 18; 1909, 10; 1910, 10; 1911, 10; 1912, 9; 1913, 9; 1914, 9; 1915, 9; 1916, 6   LAST MEMBER: Unknown

Eugene A. Colburn, for whom Post 62 at Bruce in Rusk County was named—one of the later posts formed despite its relatively low number—was a member of the First New York Cavalry during the war. He migrated to Wisconsin after the war and was a longtime resident of Bruce, succumbing in 1893, leaving three orphans.

Colburn Post was not large, never exceeding 20 members, but it remained on the rolls until 1916.

ENOS B. CORNWELL POST 63, Basswood

RICHLAND COUNTY • JANUARY 26, 1883–1901 OR 1902

CHARTER MEMBERS: Unknown

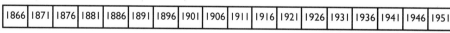

| 1866 | 1871 | 1876 | 1881 | 1886 | 1891 | 1896 | 1901 | 1906 | 1911 | 1916 | 1921 | 1926 | 1931 | 1936 | 1941 | 1946 | 1951 |

MEMBERSHIP BY YEAR (ACCOUNTED FOR): 1884, 23; 1887, 25; 1888, 28; 1889, 28
LAST MEMBER: Unknown

Basswood's G.A.R. post, Enos B. Cornwell Post 63, was named for a soldier from Bristol who died in the war. Honoring Corporal Cornwell by naming a post after him was a reminder that service did not always mean combat.

Cornwell was with Company B of the Forty-ninth Wisconsin, which was recruited in early 1865, was deployed from the state two weeks before Appomattox, and was sent to Missouri where the company lost 48 men, one mistakenly shot in the celebration over news of the fall of Richmond, and the other 47 by disease, one of whom was Cornwell, at Rolla, Missouri, on July 23, 1865.

The Basswood Post was never large and surrendered its charter in 1901 or early 1902.

THOMAS B. CRAWFORD POST 63, Westfield

MARQUETTE COUNTY • OCTOBER 9, 1906–JANUARY 25, 1924

CHARTER MEMBERS: C. E. King, Company D, Forty-third Wisconsin; G. A. Waldo, Company F, Forty-third Wisconsin; Simeon Pond, Company A, First Wisconsin Heavy Artillery; W. P. Fuller, Company E, Seventh Wisconsin; F. Meinke, Company D, Forty-fourth Wisconsin; L. M. Preston, Company A, Second Wisconsin; R. D. Mallory, Company D, Nineteenth Wisconsin; John Crawford, Company E, Sixteenth Wisconsin; Chris Schlegel, Company D, First Wisconsin; J. D. Ingraham, Company I, First Wisconsin Heavy Artillery; G. H. Woodward, Company I, Fifth New York; J. B. Crawford, Company A, First Wisconsin Heavy Artillery; David Hammel, Company D, First Wisconsin Heavy Artillery; William Holtz, Company K, One-hundred-thirty-second Illinois; Harry Gibson, Company E, Seventh Wisconsin. Several of these had also been charter members of Post 65

1866	1871	1876	1881	1886	1891	1896	1901	1906	1911	1916	1921	1926	1931	1936	1941	1946	1951

MEMBERSHIP BY YEAR (ACCOUNTED FOR): 1907, 21; 1908, 22; 1909, 20; 1910, 17; 1911, 14; 1912, 14; 1913, 14; 1914, 14; 1915, 12; 1916, 11; 1917, 11; 1918, 9; 1919, 9; 1920, 7; 1921, 7; 1922, 6; 1923, 6; 1924, 5; 1925, 5
LAST MEMBER: Unknown

Thomas B. Crawford Post of Westfield in Marquette County had an unusual history. It began in 1883 as Crawford Post 65, but it was defunct by 1902.

The veterans of Westfield came back four years later and were again chartered. This time the number available to them happened to be lower than their previous number and thus the second effort became Thomas B. Crawford Post 63.

The namesake of both posts was Thomas B. Crawford, the eldest of five brothers who went off to the Civil War from Marquette County. Thomas died in 1862 and was buried among unknown soldiers at St. Louis. His brother William also died in 1862 from illness, but the remaining three Crawfords, John, Charles and James, survived and returned to Marquette County. Two of them, John and James, were among the charter members of Post 63.

The latter, James Braden Crawford, as a member of the First Wisconsin Heavy Artillery, was stationed in the Washington defenses. On the evening of April 14, 1865, he and a friend went to Ford's Theater to see "Our American Cousin" because they heard that President Lincoln would be attending. They faced the presidential box and saw Booth as he leaped from the box after firing the fatal shot.

The "Minutes of meeting held in IOOF Hall Westfield Wis. Oct. 9, 1906, to reorganize T. B. Crawford Post G.A.R." survive and list King, Waldo, Pond, Fuller, Meinke, Schlegel, Ingraham, John Crawford, Mallory, and Preston as being present at the reorganization. The first three were elected commander, senior vice commander, and junior vice commander, respectively.

W. S. WALKER POST 64, Montello

MARQUETTE COUNTY • FEBRUARY 23, 1883–1927

CHARTER MEMBERS: John Lewis, commander; J. Daniels, senior vice commander; F. H. Hotchkiss, junior vice commander; C. F. Roskie, chaplain; M. G. Ellison, quartermaster; P. Croarken, officer of the day; William Hartwig, officer of the guard; F. A. Course, adjutant; S. Eastman, sergeant major; John Graham, quartermaster sergeant

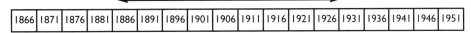

1866	1871	1876	1881	1886	1891	1896	1901	1906	1911	1916	1921	1926	1931	1936	1941	1946	1951

MEMBERSHIP BY YEAR (ACCOUNTED FOR): 1884, 27; 1887, 35; 1888, 39; 1889, 42; 1904, 17; 1905, 17; 1906, 17; 1907, 14; 1908, 14; 1909, 14; 1910, 13; 1911, 11; 1912, 11; 1913, 10; 1914, 9; 1915, 9; 1916, 8; 1917, 6; 1918, 6; 1919, 5; 1920, 6; 1921, 6; 1922, 6; 1923, 7; 1925, 6; 1926, 5   **LAST MEMBER:** Lenard Dibble

The remaining veterans in Montello on Memorial Day, 1910. From left: Sam Boone, Len Dibble, Lim Eastman, A. Wilkins, Con Maloney, Felix McPhillips, John Murphy, Lin. Stevens, Jack Ennis, Louis Fish, and Billy Hartwig.

Lenard Dibble, some years later, was the last survivor of W. S. Walker Post 64. Photo provided by the Marquette County Historical Society.

THOMAS B. CRAWFORD POST 65, Westfield

MARQUETTE COUNTY • FEBRUARY 28, 1883–JULY 1902

CHARTER MEMBERS: S D. Forbes, commander; P. Lockey, senior vice commander; J. Waldo, junior vice commander; R.D. Malloy, quartermaster; J. Crawford, sergeant at arms; L. M. Preston, chaplain; J. Perkins, officer of the day; H. M. Ormsby, guard; H. S. Ball, adjutant; C. A. Parker, sergeant major; W. Fuller, quartermaster sergeant

1866	1871	1876	1881	1886	1891	1896	1901	1906	1911	1916	1921	1926	1931	1936	1941	1946	1951

MEMBERSHIP BY YEAR (ACCOUNTED FOR): 1884, 35; 1887, 16; 1888, 33; 1889, 37
LAST MEMBER: Unknown

Thomas B. Crawford Post 65 was the first G.A.R. post in Westfield in Marquette County, chartered in 1883 during the order's booming years.

The post was active for close to 20 years, then somehow became extinct, or at least was dropped from the department rolls in 1902.

The veterans of Westfield achieved a reactivation of their post in 1906, but the post number was changed to 63, apparently the next available number under the department's policy of recycling numbers.

While the number changed, the name of the post did not. Or rather, the rechartered post chose the same name as the post that had succumbed.

For information on the post's namesake, Thomas B. Crawford, see Post 63.

Westfield's Civil War veterans pose before the town's first public library as they await the start of the Memorial Day Parade early in the twentieth century. Photo provided by the Marquette County Historical Society.

F. JACKEL POST 65, Spooner

WASHBURN COUNTY • AUGUST 26, 1903–1930

CHARTER MEMBERS: H. H. Atchison was the first commander.

1866	1871	1876	1881	1886	1891	1896	1901	1906	1911	1916	1921	1926	1931	1936	1941	1946	1951

MEMBERSHIP BY YEAR (ACCOUNTED FOR): 1904, 18; 1905, 24; 1906, 20; 1907, 8; 1908, 15; 1909, 14; 1910, 7; 1911, 7; 1912, 14; 1913, 5; 1914, 5; 1915, 6; 1916, 6; 1917, 6; 1918, 6; 1919, 6; 1920, 5; 1921, 5; 1922, 4; 1923, 4; 1924, 2; 1925, 1; 1926, 1; 1927, 1; 1928, 1; 1929, 1
LAST MEMBER: T. H. Hillman

Jackel Post 65 of Spooner was one of the later-chartered Department of Wisconsin posts. It continued until 1930.

The post received its relatively low number because the Westfield Post, which bore that number for nearly 20 years, had gone dormant the year before.

The identity of Jackel is not known. Nor is there much information about the post itself other than the annual membership numbers reported to the department. These show that it was never a large post but that its members continued loyally affiliated so long as they were able.

PLATTEVILLE POST 66
WILLIAM T. SHERMAN POST 66, Platteville

GRANTCOUNTY • FEBRUARY 6, 1883–1937

CHARTER MEMBERS: H. J. Traber, W. Homer Beebe, Fred Libert, W. J. Funston, J. S. Hammonds, Duncan McGregor, Chas. Weitenhiller, H. H. Virgin, M. T. Camp, C. H. Wannemaker, Wm. Batcheller, J. T. Davison, James Ludenstat, S. W. Traber, J. C. Danaqun, J. Ballard, J. N. McGranahan, C. G. Douly, N. Bradbury, H. L. Thomas, E. J. Buntley, J. L. Spencer, Wm. Cox, J. W. Calahan, Jessie Bray, H. S. Vaughn, Marion Rose, W. H. Oettiken, J. H. Holcomb, S. B. Spensen

1866	1871	1876	1881	1886	1891	1896	1901	1906	1911	1916	1921	1926	1931	1936	1941	1946	1951

MEMBERSHIP BY YEAR (ACCOUNTED FOR): 1887, 103; 1888, 122; 1889, 144; 1904, 97; 1905, 98; 1906, 101; 1907, 94; 1908, 91; 1909, 95; 1910, 97; 1911, 95; 1912, 95; 1913, 86; 1914, 78; 1915, 76; 1916, 69; 1917, 61; 1918, 56; 1919, 56; 1920, 49; 1921, 43; 1922, 36; 1923, 27; 1924, 22; 1925, 22; 1926, 19; 1927, 15; 1928, 12; 1929, 10; 1930, 9; 1931, 10; 1932, 7; 1933, 4; 1934, 4; 1935, 4; 1936, 4; 1937, 1   **LAST MEMBER:** John A. Blakely, died September 10, 1937.

WILLIAM T. SHERMAN

Veterans of the Grant County area around Platteville got together in a post, numbered 66, in early 1883. They chose to call it by the name of their community.

It was Platteville Post 66 until 1891 when the nation's veterans were saddened by the death of General William T. Sherman. The Platteville boys decided to honor their old comrade by naming Post 66 after him.

The Sherman Post had more than one hundred members at late as 1906. Its membership through the 1920s, in fact, stayed in the double digits even as attrition was taking scores of posts away from the department.

William Tecumseh Sherman was one of the soldiers' favorite generals, especially among those who served under him in the Atlanta Campaign, the March to the Sea, and the March into the Carolinas. He was "Uncle Billy," and his armies were an invincible force.

G.A.R. members parade past Methodist Church in Platteville on Memorial Day, 1914. Photo provided by the Grant County Historical Society.

Grant County Civil War veterans gather for a reunion in Platteville, 1924. Photo provided by the Grant County Historical Society.

About the time the Platteville Post became the William T. Sherman Post, in 1891, members posed for this picnic picture.

In the Post Room, Platteville, the G.A.R. members are feted by a Women's Relief Corps banquet in 1929. Photo provided by the Grant County Historical Society.

SAMUEL F. CURTIS POST 67, West Lima

RICHLAND COUNTY • MARCH 15, 1883–1900

CHARTER MEMBERS: George W. Shattuck, commander; Henry Todd, senior vice commander; John Carter, junior vice commander; J. H. Helm, surgeon; John Griffin, chaplain; Daniel V. DeHart, quartermaster; Franklin E. Seeley, officer of the day; Isaac Smith, officer of the guard; Jefferson M. Hankins, adjutant; Harvey D. Tillon, quartermaster sergeant; Louis Long, sergeant major; John Gomig; James Granger; Robert Drake; T. W. Payne; Jesse Beatty; C. A. Neefe; M. R. Griffin; Willet Lipley; C. A. Willey; T. R. Watts; August Zust; William Beatty

1866	1871	1876	1881	1886	1891	1896	1901	1906	1911	1916	1921	1926	1931	1936	1941	1946	1951

MEMBERSHIP BY YEAR (ACCOUNTED FOR): 1883, 23; 1887, 51; 1888, 26; 1889, 25   **LAST MEMBER:** Unknown

Samuel F. Curtis Post 67, West Lima, was organized by veterans from Richland and Vernon counties. It was never numerically strong, but continued to serve veterans in the two counties until 1900.

The post was named for Samuel F. Curtis, who enlisted in the Twentieth Wisconsin in July of 1862 and was killed in action at Prairie Grove, Arkansas, on December 7, 1862. Curtis is buried in Vernon Cemetery in the Town of Union, Richland County.

JAMES COMERFORD POST 68, Chippewa Falls

CHIPPEWA COUNTY • MARCH 15, 1883–1942

CHARTER MEMBERS: O. B. Hoard, Charles Stewart, Charles Withrow, Solomon Young, Charles E. Smith, Joseph Heskith, T. J. Kiley, B. H. Stillman, W. S. Monroe, Oswald Charpin, Birdsall Cornell, I. O. Miles, S. R. Kaiser, John R. Waring, W. H. Johnson, F. M. Clough, J. O. Donnell, William Faeh, William McDonald, R. O. Batson, J. W. Thomas, G. W. Heaverin, Alex McBean, Charles D. Gould, B. Heimelsbach, Samuel Snyder, H. Held, Thomas McBean, Elisha Ermatinger, F. H. Cutling, Willard Jarvis, Ed Fessenden, L. W. Kibbons, Alex Chisholm, Marcus Cota, Samuel Boyd, C. H. Chase

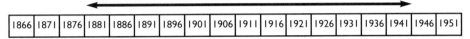

| 1866 | 1871 | 1876 | 1881 | 1886 | 1891 | 1896 | 1901 | 1906 | 1911 | 1916 | 1921 | 1926 | 1931 | 1936 | 1941 | 1946 | 1951 |

MEMBERSHIP BY YEAR (ACCOUNTED FOR): 1882, 58; 1883, 166; 1884, 215; 1885, 203; 1886, 182; 1887, 183; 1888, 169; 1889, 139; 1890, 129; 1891, 141; 1892, 112; 1893, 108; 1894, 106; 1895, 119; 1904, 87; 1905, 88; 1906, 79; 1907, 73; 1908, 66; 1909, 62; 1910, 58; 1911, 57; 1912, 55; 1913, 56; 1914, 49; 1915, 46; 1916, 45; 1917, 42; 1918, 37; 1919, 38; 1920, 36; 1921, 34; 1922, 28; 1923, 22; 1924, 19; 1925, 15; 1926, 13; 1927, 12; 1928, 10; 1929, 9; 1930, 5; 1931, 4; 1932, 2; 1933, 2; 1934, 1; 1935, 1; 1936, 1; 1937, 1; 1938, 2   **LAST MEMBER:** John Hackenbrock

James Comerford Post 68 of Chippewa Falls received a measure of fame in national Grand Army circles in that it was chosen by historian Stuart McConnell as one of three typical Grand Army posts in his 1992 study of the order titled *Glorious Contentment.* Two eastern posts exemplified the working-class post and the posts of elite veterans. Comerford Post typified a rural post, and McConnell's study is an interesting portrayal of that type of G.A.R. post that was, after all, what most posts in Wisconsin were like.

The Chippewa Falls Post was formed in 1883 and was im-mediately a very successful post, serving its area and its many veterans for decades. The post was named for James Comerford, who was county clerk of Chippewa County until his death two years before the post was organized.

Comerford, a native of Ireland, served in the war from New York. He was captured at the Battle of Ream's Station and was sent to various prisons. Though he survived his imprisonment of seven months, his health remained impaired. He came to the Chippewa Valley after the war and was in business and then county government until his death.

ERASTUS HOYT POST 69, Albany

GREEN COUNTY • MARCH 24, 1883–1906

CHARTER MEMBERS: Thomas Flint, C. W. Burns, J. T. Annis, E. F. Warren, J. W. Carver, Richard Glennon, Wm. Green, A. D. Smith, J. W. Wessel, N. B. Murray, J. E. Bartlett, J. F. Earle, S. F. Smith, F. L. Roberts, C. Wessel, James Sanderson, T. H. Alverson, J. E. Gillet, Geo. Loucks, H. C. Bump, A. W. Murray, Aaron Kellogg, Peter Benston

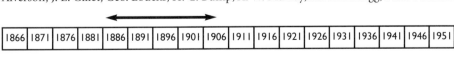

| 1866 | 1871 | 1876 | 1881 | 1886 | 1891 | 1896 | 1901 | 1906 | 1911 | 1916 | 1921 | 1926 | 1931 | 1936 | 1941 | 1946 | 1951 |

MEMBERSHIP BY YEAR (ACCOUNTED FOR): 1883, 23; 1884, 40; 1887, 36; 1888, 38; 1889, 36; 1904, 13; 1905, 12
LAST MEMBER: Unknown

The Albany G.A.R. post was named after Erastus Hoyt, a man from Albany, Green County, who was a private in Company F, Thirty-first Wisconsin. He died in Albany on August 27, 1863, of chronic diarrhea, one of the many soldiers who were so stricken, but one of the few who went home to die. He is buried in the Albany cemetery.

The post was never strong numerically, although it continued to function until into the twentieth century.

ALEXIS TALLMAN POST 70, Clinton

ROCK COUNTY • APRIL 18, 1883–1926

CHARTER MEMBERS: F. A. Ames, A. S. Isham, John M. Crotsenburg, H. H. Park, G. E. Averill, Charles Snell, H. A. Anderson, J. S. Campbell, James Kelley, T. D. Northway, W. J. Latta, James Baldwin, Amon Baldwin, Warren W. Parker, W. H. Butter, Arthur C. Stevens, John Sanders, J. M. Faver, J. F. Cleghorn, Alonzo Sawyer, George B. Turnuere, John Waugh, Ansil Flint, David Baker, Peter Bush

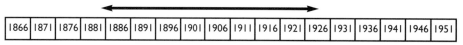

| 1866 | 1871 | 1876 | 1881 | 1886 | 1891 | 1896 | 1901 | 1906 | 1911 | 1916 | 1921 | 1926 | 1931 | 1936 | 1941 | 1946 | 1951 |

MEMBERSHIP BY YEAR (ACCOUNTED FOR): 1884, 25; 1887, 41; 1888, 51; 1889, 64; 1896, 57; 1904, 28; 1905, 31; 1906, 31; 1907, 30; 1908, 30; 1909, 27; 1910, 27; 1911, 22; 1912, 25; 1913, 21; 1914, 19; 1915, 18; 1916, 15; 1917, 14; 1918, 14; 1919, 10; 1920, 9; 1921, 8; 1922, 6; 1923, 6; 1924, 4; 1925, 4 **LAST MEMBER:** Unknown

Post 70 of Clinton in Rock County was an active small-town post for many years.

This is a picture of a memorial to General Ulysses S. Grant, following his death in 1885, in Clinton, Wisconsin. It presumably was erected by Post 70; the G.A.R. emblem is above Grant's portrait. The exact location of the memorial is not given.

It was named for Alexis W. Tallman, son of a pioneer settler of Clinton. Tallman was a private in Company I, Twenty-second Wisconsin, who was killed by a rebel sharpshooter at Acworth Station, Georgia, on June 16, 1864, just prior to the battle of Kenesaw Mountain. He is buried at Marietta, Georgia.

J. B. MOORE POST 71, Muscoda

GRANT COUNTY • MARCH 28, 1883–FEBRUARY 21, 1896

CHARTER MEMBERS: M. Dziewanowski was the first commander.

| 1866 | 1871 | 1876 | 1881 | 1886 | 1891 | 1896 | 1901 | 1906 | 1911 | 1916 | 1921 | 1926 | 1931 | 1936 | 1941 | 1946 | 1951 |

MEMBERSHIP BY YEAR (ACCOUNTED FOR): 1884, 16; 1887, 27; 1888, 30; 1889, 34
LAST MEMBER: Unknown

JOSEPH J. RIGGS COLL., USAMHI
JONATHAN B. MOORE

The name of the G.A.R. post at Muscoda, was the J. B. Moore Post 71, named after a man who led the Thirty-third Wisconsin into the war and was a prominent member of the business community afterwards.

Jonathan B. Moore was sheriff of Grant County when the war began. His regiment served in the western armies, Moore eventually rising to colonel of the Thirty-third. Moore came out a brevet brigadier general.

The post at Muscoda was never large and gave up its charter early in 1896. However, the veterans tried again in 1900 with a new post name, H. W. Lawton, and number, 279, and remained on the department rolls until 1924.

O. B. RICE POST 71, Eleva

TREMPEALEAU COUNTY • APRIL 26, 1886–1928

CHARTER MEMBERS: N. Gilbert, St. Clair Jones, Syvert Nicholson, Orvil Jones, James W. Grant, Ole Nicholson, T. L. Pratt, J. D. Cooper, J. H. Springer, F. W. Rosman, Almon Sampson, John Harrison

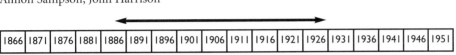

1866	1871	1876	1881	1886	1891	1896	1901	1906	1911	1916	1921	1926	1931	1936	1941	1946	1951

MEMBERSHIP BY YEAR (ACCOUNTED FOR): 1886, 12; 1904, 13; 1905, 14; 1906, 14; 1907, 14; 1908, 15; 1909, 15; 1910, 15; 1911, 13; 1912, 11; 1913, 8; 1914, 9; 1915, 9; 1916, 8; 1917, 8; 1918, 7; 1919, 7; 1920, 6; 1921, 5; 1922, 4; 1923, 3; 1924, 3; 1925, 3; 1926, 3; 1927, 3   **LAST MEMBER:** Unknown

The Grand Army post at Eleva in Trempealeau County was one of the later posts formed, being assigned a number which had just previously been surrendered.

The post, named O. B. Rice Post 71, was never large but re-mained on the department roster until 1928.

The namesake of the post is somewhat of an enigma, but there is an "Obidian Rice" buried in Eleva, his marker bearing the dates of 1832 to 1877.

A. M. HOWARD POST 72
CUSTER POST 72, Rock Elm

PIERCE COUNTY • MARCH 27, 1883–1919

CHARTER MEMBERS: Harry Britell, August Jesse, Daniel W. Dutcher, David Rice, Simon Groot, W. O. Churchill, M. C. Thompson, Milton C. Gueet, David L. White, John C. Anderson, Jamie Collett, Jacob Gove, A. H. Howard, Abraham Gossett, Peter Ahair, Chidester (first name unknown), Edmund Holt

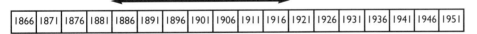

1866	1871	1876	1881	1886	1891	1896	1901	1906	1911	1916	1921	1926	1931	1936	1941	1946	1951

MEMBERSHIP BY YEAR (ACCOUNTED FOR): 1883, 17; 1884, 33; 1887, 35; 1888, 40; 1889, 33; 1904, 14; 1905, 13; 1906, 13; 1907, 12; 1908, 12; 1909, 11; 1910, 11; 1911, 11; 1912, 10; 1913, 8; 1914, 7; 1915, 8; 1916, 8; 1917, 6; 1918, 7   **LAST MEMBER:** Unknown

GEORGE A. CUSTER

The Rock Elm Post 72 in Pierce County was originally called the A. M. Howard Post. No record shows who Howard was. The roster of Wisconsin soldiers in the Civil War has no "A. Howard" as serving from Pierce County. Nor is there any indication of when and why the name was changed. But it did change, apparently sometime between 1886 and 1890.

This time the men chose to honor one of the Civil War's most flamboyant soldiers, George Armstrong Custer. Custer had fallen at Little Big Horn some years before the change. The romance attached to his name from his postwar experience may have been a factor in the choice. But his Civil War record on its own could have impressed the veterans of Rock Elm. Although he graduated last in his class at West Point in 1861, he was an able staff officer early in the war, earning a small niche in military aviation history by being sent up as the military observer in Professor Thaddeus Lowe's balloon.

Men of Custer Post 72, Rock Elm, in the Poplar Hill Cemetery, circa 1910–12. From left: John Wheeler, John Lansing, Andrew J. Weeks, Emil Leischer, Charles Condit, L. James Ingalls, Philo Kelly, John Anderson, William Churchill, and Simon Groot. Photo provided by the Pierce County Historical Society.

Post 72 members stand in reverence before the stained-glass window they donated to the Rock Elm Methodist Church, circa 1905. From left: Andrew Weeks, David Rice, Charles Condit, William Miles, Daniel Dutcher, James Ingalls, John Wheeler, William Churchill, Milton Guest, Emil Leischer, and Simon Groot. Photo provided by the Pierce County Historical Society.

JAMES S. ALBAN POST 73, Pittsville

WOOD COUNTY • MAY 10, 1883–1905

CHARTER MEMBERS: George W. Stever, James Severns, Henry Allen, Loren Shumway, Chas. Galloway, Myron F. Hubbard, Byron R. Tarbox, Frank H. Mosher, Henry W. Hitchcock, Patrick Ryan, John W. Vaughn, Samuel M. Thompson, Wm. Downing, James W. Dean, Stillman S. Snow, John P. Sharp, John Brown, John A. Brown, Orrin Gray

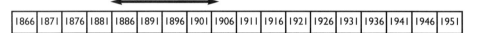

| 1866 | 1871 | 1876 | 1881 | 1886 | 1891 | 1896 | 1901 | 1906 | 1911 | 1916 | 1921 | 1926 | 1931 | 1936 | 1941 | 1946 | 1951 |

MEMBERSHIP BY YEAR (ACCOUNTED FOR): 1883, 19; 1887, 21; 1888, 22; 1889, 26; 1904, 8
LAST MEMBER: Unknown

JAMES S. ALBAN

James S. Alban was one of the leading figures in Plover, Portage County, when the Civil War began, and he was instrumental in raising the Eighteenth Wisconsin Infantry, despite having no military experience and being over 50 years old. He was appointed colonel of the regiment and lead it into its baptism of fire at the Battle of Shiloh, specifically into the vortex of battle known as the Hornet's Nest. Alban was one of those who fell to a sharpshooter's bullet that day. The new G.A.R. post at Pittsville, not far from Plover, chose to honor Alban when they selected a name. Alban Post 73 continued beyond the turn of the twentieth century, but as was typical of so many rural posts, it never had a robust membership.

EDWARD A. RAMSEY POST 74, Oconto

OCONTO COUNTY • OCTOBER 10, 1883–1938

CHARTER MEMBERS: Unknown

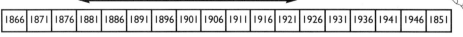

| 1866 | 1871 | 1876 | 1881 | 1886 | 1891 | 1896 | 1901 | 1906 | 1911 | 1916 | 1921 | 1926 | 1931 | 1936 | 1941 | 1946 | 1851 |

MEMBERSHIP BY YEAR (ACCOUNTED FOR): 1887, 32; 1888, 57; 1889, 85; 1895, 48; 1904, 57; 1905, 57; 1906, 51; 1907, 48; 1908, 47; 1909, 47; 1910, 46; 1911, 43; 1912, 41;

1913, 23; 1914, 21; 1915, 19; 1916, 19; 1917, 18; 1918, 17; 1919, 15; 1920, 13; 1921, 11; 1922, 11; 1923, 10; 1924, 9;
1925, 11; 1926, 8; 1927, 6; 1928, 5; 1929, 5; 1930, 4; 1931, 3; 1932, 3; 1933, 2; 1934, 2; 1935, 1; 1936, 1; 1937, 1
LAST MEMBER: George A. Baldwin

The G.A.R. post at Oconto, one of the longer-tenured posts in northern Wisconsin—its last member died in 1937—was named for, Edward A. Ramsey, an Oconto man who left for war with the "Oconto River Drivers," soon to become Company H, Fourth Wisconsin Cavalry, and rose to command the company by the end of the war.

Ramsey Post was a strong organization, a fairly large one during the order's most impressive years, and still had more than 50 members for several years into the twentieth century.

SYLVESTER WHEELER POST 75, Verona
DANE COUNTY • FEBRUARY 22, 1888–1921

CHARTER MEMBERS: Wm. Driesbock, Sam'l G. Rice, Edward Hubbard, Henry Wineland, Alfred Brader, E. S. Shuman, W. G. L. Motts, Reuben Aye, C. M. Longstreet, Patrick Goggin, Samuel Barry, M. C. Webber, John P. Cords, N. N. Merrick, John Kircher, John Casebeer, Henry Niglis, Jas. M. Gilbert, Fredrick Casebeer

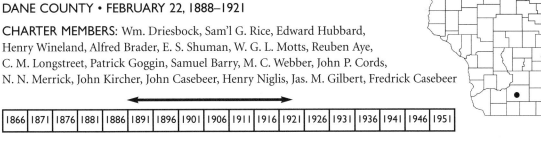

MEMBERSHIP BY YEAR (ACCOUNTED FOR): 1888, 22; 1889, 31; 1904, 15; 1905, 9; 1906, 9; 1907, 9; 1908, 9; 1909, 9; 1910, 9; 1911, 9; 1912, 9; 1913, 9; 1914, 7; 1915, 7; 1916, 7; 1917, 5; 1918, 2; 1919, 2; 1920, 2
LAST MEMBER: Unknown

Post 75 was assigned in 1888 to a new post at Verona in Dane County. It was named for Sylvester Wheeler, a Verona man who enlisted in Company E, Twenty-third Wisconsin, in August 1862. He served with his regiment in the West and suffered a fate that thousands of others suffered in that area during the war: he died of sickness at Milliken's Bend, Louisiana, on May 19, 1863. The post served Verona veterans for about 32 years.

MYRON GARDNER POST 75, Arcadia
TREMPEALEAU COUNTY • 1883–1888

CHARTER MEMBERS: Seth Putnam, commander; E.Q. Nye, senior vice commander; Joseph Failin, junior vice commander; Bishop (first name unknown), surgeon; Charles Dalle, officer of the day; Jno. Dennis, officer of the guard; Jno. D. Lewis, adjutant; T. B. Rand, sergeant major; E. M. Stanford, chaplain

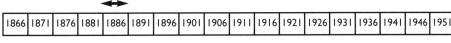

LAST MEMBER: Unknown

Myron Gardner, a youth who enlisted in the Galena Light Guards from the Arcadia area at the outbreak of the Civil War, became the first to die in the regiment, the Second Wisconsin, which had a greater proportion of men die from battlefield action than any other of the country's more than three thousand regiments. Gardner, of Company B of the Second, died from artillery fire the regiment underwent at Blackburn's Ford, a preliminary firefight to the First Battle of Bull Run. Thus he was the first of 148 killed in action and 60 more who died from wounds from the Second Wisconsin throughout the war. Gardner is buried at Centerville behind the lines of that initial battle.

This post succumbed in 1888 but was revived the following year under the number 255.

WALWORTH COUNTY POST 76, RUTHERFORD B. HAYES POST 76, Elkhorn

WALWORTH COUNTY • MAY 10, 1883–1941

CHARTER MEMBERS: Emmett McKaig, Dwight Preston, Alfred Churchill, Geo. W. Gabriel, Timothy Hall, Eli W. Garfield, S. R. Holden, O. Carswell, J. W. Gaylord, Geo. W. Wylie, O. A. Boggs, Levi E. Allen, E. C. Hollse, John Matheson, Perry Welsh, W. H. Mayhew, C. Dinsmore, L. L. Medbury, Isaac Kend, W. H. Welsh, J. C. Magill

| 1866 | 1871 | 1876 | 1881 | 1886 | 1891 | 1896 | 1901 | 1906 | 1911 | 1916 | 1921 | 1926 | 1931 | 1936 | 1941 | 1946 | 1951 |

MEMBERSHIP BY YEAR (ACCOUNTED FOR): 1883, 21; 1887, 50; 1888, 58; 1889, 62; 1904, 38; 1905, 32; 1906, 32; 1907, 37; 1908, 39; 1909, 38; 1910, 38; 1911, 37; 1912, 31; 1913, 25; 1914, 24; 1915, 21; 1916, 17; 1917, 16; 1918, 13; 1919, 12; 1920, 12; 1921, 12; 1922, 12; 1923, 10; 1924, 10; 1925, 10; 1926, 10; 1927, 10; 1928, 7; 1929, 8; 1930, 6; 1932, 6; 1933, 5; 1934, 5; 1935, 4; 1936, 4; 1937, 4; 1938, 25   **LAST MEMBER:** John Gole or J. A. Ryan

RUTHERFORD B. HAYES

The veterans of Walworth County organized their G.A.R. post at Elkhorn in 1883 and were content to be known as the Walworth County Post 76 for the next decade.

Following the death of Rutherford B. Hayes, whose controversial 1876 election as president marked the end of Reconstruction, the men chose to honor the former officer of Ohio troops who served primarily in the Shendandoah Valley. He had a successful political career after the war, culminating in his move to the White House. He died in Fremont, Ohio, on January 17, 1893.

The remaining members of Rutherford B. Hayes Post 76, Elkhorn, shown in a 1926 picture. Standing, from left: J. E. Fuller, Emmet McKaig, William O'Brien, C. H. Doane, and J. E. Lauderdale. Seated, from left: John Meadows, George H. Farrar, William H. Mayhew, G. W. Shepard, and John McGill. Photo provided by the Walworth County Historical Society.

JOHN T. FLYNN POST 77, La Crosse

LA CROSSE COUNTY • MAY 5, 1883–1936

CHARTER MEMBERS: E. B. Redfield, commander; J. D. Landis, senior vice commander; J. W. Davis, junior vice commander; E. C. Young, surgeon; J. E. Wilson, officer of the day; H. Morrison, officer of the guard; G. W. Morrison, quartermaster; L. P. Bushey, chaplain; L. M. Dolphing, adjutant; Patrick McCanley, sergeant major; R. W. McDonald, quartermaster sergeant

| 1866 | 1871 | 1876 | 1881 | 1886 | 1891 | 1896 | 1901 | 1906 | 1911 | 1916 | 1921 | 1926 | 1931 | 1936 | 1941 | 1946 | 1951 |

MEMBERSHIP BY YEAR (ACCOUNTED FOR): 1883, 33; 1887, 51; 1888, 61; 1889, 87; 1904, 58; 1905, 53; 1906, 37; 1907, 36; 1908, 30; 1909, 34; 1910, 26; 1911, 27; 1912, 27; 1913, 27; 1914, 23; 1915, 24; 1916, 17; 1917, 23; 1918, 20; 1919, 14; 1920, 12; 1921, 10; 1922, 10; 1923, 8; 1924, 7; 1925, 7; 1926, 6; 1927, 4; 1928, 4; 1929, 4; 1930, 3; 1931, 3; 1932, 3; 1933, 3; 1934, 3; 1935, 3   **LAST MEMBER:** Unknown

John T. Flynn Post 77 was originally from North La Crosse, the post office for which was discontinued the year after Post 77 was formed. This was one of southwestern Wisconsin's larger posts. It still had more than a dozen members up to 1920.

The post was named for a member of Company I, Eighth Wisconsin, recruited from La Crosse. Flynn was chosen as one of the company's corporals before it left Camp Randall in 1861. He was wounded at Corinth, but continued in service and reenlisted in 1864. However, he died from chronic sickness while home on furlough in August 1865 with his wife and two children at his side.

JOHN MATTESON POST 78, Embarrass
WAUPACA COUNTY • JULY 10, 1868–1874

CHARTER MEMBERS: J. B. Johnson, Rodney Seaver, J. P. Waite, Edwin E. Park, A. M. Cook, L. H. Stebbins, W. F. Enos, John McCannon, J. M. Vanderhoof, H. M. Fitzgerald, E. E. Hillman, Rosell S. Miner

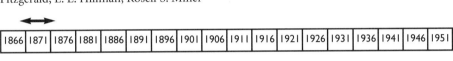

1866	1871	1876	1881	1886	1891	1896	1901	1906	1911	1916	1921	1926	1931	1936	1941	1946	1951

LAST MEMBER: Unknown

Waupaca County was the frontier when the Civil War came. Many men were working in the lumbering camps, although they came from various places. When the war broke out many enlisted from the county despite their roots elsewhere. Thus records of Waupaca County men gone to war are sketchy. One who was a "native" of the area was John Matteson, but even his service is largely unrecorded. He was killed in the war, and the veterans, about 40 of them, who returned to the Embarrass area chose to honor Matteson when they formed a post. Matteson Post 78 lasted only until 1874, perhaps a result of the inherent transient nature of these lumberjacks.

JOHN A. KELLOGG POST 78, Antigo
LANGLADE COUNTY • MAY 15, 1883–1936

CHARTER MEMBERS: E. H. Blinn, B. F. Dorr, S. W. Chamberlain, William Brainard, John A. Long, F. M. Sherman, Henry Smith, John B. Bruner, A. L. Russell, Edward Daskam, Charles Beadleston, Edward R. Dudley, H. Springstead

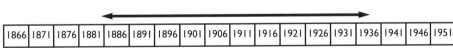

1866	1871	1876	1881	1886	1891	1896	1901	1906	1911	1916	1921	1926	1931	1936	1941	1946	1951

MEMBERSHIP BY YEAR (ACCOUNTED FOR): 1887, 56; 1888, 82; 1889, 80; 1895, 84; 1904, 54; 1905, 37; 1906, 45; 1907, 47; 1908, 47; 1909, 43; 1910, 43; 1911, 44; 1912, 39; 1913, 40; 1914, 40; 1915, 31; 1916, 35; 1917, 33; 1918, 31; 1919, 26; 1920, 22; 1921, 18; 1922, 15; 1923, 14; 1924, 12; 1925, 10; 1926, 8; 1927, 7; 1928, 6; 1929, 6; 1930, 4; 1931, 1; 1932, 1; 1933, 1; 1934, 1; 1935, 1   LAST MEMBER: John Newbury

MARC AND BETH STORCH
JOHN A.
KELLOGG

Veterans who organized the Grand Army post at Antigo chose to honor one of the leaders of the Sixth Wisconsin, John A. Kellogg.

Kellogg was the first lieutenant of Company K, the "Lemonwier Minute Men" from the Mauston area, which had been recruited by Rufus Dawes, the company's captain. Dawes rose to command of the Sixth. Kellogg was captain of Company K in the Battle of the Wilderness where he was captured and sent to South Carolina. He escaped once on the way to Charleston and was hunted down and recaptured. He escaped a second time while being moved from Charleston to Columbia, and this time he made his way for some 350 miles to federal lines. He rejoined the Sixth Wisconsin and ended the war as colonel, last commander of the Iron Brigade, and brevet brigadier general. He died in Wausau in February 1883.

Kellogg Post had a long record of serving the veterans in Langlade County, and the post had more than two dozen members until after World War I.

I. RAMSDELL POST 79, Marion

WAUPACA COUNTY • MAY 11, 1883–1896

CHARTER MEMBERS: Charles Cleveland, Joseph Chevalier, H. E. Welch, Henry Swan, Myron Taylor, Joseph Brahier, C. G. Kirberger, Israel Cannon, F. W. Lade, Ira Lake, Peter Doty, James Jordan, Robert Mountain, Myron Taylor, Charles Weed, R. H. Ha_____, E.B. Rasey, F. Herbechter, H. D. Minton, Carl Krueger, Alfred Darrell, Arnold Wheeler, James Bayard, Henry Stock, George Clark, and M. B. Hall

1866	1871	1876	1881	1886	1891	1896	1901	1906	1911	1916	1921	1926	1931	1936	1941	1946	1951

MEMBERSHIP BY YEAR (ACCOUNTED FOR): 1888, 17; 1889, 11
    W. I. Ramsdell, for whom the post was named, died in 1922.

LAST MEMBER: Dan Ramsdell, a brother of

The Marion Post was founded in 1883 and was named for Washington Irving Ramsdell, a later resident of Marion who was a Great Lakes schooner captain before the war out of Manitowoc. He chose the army rather than naval service when the war came and enlisted in the Fourteenth Wisconsin. He became a lieutenant in his unit and served from Shiloh through all of Sherman's campaigns. After the war he moved to Marion.

He died there in about 1872.

The Marion Post chose to honor Ramsdell, calling itself "I. Ramsdell Post 79." Little is on record concerning the post except that it was dropped from the department rolls in 1896 as delinquent. There is some indication that by that time its membership, never large, had dwindled considerably. Although the post was gone, three members lived on to 1911 or beyond.

GEORGE M. EMERY POST 79, Wolf Creek

POLK COUNTY • JANUARY 15, 1898–1910

CHARTER MEMBERS: A. C. Hoover was the first commander.

1866	1871	1876	1881	1886	1891	1896	1901	1906	1911	1916	1921	1926	1931	1936	1941	1946	1951

MEMBERSHIP BY YEAR (ACCOUNTED FOR): 1904, 16; 1905, 16; 1906, 15; 1907, 11; 1908, 12; 1909, 9   **LAST MEMBER:** Unknown

The Wolf Creek veterans of Polk County organized their post in 1898, being one of the later ones chartered. But the post received the number 79 because that had been most recently given up.

The post was named for George M. Emery, a soldier from Lowell, Dodge County, who was a member of Company E, Third Wisconsin. Emery died from illness on August 15, 1864, at Chattanooga, Tennessee.

ORRIN D. CHAPMAN POST 80, Gays Mills

CRAWFORD COUNTY • APRIL 24, 1883–1912

CHARTER MEMBERS: N. A. Tallman, Edward Gray, George R. Rounds, Theodore Harding, Phillip H. Moon, A. H. Frank, J. S. Dudley, Cyrus W. Shafer, C. R. Young, G. R. Twining, John Lowe, J. G. Richardson, Darius Welch, R. W. Abbey, Edwin Thompson, Charles R. Rounds, O. P. Rounds

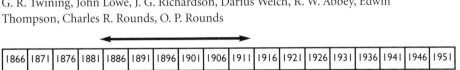

| 1866 | 1871 | 1876 | 1881 | 1886 | 1891 | 1896 | 1901 | 1906 | 1911 | 1916 | 1921 | 1926 | 1931 | 1936 | 1941 | 1946 | 1951 |

MEMBERSHIP BY YEAR (ACCOUNTED FOR): 1884, 28; 1887, 34; 1889, 44; 1904, 20; 1905, 20; 1906, 19; 1907, 10; 1908, 10; 1909, 9; 1910, 6; 1911, 6   **LAST MEMBER:** Unknown

When the men of Gays Mills formed a Grand Army Post in 1883, they chose for their name that of a man who was killed at Gettysburg.

Orrin D. Chapman was one of those men of the Iron Brigade whose heroic action on the first day at Gettysburg made possible the eventual success of Union forces over succeeding days.

Chapman had risen from the ranks of Company C, Sixth Wisconsin, and was second lieutenant of the company when it engaged the Confederates at the famous railroad cut. He was one of the many Iron Brigade soldiers killed that day.

Chapman Post 80 flourished in the prosperous days of the G.A.R. and went into sharp decline at the same time as the national order after the turn of the twentieth century. The post lasted until 1912.

WILLIAM H. HAWLEY POST 81, Shawano

SHAWANO COUNTY • MAY 4, 1883–1917

CHARTER MEMBERS: J. M. Robinson, Chris Hill, W. H. Murdock, J. M. Schweers, H. I. Walter, C. R. Klebesdal, A. Koeppen, B. B. Huntington, O. H. Huntley, M. Devlin, I. Farrell, R. K. Smith, D. Gorham Sr., J. D. Magee, C. H. Newton, J. Darrow, E. J. Munroe, A. Zerwas, F. Schweers, F. Eberlein

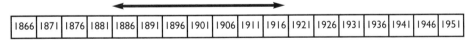

| 1866 | 1871 | 1876 | 1881 | 1886 | 1891 | 1896 | 1901 | 1906 | 1911 | 1916 | 1921 | 1926 | 1931 | 1936 | 1941 | 1946 | 1951 |

MEMBERSHIP BY YEAR (ACCOUNTED FOR): 1883, 20; 1886, 24; 1887, 10; 1889, 19; 1904, 11; 1905, 10; 1906, 10; 1907, 10; 1908, 9; 1909, 9; 1910, 9; 1911, 9; 1912, 9; 1913, 9; 1914, 7; 1915, 7; 1916, 7   **LAST MEMBER:** Unknown

WILLIAM H. HAWLEY

William H. Hawley Post 81, Shawano, was active until World War I, but was never large. Its first commander was J. M. Schweers.

The post was named for General William H. Hawley, who was the last commander of the Third Wisconsin Infantry.

He entered the war in 1861 as captain of Company K, originally known as the "Dane County Guards."

Hawley was also a soldier in the Mexican War, wounded at Chapultepec. In the Civil War he was wounded at Cedar Mountain Virginia, in 1862. Breveted a brigadier general at the close of that war, he joined the Regular Army and was first lieutenant of the Twentieth U.S. Infantry in 1868. He died in 1873.

A veterans' parade in Shawano. Photo provided by the Shawano County Historical Society.

CHARLES COLEMAN POST 82, Durand

PEPIN COUNTY • MAY 17, 1883–1924

CHARTER MEMBERS: George L. Wakefield, commander; Gilbert Dowd, senior vice commander; Allen DeGroff, junior vice commander; Dr. Hutchinson, surgeon; N. C. Bradley, chaplain; S. M. Scott, officer of the day; William Cassell, officer of the guard; Elias Vrandenburg, quartermaster; Miletus Knight, adjutant; Henry Doughty, sergeant major; E. N. Sabin, quartermaster sergeant

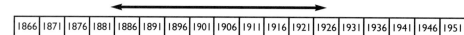

| 1866 | 1871 | 1876 | 1881 | 1886 | 1891 | 1896 | 1901 | 1906 | 1911 | 1916 | 1921 | 1926 | 1931 | 1936 | 1941 | 1946 | 1951 |

MEMBERSHIP BY YEAR (ACCOUNTED FOR): 1887, 48; 1888, 56; 1889, 60; 1904, 28; 1905, 22; 1906, 19; 1907, 16; 1908, 17; 1909, 18; 1910, 16; 1911, 19; 1912, 16; 1913, 15; 1914, 15; 1915, 11; 1916, 10; 1917, 9; 1918, 8; 1919, 7; 1920, 6; 1921, 4; 1922, 4; 1923, 4   **LAST MEMBER:** Unknown

WISCONSIN VETERANS
MUSEUM
**CHARLES
COLEMAN**

The veterans in Durand chose to name their G.A.R. post for Charles Coleman, a member of Company D, Tenth Wisconsin Infantry who was wounded at Perryville, Kentucky, in 1862 and was discharged in June 1863 because of his wounds. He returned to Durand and died in 1881.

Post 82 served its Pepin County community for more than 40 years, having 60 members in 1889, the G.A.R.'s zenith, and having more than a dozen members up to the eve of World War I.

JOHN FALLER POST 83, North Freedom

SAUK COUNTY • MAY 2, 1883–1926

CHARTER MEMBERS: John Wiggins, commander; J. B. Ashley, senior vice commander; John Rooney, junior vice commander; L. Smith, surgeon; F. Hackett, chaplain

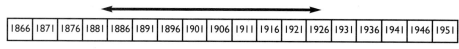

| 1866 | 1871 | 1876 | 1881 | 1886 | 1891 | 1896 | 1901 | 1906 | 1911 | 1916 | 1921 | 1926 | 1931 | 1936 | 1941 | 1946 | 1951 |

MEMBERSHIP BY YEAR (ACCOUNTED FOR): 1884, 34; 1887, 34; 1888, 34; 1889, 45; 1904, 21; 1905, 20; 1906, 20; 1907, 20; 1908, 20; 1909, 17; 1910, 16; 1911, 16; 1912, 13; 1913, 11; 1914, 11; 1915, 11; 1916, 10; 1917, 8; 1918, 8; 1919, 5; 1920, 4; 1921, 3; 1922, 2; 1923, 2; 1924, 2; 1925, 1   **LAST MEMBER:** J. Sproud

G.A.R. post 83, North Freedom, was one of many rural posts in south-central Wisconsin. It did not achieve a huge membership, but it continued to serve its veterans in that area of Sauk County so long as one was left.

The post was named for John Faller, a member of Company A., Nineteenth Wisconsin Infantry, who was taken prisoner at Fair Oaks, Virginia, on October 27, 1864. He was mustered out of service on May 17, 1865.

A. S. BENNETT POST 84, Boyceville

DUNN COUNTY • MAY 12, 1883–1919

CHARTER MEMBERS: J. W. Granger, Joseph Phillips, Thomas West, S. T. Best, Peter Bodett, E. P. Best, L. L. Sutliff, W. White, J. W. Brewer, William Steen, James S. Carver, W. P. Monteith, Henry Carman, Fred Waite, William A. Morgan, D. W. Clough, S. S. Wheeler, Frederick Wachter, Morgan D. Kinney, John Nauman, Ansel Hayes, L. J. Phillips

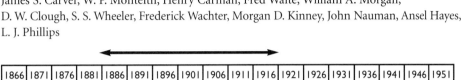

| 1866 | 1871 | 1876 | 1881 | 1886 | 1891 | 1896 | 1901 | 1906 | 1911 | 1916 | 1921 | 1926 | 1931 | 1936 | 1941 | 1946 | 1951 |

MEMBERSHIP BY YEAR (ACCOUNTED FOR): 1883, 22; 1887, 35; 1888, 33; 1889, 33; 1904, 17; 1905, 17; 1906, 10; 1907, 11; 1908, 10; 1909, 11; 1910, 10; 1911, 10; 1912, 10; 1913, 11; 1914, 10; 1915, 10; 1916, 6; 1917, 5; 1918, 5

LAST MEMBER: Unknown

Post 84 in Boyceville was named for Alfred S. Bennett, a soldier in Company A, Thirty-eighth Wisconsin. The regiment was one of the later ones raised in Wisconsin, and the soldiers were sent to the Army of the Potomac, where they saw heavy action in the late stages of the war. Bennett was missing in action on July 30, 1864, when the regiment joined the assault on Confederate lines just blown up in what became known as the Battle of the Crater. He survived the war, however, only to be killed in a skirmish with Indians after he was commissioned in the Regular Army.

Bennett Post 84 began with 22 members, with J. W. Granger as first commander. It was never large, yet it continued to exist until after World War I.

GEORGE H. THOMAS POST 9 (85), Winneconne

WINNEBAGO COUNTY • 1870–1872

CHARTER MEMBERS: W. H. Walker, post commander; T. C. Miller, senior vice commander; M. Ashley, junior vice commander; J. Ulrich, adjutant; J. J. Mathews, quartermaster; G. W. Dodge, chaplain; T. A. Clark, officer of the day; G. H. Fuller, outside guard; G. B. Noyes, surgeon

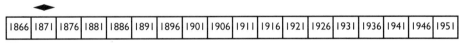

| 1866 | 1871 | 1876 | 1881 | 1886 | 1891 | 1896 | 1901 | 1906 | 1911 | 1916 | 1921 | 1926 | 1931 | 1936 | 1941 | 1946 | 1951 |

LAST MEMBER: Unknown

The officers of George H. Thomas Post 85 as noted above were installed on December 26, 1870, and may or may not have been the first officers of the post.

The newspaper account of the installation said that the post was "in a flourishing condition."

It flourished enough so that in the weeding out of posts done by the department in late 1871, Thomas Post 85 moved up in number to 9. Thereafter, apparently, it went into a decline and did not make the second cut a few years later. It was not until 1889 that the veterans in Winneconne tried again, and this new incarnation became Post 227.

For biographical information on George H. Thomas see Post 6.

JERRY TURNER POST 85, Viola
RICHLAND COUNTY • MAY 24, 1883–1927

CHARTER MEMBERS: R. H. DeLap, Salma Rodgers, W. J. Waggoner, J. B. Snow, D. B. Sommars, M. V. B. Richards, Adam Barton, Joseph Gowyer, S. D. Wiltrout, Jacob Benn, J. M. Clark, T. D. Risin, David Austin, J. M. Saubert, Thomas Morris, A. A. Wiltrout, L. C. Gates, E. C. Gill, E. B. Waggoner, G. W. Wise, James Morrow, Peter Fazel, Alonzo Clark, T. M. McCullough, J. L. Simmons, I. G. B. Ott, L. S. Kellogg, T. L. Dobson, A. E. Clark, J. S. Kanable, J. R. Campbell, B. W. Lawton, Robt. Rabbitt

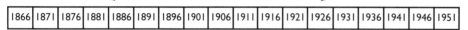

1866	1871	1876	1881	1886	1891	1896	1901	1906	1911	1916	1921	1926	1931	1936	1941	1946	1951

MEMBERSHIP BY YEAR (ACCOUNTED FOR): 1883, 33; 1887, 41; 1888, 42; 1889, 39; 1904, 23; 1905, 22; 1906, 22; 1907, 22; 1908, 23; 1909, 22; 1910, 22; 1911, 20; 1912, 21; 1913, 21; 1914, 21; 1915, 20; 1916, 18; 1917, 16; 1918, 11; 1919, 9; 1920, 9; 1921, 9; 1922, 1; 1923, 1; 1924, 1; 1925, 1; 1926, 1   **LAST MEMBER:** J. A. Loveless

Jeremiah "Jerry" Turner went off to war with the "Richland County Scott Guards" which became Company H of the Fifth Wisconsin. Turner rose to captain of the company in which capacity he was killed in action at Fredericksburg, Virginia, on May 3, 1863. That battle was part of the larger Battle of Chancellorsville under Hooker, not the forlorn Burnside assaults of December 1862.

The Jerry Turner Post 85 at Viola was begun in the great growth year of 1883. It remained a relatively strong post until World War I. It declined in the ensuing decade, in the last half of which it had a lone survivor.

COL. E. E. ELLSWORTH POST 86, Merrillan
JACKSON COUNTY • MAY 15, 1883–1920

CHARTER MEMBERS: Chas. N. Davis, Henry Martin, W. C. Eastman, John Ashton, Christian Hilty, Jacob Clark, James Delhanty, Chas. Beadle, Oliver Martin, Garry Martin, Ole A. Prestmon, E. J. Austin, M. C. Smith, A. R. Watson, B. M. Fullmer, Thomas Laughlin, A. S. Pickett, Madison Laughlin, Nelson Fields, S. W. Abbott, Clark H. Foltz, W. H. Doty, Ever Peterson, James D. Hagan, W. J. Rollse, Geo. W. LaGraves, James Murphy, Elisha Stockwell, James W. Dye, Chester Stile, R. .H. Goucher, Wm. Hartman

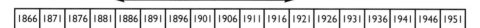

1866	1871	1876	1881	1886	1891	1896	1901	1906	1911	1916	1921	1926	1931	1936	1941	1946	1951

MEMBERSHIP BY YEAR (ACCOUNTED FOR): 1883, 32; 1884, 60; 1887, 15; 1888, 26; 1889, 36; 1904, 15; 1905, 19; 1906, 19; 1907, 19; 1908, 22; 1909, 22; 1910, 10; 1911, 15; 1912, 15; 1913, 15; 1914, 17; 1915, 15; 1916, 12; 1917, 10; 1918, 10; 1919, 8   **LAST MEMBER:** Unknown

E. E. ELLSWORTH

The first "martyr" of the War of the Rebellion was Colonel Ephriam Elmer Ellsworth. The G.A.R. post at Merrillan, Post 86, was named for him. Ellsworth was a personal friend of President Abraham Lincoln and brought a regiment of Zouaves, which he had previously organized as a crack militia outfit, to Washington in the weeks after Forth Sumter. He took his men across the Potomac to Alexandria where a rebel flag flew its defiance within view from Washington. Ellsworth personally tore the banner down and was killed by the civilian owner of the building displaying the flag on May 4, 1861. The whole nation mourned his death and he was remembered by the veterans in Merrillan more than two decades later.

PERRIN C. JUDKINS POST 87, Alma Center

JACKSON COUNTY • JUNE 15, 1883–1938

CHARTER MEMBERS: J. B. Miller, L. S. Avery, C. R. Schermerhorn, Philip Reesman, T. P. Eldridge, Wm. Bopp, John Meek, Geo. Rutherford, J. E. Most, D. H. Fuller, J. W. Stanton, A. N. Alderman, J. W. Page, Benson Hall, A. W. Merrill, C. C. Edwards, J. J. Metcalf, C. C. Durling, C. J. Carey, O. W. Irish, Geo. Gleason, L. C. V. Curtis, P. Inskip, B. Miller, D. Nolop, Geo. Meek, A. S. North, G. W. Cook, P. Cray. S. R. Raynals

1866	1871	1876	1881	1886	1891	1896	1901	1906	1911	1916	1921	1926	1931	1936	1941	1946	1951

MEMBERSHIP BY YEAR (ACCOUNTED FOR): 1887, 40; 1888, 36; 1889, 32; 1904, 26; 1905, 26; 1906, 26; 1907, 16; 1908, 16; 1909, 19; 1910, 21; 1911, 20; 1912, 17; 1913, 16; 1914, 11; 1915, 12; 1916, 10; 1917, 10; 1918, 10; 1919, 10; 1920, 9; 1921, 9; 1922, 9; 1923, 9; 1924, 9; 1925, 9; 1926, 8; 1927, 6; 1928, 5; 1929, 4; 1930, 4; 1931, 3; 1932, 3; 1933, 3; 1934, 3; 1935, 2; 1936, 2; 1937, 2; 1938, 1 **LAST MEMBER:** Mark D. Merchant

The veterans at Alma Center did not have a large post, but a few of its members had enough longevity so that the post remained on the rolls until it was down to its last member in 1938. First commander of Post 87 was J. B. Miller.

Post 87 was named for Perrin C. Judkins, a Madison man who was killed in action on May 8, 1864, while leading Company G, First United States (Berdan's) Sharpshooters, at the engagement at Todd's Tavern, Virginia. The battle was part of the Spotsylvania Campaign. He enlisted in September 1861 as a private, and he rose rapidly through the enlisted ranks, becoming second lieutenant of his company 15 months later.

Members of Judkins Post 87 of Alma Center, date unknown. Front row, from left: William Bopp, Dan Nolop, Fayette Dudley, and an unknown man. Middle row, from left: Addison Merrill, Jerome Miller, John Ashton, Carl Helwig, and Samuel Curran. Back row, from left: Carl Hauser, George Thayer, Sam Randles, and John Olson. Photo provided by the Jackson Co. Historical Society.

WILLIAM A. BARSTOW POST 88, Kendall

MONROE COUNTY • AUGUST 26, 1879–1922

CHARTER MEMBERS: J. Denton, Frank Cholvin, R. B. Dunlap, Geo. M. Evans, Daniel Newton, H. P. Waffle, Hial West, R. Leasure, D. M. Holmes, Levi Carver, R. Sherwood, John Rose, James Seiker, Jno. Baldwin, Wm. Kimmerly, W. Baxter, Samuel Buswell, Saml. McQueen, R. A. McComb, Wm. Vaughn, Wm. Lumsden, Leonard Johnson, A. Felker, John Fatherlas

1866	1871	1876	1881	1886	1891	1896	1901	1906	1911	1916	1921	1926	1931	1936	1941	1946	1951

MEMBERSHIP BY YEAR (ACCOUNTED FOR): 1883, 24; 1884, 40; 1887, 30; 1888, 22; 1889, 38; 1901, 16; 1902, 13; 1904, 11 **LAST MEMBER:** Edward John Gale, died Jan. 27, 1941

WILLIAM A. BARSTOW

William A. Barstow was the third governor of Wisconsin (1854–56), but it was not for his political success, but rather for his war service as colonel of the Third Wisconsin Cavalry that the G.A.R. boys at Kendall named Post 88 for him.

Barstow was in a sense a casualty of the war. He commanded the Third for much of its arduous service in the West. He was mustered out at Fort Leavenworth, but his health was so bad that he was unable to return to Wisconsin and died in Kansas on October 14, 1865.

Members of Barstow Post 88 line up in front of the North Western Hotel in Kendall in the early 1880s, not long after their chartering. From left: Harvey Waffle, Robert Dunlap, D. W. Holmes, Carpenter (first name unknown), Andrew Felker, Daniel Newton, Samuel McQueen, Jim Broughton, Jim Burrel, Samuel Buswell, John Rose, F. B. Webb, Robert Leasum, George Evans, Walter Baxter, an unidentified man, and John Fatherlas.

NATHAN HOYT POST 89, Woodstock

RICHLAND COUNTY • MAY 25, 1883–1905

CHARTER MEMBERS: C. A. Keefe was the first commander.

1866	1871	1876	1881	1886	1891	1896	1901	1906	1911	1916	1921	1926	1931	1936	1941	1946	1951

MEMBERSHIP BY YEAR (ACCOUNTED FOR): 1887, 11; 1888, 19; 1889, 31; 1904, 11
LAST MEMBER: Unknown

Woodstock Post 89 honored a soldier from nearby Bloom Township, Nathan Hoyt, who was first sergeant of Company D, Eleventh Wisconsin. He was killed on July 7, 1862, at Bayou Cache, Arkansas.

WESLEY W. PATTON POST 90, Brodhead

GREEN COUNTY • JUNE 4, 1883–1937

CHARTER MEMBERS: A. D. Wooster, A. N. Randall, O. S. Putman, R. Broughton, A. E. Bulson, Geo. B. Wooster, G. T. Spaulding, W. W. Roderick, H. C. Putnam, H. P. Clarke, C. C. Stone, B. W. Beebe, O. F. Smith, Elias Coombs, B. L. Rolf, Robt. Baker, C.C. Smith, J. Walkey, E. Whitmore, J. D. Cole, Levi Adams, C. L. Gilbert, R. A. Slocum, G. W. Chase, J. M. Covert, J. Macomber, Allen Whipple, Wm. Lang, John Smith, Eugene Bartlett, Chas. Gilbert, W. H. Wells, C. W. Hopkins, J. W. Douglass, A. F. Miller, T. F. Patriguin, J. P. Baker, Jerry Smith, Geo. Frarey, Abram Evans, C. A. Payne, Jacob Hartman, Joseph Thompson, James D. Lindsey, Thomas A. Jackson, Wm. Hall Jr., Wm Coldren; W. R. Balecomb, Thos. J. Minor, W. H. Murray, D. A. Towers, L. J. Hyatt, W. H. Herrington, M. Pauley. A. J. Gordon, Daniel Straw, Alvin West, Daniel Dedrick, Saml. Baldwin

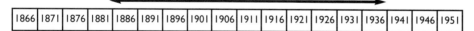

1866	1871	1876	1881	1886	1891	1896	1901	1906	1911	1916	1921	1926	1931	1936	1941	1946	1951

MEMBERSHIP BY YEAR (ACCOUNTED FOR): 1883, 59; 1884, 97; 1887, 76; 1888, 68; 1889, 78; 1904, 31; 1905, 28; 1906, 30; 1907, 50; 1908, 65; 1909, 63; 1910, 66; 1911, 68; 1912, 67; 1913, 64; 1914, 57; 1915, 55; 1916, 49; 1917, 48; 1918, 40; 1919, 37; 1920, 35; 1921, 32; 1922, 28; 1923, 27; 1924, 27; 1925, 23; 1926, 22; 1927, 17; 1928, 14; 1929, 8; 1930, 4; 1931, 4; 1932, 2; 1933, 2; 1934, 2; 1935, 2; 1936, 1 **LAST MEMBER:** Joe Bridge, 1936

WESLEY PATTON

With a rousing 59 charter members, the Wesley W. Patton Post 90 had an auspicious beginning, and it was a quite active post for most of its years. Its membership topped two dozen as late as 1924.

Post 89, for all its early strength, had some trying times. In 1896 the post considered surrendering its charter, but the veterans voted to continue Post 89 "indefinitely." Then, in the early 1900s, members from abandoned posts in the area transferred to

the Patton Post, which accounts for its unusually high membership figures approaching World War I.

The post was named for a Brodhead boy who was color sergeant of the Thirty-sixth Wisconsin and fell in the carnage at Cold Harbor on June 5, 1864.

Wesley Patton was just 21.

Members of Wesley Patton Post 90 of Brodhead, date unknown. Front row, from left: Ira Wilson, Freeman Roberts, Abner Webb, George Wooster, Isaac Young, Fred Sherman, Charles Stone, Dan Strow(?) or Straw. Second row, from left: Fred Ties, an unknown man, Winfield Pengra, Clark Williams, Ed Wessel, Taylor (first name unknown), Joe Bridge, Charles Benscoter. Third row, from left: an unknown man, Arnold Bennett, an unknown man, Tom Mack, Preston Jordan, John Keller, Bill Taylor, Ezra Stewart.

SAMUEL HARRISON POST 91, De Pere

BROWN COUNTY • JUNE 18, 1883–1937

CHARTER MEMBERS: J. R. Shepard, commander; H. E. Evans, senior vice commander; J. H. Tucker, junior vice commander; Dr. M.H. Fisk, surgeon; J. P. Weter, chaplain; S. Taylor, officer of the day; W. Croan, quartermaster; Jos. Gothica, officer of the guard; W. A. Bingham, adjutant; J. D. Tyler, sergeant major; C. Hooson, quartermaster sergeant

1866	1871	1876	1881	1886	1891	1896	1901	1906	1911	1916	1921	1926	1931	1936	1941	1946	1951

MEMBERSHIP BY YEAR (ACCOUNTED FOR): 1887, 49; 1888, 56; 1889, 57; 1904, 95; 1905, 89; 1906, 79; 1907, 79; 1908, 70; 1909, 67; 1910, 66; 1911, 64; 1912, 63; 1913, 62; 1914, 53; 1915, 52; 1916, 51; 1917, 39; 1918, 38; 1919, 40; 1920, 40; 1921, 40; 1922, 29; 1923, 25; 1924, 20; 1925, 20; 1926, 17; 1927, 16; 1928, 14; 1929, 12; 1930, 6; 1931, 4; 1932, 3; 1933, 1; 1934, 1; 1935, 1; 1936, 1   **LAST MEMBER:** Louis Vican

Company F of the Fourteenth Wisconsin was comprised primarily of men from De Pere, recruited in the fall of 1861 and sent south in early 1862 to a baptism at the Battle of Shiloh. The second lieutenant of the company was Samuel Harrison, and he soon rose to captain and the command of the company. One of the privates in the company was his son, Henry Harrison.

Captain Samuel Harrison was wounded at the Battle of

Corinth on October 3, 1862, and taken prisoner by the Confederates, who amputated his foot. He was retaken by federals the next day, but succumbed to his injuries on October 20.

When De Pere veterans organized a G.A.R. post, they chose to honor Captain Harrison. Post 91 had a long, active history, and at least numerically was strong through World War I and into the 1920s, when it counted more than three dozen members.

WILLIAM MOORE POST 92, Black River Falls

JACKSON COUNTY • JUNE 11, 1883–1935

CHARTER MEMBERS: R. D. Squires, E. F. Long, H. B. Cole, L. B. Brewer, George Moulsh, A. Meinhold, A. Erickson, Charles Franz, L. Miller, Charles Felt, S. D. Blake, J. P. Crosby, E. Quackenbush, A. Huggett, Robert Farrington, G. M. Perry, M. L. Finch, C. R. Johnson, William Bloomfeld, L. L. Dimmick, H. H. Powers, Charles Dretta, Newt Hansen, W. C. Lath, N. M. Clapp, Frank Cooper, Isaac Miles, John Marken, Lewis Clark, Daniel Spencer, William Thompson, H. C. Jones

1866	1871	1876	1881	1886	1891	1896	1901	1906	1911	1916	1921	1926	1931	1936	1941	1946	1951

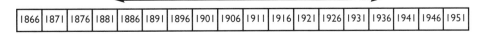

MEMBERSHIP BY YEAR (ACCOUNTED FOR): 1882, 66; 1884, 55; 1887, 104; 1888, 104; 1889, 95; 1904, 52; 1905, 50; 1906, 49; 1907, 48; 1908, 47; 1909, 42; 1910, 38; 1911, 30; 1912, 30; 1913, 24; 1914, 20; 1915, 22; 1916, 21; 1917, 19; 1918, 17; 1919, 15; 1920, 15; 1921, 15; 1922, 10; 1923, 7; 1924, 6; 1925, 6; 1926, 6; 1927, 5; 1928, 5; 1929, 4; 1930, 3; 1931, 3; 1932, 3; 1933, 1; 1934, 1   **LAST MEMBER:** C. W. Chafey

WILLIAM MOORE

William Moore Post 92, Black River Falls, was named for a Black River Falls man, captain of Company G, Tenth Wisconsin, who was killed on July 4, 1862, by guerrillas near Larkinsville, Alabama. Moore was the first Jackson County soldier killed in the war. His body was returned and is buried in the Black River Falls Cemetery.

The Moore Post was a fairly large post for its area of Wisconsin, reaching over one hundred members during the Grand Army's peak years. It was also of some interest in that it had two Mexican War veterans, C. R. Johnson and L. B. Brewer, among its charter members. It continued its strong membership well into the twentieth century.

Men of Moore Post 92, Black River Falls, date unknown. Front row, from left: Charles Franz, Ernest Quackenbush, Theodore Quackenbush, Henry Nolop, George Thompson, Frank Bathrick, and an unknown man; Standing in back, from left: Charles Reitz, Fred Reitz, another unknown man, Charles Felt, Charles Schenk, John Helbling, and Carl Helwig. Photo provided by the Jackson Co. Historical Society.

HENRY O. WATROUS POST 93, Spencer
MARATHON COUNTY • 1883–1887

CHARTER MEMBERS: Henry Siegrist, John K. Raymond, C. K. Richardson, Sam C. Sanford, John Gardner, J. P. Harvey, N. A. Gaffney, William B. McPherson, M. A. DuCate, H. K. Scott, James Vought, William Mahoney, W. H. Chariton, L. Griffeth, S. D. Graves, J . A. Newcomb, Joseph Parks, Henry Mason, S. E. Brooks, Patrick Taggart, Alfred Timmerman, G. A. Vought, Ed A. Johnson

1866	1871	1876	1881	1886	1891	1896	1901	1906	1911	1916	1921	1926	1931	1936	1941	1946	1951

MEMBERSHIP BY YEAR (ACCOUNTED FOR): 1883, 23   **LAST MEMBER:** John Miller

Post 93 at Spencer was named for Henry O. Watrous, a soldier in Company K, Fourth Cavalry, who was killed at Port Hudson, Louisiana, on May 27, 1863. The post's first commander was William Mahoney.

The Waltrous Post got off to a somewhat shaky start, and by 1888, it had expired. The state encampment journal that year had no listing for No. 93. The same year the number was assigned to a post at Osseo.

In 1895 the veterans in Spencer revived their post, using the same name, but since their old number was not available it became Post 276.

W. G. WHEELER POST 93, Osseo
TREMPEALEAU COUNTY • MAY 28, 1888–1900

CHARTER MEMBERS: Unknown

1866	1871	1876	1881	1886	1891	1896	1901	1906	1911	1916	1921	1926	1931	1936	1941	1946	1951

MEMBERSHIP BY YEAR (ACCOUNTED FOR): 1889, 27; 1890, 31
LAST MEMBER: John W. Miller, September 18, 1944

When the post number 93 became available, it was given to the next post to be organized, and that was the one at Osseo in Trempealeau County in 1888. It became W. G. Wheeler Post 93.

Not much is known of the post; it expired after just twelve years.

Scarcely more is known about its namesake, W. G. Wheeler.

There is a grave in the Osseo cemetery for W. G. Wheeler that indicates he died June 1, 1876, in a logging accident. His age then was 30, so he would have been a teenager serving in the Civil War. There was a W. G. Wheeler from Iowa County who served in 1864 and 1865 with Company F of the First Wisconsin Heavy Artillery.

OLIVER D. PEASE POST 94, Watertown
JEFFERSON COUNTY • JULY 7, 1883–1937

CHARTER MEMBERS: Fred Kusel, commander; A. Solliday, senior vice commander; John Muth, junior vice commander; D. D. Scott, chaplain; W. C. Spalding, surgeon; J. Ditschler, officer of the day; L. C. Green, officer of the guard; J. Habhegger, quartermaster; C. J. Wenck, adjutant; A. Gritzner, sergeant major

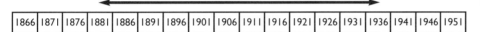

MEMBERSHIP BY YEAR (ACCOUNTED FOR): 1884, 25; 1887, 77; 1888, 75; 1889, 80; 1904, 46; 1905, 46; 1906, 46; 1907, 46; 1908, 46; 1909, 46; 1910, 46; 1911, 43; 1912, 40; 1913, 37; 1914, 33; 1915, 31; 1916, 31; 1917, 27; 1918, 25; 1919, 22; 1920, 20; 1921, 16; 1922, 16; 1923, 15; 1924, 14; 1925, 12; 1926, 12; 1927, 9; 1929, 6; 1930, 4; 1931, 4; 1932, 4; 1933, 4; 1934, 4; 1935, 1; 1936, 1   **LAST MEMBER:** A. F. Kusel

Jefferson County was part of the belt of strong commitment to the G.A.R., and Watertown contained one of the strong posts within the area, O. D. Pease Post 94. It continued until the 1930s.

Oliver D. Pease was from Watertown and was captain of Company D (originally the "Union Guards"), Sixteenth Wisconsin Infantry.

The regiment was sent to Grant's Army then encamped near Savannah, Tennessee, and it saw its first action in the Battle of Shiloh, where Pease was one of two company commanders to fall. He was wounded in the battle and died several days later from the wound. The other casualty was Captain Edward Saxe of Saxeville, Waushara County, who was killed outright.

Members of Oliver D. Pease Post 94 pose for Watertown photographer H. F. Siebert some time in the late 1800s near the height of the post's membership.

JOHN W. CHRISTIAN POST 95, Mondovi
BUFFALO COUNTY • JULY 14, 1883–1922

CHARTER MEMBERS: Thomas F. DeVany, Chas. Hebbard, James F. Brownlee, Ole Nicholson, James G. Sweet, James M. Cathcart, H. M. Nogle, W. Gilkey, C. L. Walker, John Legore, R. A. Rathburn, J. W. McKay, John D. Pace, Hubbard Gates, Daniel Van Pelt, H. C. Barrows, G. O. Bump, W. W. Wyman, M. L. Robinson, Andrew Benjamin

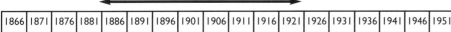

MEMBERSHIP BY YEAR (ACCOUNTED FOR): 1883, 20; 1887, 23; 1888, 28; 1889, 38; 1904, 40; 1905, 43; 1906, 42; 1907, 42; 1908, 42; 1909, 38; 1910, 36; 1911, 32; 1912, 18; 1913, 18; 1914, 18; 1915, 15; 1916, 13; 1917, 9; 1918, 10; 1919, 10; 1920, 10; 1921, 10   **LAST MEMBER:** Unknown

John W. Christian Post 95 of Mondovi was one of those posts that closed its books and transferred to other posts as membership declined in the early twentieth century.

The post was named for a private from nearby Gilmanton, John W. Christian, who, as a member of Company G, Twenty-fifth Infantry, was killed in action on July 22, 1864, at Decatur, Georgia.

UNION POST 96,
THOMAS H. OATES POST 96, Shullsburg
LAFAYETTE COUNTY • JULY 16, 1883–1927

CHARTER MEMBERS: Thomas H. Oates, commander; George Procter, senior vice commander; William J. Honeycomb, junior vice commander; Dr. C. C. Gratiot, surgeon; John Thompson, chaplain; Addison A. Townsend, officer of the day; P. Baker, officer of the guard; H. B. Chamberlain, adjutant; Thomas Teague, sergeant major; J. Henry, quartermaster sergeant

1866	1871	1876	1881	1886	1891	1896	1901	1906	1911	1916	1921	1926	1931	1936	1941	1946	1951

MEMBERSHIP BY YEAR (ACCOUNTED FOR): 1882, 66; 1884, 19; 1887, 28; 1888, 31; 1889, 43; 1904, 29; 1905, 27; 1906, 27; 1907, 27; 1908, 26; 1909, 26; 1910, 26; 1911, 26; 1912, 24; 1913, 11; 1914, 10; 1915, 10; 1916, 9; 1917, 6; 1918, 3; 1919, 3; 1920, 3; 1921, 3; 1922, 4; 1923, 3; 1924, 3; 1925, 2; 1926, 1

LAST MEMBER: Addison Townsend

MRS. ALBERT SANDEMAN
COLL. USAMHI
THOMAS H. OATES

Originally known as the Union Post 96, members of the Shullsburg G.A.R. decided in 1888 to rename their post to honor their first commander, Thomas H. Oates, a Shullsburg soldier who was with Company C, Thirty-third Wisconsin, throughout the war and was mustered out as a corporal in 1865.

WILLIAM A. NELSON POST 97, Forestville
DOOR COUNTY • AUGUST 11, 1883–1901 OR 1902

CHARTER MEMBERS: John Fetzer, commander; Richard Perry, senior vice commander; John Smith, junior vice commander; William Duwe, adjutant; Julius Bernhart, quartermaster; John Madison, officer of the guard; William Fagg, officer of the day; John Lovel, surgeon; George P. Barrandt, chaplain; Joseph Madison, sergeant major; Charles R. Doffin, quartermaster sergeant

1866	1871	1876	1881	1886	1891	1896	1901	1906	1911	1916	1921	1926	1931	1936	1941	1946	1951

MEMBERSHIP BY YEAR (ACCOUNTED FOR): 1883, 19; 1884, 20; 1887, 59; 1888, 39; 1889, 32

LAST MEMBER: Unknown

Forestville Post 97 was named for a Forestville soldier, William A. Nelson, who served in Company E, Fourteenth Wisconsin, for the first half of the war, then accepted a commission with the Eighth Louisiana Colored Troops.

The post seems to have had a number of years of activity, but went into a decline and surrendered its charter in 1901 or 1902.

JOHN E. PERKINS POST 98, Augusta

EAU CLAIRE COUNTY • AUGUST 3, 1883–1941

CHARTER MEMBERS: R. D. Campbell, W. H. Dodge, Albert Riekard, W. H. Smith, W. H. H. Coolidge, R. K. Blair, Charles A. Kirkham, G. F. Hamilton, T. D. Stone, F. N. Thomas, A. D. Hedges, Philo Baldwin, L. Beeman, John Tebo, C. W. Culbertson, Russell Hackett, J. L. Ball, C. H. Hale, J. B. Butler, William Lagrave, W. H. Tompkins, J. B. Button, M. V. Smith, H. S. Barnes

1866	1871	1876	1881	1886	1891	1896	1901	1906	1911	1916	1921	1926	1931	1936	1941	1946	1951

MEMBERSHIP BY YEAR (ACCOUNTED FOR): 1887, 53; 1888, 51; 1889, 55; 1904, 30; 1905, 30; 1906, 30; 1907, 26; 1908, 22; 1909, 26; 1910, 24; 1911, 23; 1912, 22; 1913, 24; 1914, 18; 1915, 18; 1916, 18; 1917, 18; 1918, 16; 1919, 16; 1920, 13; 1921, 9; 1922, 10; 1923, 9; 1924, 8; 1925, 6; 1926, 5; 1927, 5; 1928, 4; 1929, 3; 1930, 3; 1931, 2; 1932, 2; 1933, 1   **LAST MEMBER:** George F. Caldwell

JOHN E. PERKINS

John E. Perkins Post 98 of Augusta was chartered in 1883, but the post's headquarters burned a few years later. It received a replacement charter noting the original had burned on February 17, 1886. The new one, from which the above list of charter members is taken, was issued December 10, 1887. The post was active in the community until after World War I.

John E. Perkins, for whom the post was named, was from Eau Claire and served as captain of Company C, Eighth Wisconsin, the Eagle Company of the Eagle Regiment. Perkins, in fact, gave the eagle its name, Old Abe. Perkins was wounded at Farmington, Mississippi, and died May 11, 1862 from his wounds.

EDWIN AUSTIN POST 99, Sylvan Corners

RICHLAND COUNTY • APRIL 21, 1883–1888

CHARTER MEMBERS: Unknown

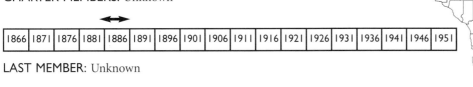

1866	1871	1876	1881	1886	1891	1896	1901	1906	1911	1916	1921	1926	1931	1936	1941	1946	1951

LAST MEMBER: Unknown

Sylvan Corners, or just Sylvan as its post office was known, is one of those tiny places where a G.A.R. post was established in the exuberance of the early 1880s, but which could not sustain enough interest for the post to put down strong roots. It was extinct in less than five years.

Nonetheless the post functioned for a time and chose as its name that of Edwin Austin, a private in Company H, Fifth Wisconsin, the "Richland County Scott Guards." Austin was killed in action May 5, 1862, at Williamsburg, Virginia.

IOLA POST 99, Iola
WAUPACA COUNTY• APRIL 21, 1888–1908

CHARTER MEMBERS: Geo. Dale, Goodman Amundson, Jacob Wipf, Nels Omut, Benj. F. Andrews, Peter Myhre, Hans Howell, Forger Gilbertson, Horace Cleaves, John Wraalstad, Juhirs? Ingelberthson, Knidt Bergern, Conrad Wipf, A. A. Bierce, Harrison Warren, H. P. Hatch, John Olson, O. P. Vallum, Jos. H. Worby, Chas. Johans, C. Torbenson, C. Jacobson, Hans A. Meyhre, H. C. Anderson, Chris Thompson, L. Jorgenson, Christian Fleck

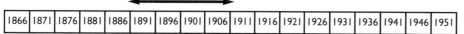

1866	1871	1876	1881	1886	1891	1896	1901	1906	1911	1916	1921	1926	1931	1936	1941	1946	1951

MEMBERSHIP BY YEAR (ACCOUNTED FOR): 1888, 27; 1889, 30; 1890, 42; 1904, 17; 1905, 14; 1906, 15; 1907, 15   **LAST MEMBER:** Unknown

Post 99 of Iola, Waupaca County, was chartered in April 1888, receiving the recycled number of the failed Sylvan Corners Post. The veterans decided to go with just the town name. It lasted with fair success until about 1908, when its members—about 15 of them—apparently affiliated with a different post.

GEORGE H. STEVENS POST 100, Fox Lake
DODGE COUNTY • AUGUST 29, 1883–1912

CHARTER MEMBERS: S. C. McDowell, C. H. Eggleston, W. Blatchley, R. L. Parker, George H. Gibson, Charles Clough, John Fanshaw, H. S. Wood, George R. Davis, S. D. Nourse, Aaron Fanshaw, John Morrison, Edmund Purdy

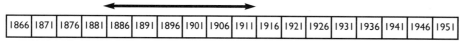

1866	1871	1876	1881	1886	1891	1896	1901	1906	1911	1916	1921	1926	1931	1936	1941	1946	1951

MEMBERSHIP BY YEAR (ACCOUNTED FOR): 1887, 28; 1888, 22; 1889, 31; 1904, 14; 1905, 13; 1906, 11; 1907, 11; 1908, 11; 1909, 11; 1910, 11; 1911, 11   **LAST MEMBER:** Solon D. Nourse

2ND WIS. INF. ASSOC.
GEORGE H. STEVENS

The milestone number of Post 100 was accorded to the veterans of Fox Lake, who organized the George H. Stevens Post in that community. The post continued until 1911 when remaining members affiliated with a neighboring post.

George H. Stevens was from Fox Lake. He raised a company, the "Citizen Guards" of Fox Lake, which became Company A of the Second Wisconsin. Stevens, then second in command of the regiment as lieutenant colonel, was mortally wounded in the Iron Brigade's heroic defense at Gettysburg on July 1, 1863. He died July 5. Stevens and one other lieutenant colonel, from New York, are the highest ranking federal casualties of the Battle of Gettysburg who are buried in the National Cemetery there.

JOHN MCDERMOTT POST 101, Boscobel

GRANT COUNTY • AUGUST 15, 1883–1941

CHARTER MEMBERS: John Stahel, William Cook, James B. Ricks, L. C. Armstrong, Charles E. Cook, John V. B. France, N. J. Francisco, J. McLaughlin, E. B. Smith, G. B. Murphy, G. C. Wurster, J. W. Nice, John Barbaux, M. Ableiter, F. Kumrein, R. B. Rice, James Grant, W. L. Huff, Isaac Woodword, James L. Taylor, D. B. Richardson, Wallis W. Young, N. E. Birchard, D. R. Lawrence, Isaac Peterson, D. W. Carley, Louis Reichel, George W. Cowan, Charles B. Miller, A. F. Henderson, M. A. Sawyer, Thomas Tuffley, A. McKinney, G. H. Winn, F. W. Dohnie, George Tuffley, W. C. Scott, A. J. Renshaw, Joseph J. Clark, William Gribble, Joseph Gribble, Amos Devoe, E. F. Devoe, Harvey Clark

1866	1871	1876	1881	1886	1891	1896	1901	1906	1911	1916	1921	1926	1931	1936	1941	1946	1951

MEMBERSHIP BY YEAR (ACCOUNTED FOR): 1883, 94; 1884, 94; 1887, 107; 1888, 53; 1889, 58; 1904, 66; 1905, 54; 1906, 52; 1907, 50; 1908, 55; 1909, 50; 1910, 50; 1911, 40; 1912, 44; 1913, 41; 1914, 44; 1915, 36; 1916, 35; 1917, 34; 1918, 33; 1919, 27; 1920, 25; 1921, 24; 1922, 20; 1923, 23; 1924, 25; 1925, 17; 1926, 16; 1927, 13; 1928, 10; 1929, 5; 1930, 10; 1931, 10; 1932, 10; 1933, 9; 1934, 9; 1935, 5; 1936, 4; 1937, 4; 1938, 1

LAST MEMBER: John Ricks, died February 15, 1942

Post 101, Boscobel, has a special status among G.A.R. posts in Wisconsin in that its meeting hall at 102 Mary Street, Boscobel, has been preserved through the continuing efforts of the Boscobel Women's Relief Corps. The building is occasionally open to public view.

Post 101 was named for John McDermott from nearby Fennimore, who was captain of Company C, Twentieth Wisconsin. McDermott was killed in action at Prairie Grove, Arkansas, on December 7, 1862, attempting to retrieve the colors from a fallen color guard.

The post began with 44 members; L. C. Armstrong was the first commander. The post's membership numbers remained high for decades. It still had more than two dozen men during the World War I years, when many other posts were withering away. In all, it served 254 men.

Fife and Drum group from Boscobel's Post 101.

Men of McDermott Post pose in front of their celebrated hall in Boscobel. The photo is not dated, but it was probably taken in the 1920s.

Members of McDermott Post 101 turn out in force for a portrait, date unknown.

187

OSCAR F. PINNEY POST 102, Monroe
GREEN COUNTY • AUGUST 28, 1883–1936

CHARTER MEMBERS: S. C. Cheney, S. E. Gardner, W. J. Miller, J. C. Hall, Nelson Darling, S. P. Shadel, A. F. Glascott, Chas. Robinson, C. E. Tanberg, J. C. Baker, M. P. Maine, F. W. Byrne, B. S. Kerr, Samuel Lewis, Geo. O. Putzash, J. C. Smith, Joseph Wetzler

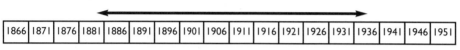

| 1866 | 1871 | 1876 | 1881 | 1886 | 1891 | 1896 | 1901 | 1906 | 1911 | 1916 | 1921 | 1926 | 1931 | 1936 | 1941 | 1946 | 1951 |

MEMBERSHIP BY YEAR (ACCOUNTED FOR): 1883, 17; 1884, 32; 1887, 110; 1888, 119; 1889, 140; 1904, 92; 1905, 92; 1906, 75; 1907, 80; 1908, 80; 1909, 74; 1910, 71; 1911, 68; 1912, 62; 1913, 56; 1914, 52; 1915, 48; 1916, 47; 1917, 42; 1918, 37; 1919, 36; 1920, 33; 1921, 30; 1922, 27; 1923, 24; 1924, 24; 1925, 18; 1926, 17; 1927, 15; 1928, 13; 1929, 9; 1930, 7; 1932, 3; 1933, 2; 1934, 1; 1935, 15   **LAST MEMBER:** William Rinehart

The Grand Army post at Monroe, Post 102, was very active for many years. As late as 1924, when some posts were disappearing, it still had two dozen members.

Post 102 was named for Oscar F. Pinney, captain of the Fifth Battery and a native of Monroe. Captain Pinney was wounded at Stone's River and died on February 17, 1863, from those wounds.

BENJAMIN I. HUMPHREY POST 103, New Richmond
ST. CROIX COUNTY • SEPTEMBER 18, 1883–1942

CHARTER MEMBERS: O. F. Brown, commander; Frank P. Chapman, senior vice commander; Harvey Law Jr., junior vice commander; Jo Turner, adjutant; H. M. Murdock, surgeon; Frank Law, chaplain; A. B. Kibbe, quartermaster; D. A. Kennedy, officer of the day; Frank LaBrash, officer of the guard; J. L. Rutty, sergeant major; A. Kribs, quartermaster sergeant

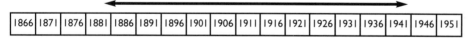

| 1866 | 1871 | 1876 | 1881 | 1886 | 1891 | 1896 | 1901 | 1906 | 1911 | 1916 | 1921 | 1926 | 1931 | 1936 | 1941 | 1946 | 1951 |

MEMBERSHIP BY YEAR (ACCOUNTED FOR): 1887, 34; 1888, 32; 1889, 38; 1904, 36; 1905, 33; 1906, 30; 1907, 34; 1908, 28; 1909, 25; 1910, 26; 1911, 19; 1912, 20; 1913, 20; 1914, 13; 1915, 8; 1916, 7; 1917, 8; 1918, 7; 1919, 7; 1920, 7; 1921, 7; 1922, 5; 1923, 5; 1924, 5; 1925, 5; 1926, 5; 1927, 5; 1928, 5; 1929, 3; 1930, 2; 1931, 2; 1932, 2; 1933, 2; 1934, 2; 1935, 1; 1936, 1; 1937, 1; 1938, 1   **LAST MEMBER:** A. B. Kibbe

It was not unheard of that a G.A.R. post should suffer a loss when its meeting hall burned. Several of them had their charters thus consumed; others suffered considerable losses of other materials. But B. I. Humphrey Post 103 of New Richmond was wiped away when a tornado leveled its hall and destroyed its contents in 1899.

Still the post managed to survive and continued serving St. Croix County veterans for another thirty-some years.

Post 103 was named after Benjamin I. Humphrey, a New Richmond private, who was with Company A, Twelfth Wisconsin, and was killed in action August 11, 1864, during the Atlanta Campaign.

WINFIELD SCOTT POST 104, Whitehall

TREMPEALEAU COUNTY • AUGUST 29, 1883–1922

CHARTER MEMBERS: George Quackenbush, commander; S. Flagler, senior vice commander; S. Parker, junior vice commander; J. Sweet, surgeon; William Lennon, chaplain; L. McNitt, quartermaster; L. Weeks, officer of the day; S. H. Breed, officer of the guard; J. P. Mallery, adjutant; A. C. Knight, sergeant major

| 1866 | 1871 | 1876 | 1881 | 1886 | 1891 | 1896 | 1901 | 1906 | 1911 | 1916 | 1921 | 1926 | 1931 | 1936 | 1941 | 1946 | 1951 |

MEMBERSHIP BY YEAR (ACCOUNTED FOR): 1887, 46; 1888, 50; 1889, 49; 1904, 24; 1905, 24; 1906, 23; 1907, 22; 1908, 22; 1909, 23; 1910, 23; 1911, 23; 1912, 22; 1913, 22; 1914, 22; 1915, 20; 1916, 20; 1917, 19; 1918, 15; 1919, 14; 1920, 14; 1921, 14   LAST MEMBER: Unknown

WINFIELD SCOTT

Post 104, Whitehall, in Trempealeau County was a relatively small post but with a stable membership. Winfield Scott Post 104 closed by 1922, surrendering its charter. Its members presumably joined neighboring posts.

Whitehall veterans chose to honor the original commanding general of the U.S. Army at the start of the Civil War. Although he was old and feeble and was derided while he was the general in chief, Winfield Scott's grand strategy pronounced at the outset to blockade the South and constrict its ability to wage war—Scott's Anaconda—was basically what was followed. Scott fought in the War of 1812 and was the hero of the Mexican War.

MAJOR WILLIAM F. DAWES POST 105, Necedah

JUNEAU COUNTY • MAY 3, 1883–1887-88

CHARTER MEMBERS: Unknown

| 1866 | 1871 | 1876 | 1881 | 1886 | 1891 | 1896 | 1901 | 1906 | 1911 | 1916 | 1921 | 1926 | 1931 | 1936 | 1941 | 1946 | 1951 |

MEMBERSHIP BY YEAR (ACCOUNTED FOR): 1883, 39; 1884, 32
LAST MEMBER: Unknown

Veterans in the Necedah area, Juneau County, organized a G.A.R. post in 1883 and named it after Major William F. Dawes.

Dawes went in as captain of Company E, Sixteenth Wisconsin, the "Adams County Guards." Dawes was from Strong's Prairie in that county. He rose to major in the Sixteenth.

Dawes Post 105 surrendered its charter at some point in 1887. Two years later the veterans revived their unit under the same name, and it was now numbered 245.

M. G. TOWNSEND POST 105, Pewaukee

WAUKESHA COUNTY • MAY 14, 1888–1904

CHARTER MEMBERS: B. F. Goss was the first commander.

| 1866 | 1871 | 1876 | 1881 | 1886 | 1891 | 1896 | 1901 | 1906 | 1911 | 1916 | 1921 | 1926 | 1931 | 1936 | 1941 | 1946 | 1951 |

MEMBERSHIP BY YEAR (ACCOUNTED FOR): 1888, 39; 1889, 41; 1904, 17
LAST MEMBER: Unknown

Townsend Post 105 in Pewaukee, Waushara County, was another of those small-town posts that served their veterans for a number of years but which eventually closed up and scattered its members to larger posts in the area.

The Pewaukee G.A.R. was named for Mandeville G. Townsend, captain of Company B, Twenty-eighth Wisconsin, who was killed in action on April 25, 1864, at Mark's Mills, Arkansas. He is buried in the National Cemetery in Little Rock.

JAMES MASON POST 106, De Soto

VERNON COUNTY • OCTOBER 16, 1883–1913

CHARTER MEMBERS: Orlando Evans, Wm. J. Hutson, Wm. Bates, James Loftus, John W. Pulver, Peter Bartholomew, Zenas T. Clark, Robt. H. Rice, Geo. L Bower, James H. Rogers, Robt. L. Ferguson, Robt. Pennel, John Campbell, Geo. P. Griffin, Josiah F. Allen, Thomas DeLacy, Wm. F. Rose, Isaac Latimore, James Davenport, Chas. F. Page, Edw. R. James, Albert E. Fosdick, Wm. M. Green, Wm. S. Cushing, Nelson Davenport, Wm. W. Miller

| 1866 | 1871 | 1876 | 1881 | 1886 | 1891 | 1896 | 1901 | 1906 | 1911 | 1916 | 1921 | 1926 | 1931 | 1936 | 1941 | 1946 | 1951 |

MEMBERSHIP BY YEAR (ACCOUNTED FOR): 1883, 26; 1887, 55; 1888, 70; 1889, 60; 1904, 21; 1905, 15; 1906, 15; 1907, 14; 1908, 14; 1909, 13; 1910, 10; 1911, 20; 1912, 10   **LAST MEMBER:** Unknown

James Mason Post 106 of De Soto was another of the large class of 1883, which flourished in the enthusiastic years of Grand Army history but which then surrendered their charters in the new century. In this case, the post shut its doors in 1912, while there were still members on the rolls but when it was increasingly difficult to maintain regular activities.

The post was named for James B. Mason, captain of Company E, Thirty-first Wisconsin, and shared the fate of some 90 men of the regiment: he died of disease. For Mason it was October 17, 1863, at Nashville.

ALLATOONA POST 107, Arena

IOWA COUNTY • SEPTEMBER 7, 1883–1917

CHARTER MEMBERS: William C. Meffert was the first commander.

| 1866 | 1871 | 1876 | 1881 | 1886 | 1891 | 1896 | 1901 | 1906 | 1911 | 1916 | 1921 | 1926 | 1931 | 1936 | 1941 | 1946 | 1951 |

MEMBERSHIP BY YEAR (ACCOUNTED FOR): 1887, 23; 1888, 16; 1889, 19; 1904, 7; 1905, 7; 1906, 6; 1907, 5; 1908, 6; 1909, 6; 1910, 6; 1911, 6; 1912, 6; 1913, 6; 1914, 6; 1915, 6; 1916, 4   **LAST MEMBER:** Unknown

Posts were named for a variety of reasons. Very often the chosen name honored a fallen comrade. Most Wisconsin G.A.R. posts did so. Others saluted national heroes; thus Lyons, Ellsworth, Sherman, Sheridan, etc. A small number commemorated an event in the military lives of members.

Post 107 at Arena in Iowa County did the latter, naming itself Allatoona Post 107 to remember the Battle of Allatoona in Georgia. Atlanta had fallen to Sherman in the latter half of 1864.

His adversary, John Hood, sought to draw him out by attacking his line of communications, and the Confederates fell upon a supply base at Allatoona north of Atlanta. The federal garrison fought off the attack with considerable losses to both sides. Part of the garrison was from Wisconsin. It helped Sherman to conclude, incidentally, to abandon the line of communication and strike off from Atlanta without one.

ANDREW J. McNURLIN POST 108, Loyd

RICHLAND COUNTY • SEPTEMBER 10, 1883–NOVEMBER, 14, 1893

CHARTER MEMBERS: Unknown

1866	1871	1876	1881	1886	1891	1896	1901	1906	1911	1916	1921	1926	1931	1936	1941	1946	1951

MEMBERSHIP BY YEAR (ACCOUNTED FOR): 1887, 39; 1888, 21; 1889, 18
LAST MEMBER: Unknown

A. J. McNurlin Post 108 at Loyd, Richland County, was chartered in 1883, but served for barely ten years.

The post was named for Andrew McNurlin, who enlisted in Company A, Thirty-sixth Wisconsin, in February 1864 and was taken prisoner at Reams Station, Virginia. He died in prison at Salisbury, North Carolina, on January 17, 1865.

JAMES LITTLE POST 108, Pepin

PEPIN COUNTY • JULY 7, 1894–1910

CHARTER MEMBERS: C. A. Allen, commander; James Hallesworth, senior vice commander; S. L. Serene, junior vice commander; Gil. Wheeler, adjutant; Claus Stoltenberg, quartermaster; George Hunter, officer of the day; O. G. Howard, officer of the guard; James Skinner, sergeant major; Henry Hogue, quartermaster sergeant; George Moore, chaplain

1866	1871	1876	1881	1886	1891	1896	1901	1906	1911	1916	1921	1926	1931	1936	1941	1946	1951

MEMBERSHIP BY YEAR (ACCOUNTED FOR): 1894, 21; 1904, 6; 1905, 6; 1906, 7; 1907, 7; 1908, 7; 1909, 7
LAST MEMBER: Unknown

The veterans of Pepin formed a Grand Army Post in 1894 and received the recycled number 108. The post started with 21 members and never gained much numerical strength; it was defunct by 1910.

The Pepin Post was named after James Little from La Crosse, who was a member of the Thirty-seventh Wisconsin and was killed in action on July 30, 1864, in the federal assault following the mine explosion under Confederate lines at Petersburg, Virginia. It was known as the Battle of the Crater.

WILLIAMSON POST 109, Dodgeville

IOWA COUNTY • SEPTEMBER 18, 1883–1931

CHARTER MEMBERS: Chris Kessler, Orville Strong, William A. Owens, O. C. Smith, William H. Roberts, John T. Jones, Thomas Bunburry, B. Thomas Jr., D. G. Jones, Ole Arneson, William R. Elliot Jr., J. R. Martin, Charles Blake, T. M. Goldsworth, William Elliot Sr., H. H. Walters, John Wiest, William Buckingham, George Beaumont, Elisha Tyrer, Peter Hubbard, Peter Crook, Joseph LaBount, James Tally, R. Carter, John Ralph, A. S. Hearn, William W. Williams

1866	1871	1876	1881	1886	1891	1896	1901	1906	1911	1916	1921	1926	1931	1936	1941	1946	1951

MEMBERSHIP BY YEAR (ACCOUNTED FOR): 1883, 28; 1887, 67; 1888, 72; 1889, 72; 1904, 34; 1905, 31; 1906, 28; 1907, 23; 1908, 21; 1909, 21; 1910, 21; 1911, 20; 1912, 19; 1913, 16; 1914, 16; 1915, 14; 1916, 13; 1917, 14; 1918, 14; 1919, 13; 1920, 12; 1921, 12; 1922, 11; 1923, 11; 1924, 8; 1925, 8; 1926, 8; 1927, 7; 1928, 6; 1929, 4; 1930, 3;   **LAST MEMBER:** Unknown

Williamson Post 109, Dodgeville, was led in its first year by R. Carter as commander. It was a strong post in that area of Wisconsin for many years. It maintained a significant number of members until well after World War I.

Dodgeville veterans named their post for one of their own, William Williamson, who left town as first sergeant of Company C., Twelfth Wisconsin, and returned after the war as its captain.

MARSHFIELD POST 110,
JAMES G. BLAINE POST 110, Marshfield
WOOD COUNTY • OCTOBER 23, 1883–1935

CHARTER MEMBERS: William H. Upham, O. R. Olin, Daniel Shahan, L. D. Wood, S. H. Phillips, David Walterbach, J. C. Davis, William Bartel, H. G. Harrower, C. B. Wood, O. F. Harkins, R. W. Franklin, George Schmall, John Clous, Abe Kantz, Jacob Becker, Christian Gukenberger, Charles Schue, George Seibert, Christian Jacobs, David Twiggs, Frank Gotschus, Willis Graves, E. G. Schmidt

1866	1871	1876	1881	1886	1891	1896	1901	1906	1911	1916	1921	1926	1931	1936	1941	1946	1951

MEMBERSHIP BY YEAR (ACCOUNTED FOR): 1887, 35; 1888, 40; 1889, 49; 1904, 17; 1905, 18; 1906, 20; 1907, 18; 1908, 17; 1909, 17; 1910, 15; 1911, 16; 1912, 15; 1913, 15; 1914, 16; 1915, 15; 1916, 17; 1917, 16; 1918, 17; 1919, 15; 1920, 12; 1921, 10; 1922, 10; 1923, 12; 1924, 12; 1925, 8; 1926, 7; 1927, 5; 1928, 4; 1930, 2; 1931, 2; 1932, 3; 1933, 1; 1934, 1   **LAST MEMBER:** Ed Dumas

JAMES G. BLAINE

Post 110 at Marshfield was known simply as the Marshfield Post of the G.A.R. for its first 10 years.

After the death of James G. Blaine in 1893, the veterans in that Wood County community chose to honor the late Republican politician.

Blaine was not a likely choice. He did not serve in the Civil War. He was elected to Congress during the war, in 1863, at the age of 33, and he rose to become a postwar power in the House, and later, in the Senate.

Perhaps the veterans admired him because he ran, and barely lost, the presidential election of 1884. He lost to Grover Cleveland, not a favorite of veterans. Blaine's razor-thin loss has been attributed to one of his supporters characterizing the Democrats as the party of "rum, Romanism and rebellion." When Cleveland was defeated in 1888, the victor, Benjamin Harrison, appointed Blaine secretary of state.

Post 110's first commander, William Upham, became department commander in 1891.

C. MCKENZIE POST 111, St. Croix Falls

POLK COUNTY • SEPTEMBER 24, 1883–1921

CHARTER MEMBERS: Unknown

1866	1871	1876	1881	1886	1891	1896	1901	1906	1911	1916	1921	1926	1931	1936	1941	1946	1951

MEMBERSHIP BY YEAR (ACCOUNTED FOR): 1887, 20; 1888, 25; 1889, 34; 1904, 12; 1905, 12; 1907, 16; 1908, 21; 1909, 21; 1910, 21; 1911, 21; 1912, 5; 1913, 4; 1914, 4; 1915, 3; 1916, 2; 1917, 2; 1918, 1; 1919, 1; 1920, 1   LAST MEMBER: Unknown

St. Croix Falls veterans who organized Post 111 in 1883 named it for Corporal C. McKenzie, a member of Company G of the First Wisconsin, the reorganized, three-year regiment that served in the western area. The company had been on active duty for about a year before it saw its first combat, suffering heavy losses at Perryville, Kentucky, in the battle between the invading rebel army of Braxton Bragg and federal forces led by Don Carlos Buell. McKenzie was one of 56 killed that day, October 8, 1862, or dying from wounds thereafter.

Post 111 was a sort of western outpost of the Wisconsin G.A.R. It gained some strength in numbers in the 1909–11 era when other posts in the region ceased. But it, too, rapidly declined in the next decade.

ISAAC N. EARL POST 112, Colby

CLARK COUNTY • DECEMBER 18, 1883–1931

CHARTER MEMBERS: Unknown

1866	1871	1876	1881	1886	1891	1896	1901	1906	1911	1916	1921	1926	1931	1936	1941	1946	1951

MEMBERSHIP BY YEAR (ACCOUNTED FOR): 1887, 34; 1888, 27; 1889, 40; 1904, 16; 1905, 15; 1906, 13; 1907, 16; 1908, 15; 1909, 15; 1910, 15; 1911, 15; 1912, 17; 1913, 17; 1914, 17; 1915, 17; 1916, 15; 1917, 9; 1918, 7; 1919, 7; 1920, 6; 1921, 4; 1922, 4; 1923, 4; 1924, 4; 1925, 4; 1926, 3; 1927, 2; 1928, 1; 1929, 1; 1930, 1   LAST MEMBER: Unknown

ISAAC N. EARL

The namesake of Colby Post 112, Isaac N. Earl, had a military career of which movies are made.

Enlisting at the outset of war in the Fourth Wisconsin, from Kilbourn, now Wisconsin Dells, he entered Company D, then commanded by Captain Joseph Bailey, the later savior of the Red River Fleet. As corporal of the company, he was captured on May 27, 1863, at Port Hudson, but escaped by outrunning the guard, jumping into the river, and swimming across to friendly forces despite two wounds suffered in the escape. He was there-upon promoted to second lieutenant of Company D and was serving as such when the Fourth was converted to cavalry. He was captured again. This time he was placed in irons. But he cut through the chains and escaped. Captured once more with the aid of bloodhounds, Earl escaped again and was again recaptured. He escaped a fourth time, was wounded in the attempt, but made his way through swamps to the Gulf coast where he got to a Union gunboat. On another expedition in November 1864, he was shot by a Confederate and sustained buckshot wounds. Again he was captured. This time the Hollywood scenario ends. He died during this final captivity from the wounds.

JOHN ROSS POST 113, Monticello
GREEN COUNTY • OCTOBER 6, 1883–1909

CHARTER MEMBERS: S. C. Taft was the first commander.

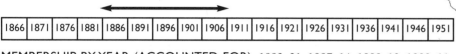

1866	1871	1876	1881	1886	1891	1896	1901	1906	1911	1916	1921	1926	1931	1936	1941	1946	1951

MEMBERSHIP BY YEAR (ACCOUNTED FOR): 1883, 21; 1887, 14; 1888, 12; 1889, 11; 1904, 8; 1905, 7; 1906, 7; 1907, 7; 1908, 7   **LAST MEMBER:** Unknown

Monticello in the town of Mt. Pleasant, Green County, was an active post, although not large, for more than two decades.

Post 113 was named for John Ross, a Mt. Pleasant boy who was a private in the Fifth Battery and died July 12, 1862, at Jacinto, Mississippi, one of the numerous victims of Mississippi's inhospitable summer climate. He died of disease.

HANS C. HEG POST 114, Waupun
DODGE COUNTY • OCTOBER 16, 1883–1934

CHARTER MEMBERS: D. R. Amidon, Fred M. Moul, H. H. Trowbridge, J. W. Oliver, J. H. Elkins, William H. Parsons, Samuel Atkins, C. H. Lindsley, Robert Paine, C. W. Page, George W. Carter, J. G. Moore, A. S. Clark, W. H. Ferris, Jacob Ferris, M. B. Tucker, J. W. Bartholomew, J. C. Reynolds, James J. Hilbert, C. T. Owens, L. B. Balcom, J. J. Roberts, W. T. Conant, Henry Brooks, E. A. Padgham, W. T. Whiting, L. E. Beardsley, L. D. Hinkley

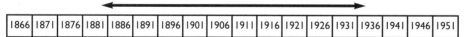

1866	1871	1876	1881	1886	1891	1896	1901	1906	1911	1916	1921	1926	1931	1936	1941	1946	1951

MEMBERSHIP BY YEAR (ACCOUNTED FOR): 1887, 47; 1888, 47; 1889, 54; 1904, 35; 1905, 34; 1906, 33; 1907, 32; 1908, 30; 1909, 18; 1910, 17; 1911, 17; 1912, 19; 1913, 20; 1914, 25; 1915, 23; 1916, 19; 1917, 18; 1918, 19; 1919, 18; 1920, 17; 1921, 16; 1922, 16; 1923, 12; 1924, 14; 1925, 11; 1926, 9; 1927, 8; 1928, 7; 1929, 7; 1930, 6; 1931, 4; 1932, 4; 1933, 3   **LAST MEMBER:** Marvin Heath

HANS C. HEG

He was one-time state prison commissioner, but best known for raising a regiment of Scandinavians—mostly Norwegians—for the Union. It was for the former credential, though, that veterans of Waupun chose the name Hans C. Heg for their Post 114.

Heg was elected prison commissioner in 1859, the first Norwegian-born man elected to public office in the country. He was elected as a Republican. After the war broke out he was the natural choice of Norwegian-Americans and other Scandinavians to raise a regiment of such brethren. The Fifteenth Wisconsin was composed almost exclusively of Scandinavians. So Norwegian was the Fifteenth that it contained 115 men named "Ole"—four Ole Olsons in Company F alone.

Heg was killed at the Battle of Chickamauga leading a brigade that included the Fifteenth Wisconsin.

A statue on the Capitol Square in Madison commemorates Heg as a Norwegian-American and Civil War leader.

CUMBERLAND POST 115, Cumberland

BARRON COUNTY • 1883–1885

CHARTER MEMBERS: Unknown

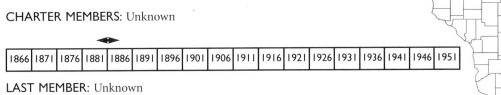

| 1866 | 1871 | 1876 | 1881 | 1886 | 1891 | 1896 | 1901 | 1906 | 1911 | 1916 | 1921 | 1926 | 1931 | 1936 | 1941 | 1946 | 1951 |

LAST MEMBER: Unknown

Post 115 of Cumberland in Barron County seems to have been an exception to the 1883 rule that the Grand Army of the Republic was at last setting roots in fertile ground. It was not that the Barron County boys gave up. But their beginning as Post 115 was somewhat tentative. They surrendered their charter by the end of 1885.

They came back, though, the following year and were chartered anew as Post 225.

BELMONT POST 115, Blaine

PORTAGE COUNTY • JUNE 18, 1888–1903

CHARTER MEMBERS: William H. Edminister, L. E. Kent, Merritt Curtis, L. H. Stark, F. L. West, Hannibal Culver, Albert Taylor, Wm. Pierce, L. D. Scott, John M. Collier, J. S. Turner, Henry Tice, J. H. Fenton, S. H. Sawyer, L. E. Buck, J. E. Lovejoy, Patrick Stinson, Willard Dearing, Archibald Marvin, C. M. Turner, Dennis Leahy, D. A. Towne, Arthur Fletcher, Christopher Bacon, Edson Casey

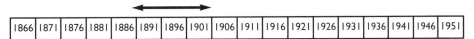

| 1866 | 1871 | 1876 | 1881 | 1886 | 1891 | 1896 | 1901 | 1906 | 1911 | 1916 | 1921 | 1926 | 1931 | 1936 | 1941 | 1946 | 1951 |

MEMBERSHIP BY YEAR (ACCOUNTED FOR): 1888, 25; 1889, 25; 1890, 27   LAST MEMBER: Unknown

Veterans of Portage County in the area of Blaine in the township of Belmont formed a post which received the vacated number 115. Their charter date was June 16, 1888. The post's history is largely unknown. Department records suggest it remained active until about 1903.

J. W. APPLETON POST 116, Black Creek

OUTAGAMIE COUNTY • OCTOBER 25, 1883–1911

CHARTER MEMBERS: C. W. Hopkins, W. H. Daniels, N. Rice, Carl Gordes, R. A. Loope, Geo. Downey, J. M. Baer, T. A. Burdick, C. M. Brainerd, John W. Wilkins, A. G. McKee, Joseph Nagreen, E. Felix, C. F. Hauff

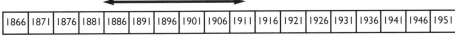

| 1866 | 1871 | 1876 | 1881 | 1886 | 1891 | 1896 | 1901 | 1906 | 1911 | 1916 | 1921 | 1926 | 1931 | 1936 | 1941 | 1946 | 1951 |

MEMBERSHIP BY YEAR (ACCOUNTED FOR): 1883, 14; 1887, 21; 1888, 23; 1889, 30; 1904, 21; 1905, 11; 1906, 10; 1907, 10; 1908, 9; 1909, 9; 1910, 7   LAST MEMBER: Unknown

The Black Creek Post 116 was named for John W. Appleton, a soldier from nearby Appleton, who was a private in Company C, First Wisconsin, and was wounded with that company. He transferred to the Twenty-first Wisconsin and served with its

Company G. Appleton was in the campaign for Atlanta and received a permanently disabling wound in the shoulder at Peach Tree Creek. In 1865 he transferred to the Veterans Reserve Corps. He was mustered out that year. Appleton went to Black Creek and engaged in milling and farming, but his war wound hastened his death on December 19, 1882.

Appleton Post 116, organized 10 months later, reached 30 members in 1889, the peak year of G.A.R. enrollment, and continued to serve until 1911.

GEORGE HALL POST 117, Beaver Dam
DODGE COUNTY • OCTOBER 29, 1883–1938

CHARTER MEMBERS: F. D. Owen, L. E. Hazen, F. S. Johnson, J. E. Lyon, W. F. Ford, A. N. Grant, Geo. Stultz, A. P. Baker, John Snorts, John Egan, James Parker, W. H. Fairbanks, O. F. Weaver, Gust. Hammer, Jos. Winebremer, H. L. Palmer, Thomas Higgins, M. G. Weeks, A. B. Cole, Peter Brown, W. H. Allard, Wm. Gunn, Phillip Staab, John Brown, Joseph Hampton, Samuel Dugan, James Powers, John Daniels, H. W. Klas, John O. Smith, Conrad Stultz, Christian Thiel, Jacob Birk, John Steward, Alex McMillian, Horace Grover, John Carroll, James Brazell, Eliziph Young, Abner Hampton, Louis Frank, J. H. Pishery, P. Weber, Timothy Skinner, O. M. Davis, W. W. Finch, Henry Kimball, Abraham Antone, M. L. Johnson, Conrad Petry

1866	1871	1876	1881	1886	1891	1896	1901	1906	1911	1916	1921	1926	1931	1936	1941	1946	1951

MEMBERSHIP BY YEAR (ACCOUNTED FOR): 1883, 52; 1887, 38; 1888, 32; 1889, 53; 1904, 14; 1905, 13; 1906, 13; 1907, 12; 1908, 11; 1909, 10; 1910, 10; 1931, 5; 1932, 4; 1933, 3; 1934, 3; 1935, 3; 1936, 3; 1937, 3
LAST MEMBER: Charles Hambright, October 4, 1938

Beaver Dam veterans (after an abortive attempt to keep a post going in the early 1870s) established George Hall Post 117 on October 29, 1883. They named their post after a recently deceased Beaver Dam veteran, George Hall, who enlisted in Company D in the renewed Fifth Wisconsin in 1864. Hall was felled by a clubbed musket in hand-to-hand fighting at Spotsylvania. He never fully recovered from the injury. He returned to Beaver Dam and worked as a carpenter when his health permitted. Hall died at age 57 on September 2, 1882, about a year before the G.A.R. post was organized.

Members of George Hall Post 117 of Beaver Dam pose at a Memorial Day gathering, presumably some time after World War I. The driver of the car appears to be wearing a Doughboy uniform. Photo provided by the Dodge County Historical Society.

ELLSWORTH POST 118, Ellsworth
PIERCE COUNTY • NOVEMBER 23, 1883–1927

CHARTER MEMBERS: H. B. Warner, commander; C. Fenton, senior vice commander; John Beatty, junior vice commander; T. L. Nelson, officer of the day; C. W. Brown, officer of the guard; M. B. Kimball, adjutant; D. W. Kinne, quartermaster; C. B. Wood, sergeant major; G. R. Thurston, quartermaster sergeant

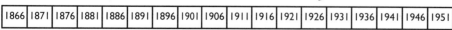

1866	1871	1876	1881	1886	1891	1896	1901	1906	1911	1916	1921	1926	1931	1936	1941	1946	1951

MEMBERSHIP BY YEAR (ACCOUNTED FOR): 1883, 12; 1887, 61; 1888, 60; 1889, 61; 1904, 34; 1905, 33; 1906, 32; 1907, 32; 1908, 26; 1909, 32; 1910, 31; 1911, 31; 1912, 32; 1913, 30; 1914, 28; 1915, 25; 1916, 22; 1917, 22; 1918, 21; 1919, 19; 1920, 18; 1921, 17; 1922, 15; 1923, 18; 1924, 12; 1925, 3; 1926, 3   **LAST MEMBER:** Unknown

What little is available in department records about Ellsworth Post 118 suggests that it was one of those fairly successful Grand Army posts serving small-town Wisconsin during the order's thriving years and on into the twentieth century.

In fact, up to World War I the post continued to serve more than two dozen members. Its precipitous decline (from 18 in

1923, to 12 in 1924, to just three members the following two years) suggests that some of the men may have affiliated with other posts.

Post 118 was one of that small number of Wisconsin G.A.R. posts content to bear the name of its community rather than to memorialize any particular comrade or famous personage.

OSCAR F. MATTICE POST 119, Waterloo
JEFFERSON COUNTY • NOVEMBER 7, 1883–1902

CHARTER MEMBERS: Peter Janisch, commander; R. J. Reamer, senior vice commander; A. T. Brown, junior vice commander; James Moorehouse, chaplain; T. A. Williams, quartermaster; D. O. Bennett, sergeant major; August Draeger, officer of the day; J. A. Wetmore, adjutant

| 1866 | 1871 | 1876 | 1881 | 1886 | 1891 | 1896 | 1901 | 1906 | 1911 | 1916 | 1921 | 1926 | 1931 | 1936 | 1941 | 1946 | 1951 |

MEMBERSHIP BY YEAR (ACCOUNTED FOR): 1887, 44; 1888, 31; 1889, 29   **LAST MEMBER:** Unknown

Post 119, the Oscar F. Mattice Post of Waterloo, Jefferson County, was one of those from the charter year of 1883 that did not survive far into the twentieth century.

What few statistics are available show that it had, in its early years, a significant number of members, but its decline was faster than actuarial tables would suggest, and it surrendered its charter by 1902.

The post was named for Captain Oscar F. Mattice, who was from Waterloo and led Company A of the Twenty-ninth Wisconsin. He was the highest ranking member of that regiment to die during the war, one of the 210 to succumb to disease. (Eighty-six others died in battle.) Captain Mattice died in New Orleans on June 3, 1864. He is buried at Waterloo.

J. B. STEADMAN POST 120, Manawa
WAUPACA COUNTY • NOVEMBER 6, 1883–1909

CHARTER MEMBERS: Unknown

| 1866 | 1871 | 1876 | 1881 | 1886 | 1891 | 1896 | 1901 | 1906 | 1911 | 1916 | 1921 | 1926 | 1931 | 1936 | 1941 | 1946 | 1951 |

J. B. STEADMAN (STEEDMAN)

MEMBERSHIP BY YEAR (ACCOUNTED FOR): 1887, 40; 1888, 28; 1889, 34; 1904, 11; 1905, 11; 1906, 11; 1907, 11; 1908, 11   **LAST MEMBER:** Unknown

The Manawa Post 120 was chartered on November 6, 1883, and chose for its name that of General James Blair Steadman, who

had died the previous month. (The name is generally spelled "Steedman," but the post used the "Steadman" spelling.)

The general was active in the western theater, where many of the Wisconsin troops served. At the Battle of Chickamauga, in which George H. Thomas won fame as the "Rock," one of the subordinates whose own actions helped save the federal forces

from disaster was General Steedman.

Post 120 was active in Manawa until about 1909. Its remaining members (11 in 1908) may have gone to other posts.

JOE MOWER POST 121, Belleville

DANE COUNTY • NOVEMBER 8, 1883–1931

CHARTER MEMBERS: J. M. Williams, Henry Goodenow, Milton Koss, Alfred Greenwood, Xavier Garviolle, W. H. Ross, Jerry Staley, Charles Croon, Fred. Duppler, John M. (last name unknown), Matthew Milam, S. A. Ross, August Francis, Elijah Ase, Rob't A. Oliver, Wm. Chatterton, J. H. Best, Wm. C. Lamore

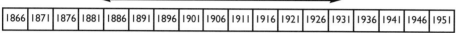

1866	1871	1876	1881	1886	1891	1896	1901	1906	1911	1916	1921	1926	1931	1936	1941	1946	1951

MEMBERSHIP BY YEAR (ACCOUNTED FOR): 1883, 18; 1887, 28; 1888, 27; 1889, 29; 1904, 18; 1905, 16; 1906, 16; 1907, 14; 1908, 14; 1909, 14; 1910, 14; 1911, 14; 1912, 14; 1913, 15; 1914, 16; 1915, 15; 1916, 10; 1917, 8; 1918, 8; 1919, 7; 1920, 6; 1921, 6; 1922, 5; 1924, 2; 1925, 2; 1927, 2; 1928, 2; 1929, 1; 1930, 1

LAST MEMBER: Martin Edwards

JOSEPH A. MOWER

Joseph A. Mower, a "GI's general" in later parlance, was best known to his men as "Joe Mower." He began the war as captain of Company A of the Eleventh Missouri and rose to colonel in short order. His regiment was brigaded with the Eighth Wisconsin, by which he became known to Wisconsin soldiers. He was a participant in most of the campaigns in the West and was frequently lauded by his superiors for his outstanding performance. He attained the rank of major general and command of the XX Corps in the campaign through the Carolinas. Mower died in New Orleans in 1870 of pneumonia while serving as commander of the Department of Louisiana.

The Belleville "boys" remembered Joe Mower and named Post 121 after him in 1883. The post was never large, but served veterans in the Belleville area up to the 1930s.

BADGERO POST 122, Friendship

ADAMS COUNTY • DECEMBER 13, 1883–1935

CHARTER MEMBERS: E. T. Hutchinson, J. B. Keyes, W. R. Newton, B. H. Powers, J. M. Harrison, H. H. Mason, Frank Higbee, John McMahon, J. W. Gunning, Wm. McFarlain, A. W. Horr, N. J. Marble, Jerome Barnett, J. J. Blower, M. E. Lawrence, Otis Hutchins, O. M. Coats, F. F. Blair, H. Rappleye, O. H. Wait, John McNabb, Philo D. Walker, E. O. Clapp, Geo. K. Wood, S. E. Lewis, W. A. Wright, James Chalmers

1866	1871	1876	1881	1886	1891	1896	1901	1906	1911	1916	1921	1926	1931	1936	1941	1946	1951

MEMBERSHIP BY YEAR (ACCOUNTED FOR): 1887, 40; 1888, 38; 1889, 42; 1904, 29; 1905, 28; 1906, 25; 1907, 24; 1908, 21; 1909, 21; 1910, 19; 1911, 16; 1912, 14; 1913, 14; 1914, 14; 1915, 12; 1916, 12; 1917, 12; 1918, 10; 1919, 8; 1920, 8; 1921, 8; 1922, 6; 1923, 5; 1924, 5; 1925, 4; 1926, 1; 1927, 1; 1928, 1; 1929, 1; 1930, 1; 1931, 1; 1932, 1; 1933, 1; 1934, 1   LAST MEMBER: William Hopper

The veterans of Adams County in the area of Friendship joined together as a G.A.R. post late in 1883 and chose to honor a Friendship boy, William W. Badgero, who enlisted in 1861 in Company D, Eighth Wisconsin, and succumbed to disease in

1863 at Vicksburg, Mississippi. The post was unusual in that it did not use the veteran's full name but was always known simply as "Badgero Post."

Yet, Badgero Post 122 was probably typical of small-town Wisconsin. The activities of the post were very much a part of life in Friendship. For instance, when the veterans and the Women's Relief Corps of Friendship decided, in early 1895, to build a meeting hall, its progress was carefully related in the local press. In March, teams went to Necedah to haul lumber for the post. A few

months later, stone for the basement was delivered and "work on the hall will be begun pretty soon." A party was held in the still unfinished Hall in August and "the citizens of Friendship were there and those who did not dance enjoyed the bountiful supper and the bright social pleasures of the evening." Plastering completed the job on the hall and the next month, October 1895, Badgero Post met for the first time in the new building. It was at Raymond and Second Streets in Friendship.

The Post remained active beyond World War I.

ORSON E. RICE POST 123, Oregon

DANE COUNTY • NOVEMBER 26, 1883–1927

CHARTER MEMBERS: Wm. Sodem, C. W. Netherwood, A. S. Parsons, E. R. Sheperd, J. T. Hayes, E. B. Whitmore, E. Jacobis, C. M. Palmer, E. S. Frary, J. D. McKee, G. M. Wilkins, A. S. Colby, Jas. A. Taylor, S. Van Etten, J. M. Getts, E. E. Fairchild, A. J. Gould, N. Hogan, N. Allen, J. M. Doolittle, Wm. McGraw

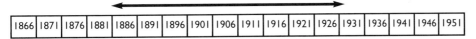

1866	1871	1876	1881	1886	1891	1896	1901	1906	1911	1916	1921	1926	1931	1936	1941	1946	1951

MEMBERSHIP BY YEAR (ACCOUNTED FOR): 1883, 21; 1887, 29; 1888, 24; 1889, 24; 1904, 15; 1905, 14; 1906, 14; 1907, 10; 1908, 9; 1909, 9; 1910, 8; 1911, 5; 1912, 5; 1913, 4; 1914, 3; 1915, 4; 1916, 3; 1917, 3; 1918, 3; 1919, 3; 1920, 4; 1921, 4; 1922, 4; 1923, 3; 1924, 3; 1925, 3; 1926, 3   **LAST MEMBER:** Unknown

The G.A.R. post at Oregon in Dane County, Post 123, was named for Orson E. Rice, an Oregon boy who joined Company B, Thirty-seventh Wisconsin, rose to sergeant and was wounded July 30, 1864, in the fighting at Petersburg. He was

moved to Rhode Island for hospitalization but died there on August 14, 1864.

Rice Post 123 was never a large post, but retained a handful of members, less than 10, from 1908 until 1927.

TIMOTHY O. HOWE POST 124, Green Bay

BROWN COUNTY • DECEMBER 29, 1883–1936

CHARTER MEMBERS: Dennis J. Murphy, Joseph Rubens, A. Howland, B. F. Garlock, Leander Blair, John Atkinson, Alex Gillis, Chas. M. Daggett, J. P. Macy, James Sprague, J. H. Leonard, J. I. Foote, Charles Enoch, E. A. Phillips, H. J. Huntington, Nicholas Gill, Edward Lefebvre, John B. Willis, Chas. Photenhauer, Michael Durocher, W. T. Moger, Julius Schraum, B. C. Brett, O. L. Harder, John M. Schoemaker, Ernst Nebel

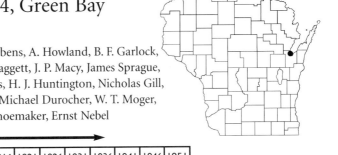

1866	1871	1876	1881	1886	1891	1896	1901	1906	1911	1916	1921	1926	1931	1936	1941	1946	1951

MEMBERSHIP BY YEAR (ACCOUNTED FOR): 1883, 26; 1887, 77; 1888, 83; 1889, 175; 1904, 107; 1905, 108; 1906, 108; 1907, 99; 1908, 102; 1909, 98; 1910, 100; 1911, 83; 1912, 81; 1913, 84; 1914, 81; 1915, 79; 1916, 72; 1917, 63; 1918, 58; 1919, 59; 1920, 52; 1921, 46; 1922, 42; 1923, 36; 1924, 34; 1925, 32; 1926, 28; 1927, 24; 1928, 22; 1929, 28; 1930, 16; 1931, 11; 1932, 6; 1933, 5; 1934, 5; 1935, 2   **LAST MEMBER:** Unknown

TIMOTHY O. HOWE

The record "class of 1883" was drawing to a close when Post 124 at Green Bay was chartered on December 29 of that year. The veterans chose to honor one of Green Bay's famous Howe brothers, Timothy Otis Howe, a prominent judge and lawyer, U.S. Senator from Wisconsin during Reconstruction, and postmaster general under President Chester Allen Arthur. Howe's long career ended with his death earlier that year, on March 25.

Post 124 was the third effort to give Green Bay a G.A.R. post and it was a highly successful one. Its ranks exceeded a hundred for decades and had more than 50 members as late as 1920. The first effort was Post 8 in the department's earliest weeks. It was gone by 1871. In 1876 Green Bay veterans tried again, Governor Harvey Post 15, but it died within two years.

GEORGE H. LEGATE POST 125, Mineral Point
IOWA COUNTY • DECEMBER 20, 1883–1938

CHARTER MEMBERS: Thomas Priestly was the first commander.

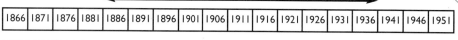

| 1866 | 1871 | 1876 | 1881 | 1886 | 1891 | 1896 | 1901 | 1906 | 1911 | 1916 | 1921 | 1926 | 1931 | 1936 | 1941 | 1946 | 1951 |

MEMBERSHIP BY YEAR (ACCOUNTED FOR): 1887, 78; 1888, 75; 1889, 79; 1904, 66; 1905, 67; 1906, 62; 1907, 64; 1908, 64; 1909, 62; 1910, 58; 1911, 55; 1912, 53; 1913, 49; 1914, 47; 1915, 44; 1916, 40; 1917, 37; 1918, 36; 1919, 36; 1920, 27; 1921, 23; 1922, 21; 1923, 20; 1924, 16; 1925, 11; 1926, 11; 1927, 9; 1928, 8; 1929, 8; 1930, 7; 1931, 7; 1932, 7; 1933, 3; 1934, 3; 1935, 3; 1936, 3; 1937, 3
LAST MEMBER: Unknown

George H. Legate Post 125 of Mineral Point, for reasons not easily explained, was chartered nine days before the one at Green Bay, but the latter received a lower number. The Mineral Point post commenced on December 20 and continued to serve its Iowa County veterans into the 1930s.

The post was named for George H. Legate, who left Mineral Point in the first rush of enlistments, joining Company I, the Miners' Guards, as they were called, in the Second Wisconsin. Legate became orderly sergeant of the company and then was named sergeant major of that famous Iron Brigade regiment. Legate fell in the Second's heroic action the first day at Gettysburg, and was not removed from the field until the next day. He died that night.

Post 125 retained a strong membership through the early years of the twentieth century, having three dozen on the rolls as late as World War I.

Members of George H. Legate Post 125 of Mineral Point stand prepared to put out Memorial Day flags on the graves of departed comrades, date unknown. Front row, holding flags, from left: George Harris, Stephen Wilkins, and William Whitford. Second row, from left: Jacobs (first name unknown), Joseph Arthur, James Hoare, Jonathan Evans, John Stoner, Charles Cox, Henry Pitts Barnell Thru[?], John S. Williams, William Kislingbury, Thomas Gardner, Jerry Humbert, and James B. Prideaux. Third row, from left: Joseph Heathcock, Sidney Shepard, George Cox, William Coad, Rogers (first name unknown), Jim Thompsons, John Perkins, Henry Tyack, John C. Martin, Ed G. Reynold, Ernest Nacf, William Skinner, an unknown man, Hack (first name unknown), George Nickelson, William J. Jones, Rev. Hurd, Wm. Williams, George Jueck. Photo provided by the Mineral Point Public Library.

MARTIN W. HELLER POST 126, Rice Lake

BARRON COUNTY • JANUARY 3, 1884–MARCH 3, 1893

CHARTER MEMBERS: Charles Bone, R. L. Young, A. M. Olds, Charles Munger, S. E. Washburn, W. T. Leonard, W. D. Bartlett, Nels Olmstead, E. C. Coleman, L. C. Sergeant, E. L. McIntosh, George C. Soper, N. Washburn, John O'Neil, E. Burby, Christ Heldstab

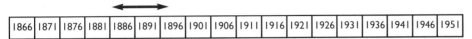

1866	1871	1876	1881	1886	1891	1896	1901	1906	1911	1916	1921	1926	1931	1936	1941	1946	1951

MEMBERSHIP BY YEAR (ACCOUNTED FOR): 1887, 24; 1888, 48; 1889, 55   **LAST MEMBER:** G. C. Soper

The first post chartered by the Department of Wisconsin in 1884, the Martin W. Heller Post 126 at Rice Lake, had as auspicious a start as any of the posts in the class of 1883, more than doubling its membership in a year at one point. But by March 13, 1893, the veterans of Heller Post surrendered their charter.

They resuscitated the post, however, the following year, and were rechartered under the same name as Post 166. Some of the men listed as charter members of that post were original members of Post 126.

The post was named for Captain Martin W. Heller of Company G, Thirty-seventh Wisconsin, who enlisted in 1864. The regiment was among those suffering heavy losses in the trenches before Petersburg.

F. A. MARDEN POST 126, King

WAUPACA COUNTY • JUNE 4, 1893–1937

CHARTER MEMBERS: Columbus Caldwell, M. H. Rice, P. H. Blodgett, N. L. Barker, H. J. D. Minton, C. C. Leonard, Erastus Disbon, Wm. Flanigan, Jas. T. Hall, Nicholas Brockel, Edward Lowth, Timothy Cronin, Oscar L. Meyers, John H. Williams, John C. Green, Geo. J. Bennett, James H. Miller, Walter Mather, Geo. L. Richardson, Thos. G. W. Morey, Joseph Watson

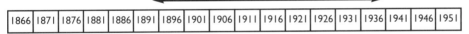

1866	1871	1876	1881	1886	1891	1896	1901	1906	1911	1916	1921	1926	1931	1936	1941	1946	1951

F. A. MARDEN

MEMBERSHIP BY YEAR (ACCOUNTED FOR): 1893, 44; 1904, 135; 1905, 140; 1906, 124; 1907, 126; 1908, 100; 1909, 104; 1910, 113; 1911, 94; 1912, 82; 1913, 79; 1914, 82; 1915, 82; 1916, 107; 1917, 116; 1918, 95; 1919, 78; 1920, 72; 1921, 60; 1922, 65; 1923, 65; 1924, 33; 1925, 31; 1926, 24; 1927, 20; 1928, 16; 1929, 14; 1930, 12; 1931, 8; 1932, 8; 1933, 5; 1934, 5; 1935, 4; 1936, 2   **LAST MEMBER:** Unknown

While the Grand Army's home near Waupaca was established in 1887, a post was not established in the town until 1893.

The new Post 126 was almost destined to be named after Dr. F. A. Marden, for it was Marden who was the primary instigator and planner of the home that was to become known as King. Marden, for instance, insisted that it accommodate wives as well as veterans, a radical departure from practices elsewhere. And it was Marden's untimely death just on the eve of the home's opening that made him the likely namesake of a future post.

Marden Post 126, numerically, was a healthy one for many years, but of course the turnover was substantial, and the health of the average member was likely to be less than comrades who were not in the veterans' home.

Marden Post, incidentally, had been gone for years when the last Civil War veteran and last G.A.R. member in Wisconsin, Lansing Wilcox, died at King in 1951.

Men of the F.A. Marden Post 126 at the Grand Army Home pose for an early spring picture on the grounds of the home at King, date unknown. Photo provided by the Wisconsin Veterans Museum, Madison.

BENJAMIN F. ALLEN POST 127, Arkansaw

PEPIN COUNTY • DECEMBER 29, 1883–1903

CHARTER MEMBERS: : Charles Richardson was the first commander.

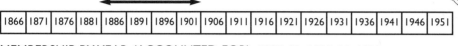

1866	1871	1876	1881	1886	1891	1896	1901	1906	1911	1916	1921	1926	1931	1936	1941	1946	1951

MEMBERSHIP BY YEAR (ACCOUNTED FOR): 1887, 18; 1888, 22; 1889,
LAST MEMBER: Unknown

BENJAMIN F.
ALLEN

B. F. Allen Post 127 was chartered December 29, 1883, making it, along with Howe Post 125 of Green Bay, the last of the posts chartered in the department's banner year.

Unlike Post 125, however, Allen Post in the community of Arkansaw in Pepin County, did not record great membership numbers nor contribute men to the department hierarchy. It lasted, in fact, for just 20 years.

The Arkansaw Post was named for Colonel Benjamin F. Allen, commander of the Sixteenth Wisconsin when it went to war in 1862. The war began for the Sixteenth at Shiloh, and it suffered many casualties, including the wounding of Colonel Allen. Allen subsequently resigned in July 1863.

ALBERT WEATHERBE POST 128, Chetek

BARRON COUNTY • JANUARY 15, 1884–1948

CHARTER MEMBERS: C. W. Moore, O. J. Hurlburt, P. Swansby, D. C. Wood, M. L. Andrus, F. E. Andrews, Owen Brady, C. A. Whitney, C. W. Meadows, L. H. Nichols, O. W. Eighmy, F. J. Banks, B. F. Tyler, S. W. Briggs, B. L. Eighmy, L. F. Locke, H. O. Field, A. D. Stacy, S. J. Packard, A. M. White, W. H. Hogeboom, A. J. Barton, G. W. Sines, A. Richal, William F. Colbert, D. M. Morley, J. Hanafain, D. A. Russell, C. H. Swan, E. Millard, H. J. Dixon, M. L. Johnson, S. N. Blatchford, A. S. Jopp

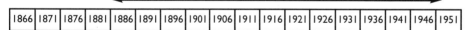

1866	1871	1876	1881	1886	1891	1896	1901	1906	1911	1916	1921	1926	1931	1936	1941	1946	1951

MEMBERSHIP BY YEAR (ACCOUNTED FOR): 1884, 33; 1887, 16; 1888, 34; 1889, 39; 1904, 24; 1905, 25; 1906, 16; 1907, 21; 1908, 20; 1909, 19; 1910, 19; 1911, 26; 1912, 27; 1913, 32; 1914, 33; 1915, 34; 1916, 32; 1917, 26; 1918, 25; 1919, 24; 1920, 23; 1921, 22; 1922, 15; 1923, 13; 1924, 13; 1925, 13; 1926, 13; 1928, 7; 1929, 5; 1930, 3; 1931, 3; 1932, 3; 1933, 1; 1934, 1; 1935, 1; 1936, 1; 1937, 1; 1938, 1; 1939, 1; 1940, 1; 1941, 1; 1942, 1; 1943, 1; 1944, 1; 1945, 1; 1946, 1; 1947, 1; 1948, 1   LAST MEMBER: Ansel Goolsbey, died 1948, age 100

The Chetek Post 128 was named for Albert Weatherbe, a private in Company H of the Second Wisconsin who was killed in the fierce battle at Brawner's Farm, the first engagement of the Black Hat Brigade of westerners which would become known as the Iron Brigade.

Weatherbe Post would be one of the longest lasting posts of the Wisconsin Department, primarily because one member remained through most of the 1930s and 1940s.

Men of the Albert Weatherbe Post 128 march to the cemetery at Chetek on Decoration Day, 1918.

HIRAM J. LEWIS POST 129, Neenah

WINNEBAGO COUNTY • JANUARY 18, 1884–1939

CHARTER MEMBERS: E. Giddings, E. W. Clark, T. T. Moulton, J. R. Barrett, H. O. Clark, J. M. Stiles, H. E. Coats, J. H. Bennett, W. B. M. Torrey, W. Lansing, C. J. Lutterman, A. J. Whitenack, H. J. Gleason, C. B . Clark, J. N. Stone, Ole O. Myhre, R. H. Klenkie, W. H. Jenkins, Wm. Clement, E. Nusdick, Geo. M. Brown, A. Smith, G. F. Thompson, D. J. Owens, Ivan Jenkins, Henry Dietz, Oscar Manley, A. T. Perry, F. T. Russell, G. T. Coats

1866	1871	1876	1881	1886	1891	1896	1901	1906	1911	1916	1921	1926	1931	1936	1941	1946	1951

MEMBERSHIP BY YEAR (ACCOUNTED FOR): 1884, 30; 1887, 67; 1888, 76; 1889, 73; 1904, 57; 1905, 53; 1906, 50; 1907, 51; 1908, 50; 1909, 60; 1910, 50; 1911, 50; 1912, 41; 1913, 39; 1914, 35; 1915, 22; 1916, 28; 1917, 26; 1918, 23; 1919, 19; 1920, 16; 1921, 13; 1922, 9; 1923, 9; 1924, 7; 1925, 6; 1926, 5; 1927, 5; 1928, 4; 1929, 4; 1930, 4; 1931, 3; 1932, 3; 1933, 2; 1934, 1; 1935, 1; 1936, 2; 1937, 2; 1938, 1

LAST MEMBER: Thad Sheerin

HIRAM J. LEWIS

The second company of Neenah soldiers recruited in the summer of 1861 became Company K of the Eleventh Wisconsin Infantry. Its captain was Hiram J. Lewis. Lewis served with the regiment for much of the war, but in 1865 he was commissioned colonel and led the Fifty-second Wisconsin for the few months it was in federal service after Appomattox.

When Neenah veterans formed a G.A.R. post in 1884, they named it, Post 129, after Lewis.

Lewis Post was an active organization for many years, both locally and in department affairs.

EDWIN A. BROWN POST 130, Fond du Lac

FOND DU LAC COUNTY • JANUARY 19, 1884–1939

CHARTER MEMBERS: Edward S. Bragg, Sumner L. Brasted, Isaac L. Hunt, Kelsey M. Adams, John B. Tripp, Wm. Zierkerick, S. E. Wade, Robt. Powrie, Frank N. Fox, Geo. D. Stanton, Napoleon Boardman, Casper Buchner, A. M. Bullock, Max Brugger, S. D. Cole, Marlin Curran, J. M. Crippen, Henry Chilcot, Elihu Coleman, Frank Derasha, Anthony Demarrar, D. Dougherty, Jacob Toutes, Fred. Weyer, John Flood, Anthony Fleischar, Frank Gowa, Geo. W. Haines, D. A. Henderson, S. S. Johnson, A. Jones, Milo B. Killam, John Lain, M. Morgan, J. P. Meisner, J. W. Meyers, W. H. Moore, James McMahon, J. W. Marsh, Geo. Perkins, J. Palmer, David Pitcher, Gerritt S. Rock, George F. Stewart, A. A. Shepard, C. H. Skinner, Geo. E. Sutherland, G. W. Townsend, L. C. Trowbridge

1866	1871	1876	1881	1886	1891	1896	1901	1906	1911	1916	1921	1926	1931	1936	1941	1946	1951

MEMBERSHIP BY YEAR (ACCOUNTED FOR): 1884, 50; 1887, 105; 1888, 176; 1889, 164; 1904, 134; 1905, 127; 1906, 112; 1907, 108; 1908, 110; 1909, 106; 1910, 98; 1911, 97; 1912, 98; 1913, 95; 1914, 93; 1915, 90; 1916, 87; 1917, 84; 1918, 75; 1919, 65; 1920, 59; 1921, 52; 1922, 48; 1923, 35; 1924, 32; 1925, 26; 1926, 28; 1927, 27; 1928, 23; 1929, 20; 1930, 18; 1931, 14; 1932, 14; 1933, 10; 1934, 10; 1935, 6; 1936, 5; 1937, 3; 1938, 1

LAST MEMBER: Albert Pride died January, 1941

EDWIN A. BROWN

Edwin A. Brown Post 130 of Fond du Lac was as intimately connected to the Iron Brigade as any G.A.R. post in the state. Its first commander was General Edward S. Bragg, last commander of that famous brigade. And its namesake was Captain Edwin A. Brown, who commanded Company E of the Sixth Wisconsin of the Iron Brigade and was killed in action in the assault through the cornfield at Antietam on September 17, 1862.

Of course not all the Fond du Lac veterans—some four hundred different men were in the post at one time or another—were from the Iron Brigade.

The Edwin A. Brown Post 130 and Women's Relief Corps were represented in this 1912 Independence Day parade in Fond du Lac.

LINCOLN COUNTY POST 131, Merrill

LINCOLN COUNTY • JANUARY 24, 1884–1941

CHARTER MEMBERS: A. C. Walker, J. B. Carr, D. C. Smith, M. H. Bryant, Spencer Wiley, David L. Anderson, John W. Bruce, H. A. Hathaway, L. LaCount, E. N. Perry, H. W. Boyer, A. Dildine, J. R. Anderson, Theador Compton, H. H. Chandler, Perry C. Hoff, Alex. Baker, Gno. Langhaff, J. .F. Cannon, Geo. P. Robinson, James Truax, L. C. Tynor, Jesse Hill, Geo. W. Longhy, H. Walther, N. L. Smith, Oley Gilbert, L. R. Manning, C. G. Brazee, C. H. Wallace, Val. Hendrick, Henry R. Allen, Philip Zipp, R. Bishop, C. C. Townsend, James Hart, W. H. Wright, J. M. Brush

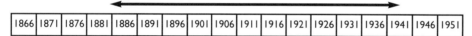

1866	1871	1876	1881	1886	1891	1896	1901	1906	1911	1916	1921	1926	1931	1936	1941	1946	1951

MEMBERSHIP BY YEAR (ACCOUNTED FOR): 1884, 38; 1887, 60; 1888, 59; 1889, 67; 1895, 74; 1904, 40; 1905, 37; 1906, 38; 1907, 40; 1908, 41; 1909, 43; 1910, 42; 1911, 38; 1912, 34; 1913, 36; 1914, 34; 1915, 28; 1916, 27; 1917, 26; 1918, 21; 1919, 16; 1920, 14; 1921, 13; 1922, 13; 1923, 13; 1924, 11; 1925, 9; 1926, 9; 1927, 6; 1928, 4; 1929, 4; 1930, 3; 1931, 4; 1932, 4; 1933, 3; 1934, 3; 1935, 3; 1936, 3; 1937, 3; 1938, 2   **LAST MEMBER:** Unknown

Lincoln Post 131 was quite content to go with the name of its county as its post name. It needed no further identification with the cause for which these veterans fought. Lincoln Post, in its early years, was a significant constituent of the social life of Merrill. It continued with a loyal membership well into the twentieth century.

THOMAS D. COX POST 132, Lancaster

GRANT COUNTY • MAY 17, 1885–1942

CHARTER MEMBERS: Alex Ivey was the first commander.

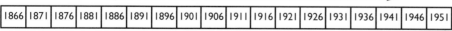

1866	1871	1876	1881	1886	1891	1896	1901	1906	1911	1916	1921	1926	1931	1936	1941	1946	1951

MEMBERSHIP BY YEAR (ACCOUNTED FOR): 1887, 56; 1888, 58; 1889, 59; 1904, 76; 1905, 74; 1906, 68; 1907, 68; 1908, 65; 1909, 64; 1910, 61; 1911, 57; 1912, 57; 1913, 54; 1914, 55; 1915, 55; 1916, 46; 1917, 38; 1918, 34; 1919, 32; 1920, 30; 1921, 27; 1922, 26; 1923, 23; 1924, 20;

1925, 17; 1926, 17; 1927, 15; 1928, 12; 1929, 12; 1930, 11; 1931, 9; 1932, 9; 1933, 5; 1934, 5; 1935, 4; 1936, 3; 1937, 3; 1938, 2   **LAST MEMBER:** Charles P. Schneider, died May 26, 1942

Thomas D. Cox Post 132, Lancaster, was named for the first Grant County soldier to die in battle in the Civil War.

Cox joined the "Grant County Grays" at the outset of the war. It became Company C of the Second Wisconsin. That "grays" designation may have been prophetic. The Second was outfitted in gray as it went into action at Bull Run, Virginia, and for a time was under "friendly fire" from confused Union troops.

Thomas Cox, whether then or later in fighting the Confederates, was killed on that battlefield.

Lancaster veterans honored Cox and began a long history as a Grand Army post. Its numbers held very steady in the early twentieth century when other posts were experiencing declines beyond natural attrition.

GEORGE D. EGGLESTON POST 133, Appleton
OUTAGAMIE COUNTY • JANUARY 1, 1884–1938

CHARTER MEMBERS: F. E. Adsit, J. G. Brown, C. H. Brown, J. H. Cook, A. M. Cole, W. H. Chilson, Jesse Couch, J. B. Cary, E. F. Decker, C. L. Fay, G. Kirchner, Fred Gass, F. W. Hoefer, H. M. Jones, L. S. Knox, W. B. Kenyon, Denis Miedam, William Marsfield, M. D. McGrath, J. H. Marston, G. W. Noble, John O'Keefe, Philip Saxton, Charles P. Palmer, J. T. Reeve, R. J. Smalley, Oscar Sterling, William Wilson, G. W. White, E. Wing, L. H. Waldo, Samuel F. Wheeler, Thomas Kelly

1866	1871	1876	1881	1886	1891	1896	1901	1906	1911	1916	1921	1926	1931	1936	1941	1946	1951

MEMBERSHIP BY YEAR (ACCOUNTED FOR): 1884, 20; 1885, 33; 1887, 119; 1888, 130; 1889, 165; 1904, 133; 1905, 135; 1906, 130; 1907, 127; 1908, 121; 1909, 117; 1910, 119; 1911, 112; 1912, 107; 1913, 96; 1914, 94; 1915, 87; 1916, 79; 1917, 72; 1918, 60; 1919, 54; 1920, 49; 1921, 44; 1922, 41; 1923, 34; 1924, 28; 1925, 22; 1926, 18; 1927, 18; 1928, 15; 1929, 12; 1930, 42; 1931, 7; 1932, 5; 1933, 5; 1934, 5; 1935, 4; 1936, 4; 1937, 3; 1938, 1
LAST MEMBER: Charles Gosha, died 1939

Appleton Post 133 was named for George D. Eggleston, who served in the Iron Brigade as second lieutenant of Company E, Sixth Wisconsin, and was wounded at two of the brigade's major battles, Antietam and Gettysburg. He continued with the Sixth until June 9, 1865, resigning due to disability. Eggleston returned to Appleton and died about 1882, two years before the post was organized.

Charles Gosha receives a plaque presented by later veterans organizations honoring him as the last member of Post 133, date unknown. Interestingly, he is wearing a United Spanish War Veterans badge.

Eggleston Post 133 had a large membership. It was estimated in 1911, when the post still had more than a hundred members, that it had had a total enrollment of 339 veterans.

WILLIAM HICKOK POST 134, Bloomington
GRANT COUNTY • FEBRUARY 8, 1884–1931

CHARTER MEMBERS: John P. Jenkins was the first commander.

1866	1871	1876	1881	1886	1891	1896	1901	1906	1911	1916	1921	1926	1931	1936	1941	1946	1951

MEMBERSHIP BY YEAR (ACCOUNTED FOR): 1887, 21; 1888, 31; 1889, 36; 1904, 31; 1905, 29; 1906, 29; 1907, 28; 1908, 26; 1909, 25; 1910, 19; 1911, 18; 1912, 17; 1913, 14;

1914, 10; 1915, 14; 1916, 13; 1917, 11; 1918, 11; 1919, 11; 1920, 10; 1921, 9; 1922, 8; 1923, 6; 1924, 4; 1925, 4; 1926, 4; 1927, 3; 1928, 3; 1929, 2; 1930, 2   **LAST MEMBER:** Unknown

William Hickok Post 134 in Bloomington was another of those Grant County rural posts which served the county's veterans for many years. Bloomington, in fact, had one of the early and unsuccessful G.A.R. posts, snuffed out by 1871.

It came back in 1884 as a post named for William Hickok, a soldier from nearby Beetown who was in Company C, Sixth Wisconsin, and served with the Iron Brigade through its early years of triumph, only to die in action in the unrelenting campaign of 1864 under U.S. Grant. Hickok was killed in action at Jericho Ford on May 23, 1864, a few weeks after the Wilderness battle began the final phase of the war in the East.

EDWARD SAXE POST 135, Wautoma

WAUSHARA COUNTY • FEBRUARY 23, 1884–1938

CHARTER MEMBERS: J. N. P. Bird, J. W. Beebe, J. C. Davies, E. E. Terrell, Chas. Daniels, B. S. Williams, J. J. Hawley, Geo. Sexton, H. C. Soule, Peter See, C. H. Taplin, Geo. Nelson, F. S. Berray, C. P. Soule, Chas. Leathart, D. W. Robinson, Fred Wandrey, John Eagan, Chris. Henke, Thomas McKeague, Aug. Nehsmer, John Sontag, Simeon Case, Joseph Lamp

1866	1871	1876	1881	1886	1891	1896	1901	1906	1911	1916	1921	1926	1931	1936	1941	1946	1951

MEMBERSHIP BY YEAR (ACCOUNTED FOR): 1884, 24; 1887, 89; 1888, 92; 1889, 104; 1904, 62; 1905, 59; 1906, 59; 1907, 42; 1908, 41; 1909, 43; 1910, 35; 1911, 37; 1912, 37; 1913, 36; 1914, 34; 1915, 31; 1916, 31; 1917, 31; 1918, 30; 1919, 26; 1920, 23; 1921, 20; 1922, 19; 1923, 17; 1924, 14; 1925, 10; 1926, 11; 1927, 7; 1928, 8; 1929, 7; 1930, 6; 1931, 6; 1932, 6; 1933, 5; 1934, 5; 1935, 2; 1936, 2; 1937, 1   **LAST MEMBER:** J. T. Sherman

WISCONSIN VETERANS MUSEUM
EDWARD SAXE

One of the most notable businessmen of Waushara County at the start of the Civil War was Edward J. Saxe, for whom the village and town of Saxeville was named. When the war began Saxe, and a good many Waushara County men, enlisted in the Sixteenth Wisconsin. Sent to Grant's army in Tennessee, Company A of the Sixteenth, led by Captain Saxe, was one of the companies on picket duty beyond the camp in Pittsburg Landing when the Confederates attacked. Captain Saxe and John Williams (Post 4, Berlin, was named after him) were killed in those opening minutes of the Battle of Shiloh.

Veterans in Waushara County's county seat, Wautoma, honored Saxe by naming their Post 135 after him. It was the third attempt in Wautoma at setting up a G.A.R. post, the first two failing in the late 1860s and early 1870s. The latter was Post 5 in 1874–75, also named for Saxe. Post 5, in fact, moved out of Wautoma and existed for a short time at Auroraville. The third time it was successful and remained chartered into the 1930s.

Men of Edward Saxe Grand Army Post 135, Wautoma, march in parade on the Main street in Wautoma. Judging from what can be seen of the automobile in the foreground, the photograph was probably taken in the early 1900s. The G.A.R. men are followed by the Women's Relief Corps. Photo provided by the Waushara County Historical Society.

BENJAMIN F. SHELDON POST 136, Brandon

FOND DU LAC COUNTY • MARCH 7, 1884–1926

CHARTER MEMBERS: M. C. Short, Chas. Herrman, Aug. Middlestaedt, Geo. W. Gee, L. Ferguson, Asa Holmes, James Connor, Ed Stickles, A. E. Austin, A. M. Bly, J. E. Gee, H. Giffy, Jac. Carter, Robt. J. Eaton, J. D. Dunning, Robt. Williams, James E. Reiley, James Patterson, Adrian Daane, Geo. W. Rogers, Chas. Reimer, James E. Thompson, F. Ausman, S. S. Spaulding

| 1866 | 1871 | 1876 | 1881 | 1886 | 1891 | 1896 | 1901 | 1906 | 1911 | 1916 | 1921 | 1926 | 1931 | 1936 | 1941 | 1946 | 1951 |

MEMBERSHIP BY YEAR (ACCOUNTED FOR): 1884, 24; 1885, 27; 1887, 35; 1888, 39; 1889, 43; 1904, 17; 1905, 16; 1906, 14; 1907, 14; 1908, 12; 1909, 19; 1910, 10; 1911, 9; 1912, 8; 1913, 7; 1914, 7; 1915, 7; 1916, 6; 1917, 6; 1918, 5; 1919, 5; 1920, 5; 1921, 5; 1922, 5; 1923, 5; 1924, 4; 1925, 4; 1926, 1
LAST MEMBER: John George Dunning, died November 18, 1926

Brandon veterans formed the Benjamin F. Sheldon Post of the G.A.R. early in 1884. Among the charter members was John Dunning, who became, 42 years later, the sole surviving member of the post (when Herman Giffy died). Three weeks later, Dunning also died, and Sheldon Post was no more. In those 42 years, Post 136 served 34 veterans in addition to the 24 charter members.

Post 136 was named for a Fond du Lac County soldier, Benjamin F. Sheldon from Metomen, who, as a corporal in Company B, Thirty-second Wisconsin, was wounded at Rivers Bridge on February 3, 1865, during Sherman's campaign in the Carolinas. He died at Hilton Head, South Carolina, five days later.

HENRY S. SWIFT POST 137, Edgerton

ROCK COUNTY • FEBRUARY 11, 1884–1936

CHARTER MEMBERS: L. K. Jessup, J. A. Perry, A. F. Rueterskivld, E. R. Squires, H. H. Robinson, James Duffy, C. H. Dickinson, Reuben Sprague, W. H. Craft, W. H. Leonard, T. L. Stillman, John Bowen, W. Hakes, T. Cook, Bradford Burdick, A. B. Campbell, J. S. Green, J. O. Webster, J. C. O'Connor, A. E. Rice, Z. H. Bowen, L. H. Maxson, Patrick Mooney, John K. White, H. G. Beach, E. C. Main, O. N. Coon, J. L. Stewart, Martin Keegan, John Cruse, Nelson Chamberlain, Thomas Young, John A. Hart

| 1866 | 1871 | 1876 | 1881 | 1886 | 1891 | 1896 | 1901 | 1906 | 1911 | 1916 | 1921 | 1926 | 1931 | 1936 | 1941 | 1946 | 1951 |

MEMBERSHIP BY YEAR (ACCOUNTED FOR): 1884, 33; 1887, 40; 1888, 35; 1889, 52; 1904, 31; 1905, 31; 1906, 30; 1907, 31; 1908, 26; 1909, 26; 1910, 26; 1911, 25; 1912, 24; 1913, 22; 1914, 20; 1915, 20; 1916, 21; 1917, 17; 1918, 14; 1919, 14; 1920, 14; 1921, 13; 1922, 10; 1923, 5; 1924, 2; 1925, 3; 1926, 3; 1927, 4; 1928, 3; 1929, 3; 1930, 3; 1931, 2; 1932, 2; 1933, 1; 1934, 1; 1935, 1   **LAST MEMBER:** John Sherman

The G.A.R. in Edgerton, Rock County, enjoyed a long history despite being relatively small. Post 137 was named for an Edgerton man, Henry S. Swift Jr., who was first lieutenant of Company E, Thirty-third Wisconsin. Swift was killed in action at Coldwater, Mississippi, on April 19, 1863. His body was returned to Edgerton and is buried in Fassett Cemetery.

JOSEPH BAILEY POST 138, Palmyra

JEFFERSON COUNTY • FEBRUARY 16, 1884–1922

CHARTER MEMBERS: Unknown

1866	1871	1876	1881	1886	1891	1896	1901	1906	1911	1916	1921	1926	1931	1936	1941	1946	1951

MEMBERSHIP BY YEAR (ACCOUNTED FOR): 1884, 30; 1887, 37; 1888, 17; 1889, 42; 1904, 37; 1905, 56; 1906, 35; 1907, 33; 1908, 33; 1909, 33; 1910, 32; 1911, 29; 1912, 27; 1913, 27; 1914, 26; 1915, 20; 1916, 20; 1917, 18; 1918, 17; 1919, 14; 1920, 12; 1921, 8; 1922, 8

LAST MEMBER: Unknown

JOSEPH BAILEY

One of the unusual heroes of the Civil War who enlisted from Wisconsin was Joseph Bailey from Kilbourn City, now Wisconsin Dells. (He was one of the town's founders.) He began as captain of Company D, Fourth Wisconsin, and rose to be a lieutenant colonel and engineering officer on the Red River Campaign. The Wisconsin soldier's engineering genius saved the naval fleet on the Red River, and he eventually was breveted major general.

Men in the Fourth remembered him after the war, and those from Jefferson County named the post at Palmyra, Post 138, for him. Bailey Post 138 had a distinctive history and was one of the posts involved in the experiment of setting out "picket posts."

Joseph Bailey, incidentally, went to Missouri after the war and was a sheriff there when, in 1867, he was killed by bushwhackers.

GEORGE M. POTTER POST 139, Cadott

CHIPPEWA COUNTY • JANUARY 14, 1884–SEPTEMBER 14, 1896

CHARTER MEMBERS: S. R. Kaiser was the first commander.

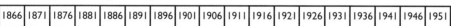

1866	1871	1876	1881	1886	1891	1896	1901	1906	1911	1916	1921	1926	1931	1936	1941	1946	1951

MEMBERSHIP BY YEAR (ACCOUNTED FOR): 1888, 24; 1889, 30

LAST MEMBER: Unknown

The post number 139 had an unusual history.

In 1884, veterans in Cadott, Chippewa County, organized a G.A.R. post, and in the ordinary course, it was designated Post 139. The veterans named the post after George M. Potter, a member of Company L, First Cavalry, who was killed in action on May 2, 1864, in Georgia.

This Cadott Post continued until 1896. It seems never to have been very large; it had just 30 members during the Grand Army's banner year of 1889.

Even so, in 1891 another post was begun in Cadott, designated Post 183, and it was only about five years later that Post 139 surrendered its charter.

That number, perhaps with a touch of irony, was subsequently issued to a second post in another small town, Berlin.

CHARLES GRAVES POST 139, Berlin
GREEN LAKE COUNTY • FEBRUARY 11, 1898–1908

CHARTER MEMBERS: Daniel Smith, Jeremiah Davis, John Hollenbeck, Patrick Dobbins, Geo. W. Thompson, Geo. W. Morton, John Mathias, Patrick O'Brien, Peter Hunt, Richard Davis, John R. Miller, Michael Larmon, Matthew Kerwin, Albert J. Bailey, Wm. E. Covill, Geo. W. Graves, Henry B. Thomas, Wm. Fink, Horace Miner, Levi D. Ruddock, Levi Eldridge, John C. Ostrone, Alex Parsons, M. B. Bailey, Gus Mosher, James Mitchell, John W. Jones, Stephen Lewis, Jefferson Perry, Dixon Work, Nels Johnson, Otto Weisander, D. C. Evans, Thomas Coleman, Geo. F. Slocum, L. C. Culver

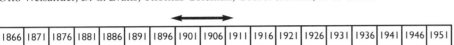

1866	1871	1876	1881	1886	1891	1896	1901	1906	1911	1916	1921	1926	1931	1936	1941	1946	1951

MEMBERSHIP BY YEAR (ACCOUNTED FOR): 1898, 36; 1904, 26; 1905, 25; 1906, 25; 1907, 27
LAST MEMBER: Alex Parsons; see Post 4.

"Fraternity, Charity, Loyalty," the three watchwords of the Grand Army of the Republic, were not always universally practiced. At least not the first two. This led to the establishment, on a few occasions, of a second G.A.R. post in a town where one had been serving the veterans for a long time.

One such was in the town where the order, from the very outset of its existence in Wisconsin, had been fervently supported by the town's veterans: Berlin.[1]

The split, and the reasons for it, were chronicled, sometimes ruefully, in the local newspaper, and it is instructive, even at this later time, because it shows some of the passions with which veterans esteemed their posts. Clearly it was important in their lives. That importance can be imputed to most posts in the state. It bubbled into print on rare occasion because sometimes two factions had different versions of that importance.

In the case of the boys at Berlin, they were extremely proud of the fact that John H. Williams Post 4 was the "oldest G.A.R. post in the world." They had finally established their claim to that honor around 1890. Not long after that, the proud veterans also succeeded in getting a monument placed in the central park in Berlin, which was—and is—a cut above the average Civil War soldier monument of the time.

From these elements arose a great schism.

In 1894 Post 4 Commander George W. Morton desired a second year at the helm, and his supporters cited his hard work, and its success in getting declared the oldest post and in getting the monument erected. At the election in November of that year, the veterans present voted Morton to a second term. But the vote provoked outrage from a significant portion of the membership, including many of the longest-standing members of Post 4. There was, they said, a tradition, an unwritten law, that

no one would be reelected commander so long as there were any other members willing to succeed to the top.

Within days the dissidents constituted themselves "Old Guard Tent No. 1 of John H. Williams Post 4." They were prepared to fight. They boycotted the installation of Morton to his new term the following January. They tried to appeal to the Department of Wisconsin but were thwarted by Morton who refused to send the appeal up through proper channels, i.e., through the post.

The disaffection remained and festered for a couple of years. The Old Guard, including four past commanders of Post 4, were loath to give up the post to go elsewhere, but it became clear that the two factions were not going to reach an accommodation. So in 1898, with Department Commander E. B. Gray making the decisions, a new post was established in Berlin with the Morton faction leaving Post 4.

CHARLES GRAVES

The new post, numbered 139, was chartered February 11, 1898. The first commander was George W. Graves. (Morton was named adjutant.)

Post 139 was named for Charles Graves, the brother of Commander Graves. Charles was a soldier in Company A, Sixteenth Wisconsin, the "Waushara and Green Lake County Rangers," who became a sergeant and was killed

GEORGE GRAVES

July 22, 1864, in the Atlanta Campaign. (Brother George Graves became a lieutenant in the same company.)

In reporting establishment of the Graves Post, the *Berlin Journal* mused: "Berlin now has the oldest and the youngest Post[s] in the world."

---

1. For a second example of a post born in fraternal strife, see John W. Scott Post 241.

GEORGE W.
MORTON

Post 139 had an auspicious start, but the old loyalty of all to the oldest post in the world prevailed. In October 1907, the commander of Post 139 surrendered the charter to department headquarters. Berliners thereafter were all affiliated with John H. Williams Post 4.

The commander of Graves Post 139 who arranged the reconciliation was former (1894–95) Post 4 Commander and future (1924) Department of Wisconsin Commander George W. Morton.

GEORGE A. CUSTER POST 140, Ashland

ASHLAND COUNTY • FEBRUARY 19, 1884–1938

CHARTER MEMBERS: C. L. Haring, John W. Meagher, W. W. Paddock, C. W. Hopkins, C. P. Pease, John H. Knight, D. G. Sampson, W. H. Clay, E. A. Shores, Peckham (first name unknown), H. Brinker, C. L. Judd, W. B. Snider, John F. Childs, C. T. Bowen, Jas. Holton, D. H. Haner, J. J. Miles

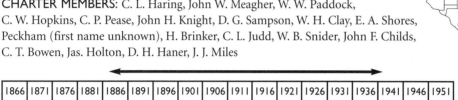

1866	1871	1876	1881	1886	1891	1896	1901	1906	1911	1916	1921	1926	1931	1936	1941	1946	1951

MEMBERSHIP BY YEAR (ACCOUNTED FOR): 1884, 18; 1887, 65; 1888, 67; 1889, 67; 1904, 23; 1905, 25; 1906, 25; 1907, 30; 1908, 30; 1909, 28; 1910, 33; 1911, 21; 1912, 26; 1913, 22; 1914, 21; 1915, 21; 1916, 21; 1917, 18; 1918, 26; 1919, 28; 1920, 28; 1921, 17; 1922, 16; 1923, 13; 1924, 13; 1925, 10; 1926, 10; 1927, 9; 1928, 6; 1929, 4; 1930, 4; 1931, 2; 1932, 1; 1933, 1; 1934, 1; 1935, 1; 1936, 1; 1937, 1   LAST MEMBER: C. L. Judd

GEORGE A. CUSTER

A few men had more than one Wisconsin Grand Army post named after them. (Governor Harvey had three.) One such favorite was George Armstrong Custer. There was already a Custer Post 72 at Rock Elm when the veterans at Ashland in the far north formed a post and chose to honor the flamboyant cavalryman from Michigan who rode into legend at Little Big Horn.

The Ashland veterans had a rather active post, especially considering their relatively sparsely settled county.

HENRY DIDIOT POST 141, Hillsboro

VERNON COUNTY • MARCH 12, 1884–1936

CHARTER MEMBERS: Roger Williams was the first commander.

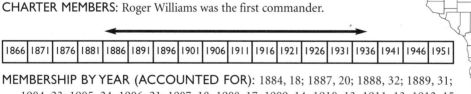

1866	1871	1876	1881	1886	1891	1896	1901	1906	1911	1916	1921	1926	1931	1936	1941	1946	1951

MEMBERSHIP BY YEAR (ACCOUNTED FOR): 1884, 18; 1887, 20; 1888, 32; 1889, 31; 1904, 23; 1905, 24; 1906, 21; 1907, 18; 1908, 17; 1909, 14; 1910, 13; 1911, 13; 1912, 15; 1913, 15; 1914, 12; 1915, 16; 1916, 16; 1917, 14; 1918, 13; 1919, 12; 1920, 12; 1921, 12; 1922, 11; 1923, 9; 1924, 8; 1925, 7; 1926, 7; 1927, 2; 1928, 2; 1929, 2; 1930, 2; 1931, 1; 1932, 1; 1933, 1; 1934, 1; 1935, 1
LAST MEMBER: Unknown

Post 141 at Hillsboro in Vernon County honored a Hillsboro soldier who was among the first to die in the Iron Brigade.

Henry Didiot was sergeant of Company I, Sixth Wisconsin. In that brigade's first battle, at Brawner's Farm on August 28, 1862, the Sixth and its companion regiments suffered tremendous losses. Among the 17 men killed from the Sixth was Sergeant Didiot.

EMERSON OPDYKE POST 142, Clear Lake

POLK COUNTY • MARCH 7, 1884–1932

CHARTER MEMBERS: D. W. Osborne was the first commander.

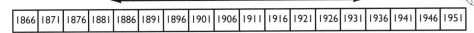

| 1866 | 1871 | 1876 | 1881 | 1886 | 1891 | 1896 | 1901 | 1906 | 1911 | 1916 | 1921 | 1926 | 1931 | 1936 | 1941 | 1946 | 1951 |

MEMBERSHIP BY YEAR (ACCOUNTED FOR): 1887, 24; 1888, 22; 1889, 25; 1904, 19; 1905, 21; 1906, 21; 1907, 21; 1908, 22; 1909, 22; 1910, 21; 1911, 21; 1912, 20; 1913, 16; 1914, 15; 1915, 14; 1916, 13; 1917, 11; 1918, 11; 1919, 11; 1920, 11; 1921, 11; 1922, 10; 1923, 8; 1924, 8; 1925, 8; 1926, 7; 1927, 7; 1928, 7; 1929, 4; 1930, 3; 1931, 3   LAST MEMBER: Unknown

EMERSON OPDYKE

Post 142 of Clear Lake chose to honor a soldier who had virtually no Wisconsin connection.

Emerson Opdyke was an Ohioan and commanded an Ohio regiment at Chickamauga, where he was among officers who stemmed the Confederate tide. He rose thereafter to brigade command. Thereafter he distinguished himself at Resaca, then at Kennesaw Mountain, and later at Franklin. His commands in these years included Wisconsin soldiers.

After the war he lived in New York, where he died in 1884, about the time the Clear Lake veterans were forming their post.

JOSEPH C. MILLER POST 143, Oxford

MARQUETTE COUNTY • MARCH 15, 1884–1926

CHARTER MEMBERS: George W. Stalker was the first commander.

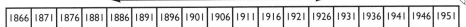

| 1866 | 1871 | 1876 | 1881 | 1886 | 1891 | 1896 | 1901 | 1906 | 1911 | 1916 | 1921 | 1926 | 1931 | 1936 | 1941 | 1946 | 1951 |

MEMBERSHIP BY YEAR (ACCOUNTED FOR): 1887, 43; 1888, 26; 1889, 25; 1904, 17; 1905, 10; 1906, 10; 1907, 10; 1908, 10; 1909, 10; 1910, 10; 1911, 5; 1912, 5; 1913, 5; 1914, 5; 1915, 5; 1916, 5; 1917, 2; 1918, 2; 1919, 2; 1920, 1; 1921, 1; 1922, 1; 1923, 1; 1924, 1; 1925, 1
LAST MEMBER: W. J. Ogle

Little is recorded on Post 143 in Oxford, Marquette County. The post was named for Joseph C. Miller, of whom little is known. A boy from Oxford, Josiah C. Miller, served with the Fourth Wisconsin Cavalry.

WILLIAM PITTS POST 144, Dallas

BARRON COUNTY • MARCH 13, 1884–1907

CHARTER MEMBERS: W. A. Kent, E. A. Keyes, Alex. Miller, John M. Goodwin, J. P. Cottington, D. W. Smith, B. Massey, B. B. Fuller, W. S. Foster, J. G. Johnson, Seth Cole, B. Kipp, Frank Vally, Geo. W. Huffnail, R. D. Brown, J. Cassell

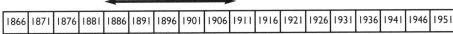

| 1866 | 1871 | 1876 | 1881 | 1886 | 1891 | 1896 | 1901 | 1906 | 1911 | 1916 | 1921 | 1926 | 1931 | 1936 | 1941 | 1946 | 1951 |

MEMBERSHIP BY YEAR (ACCOUNTED FOR): 1884, 16; 1887, 22; 1888, 21; 1889, 27; 1904, 15; 1905, 15; 1906, 15   LAST MEMBER: Unknown

Post 144 of Dallas, Barron County, was one of those posts which served Grand Army veterans in the order's prime years, but succumbed, or rather, surrendered its charter and scattered to other posts as the men grew older and less able to maintain a full-

functioning post. Its first commander was W. A. Kent.

Post 144 was named the William Pitts Post. Pitts was a soldier in Company A, Nineteenth Wisconsin. He enlisted from Baraboo, but apparently came to Barron County after the war. He is buried in Greenwood Cemetery in the Town of Dallas in that county.

Pitts Post 144 members stand before their Hall, date unknown. The fifer in the front at right, was Ole Swanson, who went to war as a fifer at age 14.

GENERAL JAMES SHIELDS POST 145, Medford

TAYLOR COUNTY • MARCH 25, 1884–1933

CHARTER MEMBERS: Fred Barrett, G. W. Adams, P. H. Mulalley, M. W. Ryan, A. J. Adams, N. L. Underhill, M. H. Mullen, James Ures, J. C. Holls, G. W. Warner, Patrick Gaghan, Lewis Brown, J. S. Curtis, Peter Cullen, George R. Doty, Joseph Linden, Jerry Haggerty, James Alexander, Washington Hogle, S. B. Smith

| 1866 | 1871 | 1876 | 1881 | 1886 | 1891 | 1896 | 1901 | 1906 | 1911 | 1916 | 1921 | 1926 | 1931 | 1936 | 1941 | 1946 | 1951 |

JAMES SHIELDS

MEMBERSHIP BY YEAR (ACCOUNTED FOR): 1887, 17; 1888, 14; 1889, 27; 1904, 15; 1905, 12; 1906, 12; 1907, 12; 1908, 12; 1909, 12; 1910, 10; 1924, 7; 1925, 6; 1926, 6; 1927, 3; 1929, 2; 1930, 2; 1931, 2; 1932, 1   **LAST MEMBER:** John Nelson

Medford veterans in Post 145 chose to honor, by giving the post his name, a Civil War general whose entire career was colorful but, as a Civil War warrior was best known for being another of the federal generals out-generalled by Stonewall Jackson.

James Shields' prewar career included service in the Blackhawk War and Mexican War, and as a lawyer in Illinois he once challenged Abraham Lincoln to a duel. The face-off never occurred, and the two became friends, helping Shields later to land a command in the Shenandoah where Jackson beat him at Port Republic.

Shields Post 145 had Fred Barrett as its first commander. It had a long history but was never large. Its distinguishing characteristic might be that it had less than a dozen members from about 1910 to its demise twenty-two years later.

The James Shield Post 145 of Medford gathered on Decoration Day, 1891, for this group picture.

FRANK A. HASKELL POST 146,
HARVEY M. BROWN POST 146, Columbus

COLUMBIA COUNTY • APRIL 10, 1884–1938

CHARTER MEMBERS: A.C. Parkinson, commander; W. G. Bresee, senior vice commander; H. D. James, junior vice commander; O. M. Dering, adjutant; H. Annis, surgeon; Harvey M. Brown, quartermaster; James O. Hutchinson, officer of the day; Christian Moll, officer of the guard

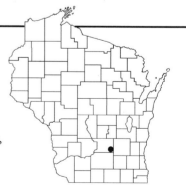

| 1866 | 1871 | 1876 | 1881 | 1886 | 1891 | 1896 | 1901 | 1906 | 1911 | 1916 | 1921 | 1926 | 1931 | 1936 | 1941 | 1946 | 1951 |

MEMBERSHIP BY YEAR (ACCOUNTED FOR): 1887, 66; 1888, 68; 1889, 78; 1904, 33; 1905, 27; 1906, 25; 1907, 23; 1908, 21; 1909, 19; 1910, 19; 1911, 17; 1912, 17; 1913, 16; 1914, 14; 1915, 14; 1916, 13; 1917, 13; 1918, 12; 1919, 11; 1920, 11; 1921, 10; 1922, 9; 1923, 9; 1924, 9; 1925, 9; 1926, 8; 1927, 8; 1928, 8; 1929, 5; 1930, 4; 1931, 4; 1932, 4; 1933, 2; 1934, 2; 1935, 1; 1936, 1; 1937, 1   **LAST MEMBER:** Theron Edwards

MARC AND BETH STORCH
FRANK HASKELL

The men of Post 146 at Columbus did an unusual thing. They changed the name of the post from one man killed in action in the war to that of a man who eventually succeeded him in commanding the same regiment.

Originally the post was named for Frank A. Haskell, who began his career in the Sixth Wisconsin in the Iron Brigade and who wrote a famous account of the climactic action at the stone wall at Gettysburg. Haskell became colonel of the Thirty-sixth Wisconsin and was killed on June 3, 1864, at Cold Harbor. About six weeks later, the major of the Thirty-sixth was wounded at Petersburg. It was this major, Harvey M. Brown, after whom the post was named around 1894.

When the post at Columbus was organized in 1884, it did not immediately chose a name, planning instead "to give it the name of the first martyr to the cause from Columbus or the vicinity, when that person could be found out." At some point thereafter it decided upon Haskell even though his tie to Columbus was somewhat tenuous. His brother, Harrison S.

PATRICIA E. DARLING
COLL. USAMHI
HARVEY M.
BROWN

Haskell, was an early lawyer in Columbus and his brother Frank may have resided with him for a time. Later Harrison went to Portage and lived there at the county seat, and brother Frank at that time did live with him. His war record made him probably the most prominent soldier to have come from Columbia County. He is buried in Silver Lake Cemetery, Portage.

It can only be conjectured what prompted the post to change its name, but in December, 1894, it chose to honor Harvey Brown. At the time Post 146 was in the midst of a campaign to procure a monument to honor "our departed heroes." News reports of the post's effort referred to it as Frank Haskell Post on December 7, and as Harvey M. Brown Post on December 21. But there was no explanation of the change.

At the dedication of that monument on Memorial Day of the next year, 1895, the unveiling was done by Miss Dorothy (Dolly) Brown, the daughter of the late Col. Harvey M. Brown. Brown, incidentally was the original quartermaster of the post.

NATHANIEL P. LYON POST 147, Bloomer

CHIPPEWA COUNTY • MARCH 31, 1884–1928

CHARTER MEMBERS: J. B. Johnson, Rodney Seaver, J. P. Waite, Edwin E. Park, A. M. Cook, L. H. Stebbins, W. F. Enos, John McCannon, J. M. Vanderhoof, H. M. Fitzgerald, E. E. Hillman, Rosell S. Miner

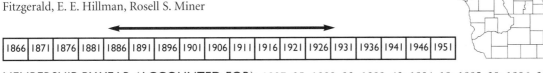

| 1866 | 1871 | 1876 | 1881 | 1886 | 1891 | 1896 | 1901 | 1906 | 1911 | 1916 | 1921 | 1926 | 1931 | 1936 | 1941 | 1946 | 1951 |

MEMBERSHIP BY YEAR (ACCOUNTED FOR): 1887, 25; 1888, 33; 1889, 43; 1904, 19; 1905, 20; 1906, 32; 1907, 31; 1908, 18; 1909, 19; 1910, 20; 1911, 18; 1912, 14; 1913, 14; 1914, 13; 1915, 13; 1916, 12; 1917, 12; 1918, 11; 1919, 11; 1920, 11; 1921, 10; 1922, 10; 1923, 8; 1924, 7; 1925, 7; 1926, 5; 1927, 4   **LAST MEMBER:** Unknown

NATHANIEL LYON

Post 147 of Bloomer was the second Wisconsin G.A.R. post to honor General Nathaniel P. Lyon, a man who is only marginally known today. But at the start of the Civil War, when Missouri hung in the balance, it was Lyon's prompt and decisive actions that kept southern sympathizers from gaining the upper hand and removing Missouri from the Union. His generalship was a bit less successful. At Wilson's Creek, Missouri, on August 10, 1861, Lyon was killed, the first general officer killed in action.

JOSEPH SHANNON POST 148, A. K. HUMPHREY POST 148, Knapp

DUNN COUNTY • APRIL 9, 1884–1902

CHARTER MEMBERS: C. E. Boynton, commander; P. L. Decker, senior vice commander; John Watson, junior vice commander; Joseph King, surgeon; Almon Hunter, chaplain; B. H. Allen, quartermaster; R. McDorman, officer of the day; Richard Adams, officer of the guard; J. F. Temple, adjutant; Simon Healy, sergeant major; C. D. Williams, quartermaster sergeant

1866	1871	1876	1881	1886	1891	1896	1901	1906	1911	1916	1921	1926	1931	1936	1941	1946	1951

MEMBERSHIP BY YEAR (ACCOUNTED FOR): 1887, 25; 1888, 27; 1889, 20   **LAST MEMBER:** Unknown

Post 148 at Knapp in Dunn County, was listed, for its first few years, as Joseph Shannon Post, although nothing is known of its namesake.

The post subsequently changed its name to Arch. K. Humphrey, after a former soldier in Company H, Sixteenth Wisconsin.

After the war Humphrey became the first postmaster of Knapp and was also the community's leading businessman until his death in 1875.

The Knapp Post started with sufficient membership, but it barely survived until the turn of the twentieth century.

PLOVER POST 149, Plover

PORTAGE COUNTY • MARCH 21, 1884–1939

CHARTER MEMBERS: A. J. Welton, commander; S. B. Carpenter, senior vice commander; F. Tyler, junior vice commander; J. D. Rogers, quartermaster; J. O. Morrison, surgeon; L. B. Farr, chaplain; J. Sellers, officer of the day; T. F. Cooley, officer of the guard; S. D. Clark, adjutant

1866	1871	1876	1881	1886	1891	1896	1901	1906	1911	1916	1921	1926	1931	1936	1941	1946	1951

MEMBERSHIP BY YEAR (ACCOUNTED FOR): 1884, 28; 1887, 53; 1888, 61; 1889, 50; 1904, 28; 1905, 29; 1906, 29; 1907, 29; 1908, 32; 1909, 26; 1910, 23; 1911, 24; 1912, 20; 1913, 19; 1914, 20; 1915, 19; 1916, 19; 1917, 15; 1918, 15; 1919, 9; 1920, 8; 1921, 9; 1922, 8; 1923, 9; 1924, 8; 1925, 6; 1926, 6; 1927, 4; 1928, 4; 1929, 2; 1930, 2; 1931, 2; 1932, 2; 1933, 1; 1934, 1; 1935, 1; 1936, 1; 1937, 1   **LAST MEMBER:** S. Whittaker

Veterans in Post 149 were quite content to keep the post name simple: Plover.

Plover Post, however, was not a simple rural post. It was quite vibrant in the days when the Grand Army was powerful. Post 149, in fact, had a fairly steady membership well into the twentieth century. It remained on the department rolls until the 1930s.

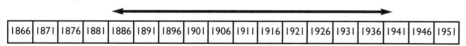

Members of Plover Post 149 pose in their meeting room, date unknown. Front row, from left: N. C. Parsons, LeRoy Shuman, Wally Parsons, Bailey (first name unknown), Stover (first name unknown), Billy Crowfoot, Tom Crowfoot, Eagleburger (first name unknown), Foss (first name unknown), and Crary (first name unknown). Middle row, from left: Volney Toppings, William Hurlbert, H. Sherman, Wm. Whili, B. F. Parker, John McGown, A. M. Blaisdell, an unknown man, and Silas Clark. Back row, from left: William Sheppard, James Bremmer, H. G. Ingersoll, H. Webster, Wally Whittaker, Hubbard Maas, Henry Johnson, and Schuyler Whittaker. Photo provided by the Portage County Historical Society.

THOMAS EUBANK POST 150, Hancock

WAUSHARA COUNTY • MARCH 26, 1884–1911

CHARTER MEMBERS: J. E. Tilton, B. L. Hales, F. B. Hamilton, W. D. Weld, Thos. Beal, W. S. Curtis, W. J. Moore, J. A. Rozell, John K. Worthing, Henry Edison, George C. Guest, J. A. Scofield, Peter H. Johnson, William Jump, L. D. Marshall, S. Ferguson, C. W. Babcock, F. R. Jones, C. W. Moors, Jas. Ordway, O. Hepburn, D. N. Green, George Hutchinson, D. W. Booth, J. R. Barker, Wm. H. Welcome, A. D. Hamilton, J. W. Greenfield, M. V. Ferdon, G. P. Bushey, John H. Ostrum, K. B. Wilkinson

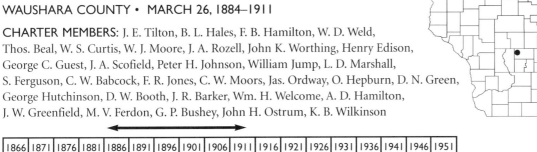

1866	1871	1876	1881	1886	1891	1896	1901	1906	1911	1916	1921	1926	1931	1936	1941	1946	1951

MEMBERSHIP BY YEAR (ACCOUNTED FOR): 1884, 32; 1885, 50; 1887, 92; 1888, 93; 1889, 83; 1904, 27; 1905, 29; 1906, 27; 1907, 26; 1908, 25; 1909, 25; 1910, 18   **LAST MEMBER:** Unknown

THOMAS EUBANK

Thomas Eubank was a postwar businessman in Hancock, operating the Eubank House. During the war he was a member of the Iron Brigade and was wounded and captured at that brigade's inaugural fight at Brawner's Farm. He was later released and returned to his unit in the Seventh Wisconsin. He was mustered out in July 1865.

Eubank Post 150 of Hancock met in a number of locations, including at the Eubank House, but in 1894 it built its own post building. The building still stands in Hancock. The post closed in 1911, its remaining members going elsewhere. The post hall is about as it was in 1911.

Thomas Eubank Post 150 of Hancock built this post hall in 1894. The addition in the back was completed in 1897. The building has been maintained by the Village of Hancock.

EDWIN A. CLAPP POST 151, Hudson

ST. CROIX COUNTY • MARCH 24, 1884–1938

CHARTER MEMBERS: Merton Herrick, A. A. Kelley, J. H. Harrington, Theo. F. Young, Jas. A. Andrews, Otis Hoyt, T. F. Cleveland, H. F. Dinsmore, Andrew Kees, R. R. Young, T. J. Cleveland, P. W. Oakley, David Buckwheat, H. B. Jagger, H. D. Hodges, A. Curtis, Geo. C. Stone, J. D. Hamlin, John Orr, E. T. Rice, A. Swansen, Peter Olisk, W. H. McDermaid

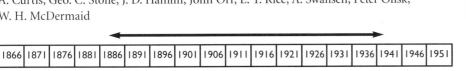

1866	1871	1876	1881	1886	1891	1896	1901	1906	1911	1916	1921	1926	1931	1936	1941	1946	1951

MEMBERSHIP BY YEAR (ACCOUNTED FOR): 1887, 54; 1888, 58; 1889, 56; 1904, 40; 1905, 38; 1906, 36; 1907, 35; 1908, 30; 1909, 29; 1910, 29; 1911, 25; 1912, 22; 1913, 22; 1914, 21; 1915, 19; 1916, 20; 1917, 19; 1918, 17; 1919, 16; 1920, 15; 1921, 14; 1922, 13; 1923, 11; 1924, 10; 1925, 10; 1926, 10; 1927, 10; 1928, 8; 1929, 6; 1930, 2; 1931, 4; 1932, 2; 1933, 1; 1934, 1; 1935, 1; 1936, 1; 1937, 1   **LAST MEMBER:** Anton Swanson

EDWIN A. CLAPP

Hudson Post 151, established in 1884 in an area known for its rabid postwar republicanism, was thriving for the many years the G.A.R. was most active. Edwin A. Clapp Post 151 served its St. Croix County veterans and maintained substantial numbers on its rolls well into the twentieth century.

The post was named for First Lieutenant Edwin A. Clapp, a Hudson soldier who served with Company G, Fourth Wisconsin Infantry. Clapp was killed at Port Hudson, Louisiana, on May 27, 1863, several months before the regiment was converted to cavalry.

PHIL DAVENPORT POST 152, Soldiers Grove
CRAWFORD COUNTY • MAY 3, 1884–1920

CHARTER MEMBERS: Geo. C. Baker, J. H. Salsbury, A. L. Lee, John Miller, Jr., J. Whitemore, A. Montgomery, Peter Peterson, Chas. H. Rinehart, Geo. W. Collins, Geo. A. Smith, Chas. M. Poff, Joseph Randall, Lewis D. Kellogg, M. Bonham, Wm. W. Phillips, J. M. Bown, C. W. Baker, Elisha Moore, John Sutherland, Thomas Kissack, S. Nicholson, Peter Nelson, John S. Rogers

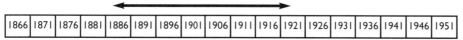

MEMBERSHIP BY YEAR (ACCOUNTED FOR): 1884, 23; 1887, 47; 1888, 24; 1889, 30; 1904, 31; 1905, 32; 1906, 31; 1907, 32; 1908, 30; 1909, 20; 1910, 20; 1911, 20; 1912, 20; 1913, 15; 1914, 15; 1915, 14; 1916, 10; 1917, 6; 1918, 9; 1919, 8   **LAST MEMBER:** Unknown

The veterans of Soldiers Grove in Crawford County named their post for Phillip Davenport, a member of Company I, Twelfth Wisconsin. Davenport was from Rolling Ground, a small community a few miles from Soldiers Grove. He survived the war and was mustered out on May 31, 1865.

Davenport Post 152 remained active until after World War I.

PHILO C. BUCKMAN POST 153, Stoughton
DANE COUNTY • MARCH 29, 1884–1934

CHARTER MEMBERS: J. E. Wright, Nels Thompson, Wm. S. Sylvester, J. M. Estes, John Thornton, J. M. Burnett, O. N. Falk, Thomas Beattie, John W. Shetter, M. H. Doty, W. B. Atkinson, C. O. Harrington, Osman Halverson, O. M. Turner, R. B. McComb, W. O. Wettleson, A. E. Anderson

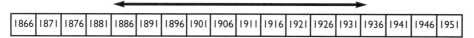

MEMBERSHIP BY YEAR (ACCOUNTED FOR): 1884, 17; 1887, 59; 1888, 51; 1889, 49; 1904, 31; 1905, 32; 1906, 32; 1907, 30; 1908, 31; 1909, 28; 1910, 29; 1911, 30; 1912, 28; 1913, 26; 1914, 21; 1915, 19; 1916, 17; 1917, 15; 1918, 15; 1919, 13; 1920, 13; 1921, 13; 1922, 9; 1923, 7; 1924, 6; 1925, 6; 1926, 6; 1927, 4; 1928, 2; 1929, 2; 1930, 2; 1931, 1; 1932, 1; 1933, 1   **LAST MEMBER:** W. B. Atkinson

CRAIG JOHNSON, TOWSON, MD.
PHILO C. BUCKMAN

Stoughton's G.A.R. Post 153 was named for a Stoughton soldier who was killed in the action of the Seventh Wisconsin at Brawner's Farm during the Iron Brigade's inaugural fight on August 28, 1862.

Philo C. Buckman had enlisted in Company D of the Seventh.

Post 153, one of the many long-standing posts in Dane County, was by no means the largest, but it lasted longer than the other nine save one: Madison's Fairchild Post 11.

The twenty-one surviving members of Buckman G.A.R. Post 153, Stoughton, posed for this picture in April of 1914. Photo provided by the Wisconsin Veterans Museum, Madison.

ALLEN MCVEY POST 154, Star/La Farge
VERNON COUNTY • APRIL 23, 1884–1938

CHARTER MEMBERS: C. W. Lawton, C. G. Stebbens, Robt. Parker, Marvin Wood, Joseph Cather, E. O. Pelton, Joseph Cowan, Cal. Rush, John Cowle, John Wood, W. F. Adams, John Snyder, W. J. Roberts, Wm. Strait, J. W. Sinclair, J. W. Marshall, Thomas Bryant, A. H. Rolfe, Nathan Wilson, D. H. Burgduff

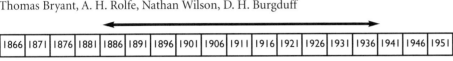

1866	1871	1876	1881	1886	1891	1896	1901	1906	1911	1916	1921	1926	1931	1936	1941	1946	1951

MEMBERSHIP BY YEAR (ACCOUNTED FOR): 1884, 20; 1887, 35; 1888, 35; 1889, 21; 1904, 15; 1905, 15; 1906, 9; 1907, 11; 1908, 11; 1909, 11; 1910, 14; 1911, 14; 1912, 14; 1913, 17; 1914, 17; 1915, 18; 1916, 20; 1917, 15; 1918, 13; 1919, 13; 1920, 12; 1921, 12; 1922, 11; 1923, 11; 1924, 10; 1925, 8; 1926, 7; 1927, 7; 1928, 4; 1929, 4; 1930, 4; 1931, 3; 1932, 3; 1933, 3; 1934, 3; 1935, 2; 1936, 2; 1937, 2   **LAST MEMBER:** Unknown

The community was Star when veterans in eastern Vernon County established G.A.R. Post 154. The designation was changed to La Farge, a nearby community equally as small, after the turn of the twentieth century. By 1902 the Star post office was closed and La Farge was the successful town. La Farge's G.A.R. post, Allen McVey Post 154, was also successful in serving the area. Bucking the trend, the post increased in membership numbers around World War I, as a result of the closing of other nearby posts.

Allen McVey, the soldier honored by the men of Post 154, was a member of Company I, Twelfth Wisconsin, who was wounded in the Atlanta Campaign and was mustered out October 31, 1864.

JOHN M. READ POST 155, Kewaunee
KEWAUNEE COUNTY • MAY 6, 1884–1919

CHARTER MEMBERS: Frank Stelskal, commander; Vitalis Miller, senior vice commander; John Wrabetz, junior vice commander; R. L. Wing, officer of the day; James McIntosh, officer of the guard; Valentine Hoffman, chaplain; Henry Tisch, adjutant; Thomas Hlawacek, sergeant major; Lorenz Lutz, quartermaster; Peter Bregger, quartermaster sergeant

1866	1871	1876	1881	1886	1891	1896	1901	1906	1911	1916	1921	1926	1931	1936	1941	1946	1951

MEMBERSHIP BY YEAR (ACCOUNTED FOR): 1887, 51; 1888, 64; 1889, 59; 1904, 31; 1905, 20; 1906, 17; 1907, 20; 1908, 16; 1909, 11; 1910, 10; 1911, 10; 1912, 10; 1913, 10; 1914, 10; 1915, 9; 1916, 8; 1917, 8; 1918, 8
LAST MEMBER: Unknown

JOHN M. READ

John M. Read Post 155 of Kewaunee was named for a prominent member of the Kewaunee community who also had a distinguished career in the war.

Read enlisted at Manitowoc in October 1861, in Company E, Fourteenth Infantry. He was soon made sergeant, then became adjutant of his regiment, and later served on the brigade staff.

Read served in many battles and was wounded, a second time, at Spanish Fort, Alabama, a week before Appomattox. He returned eventually to Kewaunee, where he was editor of the Kewaunee Enterprise. He died in 1881 from sickness he contracted during the war.

Post 155 maintained strong membership numbers until after the turn of the twentieth century. The post was extinct by 1919, its surviving members presumably going to other posts.

STEVENS POINT POST 156, Stevens Point

PORTAGE COUNTY • APRIL 9, 1884–1938

CHARTER MEMBERS: James O. Raymond, Owen Clark, Jefferson Wright,. E. M. Copps, A. J. Empy, Marshall A. Dille, Edwin R. Herren, J. H. Bellinger, J. R. Luce, James Sheron, Harry Isherwood, Benjamin L. Roe, W. L. Tucker, A. B. Dwinnell, H. C. Day, John Knauf, Peter Gordon, Hiram E. Gee, R. M. Griswold, J. O. Johnson, D. Lloyd Jones, John Stumpf, Henry Curran , Charles E. Harris, S. Wright, Ed McGlacklin, E. J. Hildreth

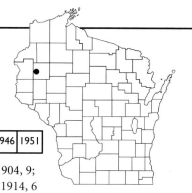

| 1866 | 1871 | 1876 | 1881 | 1886 | 1891 | 1896 | 1901 | 1906 | 1911 | 1916 | 1921 | 1926 | 1931 | 1936 | 1941 | 1946 | 1951 |

MEMBERSHIP BY YEAR (ACCOUNTED FOR): 1887, 60; 1888, 70; 1889, 126; 1904, 34; 1905, 33; 1906, 40; 1907, 40; 1908, 39; 1909, 37; 1910, 25; 1911, 25; 1912, 25; 1913, 21; 1914, 22; 1915, 19; 1916, 19; 1917, 19; 1918, 20; 1919, 20; 1920, 16; 1921, 11; 1922, 11; 1923, 10; 1924, 7; 1925, 7; 1928, 2; 1929, 3; 1930, 3; 1931, 3; 1932, 3; 1933, 3; 1934, 3; 1935, 2; 1936, 3; 1937, 3   **LAST MEMBER:** Unknown

EDWIN R. HERREN

Not unlike their neighbors in Plover, members of Stevens Point Post 156 were content to have their post called by the name of their town.

Post 156 was the larger of the two, and, in the Grand Army's banner year of 1889, Stevens Point had 126 members. In 1902, Stevens Point was host to the annual state encampment.

Post 156 had more than 18 men on the rolls past World War I.

Major Edwin R. Herren, an associate of Joseph Bailey in Kilbourn City (Wisconsin Dells) before the war, was one of the founders of Post 156. He became second lieutenant of the Colombia County Rifles of the Fourth Wisconsin of which Bailey, of later Red River fame, was captain. After the war, he moved to Stevens Point and became a prominent member of the community as an official of a lumber company.

W. W. OLDS POST 157, Turtle Lake

BARRON COUNTY • APRIL 23, 1884–1915

CHARTER MEMBERS: Unknown

| 1866 | 1871 | 1876 | 1881 | 1886 | 1891 | 1896 | 1901 | 1906 | 1911 | 1916 | 1921 | 1926 | 1931 | 1936 | 1941 | 1946 | 1951 |

MEMBERSHIP BY YEAR (ACCOUNTED FOR): 1887, 10; 1888, 17; 1889, 20; 1904, 9; 1905, 10; 1906, 7; 1907, 7; 1908, 7; 1909, 7; 1910, 7; 1911, 6; 1912, 6; 1913, 6; 1914, 6
LAST MEMBER: Unknown

Turtle Lake in Barron County was the site of G.A.R. W. W. Olds Post 157.

The group was chartered on April 25, 1884, and was on the department rolls for the succeeding 30 years.

But little is otherwise recorded about it or about the man for which the post was named.

JAMES WILLIAMS POST 158, Ontario
VERNON COUNTY • APRIL 19, 1884–1917

CHARTER MEMBERS: Thomas B. Marsden, Lafayette Boring, Chas. C. Haskell, Horace H. Stedman, Perry Walker, Newton M. Baldwin, Thomas L. DeLap, Allen P. Hobbs, James C. Gordon, John W. Latamore, John James Taylor, James Hutchinson, Isaac Roberts, John P. Floyd, John W. Revels, Wm. L. Bodon, Wm. R. Parrish, John Shields, Samuel L. Boldon, Daniel Whitinger, David E. Lumley, Walter Goodnough, James Mooney, Nathan Culver, Wm. Fuller, Millin Graham, Geo. W. DeLap, Wm. L. Carter, Wm. G. Downing, Samuel Walden, Livingston Rhone

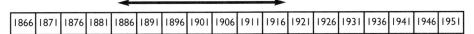

1866	1871	1876	1881	1886	1891	1896	1901	1906	1911	1916	1921	1926	1931	1936	1941	1946	1951

MEMBERSHIP BY YEAR (ACCOUNTED FOR): 1884, 31; 1887, 40; 1888, 32; 1889, 44; 1904, 29; 1905, 37; 1906, 31; 1907, 27; 1908, 26; 1909, 23; 1910, 23; 1911, 18; 1912, 26; 1913, 26; 1914, 25; 1915, 12; 1916, 12
LAST MEMBER: Thomas Sullivan, 1936

James Williams Post 158 of Ontario was organized in 1884 and served until the eve of World War I. Its members thereafter went to Post 154 at La Farge. The Ontario Post was named for an Ontario boy who joined Company H, Sixth Wisconsin. Corporal James Williams was wounded at Antietam. He was discharged for disability in February 1863.

FORT ATKINSON POST 159, Fort Atkinson
JEFFERSON COUNTY • APRIL 24, 1884–1923

CHARTER MEMBERS: Samuel A. Bridges, W. H. Rogers, Asa Foote, John W. Foote, L. W. Lastead, George Coppins, Wellington Case, Frank Holmes, Hiram Drake, Herman Seigner, Isaac W. Spoor, David W. Curtis, Peter Irnig, Wm. Schafer, Geo. W. Turner, Samuel Frasier, John C. Damuth, Alonzo E. Jaycox, Chas. Hummel, Chas. LaPlant, Herman A. Alling, Dolphus S. Damuth, Milton Sherman, Phillip Pfeiffer, Albert R. Thatcher, Johil Jackson, Joseph C. Sawyer, Will Noel, Lewis C. Bickwell, James Atwood, Geo. W. Burchard, John Preston, Samuel Plumb, Ignaz Koser, Chas. Dodge

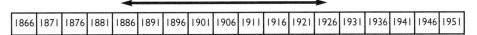

1866	1871	1876	1881	1886	1891	1896	1901	1906	1911	1916	1921	1926	1931	1936	1941	1946	1951

MEMBERSHIP BY YEAR (ACCOUNTED FOR): 1884, 35; 1887, 49; 1888, 37; 1889, 56; 1904, 30; 1905, 30; 1906, 28; 1907, 28; 1908, 27; 1909, 27; 1910, 24; 1911, 23; 1912, 23; 1913, 23; 1914, 24; 1915, 20; 1916, 19; 1917, 18; 1918, 16; 1919, 16; 1920, 15; 1921, 14; 1922, 11   LAST MEMBER: Unknown

Fort Atkinson Post 159 served its Jefferson County community's veterans until after World War I, and then those veterans remaining—11 in 1922—transferred to nearby posts.

HIRAM RUSSELL POST 160, Fremont

WAUPACA COUNTY • APRIL 30, 1884–1931

CHARTER MEMBERS: C. P. Barnes, C. Kinsman, H. C. Pitt, J. G. Hickman, H. Spindler, Wm. Barr, Byron Albee, J. Steiger, C. U. Isbell, Lancellott Pickle, Eugene Fuller, John Hoofberger, J. W. Holmes, John McKinley

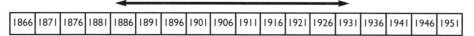

| 1866 | 1871 | 1876 | 1881 | 1886 | 1891 | 1896 | 1901 | 1906 | 1911 | 1916 | 1921 | 1926 | 1931 | 1936 | 1941 | 1946 | 1951 |

MEMBERSHIP BY YEAR (ACCOUNTED FOR): 1884, 14; 1887, 38; 1888, 38; 1889, 40; 1904, 22; 1905, 17; 1930, 1
LAST MEMBER: John Dicke

Fremont veterans got together to form G.A.R. Post 160 in 1884. The post was never large, but the sole member survived until 1930.

The post was named for Hiram Russell, a Fremont business-man before the war, who was captain of Company B of the Twenty-first Wisconsin. Russell was wounded and taken prisoner at Chickamauga. He resigned from the army in 1864 for disability. Russell died on November 17, 1879.

ELIJAH H. AMIDON POST 161, Melrose

JACKSON COUNTY • MAY 1, 1884–1910

CHARTER MEMBERS: James F. Austin, J. L. Button, F. M. Brist, Arad Stebbins, C. W. Chafey, F. W. Behm. Thomas McClean, Erick Trondson, Jacob Harris, F. H. White, George Ralston, Silas W. Amidon, John Shuman

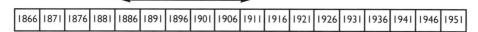

| 1866 | 1871 | 1876 | 1881 | 1886 | 1891 | 1896 | 1901 | 1906 | 1911 | 1916 | 1921 | 1926 | 1931 | 1936 | 1941 | 1946 | 1951 |

MEMBERSHIP BY YEAR (ACCOUNTED FOR): 1887, 21; 1888, 16; 1889, 19; 1904, 12; 1905, 10; 1906, 10; 1907, 10; 1908, 10; 1909, 10   **LAST MEMBER:** William Sholes

Elijah Amidon Post 161 of Melrose, Jackson County, was a post which was destined not to be large nor long-lived.

It had less than two dozen members in any year for which numbers are known, and in its final year, 1909, it still had 10. Presumably some went to other posts.

Elijah Amidon was one of three Melrose brothers who served in the war. Elijah was in the Thirty-sixth Wisconsin and was wounded in the siege of Petersburg. He died within a month, on July 9, 1864, at Annapolis. His brother, George, also did not return from the war. The third brother, Silas, survived and was a member of Post 161.

The last nine men of Amidon Post 161 are shown in front of their post hall, date unknown. From left: Fred White, Joe LaVannaway, Leland Amidon, Hiram Finch, William Sholes, Jefferson Burton, Matthew K. Pynn, Marcus Finch, and Robert Farrington. Photo provided by the Jackson Co. Historical Society.

ARTHUR C. ELLIS POST 162, Eau Claire

EAU CLAIRE COUNTY • JULY 21, 1884–1886 OR 1887

CHARTER MEMBERS: William F. Bailey was the first commander.

1866	1871	1876	1881	1886	1891	1896	1901	1906	1911	1916	1921	1926	1931	1936	1941	1946	1951

LAST MEMBER: Unknown

CHIPPEWA VALLEY
MUSEUM
ARTHUR C. ELLIS

Post 162 at Eau Claire is one of those posts with little on record yet with tantalizing questions. It was formed in 1884, although Eagle Post 52 already existed in Eau Claire. Was it a breakaway group? And when in 1887 or so it gave up its charter, did they heal whatever wounds and return to Eagle Post?

What is known about the post is that it was named for Arthur C. Ellis, who joined the Sixth Wisconsin shortly after he came to Eau Claire. Ellis was wounded in the Battle of South Mountain at which the Iron Brigade won its name and transferred to the veterans reserve corps. Ellis stayed in service until 1867 and then returned to Eau Claire, practicing law there from 1870 to 1880. He was a judge the last seven years of that time. Ellis died in 1883 from complications arising from his war wound.

BELKNAP FUQUA POST 162, Potosi

GRANT COUNTY • AUGUST 26, 1889–1923

CHARTER MEMBERS: Unknown

1866	1871	1876	1881	1886	1891	1896	1901	1906	1911	1916	1921	1926	1931	1936	1941	1946	1951

MEMBERSHIP BY YEAR (ACCOUNTED FOR): 1889, 27; 1890, 22; 1904, 26; 1905, 24; 1906, 24; 1907, 23; 1908, 23; 1909, 21; 1910, 18; 1911, 14; 1912, 14; 1913, 14; 1914, 11; 1915, 11; 1916, 9; 1917, 9; 1918, 9; 1919, 8; 1920, 8; 1921, 8; 1922, 7   LAST MEMBER: Unknown

The second Post 162 was the Belknap Fuqua Post of Potosi, chartered around 1889. The post was named for a Grant County soldier from Rockville who was wounded and taken prisoner at the first Battle of Bull Run. The corporal from Company C, Second Wisconsin, died at Richmond, Virginia, on August 18, 1861.

Belknap Fuqua Post in 1880.

FRANCIS ASBRA WELLCOME POST 163, Thorpe

CLARK COUNTY • MAY 12, 1884–1911

CHARTER MEMBERS: G. Howard, Z. Worden, E. W. Bradburg. J. Adams, M. A. Hubbard, Frank Smith, J. H. Sargent, W. R. Phillips, J. N. Norton, V. R. Mead, G. W. Courter, M. Ducale, P. Schroder, Victor Fellows, H. J. Ferrenden

1866	1871	1876	1881	1886	1891	1896	1901	1906	1911	1916	1921	1926	1931	1936	1941	1946	1951

MEMBERSHIP BY YEAR (ACCOUNTED FOR): 1884, 15; 1887, 16; 1888, 12; 1889, 24; 1904, 23; 1905, 20; 1906, 19; 1907, 17; 1908, 14; 1909, 15; 1910, 15 **LAST MEMBER:** Unknown

Veterans in Thorpe organized their G.A.R. post in 1884 and named it for Francis Asbra Wellcome, a soldier from nearby La Crosse County who was in Company H, Sixteenth Wisconsin. In the campaign around Atlanta, the Federals followed up their win at Peachtree Creek by assaulting and capturing Bald Hill, from which they had a full view of Atlanta. Wellcome did not see the view; he was killed in the assault.

Post 163 gave up its charter in 1910, its approximately 15 members at the time presumably going to other posts.

CARMI P. GARLICK POST 164, Osceola Mills

POLK COUNTY • MAY 22, 1884–1900

CHARTER MEMBERS: Unknown

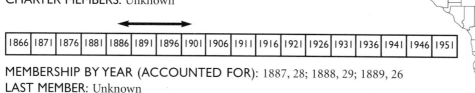

1866	1871	1876	1881	1886	1891	1896	1901	1906	1911	1916	1921	1926	1931	1936	1941	1946	1951

MEMBERSHIP BY YEAR (ACCOUNTED FOR): 1887, 28; 1888, 29; 1889, 26
LAST MEMBER: Unknown

Veterans in Osceola Mills organized G.A.R. Post 164 in 1884, but the organization apparently was never really robust.

Post 164 was suspended in the 1890s, but was reinstated in 1895. By 1900, however, it was permanently off the Department of Wisconsin rolls.

The post was named for Carmi P. Garlick, an Osceola Mills man, who was assistant surgeon of the Thirty-fifth Wisconsin. Garlick is buried in Mount Hope Cemetery at Osceola.

GEORGE M. WEST POST 165, Hartford

WASHINGTON COUNTY • MAY 31, 1884–1938

CHARTER MEMBERS: Dr. E. M. Rogers, commander; William J. Le Count, senior vice commander; Wallace Chapman, junior vice commander; A. L. Williams, quartermaster; John White, quartermaster sergeant; C. L. Brink, chaplain; J. H. Simon, surgeon; J. P. Gould, officer of the day; Leo Laverence, officer of the guard; D. A. Bradford, adjutant; Stephen Reundi, adjutant assistant

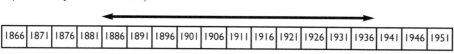

1866	1871	1876	1881	1886	1891	1896	1901	1906	1911	1916	1921	1926	1931	1936	1941	1946	1951

MEMBERSHIP BY YEAR (ACCOUNTED FOR): 1884, 25; 1887, 55; 1888, 56; 1889, 56; 1904, 27; 1905, 27; 1906, 25; 1907, 24; 1908, 24; 1909, 22; 1910, 22; 1911, 22; 1912, 22; 1913, 20; 1914, 20; 1915, 17; 1916, 15; 1917, 14; 1918, 13; 1919, 13; 1920, 12; 1921, 11; 1922, 11; 1923, 9; 1924, 8; 1925, 8; 1926, 7; 1927, 4; 1928, 4; 1929, 3; 1930, 3; 1931, 3; 1932, 3; 1933, 3; 1934, 3; 1935, 2; 1936, 2; 1937, 2 **LAST MEMBER:** John Kauper died in 1939.

Hartford veterans formed Post 165 in 1884, naming it for George M. West, a Hartford man, who enlisted as second lieutenant of Company E, Tenth Wisconsin. He was captain of that company when he was killed on September 20, 1863, at Chickamauga.

George M. West Post 165 served Hartford veterans for many years. It had a dozen members as late at 1920. Although it was off department rolls by 1938, the last G.A.R. man in Hartford died the following year.

MAJOR NATHAN PAINE POST 166, Fairchild

EAU CLAIRE COUNTY • JUNE 19, 1884–AUGUST 12, 1893

CHARTER MEMBERS: Unknown

1866	1871	1876	1881	1886	1891	1896	1901	1906	1911	1916	1921	1926	1931	1936	1941	1946	1851

MEMBERSHIP BY YEAR (ACCOUNTED FOR): 1887, 19; 1888, 23; 1889, 24

LAST MEMBER: Unknown

NATHAN PAINE

Nathan Paine Post 166 was begun by veterans in Fairchild, Eau Claire County, in 1884, but it failed to take firm root. It surrendered its charter in August 1893. Presumably its members went to other Eau Claire area posts.

The Fairchild Post was named for Major Nathan Paine, a leader of the First Wisconsin Cavalry who returned home to Oshkosh from an eastern college when the war broke out and immediately joined the Cavalry then forming at Ripon.

Paine was a popular leader with the unit. His death on July 28, 1864, in a skirmish at Campbellton, Georgia, during a gallant but futile charge (which won even the admiration of his adversaries, who buried Paine with great care), was much mourned by his comrades. He was the highest ranking officer in the First Cavalry to be killed in action.

MARTIN W. HELLER POST 166, Rice Lake

BARRON COUNTY • AUGUST 1, 1894–1934

CHARTER MEMBERS: A. S. Jopp, R. L. Young, Ephraim Burby, John Deitz, W. B. Slick, D. W. McClench, H. W. Richardson, Gottlieb Frion, W. W. Bordwell, A. W. Bailey, C. Z. Stevenson, C. A. Bunce, F. R. Conn, E. L. Everts, J. W. Rogers, W. C. Porter, Ebenezer Bassett, J. W. Henderson, T. E. Richards, C. F. Bone, Alfred Locey, W. H. Luce, T. A. Ross, N. E. Leach, M. P. Barry, J. H. Hogenboom, G. C. Soper

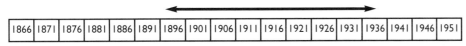

1866	1871	1876	1881	1886	1891	1896	1901	1906	1911	1916	1921	1926	1931	1936	1941	1946	1951

MEMBERSHIP BY YEAR (ACCOUNTED FOR): 1904, 31; 1905, 30; 1906, 28; 1907, 29; 1908, 29; 1909, 29; 1910, 29; 1911, 25; 1912, 23; 1913, 21; 1914, 21; 1915, 16; 1916, 15; 1917, 14; 1918, 10; 1919, 11; 1920, 10; 1921, 8; 1922, 6; 1923, 6; 1924, 4; 1925, 4; 1926, 4; 1927, 3; 1928, 3; 1929, 3; 1930, 3; 1931, 1; 1932, 1; 1933, 1

LAST MEMBER: G. C. Soper

M. W. Heller Post was reformed in Rice Lake in 1894 and continued to serve that Barron County area until 1934. It had begun as Post 126 but was given up in early 1893. They rechartered as Post 166 and retained the original name, which honored Martin W. Heller, who served with Company K, Fifth Wisconsin in the early years of the war. In May 1864, when new regiments were being put together, Heller was commissioned captain of Company G, Thirty-seventh Wisconsin. By November 1864 he was discharged on disability.

FRANK BIGELOW POST 167, Eagle

WAUKESHA COUNTY • FEBRUARY 21, 1884–1887

CHARTER MEMBERS: J. A. Lins was the first commander.

1866	1871	1876	1881	1886	1891	1896	1901	1906	1911	1916	1921	1926	1931	1936	1941	1946	1951

LAST MEMBER: Unknown

Among the Grand Army posts chartered in the record years of 1883–84, it was perhaps remarkable that the great majority of them succeeded, unlike the flurry of posts and failures in 1867–70.

One of the few that did not succeed from the class of 1884 was the Franklin Bigelow Post 167 in Eagle, Waukesha County. Virtually nothing is on record regarding this post, but it is clear that it had ceased as a member of the Department of Wisconsin by 1887.

It is known, though, that the post was named for Franklin Bigelow from Eagle, who was a private in Company G, Thirty-seventh Wisconsin. (His company was commanded by Martin W. Heller, after whom Post 166 was named.) Bigelow as one of 31 officers and men of the Thirty-seventh killed in the ill-fated Battle of the Crater before Petersburg on July 30, 1864.

Veterans in the Eagle area were later served (around 1894), for a short time, by a "picket post" sponsored by Post 138, Palmyra.

LUCIUS H. DRURY POST 167, Eagle River

VILAS COUNTY • JULY 21, 1888–1890

CHARTER MEMBERS: Unknown

1866	1871	1876	1881	1886	1891	1896	1901	1906	1911	1916	1921	1926	1931	1936	1941	1946	1951

MEMBERSHIP BY YEAR (ACCOUNTED FOR): 1889, 16   **LAST MEMBER:** Unknown

If Post 167 of Eagle had a short history, its successor Post 167, at Eagle River, was even shorter.

It was, perhaps due to the small population of Vilas County. Though the charter members in 1888 are not known, the enrollment for the succeeding year is recorded: the post had only 16 men in the year of the Grand Army's greatest membership.

By the end of that year, or just into the next, the Lu H. Drury Post 167 of Eagle River was defunct.

The post was named for Major Lucius H. Drury of Berlin, major of the First Regiment of Heavy Artillery. He served through the entire war.

JOHN GREEN POST 167, Eau Galle

DUNN COUNTY • FEBRUARY 27, 1890–1913

CHARTER MEMBERS: J. B. Johnson, Rodney Seaver, J. P. Waite, Edwin E. Park, A. M. Cook, L. H. Stebbins, W. F. Enos, John McCannon, J. M. Vanderhoof, H. M. Fitzgerald, E. E. Hillman, Rosell S. Miner

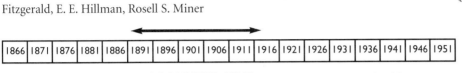

1866	1871	1876	1881	1886	1891	1896	1901	1906	1911	1916	1921	1926	1931	1936	1941	1946	1951

MEMBERSHIP BY YEAR (ACCOUNTED FOR): 1890, 18; 1904, 20; 1905, 20; 1906, 15; 1907, 14; 1908, 14; 1909, 12; 1910, 11; 1911, 11; 1912, 9; 1913, 7   LAST MEMBER: Unknown

John Green Post 167 of Eau Galle, Dunn County, was like its predecessor posts with the 167 number in that it was never a large organization. Unlike the other two, however, it had some staying power and was carried on the department rolls until the eve of World War I.

This Post 167 was named for an Eau Galle boy, John Green, who became a corporal in Company G, Fifth Wisconsin. On November 4, 1863, in one of several skirmishes marking the Army of the Potomac's maneuvers to straighten its lines along the Rappahannock, the Fifth was engaged and Corporal Green was killed.

HOWARD F. PRUYN POST 168, Dorchester

CLARK COUNTY • JULY 9, 1884–1928

CHARTER MEMBERS: August Homsted was the first commander.

1866	1871	1876	1881	1886	1891	1896	1901	1906	1911	1916	1921	1926	1931	1936	1941	1946	1951

MEMBERSHIP BY YEAR (ACCOUNTED FOR): 1887, 21; 1888, 23; 1889, 23; 1904, 12; 1905, 10; 1906, 10; 1907, 9; 1908, 9; 1909, 9; 1910, 7; 1911, 6; 1912, 5; 1913, 5; 1914, 3; 1915, 2; 1916, 2; 1917, 2; 1918, 2; 1919, 2; 1920, 2; 1921, 2; 1922, 2; 1923, 2; 1924, 2; 1925, 1; 1926, 1; 1927, 1   LAST MEMBER: Charles Beyreis

HOWARD F. PRUYN

From 1884 to 1928, Howard F. Pruyn Post 168 served the veterans of Dorchester in Clark County. The post was never large, but its handful of veterans from the 1910s and 1920s kept the post in good standing with the department.

Post 168 was named for Howard Pruyn, first lieutenant of Company A, Sixth Wisconsin, from Baraboo. Pruyn was in command of the company at Gettysburg on July 1, 1863, and he was wounded in the regiment's charge at the railroad cut. He recovered and served with the Sixth until he was killed in action on May 8, 1864, at Laurel Hill, Virginia, in an opening engagement of the Battle of Spotsylvania Court House.

JOHN ECHTERNOCH POST 169, Theresa

DODGE COUNTY • JULY 10, 1884–1901

CHARTER MEMBERS: Unknown

1866	1871	1876	1881	1886	1891	1896	1901	1906	1911	1916	1921	1926	1931	1936	1941	1946	1951

MEMBERSHIP BY YEAR (ACCOUNTED FOR): 1887, 10; 1888, 11; 1889, 13

LAST MEMBER: Unknown

Theresa veterans honored a Theresa soldier when they named their G.A.R. Post 169. He was John Echternoch, a sergeant in Company K of the Thirty-fifth Wisconsin. The regiment lost only two men from combat, and both of those were in action in Alabama in the last month of the war. But the Thirty-fifth had 259 soldiers die of disease. One of them was Sergeant Echternoch, on July 1, 1864, at Port Hudson, Louisiana.

Post 169, similar to dozens of other small-town G.A.R. posts begun in the 1880s, was never large. It was listed in department records as existing in 1900 but was extinct within a year.

ALONZO PALMER POST 170, Superior

DOUGLAS COUNTY • AUGUST 9, 1884–1942

CHARTER MEMBERS: J. Lute Christe, commander; J. D. Robie, senior vice commander; L. T. Slayton, junior vice commander; A. B. Lord, surgeon; A. A. Maxim, quartermaster; D. W. Head, quartermaster sergeant; H. Barney, officer of the day; F. B. Wight, officer of the guard; S. E. Tubbs, adjutant; J. G. Scripter, sergeant major

1866	1871	1876	1881	1886	1891	1896	1901	1906	1911	1916	1921	1926	1931	1936	1941	1946	1951

MEMBERSHIP BY YEAR (ACCOUNTED FOR): 1887, 15; 1888, 18; 1889, 50; 1904, 150; 1905, 150; 1906, 145; 1907, 132; 1908, 135; 1909, 119; 1910, 110; 1911, 108; 1912, 87; 1913, 72; 1914, 69; 1915, 67; 1916, 65; 1917, 64; 1918, 62; 1919, 51; 1920, 42; 1921, 34; 1922, 36; 1923, 31; 1924, 25; 1925, 26; 1926, 18; 1927, 17; 1928, 17; 1929, 13; 1930, 10; 1931, 8; 1932, 7; 1933, 7; 1934, 7; 1935, 7; 1936, 5; 1937, 5; 1938, 2

LAST MEMBER: C. L. Hooker

Alonzo Palmer Post 170 Drum Corps., West Superior.

Alonzo Palmer Post 170 of Superior might be called the premier post of the North. It also had a membership curve unlike most other Department of Wisconsin posts. It began, in 1884, on a relatively small scale as state demographics of the time would suggest. But by the turn of the twentieth century, when many other posts had passed their peak, Post 170 hit its stride.

Post 170, in fact, was host to the state encampment in 1900, only the third state gathering north of Oshkosh up until that time. (Green Bay, 1895, and Eau Claire, 1897, began the pattern of encampments moving outside southeastern Wisconsin from time to time.)

At the post's chartering (attended by half a dozen Duluth G.A.R. men who rowed a boat across to attend), the men chose the name of Alonzo Palmer, who was identified in the newspaper as "a fallen hero . . . whose remains molder in our cemetery on the banks of the Nemadji." Palmer served four years with an Illinois regiment, the Fifteenth, and returned to the Duluth area after the war where he died from injuries he sustained in service.

HENRY CONCKLIN POST 171, East Troy

WALWORTH COUNTY • AUGUST 16, 1884–1929

CHARTER MEMBERS: S. B. Tullar was the first commander.

1866	1871	1876	1881	1886	1891	1896	1901	1906	1911	1916	1921	1926	1931	1936	1941	1946	1951

MEMBERSHIP BY YEAR (ACCOUNTED FOR): 1887, 31; 1888, 32; 1889, 43; 1904, 39; 1905, 38; 1906, 34; 1907, 33; 1908, 27; 1909, 24; 1910, 24; 1911, 21; 1912, 22; 1913, 22; 1914, 21; 1915, 20; 1916, 16; 1917, 13; 1918, 13; 1919, 13; 1920, 12; 1921, 12; 1922, 11; 1923, 9; 1924, 7; 1925, 6; 1926, 6; 1927, 5; 1928, 5 **LAST MEMBER:** Unknown

The Henry Concklin Post of East Troy, Post 171, served its members from 1884 until 1929. It was one of those posts that maintained a relatively stable membership until time claimed the men.

It was named for Henry L. Concklin, a private in Company A, Tenth Wisconsin. The company, raised in Elkhorn and Delavan, known as the Walworth County Guards, was recruited in September 1861. The Tenth was in service for almost a year when it marched to Perryville, Kentucky, where the company was heavily engaged in battle against Braxton Bragg's army. Among those killed in that battle was Private Concklin.

MARTIN WATSON POST 172, Barron

BARRON COUNTY • AUGUST 6, 1884–1931

CHARTER MEMBERS: J. J. Smith, Ole Christopherson, J. B. Thurston, J. P. Briggs, Levi Miller, Chas. Jenks, John N. Conner, John Post, J. C. Beckwith, William Miller, Thomas Bourke, A. Blodgett, D. G. Harris

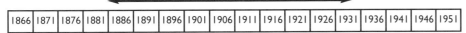

1866	1871	1876	1881	1886	1891	1896	1901	1906	1911	1916	1921	1926	1931	1936	1941	1946	1951

MEMBERSHIP BY YEAR (ACCOUNTED FOR): 1887, 28; 1888, 26; 1889, 28; 1904, 21; 1905, 19; 1906, 24; 1907, 26; 1908, 24; 1909, 29; 1910, 30; 1911, 36; 1912, 33; 1913, 34; 1914, 32; 1915, 28; 1916, 22; 1917, 20; 1918, 14; 1919, 10; 1920, 9; 1921, 8; 1922, 8; 1923, 8; 1924, 8; 1925, 6; 1926, 6; 1927, 3; 1928, 3; 1929, 3; 1930, 2
LAST MEMBER: Unknown

Members of the Barron Post 172 honored a soldier from out of state, Martin Watson, a postwar member of the Barron community who died just a year before the veterans got together to form a G.A.R. post. First commander of the Watson post was John Post.

Martin Watson Post 172 was a relatively successful one over the years. In fact, it increased its membership rolls in the years 1908–15, presumably by accommodating members from other declining posts.

Watson was a soldier with the Seventy-third Indiana Infantry. He enlisted in August 1862 and was discharged in December of that same year for disability. He farmed in Indiana after the war and moved to Barron County in 1880. He died in the Town of Maple Grove in Barron County on July 1, 1883.

Post 172 on Memorial Day, 1923. Photo provided by the Barron County Historical Society.

SAM MONTIETH POST 173, Fennimore

GRANT COUNTY • AUGUST 12, 1884–1934

CHARTER MEMBERS: John Montieth, commander; Matthew Burcherd, senior vice commander; D. O. Pickard, junior vice commander; Joseph Morrison, surgeon; B. W. Niehaus, chaplain; J. W. Vetter, quartermaster; Charles A. Willison, officer of the day; Sylvester Moody, officer of the guard; Martin Oswald, adjutant

1866	1871	1876	1881	1886	1891	1896	1901	1906	1911	1916	1921	1926	1931	1936	1941	1946	1951

MEMBERSHIP BY YEAR (ACCOUNTED FOR): 1884, 24; 1887, 49; 1888, 35; 1889, 28; 1904, 37; 1905, 35; 1906, 36; 1907, 35; 1908, 33; 1909, 35; 1910, 34; 1911, 34; 1912, 34; 1913, 20; 1914, 17; 1915, 15; 1916, 14; 1917, 10; 1918, 10; 1919, 10; 1920, 10; 1921, 10; 1922, 7; 1923, 6; 1924, 7; 1925, 7; 1926, 7; 1927, 6; 1928, 4; 1929, 2; 1930, 2; 1931, 2; 1932, 2; 1933, 1; 1934, 1   **LAST MEMBER:** Amos W. Hadlock, died 1934

Sylvester Kitelinger, a member of Post 173, wears his parade badge.

Grant County provided its share of soldiers in the Civil War and had its share of Grand Army Posts thereafter. One was the Sam Montieth Post 173 at Fennimore.

Although the 24 charter members are not all on record, two of the men served the post in an official capacity from its founding in 1884 until they died. Ben W. Niehaus was chaplain and then adjutant until 1926, and Charles A. Willison served as officer of the day and then quartermaster until 1915.

In its long history, Post 173 served 104 veterans. It continued until 1934.

The post was named for Sam Montieth, who was from Vernon rather than Grant County and was a sergeant of Company H, Seventh Wisconsin, in which many Fennimore men served. Montieth was killed in the Iron Brigade's attack through the cornfield at Antietam on September 17, 1862.

A. D. THORNBURG POST 174, Lime Ridge

SAUK COUNTY • AUGUST 11, 1888–1908

CHARTER MEMBERS: Chas. Hohman, David Rowe, P. R. Baldwin, Martin Rogers, J. A. Hill, Jas. B. Poole, E. Reynolds, A. Rist, F. Tyler, Gilbert Wheeler, J. Sweet, W. A. White, Right Brown, J. W. Settle, Frank Conklin, Wm. Blackman, Fred Rowe, W. H. Shaw, P. Walker, Lyman Terry, Z. B. Frye, F. A. Price, A. M. Lee, Clark R. Buell

1866	1871	1876	1881	1886	1891	1896	1901	1906	1911	1916	1921	1926	1931	1936	1941	1946	1951

MEMBERSHIP BY YEAR (ACCOUNTED FOR): 1887, 19; 1888, 24; 1889, 35; 1904, 23; 1905, 24; 1906, 18; 1907, 18; 1908, 17   **LAST MEMBER:** Unknown

Sauk County was one of the places where G.A.R. interest ran high, and even such a small town as Lime Ridge started a post, known as A. D. Thornburg Post 174.

Thornburg Post was quite active in the years that the order was booming. But when numbers began sliding, the veterans at Lime Ridge decided to close their post, even though there were 17 of them in 1908, the post's last year. They presumably went to nearby Sauk County posts.

Post 174 was named for Addison D. Thornburg, a private in Company K, Twenty-third Wisconsin. Thornburg died at Memphis on February 5, 1863, from disease.

GEORGE W. HOLLOWAY POST 175, Beetown

GRANT COUNTY • AUGUST 16, 1884–APRIL 1, 1893

CHARTER MEMBERS: H. L. Sprague was the first commander.

1866	1871	1876	1881	1886	1891	1896	1901	1906	1911	1916	1921	1926	1931	1936	1941	1946	1951

MEMBERSHIP BY YEAR (ACCOUNTED FOR): 1887, 16; 1888, 28; 1889, 15
LAST MEMBER: Unknown

GEORGE
HOLLOWAY

Beetown, Grant County, formed a G.A.R. post in 1884, and named it for one of their townsmen who went to war and did not return.

George W. Holloway enlisted at the news of the firing on Fort Sumter and was a corporal with Company C, the "Grant County Grays," in the Second Wisconsin.

Holloway, like dozens of Iron Brigade men that day, fell in the cornfield striving to reach the Dunker Church on the battlefield of Antietam on September 17, 1862. It was the sad lot of his younger brother, William, a private in the Sixth Wisconsin, to identify the five-times minié-pierced body.

The veterans of Beetown surrendered their G.A.R. charter on April 1, 1893.

RUFUS KING POST 175, South Milwaukee

MILWAUKEE COUNTY • NOVEMBER 15, 1893–1922

CHARTER MEMBERS:[1] Edward Oertel, Silas Stewart, Augustus Haybringer, Joseph Whalen, H. B. Warner, Geo. C. Bush, John C. Williams, Joseph G. Davies, F. W. King, E. A. Bunn, John Sweeney, John Leonard, Geo. McCreedy, O. B. Peterson, Livingston B. Gregory, J. J. Rinehart, John Rapple

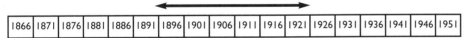

1866	1871	1876	1881	1886	1891	1896	1901	1906	1911	1916	1921	1926	1931	1936	1941	1946	1951

MEMBERSHIP BY YEAR (ACCOUNTED FOR): 1893, 17; 1904, 13; 1905, 12; 1906, 12; 1907, 11; 1908, 9; 1909, 7; 1910, 7; 1911, 7; 1912, 7; 1913, 5; 1914, 5; 1915, 5; 1916, 5; 1917, 3; 1918, 3; 1919, 3; 1920, 3; 1921, 3   LAST MEMBER: Unknown

COURTESY JIM SCHMIDT
RUFUS KING

One of the peculiar phenomena of G.A.R. growth in Wisconsin is that for a long time only three posts existed in Milwaukee County: Numbers 1, 2, and 8. None were added in the 1883–84 boom years. But after that, six posts, Numbers 175, 211, 223, 240, 250, and 274, were added.

The second to the last of these was Rufus King Post 175 in South Milwaukee, chartered in 1893. It was named for the one-time *Milwaukee Sentinel* editor, West Point graduate (in class of 1833 with U. S. Grant), strong abolitionist, and original commander of the brigade that would become the Iron Brigade.

1. "Dec. 6, 1894 – This duplicate charter is issued to replace the original which was destroyed by fire Oct. 7, 1894. Original signed by E. A. Shores, Dept. Commander, & D. G. Sampson, AAG. Dates as above."

CULLIN POST 176,
JOHN BRAGG POST 176, Gratiot
LAFAYETTE COUNTY • AUGUST 8, 1884–1922

CHARTER MEMBERS: J. B. Johnson, Rodney Seaver, J. P. Waite, Edwin E. Park, A. M. Cook, L. H. Stebbins, W. F. Enos, John McCannon, J. M. Vanderhoof, H. M. Fitzgerald, E. E. Hillman, Rosell S. Miner

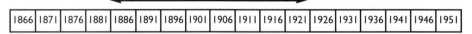

1866	1871	1876	1881	1886	1891	1896	1901	1906	1911	1916	1921	1926	1931	1936	1941	1946	1951

MEMBERSHIP BY YEAR (ACCOUNTED FOR): 1879, 12; 1884, 17; 1887, 18; 1888, 22; 1889, 28; 1904, 17; 1905, 16; 1906, 16; 1907, 15; 1908, 15; 1909, 14; 1910, 13; 1911, 9; 1912, 8; 1913, 10; 1914, 10; 1915, 10; 1916, 10; 1917, 7; 1918, 7; 1919, 7; 1920, 7; 1921, 5   **LAST MEMBER:** Unknown

The veterans of Gratiot, Lafayette County, did an unusual (but not entirely unprecedented) thing; they changed the name of their Post 176 after several years of their existence.

Post 176 began as Cullen Post, in honor of two brothers, John and James Cullen, brothers in Company I, Second Wisconsin Cavalry. John Cullen died August 4, 1864 of disease at Vicksburg, and four months later, December 1, James Cullen was killed in action at Yazoo City, Mississippi.

In 1898, Post 176 changed its name to John F. Bragg Post, honoring a soldier from Monticello in neighboring Green County, who was in Company I of the Fifth Wisconsin and was killed on April 5, 1865, as the Army of the Potomac began pursuing Lee's troops toward Appomattox.

I. N. NICHOLS POST 177, *River Falls*
PIERCE COUNTY • AUGUST 23, 1884–1934

CHARTER MEMBERS: A. D. Andrews, W. A. Burnett, Hugh Cameron, Thomas Cusick, C. R. Ellis, J. D. Fisher, Wm. Fisher, H. G. Godfrey, Ezra Healy, John Jellings, D. Kribbs, J. H. Langdon, Pat Lovell, G. B. Merrick, W. H. Nichols, G. E. Pratt, J. D. Putnam, A. W. Preston, J. W. Reynolds, Luther Spalding, W. W. Shafer, A. J. Shorborn, W. H. Williams, W. H. Winchester, W. H. Ward

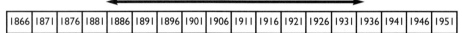

1866	1871	1876	1881	1886	1891	1896	1901	1906	1911	1916	1921	1926	1931	1936	1941	1946	1951

MEMBERSHIP BY YEAR (ACCOUNTED FOR): 1884, 25; 1887, 55; 1888, 55; 1889, 58; 1904, 67; 1905, 63; 1906, 61; 1907, 54; 1908, 54; 1909, 54; 1910, 52; 1911, 49; 1912, 46; 1913, 51; 1914, 44; 1915, 42; 1916, 42; 1917, 42; 1918, 42; 1919, 34; 1921, 10; 1922, 26; 1923, 18; 1924, 19; 1925, 14; 1926, 7; 1927, 4; 1928, 2; 1929, 2; 1930, 1; 1931, 2; 1932, 1; 1933, 1   **LAST MEMBER:** Martin Iverson

I. N. Nichols Post 177, River Falls, had a substantial membership through much of its history. John Putnam was the first commander. Its annual figures in the first two decades of the twentieth century remained relatively high, and it had three dozen members as late as World War I.

The post was named for I. N. Nichols, a sergeant with Company F of the reorganized First Wisconsin. Sergeant Nichols was killed on October 8, 1862, in the Battle of Perryville, Kentucky. He was the first soldier from River Falls to die in battle.

CHELSEA POST 178, Chelsea

TAYLOR COUNTY • SEPTEMBER 27, 1884–1888

CHARTER MEMBERS: Unknown

1866	1871	1876	1881	1886	1891	1896	1901	1906	1911	1916	1921	1926	1931	1936	1941	1946	1951

LAST MEMBER: Unknown

The veterans in Chelsea, Taylor County, were chartered as Post 178 in the autumn of 1884. They called it simply the Chelsea Post. It did not succeed and was off the department rolls by 1888.

HENRY C. ISBELL POST 178, Birnamwood

SHAWANO COUNTY • DECEMBER 18, 1888–1932

CHARTER MEMBERS: Unknown

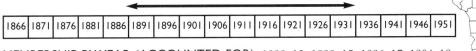

1866	1871	1876	1881	1886	1891	1896	1901	1906	1911	1916	1921	1926	1931	1936	1941	1946	1951

MEMBERSHIP BY YEAR (ACCOUNTED FOR): 1888, 13; 1889, 15; 1896, 17; 1904, 18; 1905, 15; 1906, 14; 1907, 11; 1908, 11; 1909, 8; 1910, 8; 1911, 8; 1912, 8; 1913, 8; 1914, 8; 1915, 8; 1916, 6; 1917, 6; 1918, 6; 1919, 6; 1920, 5; 1921, 3; 1922, 3; 1923, 3; 1924, 2; 1925, 2; 1926, 2; 1928, 1; 1929, 1; 1930, 1; 1931, 1 LAST MEMBER: Sam Hunter or A. J. Hunter

MARC AND BETH STORCH
HENRY C. ISBELL

A new post in Birnamwood, Shawano County, succeeded to Post Number 178 in 1888, and it was named after Henry C. Isbell.

The village had been settled only seven years earlier, with many of the first men being Civil War veterans.

Some of those veterans may have moved up from the Waupaca area since they gave their post the name of a Fremont soldier who was a sergeant in Company B, Third Wisconsin.

Henry Isbell was wounded in the famous cornfield at Antietam. The Third Wisconsin was among later regiments contesting that day before Dunker Church after the Iron Brigade had been repulsed. Isbell survived the war and was mustered out July 18, 1865.

Although it was never a large post, Post 178 survived for decades, into the 1930s.

HORACE T. SANDERS POST 179, Norwalk

MONROE COUNTY • SEPTEMBER 5, 1884–1931

CHARTER MEMBERS: William Meeny was the first commander.

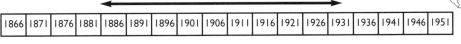

1866	1871	1876	1881	1886	1891	1896	1901	1906	1911	1916	1921	1926	1931	1936	1941	1946	1951

MEMBERSHIP BY YEAR (ACCOUNTED FOR): 1887, 46; 1888, 50; 1889, 51; 1924, 2; 1925, 2; 1926, 2; 1928, 1; 1929, 1; 1930, 1 LAST MEMBER: H. Steinhoff

ROGER D. HUNT COLL.
USAMHI
HORACE T. SANDERS

The history of Horace T. Sanders Post 179, Norwalk, raises a considerable number of questions. It is carried on the department records by 1884, and appears with membership figures in the late 1880s when such numbers were generally available. In the subsequent era the figures were not available, until 1904, that is. But then Sanders Post 179 does not appear in department lists again until 1924, when it was down to two members.

So the history of the post has substantial gaps in knowledge. Yet it apparently existed until 1930.

The post was named for Horace T. Sanders, a Racine lawyer who was commissioned by the War Department (rather than the governor) to raise a regiment, the Nineteenth Wisconsin, which did service in the East but generally not with the Army of the Potomac. Sanders was breveted a brigadier general, but was in ill health and survived the war by only six months.

ANDREW CHAMBERS POST 180, Weyauwega
WAUPACA COUNTY • SEPTEMBER 6, 1884–1920

CHARTER MEMBERS:[1] Andrew Gasman, John Mack, John Borngester, P. L. VanEpps, Albert Smith, John L. Rohde, David Wafler, Berny Vincent, Chas. H. Goodnove, Wm. Rease, T. P. Syphyer, Myron Sherman, Daniel Higgins, Enoch Smith, Daniel Buck, Ephraim Smith, Warren Rice, Norman Libby

1866	1871	1876	1881	1886	1891	1896	1901	1906	1911	1916	1921	1926	1931	1936	1941	1946	1951

Emery Ensign, member of Post 180

MEMBERSHIP BY YEAR (ACCOUNTED FOR): 1884, 18; 1887, 29; 1888, 32; 1889, 37; 1904, 33; 1905, 33; 1906, 24; 1907, 28; 1908, 27; 1909, 26; 1910, 26; 1911, 22; 1912, 15; 1913, 16; 1914, 15; 1915, 15; 1916, 9; 1917, 11; 1918, 11; 1919, 8   **LAST MEMBER:** Unknown

Post 180 was chartered at Weyauwega in autumn of 1884. It was named for Andrew Chambers, who was among the first Weyauwega men to volunteer, serving with Company B, Fourteenth Wisconsin, the first company from Waupaca County. He left as corporal of the company, became a sergeant and then second lieutenant. Chambers returned to Weyauwega after the war but died there August 29, 1865.

PHILLIPS POST 181,
ALLEN JACKSON POST 181, Phillips
PRICE COUNTY • SEPTEMBER 7, 1884–1938

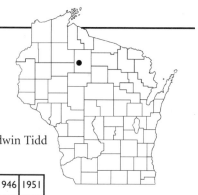

CHARTER MEMBERS: M. Oudinot, F. W Sackett, Peter Kuhn, H. B. Woodhouse, August Kraimer, William Houghton, C. H. Silvernail, Frank Prosser, John Davis, Edwin Tidd

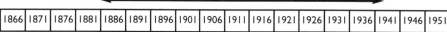

1866	1871	1876	1881	1886	1891	1896	1901	1906	1911	1916	1921	1926	1931	1936	1941	1946	1951

"This charter is granted [April 17, 1908] to take the place of the original charter which was burned in their post hall, Sunday morning between 6 and 7 a.m. March 25, 1906."

MEMBERSHIP BY YEAR (ACCOUNTED FOR): 1884, 10; 1887, 17; 1888, 19; 1889, 19; 1895, 9; 1904, 10; 1905, 10; 1906, 10; 1907, 10; 1908, 9; 1909, 9; 1910, 9; 1913, 8; 1914, 8; 1915, 8; 1916, 8; 1917, 8; 1918, 5; 1919, 5; 1920, 5; 1921, 6; 1922, 5; 1923, 1; 1924, 1; 1925, 1; 1926, 1; 1928, 3; 1929, 3; 1930, 3; 1931, 3; 1932, 2; 1933, 3; 1934, 3; 1935, 3; 1936, 3; 1937, 3 **LAST MEMBER:** Unknown

The story of Post 181 in Price County is a story not just of veterans, but of veterans who chose to move to the frontier after the war.

Post 181 was located in Phillips and went by the name of the town for many years. Its chartering in 1884 was eight years after the town was platted and just five years after Price County was established. M. Oudinot was the first commander of the Phillips Post.

One of the original men in all three—town, county, and G.A.R. post—was Allen Jackson. Jackson had served in the Twenty-eighth Maine during the war, then came to frontier Wisconsin in 1867, finally moving in 1876 to the new settlement rising in what would be Price County. His career there was varied, but entailed a good deal of public service, as well as business and farming.

Jackson died in 1917, and about three years later, after some 36 years as Phillips Post 181, it became Allen Jackson Post 181.

Post 181 remained on department rolls until well into the 1930s.

SIDNEY A. BEAN POST 182, Hammond
ST. CROIX COUNTY • SEPTEMBER 17, 1884–1901 OR 1902

CHARTER MEMBERS: Unknown

| 1866 | 1871 | 1876 | 1881 | 1886 | 1891 | 1896 | 1901 | 1906 | 1911 | 1916 | 1921 | 1926 | 1931 | 1936 | 1941 | 1946 | 1951 |

MEMBERSHIP BY YEAR (ACCOUNTED FOR): 1887, 31; 1888, 30; 1889, 40
LAST MEMBER: Unknown

SIDNEY A. BEAN

Sidney A. Bean Post 182 in Hammond, in the center of St. Croix County, had a fairly auspicious start for a post on the frontier in 1884, enjoying up to 40 members by 1889. But it was unable to sustain itself and surrendered its charter in 1901 or 1902.

The post was named for the colonel of the Fourth Wisconsin Cavalry (originally Infantry), who was a noted educator (Carroll College), mathematician, and linguist before the war. Colonel Bean was also an outspoken abolitionist, which was not universally admired by his superiors.

Bean was leading his regiment, which was then still infantry, in the effort to subdue Port Hudson when he was killed by a Confederate sharpshooter on May 29, 1863.

JOHN B. DOUGHTY POST 183, Colfax
DUNN COUNTY • OCTOBER 15, 1884–1891

CHARTER MEMBERS: Unknown

| 1866 | 1871 | 1876 | 1881 | 1886 | 1891 | 1896 | 1901 | 1906 | 1911 | 1916 | 1921 | 1926 | 1931 | 1936 | 1941 | 1946 | 1951 |

MEMBERSHIP BY YEAR (ACCOUNTED FOR): 1887, 27; 1888, 28; 1889, 31
LAST MEMBER: Ebert Sorkness

John B. Doughty Post 183 was chartered at Colfax in Dunn County in 1884. It survived only until 1891.

The post was named for a captain in the reorganized Fifth Wisconsin, Company A's John B. Doughty.

On the day that the Army of Northern Virginia began withdrawing from Richmond, the Fifth was in a heavy fight before Petersburg. Doughty and 11 enlisted men were killed in that action on April 2, 1865.

GEORGE C. GINTY POST 183, Cadott

CHIPPEWA COUNTY • DECEMBER 28, 1891–1934

CHARTER MEMBERS: Unknown

1866	1871	1876	1881	1886	1891	1896	1901	1906	1911	1916	1921	1926	1931	1936	1941	1946	1951

MEMBERSHIP BY YEAR (ACCOUNTED FOR): 1904, 23; 1905, 24; 1906, 20; 1907, 16; 1908, 12; 1909, 11; 1910, 10; 1911, 10; 1912, 8; 1913, 10; 1914, 12; 1915, 11; 1916, 10; 1917, 10; 1918, 10; 1919, 9; 1920, 8; 1921, 7; 1922, 7; 1923, 3; 1924, 3; 1925, 2; 1926, 1; 1927, 1; 1928, 1; 1929, 1; 1930, 1; 1932, 1; 1933, 1

COURTESY JIM PETERSON
GEORGE C. GINTY

LAST MEMBER: Landing A. Wilcox, Wisconsin's last Civil War veteran, died September 30, 1951. He has been a member of Post 183, but the post had long been extinct by the time of his death.

The second post to carry the number 183 was chartered at Cadott in Chippewa County on December 28, 1891, and for years it would be the home post of the man who eventually became, in 1951, the last member of the Grand Army of the Republic in Wisconsin, Lansing A. Wilcox. The post itself, however, had expired nearly 18 years before his death.

The post in Cadott was named the George C. Ginty Post 183, honoring the colonel of the Forty-seventh Wisconsin. Colonel Ginty's command entered service in February 1865, and was on guard duty in Tennessee until August. He was breveted a brigadier general when the regiment was discharged in September.

LUTHER T. PARK POST 184, Black Earth

DANE COUNTY • OCTOBER 18, 1884–1920

CHARTER MEMBERS: U. D. Wood was the first commander.

1866	1871	1876	1881	1886	1891	1896	1901	1906	1911	1916	1921	1926	1931	1936	1941	1946	1951

MEMBERSHIP BY YEAR (ACCOUNTED FOR): 1887, 32; 1888, 34; 1889, 37; 1904, 7; 1905, 7; 1906, 8; 1907, 8; 1908, 10; 1909, 7; 1910, 6; 1911, 6; 1912, 6; 1913, 6; 1914, 4; 1915, 5; 1916, 5; 1917, 5 LAST MEMBER: Unknown

Black Earth veterans obtained a charter in 1884 and named their post, number 184, for a soldier from Black Earth, Luther T. Park.

In September 1861, Park enlisted in Company A, Eleventh Wisconsin. He was sergeant, then first sergeant, and finally first lieutenant, promoted to the latter in June 1863. He was mustered out after the war.

Park Post 184 maintained a loyal membership initially, but by 1904, when the state kept such data after foregoing those statistics after 1889, the Black Earth Post was down to just seven members, a bit low, even for those days. But it kept going, with rather few members, until almost 1920.

MORRIS E. SEXTON POST 185, Sextonville

RICHLAND COUNTY • OCTOBER 7, 1884–1918

CHARTER MEMBERS: C. H. Pierce was the first commander.

1866	1871	1876	1881	1886	1891	1896	1901	1906	1911	1916	1921	1926	1931	1936	1941	1946	1951

MEMBERSHIP BY YEAR (ACCOUNTED FOR): 1887, 18; 1888, 19; 1889, 21; 1904, 16; 1905, 16; 1906, 14; 1907, 15; 1908, 13; 1909, 12; 1910, 12; 1911, 8; 1912, 8; 1913, 8; 1914, 8; 1915, 4; 1916, 4; 1917, 4   LAST MEMBER: Unknown

Veterans at Sextonville, Richland County, named their post for Morris E. Sexton, who entered the army from Richland Center in Company B, Twentieth Wisconsin.

Sexton was killed in action at Prairie Grove, Arkansas, when federal forces were attacked by Confederates but drove the rebels off and maintained control over northwestern Arkansas.

Morris E. Sexton Post 185 served its area until World War I, although it was never large.

WILLIAM PAYNE POST 186, Pardeeville

COLUMBIA COUNTY • OCTOBER 6, 1884–1938

CHARTER MEMBERS: Unknown

1866	1871	1876	1881	1886	1891	1896	1901	1906	1911	1916	1921	1926	1931	1936	1941	1946	1951

MEMBERSHIP BY YEAR (ACCOUNTED FOR): 1887, 62; 1888, 59; 1889, 72; 1904, 52; 1905, 52; 1906, 42; 1907, 42; 1908, 31; 1909, 35; 1910, 33; 1911, 35; 1912, 31; 1913, 29; 1914, 28; 1915, 30; 1916, 27; 1917, 23; 1918, 23; 1919, 23; 1920, 21; 1921, 18; 1922, 13; 1923, 7; 1924, 6; 1925, 6; 1926, 6; 1927, 6; 1928, 3; 1929, 2; 1930, 2; 1931, 2; 1932, 2; 1933, 2; 1934, 2; 1935, 1; 1936, 1; 1937, 1
LAST MEMBER: B. F. Hail

Post 186 at Pardeeville, begun in the autumn of 1884, was named for William Payne.

Payne was a private in Company E, Second Wisconsin Cavalry. He was killed on April 21, 1862, when his unit skirmished with Confederates at Red Bone, Mississippi.

Payne Post 186 was an active post well into the twentieth century. It remained on the department roster until its last member died in 1938.

GUSTAVUS WINTERMEYER POST 187, Sheboygan

SHEBOYGAN COUNTY • NOVEMBER 28, 1884–1938

CHARTER MEMBERS: Watson D. Crocker, J. H. Abraham, A. Feuerstake, T. Suffronn, Fred Raush, David Wittner, Aug. Knocke, M. O. Younge, A. D. Crocker, William Konig, Jak. Kommers, J. Feldhussen, Adolf Ziegler, L. Overbeck, L. Hoberg, S. Hanchett, H. Look, Peter Dix, Charles Osthelder, A. Lupinski, Herm. Stroesser, Christ Otten, B. Renzelmann, A. Grupe, K. Knocke, Jos. Hoffmann, Ph. Kramme H. Stocks, F. Hironimus, Fred Kuck, John Rohwer, Fred Kaehling, Anton Maas, Chas. Grasse, Ernst Aldag, J. Hilpertshauser, F. Zachow, Wm. Nack, H. Bowe, Ed. Thimmig, Wm. Schroeder, Fred Mallman, Fred Schneller, Aug. Froehlich

| 1866 | 1871 | 1876 | 1881 | 1886 | 1891 | 1896 | 1901 | 1906 | 1911 | 1916 | 1921 | 1926 | 1931 | 1936 | 1941 | 1946 | 1951 |

MEMBERSHIP BY YEAR (ACCOUNTED FOR): 1887, 111; 1888, 112; 1889, 116; 1900, 91; 1904, 73; 1905, 65; 1906, 63; 1907, 53; 1908, 63; 1909, 62; 1910, 62; 1911, 58; 1912, 57; 1913, 53; 1914, 51; 1915, 46; 1916, 50; 1917, 46; 1918, 44; 1919, 38; 1920, 36; 1921, 34; 1922, 32; 1923, 27; 1924, 24; 1925, 19; 1926, 14; 1927, 14; 1928, 12; 1929, 10; 1930, 10; 1931, 9; 1932, 9; 1933, 6; 1934, 6; 1935, 3; 1936, 2; 1937, 2   **LAST MEMBER:** Unknown

GUSTAVUS
WINTERMEYER

Gustavus Wintermeyer Post 187, Sheboygan, was one of the more successful posts of Wisconsin in terms of numbers and in hosting the state encampment. It welcomed comrades from around the state in 1901, again in 1925, and finally in 1933. (The 1944 encampment was also in Sheboygan, but Post 187 had by then expired.)

Post 187 organized an annual reunion of veterans in Sheboygan County, hosting it alternately with neighboring posts at Sheboygan Falls, Plymouth, and Cascade.

Gustavus Wintermeyer was a lieutenant in the Fourth Wisconsin Cavalry (while it was still infantry) who was killed in the attempt to storm Port Hudson on June 14, 1863. He had begun the war as a private.

WILLIAM J. KERSHAW POST 188, Briggsville

MARQUETTE COUNTY • OCTOBER 27, 1884–1930

CHARTER MEMBERS: Unknown

| 1866 | 1871 | 1876 | 1881 | 1886 | 1891 | 1896 | 1901 | 1906 | 1911 | 1916 | 1921 | 1926 | 1931 | 1936 | 1941 | 1946 | 1951 |

MEMBERSHIP BY YEAR (ACCOUNTED FOR): 1884, 25; 1887, 37; 1888, 41; 1889, 44; 1904, 22; 1906, 21; 1907, 21; 1908, 20; 1909, 19; 1910, 19; 1911, 18; 1912, 18; 1913, 18; 1914, 16; 1915, 16; 1916, 13; 1917, 13; 1918, 8; 1919, 10; 1920, 9; 1921, 7; 1922, 3; 1923, 3; 1924, 3; 1925, 2; 1926, 2; 1927, 2; 1928, 2; 1929, 1   **LAST MEMBER:** Unknown

William J. Kershaw, a major with the Thirty-seventh Wisconsin, was honored by the veterans of Briggsville, Marquette County, who named their G.A.R. post after him.

Post 188 served its largely rural area in Marquette and Columbia Counties until 1930.

The Thirty-seventh Wisconsin is the archetype of those reg-

iments raised in 1864 and sent to the Army of the Potomac to make up for losses it sustained from the Wilderness to Cold Harbor. Major Kershaw was wounded in an assault on Petersburg on June 17, 1864, before the siege of that city began. He was breveted a lieutenant colonel and left service that autumn.

ROLLIN P. CONVERSE POST 189, Prescott

PIERCE COUNTY • DECEMBER 16, 1884–1929

CHARTER MEMBERS: D. J. Doll was the first commander.

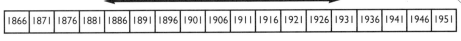

1866	1871	1876	1881	1886	1891	1896	1901	1906	1911	1916	1921	1926	1931	1936	1941	1946	1951

MEMBERSHIP BY YEAR (ACCOUNTED FOR): 1887, 37; 1888, 31; 1889, 26; 1904, 18; 1905, 18; 1906, 16; 1907, 15; 1908, 14; 1909, 13; 1910, 13; 1911, 12; 1912, 12; 1913, 11; 1914, 11; 1915, 10; 1916, 10; 1917, 10; 1918, 7; 1919, 7; 1920, 6; 1921, 5; 1922, 5; 1923, 4; 1924, 3; 1925, 3; 1926, 3; 1927, 3; 1928, 2;   **LAST MEMBER:** Unknown

CRAIG JOHNSON
ROLLIN CONVERSE

The "Prescott Guards" left Prescott at the start of the war, becoming Company B of the Sixth Wisconsin.

Men of Prescott remembered one of their own, Rollin P. Converse, and named Post 189 after him.

Converse survived the many heavy engagements of the Iron Brigade and be- came captain of the Prescott company. He remained with the Sixth after its three-year enlistment expired. His luck ran out in the fourth year when he was wounded and taken prisoner during the Battle of the Wilderness. He was treated at a Confederate hospital but died from his wounds on May 7, 1864.

Converse Post 189 was never a large post, but its members remained involved. Their numbers diminished with typical steadiness, and the post left the department rolls, finally, in 1929.

GENERAL LYTLE POST 190, Kiel

MANITOWOC COUNTY • DECEMBER 27, 1884–1926

CHARTER MEMBERS: Peter Ingenheimer was the first commander.

1866	1871	1876	1881	1886	1891	1896	1901	1906	1911	1916	1921	1926	1931	1936	1941	1946	1951

MEMBERSHIP BY YEAR (ACCOUNTED FOR): 1887, 27; 1888, 27; 1889, 27; 1904, 16; 1905, 16; 1906, 14; 1907, 12; 1908, 11; 1909, 11; 1910, 10; 1911, 7; 1912, 7; 1913, 7; 1914, 7; 1915, 7; 1916, 4; 1917, 4; 1918, 4; 1919, 4; 1920, 4; 1921, 4; 1922, 2; 1923, 2; 1924, 2; 1925, 2
LAST MEMBER: Jacob Mahloch

WILLIAM H. LYTLE

A general who was known and re- spected in the North and the South as a poet was honored by the veterans of Kiel when they chartered their G.A.R. Post 190 in the last week of 1884.

Post 190 was named the General Lytle Post, remembering Brigadier General William H. Lytle who fell while urging his brigade to stave off the Confederate onslaught at Chickamauga. One of the regiments of his brigade was the Twenty-fourth Wisconsin.

A lawyer by profession, he amused himself and friends by writing poetry. One, titled "Antony and Cleopatra," was published in 1858 and was a huge success. He was nationally acclaimed for his poetic talent.

Lytle was commissioned from Ohio and rose in the western armies. He earned a reputation as both a fighter and a man of chivalry. When he was killed on September 20, 1863, Confederate officers on the field mourned Lytle's death and saw to it that his body and personal effects were sent North.

LORENZO A. DIXON POST 191, Mount Horeb
DANE COUNTY • MARCH 25, 1885–1938

CHARTER MEMBERS: Ole Grimsvedt, Lawrence Post, John C. Johnson, H. O. Grinder, K. K. Syvrud, Ole Peterson, Syver Erikson, Ole Barton, John Everson, O. H. Rindy, A. O. Huset, Christian Thoreson, H. O. Opsol, P. G. Krogh, W. J. Helmenstein, W. T. Howery, Martin Anderson, Joseph Harmon, J. H. Scott, W. R. Campbell, Hans Everson, John W. Smith

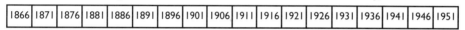

1866	1871	1876	1881	1886	1891	1896	1901	1906	1911	1916	1921	1926	1931	1936	1941	1946	1951

MEMBERSHIP BY YEAR (ACCOUNTED FOR): 1885, 22; 1887, 28; 1888, 28; 1889, 29; 1904, 28; 1905, 25; 1906, 22; 1907, 21; 1908, 19; 1909, 17; 1910, 17; 1911, 17; 1912, 18; 1913, 16; 1914, 15; 1915, 14; 1916, 14; 1917, 14; 1918, 14; 1919, 13; 1920, 12; 1921, 12; 1922, 11; 1923, 9; 1924, 8; 1925, 7; 1926, 7; 1927, 6; 1928, 5; 1929, 5; 1930, 6; 1931, 5; 1932, 5; 1933, 4; 1934, 4; 1935, 4; 1936, 4; 1937, 4; 1938, 2   **LAST MEMBER:** Unknown

Mt. Horeb's Post 191 was named for an officer of the Third Wisconsin Cavalry, Lorenzo A. Dixon. Dixon was first lieutenant of Company M of the Third Wisconsin.

Post 191 shortened "Lorenzo" to "Ren.," presumably as Dixon was known before he died on October 29, 1864, from wounds he had received in action near Independence, Missouri. Post 191 was quite successful and remained on the department rolls until 1938.

Members of Post 191 some time before 1900. Photo provided by the Wisconsin Veterans Museum, Madison.

ABNER O. HEALD POST 192, Cascade
SHEBOYGAN COUNTY • FEBRUARY 26, 1885–1921

CHARTER MEMBERS: Richard Phelen, commander; W. J. Hellenbolt, senior vice commander; A. E. Brown, junior vice commander; M. Murray, quartermaster; James Nichols, officer of the day; M. Keyes, officer of the guard; Stephen Payne, chaplain; Henry S. Averill, adjutant; Charles E. Copley, sergeant major; Ed. O'Hearn, quartermaster sergeant

1866	1871	1876	1881	1886	1891	1896	1901	1906	1911	1916	1921	1926	1931	1936	1941	1946	1951

MEMBERSHIP BY YEAR (ACCOUNTED FOR): 1885, 35; 1887, 50; 1888, 65; 1889, 65; 1904, 48; 1905, 48; 1906, 44; 1907, 42; 1908, 42; 1909, 41; 1910, 38; 1911, 28; 1912, 36; 1913, 34; 1914, 33; 1915, 34; 1916, 32; 1917, 27; 1918, 24; 1919, 19; 1920, 16   **LAST MEMBER:** Unknown

ABNER HEALD

The first G.A.R. post chartered in the year 1885 was the Abner O. Heald Post 192 at Cascade in Sheboygan County. (Post 191 has a later charter date by a month.) The Cascade Post was founded on February 26.

These veterans chose their post name to honor Heald, a local flourmill operator who was elected first lieutenant of Company I, First Wisconsin when it became a three-year regiment. He was promoted to captain of the company, which was virtually surrounded at Chickamauga on September 19, 1863, fired upon by Federals as well as Confederates. Heald was among the killed. His body was not recovered.

Post 192 enjoyed a substantial membership in its first

decades, and, indeed, in the year before it left the department rolls, it had 16 members. Cascade and the other posts in Sheboygan County enjoyed good rapport over the years, and presumably the Cascade veterans affiliated with nearby posts.

ANDREW J. FULLERTON POST 193, West Bend
WASHINGTON COUNTY • MARCH 21, 1885–1927

CHARTER MEMBERS: C. L. Powers, J. R. Kohlsdorf, John Thielges, Richard Rohn, Charles Silberzahn, N. N. Emery, Joseph Huber, George W. Jones, George Emmett, Albert Storey, August Neumeier, Elias Smith, Charles Hantkee, Andrew Schmidt, Wareham P. Rix, John Emmett, John Koester

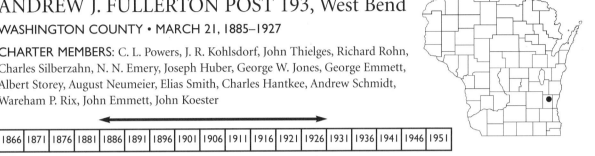

1866	1871	1876	1881	1886	1891	1896	1901	1906	1911	1916	1921	1926	1931	1936	1941	1946	1951

MEMBERSHIP BY YEAR (ACCOUNTED FOR): 1885, 17; 1887, 40; 1888, 41; 1889, 69; 1904, 58; 1905, 56; 1906, 53; 1907, 47; 1908, 45; 1909, 42; 1910, 37; 1911, 37; 1912, 35; 1913, 33; 1914, 31; 1915, 28; 1916, 26; 1917, 23; 1918, 21; 1919, 18; 1920, 17; 1921, 17; 1922, 16; 1923, 8; 1924, 5; 1925, 4; 1926, 4   **LAST MEMBER**: Unknown

Post 193 at West Bend was chartered in March 1885, and the veterans chose the name of Andrew J. Fullerton, a soldier from West Bend, who served with the sometimes ill-fated Twenty-sixth Wisconsin.

The Twenty-sixth was a largely German regiment recruited principally in southeastern Wisconsin. It was involved in the rout of the Eleventh Corps at Chancellorsville and was engaged on the first day at Gettysburg. It subsequently was transferred with the rest of its corps to the West, where the regiment finished the war.

Fullerton was first sergeant of Company F at the time of the transfer, was commissioned first lieutenant of the company on June 8, 1864, and was captain of the company from October 19, 1864, until it was mustered out at the close of hostilities. He died at Shawano about two years before Post 193 was organized.

First commander of Fullerton Post 193 was J. R. Kohlsdorf. The post enjoyed a very large membership during the order's booming years and well after that: it still had 18 members at the end of World War I.

HENRY BERTRAM POST 194, Oconomowoc
WAUKESHA COUNTY • MARCH 26, 1885–1921

CHARTER MEMBERS: J. M. Alvord, J. C. Barnum, Wm. H. Bolson, E. C. Catherwood, Eugene Dodge, James J. Hall, J. F. Jones, Hiram F. Lyke, D. McL. Miller, Warham Parks, Chas. W. Wood, James Reavley, J. H. Rector, Albert J. Rockwell, P. K. Tucker, D. J. Thompson

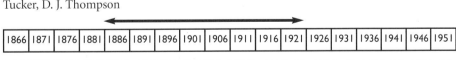

1866	1871	1876	1881	1886	1891	1896	1901	1906	1911	1916	1921	1926	1931	1936	1941	1946	1951

MEMBERSHIP BY YEAR (ACCOUNTED FOR): 1887, 54; 1888, 65; 1889, 85; 1904, 35; 1905, 34; 1906, 35; 1907, 26; 1908, 23; 1909, 24; 1910, 24; 1911, 20; 1912, 13; 1913, 11; 1914, 12; 1915, 14; 1916, 13; 1917, 13; 1918, 13; 1919, 11; 1920, 10   **LAST MEMBER**: James F. Jones

NEVILLE PUBLIC MUSEUM
HENRY BERTRAM

Henry Bertram Post 194 was chartered at Oconomowoc in 1885. The post was active for several decades, and even its last roster, in 1920, included 10 members.

The Oconomowoc veterans honored the colonel of the Twentieth Wisconsin, Henry Bertram. He began the war as a second lieutenant in the Third Wisconsin, but when the Twentieth was organized, Bertram was commissioned its lieutenant colonel.

He headed the regiment as its colonel at the end of the war and was breveted a brigadier general shortly before the war's close.

GEORGE PARSONS POST 195, Merrimac

SAUK COUNTY • APRIL 25, 1885–1923

CHARTER MEMBERS: Henry Pigg was the first commander.

1866	1871	1876	1881	1886	1891	1896	1901	1906	1911	1916	1921	1926	1931	1936	1941	1946	1951

MEMBERSHIP BY YEAR (ACCOUNTED FOR): 1887, 23; 1888, 21; 1889, 22; 1904, 12; 1905, 12; 1906, 10; 1907, 20; 1908, 9; 1909, 8; 1910, 6; 1911, 4; 1912, 3; 1913, 3; 1914, 3; 1915, 3; 1916, 3; 1917, 3; 1918, 2; 1919, 1; 1920, 1; 1921, 1; 1922, 1   **LAST MEMBER:** Unknown

Veterans at Merrimac in Sauk County received a charter in the Spring of 1885 and named their new post George Parsons Post 195.

Post 195 was never large, but it functioned beyond the turn of the twentieth century as a viable post, and thereafter its membership dwindled. It remained on the department rolls until 1922.

The namesake of Post 195, George Parsons, was from Merrimac and served in Company H, Eleventh Wisconsin, receiving promotion to corporal. Parsons died on December 1, 1862, at Ironton, Missouri, of illness.

CHRISTOPHER FIMIAN POST 196, Alma

BUFFALO COUNTY • MAY 25, 1885–1914

CHARTER MEMBERS: Richard B. Kempter, J. A. Tester, Robert Lees, D. W. Hussong, J. M. Pratt, Phil Philippi, Jacob Haug, Louis Mueller, Halvor A. Lee, Jacob May, Jacob Bollinger, Lutze Tscharner, John Henrich, D. B. Pember, Geh. Gesell, Christopher Schwedes, N. McVey, Anton Liesch, Martin Polin

1866	1871	1876	1881	1886	1891	1896	1901	1906	1911	1916	1921	1926	1931	1936	1941	1946	1951

MEMBERSHIP BY YEAR (ACCOUNTED FOR): 1885, 19; 1887, 39; 1888, 38; 1889, 39; 1904, 26; 1905, 26; 1906, 26; 1907, 23; 1908, 21; 1909, 12; 1910, 13; 1911, 10; 1912, 10; 1913, 8   **LAST MEMBER:** Unknown

The veterans in Alma, Buffalo County, came together and formed a G.A.R. post in May 1885. It was Fimian Post 196.

The post honored Christopher Fimian, who volunteered from Alma at the outbreak of the war. He became a corporal of Company H, Sixth Wisconsin, which would become part of the Iron Brigade. Fimian, however, was not in the brigade's famous battles; he was discharged on disability on December 31, 1862.

Post 196 had a steady membership into the early part of the twentieth century, but gave up its charter by 1914.

WALTER WATERMAN POST 197, Plainfield

WAUSHARA COUNTY • AUGUST 22, 1885–1937

CHARTER MEMBERS: J. B. Mitchell, Henry McCallin, H. B. Holmes, J. C. Rowsam, Peter Mitchell, Frank Rathermel, L. S. Walker, J. P. Lane, L. D. Stilwell, S. S. Mils, E. M. Pickering, A. M. Pierce, Geo. B. Fox, Henry Washburn, Frank Briggs, H. C. Wood, C. B. Fox, W. W. Gillett, G. D. Foss, John Metier, R. R. Crowe, B. F. Powell, George D. Ball, Joseph Waters, B. B. Borden, Gideon Crowe, A. Allen, Andrew Lutz, George Goult, Jas. Rozell, A. D. Dewitt, Louis Thiele, John Tibbetts, S. Bentley, I. N. Copeland, E. G. Eaton, W. A. Rozell, A. Stevens, W. W. Stilwell, D. B. Culbertson, R. H. Runcorn, B. R. Hutchinson, I. C. Herrick John Townsend, R. D. Sparks, Joseph Sherman, Arad Lakin, S. C. Waterman, John E. Wilson, John Peevy

1866	1871	1876	1881	1886	1891	1896	1901	1906	1911	1916	1921	1926	1931	1936	1941	1946	1951

MEMBERSHIP BY YEAR (ACCOUNTED FOR): 1885, 50; 1887, 66; 1888, 50; 1889, 62; 1904, 48; 1905, 41; 1906, 42; 1907, 37; 1908, 39; 1909, 38; 1910, 38; 1911, 40; 1912, 37; 1913, 35; 1914, 30; 1915, 30; 1916, 24; 1917, 21; 1918, 14; 1919, 12; 1920, 10; 1921, 9; 1922, 7; 1923, 8; 1924, 7; 1925, 6; 1926, 6; 1927, 3; 1929, 3; 1930, 2; 1932, 3; 1933, 3; 1934, 3; 1935, 3; 1936, 3   **LAST MEMBER:** Unknown

WALTER WATERMAN

Plainfield veterans named their G.A.R. post for Walter William Waterman, one of the two sons of Plainfield founder E. C. Waterman to join Company I of the Seventh Wisconsin. Son Sidney survived the war and was a charter member of the post when it was organized in the summer of 1885. Walter did not survive his Iron Brigade experience: he was killed in the opening day of the Battle of the Wilderness on May 5, 1864.

Waterman Post 197 was one of the most active posts in Waushara County and remained on department rolls until 1938.

Company I, Seventh Wisconsin, was recruited from Dodge, Green Lake, and Waushara counties; they called themselves "Northwestern Tigers." In 1909 members of the company got together in Plainfield. Sidney Waterman, standing, left, was the host. He was the brother of Walter Waterman, for whom the Plainfield Post 197 was named. Walter was a member of Company I, also, but was killed in the Battle of the Wilderness. Standing, from left: Sidney Waterman, A. Dudley, J. J. Phillips, Charles Harris, and D. W. Greenfield. Seated, from left: B. S. Williams, John W. Roe, and S. Weldon. Photo provided by the courtesy of Don Stube.

JOHN GRANZO POST 198, Seymour

OUTAGAMIE COUNTY • JUNE 24, 1885–1916

CHARTER MEMBERS: D. A. Kenyon was the first commander.

1866	1871	1876	1881	1886	1891	1896	1901	1906	1911	1916	1921	1926	1931	1936	1941	1946	1951

MEMBERSHIP BY YEAR (ACCOUNTED FOR): 1887, 30; 1888, 23; 1889, 35; 1904, 10; 1905, 8; 1906, 8; 1907, 8; 1908, 8; 1909, 12; 1910, 12; 1911, 11; 1912, 9; 1913, 9; 1914, 9; 1915, 7; 1916, 4   **LAST MEMBER:** Unknown

John Granzo Post 198 in Seymour, in the rural northern portion of Outagamie County, is somewhat typical of rural posts that served its community while able, and then slipped into oblivion without imprinting history with much information about itself.

Very little is known, in fact, about the namesake, John

Granzo. He was with the Fourth Infantry from his enlistment on April 23, 1861, until he was killed on May 27, 1863, at Port Hudson, a few months before the Fourth was reequipped and redesignated the Fourth Cavalry.

Post 198 began in the summer of 1885, and what data there is in department records suggests an early history of some substance. By the first decade of the twentieth century, the

Granzo Post was experiencing the typical decline in membership of that time. Then in 1909 its rolls showed a 50 percent gain to an even dozen, hinting that the post benefited from the demise of other posts in the area (possibly Black Creek).

A 1911 history of Outagamie County says merely that "John Granzo Post, No. 198, instituted June 24, 1885, still exists at Seymour."

H. S. EGGLESTON POST 199, Ripon

FOND DU LAC COUNTY • JUNE 13, 1885–1938

CHARTER MEMBERS: H. C. Welcome was the first commander.

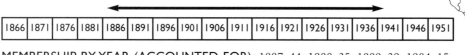

MEMBERSHIP BY YEAR (ACCOUNTED FOR): 1887, 44; 1888, 35; 1889, 39; 1904, 15; 1905, 15; 1906, 14; 1907, 15; 1908, 12; 1909, 15; 1910, 15; 1911, 16; 1912, 15; 1913, 15; 1914, 11; 1915, 15; 1916, 15; 1917, 15; 1918, 14; 1919, 14; 1920, 13; 1921, 13; 1922, 11; 1923, 13; 1924, 10; 1925, 10; 1926, 9; 1927, 7; 1928, 4; 1929, 3; 1930, 6; 1931, 6; 1932, 5; 1933, 3; 1934, 3; 1935, 1; 1936, 1; 1937, 1   LAST MEMBER: Lewis Hyde

WISCONSIN VETERANS MUSEUM
H. S. EGGLESTON

In the bright, early days of the Department of Wisconsin, the veterans at Ripon played a significant role in the order. They were chartered second after Madison, and Ripon survived the first "cut" of posts in 1871, retaining the number of Post 2. Not long after 1871, however, the post succumbed, and it was not until 1885 that com-

rades began a new post at Ripon.

This was H. S. Eggleston Post 199, and it stayed, this time, until its last member died in 1938.

Henry S. Eggleston began the war as captain of Company B of the First Wisconsin Cavalry as it rendezvoused at Ripon in the summer of 1861. The regiment saw service in Missouri initially. Eggleston rose to the rank of major, but he was struck by disease and died December 11, 1862. Eggleston is buried in the City Cemetery at Ripon.

ALEXANDER RICKEY POST 200, Hersey

ST. CROIX COUNTY • JANUARY 8, 1886–1911

CHARTER MEMBERS: Richard Adams was the first commander.

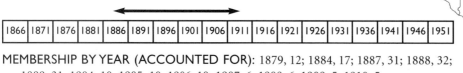

MEMBERSHIP BY YEAR (ACCOUNTED FOR): 1879, 12; 1884, 17; 1887, 31; 1888, 32; 1889, 31; 1904, 10; 1905, 10; 1906, 10; 1907, 6; 1908, 6; 1909, 5; 1910, 5
LAST MEMBER: Unknown

The milestone number 200—for some reason "reserved" and unused in the second half of 1885—was given to the first post chartered in 1886, that being the Alexander Rickey Post at Hersey in St. Croix County.

It served until about 1911.

Post 200 was named for Alexander Rickey, a private in Company A, First Wisconsin (three years). Rickey was discharged on June 20, 1862, for disability.

MARTIN LUTHER CRANE POST 201, Burlington

RACINE COUNTY • AUGUST 6, 1885–1931

CHARTER MEMBERS: Andrew Bettzuech, George S. Bradshaw, Alex. Creitz, Ben David, George C. Denniston, Martin Freeney, John Gill, Simon Green, John Grosskopf, H. B. Haight, James B. Hall, William Hockings, Fred Jantzen, George Jones, J. C. Kies, Fred Krakofsky, William Laske, J. A. McIntosh, J. G. Meadows, John Nehls, Charles Pagel, August Reuschlein, Theodore Riel, William Saloman, Julius Schuke, George Schumann, H. S. Scofield, H. A. Sheldon, George Smith, Charles Spoor, Jacob Weyrough, Fred Wilhoeft, C. W. Wood, Michael Zimmer

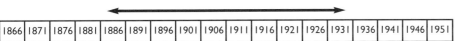

1866	1871	1876	1881	1886	1891	1896	1901	1906	1911	1916	1921	1926	1931	1936	1941	1946	1951

MEMBERSHIP BY YEAR (ACCOUNTED FOR): 1885, 34; 1887, 49; 1888, 58; 1889, 77; 1904, 70; 1905, 69; 1906, 64; 1907, 56; 1908, 54; 1909, 54; 1910, 48; 1911, 48; 1912, 45; 1913, 45; 1914, 43; 1915, 34; 1916, 37; 1917, 36; 1918, 28; 1919, 18   **LAST MEMBER:** Unknown

Martin Luther Crane Post 201 of Burlington was named for a Burlington soldier who joined Company C of the First Wisconsin (three years); he was corporal of the company. Crane was wounded at Chaplin Hills and was discharged on January 16, 1863, due to disability.

Post 201 enjoyed considerable success during its existence. It had more than two dozen members when World War I broke out. The post, however, was extinct by 1920. Presumably members went to other posts. Racine's Harvey Post 17 was still active.

ELISHA HARRISON RANDALL POST 202, Green Lake

GREEN LAKE COUNTY • SEPTEMBER 5, 1885–1931

CHARTER MEMBERS: Daniel Reilly, Henry H. Marshall, Christian Brisval, Charles F. Taylor, David Wilson, Thomas B. Davis, Lester Clawson, Charles A. Brown, James C. Boice, Joseph Taylor, James H. Prume, Nathaniel Pierce Jr., A. Eugene Dunlap

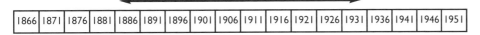

1866	1871	1876	1881	1886	1891	1896	1901	1906	1911	1916	1921	1926	1931	1936	1941	1946	1951

MEMBERSHIP BY YEAR (ACCOUNTED FOR): 1887, 2; 1888, 21; 1889, 19; 1904, 17; 1905, 16; 1906, 14; 1907, 10; 1908, 12; 1909, 10; 1910, 9; 1911, 9; 1912, 9; 1913, 8; 1914, 7; 1915, 6; 1916, 4; 1917, 4; 1918, 4; 1919, 3; 1920, 3; 1921, 3; 1922, 3; 1923, 1; 1924, 1; 1925, 1; 1926, 1; 1927, 1; 1928, 1; 1929, 1; 1930, 1   **LAST MEMBER:** M. F. Spencer

Harry Randall Post 202, Dartford, Green Lake County—it is now the City of Green Lake—was named for a soldier of the Fourth Wisconsin, killed while the regiment was still infantry. Harry Randall was actually Elisha Harrison Randall, a Dartford boy who was a private in Company B.

Randall was acting as a sharpshooter on the gunboat Tyler on the Yazoo River in Mississippi on July 5, 1862, when a Confederate shell struck nearby and killed him.

Post 202 was never large, but it remained on the rolls until 1931, the last member carrying on alone for eight years.

Members of Post 202, date unknown. From left: Harry B. Lowe, Joe Taylor, Charley Brown, Lester Clawson, Francis Spencer, and Gus Palmer. Spencer was the last member.

GRANTSBURG POST 203, Grantsburg

BURNETT COUNTY • SEPTEMBER 25, 1885–1889

CHARTER MEMBERS: J. A. Richardson was the first commander.

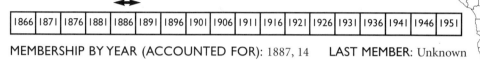

1866	1871	1876	1881	1886	1891	1896	1901	1906	1911	1916	1921	1926	1931	1936	1941	1946	1951

MEMBERSHIP BY YEAR (ACCOUNTED FOR): 1887, 14   **LAST MEMBER:** Unknown

The Department of Wisconsin's westernmost outpost was at Grantsburg in Burnett County, only half a dozen miles from the St. Croix River, the Minnesota border. It was definite wilderness when the war was on, but by 1885 a number of veterans were residing there and wanted a G.A.R. post.

Grantsburg Post 203, chartered in the autumn of 1885, was not successful and it surrendered its charter by 1889.

The men of that frontier did not give up entirely and got a new charter in 1902, the W. S. Rosecrans Post 49.

CHARLES A. BLAIR POST 203, FRED RICHTER POST 203, Lowell

DODGE COUNTY • MAY 25, 1889–1934

CHARTER MEMBERS: Fred Arndt, John W. Burgess, P. B . Coleman, George Etscheid, J. W. Ganes, David Jilson, John Katzamuller, J. C. Miller, Michal Nash, Wm. O'Connors, Daniel Piper, John Schaller, August Schoenwetter, Ernst Schwanitz, G. W. W. Tanner, C. Weille

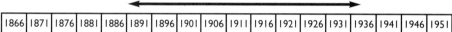

1866	1871	1876	1881	1886	1891	1896	1901	1906	1911	1916	1921	1926	1931	1936	1941	1946	1951

MEMBERSHIP BY YEAR (ACCOUNTED FOR): 1890, 23; 1904, 15; 1905, 11; 1906, 10; 1907, 12; 1908, 11; 1909, 11; 1910, 10; 1911, 10; 1912, 8; 1913, 7; 1914, 6; 1915, 6; 1916, 6; 1917, 6; 1918, 5; 1919, 5; 1920, 5; 1921, 5; 1922, 5; 1923, 5; 1924, 5; 1925, 4; 1926, 4; 1927, 3; 1928, 3; 1929, 2; 1930, 1; 1931, 1; 1932, 1; 1933, 1
LAST MEMBER: Fred Arndt

The second Post 203 had a fairly long history, notwithstanding that its charter membership was not much more than its Grantsburg predecessor four years earlier.

This Post 203 was at Lowell, a small Dodge County community. Its name at chartering in 1889 was the Charles A. Blair Post, named for a private of Company D, First Cavalry, from nearby Beaver Dam. Blair was captured by Confederates and died in Andersonville.

The post changed its name in 1907, this time memorializing another private of Company D, First Cavalry, Frederick Richter. Richter served throughout his term and was mustered out September 1, 1864. Richter is not listed as a charter member, but may have been a member of the post at one time.

One who was a charter member was Fred Arndt, and he outlived all the others to carry the post down to 1934.

U. S. GRANT POST 204, Maiden Rock

PIERCE COUNTY • AUGUST 1, 1885–1901

CHARTER MEMBERS: A. S. Otis, commander; A. W. Ogilvie, senior vice commander; Henry Series, junior vice commander; George Davis, surgeon; Oscar Thomas, adjutant; L. P. Carson, officer of the day; J. K. Alters, officer of the guard; O. A. Warren, chaplain; E. A. Seaman, sergeant major; Charles Wheeler, quartermaster sergeant

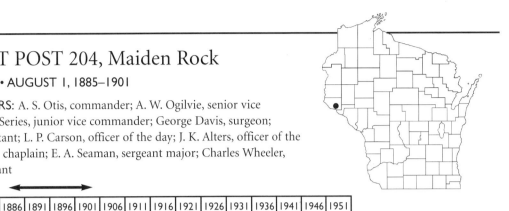

1866	1871	1876	1881	1886	1891	1896	1901	1906	1911	1916	1921	1926	1931	1936	1941	1946	1951

U. S. GRANT

MEMBERSHIP BY YEAR (ACCOUNTED FOR): 1887, 30; 1888, 30; 1889, 35
LAST MEMBER: Unknown

The name of the new G.A.R. post at Maiden Rock was perhaps foreordained. Post 204 was chartered August 1, 1885, exactly one week after the nation learned of the death of General U. S. Grant from cancer on July 25, 1885. Veterans every-where were mourning the loss of their old commander, and the Pierce County veterans naturally seized the opportunity to pay their tribute by naming their new post the U. S. Grant Post 204.

The post was successful for a few years, but its numbers were never large and by 1901 it surrendered its charter.

CHILTON POST 205,
JOSEPH B. REYNOLDS POST 205, Chilton

CALUMET COUNTY • AUGUST 28, 1885–1933

CHARTER MEMBERS: Joseph B. Reynolds was the first commander.

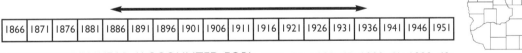

1866	1871	1876	1881	1886	1891	1896	1901	1906	1911	1916	1921	1926	1931	1936	1941	1946	1951

MEMBERSHIP BY YEAR (ACCOUNTED FOR): 1885, 30; 1887, 65; 1888, 61; 1889, 69; 1904, 49; 1905, 50; 1906, 44; 1907, 40; 1908, 35; 1909, 32; 1910, 30; 1911, 29; 1912, 26; 1913, 29; 1914, 29; 1915, 28; 1916, 28; 1917, 28; 1918, 19; 1919, 21; 1921, 17; 1922, 17; 1923, 17; 1924, 15; 1925, 15; 1926, 11; 1927, 9; 1928, 8; 1929, 7; 1930, 4; 1931, 4; 1932, 1   **LAST MEMBER:** Bernard Schimmer

RONALD ZARLING,
NEW HOLSTEIN
JOSEPH B.
REYNOLDS

The veterans at Chilton formed a G.A.R. post in August 1885, and they were quite content to go by the name of Chilton Post 205 for nearly 20 years. But in 1905 they decided to honor their newly deceased first post commander.

Joseph B. Reynolds led some of the Chilton soldiers off to war. He went into the war as second lieutenant of the Calumet Rifles, or Company K, Fourth Wisconsin, later Cavalry. Reynolds rose to captain of the company and was discharged due to disability on September 19, 1863. He became a founder of the G.A.R. in Chilton. Reynolds became a lawyer and practiced in Chilton for many years, but his declining health forced him to give up his practice.

COLWERT PIER POST 206, Argyle

LAFAYETTE COUNTY • DECEMBER 2, 1885–1915

CHARTER MEMBERS: C. B. Wright, Coleman Westcott, Thomas Lathrop, G. A. Penniston, C. C. Eldred, W. H. Thurston, A. Wescott, James Smith, Thomas Wright, David Arnold, John Powell, F. Wyman, W. A. Sisson, David Penniston

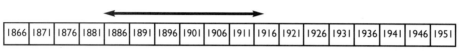

MEMBERSHIP BY YEAR (ACCOUNTED FOR): 1885, 14; 1887, 20; 1888, 20; 1889, 20; 1904, 11; 1905, 10; 1906, 10; 1907, 10; 1908, 10; 1909, 10; 1910, 10; 1911, 10; 1912, 9; 1913, 8; 1914, 6   LAST MEMBER: Unknown

COLWERT PIER

The Argyle G.A.R. Post 206 was chartered late in 1885. It chose the name of Colwert K. Pier of Fond du Lac for its post.

Pier was perhaps honored for his postwar veterans affairs activities as much as for his service during the war. It was Pier who was president of the Soldiers and Sailors Reunion organization, which staged the giant reunion in Milwaukee in 1880 and gave impetus to rejuvenated Grand Army recruiting.

Nonetheless, Pier had a good war record. He served as a private in the First Wisconsin (three months) and later was lieutenant colonel of the Thirty-eighth Wisconsin before Petersburg, where he was wounded in June 1864.

Post 206 remained active for several decades.

SAMUEL H. SIZER POST 207, Marinette

MARINETTE COUNTY • SEPTEMBER 14, 1885–1942

CHARTER MEMBERS: Chas. J. Ellis, A. M. Fairchild, J. K. Wright, Thomas Tookey, James Ellis, Orlin Reeves, H. E. Mann, A. R. Lang, A. V. Howe, John Stratton, Geo. W. Bander, J. A. Rappe, John W. Miner, J. C. Tyrrell, Amos Halgate

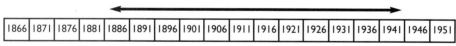

MEMBERSHIP BY YEAR (ACCOUNTED FOR): 1885, 15; 1887, 31; 1888, 68; 1889, 85; 1895, 62; 1904, 68; 1905, 41; 1906, 60; 1907, 61; 1908, 55; 1909, 51; 1910, 51; 1911, 51; 1912, 47; 1913, 46; 1914, 46; 1915, 40; 1916, 33; 1917, 29; 1918, 27; 1919, 26; 1920, 25; 1921, 25; 1922, 21; 1923, 20; 1924, 17; 1925, 17; 1926, 15; 1927, 12; 1928, 11; 1929, 10; 1930, 7; 1931, 7; 1932, 7; 1933, 6; 1934, 6; 1935, 4; 1936, 3; 1937, 3   LAST MEMBER: Unknown

Samuel H. Sizer Post 207, Marinette, chartered in 1885, had a rather successful history. The post was host to the state encampment in 1906 at a time when the department was beginning its decline but was still vibrant.

So was Sizer Post 207. It remained the premier post in the northeast beyond Green Bay into the 1920s.

The post was named for Samuel H. Sizer, a native of Michigan. Sizer enlisted in Company A, Seventeenth Michigan, in 1862, and he was mustered out in 1865 as a first lieutenant.

After the war he moved to Marinette and subsequently died there.

WILLIAM H. HAMILTON POST 208, Sun Prairie

DANE COUNTY • SEPTEMBER 18, 1885–1906

CHARTER MEMBERS: E. W. Cornes, C. L. Long, J. O. Flynn, W. F. Evans, John Hecker, Cyrus Stowe, Ferdinand Eske, M. H. Welton, James T. Gilbert, Oliver Vansant, C. G. Crosse, Henry Beecham, Thomas C. Hayden, James Sweeney, Marvin J. Vincent, E. A. W. (last name unknown), W. E. Angell, Nicholas Kline, F. A. Brewer, Louis Berghard, W. M. Small

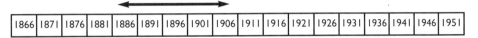

1866	1871	1876	1881	1886	1891	1896	1901	1906	1911	1916	1921	1926	1931	1936	1941	1946	1951

MEMBERSHIP BY YEAR (ACCOUNTED FOR): 1885, 21; 1886, 31; 1887, 24; 1888, 33; 1904, 15; 1905, 13
LAST MEMBER: Unknown

Post 208 of Sun Prairie was chartered September 18, 1885, and honored a Dane County officer who had a distinguished record.

William H. Hamilton had served with the Sixth Wisconsin Battery early in the war but was commissioned captain of A Company, Thirty-sixth Wisconsin Infantry, when it was organized at Madison in 1864 under Colonel Frank Haskell of Gettysburg fame. Hamilton was promoted to major of the Thirty-sixth in July 1864. He was wounded at Deep Bottom, Virginia, on August 14, 1864. Hamilton was subsequently promoted to lieutenant colonel of the regiment and was mustered out as such in July 1865.

Post 208 was active in the order's busy years, but by 1906 it was extinct, its remaining dozen or so members probably joining other Dane County posts.

Photo provided by Rod Dary.

PLUM CITY POST 209, Plum City

PIERCE COUNTY • 1885–1888

CHARTER MEMBERS: James H. Parsons was the first commander.

1866	1871	1876	1881	1886	1891	1896	1901	1906	1911	1916	1921	1926	1931	1936	1941	1946	1951

MEMBERSHIP BY YEAR (ACCOUNTED FOR): 1887, 13   **LAST MEMBER:** Unknown

The early years of the Grand Army of the Republic Department of Wisconsin were replete with mystery posts. Dozens came and went with scarcely a trace. But the record-keeping got better, as did the recruiting and retention of members and posts.

Still a mystery post appears even in those later years on rare occasion. And one of these was the Post at Plum City, Pierce County, numbered 209. Even its date of chartering is unknown. It appears in the 1886 encampment journal as mustered in 1885, and it is shown in the 1887 figures as having thirteen members. But by 1888 it is gone from department records, never to reappear.

ENNIS T. REED POST 209, White Creek

ADAMS COUNTY • MARCH 23, 1889–1936

CHARTER MEMBERS: John. A. Henry was the first commander.

1866	1871	1876	1881	1886	1891	1896	1901	1906	1911	1916	1921	1926	1931	1936	1941	1946	1951

MEMBERSHIP BY YEAR (ACCOUNTED FOR): 1889, 18; 1904, 15; 1905, 15; 1906, 13; 1907, 12; 1908, 12; 1909, 11; 1910, 13; 1911, 14; 1912, 13; 1913, 12; 1914, 9; 1915, 10; 1916, 9; 1917, 8; 1918, 6; 1919, 6; 1920, 5; 1921, 3; 1922, 3; 1923, 3; 1924, 3; 1925, 3; 1926, 3; 1927, 3; 1928, 2; 1929, 2; 1930, 2; 1931, 2; 1932, 2; 1933, 2; 1934, 2; 1935, 2   **LAST MEMBER:** Unknown

White Creek, just a few miles from the Wisconsin River in Adams County, received its charter on March 23, 1889, receiving the recycled number 209.

Ennis T. Reed Post 209 was highly successful for a town of White Creek's size. Reed Post continued in existence until 1936, although it never had a large number on the rolls.

The post was named for Ennis T. Reed from nearby Friendship. Reed was a sergeant in Company D., Eighth Wisconsin. He died on April, 22, 1862. Reed is buried in White Creek Cemetery.

Members of Post 209, date unknown. From left: Silas Lamphear, Jim Bidwell, Frank Jencks, H. H. Howard, Jef Pishion, H. Walrath, Myron Mosley, Amos Brown, Will Garthwait, Wm. Risk, A. J. Henry.

FRANCIS STEFFEN POST 210, Hortonville

OUTAGAMIE COUNTY • SEPTEMBER 29, 1885–1931

CHARTER MEMBERS: S. S. Given, commander; L. Jacquot, senior vice commander; H. T. Hunt, junior vice commander; John McMurdo, quartermaster; J. H. McMurdo, surgeon; F. J. Nye, chaplain.

At the post's reorganization in 1889, officers were: S. C. Torry, commander; H. Hunt, senior vice commander; Dan Lamb, junior vice commander; Joseph Brooks, chaplain; N. Rideout, officer of the day; Frank Smith, quartermaster; Charles T. Buck, adjutant; Gustave Schwabs, surgeon; E. Kellogg, officer of the guard; Conrad Peters, sergeant major; H. Hough, quartermaster sergeant

1866	1871	1876	1881	1886	1891	1896	1901	1906	1911	1916	1921	1926	1931	1936	1941	1946	1951

MEMBERSHIP BY YEAR (ACCOUNTED FOR): 1888, 49; 1889, 75; 1904, 45; 1905, 37; 1906, 36; 1907, 29; 1908, 33; 1909, 32; 1910, 32; 1911, 35; 1912, 32; 1913, 34; 1914, 30; 1915, 29; 1916, 27; 1917, 23; 1918, 21; 1919, 16; 1920, 14; 1921, 12; 1922, 9; 1923, 10; 1924, 6; 1925, 6; 1927, 5; 1928, 5; 1929, 4; 1930, 35   **LAST MEMBER:** Unknown

FRANCIS STEFFEN

Hortonville veterans in 1885 organized a G.A.R. post and named it for Francis Steffen, a veteran and postwar leader of Outagamie County politics. Post 210 got off to a shaky start, but reorganized in 1889 and continued into the 1930s.

Post 210's namesake was a sergeant of Company I, Thirty-second Wisconsin. (His brother in the same company, Jacob, succumbed to disease.) Francis Steffen survived the war and returned to the Hortonville area, where he farmed and was active in town and county affairs. He was considered the town's most prominent citizen.

E. E. ELLSWORTH POST 211, Fish Creek
DOOR COUNTY • OCTOBER 24, 1885–1896

CHARTER MEMBERS: Unknown

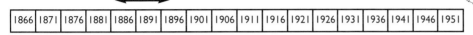

1866	1871	1876	1881	1886	1891	1896	1901	1906	1911	1916	1921	1926	1931	1936	1941	1946	1951

MEMBERSHIP BY YEAR (ACCOUNTED FOR): 1887, 23; 1888, 22; 1889, 24
LAST MEMBER: Unknown

E. E. Ellsworth Post 211 of Fish Creek was chartered in the autumn of 1885, and after a few years of some success, the post's membership declined. Post 211 was classed as delinquent in 1896. In all probability it had ceased to function by 1894.

Post 211 was named for Elmer E. Ellsworth, one of the war's first heroes. At the time of Post 211's founding, there already was a post named for him in Wisconsin, Merrillan Post 86. See Post 86 for a picture and biographical material on Ellsworth.

OLD GUARD POST 211, Milwaukee
MILWAUKEE COUNTY • MAY 17, 1898–1906

CHARTER MEMBERS: Almon Clarke, A. O'Connell, Elijah Baker, Thomas L. Pollock, John Allen, Wm. Waring, Wm. H. Hull, John C. Rozas, James A. Coombes, W. H. Hassinger, Martin Guilfoil, Seneca S. Bragg, Fergus Potter, John W. Clifford, Royal D. Davis, Samuel Brockway, Henry Gorman, Chas. A. Butler, Alfred Langen, DeWitt Brownson

1866	1871	1876	1881	1886	1891	1896	1901	1906	1911	1916	1921	1926	1931	1936	1941	1946	1951

MEMBERSHIP BY YEAR (ACCOUNTED FOR): 1904, 63; 1905, 38; 1906, 37   **LAST MEMBER:** Unknown

Old soldiers at the National Home in Milwaukee organized another G.A.R. post in 1898, receiving the recycled number 211.

The veterans chose to call themselves the Old Guard Post. The name probably was a comparison to what was happening at that time. The "new guard," specifically the new Wisconsin National Guard, was busy recruiting and preparing to depart for the Spanish-American War at the time.

Although it got off to a good start numerically and sustained those numbers for about eight years, the Old Guard Post ceased functioning by 1907.

HENRY P. DAVIDSON POST 212, Plymouth
SHEBOYGAN COUNTY • NOVEMBER 9, 1885–1938

CHARTER MEMBERS: Julius Schlaich, Otto Puhlmann, Adam Wolf, Ira J. Bradford, August Scheibe, Gustav Kappe, Charles Corbett, August Hein, Henry Scheldon, Michael Schneider, Andrew Henkel, August Schmidt, F. W. McNally, Sebastian Fuchs, Conrad Liese, Rial R. Wilson, Hiram H. Bowers, Anthony Gaffron, John Frick, Albert Witte, Joseph Ickstadt, William Breitung, John Knowd, Morgan L. Jones, Arthur F. Gilman, William Chaplin, Michael Sweet

1866	1871	1876	1881	1886	1891	1896	1901	1906	1911	1916	1921	1926	1931	1936	1941	1946	1951

MEMBERSHIP BY YEAR (ACCOUNTED FOR): 1885, 27; 1887, 36; 1888, 33; 1889, 60; 1900, 64; 1904, 57; 1905, 55; 1906, 53; 1907, 53; 1908, 51; 1909, 50; 1910, 46; 1911, 43; 1912, 38; 1913, 38; 1914, 38; 1915, 37; 1916, 33; 1917, 26; 1918, 26; 1919, 26; 1921, 10; 1922, 7; 1923, 6; 1924, 6; 1925, 6; 1926, 6; 1927, 6; 1928, 5; 1929, 5; 1930, 4; 1931, 4; 1932, 4; 1933, 3; 1934, 3; 1935, 3; 1936, 2; 1937, 2   **LAST MEMBER:** Unknown

H. P. Davidson Post 212 of Plymouth was another of Sheboygan County's quite active posts. Its first commander was August Scheibe. Although its chartering in 1885 was one of the later ones, the post remained active into the 1930s.

Post 212 was named for a Plymouth boy, Henry P. Davidson, who was a corporal in Company E of the Thirty-sixth Wisconsin.

In the summer of 1864, U. S. Grant was trying to outflank Lee's Army of Northern Virginia. On June 1, the federals arrived in the vicinity of Cold Harbor only to find Lee had arrived first. Nonetheless the federals tried to assault the entrenchments that day, and Corporal Davidson was one of 32 soldiers in the Thirty-sixth Wisconsin killed in the effort. The battle at Cold Harbor got worse the next two days, and Grant regretted ordering the final assault on June 3. But June 1 and 2 had been bad enough.

Post 212 joined with the older Sheboygan posts in holding an annual reunion of Sheboygan County veterans for many years. Davidson Post was honored in 1926 with the selection of one of its members, Henry Stannard, as department commander.

JOE MOWER POST 213, Wrightstown
BROWN COUNTY • OCTOBER 20, 1885–1887 OR 1888

CHARTER MEMBERS: L. M. Pippinger was the first commander.

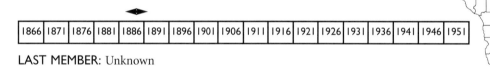

1866	1871	1876	1881	1886	1891	1896	1901	1906	1911	1916	1921	1926	1931	1936	1941	1946	1951

LAST MEMBER: Unknown

Joe Mower Post 213 had an abbreviated history. Chartered at Wrightstown, a town on the Fox River in Brown County, in October 1885, it was extinct within about two years.

Joe Mower, the namesake of Post 213, had previously been honored by the veterans of Post 121 at Belleville. See Post 121 for a picture and biographical material on Mower.

JOHN A. EATON POST 213, Greenwood
CLARK COUNTY • OCTOBER 20, 1888–1919

CHARTER MEMBERS: Unknown

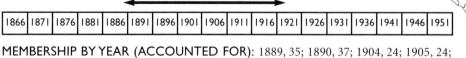

1866	1871	1876	1881	1886	1891	1896	1901	1906	1911	1916	1921	1926	1931	1936	1941	1946	1951

MEMBERSHIP BY YEAR (ACCOUNTED FOR): 1889, 35; 1890, 37; 1904, 24; 1905, 24; 1906, 24; 1907, 22; 1908, 20; 1909, 20; 1910, 21; 1911, 19; 1912, 15; 1913, 16; 1914, 14; 1915, 14; 1916, 13; 1917, 12; 1918, 12   **LAST MEMBER:** Unknown

The John A. Eaton Post 213, Greenwood, Clark County, was chartered in 1888, but veteran activities were taking place in the area well before that.

Newspaper coverage of the 1880 reunion in Milwaukee reported that "Capt. A. S. Eaton of Company H, Tenth Regiment of New Hampshire, . . . secured quarters for 100 men from Clark County. . . . These men are old veterans who have congregated in the pineries of Northwestern Wisconsin from all quarters of the Union, and the regiments they represent are as diversified as the loyal states will admit of their being."

The reunion was eight years before the Greenwood Post was chartered. Presumably, Captain Eaton was a charter member. He was listed in later histories as one of the important members of the post. However, it is not clear who John A. Eaton was. There is no information available on him.

Eaton Post 213 enjoyed many years of activity.

Men of John A. Eaton Post 213, Greenwood, pose on Memorial Day, 1907. Seated, from left: John Booth, Jess Crane, Paul Rossman, Charles Richelieu, and Charles Cummings. Standing, from left: William Oelig, Pascal Wallis, John Scovel, John Foust, John McCarty, and Tom Vine.

JOHN HAZEN POST 214, Cashton

MONROE COUNTY • FEBRUARY 11, 1886–1900

CHARTER MEMBERS: T. F. Caffey was the first commander.

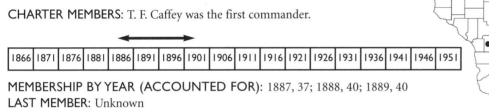

1866	1871	1876	1881	1886	1891	1896	1901	1906	1911	1916	1921	1926	1931	1936	1941	1946	1951

MEMBERSHIP BY YEAR (ACCOUNTED FOR): 1887, 37; 1888, 40; 1889, 40
LAST MEMBER: Unknown

Some of the posts of the Wisconsin G.A.R. leave present-day students with more questions than answers, and a few invite all sorts of speculation. Post 214 at Cashton in Monroe County is one for which speculation is inevitable.

Post 214 was named the John Hazen Post, and it lasted for about 14 years, although it left little evidence of its existence. In addition, no record has emerged as to who John Hazen was.

Yet there are tantalizing nuggets in the few available details about the post. Cashton, before it was so named, was known as

Hazen Corners. It was founded shortly before the war by one Jacob Hazen. Cashton was begun nearby (and Hazen Corners disappeared) about 1879. The next year, Jacob Hazen sold Hazen Corners, actually his farm.

There is nothing to indicate, however, whether Jacob was known as John, or whether Jacob was in the war. By 1886, when Hazen Post was established, Hazen Corners was history. What, if any, was the relationship?

GEORGE B. LINCOLN POST 215, Union Grove

RACINE COUNTY • JANUARY 26, 1886–1920

CHARTER MEMBERS: L. C. Canfield, J. Hay, Homer Adams, John Kinie, H. J. Powles, D. Benton, J. McKune, A. H. Hewlett, P. Myers, W. H. Servis, D. H. Collier, D. M. Jones, Ellis Seed, L. Friedenburg, J. M. Johnson, J. E. Perrigo, H. Morey, J. W. Leach, A. Gilmore, Robt. Blackburn

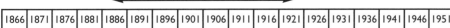

1866	1871	1876	1881	1886	1891	1896	1901	1906	1911	1916	1921	1926	1931	1936	1941	1946	1951

MEMBERSHIP BY YEAR (ACCOUNTED FOR): 1886, 20; 1887, 25; 1888, 24; 1889, 25; 1904, 20; 1905, 18; 1906, 15; 1907, 12; 1908, 12; 1909, 12; 1910, 10; 1911, 9; 1912, 9; 1913, 9; 1914, 8; 1915, 8; 1916, 7; 1917, 5; 1918, 5; 1919, 4   **LAST MEMBER:** Unknown

Post 215 members in 1914. From left: T. D. Manchester, Edwin Buchan, John Hay, Daniel Jones, D. N. Collar, Abram Gilmore, Guy Nicholson, Harrison Morey.

One of the men to respond to President Lincoln's initial call for troops after Fort Sumter was a Racine boy, George B. Lincoln.

He joined Company F, Second Wisconsin, the Belle City Rifles. He became corporal of the company. Lincoln was killed in the engagement at Brawner's Farm on August 28, 1862.

When Union Grove veterans formed Post 215 in 1886, they honored George Lincoln.

Lincoln Post maintained an active body for many years, but finally succumbed in 1920.

CHARLES GREEN POST 216, Seneca

CRAWFORD COUNTY • MARCH 27, 1886–1901

CHARTER MEMBERS: Gilbert Stewart was the first commander

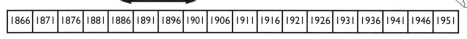

| 1866 | 1871 | 1876 | 1881 | 1886 | 1891 | 1896 | 1901 | 1906 | 1911 | 1916 | 1921 | 1926 | 1931 | 1936 | 1941 | 1946 | 1951 |

MEMBERSHIP BY YEAR (ACCOUNTED FOR): 1887, 27; 1888, 36; 1889, 42
LAST MEMBER: Unknown

Charles Green Post 216 began, apparently, in Lynxville, Crawford County, but transferred to Seneca about 15 miles away. It enjoyed some success in the G.A.R.'s active years, but by the turn of the twentieth century, it was in a steep decline. And the post surrendered its charter by 1901.

Charles Green was a Seneca boy who served with Company I, Eighth Wisconsin, from 1861 to the end of the war.

UNITY POST 217, Unity

MARATHON COUNTY • MAY 20, 1886–1896

CHARTER MEMBERS: J. C. Boudell was the first commander.

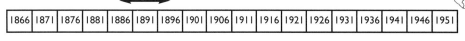

| 1866 | 1871 | 1876 | 1881 | 1886 | 1891 | 1896 | 1901 | 1906 | 1911 | 1916 | 1921 | 1926 | 1931 | 1936 | 1941 | 1946 | 1951 |

MEMBERSHIP BY YEAR (ACCOUNTED FOR): 1887, 26; 1888, 10; 1889, 37
LAST MEMBER: Unknown

Veterans at Unity were content to call their Post Unity when they formed a G.A.R. unit in 1886. Unity Post 217 was chartered May 20 of that year.

The few department references to Post 217 suggest that it may have been a bit shaky from the start. Its membership went from 26 in 1887 down to just 10 the following year, but then bounced back up to 37 in 1890, its fourth year of existence.

The surge might have marked a turnaround, except that in six more years, Post 217 was defunct.

J. MUELLER POST 218, Cassville

GRANT COUNTY • JUNE 19, 1886–1901 OR 1902

CHARTER MEMBERS: Stephen Schniring, E. Kleinpell, Vinton Raney, John Engler, Davis Williams, Charles Wamsly, A. C. Fowler, Lambert Wahl, John Fry, Mattis Schliert, Gust. Chandler, John Woodington, James Schinde, S. R. Garner, Alfred Diedrich, Isaac Day

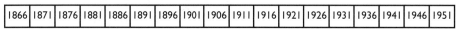

| 1866 | 1871 | 1876 | 1881 | 1886 | 1891 | 1896 | 1901 | 1906 | 1911 | 1916 | 1921 | 1926 | 1931 | 1936 | 1941 | 1946 | 1951 |

MEMBERSHIP BY YEAR (ACCOUNTED FOR): 1886, 16; 1887, 20; 1888, 23; 1889, 25
LAST MEMBER: Unknown

Post 218 at Cassville in Grant County was chartered June 19, 1886. Davis Williams was its first commander.

What little is on record suggests that the post was never large and perhaps surrendered its charter in 1901 or 1902 in order to affiliate with other Grant County posts.

Cassville veterans, while they had their own post, honored the memory of Joseph Mueller (sometimes given as Miller), a Cassville soldier who joined the Ninth Wisconsin in 1861. It was the only post named for a Ninth Wisconsin soldier. Perhaps symbolic of the Ninth's role (and the role of so many other regiments and soldiers) was that Mueller was killed in action in a little-known engagement on September 20, 1862, one of six such minor engagements that day: three in Kentucky, one in Tennessee, another in Virginia, and involving the Ninth Wisconsin one at Newtonia, Missouri.

JOE RANKIN POST 219, Two Rivers
MANITOWOC COUNTY • JUNE 16, 1886–1918

CHARTER MEMBERS: Henry Wieman, Francis St. Peter, Wm. Hurst, John Miller, Phillip Newman, W. T. Nash, Louis Hartung, Frank Laford, Henry Beck, Frederick Sonntag, Otto Kahlenberg, John Neuman, Otto Gauthier, Henry Thiele, August Ahrend, Henry Allen, Chris Miller, Anton Dietz, Charles Reimers, Peter Lefleuer, Jacob Mohr, Wm. Rediger, Michael Laford

1866	1871	1876	1881	1886	1891	1896	1901	1906	1911	1916	1921	1926	1931	1936	1941	1946	1951

MEMBERSHIP BY YEAR (ACCOUNTED FOR): 1887, 29; 1888, 29; 1889, 27; 1904, 35; 1905, 30; 1906, 25; 1907, 20; 1908, 19; 1909, 18; 1910, 17; 1911, 17; 1912, 15; 1913, 14; 1914, 12; 1915, 11; 1916, 10; 1917, 10
LAST MEMBER: Unknown

JOSEPH RANKIN

Joe Rankin Post 219, of Two Rivers, began in the summer of 1886 and was active until the end of World War I. It was named for Joseph Rankin, a Manitowoc captain who took Company D of the Twenty-seventh Wisconsin from the Manitowoc area into war in 1862, led it through three years of war including the siege of Vicksburg and later combat in Arkansas, and brought it home again in 1865. Company D suffered only one combat death, but a fair number died from disease in those three years.

After the war, Rankin entered politics. He served in the Wisconsin legislature as a Democrat from 1872 until he was elected to Congress in 1883. He died in Washington at the beginning of his second term, on January 24, 1886, half a year before Post 219 was chartered.

Rankin Post 219 was quite successful in its first several decades and still had 10 on its roster when it yielded its charter.

JOHN A. HAUFF POST 220, Horicon
DODGE COUNTY • JUNE 15, 1886–1938

CHARTER MEMBERS: S. E. Davis, E. N. Palmer, C. W. Rehfeld, Jacob Quick, Peter Quick, Julius Quick, George Williams, August Wendorf, H. S. Jones, John Bacon, Charles Discher

1866	1871	1876	1881	1886	1891	1896	1901	1906	1911	1916	1921	1926	1931	1936	1941	1946	1951

MEMBERSHIP BY YEAR (ACCOUNTED FOR): 1887, 16; 1888, 20; 1889, 24; 1904, 12; 1905, 12; 1906, 10; 1907, 9; 1908, 8; 1909, 10; 1910, 9; 1911, 8; 1912, 7; 1913, 6; 1914, 6; 1915, 6; 1916, 6; 1917, 6; 1918, 5; 1919, 5; 1920, 5; 1921, 5; 1922, 4; 1923, 4; 1924, 4; 1925, 4; 1926, 2; 1928, 2; 1929, 2; 1930, 2; 1931, 2; 1932, 2; 1933, 2; 1934, 2; 1935, 1; 1936, 1; 1937, 1   **LAST MEMBER:** Charles Dischler

John Hauff Post 220 was organized in the summer of 1886 at Horicon. The largely rural area of Dodge County never provided huge numbers for membership, and by 1923, when the post handed its records to the American Legion for safekeeping, but four members remained. Hauff Post remained on the department rolls, though, into the 1930s.

The post was named for John A. Hauff, a sergeant with Company C, Twenty-ninth Wisconsin. Hauff was killed in the battle of Champion's Hill, Mississippi, on May 16, 1863. This battle sealed the fate of the Confederate army defending Vicksburg.

C. MCCARTHY POST 221, Rockbridge
RICHLAND COUNTY • AUGUST 27, 1886–1908

CHARTER MEMBERS: M. Cunningham, P. McCarthy. R. M. Stockwell, Geo. Fogo, T. C. Stockwell, B. M. Jarvis, Nelson Moore, John Fitzpatrick, Wm. Drea, John Donahue, Wm. Cockraft, Sidney Rose, Wm. Newkirk, John McGrath, J. M. Garfield, Wm. Moore, John Barto, John Nicholson, James Kennedy, James Washburn, Newton Chessmore, J. W. Watts, Wm. Nichols, G. W. Richardson

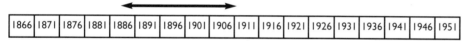

| 1866 | 1871 | 1876 | 1881 | 1886 | 1891 | 1896 | 1901 | 1906 | 1911 | 1916 | 1921 | 1926 | 1931 | 1936 | 1941 | 1946 | 1951 |

MEMBERSHIP BY YEAR (ACCOUNTED FOR): 1886, 24; 1887, 26; 1888, 24; 1889, 23; 1904, 10; 1905, 10; 1906, 10; 1907, 10   **LAST MEMBER:** Unknown

The post organized by veterans at Rockbridge in Richland County in the late summer of 1886 was named for a Richland County soldier who distinguished himself with the Eleventh Wisconsin early in the war.

Cornelius McCarthy was a corporal with Company D, the "Richland County Plow-Boys." In early July 1862 the Eleventh engaged Confederates at Bayou Cache, Arkansas, where the regiment suffered severe casualties. One of the wounded was McCarthy, who was shot in three places. He was made a brevet captain for his gallantry in that battle, but the wounds forced his discharge on September 11, 1862.

McCarthy was from Henrietta, about six miles from Rockbridge.

McCarthy Post 221 remained on the department roster until 1908 and still had 10 members its last year. Interestingly, it was listed as "McArthur" Post on department lists in 1890, 1891, 1892, and 1900, but as "McCarthy" Post on other department reports.

HIRAM M. GIBBS POST 222, Brillion
CALUMET COUNTY • SEPTEMBER 18, 1886–1917

CHARTER MEMBERS: Peter Ruther was the first commander.

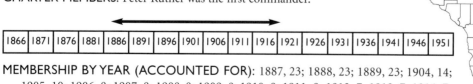

| 1866 | 1871 | 1876 | 1881 | 1886 | 1891 | 1896 | 1901 | 1906 | 1911 | 1916 | 1921 | 1926 | 1931 | 1936 | 1941 | 1946 | 1951 |

MEMBERSHIP BY YEAR (ACCOUNTED FOR): 1887, 23; 1888, 23; 1889, 23; 1904, 14; 1905, 10; 1906, 8; 1907, 8; 1908, 8; 1909, 8; 1910, 8; 1911, 8; 1912, 7; 1913, 7; 1914, 7; 1915, 7; 1916, 6   **LAST MEMBER:** Joseph Barth, died July 27, 1930

In the autumn of 1886 veterans in the Brillion area of Calumet County formed G.A.R. Post 222.

Although by then it was nearly a quarter century after the war began, they remembered Hiram M. Gibbs, a captain who led a company from Calumet County, which was mustered in on September 5, 1862. He was killed leading those men in their first action little more than a month later.

Gibbs, from Chilton, led Company E of the Twenty-first

Wisconsin. Mustered in at Oshkosh, the regiment was sent directly to Kentucky, where the Twenty-third was in the thick of the fight at Perryville on October 8. Gibbs was one of four officers and 38 men to succumb that day.

Gibbs Post 222 remained on the department roster for several decades. Its story is probably typical of rural posts. Attrition made its mark in the early years of the twentieth century, and Post 222 gave up its charter about 1917.

GEORGE C. DRAKE POST 223, Milwaukee

MILWAUKEE COUNTY • AUGUST 18, 1886–1938

CHARTER MEMBERS: Charles H. Gardner was the first commander.

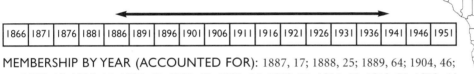

| 1866 | 1871 | 1876 | 1881 | 1886 | 1891 | 1896 | 1901 | 1906 | 1911 | 1916 | 1921 | 1926 | 1931 | 1936 | 1941 | 1946 | 1951 |

MEMBERSHIP BY YEAR (ACCOUNTED FOR): 1887, 17; 1888, 25; 1889, 64; 1904, 46; 1905, 49; 1906, 46; 1907, 45; 1908, 50; 1909, 56; 1910, 54; 1911, 51; 1912, 51; 1913, 44; 1914, 48; 1915, 43; 1916, 60; 1917, 53; 1918, 40; 1919, 45; 1920, 40; 1921, 35; 1922, 32; 1923, 24; 1924, 43; 1925, 56; 1926, 50; 1927, 52; 1928, 50; 1929, 48; 1930, 42; 1931, 25; 1932, 18; 1933, 11; 1934, 11; 1935, 9; 1936, 5; 1937, 5   **LAST MEMBER:** Unknown

GEORGE C. DRAKE

President Lincoln's call for volunteers on the news of Fort Sumter brought an overwhelming response in Wisconsin; men were afraid that they would miss the thrilling experience if they did not rush to join. Men who became the First Wisconsin felt that they were chosen to lead the way to the honors and glory sure to come.

The First was first to go, the first to see combat, and the first to learn the reality that lay ahead for thousands of Wisconsin men to follow. Private George C. Drake, Company A, First Wisconsin, was killed in action on July 2, 1861, at Falling Waters, Virginia.

Drake would not be forgotten. When another Milwaukee G.A.R. Post was chartered in 1886, the men chose the name of George C. Drake for Post 223.

Post 223 was no fleeting gathering, as some Milwaukee Posts were. It carried two dozen men on its rolls as late as 1931 and kept its charter until 1938.

G. L. PARK POST 224, Boyd

CHIPPEWA COUNTY • OCTOBER 27, 1886–1888

CHARTER MEMBERS: Unknown

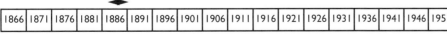

| 1866 | 1871 | 1876 | 1881 | 1886 | 1891 | 1896 | 1901 | 1906 | 1911 | 1916 | 1921 | 1926 | 1931 | 1936 | 1941 | 1946 | 1951 |

LAST MEMBER: Unknown

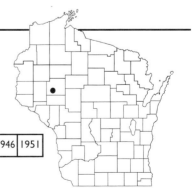

Late in December in 1886, veterans at Boyd, Chippewa County, were chartered as G. L. Park Post 224.

In simple fact, the effort did not take hold.

The 1887 roster of G.A.R. posts showed Post 224 at Boyd, but the following year, the roster shows that it was no longer operating. The post survived for a year at most.

Nonetheless, some information about the man for whom the post was named is known. He was Gilbert L. Park, the mayor of Stevens Point when the war started. He resigned to join the Eighteenth Wisconsin, which was commanded by his former law partner, James S. Alban. Park became captain of Company G, Eighteenth Wisconsin, until the close of the war. After the war, he served as a judge.

JOHN E. GURLEY POST 224, Blanchardville

LAFAYETTE COUNTY • DECEMBER 27, 1888–1931

CHARTER MEMBERS: J. B. Johnson, Rodney Seaver, J. P. Waite, Edwin E. Park, A. M. Cook, L. H. Stebbins, W. F. Enos, John McCannon, J. M. Vanderhoof, H. M. Fitzgerald, E. E. Hillman, Rosell S. Miner

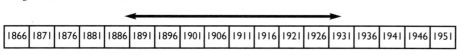

1866	1871	1876	1881	1886	1891	1896	1901	1906	1911	1916	1921	1926	1931	1936	1941	1946	1951

MEMBERSHIP BY YEAR (ACCOUNTED FOR): 1889, 21; 1890, 32; 1904, 19; 1905, 17; 1906, 15; 1907, 13; 1908, 13; 1909, 10; 1910, 9; 1911, 10; 1912, 8; 1913, 8; 1914, 8; 1915, 8; 1916, 6; 1917, 6; 1918, 4; 1919, 4; 1920, 4; 1921, 4; 1929, 1; 1930, 1   **LAST MEMBER:** Andrew Hanson

Two years to the day after the original Post 224 was chartered at Boyd, a new Post 224 was given a charter. This was at Blanchardville in Lafayette County, and this Post 224 was quite successful.

Its success would not be measured in huge numbers, for this post never accumulated such a roster, but its members stayed affiliated into the 1930s.

Blanchardville's Post 224 was named for John E. Gurley, a soldier from nearby Shullsburg who was captain of Company C, Thirty-third Wisconsin. He ended the war as a colonel.

CUMBERLAND POST 225, Cumberland

BARRON COUNTY • SEPTEMBER 20, 1886–1937

CHARTER MEMBERS: J. W. Chase was the first commander.

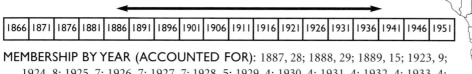

1866	1871	1876	1881	1886	1891	1896	1901	1906	1911	1916	1921	1926	1931	1936	1941	1946	1951

MEMBERSHIP BY YEAR (ACCOUNTED FOR): 1887, 28; 1888, 29; 1889, 15; 1923, 9; 1924, 8; 1925, 7; 1926, 7; 1927, 7; 1928, 5; 1929, 4; 1930, 4; 1931, 4; 1932, 4; 1933, 4; 1934, 4; 1935, 4; 1936, 4   **LAST MEMBER:** Unknown

Cumberland Post 225 is one of those posts that can be characterized as an enigma. It was chartered in 1886 and was quite content to go by the name of its Barron County community.

Post 225 disappeared from the rolls of the Department of Wisconsin in the early years of the twentieth century. It reappeared on the department roster in 1923, again listed as Cumberland Post 225 with nine members on call. Thereafter Cumberland figures appear each year until 1937, when the post is listed as extinct.

H. SMITH SCHUYLER POST 226, Sturgeon Bay

DOOR COUNTY • OCTOBER 16, 1886–1919

CHARTER MEMBERS: James Harris Jr. was the first commander.

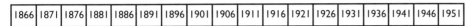

1866	1871	1876	1881	1886	1891	1896	1901	1906	1911	1916	1921	1926	1931	1936	1941	1946	1951

MEMBERSHIP BY YEAR (ACCOUNTED FOR): 1887, 49; 1888, 66; 1889, 61; 1904, 28; 1905, 23; 1906, 25; 1907, 23; 1908, 28; 1909, 30; 1910, 27; 1911, 26; 1912, 22; 1913, 20; 1914, 22; 1915, 19; 1916, 16; 1917, 16; 1918, 9   **LAST MEMBER:** Unknown

Alex Templeton of Post 226 in 1909

Post 226 at Sturgeon Bay was chartered in October 1886. The post was named for Henry Smith Schuyler, an officer from Sturgeon Bay.

Schuyler was a sergeant of Company I, First Wisconsin Cavalry, promoted to first lieutenant, when he resigned in April 1864 because of disability. He was also the first returning Door County soldier to die from his wartime illness.

Schuyler Post 226 was quite successful for a northern post. Door County was largely rural (having had a total population during the war years of less than three thousand), yet Schuyler Post 226 was quite active up to World War I.

SOLOMON MEREDITH POST 227, Hayward

SAWYER COUNTY • OCTOBER 6, 1886–1888

CHARTER MEMBERS: F. D. Stone, commander; M. Daniels, senior vice commander; J. A. McCoy, junior vice commander; W. Ferguson, officer of the day; B. F. Coe, quartermaster; D. R. Deumond, surgeon; W. Holway, chaplain; H. Wilson, adjutant; H. F. Townsend, officer of the guard

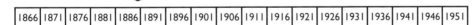

1866	1871	1876	1881	1886	1891	1896	1901	1906	1911	1916	1921	1926	1931	1936	1941	1946	1951

LAST MEMBER: Unknown

CRAIG JOHNSON
SOLOMON MEREDITH

On October 6, 1886, veterans in Sawyer County organized a G.A.R. post and chose to honor one of the men who commanded the Iron Brigade, Indianan Solomon Meredith.

Meredith Post 227 of Hayward, unfortunately, did not last and was extinct by 1888.

Meredith was one of the few southern-born men after whom a Wisconsin G.A.R. post was named. He was born and grew up in North Carolina, moving to Indiana at age 19 where his natural leadership qualities brought him early recognition and a political career. At the start of the war he was appointed colonel of the Nineteenth Indiana, which was brigaded with the Second, Sixth, and Seventh Wisconsin to become the Iron Brigade. When the brigade's leader, John Gibbon (another North Carolinian), was promoted, Meredith was given command of the brigade. At six feet, seven inches, Meredith was the tallest general in the Union army.

AZRO YOUNG POST 227, Winneconne

WINNEBAGO COUNTY • JANUARY 14, 1889–1934

CHARTER MEMBERS: John McCabe, Edgar Vrendenburg, Dr. G. Noyes, L. M. Bennett, J. J. Matthews, H. Trefethin, D. Converse, H. H. Hoffman, C. W. Johnston, Thos. O'Reiley, Andrew Olen, M. J. Manta, A. Doughty, W. G. Thorpe, S. Swinson, Geo. Olmsted, Wm. Crouse, Z. M. Sumner, R. R. Johnston, Owen Brady, J. Leicher, Ambrose Labord, J. B. Grignon, A. B. Dodge, Andrew Grignon, Frank Leroy, John Bersch, J. C. Bronson, J. Yager, F. M. Stowe, A. O'Reiley, D. S. Cross, W. H. Rogers, N. Bersch, Wm. Leidenburg, Frederick Lueck, C. Browning, John Alyea

1866	1871	1876	1881	1886	1891	1896	1901	1906	1911	1916	1921	1926	1931	1936	1941	1946	1951

MEMBERSHIP BY YEAR (ACCOUNTED FOR): 1890, 58; 1904, 20; 1905, 23; 1906, 20; 1907, 20; 1908, 21; 1909, 18; 1910, 17; 1911, 17; 1912, 16; 1913, 44; 1914, 13; 1915, 13; 1916, 13; 1917, 12; 1918, 12; 1919, 11; 1920, 10; 1921, 8; 1922, 8; 1923, 6; 1924, 5; 1925, 4; 1926, 4; 1927, 4; 1928, 3; 1929, 3; 1930, 3; 1931, 3; 1932, 3; 1933, 3; 1934, 3

LAST MEMBER: Andrew Olen, died in 1934.

Winneconne had been one of the towns where veterans eagerly joined the G.A.R. in its earliest days. The Winneconne Post was numbered 85 in the original listing, then moved up to George H. Thomas Post 9 in the housecleaning of 1871. But Post 9 faltered within a few years. In January 1889, a new post was chartered at Winneconne, Azro Young Post 227.

This post succeeded and lasted until 1934, playing a major factor in Winneconne life for many of those years.

Post 277 was named for Azro Young, a soldier from nearby Winchester, who served in Company I, Thirty-second Wisconsin, and was wounded on February 1, 1865, at River's Bridge, South Carolina. He was mustered out in September 1865.

WALLACE DANTZ POST 228, Princeton

GREEN LAKE COUNTY• OCTOBER 8, 1886–1913

CHARTER MEMBERS: A. Eggersbroad, commander; G. T. Hamer, senior vice commander; August Mittelstadt, junior vice commander; William J. Frank, quartermaster; Henry Rose, chaplain; Frank S. Merrill, officer of the day; Philo J. Heskins, surgeon; August Kleiner, officer of the guard; Edward Harroun, adjutant; Henry Crowthe, sergeant major; M. C. Russell, quartermaster sergeant; Silsby Stevens; George Leiches; Caleb Washburn; Peter Zelner; Frank Tucker; William Santo; Julius Rimples; Loren N. Bennett

1866	1871	1876	1881	1886	1891	1896	1901	1906	1911	1916	1921	1926	1931	1936	1941	1946	1951

MEMBERSHIP BY YEAR (ACCOUNTED FOR): 1886, 19; 1887, 25; 1888, 26; 1889, 28; 1904, 11; 1905, 11; 1906, 11; 1907, 9; 1908, 8; 1909, 8; 1910, 8; 1911, 8; 1912, 7   **LAST MEMBER:** Unknown

Princeton veterans formed their G.A.R. post in the autumn of 1886, choosing to honor William Wallace Dantz, a soldier from Company F, Thirty-sixth Wisconsin, who was wounded at Ream's Station and lost a leg. He was brevetted captain on August 25, 1864, and he was discharged in January 1866. Dantz was a member of a prominent family in the county and died some time after the war. Dantz Post 228 served the Princeton area of Green Lake County until 1913.

FRANKLIN H. POTTER POST 229, Cambridge

DANE COUNTY • JANUARY 5, 1887–1928

CHARTER MEMBERS: A. H. Krogh was the first commander.

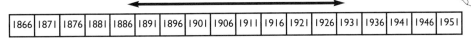

1866	1871	1876	1881	1886	1891	1896	1901	1906	1911	1916	1921	1926	1931	1936	1941	1946	1951

MEMBERSHIP BY YEAR (ACCOUNTED FOR): 1887, 20; 1888, 25; 1889, 28; 1904, 13; 1905, 13; 1906, 13; 1907, 12; 1908, 12; 1909, 12; 1910, 10; 1911, 10; 1912, 10; 1913, 10; 1914, 10; 1915, 9; 1916, 9; 1917, 9; 1918, 9; 1919, 9; 1920, 9; 1921, 9; 1922, 9; 1923, 9; 1924, 6; 1925, 5; 1926, 4; 1927, 3   **LAST MEMBER:** Unknown

By the latter half of the 1880s, the pace of chartering new posts in the Wisconsin Department was perceptibly slowing, even though the peak years for membership totals were just arriving. The first new post in several months—and the first in 1887—was chartered as Frank H. Potter Post 229 at Cambridge in Dane County on January 5.

Potter had been a member of the First Wisconsin Heavy Artillery, Company E, from August 1864 to his mustering out in June 1865. He was from Oakland in Jefferson County, not far from Cambridge.

Potter Post 229 served southeastern Dane County and southwestern Jefferson County. The post survived until 1928.

FREDERICK S. LOVELL POST 230, Kenosha

KENOSHA COUNTY • APRIL 11, 1887–1942

CHARTER MEMBERS: James H. Howe, John W. Becker, A. C. Warriner, L. N. DeDiemar, C. F. Stemm, Michael D. Ernst, Henry Christman, A. C. Sherwood, C. H. Foggett, Benj. F. DeDiemar, Chas. Frantz, Ernst, G. Timme, Geo. Hale, Geo. C. Limpert, Wm. Burt, Bernhard Schloeder, Dennis Langin, A. A. Carter, Warren T. Wilder, Alfred Miller, Chas. Weller, Timothy McIntyre, Jacob Jacobs, Abraham Dupons, Walter Cook, John M. Miller, Emil Senne, John Clifford, Chas. A. Blood, A. B. Wattles, John C. Mitchell, Chas. Wotters, Rudolph Kriofski, J. White, John Bailey, Martin Adamson, John Schultz, Jerome White

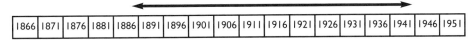

1866	1871	1876	1881	1886	1891	1896	1901	1906	1911	1916	1921	1926	1931	1936	1941	1946	1951

MEMBERSHIP BY YEAR (ACCOUNTED FOR): 1887, 81; 1888, 84; 1889, 96; 1890, 117; 1895, 71; 1904, 86;1905, 78; 1906, 75; 1907, 78; 1908, 78; 1909, 87; 1910, 97; 1911, 97; 1912, 81; 1913, 72; 1914, 66; 1915, 64; 1916, 62; 1917, 57; 1918, 57; 1919, 45; 1921, 31; 1922, 25; 1923, 23; 1924, 18; 1925, 11; 1926, 10; 1927, 7; 1928, 7; 1929, 6; 1930, 4; 1931, 4; 1932, 4; 1933, 3; 1934, 3; 1935, 3; 1936, 2; 1937, 2; 1938, 1   **LAST MEMBER:** Charles A. Leonard

Although it was founded later than many posts, Fred S. Lovell Post 230 of Kenosha was one of the larger and most active posts in the twentieth century. In fact, it had more than 50 members in 1917, the year Lovell Post was host to the state encampment.

Frederick S. Lovell was one of the prominent attorneys in Kenosha when he was appointed lieutenant colonel of the Thirty-third Wisconsin. He had been a member of the convention that drew up the state Constitution, and he was speaker of the Assembly in 1858–59. He proved to be a good officer for preparing troops and was named colonel of the Forty-sixth Wisconsin.

JAMES S. EWING POST 231, Poy Sippi

WAUSHARA COUNTY • APRIL 11, 1887–1929

CHARTER MEMBERS: F. E. Noyes was the first commander.

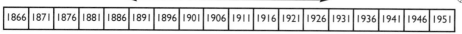

1866	1871	1876	1881	1886	1891	1896	1901	1906	1911	1916	1921	1926	1931	1936	1941	1946	1951

MEMBERSHIP BY YEAR (ACCOUNTED FOR): 1887, 30; 1888, 38; 1889, 36; 1904, 25; 1905, 25; 1906, 20; 1907, 20; 1908, 17; 1909, 16; 1910, 12; 1911, 12; 1912, 11; 1913, 11; 1914, 10; 1915, 9; 1916, 8; 1917, 8; 1918, 8; 1919, 7; 1920, 7; 1921, 7; 1922, 9; 1923, 7; 1924, 4; 1925, 3; 1926, 2; 1927, 2; 1928, 2   **LAST MEMBER:** Unknown

James S. Ewing Post 231, chartered in the spring of 1887, was another of those rural posts that thrived because they were viewed as the most important organization in the community.

Ewing Post was in Poy Sippi, not far from Berlin, and its members shared the special affection for the G.A.R. that motivated many east-central Wisconsin posts.

James Ewing was from Poy Sippi and had served as assistant surgeon with the Fifth Wisconsin.

Post 231's membership was never large, but the post remained on the department rolls until 1929.

This 1910 view of Main Street in Poy Sippi, Waushara County, shows the G.A.R. Hall of James S. Ewing Post 231. The town was typical of many small communities in Wisconsin during the early twentieth century when the Grand Army of the Republic was one of the mainstays of social and cultural activities.

JOHN A. LOGAN POST 232, Rhinelander

ONEIDA COUNTY • MAY 5, 1887–1908

CHARTER MEMBERS: E. B. Crowfoot, T. G. McLaughlin, F. A. Noble, Amos Decanter, Leonard Norr, W. Aldrich, D. A. Reed, W. W. Crowfoot, W. W. Wright, S. T. DeVoin, Jas. O'Connor

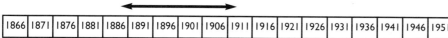

1866	1871	1876	1881	1886	1891	1896	1901	1906	1911	1916	1921	1926	1931	1936	1941	1946	1951

MEMBERSHIP BY YEAR (ACCOUNTED FOR): 1887, 11; 1888, 13; 1889, 20; 1904, 26; 1905, 22; 1906, 20; 1907, 19
LAST MEMBER: Unknown

JOHN A. LOGAN

John A. Logan was an early legend in the Grand Army of the Republic, so it is not surprising that he would be memorialized by comrades. John A. Logan Post 232 was chartered at Rhinelander in northern Wisconsin in 1887.

Logan had been the second national commander of the G.A.R., and he left a lasting imprint—particularly his institution of Memorial Day—upon the organization and upon the nation as a whole.

The post named in his honor seems not to have had that type of imprint upon the G.A.R. Department of Wisconsin. It was off the rolls by 1908, its 19 members presumably transferred to other posts.

NELSON QUIGGLE POST 233, Mindoro

LA CROSSE COUNTY • JUNE 3, 1887–JANUARY 1, 1898

CHARTER MEMBERS: Unknown

1866	1871	1876	1881	1886	1891	1896	1901	1906	1911	1916	1921	1926	1931	1936	1941	1946	1951

MEMBERSHIP BY YEAR (ACCOUNTED FOR): 1887, 17; 1888, 20; 1889, 25
LAST MEMBER: Unknown

Nelson Quiggle Post 233 of Mindoro in La Crosse County struggled for a number of years to keep going, but its membership did not grow, and, by the beginning of 1898, it was defunct.

The post was named for Nelson Quiggle, a man from the Town of Farmington who was a private in Company I, Eighth Wisconsin. Quiggle was wounded at Corinth, Mississippi. He returned to the Mindoro area and died from his wounds on February 13, 1864.

OSCAR F. BROWN POST 233, Glenwood

ST. CROIX COUNTY • DECEMBER 3, 1898–1918

CHARTER MEMBERS: H. J. Wull, J. M. Blakely, J. R. Hoagland, O. M. Allen, D. R. LeGrant, J. R. Wheelen, J. Zimmermann, J. L. Rutty, Gilbert Northrup, Albert J. Payne, H. N. Weston, Benj. Goodison, Wm. Hartshorn, Chas. Nitshey, Wm. Randolph, W. D. Brown

1866	1871	1876	1881	1886	1891	1896	1901	1906	1911	1916	1921	1926	1931	1936	1941	1946	1951

MEMBERSHIP BY YEAR (ACCOUNTED FOR): 1906, 16; 1907, 11; 1908, 14; 1909, 14; 1910, 13; 1911, 12; 1912, 12; 1913, 10; 1914, 7; 1915, 7; 1916, 5; 1917, 6   LAST MEMBER: Unknown

The men who chartered O. F. Brown Post 233 in Glenwood, St. Croix County, had already seen one post in town falter. Post 272 lasted there from 1891 to 1893. Nonetheless, they tried again.

Brown Post 233 itself had a rather shaky existence. It was listed as extinct in the 1901 state roster, although it remained active on a small scale for another 17 years.

The post was named for Captain Oscar F. Brown from Hudson, who commanded Company A of the Forty-fourth Wisconsin.

CYPRIAN DOWNER POST 234, Bangor

LA CROSSE COUNTY • MAY 28, 1887–1936

CHARTER MEMBERS: W. E. Hewett, U. S. Sisson, A. B. Newton, Hiram Sweet, C. H. Newton, James Wright, Halsey Cass, David Jenkins, Luther Larkin, B. Ferrell, A. R. Benzie, Almon Dayton, David R. Lewis, U. Bowen, Joseph Pinkerton, John Pinkerton, James Capper, Sever Anderson, John Draper, Samuel C. Fauver, J. W. Berg, Chas. F. Miller, James Benzie, J. C. Hewett, Geo. McElroy, J. B. Parsons, Simon Newton, Theodore Schmitz, Walter Green, John Stintzie, Elias Wheldon, Abrams Towsen, S. L. Hall, A. S. Daniels, A. D. Goodrich

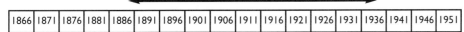

1866	1871	1876	1881	1886	1891	1896	1901	1906	1911	1916	1921	1926	1931	1936	1941	1946	1951

MEMBERSHIP BY YEAR (ACCOUNTED FOR): 1887, 35; 1888, 40; 1889, 37; 1904, 18; 1905, 18; 1906, 18; 1907, 17; 1908, 15; 1909, 13; 1910, 14; 1911, 10; 1912, 9; 1913, 8; 1914, 7; 1915, 7; 1916, 7; 1917, 7; 1918, 5; 1919, 4; 1920, 4; 1921, 4; 1922, 4; 1923, 2; 1924, 1; 1925, 1; 1926, 1; 1927, 1; 1928, 5; 1929, 1; 1930, 1; 1931, 1; 1932, 1; 1933, 1; 1934, 1; 1935, 15   **LAST MEMBER:** Samuel C. Fauver

Cyprian Downer Post 234 was chartered May 28, 1887, by veterans in Bangor, La Crosse County.

The post was named for Cyprian Dower, who was a member of Company I, Eighth Wisconsin, and served until his term expired on September 16, 1864. He died in 1872.

GEORGE A. FISK POST 235, Cataract
MONROE COUNTY • JUNE 4, 1887–1896

CHARTER MEMBERS: H. H. Atchinson was the first commander.

1866	1871	1876	1881	1886	1891	1896	1901	1906	1911	1916	1921	1926	1931	1936	1941	1946	1951

MEMBERSHIP BY YEAR (ACCOUNTED FOR): 1887, 21; 1888, 23; 1889, 24
LAST MEMBER: Unknown

G. A. Fisk Post 235, was established in Cataract, Monroe County, in the summer of 1887.

The post was named for George A. Fisk, a soldier from Sparta who was captain of Company C, Thirty-sixth Wisconsin, in which 13 Cataract men served. Early in the war, he was captured at Shiloh and later served also in the siege of Vicksburg. After he was commissioned with the Thirty-sixth he was involved in the fighting before Petersburg. Fisk died the year before the Cataract Post was organized.

Post 235 remained on the department rolls until 1896 when it was dropped as delinquent.

CHARLES R. GILL POST 236, Loyal
CLARK COUNTY• AUGUST 5, 1887–1911

CHARTER MEMBERS: J. H. Welch was the first commander.

1866	1871	1876	1881	1886	1891	1896	1901	1906	1911	1916	1921	1926	1931	1936	1941	1946	1951

MEMBERSHIP BY YEAR (ACCOUNTED FOR): 1887, 16; 1888, 29; 1889, 31; 1904, 26; 1905, 24; 1906, 24; 1907, 16; 1908, 13; 1909, 13; 1910, 12
LAST MEMBER: Albert Darton

Veterans of Loyal in Clark County formed a G.A.R. post in 1887 and named it for the commander of the Twenty-ninth Wisconsin, Charles R. Gill.

Gill Post 236 was active for several decades, but relinquished its charter in 1911 while there were still nearly a dozen men on the roster. Presumably many of them affiliated with other posts.

The man for whom the post was named, Colonel Charles R. Gill, headed the Twenty-ninth of the western armies. Gill was involved in the siege of Vicksburg but resigned his commission because of poor health. He returned to Wisconsin and was elected state attorney general in 1865.

Veterans in Loyal, circa 1895.

AUGUST ROEMHILD POST 237, Prairie Farm

BARRON COUNTY • JULY 16, 1887–1923

CHARTER MEMBERS: Unknown

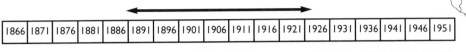

1866	1871	1876	1881	1886	1891	1896	1901	1906	1911	1916	1921	1926	1931	1936	1941	1946	1951

MEMBERSHIP BY YEAR (ACCOUNTED FOR): 1879, 15; 1884, 20; 1887, 20; 1904, 28; 1905, 26; 1906, 25; 1907, 17; 1908, 16; 1909, 13; 1910, 13; 1911, 13; 1912, 12; 1913, 11; 1914, 10; 1915, 8; 1916, 8; 1917, 8; 1918, 8; 1919, 6; 1920, 5; 1921, 3; 1922, 2

LAST MEMBER: Unknown

BARRON COUNTY
HISTORICAL SOCIETY
(CARL) AUGUST
ROEMHILD

One of the pioneer settlers of the Town of Prairie Farm, Barron County, was honored by the veterans of that town who named their G.A.R. Post 237 for him. He was Carl August Roemhild. He tended to drop his first name and, hence, so did the post.

Roemhild had joined Company I, Forty-second Wisconsin, in September 1864 and served in that unit for the balance of the war. After that he moved to the Prairie Farm area and was active in town development and town government. Roemhild died in 1883.

Roemhild Post 237 was active for several decades even as its membership dwindled. Its quarterly "bean bakes" were community events. The post finally succumbed in 1923.

JOHN A. OTIS POST 238, Trimbelle

PIERCE COUNTY • AUGUST 11, 1887–1908

CHARTER MEMBERS: : M. F. Harris was the first commander.

1866	1871	1876	1881	1886	1891	1896	1901	1906	1911	1916	1921	1926	1931	1936	1941	1946	1951

MEMBERSHIP BY YEAR (ACCOUNTED FOR): 1887, 17; 1888, 24; 1889, 24; 1904, 20; 1905, 15; 1906, 13; 1907, 12; LAST MEMBER: Unknown

A Trimbelle boy who died in the war was honored by Trimbelle veterans when they organized G.A.R. Post 238 in 1887. The post was named for John A. Otis, who had enlisted in Company A, Twelfth Wisconsin, and had succumbed to disease in Rome, Georgia, on June 11, 1864.

Otis Post served its veterans into the twentieth century, but left the department rolls in 1908. Presumably a number of its nearly dozen members enrolled in other posts.

CHESTER A. ARTHUR POST 239, Ogdensburg

WAUPACA COUNTY • NOVEMBER 3, 1887–JULY 16, 1896

CHARTER MEMBERS: D. M. Russell was the first commander.

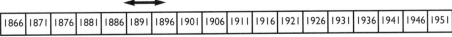

1866	1871	1876	1881	1886	1891	1896	1901	1906	1911	1916	1921	1926	1931	1936	1941	1946	1951

MEMBERSHIP BY YEAR (ACCOUNTED FOR): 1887, 24; 1888, 36; 1889, 40
LAST MEMBER: Unknown

CHESTER A. ARTHUR

Just about a year after he died, President Chester Allen Arthur was chosen as namesake of a new G.A.R. post at Ogdensburg in Waupaca County.

Post 238 was chartered November 3, 1887. Arthur had died November 18, 1886, within a year after he left the White House.

Arthur had come to the White House on the assassination of James A. Garfield in 1881. (A post named for Garfield also existed in Waupaca County, Post 21, Waupaca.)

Arthur had no particular affiliation with the Civil War but was a long-time New York Republican.

Chester A. Arthur Post 239 was active for about 10 years, relinquishing its charter in the summer of 1896.

RANK & FILE POST 240, Milwaukee
MILWAUKEE COUNTY • JANUARY 7, 1888–1919

CHARTER MEMBERS: Henry P. Fischer, Albert Bleml, Erich Westenhagen, Peter Schoenberger, Joseph Duke, James B. Wright, J. C. H. Van Schlen, John Hanson, Thomas Litter, Charles Strothmann, John Martin, Ferdinand Achtenhagen, William Herb, John Hegelmeyer, John Walker, Louis Schadigg, Peter Treaumer, Charles Margenroth, Theo. O. Hartmann, Joseph Beeb, John McGreen, A. T. Ames, Thomas S. Lawton, John Henken, George Schuele, T. W. Brinkmeyer, Joseph Gochelmann

1866	1871	1876	1881	1886	1891	1896	1901	1906	1911	1916	1921	1926	1931	1936	1941	1946	1951

MEMBERSHIP BY YEAR (ACCOUNTED FOR): 1887, 28; 1888, 37; 1889, 56; 1904, 43; 1905, 41; 1906, 41; 1907, 42; 1908, 43; 1909, 46; 1910, 44; 1911, 42; 1912, 37; 1913, 37; 1914, 26; 1915, 27; 1916, 17; 1917, 13; 1918, 12

LAST MEMBER: Unknown

Nothing ostentatious about G.A.R. Post 240. The veterans who chartered it in January 1888, comprised mainly of transfers from Chivas Post 2, called themselves the Rank and File Post.

It was the eighth post chartered in Milwaukee (five of which were still in existence at the time Post 240 was founded.) Their parting from Chivas Post was apparently amicable; installing officer was George Staff of the parent post.

Rank & File Post 240 had a fairly successful run. It never counted the number of members of Wolcott Post 1, but it had more than three dozen members on the eve of World War I.

It had, in fact, a dozen on its final roster, in 1918. Many of them presumably went to other Milwaukee posts.

First commander of Post 240 was Henry P. Fischer, who had, in 1886, succeeded Lucius Fairchild as commander of the Department of Wisconsin when Fairchild moved up to national commander.

JOHN W. SCOTT POST 241, Oshkosh
WINNEBAGO COUNTY • DECEMBER 22, 1887–1923

CHARTER MEMBERS: Gabe Bouck, Thomas S. Allen, Wm. Sharpe, R. A. Spink, J Staudenraus, C. W. Felker, G. W. Neuman, W. B. Greenwood, Conrad Schini, S. Ostertag, G. W. Buckstaff, Phillip Blake, J. F. Harnish, Wm. Hubbard, John Banderob, John McCabe, Robt. Brand, Wm. Spikes, D. H. Hines, O. G. Gary, Wm. Perry, E. M. Lull, James Freeman, Eli Seeley, John Chase, D. McKeney, G. W. Briggs, C. W. Johnston, A. F. Baehr, W. A. Gordon, Casper Schmidt, George Loper, Wm. Wadkins, E. E. White, Mat Weitzel, John Strasser, G. H. Robinson, Thos. Roache, L. B. Reed. Gus Behrand, Sigfred Kuhn, Charles Noe, Charles Rahr, Lewis Genter, Louis De Foe, George Bauman, Henry Zinn, Robt. Fetigs, John Licks, J. H. Jenkins, M. M. Morgan, Wm. Spiegelberg, C. O. Dell, August Huse, Emil Schmidt, G. Gebauer, H. B. Jackson,

P. McDermott, L. Littlefield, Gotlieb Velte, L. D. Harmon, John Kinsler, J. T. Streeter, O. L. Brown, Charles Reynolds, John Blake, E. Brooks, G. R. Belknap, George Cressey, R. H. Bingham, Willard Clough, Henry Bailey, George Hasbrouck, A. Belanger, A. C. Rasmussen, J. J. Sprague, Charles Doberkuhl, Julius Kushee, John Cowling, John Rhyner, H. B. Harshaw, August Porath, Jeffrey Riordan, T. C. Miller, John Daggett, Truman Hurlbut, Henry Steven, J. H. Sharp, Herman Mayer, John Brockway, F. M. Pieper, Adolph Priebe

1866	1871	1876	1881	1886	1891	1896	1901	1906	1911	1916	1921	1926	1931	1936	1941	1946	1951

MEMBERSHIP BY YEAR (ACCOUNTED FOR): 1887, 96; 1888, 119; 1889, 130; 1904, 76; 1905, 80; 1906, 82; 1907, 91; 1908, 85; 1909, 75; 1910, 61; 1911, 55; 1912, 55; 1913, 56; 1914, 56; 1915, 57; 1916, 51; 1917, 41; 1918, 32; 1919, 27; 1920, 24; 1921, 23; 1922, 20; 1923, 18   **LAST MEMBER:** Unknown

JOHN W. SCOTT

A long-simmering dispute in one of the oldest and largest posts of the Department of Wisconsin resulted in the division of Oshkosh Post 10 into two parts at the end of 1887. One part remained Post 10. The other faction—which included one of the founders of the Department of Wisconsin, General Thomas S. Allen—formed the new John W. Scott Post 241.

The root of the dispute may seem difficult at this time to fathom, but it brought the "boys" to the boiling point more than once in the almost year-long discussion of where to hold the post meetings. Minutes of Post 10 document some of the debates that went on over the issue, yet do not really tell why some members wanted to quit renting the hall from Post Adjutant R. J. Weisbrod, while others wanted to retain that location. It is clear that the issue was not over the cost of the space. The alternate hall had a higher price.

Nonetheless, according to the minutes "a considerable amount of sparring and wasting of a good deal of wind on both sides of the house" accompanied the debate. At one point, early in spring, the issue brought out more than 150 members to the meeting, and the Weisbrod faction narrowly prevailed. But by summer the dissidents won their point on another vote and, against the adamant objections of Commander Joseph Arnold,

marched the post down the street to their favored hall.

The minutes are silent on what happened next, but Post 10 was back at Weisbrod's Hall the next meeting.

The factions continued to seethe, however, so by October the top men of both sides were appointed "to settle the difficulties existing in this Post." The settlement, achieved in December, was the withdrawal of the "Weisbrod" faction from Post 10 to establish a new post. Among those who withdrew were General Allen and Colonel Gabe Bouck, who had served two years on the national G.A.R. Council of Administration in the early years. Bouck had raised a company from Oshkosh in the first months of the war. It went into the Second Wisconsin.

Raising another Oshkosh company at the same time was John W. Scott, a Mexican War veteran and something of a hero there. He was one of the first Americans to enter Mexico City. The company he raised entered the Third Wisconsin.

The new post, No. 241, was named for Scott. As a veteran with some war experience, Scott was a rarity in those early days of the war. He rose the ranks to become lieutenant colonel of the Third. As such, he was killed by a sharpshooter's bullet about the time the battle of Chancellorsville opened.

Scott Post 241 started out with a strong roster of members and unlike the dissident faction, which later split Post 4 to become Post 139,[1] did not return to the fold in a matter of a few years. Posts 10 and 241 only rejoined about 1923 when both posts had diminished to mere shadows of their past.

---

1. For the history of that split, see Graves Post 139.

JOSEPH ANDEREGG POST 242, Algoma
KEWAUNEE COUNTY • JANUARY 11, 1888–1912

CHARTER MEMBERS: F. K. Wapil, commander; John Indenteld, senior vice commander; George Matt, junior vice commander; D. W. Stubbins, quartermaster; I. W. Elliot, adjutant; M. McDonald, officer of the day; George Barrand, officer of the guard; James Flynn, chaplain; John Pfluger, surgeon

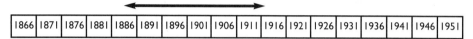

1866	1871	1876	1881	1886	1891	1896	1901	1906	1911	1916	1921	1926	1931	1936	1941	1946	1951

MEMBERSHIP BY YEAR (ACCOUNTED FOR): 1887, 15; 1888, 20; 1889, 33; 1904, 17; 1905, 17; 1906, 17; 1907, 17; 1908, 17; 1909, 15; 1910, 10; 1911, 10   **LAST MEMBER:** Irving W. Elliott, died December 23, 1941

Veterans in Kewaunee County formed a G.A.R. post in 1866, among the first in the Department of Wisconsin, at Ahnapee, which later became known as Algoma. It failed.

The Ahnapee veterans tried again in 1888, and this time the post, numbered 242, succeeded.

Post 242 was named for Joseph Anderegg from Kewaunee County, who enlisted in Company A, Twenty-seventh Wisconsin.

He was discharged as disabled on August 17, 1864, two years and two days after enlisting.

The post began in one of the order's peak years and continued to serve Kewaunee County veterans until 1912. A few veterans remained in the county for a number of years after that, however.

NEWTON S. GREEN POST 243, Shell Lake
WASHBURN COUNTY • JANUARY 28, 1888–1917

CHARTER MEMBERS: Wm. Beede, Floyd Gay, Alpheus Currant, W. H. Cantly, Chas. Mitchell, Oliver Presely, Woodward Wells, James Endicott, Joseph A. Lutes, Freeman Dussel, Josiah Lielball, Alexander Baldwin, R. C. Custurd, Hiram Prickett, Nat. A. Kent, Harrison Smith, Isaac Slover, Loren Moody, James Woodford, Leander Thomas, M. G. Thomas, Geo. Westermary

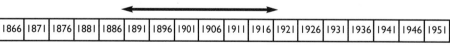

1866	1871	1876	1881	1886	1891	1896	1901	1906	1911	1916	1921	1926	1931	1936	1941	1946	1951

MEMBERSHIP BY YEAR (ACCOUNTED FOR): 1888, 22; 1889, 25; 1890, 26; 1895, 17; 1904, 10; 1905, 10; 1906, 10; 1907, 11; 1908, 10; 1909, 8; 1910, 6; 1911, 8; 1912, 9; 1913, 8; 1914, 8; 1915, 7; 1916, 12
LAST MEMBER: Unknown

The post at Shell Lake in Washburn County was chartered in January 1888 by 22 veterans. The charter gives the name of the post as Nat Green.

The post is apparently named for Newton S. Green, a member of the Eighth Wisconsin Battery who died of illness at St. Louis, Missouri, on April 3, 1862.

Green Post 243 served the veterans in its area well into the twentieth century; 12 members were listed in 1916. But the post was considered extinct in 1917 department records.

WINFIELD SCOTT HANCOCK
POST 244, Cedarburg
OZAUKEE COUNTY • JANUARY 21, 1889–1920

CHARTER MEMBERS: John Grundke, commander; Walter Zastrow, senior vice commander; W. H. Rintelman, junior vice commander; Charles Gottschalk, quartermaster; Hugo Bacla, surgeon; C. W. Lehman, chaplain; W. Liesenberg, officer of the day; John Hoehmann, officer of the guard; Henry Ropeter, adjutant; W. Roepken, sergeant major; H. Roth, quartermaster sergeant

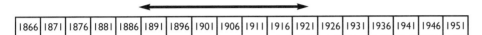

1866	1871	1876	1881	1886	1891	1896	1901	1906	1911	1916	1921	1926	1931	1936	1941	1946	1951

MEMBERSHIP BY YEAR (ACCOUNTED FOR): 1889, 24; 1905, 10; 1906, 10; 1907, 10; 1908, 10; 1909, 8; 1910, 8; 1911, 8; 1912, 8; 1913, 6; 1914, 4; 1915, 4; 1916, 3; 1917, 3; 1918, 1; 1919, 1
LAST MEMBER: Unknown

W. S. HANCOCK

Cedarburg veterans, when they organized their G.A.R. post in 1889, reached back to one of the popular Army of the Potomac generals who starred particularly at Gettysburg. Winfield Scott Hancock Post 244 served Ozaukee County veterans until 1920.

The post honored one of the illustrious leaders of the war. Hancock was one of 15 army officers in the war later voted the Thanks of Congress for his service.

Hancock was named after Winfield Scott, the War of 1812 and Mexican War hero who was still in command of the army in 1861. Hancock followed Scott's footsteps and went to West Point. After the war, Hancock remained in the regular army. He ran as the Democratic Party nominee for president in 1880, losing to James A. Garfield. Hancock died in 1886.

W. F. DAWES POST 245, Necedah
JUNEAU COUNTY • FEBRUARY 9, 1889–1931

CHARTER MEMBERS: D. Clemmons was the first commander.

1866	1871	1876	1881	1886	1891	1896	1901	1906	1911	1916	1921	1926	1931	1936	1941	1946	1951

MEMBERSHIP BY YEAR (ACCOUNTED FOR): 1889, 38; 1905, 29; 1906, 29; 1907, 28; 1908, 26; 1909, 25; 1910, 23; 1911, 20; 1912, 20; 1913, 19; 1914, 19; 1915, 16; 1916, 16; 1917, 16; 1918, 13; 1919, 11; 1920, 10; 1921, 9; 1922, 6; 1923, 6; 1924, 3; 1925, 3; 1926, 2; 1927, 2; 1928, 2; 1929, 2; 1930, 1   **LAST MEMBER:** J. J. Eggman

It took two tries, but the veterans of Juneau County in Necedah had a highly successful post. Or rather, two posts, both named for Major William F. Dawes.

The first post was chartered in 1883 and was numbered 105. But they gave it up in late 1887 or early 1888. It was listed in department records from 1888 as extinct.

The Necedah veterans did not give up their intention to have a post, and in February 1889, the Dawes Post was rechartered, this time with the number 245.

This revised post went on to serve the veterans for many years, finally succumbing when the last veteran expired by 1931.

For information on the man for whom the posts were named, see Post 105.

ISAAC HENDRICKS POST 246, Campbellsport
FOND DU LAC COUNTY • FEBRUARY 7, 1889–1919

CHARTER MEMBERS: J. B. Hughes was the first commander.

1866	1871	1876	1881	1886	1891	1896	1901	1906	1911	1916	1921	1926	1931	1936	1941	1946	1951

MEMBERSHIP BY YEAR (ACCOUNTED FOR): 1889, 31; 1905, 19; 1906, 18; 1907, 17; 1908, 15; 1909, 12; 1910, 11; 1911, 10; 1912, 10; 1913, 8; 1914, 8; 1915, 8; 1916, 4; 1917, 4; 1918, 4 **LAST MEMBER:** Unknown

The community of Campbellsport established a G.A.R. post in early 1889, naming it for a Fond du Lac soldier who died in the war. Isaac Hendricks Post 246 was chartered with 31 members and served the southeastern portion of Fond du Lac County until 1919 when it was dropped from department rolls.

Isaac Hendricks had been sergeant of Company A, Fourteenth Wisconsin. He was killed in action at Vicksburg on May 22, 1863, in U. S. Grant's second assault on that bastion before the general settled into a formal siege.

PAUL H. BEAULIEU POST 247, Kaukauna
OUTAGAMIE COUNTY • FEBRUARY 15, 1889–1934

CHARTER MEMBERS: H. M. Frambaugh, commander; Thomas Rees, senior vice commander; C. A. Walker, junior vice commander; David J. Brothers, quartermaster; J. H. Chamberlain, chaplain; Albert Gates, officer of the day; James Conway, officer of the guard; G. M. Raught, surgeon; T. H. Mitchell, adjutant; A. A. Kirn; Peter Nettekoven; Abram Brower; E. Lown; Andrew Brower; Fred Lindauer; I. W. Acker; G. D. Kemp; James Hamilton; Herman Pauli; J. R. Phelps; and Thomas Walsh

1866	1871	1876	1881	1886	1891	1896	1901	1906	1911	1916	1921	1926	1931	1936	1941	1946	1951

MEMBERSHIP BY YEAR (ACCOUNTED FOR): 1889, 44; 1905, 20; 1906, 20; 1907, 20; 1908, 20; 1909, 20; 1910, 22; 1911, 22; 1912, 21; 1913, 20; 1914, 20; 1915, 19; 1916, 20; 1917, 18; 1918, 15; 1919, 12; 1920, 12; 1921, 11; 1922, 9; 1923, 7; 1924, 7; 1925, 6; 1926, 6; 1927, 5; 1928, 3; 1929, 2; 1930, 2; 1931, 1; 1932, 1; 1933, 15
LAST MEMBER: John D. Lawe

PAUL BEAULIEU

Paul H. Beaulieu Post 247 was organized in Kaukauna in February 1889, at the height of Grand Army power and prestige.

The post was named for Paul Beaulieu, who enlisted from Kaukauna in Company F, Thirty-second Wisconsin in September 1862. He died of malaria on October 14, 1863. His body was returned to Kaukauna, the first soldier of the war to be buried there.

Post 247 enjoyed many years of activity, although it never grew large. Over the course of its history it served some 94 veterans.

WILLIAM TAYLOR POST 248, Peshtigo

MARINETTE COUNTY • FEBRUARY 16, 1889–APRIL 12, 1893

CHARTER MEMBERS: W. Kittle, commander; J. R. Roe, senior vice commander; D. Heidenworth, junior vice commander; Allen Moran, officer of the day; William Dieck, quartermaster; William Stewart, chaplain; W. Seymour, surgeon; C. P. G. Gordon, inside guard

1866	1871	1876	1881	1886	1891	1896	1901	1906	1911	1916	1921	1926	1931	1936	1941	1946	1951

MEMBERSHIP BY YEAR (ACCOUNTED FOR): 1889, 28   LAST MEMBER: Unknown

WILLIAM R. TAYLOR

The veterans in Peshtigo in Marinette County, organizing a G.A.R. post in 1889, made an interesting choice for a name. They named theirs the William R. Taylor Post 248, after a governor of Wisconsin who ended a long line of Republican and veteran-backed governors.

In fact, Taylor, a Democrat, defeated the incumbent in 1873 for whom the Madison G.A.R. Post 11 was for a time named, C. C. Washburn.

Taylor had strong credentials as a civic leader in Dane County. His closest association with the war, however, was that he was the first man in Dane County to offer a bounty for volunteer enlistments.

Taylor Post 248 was not on firm ground, however. Organized February 16, 1889, it surrendered its charter a little more than four years later on April 12, 1893.

ESTRICK BURBANK POST 248, Mather

JUNEAU COUNTY • NOVEMBER 11, 1893–1903

CHARTER MEMBERS: John M. Sanborn was the first commander.

1866	1871	1876	1881	1886	1891	1896	1901	1906	1911	1916	1921	1926	1931	1936	1941	1946	1951

MEMBERSHIP BY YEAR (ACCOUNTED FOR): 1893, 11   LAST MEMBER: Unknown

The Grand Army of the Republic was past its prime when the veterans in the area of the community of Mather in Juneau County, adjacent to southeast Jackson and northeast Monroe counties, got together for a new post. They received their charter in November of 1893, recycled from the failed Peshtigo Post, No. 248.

The new 248 was named for Estrick Burbank, a Juneau County soldier (New Lisbon) who enlisted in the Tenth Battery of light artillery in January 1864, and served until the close of the war.

Burbank Post 248 started with 11 members and managed to survive only until 1903.

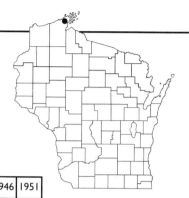

AMBROSE E. BURNSIDE POST 249, Bayfield
BAYFIELD COUNTY • MARCH 24, 1889–1927

CHARTER MEMBERS: Robert Inglis, commander; F. M. Herrick, senior vice commander; Frank Shaw, junior vice commander; M. B. Conklin, quartermaster; P. F. Rumrill, chaplain; John Gonnon, adjutant; John Pasque, surgeon; Rolla Baker, officer of the day; Charles Van Buren, officer of the guard

1866	1871	1876	1881	1886	1891	1896	1901	1906	1911	1916	1921	1926	1931	1936	1941	1946	1951

MEMBERSHIP BY YEAR (ACCOUNTED FOR): 1889, 23; 1905, 18; 1906, 18; 1907, 17; 1908, 16; 1909, 16; 1910, 14; 1911, 14; 1912, 15; 1913, 16; 1914, 15; 1915, 14; 1916, 15; 1917, 13; 1918, 12; 1919, 9; 1920, 9; 1921, 9; 1922, 11; 1923, 11; 1924, 6; 1925, 5; 1926, 5   **LAST MEMBER:** Unknown

AMBROSE E. BURNSIDE

While historians have not been kind to Ambrose E. Burnside for two rather good reasons—Fredericksburg and the Crater—many of his soldiers were more understanding.

And in 1889, old soldiers migrated to Bayfield in the far North and honored Burnside by naming their new post, No. 249, after him.

Possibly it was as much for his postwar career as for his war record, that they honored him. Burnside became Rhode Island governor and a senator from that state, and more importantly, he was the third commander of the Grand Army of the Republic (succeeding John A. Logan), serving two terms, 1872 and 1873.

Burnside Post 249 enjoyed a relatively lengthy history, considering the sparsely populated nature of its constituency, holding on until 1927.

ROBERT MUELLER POST 250, Milwaukee
MILWAUKEE COUNTY • APRIL 8, 1889–1923

CHARTER MEMBERS: August Loebel was the first commander.

1866	1871	1876	1881	1886	1891	1896	1901	1906	1911	1916	1921	1926	1931	1936	1941	1946	1951

MEMBERSHIP BY YEAR (ACCOUNTED FOR): 1889, 63; 1904, 58; 1905, 53; 1906, 53; 1907, 51; 1908, 45; 1909, 43; 1910, 45; 1911, 40; 1912, 41; 1913, 35; 1914, 34; 1915, 33; 1916, 24; 1917, 17; 1918, 16; 1919, 14; 1920, 12; 1921, 11; 1922, 11   **LAST MEMBER:** Unknown

The year 1889 was the top year for membership in the G.A.R., which may explain why a new post, numbered 250, was chartered in Milwaukee. There were veterans in the metropolis to be served.

Robert Mueller Post 250 did that, and possibly more. It started with 63 members, and the post was sustained on the department rolls with a dozen or more members until after World War I.

Mueller Post 250, in fact, survived longer than all the other Milwaukee posts except two: Wolcott Post 1 and Drake Post 223. Mueller surrendered its charter after 1922, even though it still had 11 members.

Post 250 was named for Robert Mueller from Milwaukee, who enlisted in Company C, Fifth Wisconsin, on April 21, 1861, and served until August 3, 1864, when his term expired.

HENRY E. HESS POST 251, Eureka
WINNEBAGO COUNTY • APRIL 19, 1889–1926

CHARTER MEMBERS: H. H. G. Bradt, commander; Wm. J. McLaughlin, senior vice commander; T. M. Fishbeck, junior vice commander; A. A. Parsons, chaplain; Wm. M. Martin, adjutant; A. L. H. Walpot, quartermaster; L. M. Butler, officer of the day; C. F. Apply, quartermaster sergeant; George Gifford, sergeant major; C. C. Brown, surgeon

1866	1871	1876	1881	1886	1891	1896	1901	1906	1911	1916	1921	1926	1931	1936	1941	1946	1951

MEMBERSHIP BY YEAR (ACCOUNTED FOR): 1889, 25; 1905, 19; 1906, 19; 1907, 19; 1908, 17; 1909, 17; 1910, 15; 1911, 15; 1912, 13; 1913, 13; 1914, 12; 1915, 12; 1916, 9; 1917, 9; 1918, 6; 1919, 5; 1920, 5; 1921, 5; 1922, 5; 1923, 5; 1925, 3   **LAST MEMBER:** Unknown

With the men of nearby Berlin Post 4 assisting, the veterans around Eureka formed a G.A.R. post in the spring of 1889 that became Post 251.

The post was named for Henry E. Hess, a Eureka boy who joined the Third Battery, Light Artillery, and was taken prisoner at Chickamauga on September 20, 1863. Hess died in prison at Danville, Virginia, of malnutrition on February 24, 1864.

Hess Post 251 remained on the department rolls through 1925.

GOUVERNEUR K. WARREN POST 252, Nelson
BUFFALO COUNTY • APRIL 23, 1889–1910

CHARTER MEMBERS: A. H. DeGroff was the first commander.

1866	1871	1876	1881	1886	1891	1896	1901	1906	1911	1916	1921	1926	1931	1936	1941	1946	1951

MEMBERSHIP BY YEAR (ACCOUNTED FOR): 1889, 25; 1905, 13; 1906, 11; 1907, 9; 1908, 9; 1909, 9   **LAST MEMBER:** Unknown

GOUVERNEUR WARREN

Those who like to play "what if" with history can have a field day with Gouverneur K. Warren.

Perhaps the veterans at Nelson in Buffalo County were such speculators when they chose to name their G.A.R. Post 252 after the savior of Union fortunes at Gettysburg.

What if, the game goes, Warren had not, as the army's engineering officer, gone down to the end of the line July 2 and found it completely vulnerable. What if, as a staff, rather than field officer, he had gone through channels to report his finding. What if, since he was staff and not in command of anything, the units he found had waited for proper authority to go where he wanted them. What if, in short, Little Round Top had not been defended. The Battle of Gettysburg could well have been lost that day, and all the players of "what if" can carry on from there.

Gouverneur K. Warren Post 252 remained a small but active post from its founding until 1909, and even in that final year had nine men on its roster.

GUSTAVUS H. BRYANT POST 253, Lake Mills

JEFFERSON COUNTY • MAY 28, 1889–1923

CHARTER MEMBERS: O. L. Ray, commander; C. J. Millard, senior vice commander; W. S. Howe, junior vice commander; W. W. Seely, chaplain; J. W. Hanson, adjutant; Frank Foote, quartermaster; O. Pixley, sergeant; Col. Parsons, sergeant major; L. B. Leonard, officer of the day; R. Van Slyke, surgeon

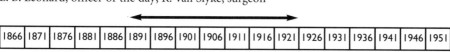

1866	1871	1876	1881	1886	1891	1896	1901	1906	1911	1916	1921	1926	1931	1936	1941	1946	1951

MEMBERSHIP BY YEAR (ACCOUNTED FOR): 1889, 27; 1905, 20; 1906, 20; 1907, 19; 1908, 19; 1909, 16; 1910, 15; 1911, 13; 1912, 13; 1913, 11; 1914, 11; 1915, 10; 1916, 10; 1917, 10; 1918, 10; 1919, 9; 1920, 8; 1921, 8; 1922, 8; 1923, 8   **LAST MEMBER:** Frank Foote

GUSTAVUS BRYANT

Gustavus H. Bryant, for whom G.A.R. Post 253 at Lake Mills was named, was a native of that town. As captain of Company D, Twenty-ninth Wisconsin, he was wounded at Sabine Cross Roads, Louisiana.

Bryant was breveted a major at the end of the war and was mustered out June 22, 1865.

Bryant Post 253, chartered May 28, 1889, was an active post well into the twentieth century. Its charter year was at the height of Grand Army power and activity. Lake Mills veterans seemed to stay with the order even as some other posts were losing members because of declining interest. Bryant Post remained on the rolls until 1923. It still had eight members its final year. They probably affiliated with other Jefferson County posts.

FRANK ELLENBECKER POST 254, Port Washington

OZAUKEE COUNTY • JUNE 25, 1889–1894

CHARTER MEMBERS: John Schroeling was the first commander.

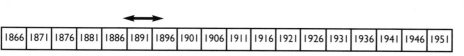

1866	1871	1876	1881	1886	1891	1896	1901	1906	1911	1916	1921	1926	1931	1936	1941	1946	1951

MEMBERSHIP BY YEAR (ACCOUNTED FOR): 1889, 35; 1890, 31   **LAST MEMBER:** Unknown

In mid-1889 Port Washington veterans applied for and received a charter for a G.A.R. post, which they named Frank Ellenbecker Post 254.

Although its chartering was in the midst of the Grand Army's most productive years, Ellenbecker Post proved that a post was still capable of failing. It was on the roster for about five years and then disappeared.

Frank Ellenbecker was a Port Washington soldier, a private in Company H, Twenty-fourth Wisconsin, who rose to corporal and then to sergeant. Ellenbecker was killed in action on May 17, 1864, at Adairsville, Georgia, in a skirmish with General Joe Johnston's forces that were withdrawing under pressure from Sherman.

MOSES H. HULL POST 254, Washburn

BAYFIELD COUNTY • DECEMBER 20, 1895–1900

CHARTER MEMBERS: I. I. Anderson, Charles Arnold, Russell Brown, R. A. Campbell, J. H. Cole, Nels N. Hanson, J. M. Harris, Rev. Stanley Lathrop, John Leighton, Dr. William T. Leonard, George Morris, Peter Nelson, Capt. Wm. O'Neil, M. R. Potts, Hosea Rood

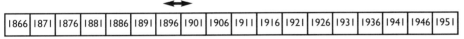

| 1866 | 1871 | 1876 | 1881 | 1886 | 1891 | 1896 | 1901 | 1906 | 1911 | 1916 | 1921 | 1926 | 1931 | 1936 | 1941 | 1946 | 1951 |

LAST MEMBER: Unknown

Moses Hull Post in Washburn, Bayfield County, succeeded to the number of the Port Washington Post, 254.

And it had no better luck in keeping the order going. By 1900, about five years after its chartering late in 1895, it was extinct, most of the men then joining Burnside Post 249 at Bayfield.

Hull Post 254 may have one claim to distinction, however. Its commander in 1898 was Hosea Rood, school principal in Washburn at the time, who would become, in a few years, the patriotic instructor for the Department of Wisconsin and unques-

tionably the most influential man in the state Grand Army in the twentieth century.

Moses H. Hull, namesake of Post 254, was a soldier from Greenbush, Sheboygan County, who served throughout the war in Company K, Twentieth Wisconsin. After the war he went to St. Croix County, then to Washburn in 1887, where his brother-in-law was editor of the local newspaper. He died there in 1888 and was the first Civil War veteran buried at Washburn.

MYRON GARDNER POST 255, Arcadia

TREMPEALEAU COUNTY • JUNE 28, 1889–1922

CHARTER MEMBERS: Seth Putnam, commander; Joseph Farlin, senior vice commander; S. Colburn, junior vice commander; John Faulds, officer of the day; J. P. Penny, officer of the guard; George Webb, quartermaster; E. J. Nichols, surgeon; T. A. Simpson, chaplain; John C. Mair, adjutant; C. E. Richardson, sergeant major; James R. Davis, quartermaster sergeant

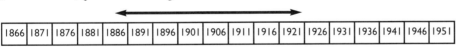

| 1866 | 1871 | 1876 | 1881 | 1886 | 1891 | 1896 | 1901 | 1906 | 1911 | 1916 | 1921 | 1926 | 1931 | 1936 | 1941 | 1946 | 1951 |

MEMBERSHIP BY YEAR (ACCOUNTED FOR): 1889, 28; 1905, 12; 1906, 14; 1907, 14; 1908, 13; 1909, 12; 1910, 9; 1911, 9; 1912, 7; 1913, 8; 1914, 8; 1915, 8; 1916, 8; 1917, 8; 1918, 8; 1919, 8; 1920, 7; 1921, 6
LAST MEMBER: Unknown

The Arcadia Post of the G.A.R. faltered in 1888, just five years after it was chartered as Post 75.

These Trempealeau County veterans were a determined lot, however, and they secured a new charter the following year. They kept the same name they had as Post 75, Myron Gardner Post, and indeed, named Seth Putnam, who had been commander of

Post 75 its first year, as commander again. This time, however, the post number was 255.

For biographical information on Gardner, see Post 75.

This latter Gardner Post remained active, albeit, never really large, until it disbanded in the 1920s.

EDMOND W. LONG POST 256, Wittenberg

SHAWANO COUNTY • JUNE 29, 1889–1902

CHARTER MEMBERS: F. A. Miller was the first commander.

| 1866 | 1871 | 1876 | 1881 | 1886 | 1891 | 1896 | 1901 | 1906 | 1911 | 1916 | 1921 | 1926 | 1931 | 1936 | 1941 | 1946 | 1951 |

MEMBERSHIP BY YEAR (ACCOUNTED FOR): 1889, 15   LAST MEMBER: Unknown

E. W. Long Post 256 of Wittenberg, was chartered in 1889, but never gained much membership—it had 15 veterans in its charter year—and was extinct by 1900.

Post 256 was named for Edmond Long from Farmington, a private in Company G, Thirty-seventh Wisconsin. He succumbed to a Confederate bullet on July 24, 1864, before Petersburg, Virginia, one of the growing list of individual victims of the new phenomenon: trench warfare.

PETER WEBER POST 257, Fountain City

BUFFALO COUNTY • JULY 15, 1889–1938

CHARTER MEMBERS: John Schmitz was the first commander.

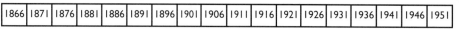

| 1866 | 1871 | 1876 | 1881 | 1886 | 1891 | 1896 | 1901 | 1906 | 1911 | 1916 | 1921 | 1926 | 1931 | 1936 | 1941 | 1946 | 1951 |

MEMBERSHIP BY YEAR (ACCOUNTED FOR): 1889, 23; 1905, 21; 1906, 21; 1907, 17; 1908, 17; 1909, 17; 1910, 17; 1911, 15; 1912, 15; 1913, 10; 1914, 14; 1915, 15; 1916, 13; 1917, 11; 1918, 12; 1919, 9; 1920, 8; 1921, 8; 1922, 8; 1923, 7; 1924, 5; 1925, 4; 1926, 4; 1927, 4; 1928, 3; 1929, 3; 1930, 3; 1931, 2; 1932, 2; 1933, 2; 1934, 2; 1935, 2; 1936, 2; 1937, 2   LAST MEMBER: Unknown

Fountain City veterans formed G.A.R. Post 257 in the summer of 1889, having a total of 23 members that year, according to department records.

Although the post, named Peter Weber Post 257, maintained a loyal membership over the years, it was never large. Yet it had a dozen men on its rolls at the end of World War I, and remained on the department lists until 1938.

The namesake of Post 257, Peter Weber, was a Fountain City boy who enlisted in Company H, Sixth Wisconsin, and was wounded in the Iron Brigade's fierce fighting around the cornfield at Antietam. He died of his wound on Oct. 23, 1862, at Frederick, Maryland.

CHARLES H. FORD POST 258, Galesville

TREMPEALEAU COUNTY • JULY 24, 1889–1933

CHARTER MEMBERS: D. H. Howel, James Gillies, D. D. Chappell, C. A. Bugbee, T. D. Wilcox, John Bohrustedt, Parly P. Stoner, William Mars, C. F. Cole, Iver Pederson, F. T. Shrake, Allen Bright, John Gould, S. Shinner, Edwin Elkins, B. F. Robinson, J. B. Ilgin, John Raichle, Walter Glassford, T. F. Funston, William Kribs, Jame Smith, Daniel McCullity, John Dettinger, Herman Sacia, Peter G. Huff, Michael Larson, Walter Wall, Myron Bullock, Arne Olson, Ed Johnson, Andrew Larson, H. W. Beecher, J. Cleveland, H. A. Towner, James Merwin, J. Curtis, John Gladson, A. Tibbitts, Duke Porter, H. W. Church, J. G. Klees, E. L. Wilber, Henry Webb, Ole Onsrud, M. K. Pynn, John O'Neil, William McKeeth, Dudley Phelps, John Pickering, John Beeman,

I. S. Farrand, A. A. Arnold, A. A. Beck, C. R. McCullom, Loran Olds, C. T. Silk, Charles Boulin, D. O. Van Slyke, Sylvester Lynne, Isaac Greimes, Hiram Drake, John Pederson, James Emerson, Peter Olson, Sever Olson, Simon Gergenson

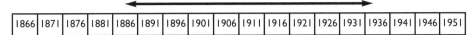

1866	1871	1876	1881	1886	1891	1896	1901	1906	1911	1916	1921	1926	1931	1936	1941	1946	1951

MEMBERSHIP BY YEAR (ACCOUNTED FOR): 1889, 62; 1905, 20; 1906, 20; 1907, 20; 1908, 19; 1909, 18; 1910, 15; 1911, 15; 1912, 15; 1913, 15; 1914, 18; 1915, 18; 1916, 16; 1917, 15; 1918, 11; 1919, 11; 1920, 8; 1921, 7; 1923, 6; 1924, 6; 1925, 6; 1926, 5; 1927, 3; 1928, 3; 1929, 3; 1930, 2; 1931, 2; 1932, 1   **LAST MEMBER:** A. A. Beck

Galesville-area veterans formed Charles H. Ford Post 258 in the summer of 1889, and like the Grand Army of the Republic itself that year, had good success. In its first year, the post recorded 62 members. Ford Post 258, in fact, had a long history of service to its veterans, and to its community.

Interestingly, it was the second post in the area named for

Charles H. Ford, a soldier from nearby Trempealeau, who served with the Forty-fifth Wisconsin.

The first Ford Post, numbered 13, had a less auspicious record. It existed from around 1873 to 1875 in Ford's home town, which was located less than a dozen miles from Galesville.

JAMES S. ALBAN POST 259, Hurley

IRON COUNTY • JULY 30, 1889–JUNE 30, 1896

CHARTER MEMBERS: George A. Alexander was the first commander.

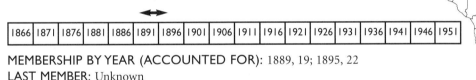

1866	1871	1876	1881	1886	1891	1896	1901	1906	1911	1916	1921	1926	1931	1936	1941	1946	1951

MEMBERSHIP BY YEAR (ACCOUNTED FOR): 1889, 19; 1895, 22
LAST MEMBER: Unknown

Although there was already a post named for James S. Alban (at Pittsville in Wood County), veterans in Iron County chose to honor the man when they organized a G.A.R. post at Hurley.

This latter Alban Post, numbered 259, in fact, did not last as

long as did the Pittsville Post. The Hurley Post succumbed in 1896 and the Pittsville Post about 1905.

For biographical data on James S. Alban, see the Pittsville Post 73.

SOLOMON MEREDITH POST 260, Hayward

SAWYER COUNTY • AUGUST 20, 1889–1938

CHARTER MEMBERS: C. E. Rogers, commander; Louis Mishier, senior vice commander; W. H. Marquette, junior vice commander; D. I. Miner, quartermaster; James Adams, chaplain; Watson Holway, surgeon; F. H. Tuttle, officer of the day; J. W. Jones, officer of the guard; Henry Beal, adjutant; Dewitt Ramsdell, quartermaster sergeant; S. R. Brown sergeant major

1866	1871	1876	1881	1886	1891	1896	1901	1906	1911	1916	1921	1926	1931	1936	1941	1946	1951

MEMBERSHIP BY YEAR (ACCOUNTED FOR): 1889, 18; 1895, 12; 1905, 18; 1906, 18; 1907, 18; 1908, 13; 1909, 12; 1910, 11; 1911, 10; 1912, 8; 1913, 6; 1914, 6; 1915, 6; 1916, 6; 1917, 6; 1918, 6; 1919, 6; 1920, 6; 1921, 6; 1922, 6; 1923, 5; 1924, 5; 1925, 3; 1926, 3; 1927, 3; 1928, 3; 1929, 3; 1930, 3; 1931, 3; 1932, 2; 1933, 2; 1934, 2; 1935, 1; 1936, 1; 1937, 1   **LAST MEMBER:** Unknown

Exactly why veterans in Hayward, Sawyer County, were unable to hold their G.A.R. post together and subsequently went out of existence as Post 227 in 1888 is not known.

But the fact that they came back the following year and kept this Post 260 going into the 1930s does testify to the tenacity of these veterans. Installing officer for Post 260's first officers was James H. Cole, a past commander of Post 227. Only Watson

Holway was an officer at the chartering of both posts. He was first chaplain of Post 227 and first surgeon of Post 260.

The resurrected organization assumed the same name as its predecessor: Solomon Meredith Post 260.

For a picture and biographical information on Meredith, see Post 227.

JOSEPH A. LEDERGERBER POST 261, Keshena

MENOMINEE COUNTY • AUGUST 16, 1889–1933

CHARTER MEMBERS: J. A. Venus was the first commander.

1866	1871	1876	1881	1886	1891	1896	1901	1906	1911	1916	1921	1926	1931	1936	1941	1946	1951

MEMBERSHIP BY YEAR (ACCOUNTED FOR): 1889, 29; 1892, 50; 1905, 18; 1906, 9; 1907, 10; 1908, 10; 1909, 10; 1910, 10; 1911, 8; 1912, 10; 1913, 10; 1914, 11; 1915, 10; 1916, 13; 1917, 13; 1918, 11; 1919, 11; 1920, 10; 1921, 9; 1922, 7; 1923, 5; 1924, 4; 1925, 4
LAST MEMBER: Unknown (April 5, 1933.)

When Joseph A. Ledergerber Post 261 was chartered August 16, 1889, it was a national event, of sorts. Friends in St. Louis, Missouri, arranged to present the post with an American flag.

Post 261 was not an ordinary one; it was the first post in the nation consisting entirely of American Indians.

Ledergerber Post was at Keshena on the Menominee Reservation. Its 29 charter members had left the reservation during the Civil War to fight for the United States.

The namesake of the post was not a Menominee. Joseph Ledergerber was an officer of a Missouri regiment who later commanded a brigade that included the Seventeenth Wisconsin, in which some 22 Menominees served. Ledergerber was wounded in the Atlanta Campaign and died of his wounds on November 27, 1863. It was in honor of their commander that the Keshena veterans named their post. Veterans in Missouri who had served with these men under Ledergerber arranged to present the new post with its flag.

The motives which sent these men from the reservation into the Civil War were perhaps a bit more complex, but no less patriotic, that those that moved other men of Wisconsin to go. At the time, Wisconsin was still frontier, and the tribes in the state were diverse and had their own tribal interests to consider. Generally the American Indians on the frontier, whether in Oklahoma, Iowa, Minnesota, or Wisconsin, were aware of the impact that the war was having on the United States. They were aware that a Confederate victory could impact them more beneficially, perhaps, than a Union win.

This, rather than strict geography, must be borne in mind.

Men of Ledergerber Post 261 at Keshena pose
with their flags early in the twentieth century.

In the southern area of the frontier, many American Indians did cast their lot with the Confederacy. The Sioux Uprising in Minnesota in 1862 was in part a recognition by the Sioux of the vulnerability of the government because of the Civil War. That uprising brought fear to the frontier areas of Wisconsin, not entirely without reason.

Emissaries of Winnebago Chief Dandy approached the Menominees to become part of a confederation of tribes to help the South, threatening the Menominees with destruction along with their white neighbors if they did not.

The plea was rejected, and the Menominees protested the presence of Potawatomis and Winnebagos, who were then roaming the forests of the region, on their lands. And they were as frightened as their white neighbors of any uprising, knowing they would be blamed, too.

Elders of the tribe wanted to show their loyalty and surrendered six highly prized medals they had received from the British. They had guessed wrong in the War of 1812 and backed the British.

Some men of the reservation had already joined the Union cause and others would follow; a total of 125 men served, including a large contingent in the Thirty-seventh Wisconsin that fought before Petersburg and Richmond.

Post 261 received some national recognition in G.A.R. publications for being the only American Indian post. It had as many as 50 members at one time and remained a viable group for many years.

NICHOLAS FRIDDLE POST 262, Rome

JEFFERSON COUNTY • AUGUST 24, 1889–1910

CHARTER MEMBERS: L. C. Sears was the first commander.

1866	1871	1876	1881	1886	1891	1896	1901	1906	1911	1916	1921	1926	1931	1936	1941	1946	1951

MEMBERSHIP BY YEAR (ACCOUNTED FOR): 1889, 17; 1905, 19; 1906, 15; 1907, 14; 1908, 9; 1909, 8   LAST MEMBER: Unknown

Romans in Jefferson County named their town's Nicholas Friddle Post 262 after a cavalryman who was killed in Arkansas in 1862.

Friddle was in Company L of the First Cavalry, and he was killed in a minor skirmish at L'Anguille, one of three such small clashes with Confederates in Arkansas that day.

Friddle Post, established in 1889 at the height of G.A.R. power, was never a large post, but remained active through the first decade of the twentieth century

DANIEL CHAPLIN POST 263, Amery

POLK COUNTY • OCTOBER 25, 1889–1904

CHARTER MEMBERS: G. N. Tanner, commander; J. R. Schuffner, senior vice commander; H. R. Preston, junior vice commander; W.H. Robbins, adjutant; W. H. Fox, quartermaster; W. E. Jones, officer of the day; Sam Fox, officer of the guard; Dan Fox, chaplain; J. W. Palmer, surgeon; J. P. Quinlen, quartermaster sergeant; J. P. Crowley, sergeant major

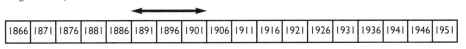

1866	1871	1876	1881	1886	1891	1896	1901	1906	1911	1916	1921	1926	1931	1936	1941	1946	1951

MEMBERSHIP BY YEAR (ACCOUNTED FOR): 1889, 15   LAST MEMBER: Unknown

Daniel Chaplin Post 263 was chartered October 25, 1889, at Amery in Polk County, and survived for a number of years, but left scarcely any tracks in the department. The charter officers given above are from the Amery newspaper of the time.

Even the identity of Daniel Chaplin escapes record. The Chaplin Post began with 15 members and was still listed by the department after the turn of the twentieth century, but it dropped even from that mention in 1904.

BENJAMIN S. DAVIS POST 264, Pedee
GREEN COUNTY • FEBRUARY 12, 1890–1906

CHARTER MEMBERS: Fred Ties was the first commander. One other charter member is known: Austin Chapel.

1866	1871	1876	1881	1886	1891	1896	1901	1906	1911	1916	1921	1926	1931	1936	1941	1946	1951

MEMBERSHIP BY YEAR (ACCOUNTED FOR): 1889, 21; 1905, 19
LAST MEMBER: Unknown

The first post chartered in the year 1890, on February 12, was at Pedee in Green County. (The name of the town was also spelled Peedee.)

The post, numbered 264, was known as the Ben Davis Post, named for private Benjamin S. Davis from Oakley, a town about five miles from Pedee.

Davis, a member of Company B, Eighteenth Wisconsin, was killed in action on May 14, 1863, as Confederates tried vainly to prevent Grant's capture of Jackson, Mississippi.

An unidentified member of Davis Post 264 displays the Davis Post Badge, date unknown.

Ben Davis Post was listed as having 19 members in 1905, but was extinct the next year. The 1905 membership figure may have been in error.

BRADFORD PHILLIPS POST 265, Royalton
WAUPACA COUNTY • FEBRUARY 16, 1891–1899

CHARTER MEMBERS: W. R. Craig was the first commander.

1866	1871	1876	1881	1886	1891	1896	1901	1906	1911	1916	1921	1926	1931	1936	1941	1946	1951

MEMBERSHIP BY YEAR (ACCOUNTED FOR): 1891, 16   **LAST MEMBER:** Unknown

The first Wisconsin G.A.R. post of 1891 was at Royalton in Waupaca County.

Post 265 was named for Bradford Phillips, a Royalton soldier who became first sergeant of Company A, Eighth Wisconsin. Phillips died on October 19, 1862, at Corinth, Mississippi, from sickness. A person with the name Bradford Phillips was the first postmaster of Royalton in 1853. It is uncertain if that was the man for whom the post was named, but the rapid rise of Phillips to first sergeant of his company suggests that he may have been a community leader before the war. It is possible, however, that he was a son of the postmaster.

Phillips Post 265 began with 16 members, but it did not grow and was listed as expired in department records for 1899.

WILLIAM O. TOPPING POST 266, Hazel Green

GRANT COUNTY • APRIL 22, 1891–1922

CHARTER MEMBERS: Edward O'Neil was the first commander.

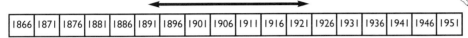

1866	1871	1876	1881	1886	1891	1896	1901	1906	1911	1916	1921	1926	1931	1936	1941	1946	1951

MEMBERSHIP BY YEAR (ACCOUNTED FOR): 1891, 15; 1904, 19; 1905, 20; 1906, 20; 1907, 21; 1908, 20; 1909, 20; 1910, 18; 1911, 15; 1912, 15; 1913, 12; 1914, 12; 1915, 12; 1916, 12; 1917, 8; 1918, 8; 1919, 8; 1920, 8; 1921, 8   LAST MEMBER: Unknown

Hazel Green veterans formed a William O. Topping Post 266 in April of 1891, and it became a successful organization in their Grant County community for several decades.

The veterans were honoring Second Lieutenant William O. Topping of Company C, Seventh Wisconsin. Topping was killed in a minor engagement at Fitzhugh's Crossing on April 29, 1863, as General Joe Hooker began maneuvering his army as a prelude to what became the Battle of Chancellorsville.

Topping Post 266 maintained a steady membership in the early part of the twentieth century, but finally yielded its charter around 1922 despite still having more than half a dozen members.

WILLIAM ATKINSON POST 267, Marcellon

COLUMBIA COUNTY • MAY 23, 1891–1903

CHARTER MEMBERS: Jonathan Whitney, commander; John H. Davis, senior vice commander; M. W. Prescott, junior vice commander; George Reid, adjutant; K. B. Cook, quartermaster; W. W. Dates, officer of the day; Levi Reeves, surgeon; Christopher Cole, chaplain; John Beakerman, officer of the guard; G. W. Purris, sergeant major; Sidney Gifford, quartermaster sergeant

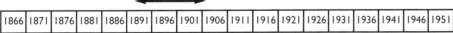

1866	1871	1876	1881	1886	1891	1896	1901	1906	1911	1916	1921	1926	1931	1936	1941	1946	1951

LAST MEMBER: Unknown

William Atkinson Post 267 was formed at Marcellon, northern Columbia County, in the spring of 1891.

Atkinson was from nearby Pardeeville and served in Company C, Second Wisconsin Cavalry. The company contained many members from Marcellon and surrounding areas of Columbia County. Atkinson was taken prisoner in April 1864 and died in prison at Florence, South Carolina, on November 19 of that year.

Little is recorded about Post 267. It existed, according to department records, through 1902, after which it ceased to be listed.

JOSEPH DUPONT POST 268, Florence

FLORENCE COUNTY • JUNE 30, 1891–1928

CHARTER MEMBERS: Omer Huff, George Baird, William H. Clark, T. C. Tully, S. Stokes, Robert Mitchell, A. M. Parmenter, John Ronan, W. P. Carr, George H. Keyes, J. C. Van Marter, J. H. Mosher, R. F. Andrews, E. L. Fraser, Thomas Penrose, W. O. Torigson, Julius Miesel

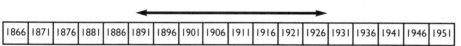

1866	1871	1876	1881	1886	1891	1896	1901	1906	1911	1916	1921	1926	1931	1936	1941	1946	1951

MEMBERSHIP BY YEAR (ACCOUNTED FOR): 1895, 16; 1904, 12; 1905, 12; 1906, 12; 1907, 10; 1908, 11; 1909, 11; 1910, 9; 1911, 6; 1912, 4; 1913, 4; 1914, 3; 1915, 3; 1916, 3; 1917, 3; 1918, 3; 1919, 3; 1920, 3; 1921, 3; 1922, 2; 1923, 1; 1924, 1; 1925, 1; 1926, 1; 1927, 1   **LAST MEMBER:** G. W. Baird

One of the later north woods posts was Joseph Dupont Post 268 at Florence, about five miles from the Michigan border in Florence County.

Chartered June 30, 1891, the post was named for Joseph Dupont from Chippewa Falls, a private in Company G, Thirty-seventh Wisconsin.

Dupont was wounded in the final assault that cracked Confederate lines in front of Petersburg. Although the wound did not claim him, he died of disease at Stanton, Virginia, in a Union hospital on September 2, 1865.

Dupont Post 268 was steadfast, despite its limited membership. The department included it on the roster of posts through 1927.

ARCHIBALD WHEELER POST 269, Coloma

WAUSHARA COUNTY • JULY 7, 1891–MAY 14, 1894

CHARTER MEMBERS: Lafayette Bishop was the first commander.

1866	1871	1876	1881	1886	1891	1896	1901	1906	1911	1916	1921	1926	1931	1936	1941	1946	1951

LAST MEMBER: Unknown

Archibald Wheeler, a Coloma boy who joined the Seventh Wisconsin (Company E) and was wounded in the Iron Brigade's baptism of fire at Brawner's Farm, was chosen by Coloma veterans as the honoree of their new G.A.R. Post 269 in 1891.

Wheeler survived that affair only to succumb to disease about a year later at Alexandria, Virginia.

Wheeler Post 269 survived somewhat longer. The Coloma veterans surrendered their charter on May 14, 1894.

EDWARD WINSLOW HINCKS
POST 269, New Cassel
FOND DU LAC COUNTY • AUGUST 24, 1894–1898

CHARTER MEMBERS: C. W. Brigham, commander; P. Brennan, senior vice commander; E. Rouch, junior vice commander; S. M. Kuter, adjutant; A. Laird, surgeon; M. S. Thayer, chaplain; W. R. Foltz, quartermaster; G. Rouch, officer of the day; J. Gorey, officer of the guard; J. Smith, sergeant major; C. Hanz, quartermaster sergeant

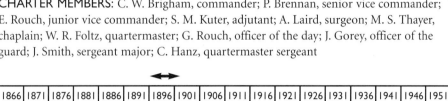

1866	1871	1876	1881	1886	1891	1896	1901	1906	1911	1916	1921	1926	1931	1936	1941	1946	1951

LAST MEMBER: Unknown

EDWARD HINCKS

Number 269, given up by the Coloma Post in 1894, was hastily given, about three months later, to a new post in Fond du Lac County at New Cassel. This was in spite of the fact that a new G.A.R. post, No. 246, had been chartered at nearby Campbellsport a few years earlier.

The new Post 264 took the name of General Edward W. Hincks, a Maine politician who achieved a commission in the army, partly through the influence of General Benjamin F. Butler. Hincks served with some distinction in a variety of combat and noncombat rolls. It was not for his military record, however, that the New Cassel veterans honored him. After the war, from 1873 to 1880, Hincks was in charge of the National Veterans Home in Milwaukee. He died in 1894, half a year before Post 269 was chartered.

Hincks Post lasted little longer than its predecessor at Number 269. It was dropped from department rolls in 1899.

Possibly its members were absorbed by the Campbellsport Post as, eventually, the New Cassel Post also was.

DUANE PATTEN POST 270, Sharon
WALWORTH COUNTY • JULY 9, 1891–1919

CHARTER MEMBERS: J. W. Brownson, David McDonald, Joe P. Miller, C. N. Burton, W.H. Knaub, A. Schellinger, Jacob Newman, Mahlon Piper, J. D. Shufelt, Rudolph Stoll, Geo. Wheeler, Volney Boyce, G. C. Loses, Burgett Banner, H. G. Bardwell, N. F. Truax, John H. Welch, L. H. Dougall, P. J. Bogardez, Frank Cole, Calvin J. N(V?)eiglue, J. H Rodawalt, Charles A. Wilson, N. Cline, Daniel Bollinger, Robt. Pearson

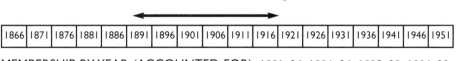

1866	1871	1876	1881	1886	1891	1896	1901	1906	1911	1916	1921	1926	1931	1936	1941	1946	1951

MEMBERSHIP BY YEAR (ACCOUNTED FOR): 1891, 26; 1904, 26; 1905, 28; 1906, 23; 1907, 22; 1908, 20; 1909, 20; 1910, 19; 1911, 14; 1912, 13; 1913, 14; 1914, 14; 1915, 10; 1916, 10; 1917, 10; 1918, 10   **LAST MEMBER:** Unknown

Veterans at Sharon, Walworth County, organized a G.A.R. post in 1880. It lasted only three years. For its brief history see McPherson Post 12.

While that early effort was unsuccessful, the men tried again in the summer of 1891, and this post, Duane Patten Post 270, had considerably more staying power. The membership remained steady until the post closed in 1919. Presumably some of the 10 members the previous year transferred to other Walworth posts.

Duane Patten, the man for whom this post was named, was a son of a prominent Sharon area farmer, Benjamin Patten, who moved there after the war. Duane Patten was in the Seventh Michigan Infantry and was killed in the Wilderness campaign in 1864.

GEORGE H. BRAYTON POST 271, Fall River

COLUMBIA COUNTY • SEPTEMBER 28, 1891–1936

CHARTER MEMBERS: M. C. Hobart was the first commander.

1866	1871	1876	1881	1886	1891	1896	1901	1906	1911	1916	1921	1926	1931	1936	1941	1946	1951

MEMBERSHIP BY YEAR (ACCOUNTED FOR): 1904, 20; 1905, 20; 1906, 20; 1907, 19; 1908, 18; 1909, 17; 1910, 17; 1911, 16; 1912, 15; 1913, 12; 1914, 12; 1915, 11; 1916, 10; 1917, 9; 1918, 9; 1919, 8; 1920, 6; 1921, 4; 1922, 3; 1923, 1; 1924, 1; 1925, 1; 1926, 1; 1927, 1; 1928, 1; 1929, 1; 1930, 1; 1931, 1; 1932, 1; 1933, 1; 1934, 1; 1935, 1 **LAST MEMBER:** Washington Loomis

CRAIG JOHNSON, TOWSON, MD.
GEORGE H. BRAYTON

Although the Fall River (Columbia County) G.A.R. Post came into being a little past the order's prime, it was one of those stalwart small-town posts that took pride in its standing in the community. Thanks to the longevity of one of its members, it remained on the Department rolls until 1935. Washington Loomis outlived the other comrades of George H. Brayton Post 271 by 13 years.

The post was named for a captain from Fall River who commanded Company B, Seventh Wisconsin, in its first engagement at Brawner's Farm and was killed that August 28, 1862. The post namesake was a half-brother of the founder of Fall River, Alfred Brayton. He is probably buried in a mass grave at Arlington National Cemetery where many unknown soldiers who fell at Brawner's Farm and other northern Virginia battles are buried.

Members of Fall River Post 271, 1911. Washington Loomis, third from right, outlived all the others by 13 years. Photo provided by the Wisconsin Veterans Museum, Madison.

OTIS HOYT POST 272, Glenwood

ST. CROIX COUNTY • NOVEMBER 12, 1891–JULY 7, 1893

CHARTER MEMBERS: O. F. Brown was the first commander.

1866	1871	1876	1881	1886	1891	1896	1901	1906	1911	1916	1921	1926	1931	1936	1941	1946	1951

LAST MEMBER: Unknown

The veterans of Glenwood in eastern St. Croix County chartered their G.A.R. post on November 12, 1891, naming it Otis Hoyt Post 272.

The post never really got started, however, and the men surrendered their charter in little more than a year and a half. It ceased to exist in July 1893. The veterans in Glenwood tried again in 1898, and that Post 233 lasted two decades.

The post was named for Otis Hoyt from Hudson in St. Croix County, who served as surgeon of the Thirtieth Wisconsin until the end of the war. He was not only in the Civil War but also had served in the Mexican War. One of the earliest physicians in St. Croix County, he died in 1885.

JEREMIAH RUSK POST 272, Spring Valley

PIERCE COUNTY • JANUARY 21, 1895–1929

CHARTER MEMBERS: Col. W. W. Robinson, J. K. Preston, J. C. Anderson, E. Blaisdel, J. A. Hess, D. L. White, S. Sanders, F. Chambers, G. R. Whitbeck, M. Tio, J. Stever, C. D. Gorman, Wm. Hosmer

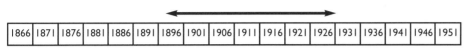

1866	1871	1876	1881	1886	1891	1896	1901	1906	1911	1916	1921	1926	1931	1936	1941	1946	1951

MEMBERSHIP BY YEAR (ACCOUNTED FOR): 1895, 12; 1905, 10; 1906, 10; 1907, 10; 1908, 10; 1909, 12; 1910, 15; 1911, 18; 1912, 16; 1913, 17; 1914, 18; 1915, 22; 1916, 20; 1917, 22; 1918, 21; 1919, 20; 1921, 16; 1922, 17; 1923, 14; 1924, 10; 1925, 9; 1926, 6; 1927, 9; 1928, 5   **LAST MEMBER:** Richard Palmer, died December 24, 1935.

JEREMIAH RUSK

Of the six governors of Wisconsin honored by veterans' naming their local post after them, the last, and in some ways, the most popular, was Jeremiah Rusk, chosen by Spring Valley men when they formed Post 272 in 1895.

"Jerry" Rusk, governor for seven years beginning in 1885, was in some ways a precursor of twentieth-century populist politicians, right up to preferring the familiar "Jerry" to his formal first name. He had a very successful political career beginning even before the Civil War. He served with the Twenty-fifth Wisconsin and rose to brevet brigadier general. Immediately after he resumed his political career and became state bank comptroller, then an elected office, in 1866. Given his political status and war record, it was natural for him to be one of the founders of the Grand Army of the Republic in Wisconsin.

Spring Valley succeeded to the number 272 in early 1895. The post was quite successful and remained on the rolls of the department until 1929.

Surviving members of Jeremiah Rusk Post 272, Spring Valley, 1920. Seated, from left: Fred Chambers, David L White, Jacob Gore, John Young, and Philo Kelley. Standing, from left: Henry Couch, an unknown man, John Anderson, and J. S. Hanes. Photo provided by Doug Blegen, Spring Valley.

GEORGE WILLICH POST 273, Boyd

CHIPPEWA COUNTY • JULY 1, 1892–SEPTEMBER 24, 1892

CHARTER MEMBERS: J. B. Johnson, Rodney Seaver, J. P. Waite, Edwin E. Park, A. M. Cook, L. H. Stebbins, W. F. Enos, John McCannon, J. M. Vanderhoof, H. M. Fitzgerald, E. E. Hillman, Rosell S. Miner

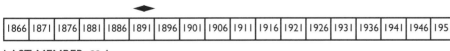

1866	1871	1876	1881	1886	1891	1896	1901	1906	1911	1916	1921	1926	1931	1936	1941	1946	1951

LAST MEMBER: Unknown

The boys in Boyd were doubly vexed. Their Grand Army Post 273 was one of the shortest tenured in the Department of Wisconsin, lasting less than two months. And this was their second effort.

The Chippewa County community had G. L. Park Post 224 from 1886 to 1888

Then on July 1, 1892, it tried again. This was the George Willich Post 273. Nothing is known about the man for whom the post was named.

Its entire history apparently is encapsulated in the *1893 Proceedings of the Twenty-seventh Annual Encampment:*

"George Willich Post #273, Boyd, Wis., was chartered July 1, 1892 and surrendered its charter September 24, 1892. The Post did not live long enough to make its first report."

J. D. ROBIE POST 273, Superior

DOUGLAS COUNTY • JANUARY 25, 1893–1904

CHARTER MEMBERS: A. H. Wheldon, E. R. Otis, George R. Hughes, John Ruggles, B. C. Alford, A. A. Wilson, N. M. Reynolds, A. A. Maxim, C. C. Edwards, George Maxfield, R. W. Sanborn, Ehrism Romine, Octave Robert, N. Lucius Sr.

1866	1871	1876	1881	1886	1891	1896	1901	1906	1911	1916	1921	1926	1931	1936	1941	1946	1951

MEMBERSHIP BY YEAR (ACCOUNTED FOR): 1893, 13   **LAST MEMBER:** Unknown

Among the Wisconsin cities having two G.A.R. posts, the evidence points clearly to dissention in the ranks of the elder post in two instances (Oshkosh and Berlin), and is ambivalent as to why there were two in Eau Claire. In the fourth instance, La Crosse, evidence is that the second post was originated in a community, West La Crosse, which at the time was distinct. Only in the case of Superior does it seem clear that the second post was the result of the growth of the community itself. Members of the elder post, Alonzo Palmer Post 170, in fact, were prominent in the installation of the new J. D. Robie Post 273 in 1893. The Palmer Post met in the western part of Superior and the Robie Post in the eastern part. They held their meetings on different nights specifically to facilitate visits between the two clubs.

The new post, No. 273, was named for a deceased member of the Palmer Post, James Dudley Robie, who had been its original senior vice commander and a later commander. Robie was perhaps typical of Grand Army men in the great northwest part of Wisconsin. He was not a native. He was, in fact, from Maine and served in the Twenty-eighth Maine as a commissioned officer.

It was after the war that he came West, as so many other veterans did. He went first to Minnesota and then to Superior in 1880 and became prominent through dealing in real estate. Robie died in Superior in 1892, just about nine months before Post 273 was organized.

The experiment of having a second post in Superior was understandable in that the region was a growing part of the state in the 1890s. But in fact, Robie Post had the disadvantage of being smaller and always trailed behind the Palmer Post. It managed to serve for about a decade before it surrendered its charter. Presumably the veterans from the younger post transferred to the older one, for Palmer Post, in 1904, with membership of 150, was one of the stronger posts in state.

Among the communities that had more than one post at one time (Milwaukee, for obvious reasons, is discounted here) only two had them a considerable period of time. La Crosse had two posts for the longest time, 53 years. Oshkosh had two for 36 years. Superior and Berlin each had them for 10 years, and Eau Claire for only about two years.

WILLIAM STEINMEYER POST 274, Milwaukee

MILWAUKEE COUNTY • JULY 26, 1892–1909

CHARTER MEMBERS: F. T. Zetteler was the first commander.

1866	1871	1876	1881	1886	1891	1896	1901	1906	1911	1916	1921	1926	1931	1936	1941	1946	1951

MEMBERSHIP BY YEAR (ACCOUNTED FOR): 1892, 27; 1904, 22; 1905, 20; 1906, 21; 1907, 18; 1908, 17   **LAST MEMBER:** Unknown

WISCONSIN VETERANS MUSEUM
WILLIAM STEINMEYER

The last post chartered to serve the veterans of the Milwaukee area was William Steinmeyer Post 274. The post was chartered July 26, 1892. At the time, there were already seven other posts in Milwaukee and one in South Milwaukee.

While statistics show that the order was beginning its numeric decline by 1892, it was not really perceptible at that time, and Post 274, with 27 charter members, began an active decade and a half before it became the second of those seven Milwaukee Posts to surrender its charter, in 1909, still having seventeen members.

The post was named for Milwaukeean William Steinmeyer, who enlisted in Company B, Twenty-sixth Wisconsin, in 1862 and rose through the ranks to become its captain in June 1864. A month later, he was wounded at Peach Tree Creek, but he survived and was mustered out at the close of the war.

OLIVER A. HEGG POST 275, Independence
TREMPEALEAU COUNTY • JANUARY 26, 1893–1898

CHARTER MEMBERS: G. W. Cook, commander; W. J. Carlton, senior vice commander; G. L. Lintz, junior vice commander; M. F. Whitney, adjutant; A. D. Fay, surgeon; T. J. Bramwell, chaplain; J. J. Zimmer, quartermaster; Wm. E. Markham, officer of the day; D. C. Hare, officer of the guard

1866	1871	1876	1881	1886	1891	1896	1901	1906	1911	1916	1921	1926	1931	1936	1941	1946	1951

MEMBERSHIP BY YEAR (ACCOUNTED FOR): 1893, 21   **LAST MEMBER:** Unknown

OLIVER A. HEGG

Oliver A. Hegg Post 275, Independence, Trempealeau County, was chartered January 26, 1893. Twenty-one men were initially in the post.

This was another of those latter-day posts which was chartered in a small community and found it impossible to sustain itself for any length of time. Post 275 was dropped from department rolls in 1898.

The Independence Post was named for Oliver A. Hegg, quartermaster sergeant of the Third Wisconsin. Hegg was promoted to first lieutenant of Company B in September 1864, and he was mustered out at the end of the war. He returned to Trempealeau County, where he farmed and taught. He was county board chairman one year and later was appointed clerk of the Trempealeau Circuit Court.

HENRY O. WATROUS POST 276, Spencer
MARATHON COUNTY • JANUARY 19, 1895–1921

CHARTER MEMBERS: S. D. Graves, Wesley Vanderhoof, Thos. H. Box, Henry Seagrist, S. C. Brooks, Jos. Arks, J. K. Lum, A. K. Hungerford, Jos. Whitmore, Henry Mason, Jos. Damon, C. K. Richardson, M. P. Hartford, J. S. Burnside, Collins Williams, Septimus Plomer, H. R. Crowell, H. L. Whipple, Erastus Trumbull, Geo. I. Follett, Jerome B. Van Horn, Benj. S. Bradley, J. B. Upson, Ward Vanderhoof

1866	1871	1876	1881	1886	1891	1896	1901	1906	1911	1916	1921	1926	1931	1936	1941	1946	1951

MEMBERSHIP BY YEAR (ACCOUNTED FOR): 1895, 24; 1904, 15; 1905, 14; 1906, 12; 1907, 13; 1908, 15; 1909, 11; 1910, 12; 1911, 15; 1912, 13; 1913, 13; 1914, 12; 1915, 15; 1916, 13; 1917, 8; 1918, 8; 1919, 8; 1920, 7
LAST MEMBER: Albert Darton

This second try by the veterans in Spencer to have a G.A.R. post was more successful than their first. That was Post 93, and it lasted four years, from 1883 to 1887. This was Post 276, chartered January 19, 1895, and it had a successful history serving southwest Marathon County and adjoining Clark and Wood Counties.

As was Post 93, this post was named for a member of the Fourth Wisconsin. Henry O. Watrous was killed in the assault on Port Hudson, Louisiana, on May 27, 1863, when the Fourth was still an infantry regiment.

WAUSAUKEE POST 277, Wausaukee

MARINETTE COUNTY • AUGUST 12, 1899–1901 OR 1902

CHARTER MEMBERS: G. M. Rickaby was the first commander.

1866	1871	1876	1881	1886	1891	1896	1901	1906	1911	1916	1921	1926	1931	1936	1941	1946	1951

LAST MEMBER: Unknown

The G.A.R. came to Wausaukee in Marinette County in 1899, but it did not "take." Wausaukee Post 277 was chartered on August 12, 1899, and that is about the only information about the post that survives.

It apparently lasted for more than a year. The department list for 1900 includes Post 277, but the following year there was no mention of the post, and the 1902 encampment journal reports that the charter had been surrendered.

ONEIDA POST 278, Oneida

BROWN COUNTY • SEPTEMBER 21, 1899–1926

CHARTER MEMBERS: Peter Bread was the first commander.

1866	1871	1876	1881	1886	1891	1896	1901	1906	1911	1916	1921	1926	1931	1936	1941	1946	1951

MEMBERSHIP BY YEAR (ACCOUNTED FOR): 1879, 12; 1884, 17; 1887, 18; 1888, 22; 1889, 28; 1904, 17; 1905, 16; 1906, 16; 1907, 15; 1908, 15; 1909, 14; 1910, 13; 1911, 9; 1912, 8; 1913, 10; 1914, 10; 1915, 10; 1916, 10; 1917, 7; 1918, 7; 1919, 7; 1920, 7; 1921, 5

LAST MEMBER: Ge Gur Kel, c. 1925

It did not gain the notice that the earlier Menominee Grand Army Post achieved, but Oneida Post 278, chartered September 21, 1899, was the second all-American Indian post in Wisconsin, and possibly in the nation.

The Oneida Post chose to be known simply by its tribal name. But like the Menominees of Post 261, Oneida Post served its tribal Civil War veterans through their advancing years.

Although they both were relatively late additions to the Wisconsin Department lists—261 in 1889 and 278 in 1899— they both served their members and their communities for many years.

The Oneidas were scarcely less involved in the Civil War than the Menominees. The latter had 125 men in the army; the Oneidas, 111.

Although these were the only two all-American Indian posts, Wisconsin's roster of Civil War soldiers contains any num-

Last surviving Post 278 member Ge Gur Kel in American Indian dress and Grand Army badge, date unknown. Photo provided by the Wisconsin Veterans Museum, Madison.

Members of Oneida Post 278, Grand Army of the Republic, are show in front of the Parish Hall at Oneida about 1907. Photo provided by the Wisconsin Veterans Museum, Madison.

ber of Indian volunteers. The Stockbridge of Calumet County were well represented. The Seventh Wisconsin had a representation of American Indians. A number of Chippewas were serving in the later stages of the war with Company E of the Third Wisconsin. In Sherman's March to the Sea, the Third had a minor clash with a Confederate cavalry detachment and killed two. The Chippewas of Company E had to be dissuaded from claiming their scalps. Indians served in many regiments and were probably G.A.R. members in individual instances.

H. W. LAWTON POST 279, Muscoda

GRANT COUNTY • MARCH 1, 1900–1924

CHARTER MEMBERS: Wilder B. Jacobs was the first commander.

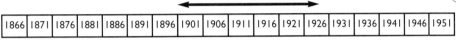

1866	1871	1876	1881	1886	1891	1896	1901	1906	1911	1916	1921	1926	1931	1936	1941	1946	1951

MEMBERSHIP BY YEAR (ACCOUNTED FOR): 1904, 28; 1905, 23; 1906, 23; 1907, 25; 1908, 21; 1909, 19; 1910, 20; 1911, 19; 1912, 17; 1913, 11; 1914, 10; 1915, 7; 1916, 8; 1917, 6; 1918, 6; 1919, 6; 1920, 5; 1921, 5; 1922, 3; 1923, 3 **LAST MEMBER:** Unknown

After one failed attempt to provide their area of Grant County with a G.A.R. post (see Post 71), Muscoda's old soldiers chartered H. W. Lawton Post 279.

While this post was never large, the veterans were able to maintain activities and membership for several decades. The post finally succumbed in 1924.

Unfortunately, virtually nothing is known of the post's history, nor of the identity of H. W. Lawton.

JOHN E. TOURTELLOTE POST 280, RUSK COUNTY POST 280, Ladysmith

RUSK COUNTY • AUGUST 7, 1906–1940

CHARTER MEMBERS: Alfred Prouty, R. S. Reeves, J. C. Miller, Robt. Corbett, Joseph Demars, T. F. Armstrong, Frank Sherin Jr., G. W. Holt, A. D. Putney, John Corbett, R. O. Sinclair, C. P. Soule, Joseph F. Andrus

1866	1871	1876	1881	1886	1891	1896	1901	1906	1911	1916	1921	1926	1931	1936	1941	1946	1951

MEMBERSHIP BY YEAR (ACCOUNTED FOR): 1906, 13; 1907, 14; 1908, 15; 1909, 19; 1910, 28; 1911, 23; 1912, 20; 1913, 19; 1914, 21; 1915, 19; 1916, 20; 1917, 20; 1918, 16; 1919, 15; 1920, 13; 1921, 12; 1922, 12; 1923, 11; 1924, 11; 1925, 10; 1926, 6; 1927, 4; 1928, 4; 1929, 3; 1930, 3; 1931, 3; 1932, 3; 1933, 2; 1934, 2; 1935, 1; 1936, 1; 1937, 1; 1938, 1; 1939, 1; 1940, 1 **LAST MEMBER:** Truman D. Goodrich, died July 19, 1940

The final Grand Army Post chartered by the Department of Wisconsin was at Ladysmith in Rusk County, founded August 7, 1906.

The post, numbered 280, did something quite unusual. It started its tenure with a name, John E. Tourtellotte Post 280, but in March of 1910 went to the more general name of Rusk County Post.

John E. Tourtellotte had no direct Wisconsin connection. He served on Sherman's staff and died in 1891. He had a nephew who was a prominent lawyer and landowner in western Wisconsin in the late nineteenth century.

Rusk County Post 280, as it was known for the subsequent 30 years, survived on the longevity of a couple of its members for the final half dozen years. Its last man, Truman Goodrich, attended the seventy-fifth anniversary at Gettysburg in 1938, where he was able to dance a jig.

PICKET POSTS AND THE
CENSUS OF 1895

As the "boys" grew older and the order started to feel the pinch of attrition that necessarily comes with age, the Department of Wisconsin sought ways to make the Grand Army of the Republic more accessible to veterans.

With this goal in mind, the order experimented with "picket" posts, in which men could be members of the G.A.R. even if they were living some distance from a post. Picket duty could bring back their wartime experience of being away from the main body but being every bit a part of that body.

The issue was not simple. In 1893, J. H. Whitney, the adjutant general of the department that year, told the encampment that it was fine to try to accommodate comrades, but it had to be done in a way that accommodated the greatest number of comrades.

Establishing a post is warranted when numbers are sufficient and it does no material injury to existing posts, he said, but too often there is a "tendency to leave existing Posts for insufficient reasons," and it is rare when conditions are right for new posts "except in the northern parts of the state."

The next year, Whitney's successor, D. G. Sampson, echoed his sentiments, but Sampson was happy to report that "the ice is broken" on the idea tossed around informally for a year or two, that is, "establishing picket out-posts or videttes in sparsely settled districts, too far away from established Posts for Comrades to attend their Post meetings."

"The 'Delton Pickets,' comprising 28 Comrades and commanded by Comrade J. Freer, have the honor of being the senior organization of this kind in this Department," he told the 1894 encampment.

"It is located in Sauk County, is an adjunct of Posts Nos. 49 [A. A. Matthews, LaValle] and 50 [John Gillespie, Wisconsin Dells], and organized in December last.

"From this small beginning," beamed the adjutant general, "may it not be hoped that the large numbers of Veterans who yet remain outside of our order, by reason of their great distance from any Post, may now be brought into comradeship of the order?"

Sampson urged, "Let this Department be the first in this movement, as it has in all others in which the welfare of the Veterans has been sought."

The encampment ordered a committee of three to study the picket post idea and to report at the 1895 encampment. If the comrades at that encampment were expecting great new

things to come forth from this picket post endeavor, they were to be disappointed next year by the report. The committee—headed by James E. Jones of Gillespie Post 50—did not put any effort into studying the concept, and when it was time to report to the 1895 encampment, Jones was anything but enthusiastic.

"The only experiment in that line I know of in the Department is within our Post, and while as a local arrangement it might accommodate some country Comrades, it would unnecessarily and seriously complicate the Department if it should become officially recognized. The tendency of that would be the institution of Picket Posts by disgruntled factions who could not get a charter for a new Post in the G.A.R., and the existence of organizations within the order, not constitutional or in the interest of the fundamental principles.

"Once adopted, it would obtain a dangerous and insidious influence that would weaken the existing structure and encourage dissentions and partitions in the common family. There are a few favorable points toward permitting Picket Posts, it is true, but all are of local character and could not apply generally."

Jones could see such posts in a few circumstances if they were under the strict control of the sponsoring post and subject to disbandment if the sponsoring post saw fit. It would be unwise, he concluded "for the Department to take any official cognizance of local Picket Posts except to tacitly and uncompromisingly leave the matter to the discretion and privilege of individual Posts."

Because it was generally understood that picket posts would be quite outside the normal organization of the Grand Army of the Republic, the subject thereafter was not often broached in the annual encampment and thus what happened to the idea is not well documented.

Nonetheless it is clear that Comrade Jones's admonitions, while having some effect, did not put the matter to rest.

In fact, State Commander E. B. Gray, a perennial leader in Department of Wisconsin affairs, spoke with some pride in his commander's address in 1898 about the status of picket posts.

"Pickets have been established in several localities and are becoming a feature of this Department." Although the department did not have full knowledge of where and how they were organized, they knew of something like 14 or 15 of the outposts. He listed nine posts as sponsoring posts (and interestingly did not mention the LaValle or Wisconsin Dells posts among them).

Unfortunately, the commander's report did not mention

the locations of the picket posts, except in three instances: Iron River, offspring of the post at Washburn; Spooner, the outpost of Shell Lake; and Eagle, an offshoot of Palmyra (Gray's home post). Those three plus Delton are the only recorded locations of the picket posts. The picket post at Eagle, the commander was happy to relate, had even arranged to hold Memorial Day services at Eagle, "and the 15 members of that Picket have invited the parent Post to join them in observing the day, which invitation has been accepted."

The records are sparse on picket posts thereafter. At least one, however, was added a couple years after Gray's enthusiastic report. In 1900, members of Rank and File Post 240, Milwaukee, sponsored such an adjunct at Muskego. It was begun on July 29 with former state commander Henry Fischer enrolling the 21 members. Rank and File's minutes show, in fact, that the post and its offspring got together from time to time, and as late as 1908 they held a joint Memorial Day program at Muskego.

Still picket posts, altogether, remain rather a mystery. The department did not even view their locations as important enough to have been recorded. There are no references to them in the encampment journals after 1898. The sponsoring posts, at least those that are known, are indicated on the map below. The map illustrates that the picket post idea was tried in a wide variety of places and circumstances.

(7) Bangor Post, with one picket post, location unknown.
(8) Sextonville Post, with two picket posts, locations unknown.
(9) LaVille Post and (10) Wisconsin Dells Post, shared picket post at Delton.
(11) Palmyra Post, one picket post in Eagle.
(12) Rank and File Post, Milwaukee, with one picket post at Muskego.

In his 1894 report commending establishment of the first picket post, Adjutant General D. G. Sampson also noted that veterans of the Civil War "who yet remain outside of our order" were a constant concern of the Department of Wisconsin, with fair reason. The order was declining in numbers. It was manifestly true that there were lots of veterans who benefited from the G.A.R.'s pension successes, but many remained steadfastly unaffiliated.

As it happened, the following year, the State of Wisconsin's census included information about veterans living in the state. This census data gave the order irrefutable evidence that there were plenty of veterans to recruit. The following map indicates counties where the census showed that the order was strong (the darker the shading, the greater the percentage of members among the counted veterans) and where, manifestly, it was weak.

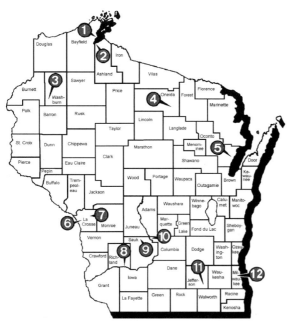

(1) Washburn Post with picket post at Iron River.
(2) Ashland Post with two picket posts, locations unknown.
(3) Shell Lake Post with picket post at Spooner.
(4) Rhinelander Post with three picket posts, locations unknown.
(5) Oconto Post with two picket posts, locations unknown.
(6) La Crosse Post with two picket posts , locations unknown.

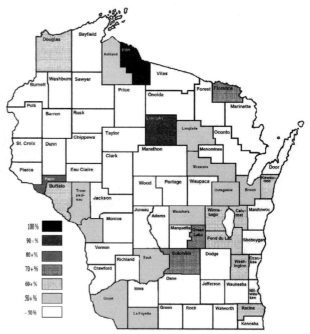

The strength of the order can be seen to run diagonally across the state, roughly along the old Fox-Wisconsin waterway route. Most of the counties on that line had memberships of 50 percent or more of eligible men. Some counties along the Mississippi River, too, were strong. Twenty-seven counties had enrolled more than half their veterans.

Milwaukee County had the weakest showing. The percentage of member veterans there was only 23.5, compared to an average of 44.3 percent statewide. Among the five counties (excluding Milwaukee) having the largest number of veterans, Winnebago had the most members, 531 or 62.6 percent, followed by Grant with 455 or 54.1 percent.

The census of 1895 provided a unique "snapshot" of the state's veterans, and by extension, of the G.A.R., disclosing its strengths and where it presumably had major influence, that year and for years to follow.

CENSUS OF 1895			
Counties	Veterans	G. A. R.	%
Adams	200	67	33.5
Ashland	92	52	56.5
Barron	343	148	43.1
Bayfield	89	33	37
Brown	484	287	59.2
Buffalo	237	143	60.3
Burnett	35	0	0
Calumet	213	132	61.9
Chippewa	354	168	47.4
Clark	401	149	37.1
Columbia	485	340	70.1
Crawford	399	97	24.3
Dane	762	356	46.7
Dodge	410	145	35.3
Door	159	71	44.6
Douglas	186	116	62.3
Dunn	393	127	32.3
Eau Claire	450	168	37.3
Fond du Lac	506	323	63.8
Florence	22	16	72.7
Forest	24	0	0
Grant	841	455	54.1
Green	428	197	46
Green Lake	216	154	71.2
Iowa	281	131	46.6
Iron	20	22	100.1
Jackson	302	140	46.3
Jefferson	381	230	60.3
Juneau	459	198	43.1
Kenosha	176	71	40.3
Kewaunee	130	88	67.6
La Crosse	441	245	56.2
Lafayette	292	170	58.2
Lincoln	75	74	98.6
Langlade	150	84	56
Manitowoc	421	179	42.5
Marathon	200	72	36

Counties	Veterans	G. A. R.	%
Marinette	150	62	41.3
Marquette	197	94	47.7
Milwaukee	3,934	926	23.5
Monroe	533	225	42.2
Oconto	227	48	21.1
Oneida[1]	57	0*	0*
Outagamie	547	305	55.7
Ozaukee	133	29	21.8
Pepin	123	100	81.3
Pierce	415	203	48.9
Polk	218	86	39.4
Portage	409	144	35.2
Price	63	9	14.2
Racine	447	280	62.6
Richmond	591	235	39.7
Rock	812	385	47.4
Sauk	697	377	54
Sawyer	38	12	31.5
Shawano	170	86	50.5
Sheboygan	524	280	53.4
St. Croix	386	158	40.9
Taylor	76	24	31.5
Trempealeau	215	127	59
Vernon	565	191	33.8
Vilas	20	0	0
Washburn	68	17	25
Washington	216	135	62.6
Walworth	534	258	48.3
Waukesha	409	194	47.4
Waupaca	802	314	39.1
Waushara	468	276	58.9
Winnebago	843	531	62.9
Wood	268	119	44.4
Totals	26,307	11,678	44.3

1. Department data seems to be in error. Rhinelander Post 232 was then active and had 26 members as late as 1904.

IRON BRIGADE ASSOCIATION

In the mid-nineteenth century, joining multiple associations and organizations, fraternal or otherwise, was a quite common phenomenon, and Civil War veterans did this as much as anyone. They were as prone to become Masons or Knights Templar or Odd Fellows as the next man. But they also had, as veterans, eligibility to organizations that did not include that "next man."

As veterans they were eligible for membership in the Grand Army of the Republic. They were also veterans with a particular history, and so they were eligible for an array of organizations in addition to the G.A.R. Many of these organizations were unit associations, mostly at the regimental level. These had a special significance to the men because they represented intimately shared experiences.

Regimental associations usually held annual meetings at which veterans were able to get together with the actual men with whom they had experienced all the privations and triumphs of wartime. These associations frequently encouraged their members to commit to writing their remembrances. The results, in some cases, were regimental histories of value today for portraying the historical record of, say, the Third Wisconsin, or some other Wisconsin unit. Some of them were heavy on anecdotal material, giving future readers some sample or flavor of soldier life in the tumultuous years of the Rebellion.

The essential element, however, was the continuation of the bonding those men had experienced in their cherished regiment or other unit.

Probably the most important of these unit associations was the one that went a step higher to the brigade level, specifically, the Iron Brigade Association.

The Iron Brigade Association had something of a special relationship with the Grand Army of the Republic. Not only was it born in that organizational surge which began with the calling of the great Soldiers and Sailors Reunion in Milwaukee in 1880 (a reunion in which the G.A.R. was the underlying force), but also, in the G.A.R.'s later years, Iron Brigade Association gatherings were concurrent with the annual encampment of the Department of Wisconsin.

Most of the unit associations were born from that 1880 reunion. The reunion was organized along regimental lines: the organizers got the ranking man of each Wisconsin regiment or battery to call upon his officers to respond to the reunion call and to urge upon their men, the enlisted men, to come to

Milwaukee that summer. And they gathered there, naturally, in their old company and regimental formations. A reunion, after all, is a gathering of people who have shared a past, and the joy of reuniting is to see the individuals with whom the past was shared. These were company and regimental pasts they were reuniting to share—much more than Army of the Cumberland or Army of the Potomac experiences, which were too vast to have the necessary intimacy.

Once these middle-aged soldiers had experienced the elation that comes with such reunions, a good many of them resolved to continue getting together from time to time, not in a grand and almost overwhelming setting such as they had seen in 1880, but just as members of the old Twenty-first Wisconsin or the Thirty-eighth Wisconsin or whatever their unit had been.

Because three of Wisconsin's regiments had been brigaded together, and moreover, were representing the West in the closely watched Eastern Army of the Potomac, the idea was hatched very early in the preparations for the 1880 reunion to bring together those three regiments, the Second, Sixth, and Seventh, along with their Iron Brigade comrades from Indiana (the Nineteenth Indiana) and Michigan (Twenty-fourth Michigan), acceding to the urging of Colonel Rufus Dawes of

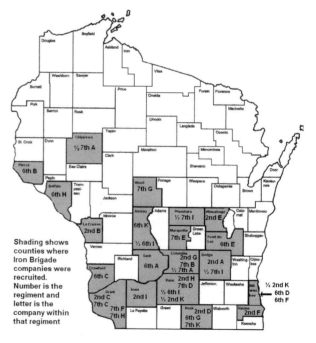

Shading shows counties where Iron Brigade companies were recruited. Number is the regiment and letter is the company within that regiment

the Sixth Wisconsin that "there should, if possible, be at least one reunion of the old brigade."

It would be arranged. General Edward S. Bragg of Fond du Lac, last commander of the Iron Brigade, issued the call for officers and men of the Second Wisconsin, Sixth Wisconsin, Seventh Wisconsin, Nineteenth Indiana, and Twenty-fourth Michigan to gather in Milwaukee at the grand reunion that summer of 1880. The Nineteenth and Twenty-Fourth were the only regiments from outside the state of Wisconsin invited to the state reunion.

The three Iron Brigade regiments from Wisconsin represented a broad cross section of the state, not only geographically, as the map shows, but also signifying the breadth of the outpouring of patriotic sentiment at the outset of the war. The Second, Sixth, and Seventh Regiments were recruited in the first months after Fort Sumter. Those three and the First, Third, Fourth, and Fifth Regiments were all in federal service by the summer of 1861.

As it happened, the Second, Sixth, and Seventh were brigaded together in what was to become the Army of the Potomac. (The Fifth Wisconsin was briefly in that brigade but was transferred out—rather than the Nineteenth Indiana—when the Seventh Wisconsin was added. This frustrated Wisconsin's ambition of furnishing an entire brigade to the East.)

And as it happened, this brigade of three Wisconsin and one Indiana regiments—the Twenty-fourth Michigan was added later—would become the hardest-fighting brigade in the Union Army, suffering more battlefield casualties than any other Union brigade. It was, quite literally, a legend in its time, famed throughout the army and recognized by its adversaries for its fearsome abilities.

The legend persisted after the war. Communities that furnished companies to the Iron Brigade took special pride in these veterans—not to the exclusion of others, of course—and the legend was powerful even as the years rolled on.

Lucius Fairchild, Edward S. Bragg and John Gibbon at Iron Brigade Association reunion about 1885. Photo provided by E. R. Curtis/ Wisconsin Veterans Museum, Madison.

Rufus Dawes, who was an Ohioan who happened to be residing for a short time in Wisconsin when the war came and thus enlisted in the Sixth Wisconsin, had returned to Ohio to resume his life, but when word came of planning for a reunion, he was eager. "There should, if possible, be at least one reunion of the old brigade. I doubt if our own or any other war affords a service record parallel with its history. For the old Iron Brigade was literally destroyed on the field of battle."

While the birth of the Iron Brigade Association was thus intimately tied to the resurgence of the Grand Army's Department of Wisconsin in 1880 and beyond, they were initially quite separate. In fact, because of some machinations that went on in that era of robust politicking, the two organizations often stayed deliberately apart. It was natural that the Iron Brigade Association would have at its head the man who had created it and made it the distinctive fighting unit that it was. In other words, the veterans chose as their president General John Gibbon.

But Gibbon was still on active duty with the army, so his leadership was very much figurative rather than actual. In reality, the association was to be run by the vice president, who would handle the details, such as setting the time and place for reuniting. That office was given to General Bragg, the Brigade's last commander. Bragg had returned to Fond du Lac after the war and resumed his career as a leading Democratic politician.

Bragg did not think of the organization as anything like an adjunct to the G.A.R. Quite the opposite, he wanted to avoid any apparent alliance, for the G.A.R. still had the aura of being a Republican vehicle. He was criticized, in fact, for setting the Iron Brigade Association meetings at the same time of year but in a different location from the G.A.R. annual encampment.

The two organizations thus went separate ways for a number of years. Obviously, with members outside Wisconsin, the association had reason to meet some years in locales away from the state. But it was not an ongoing effort to keep an arm's length between the two groups. In 1889, for instance, the Iron Brigade Association meeting was in conjunction with the G.A.R. national encampment in Milwaukee.

Gradually, as the men grew older, the focus of the Iron Brigade Association moved more and more to the common heritage it had with the Grand Army of the Republic. By the late 1920s, the Wisconsin Department began to treat the Iron Brigade Association as being much like the Women's Relief Corps, the Sons of Union Veterans, and other such groups as affiliated bodies. And the Iron Brigade Association, for its part, held annual meetings—by now they could hardly be classed as reunions—in the same location as the department encampment.

In 1927, for example, the association and G.A.R. convened in June at Fond du Lac. By then the membership numbers in both organizations were depleted. Only references to the former in the latter's journals of the encampments recorded the gathering of Iron Brigade veterans at Fond du Lac. And that might be rather obliquely. The 1929 Iron Brigade Association meeting is recorded only by the fact that the 1930 meeting in Eau Clare mentions the acceptance of minutes for the 1929 meeting in Beloit.

At that meeting, Albert Morse, Lancaster, was named president of the association. The following year, at the La Crosse encampment, Morse addressed the comrades of the G.A.R., somewhat disjointedly, "I am the commander of the Iron Brigade Association. We have no headquarters. I can see the necessity of closing this up and I would like to do it officially some way so that what we did can be placed with the G.A.R. headquarters in Madison. I have no place assigned to give notice that we have a meeting. The last of March I reported, I think, that there are 153 still living of the Iron Brigade, scattered from coast to coast. Quite a large percent are in California. I cannot see any prospect of keeping this organization together. I'd like to turn over what we have to the G.A.R."

It was ordered done. Thus in some respects, the Iron Brigade Association might be viewed as ended in 1931. Just three members were at the meeting—Morse and fellow Seventh Wisconsin survivor George Leonard, as well as W. H. Ellis of the Second Wisconsin.

Still, in 1932 at Waukesha, the G.A.R. encampment journal had a report on the Iron Brigade Association, listing officers and indicating that there were still 112 survivors of the Brigade living. Only Morse and William L. Riley, however, attended the encampment. In 1933, it was only Riley on the rolls as attending the encampment and the journal gave scant attention to the Iron Brigade Association as an affiliated group, including no record as to how many survived. At the Appleton Encampment in 1934 there was no suggestion of the Iron Brigade as an organization. Riley was the only man on the list of G.A.R. attendees who had served with an Iron Brigade regiment. The association was effectively gone.[1]

William Riley, incidentally, is considered to have been the last survivor of the Iron Brigade. He was a resident of the Soldier's Home in Milwaukee at the time of his death, at age 98, on March 23, 1939. Riley had served four years with Company I, Sixth Wisconsin. Officials of the Home said he was the last, by several years, of the 7,259 soldiers who served in the regiments of the Iron Brigade.

While it was a vibrant organization, the Iron Brigade Association had the full enthusiasm of its hundreds of members and attracted public adulation at its reunions because of its widespread fame as the best of the Union's fighting units. It got together, after 1880, almost every year for the next two decades. But as time was exacting its toll on its members, the organization may have gone into a period of inactivity. Between 1903 and 1920 there is scant evidence of the association's existence. In fact, only a reunion in Kansas City in 1916 is presently known to have been held. After 1920, the Iron Brigade Association became closely allied to the Grand Army of the Republic.

The table on the following page lists, as well as can be gleaned from records and surviving ribbons or other paraphernalia, the dates and locations of reunions. It is not definitive.

---

1. The Iron Brigade Association still exists. At the I.B.A. reunion at La Crosse in 1897, members voted to give membership to their children and grandchildren. Two of those children, William Upham and James F. Sullivan, decided in 1990 to reinstitute the organization and issued a call for a "reunion of the Iron Brigade Association" that year. Upham and Sullivan turned the organization over to the Milwaukee Civil War Round Table after opening membership to anyone interested in affiliating. The restored organization is convened at irregular intervals.

REUNIONS

Year	Dates	Location	Notes
1880	June 7-12	Milwaukee	Soldiers and Sailors Reunion
1881		No meeting	Antietam anniversary
1882	Sept. 20	Milwaukee	Army of Cumberland reunion
1883	Sept. 13-14	La Crosse	
1884	Aug. 28	Lancaster	
1885	Sept. 16-17	Madison	
1886	Aug. 31-Sept.2	Oshkosh	
1887	Sept.	Milwaukee	
1888			
1889	August	Milwaukee	G.A.R. encampment
1890	Aug. 6-7	Detroit	
1891	April 14-16	Dubuque	
1892	Sept. 16-17	Muncie	
1893			Gibbon issued no call
1894			
1895			
1896	Sept. 16-17	Baraboo	Devil's Lake
1897	Oct. 20-21	La Crosse	
1898	Aug. 30-31	Milwaukee	
1899	Sept. 14-15	Racine	
1900	Aug. 27	Chicago	President McKinley attended
1901			
1902		Washington	
1916	Aug. 28-Sept. 1	Kansas City	
1921		Milwaukee	
1922	Sept. 25	Des Moines	G.A.R. National Encampment
1923	Sept. 5	Milwaukee	G.A.R. National Encampment
1924	Jun. 17	Janesville	Department G.A.R. Encampment
1925	Jun. 16	Sheboygan	Department G.A.R. Encampment
1925	Aug.31	Grand Rapids	G.A.R. National Encampment
1926	Jun. 14-17	Racine	Department G.A.R. Encampment
1926	Sept. 21	Des Moines	G.A.R. National Encampment
1927	Jun. 14	Fond du Lac	Department G.A.R. Encampment
1928	Jun. 12-15	Madison	Department G.A.R. Encampment
1929	Jun. 25	Beloit	Department G.A.R. Encampment
1930	Jun. 6-10	Eau Claire	Department G.A.R. Encampment
1931	Jun. 16	La Crosse	Department G.A.R. Encampment
1932	Jun. 13-16	Waukesha	Department G.A.R. Encampment
1933	Jun. 12-14	Sheboygan	Department G.A.R. Encampment

DEPARTMENT OFFICERS AND MEMBERSHIP FIGURES

The Department of Wisconsin's smooth functioning over the decades can be attributed largely to the dedication of men who seldom aspired to be the leader of the order, but who were happy to serve in one of the many offices filled by appointment. A number of them served year after year as assistant adjutant general or assistant quartermaster general or judge advocate or medical officer.

Occasionally one might be a department commander during his career, but more often they simply worked diligently and were not especially heralded in those offices that gave continuity to the Department of Wisconsin.

The offices which were part of the setup of the Grand Army of the Republic from the first were: assistant adjutant general, assistant quartermaster general ("assistants" to the national adjutant and quartermaster generals), judge advocate, chaplain, medical officer, and inspector. The incoming commander made these appointments each year. Some of the offices were especially important, particularly adjutant. He maintained the records and handled the business of the department year-round. He was often a friend of the incoming commander and a resident of the commander's hometown, meaning they often could work closely together. The quartermaster as the fiscal officer was likewise important.

In the earlier years, the other offices held quite some importance. The medical officer, in fact, sometimes supplied doctoring for destitute comrades, and he later kept records detailing the decline of membership through the attrition of time. The inspector was also important in the robust years of the Grand Army. He kept the department in contact with the local posts. For years, while there were plenty of posts on the rolls, the inspector had a host of assistants helping him. Regular, frequent contact was important to the health of the order.

The military nature of the Grand Army required a judge advocate to see to it that everything was done according to the rules of the order. Members of the G.A.R. were subject to court martial for serious breaches.[1] Such proceedings, however, were rare. The judge advocate was kept more or less busy applying Grand Army rules to particular circumstances arising at the post

level, or bearing on the relationship of individuals to their posts and to the order.

The office of chaplain is self-explanatory. The chaplain was more active in the years when the membership was high. He kept liaison with chaplains of the posts.

On the pages following is a year-by-year list of officers of the Department of Wisconsin, headed by the three elected officers—commander, senior vice commander, and junior vice commander—and then followed by the appointees to the specified offices. Each year's roster of department membership gives the number of members for the year and shows where that year's figures placed them in relation to the whole picture.

There is a huge, but necessary, gap in the portrayal of those men who served the Department of Wisconsin in appointed capacities. In addition to the offices detailed above, the Department of Wisconsin, and the Grand Army itself, instituted a few others during this time. For instance, the department named a "transportation officer" for a number of years, whose duties included working with the railroads to get the most advantageous fares for Grand Army men traveling to encampments. When such travel arrangements began to lose their importance because there were few men left, the job of transportation officer was dropped. In addition, when there were numbers warranting the post, the department had a "chief mustering officer," who also had assistants to aide in carrying out his duties around the state.

Another office, which was not instituted until the twentieth century, was that of "patriotic instructor." It is impossible to overstate the importance of this office—or of the man who held the office for most of its existence, Hosea Rood. Rood's service to the Grand Army of the Republic, Department of Wisconsin, made him, hands down, the most important G.A.R. man in the second half of the department's history.

HOSEA ROOD

The office was instituted nationally (at the behest of the Department of Wisconsin), and Rood took the state post in

1906, serving as such until 1929. And he resumed the position in 1931 when his successor died. He was still patriotic instructor in 1933 when he died at the age of 88.

Though Rood was a towering figure in the department in those declining decades, there were others, both before him and during his long record of service, who were noteworthy for the years of devotion they applied to the functioning of the Department of Wisconsin.

The man who, after Rood, devoted more years to department office than anyone else was Frederick A. Bird of Madison. From 1898 to 1916, he held office, primarily assistant quartermaster general (1898–1901 and 1903–16). In 1902 he served as assistant adjutant general. And finally, in 1915 and 1916 he was

both assistant adjutant general and assistant quartermaster general. Apparently the demands of office had slowed enough so the department combined the two offices, making Bird and his successors for the next several years what would now be called "executive secretary."

Bird's years, of course, were among the most important in the department's history. It had passed its peak but was still strong.

FREDERICK BIRD

Bird was followed in both posts by W. J. McKay of Madison, who served from 1917 through 1920. He was succeeded by E. B. Heimstreet of Lake Mills. Heimstreet carried on the combined offices' executive functions from 1922 through 1925, again in 1928 and 1929, and yet again in 1931 and 1932. By this time, Department of Wisconsin membership was barely five hundred men.

The first man given consecutive terms as assistant adjutant general in recognition of the fact that the department had need

at the time for continuity in its affairs was Edmund B. Gray of Palmyra. He served four terms, 1888 to 1891, and then was given another term in 1901. Gray was the first department officer seen as being in "career" service rather than as someone to be honored by the conferring of office. Gray capped that "career" by being elected department commander in 1897.

There was one man prior to

EDMUND B. GRAY

Gray, though, who served a number of consecutive terms. T. B.

Russell of Berlin was medical officer from 1877 to 1881.

After Rood, Bird, and Gray, another servant of the department stands out, although it was later in time than these, and the demands were not so large on officeholders as they once were. This was Henry Held of Milwaukee who filled a greater number of offices than anyone else in department history.

Held was elected junior vice commander for 1928 and moved up to senior vice commander when the man in that position, Edward D. Town, died. In a few years Held was elected department commander, serving in 1933. After leaving the top spot, he was named assistant adjutant general and assistant quartermaster general in 1934 and again in 1935. A few

HENRY HELD

years later, in 1938, he was named judge advocate, and that year and the next he also served as department chaplain.

One man, Charles Henry of Eau Claire, served a record number of times as judge advocate. He was in that office from 1924 through 1927, and again from 1929 through 1935.

The most noteworthy chaplain in the department was Alexander Hood of Milwaukee, who served in 1913, and again from 1915 through 1921. The next longest service was by Alfred Eaton of Superior, 1928 through 1931.

George D. Breed of Chilton served the department as commander in 1918. Then from 1923 through 1929 he held the office of inspector. Another inspector who served five terms was George Pietzsch of Monroe. He held the office in 1905 and was returned to it in 1917 through 1920.

One other member served the department for four consecutive appointive terms. He was Henry G. Rogers of Milwaukee, who was assistant quartermaster general from 1871 through 1874. In contrast to most men appointed to department office, Rogers headed for the top. He was elected junior vice commander in 1875—this was when state membership hovered around three hundred men—went up to senior vice commander in 1876 and state commander in 1877.

These men put in a good deal of unheralded work on behalf of the Department of Wisconsin. Just consider the miles the inspector might travel during his year in office carrying out his duty of providing liaison between the department and the local posts.

There were hundreds of men who breathed life into the workaday operations of the Department of Wisconsin during its history.

OFFICERS

～1866～

Commander: James Kerr Proudfit, Madison
Assistant Adjutant General: George F. Rowell, Madison
Assistant Quartermaster General: Edward Coleman, Madison
Medical Officer: L. H. Cary

Membership: 17

～1867～

Commander: Henry Arthur Starr, Madison
Senior Vice Commander: W. A. Bugh, Berlin
Junior Vice Commander: D. A. Reed
Assistant Adjutant General: J. T. Bull, Madison
Assistant Quartermaster General: Edward Coleman, Madison

Membership: Unknown

～1868～

Commander: Jeremiah McClain Rusk, Madison
Senior Vice Commander: C. L. Dering, Portage
Junior Vice Commander: A. J. Langworthy, Milwaukee
Assistant Adjutant General: J. M. Bull, Madison
Assistant Quartermaster General: C. G. Mayers, Madison

Membership: Unknown

～1869～

Commander: Thomas Scott Allen, Madison
Senior Vice Commander: Edward Ferguson, Milwaukee
Junior Vice Commander: N. O. Adams
Assistant Adjutant General: J. M. Bull, Madison
Assistant Quartermaster General: C. G. Mayers, Madison
Chaplain: Reverend Peck, Waupaca
Medical Officer: J. B. H. Baxter
Inspector: A. J. McCoy, Beaver Dam

Membership: Unknown

～1870～

Commander: Thomas Scott Allen, Madison
Senior Vice Commander: Edward Ferguson, Milwaukee
Junior Vice Commander: A. J. McCoy, Beaver Dam
Assistant Adjutant General: J. M. Bull, Madison
Assistant Quartermaster General: C. G. Mayers, Madison
Chaplain: J. H. McNees
Medical Officer: A. J. Ward, Madison

Membership: Unknown

～1871～

Commander: Edgar Ferguson, Milwaukee
Senior Vice Commander: A. J. McCoy, Beaver Dam
Junior Vice Commander: J. M. Bull, Madison

Assistant Adjutant General: George R. Wright, Milwaukee
Assistant Quartermaster General: H. G. Rogers, Milwaukee
Judge Advocate: John F. Hanser, Alma
Chaplain: E. A. Ludwick, Milwaukee
Medical Officer: A. J. Ward, Madison
Inspector: Griff J. Thomas, Berlin

Membership: 297

～1872～

Commander: Edgar Ferguson, Milwaukee
Senior Vice Commander: A. J. McCoy, Beaver Dam
Junior Vice Commander: James Bennett, Madison

Assistant Adjutant General: George A. Hannaford, Milwaukee
Assistant Quartermaster General: H. G. Rogers, Milwaukee
Chaplain: Samuel Fallows, Milwaukee
Medical Officer: A. J. Ward, Madison

Membership: 219

～1873～

Commander: Andrew J. McCoy, Beaver Dam
Senior Vice Commander: George A. Hannaford, Milwaukee
Junior Vice Commander: A. L. Tucker, Berlin
Assistant Adjutant General: A. M. Burns
Assistant Quartermaster General: H. G. Rogers, Milwaukee
Chaplain: T. S. Johnson, Beaver Dam
Medical Officer: S. L. Fuller, Milwaukee

Membership: 156

～1874～

Commander: George A. Hannaford, Milwaukee
Senior Vice Commander: Michael Larkin, Milwaukee
Junior Vice Commander: Z. C. Hamilton, Berlin
Assistant Adjutant General: W. F. Angevine, Milwaukee
Assistant Quartermaster General: H. G. Rogers, Milwaukee
Chaplain: William Zickerick, Berlin
Medical Officer: S. L. Fuller, Milwaukee

Membership: 300

～1875～

Commander: George A. Hannaford, Milwaukee
Senior Vice Commander: John Hancock, Oshkosh
Junior Vice Commander: Henry G. Rogers, Milwaukee
Assistant Adjutant General: S. W. Rhodes, Milwaukee
Assistant Quartermaster General: Samuel Martin, Milwaukee
Judge Advocate: C. D. Cleveland, Oshkosh
Chaplain: Myron W. Reed, Milwaukee
Medical Officer: W. A. Gordon, Oshkosh

Membership: 321

1876

Commander: John Hancock, Oshkosh
Senior Vice Commander: H. G. Rogers, Milwaukee
Junior Vice Commander: Griff J. Thomas, Berlin
Assistant Adjutant General: William Wall, Oshkosh
Assistant Quartermaster General: R. J. Weisbrod, Oshkosh
Judge Advocate: T. C. Ryan
Chaplain: Myron W. Reed, Milwaukee
Medical Officer: J. H. Stearns, Milwaukee

Membership: 353

1877

Commander: Henry G. Rogers, Milwaukee
Senior Vice Commander: William Wall, Oshkosh
Junior Vice Commander: A. G. Dinsmore, Oshkosh
Assistant Adjutant General: S. F. Hammond, Milwaukee
Assistant Quartermaster General: H. E. Blanchard, Milwaukee
Judge Advocate: George B. Goodwin, Milwaukee
Chaplain: Myron W. Reed, Milwaukee
Medical Officer: T. B. Russell, Berlin

Membership: 273

1878

Commander: Samuel F. Hammond, Milwaukee
Senior Vice Commander: J. P. Luther, Berlin
Junior Vice Commander: Henry Bailey, Oshkosh
Assistant Adjutant General: Michael Larkin, Milwaukee
Assistant Quartermaster General: H. E. Blanchard, Milwaukee
Chaplain: William Zickerick, Berlin
Medical Officer: T. P. Russell, Berlin

Membership: 308

1879

Commander: Griffith J. Thomas, Berlin
Senior Vice Commander: J. M. Vanderhoff, Darien
Junior Vice Commander: George C. Staff, Milwaukee
Assistant Adjutant General: John D. Galloway, Berlin
Assistant Quartermaster General: Nathaniel Pierce, Berlin
Judge Advocate: Henry B. Harshaw, Oshkosh
Chaplain: Charles T. Susan, Berlin
Medical Officer: T. P. Russell, Berlin

Membership: 135

1880

Commander: Griffith J. Thomas, Berlin
Senior Vice Commander: C. D. Cleveland, Oshkosh
Junior Vice Commander: George C. Staff, Milwaukee
Assistant Adjutant General: John D. Galloway, Berlin
Assistant Quartermaster General: Z. C. Hamilton, Berlin
Judge Advocate: Henry B. Harshaw, Oshkosh

Chaplain: Joel Clark
Medical Officer: T. B. Russell, Berlin
Inspector: Charles Perkins, Milwaukee

Membership: 505

1881

Commander: Griffith J. Thomas, Berlin
Senior Vice Commander: George C. Staff, Milwaukee
Junior Vice Commander: J. M. Vanderhoff, Darien
Assistant Adjutant General: John D. Galloway, Berlin
Assistant Quartermaster General: Z. C. Hamilton, Berlin
Judge Advocate: H. D. Bullard, Delavan
Chaplain: Charles T. Susan, Berlin
Medical Officer: T. B. Russell, Berlin

Membership: 858

1882

Commander: Herbert Merton Enos, Waukesha
Senior Vice Commander: J. M. Vanderhoff, Darien
Junior Vice Commander: J. H. Wordsworth, Waupaca
Assistant Adjutant General: F. H. Putney (resigned)
　　　　R. L. Grove, Waukesha
Assistant Quartermaster General: Griff J. Thomas, Berlin
Judge Advocate: George W. Bird, Jefferson
Chaplain: J. H. Whitney, Reedsburg
Medical Officer: Henry Palmer

Membership: 2,486

1883

Commander: Phillip Cheek, Jr., Baraboo
Senior Vice Commander: R. J. Flint, Menominee
Junior Vice Commander: E. W. Steele, Whitewater
Assistant Adjutant General: J. H. Whitney, Baraboo
Assistant Quartermaster General: Griff J. Thomas, Berlin
Judge Advocate: George Graham, Tomah
Chaplain: A. C. Barry, Lodi
Medical Officer: J. G. Pelton, Spring Green
Inspector: T. W. Haight, Waukesha

Membership: 5,979

1884

Commander: Phillip Cheek, Jr., Baraboo
Senior Vice Commander: E. A. Calkins, Milwaukee
Junior Vice Commander: E. M. Rogers, Viroqua
Assistant Adjutant General: J. H. Whitney, Baraboo
Assistant Quartermaster General: Herman Albrecht, Baraboo
Judge Advocate: George W. Bird, Jefferson
Chaplain: W. W. Hurd, La Crosse
Medical Officer: Alex McBean, Chippewa Falls

Inspector: William S. Stanley Jr., Milwaukee

Membership: 9,165

☙1885☙
Commander: James Davidson, Sparta
Senior Vice Commander: E. M. Rogers, Viroqua
Junior Vice Commander: T. W. Haight, Waukesha
Assistant Adjutant General: Phillip Cheek, Baraboo
Assistant Quartermaster General: L. M. Stevens, Sparta
Judge Advocate: M. Griffin, Eau Claire
Chaplain: J. W. Sanderson, Milwaukee
Medical Officer: T. W. Byers, Monroe
Inspector: William S. Stanley Jr., Milwaukee

Membership: 10,242

☙1886☙
Commander: Lucius Fairchild, Madison
Senior Vice Commander: Henry P. Fisher*, Milwaukee
Junior Vice Commander: J. P. Briggs, Warsaw
Assistant Adjutant General: Phillip Cheek, Baraboo
Assistant Quartermaster General: Thomas Priestly,
    Mineral Point
Judge Advocate: Michael Griffin, Eau Claire
Chaplain: William Zickerick, Fond du Lac
Medical Officer: Charles Ottilie, La Crosse
Inspector: Charles E. Estabrook, Manitowoc

Membership: 11,939

☙1887☙
Commander: Michael Griffin, Eau Claire
Senior Vice Commander: Benjamin F. Bryant, La Crosse
Junior Vice Commander: Robert Inglis, Bayfield
Assistant Adjutant General: George A. Barry, Eau Claire
Assistant Quartermaster General: Charles W. Mott, Milwaukee
Judge Advocate: William H. Beebe, Platteville
Chaplain: William J. Fisher, Horicon
Medical Officer: F. A. Marden (died in office), Milwaukee
    A. J. Ward, Madison
Inspector: Leander Ferguson, Brandon

Membership: 10,534

☙1888☙
Commander: Augustus Gordon Weissert, Milwaukee
Senior Vice Commander: R. L. Wing, Kewaunee
Junior Vice Commander: William A. Browne, Racine
Assistant Adjutant General: Edmund B. Gray, Palmyra
Assistant Quartermaster General: W. A. Wyse, Reedsburg
Judge Advocate: C. D. Cleveland, Oshkosh

* Moved up to Commander.

Chaplain: William J. Fisher, Horicon
Medical Officer: Almon Clark, Sheboygan
Inspector: George A. Barry, Eau Claire

Membership: 11,953

☙1889☙
Commander: Augustus Gordon Weissert, Milwaukee
Senior Vice Commander: Leander Ferguson*, Brandon
Junior Vice Commander: D. G. James, Richland Center
Assistant Adjutant General: Edmund B. Gray, Milwaukee
Assistant Quartermaster General: William Mahoney, Wausau
Judge Advocate: J. V. Quarles, Racine
Chaplain: F. L. Wharton, Fond du Lac
Medical Officer: George Dale, Iola
Inspector: James Matheson, Elkhorn

Membership: 13,982

☙1890☙
Commander: Benjamin F. Bryant, La Crosse
Senior Vice Commander: John Meehan, Darlington
Junior Vice Commander: James K. P. Coon, Merrill
Assistant Adjutant General: Edmund B. Gray, Palmyra
Assistant Quartermaster General: Theodore Reil, Burlington
Judge Advocate: E. Q. Nye, Milwaukee
Chaplain: J. H. Whitney, Baraboo
Medical Officer: O. W. Carlson, Milwaukee
Inspector: Daniel Webster, Prairie du Chien

Membership: 13,785

☙1891☙
Commander: William Henry Upham, Marshfield
Senior Vice Commander: J. A. Ruby, Oshkosh
Junior Vice Commander: A. H. De Groff, Alma
Assistant Adjutant General: Edmund B. Gray, Palmyra
Assistant Quartermaster General: John Beth, Green Bay
Judge Advocate: D. Lloyd Jones, Stevens Point
Chaplain: Judson Titsworth, Milwaukee
Medical Officer: A. J. Ward, Madison
Inspector: S. W. Eager, Racine

Membership: 13,676

☙1892☙
Commander: Chauncey B. Welton, Madison
Senior Vice Commander: P. S. Fenton, Janesville
Junior Vice Commander: Sidney E. Tubbs, Superior
Assistant Adjutant General: J. H. Whitney, Baraboo
Assistant Quartermaster General: Charles A. Carter, Milwaukee
Judge Advocate: F. S. Veeder, Mauston
Chaplain: Milton Wells, Richland Center
Medical Officer: B. Bantley, Milwaukee

Membership: 13,240

≈1893≈

Commander: Eugene A. Shores, Ashland
Senior Vice Commander: William T. Symons, La Crosse
Junior Vice Commander: Theodore Riel, Burlington
Assistant Adjutant General: D. G. Sampson, Ashland
Assistant Quartermaster General: Richard Carter, Dodgeville
Judge Advocate: C. K. Erwin, Tomah
Chaplain: J. E. Webster, Black Earth
Medical Officer: H. B. Cole, Black River Falls
Inspector: Henry A. Heath, Milwaukee

Membership: 12,761

≈1894≈

Commander: Jerome Anthony Watrous, Milwaukee
Senior Vice Commander: Richard Carter, Dodgeville
Junior Vice Commander: C. H. Russell, Berlin
Assistant Adjutant General: S. H. Tallmadge, Milwaukee
Assistant Quartermaster General: Charles A. Carter,
    Milwaukee
Judge Advocate: J. B. Reynolds, Chilton
Chaplain: W. H. Thompson, Green Bay
Medical Officer: J. B. Whiting, Janesville
Inspector: W. S. Munroe, Cadott

Membership: 12,411

≈1895≈

Commander: William D. Hoard, Fort Atkinson
Senior Vice Commander: H.W. Thompson, Green Bay
Junior Vice Commander: W. J. Blinn, Antigo
Assistant Adjutant General: S. H. Tallmadge, Milwaukee
Assistant Quartermaster General: D. W. Curtis, Fort Atkinson
Judge Advocate: P. J. Clawson, Monroe
Chaplain: W. D. Gibson, Appleton
Medical Officer: J. T. Reeves, Appleton
Inspector: George B. Merrick, Madison

Membership: 11,650

≈1896≈

Commander: D. Lloyd Jones, Stevens Point
Senior Vice Commander: H. J. Smith, Racine
Junior Vice Commander: F. M. Mason, Rhinelander
Assistant Adjutant General: George B. Merrick, Madison
Assistant Quartermaster General: Edward McGlachlin,
    Stevens Point
Judge Advocate: George B. Carter, Lancaster
Chaplain: M. B. Balch, Mauston
Medical Officer: J. T. Reeves, Appleton
Inspector: Joseph Harris, Sturgeon Bay

Membership: 11,093

≈1897≈

Commander: Edmund B. Gray, Palmyra
Senior Vice Commander: E. M. Bartlett, Eau Claire
Junior Vice Commander: Henry A. Heath, Milwaukee
Assistant Adjutant General: W. H. Bennett, Mineral Point
Assistant Quartermaster General: H. D. Barnes, Elkhorn
Judge Advocate: J. S. Anderson, Manitowoc
Chaplain: W. W. Hurd, La Crosse
Medical Officer: J. T. Reeves, Appleton
Inspector: Joseph Harris, Sturgeon Bay

Membership: 10,644

≈1898≈

Commander: Charles H. Russell, Berlin
Senior Vice Commander: William C. Wilson, Appleton
Junior Vice Commander: James H. Agen, Superior
Assistant Adjutant General: Z. C. Hamilton, Berlin
Assistant Quartermaster General: Frederick A. Bird, Madison
Judge Advocate: Hollan Richardson, Chippewa Falls
Chaplain: D. O. Sanborn, De Pere
Medical Officer: J. C. Noyes, Oshkosh
Inspector: Allen H. DeGroff, Nelson

Membership: 10,563

≈1899≈

Commander: Henry Harnden, Madison
Senior Vice Commander: S. H. Talmadge*, Milwaukee
Junior Vice Commander: B. N. Robinson, Baraboo
Assistant Adjutant General: C. A. Curtis, Madison
Assistant Quartermaster General: Frederick A. Bird, Madison
Judge Advocate: W. R. Hoyt, Chippewa Falls
Chaplain: D. O. Sanborn, De Pere
Medical Officer: J. C. Noyes, Oshkosh
Inspector: R. B. Showalter, Lancaster

Membership: 10,175

≈1900≈

Commander: David J. James, Richland Center
Senior Vice Commander: James H. Agen, Superior
Junior Vice Commander: P. H. Saylor, Green Bay
Assistant Adjutant General: J. C. McFarlin, Richland Center
Assistant Quartermaster General: Frederick A. Bird, Madison
Judge Advocate: F. S. Veeder, Mauston
Chaplain: D. O. Sanborn, De Pere
Medical Officer: George Dale, Iola
Inspector: J. C. Smelker, Platteville

Membership: 9,746

* Moved up to Commander.

1901

Commander: Allen H. DeGroff, Nelson
Senior Vice Commander: William M. Root, Sheboygan
Junior Vice Commander: George W. Morton, Berlin
Assistant Adjutant General: Edmund B. Gray, Madison
Assistant Quartermaster General: Frederick A. Bird, Madison
Judge Advocate: J. S. Anderson, Manitowoc
Chaplain: George W. Case, Monroe
Medical Officer: E. E. Berry, Lancaster
Inspector: J. M. Whitley, De Pere

Membership: 9,516

1902

Commander: James H. Agen, Superior
Senior Vice Commander: Owen Clark, Stevens Point
Junior Vice Commander: C. E. Morley, Viroqua
Assistant Adjutant General: Frederick A. Bird, Madison
Assistant Quartermaster General: B. N. Robinson, Baraboo
Judge Advocate: R. E. Bradford, Chippewa Falls
Chaplain: C. T. Brumley, Hudson
Medical Officer: B. C. Brett, Green Bay
Inspector: J. M. Whitley, De Pere

Membership: 9,447

1903

Commander: Joseph P. Rundle, Milwaukee
Senior Vice Commander: E. E. Clough, Chippewa Falls
Junior Vice Commander: J. M. Whitley , De Pere
Assistant Adjutant General: Wade H. Richardson, Milwaukee
Assistant Quartermaster General: Frederick A. Bird, Madison
Judge Advocate: P. J. Clawson, Monroe
Chaplain: Stanley Lathrop, Ashland
Medical Officer: Hugo Philler, Waukesha
Inspector: H. W. Howleson, Chippewa Falls

Membership: 8,908

1904

Commander: Pliny Norcross, Janesville
Senior Vice Commander: George S. Martin, Madison
Junior Vice Commander: B. S. Williams, Wautoma
Assistant Adjutant General: E. O. Kimberley, Janesville
Assistant Quartermaster General: Frederick A. Bird, Madison
Judge Advocate: E. M. Bartlett, Eau Claire
Chaplain: L. G. Carr, Fond du Lac
Medical Officer: Hugo Philler, Milwaukee

Membership: Unknown

---

* Moved up to Commander.

1905

Commander: Frederick Alden Copeland, La Crosse
Senior Vice Commander: A. L. Tucker, Berlin
Junior Vice Commander: H. R. Allen, Merrill
Assistant Adjutant General: W. L. Osborne, La Crosse
Assistant Quartermaster General: Frederick A. Bird, Madison
Judge Advocate: M. Herrick, Hudson
Chaplain: O. A. Britton, Superior
Medical Officer: F. R. Garlock, Racine
Inspector: George O. Pietzsch, Monroe

Membership: 7,518

1906

Commander: John Wesley Ganes, Lowell
Senior Vice Commander: Jason K. Wright, Marinette
Junior Vice Commander: L. A. Brace, Eau Claire
Assistant Adjutant General: C. A. Pettibone, Juneau
Assistant Quartermaster General: Frederick A. Bird, Madison
Judge Advocate: George Burnell, Oshkosh
Chaplain: O. A. Britton, Superior
Medical Officer: F. R. Garlock, Racine
Inspector: R. B. Showalter, Lancaster

Membership: 7,801

1907

Commander: John Cobin Martin, Mineral Point
Senior Vice Commander: E. T. Ellsworth, Oshkosh
Junior Vice Commander: W. H. Getts, Grand Rapids
Assistant Adjutant General: W. W. Williams, Mineral Point
Assistant Quartermaster General: Frederick A. Bird, Madison
Judge Advocate: E. Q. Nye, Milwaukee
Chaplain: George W. Case, Portage
Medical Officer: Samuel Bell, Beloit
Inspector: I. N. Stewart, Appleton

Membership: 7,311

1908

Commander: Edward D. Coe, Whitewater
Senior Vice Commander: R. B. Lang*, Racine
Junior Vice Commander: David J. Dill, Prescott
Assistant Adjutant General: J. A. Watrous, Whitewater
Assistant Quartermaster General: Frederick A. Bird, Madison
Judge Advocate: John A. Barney, Mayville
Chaplain: W. J. McKay, Madison
Medical Officer: Samuel Bell, Beloit
Inspector: James S. Anderson, Manitowoc

Membership: 7,197

1909

Commander: William H. Grinnell, Beloit
Senior Vice Commander: L. A. Brace, Eau Claire

Junior Vice Commander: Thomas Steele, De Pere
Assistant Adjutant General: W. J. McKay, Madison
Assistant Quartermaster General: Frederick A. Bird, Madison
Judge Advocate: George S. Martin, Madison
Chaplain: S. S. Auch Moedy, Milwaukee
Medical Officer: Samuel Bell, Beloit
Inspector: W. H. Howieson, Chippewa Falls

Membership: 6,927

✑1910✑

Commander: Frank Augustin Walsh, Milwaukee
Senior Vice Commander: A. G. Purdy, Fond du Lac
Junior Vice Commander: C. E. Likes, Kenosha
Assistant Adjutant General: J. A. Watrous, Milwaukee
Assistant Quartermaster General: Frederick A. Bird, Madison
Judge Advocate: A. S. Douglas, Monroe
Chaplain: S. S. Auch Moedy, Milwaukee
Medical Officer: Samuel Bell, Beloit
Inspector: Hiram J. Smith, Racine

Membership: 6,734

✑1911✑

Commander: Hiram J. Smith, Racine
Senior Vice Commander: J. W. Hinkley, Green Bay
Junior Vice Commander: E. O. Kimberly, Janesville
Assistant Adjutant General: F. H. Lyman, Kenosha
Assistant Quartermaster General: Frederick A. Bird, Madison
Judge Advocate: F. S. Veeder, Mauston
Chaplain: W. R. Brown, Milwaukee
Medical Officer: Herbert R. Bird, Madison
Inspector: W. H. Starkweather, Milwaukee

Membership: 6,109

✑1912✑

Commander: George W. Spratt, Sheboygan Falls
Senior Vice Commander: W. S. Carr, Antigo
Junior Vice Commander: William Handeyside, De Pere
Assistant Adjutant General: J. A. Watrous, Milwaukee
Assistant Quartermaster General: Frederick A. Bird, Madison
Judge Advocate: James S. Anderson, Manitowoc
Chaplain: W. R. Brown, Milwaukee
Medical Officer: Herbert R. Bird, Madison
Inspector: J. W. Cochrane, Grand Rapids

Membership: 6,040

✑1913✑

Commander: Charles H. Henry, Eau Claire
Senior Vice Commander: A. P. Jackson, Menasha
Junior Vice Commander: George D. Breed, Chilton
Assistant Adjutant General: R. B. Rathbun, Eau Claire
Assistant Quartermaster General: Frederick A. Bird, Madison

Chaplain: Alexander J. Hood, Muscoda
Medical Officer: Herbert R. Bird, Madison

Membership: 5,703

✑1914✑

Commander: Samuel Andrew Cook, Neenah
Senior Vice Commander: Walter O. Pietzsch, Baraboo
Junior Vice Commander: H. L. Farr, Madison
Assistant Adjutant General: Frederick A. Bird, Madison
Assistant Quartermaster General: Frederick A. Bird, Madison
Judge Advocate: E. Q. Nye, Milwaukee
Chaplain: E. C. Barnard, Whitewater
Medical Officer: B. C. Brett, Green Bay
Inspector: J. M. Whitley, De Pere

Membership: 5,200

✑1915✑

Commander: William J. McKay, Madison
Senior Vice Commander: D. M. Maxson, Wausau
Junior Vice Commander: William A. Kent, Barron
Assistant Adjutant General: Frederick A. Bird, Madison
Assistant Quartermaster General: Frederick A. Bird, Madison
Judge Advocate: Benjamin F. Bryant, King
Chaplain: Alexander J. Hood, Milwaukee
Medical Officer: B. C. Brett, Green Bay
Inspector: C. J. Brazee, Merrill

Membership: 5,137

✑1916✑

Commander: Omer Levi Rosenkrans, Milwaukee
Senior Vice Commander: L. E. Reed, Ripon
Junior Vice Commander: A. N. Lent, Superior
Assistant Adjutant General: Frederick A. Bird, Madison
Assistant Quartermaster General: Frederick A. Bird, Madison
Judge Advocate: George W. Burnell, Oshkosh
Chaplain: Alexander J. Hood, Milwaukee
Medical Officer: B. C. Brett, Green Bay
Inspector: David Evans Jr., Berlin

Membership: 5,293

✑1917✑

Commander: William A. Wyse, Reedsburg
Senior Vice Commander: Charles Likes, Kenosha
Junior Vice Commander: William H. Howieson,
        Chippewa Falls
Assistant Adjutant General: W. J. McKay, Madison
Assistant Quartermaster General: W. J. McKay, Madison
Judge Advocate: Benjamin F. Bryant, King
Chaplain: Alexander J. Hood, Milwaukee
Medical Officer: Herbert R. Bird, Madison

Inspector: George O. Pietzsch, Monroe

Membership: 4,960

❧1918❧
Commander: George DeWitt Breed, Chilton
Senior Vice Commander: Robert Inglis, Bayfield
Junior Vice Commander: Almon Baldwin, Clinton
Assistant Adjutant General: W. J. McKay, Madison
Assistant Quartermaster General: W. J. McKay, Madison
Judge Advocate: Benjamin F. Bryant, King
Chaplain: Alexander J. Hood, Muscoda
Medical Officer: Herbert. R. Bird, Madison
Inspector: George O. Pietzsch, Monroe

Membership: 3,776

❧1919❧
Commander: Robert R. Campbell, Green Bay
Senior Vice Commander: M. L. Snyder, Waukesha
Junior Vice Commander: Alvin Alder, Edgerton
Assistant Adjutant General: W, J. McKay, Madison
Assistant Quartermaster General: W. J. McKay, Madison
Judge Advocate: Melancthon J. Briggs, Dodgeville
Chaplain: Alexander J. Hood, Muscoda
Medical Officer: Herbert R. Bird, Madison
Inspector: George O. Pietzsch, Monroe

Membership: 3,113

❧1920❧
Commander: Walter O. Pietzsch, Baraboo
Senior Vice Commander: M. L. Snyder, Waukesha
Junior Vice Commander: Dennis Meidam, Appleton
Assistant Adjutant General: W. J. McKay, Madison
Assistant Quartermaster General: W. J. McKay, Madison
Judge Advocate: Melancthon J. Briggs, Dodgeville
Chaplain: Alexander J. Hood, Muscoda
Medical Officer: Herbert R. Bird, Madison
Inspector: George O. Pietzsch, Monroe

Membership: 3,484

❧1921❧
Commander: Mathias L. Snyder, Waukesha
Senior Vice Commander: Hiram H. Ward, Antigo
Junior Vice Commander: Harvey F. Myers, Hillsboro
Assistant Adjutant General: Jerome A. Watrous, Milwaukee
Assistant Quartermaster General: Jerome A. Watrous, Milwaukee
Judge Advocate: George D. Breed, Chilton
Chaplain: Alexander J. Hood, Muscoda
Medical Officer: Herbert R. Bird, Madison

Inspector: Alfred S. Eaton, Superior

Membership: 2,701

❧1922❧
Commander: James F. Carle, Janesville
Senior Vice Commander: Robert K. Boyd, Eau Claire
Junior Vice Commander: Tom L. Johnson, Milwaukee
Assistant Adjutant General: E. B. Heimstreet, Lake Mills
Assistant Quartermaster General: E. B. Heimstreet, Lake Mills
Judge Advocate: M. L. Snyder, Waukesha
Chaplain: Orrin A. Britton, Superior
Medical Officer: Herbert R. Bird, Madison
Inspector: Alfred S. Eaton, Superior

Membership: 2,354

❧1923❧
Commander: Alfred S. Eaton, Superior
Senior Vice Commander: A. G. Dinsmore, Oshkosh
Junior Vice Commander: Frank N. Fox, Milwaukee
Assistant Adjutant General: E. B. Heimstreet, Lake Mills
Assistant Quartermaster General: E. B. Heimstreet, Lake Mills
Judge Advocate: Charles H. Henry, Eau Claire
Chaplain: E. O. Britton, Superior
Medical Officer: S. S. Hall, Ripon
Inspector: George D. Breed, Chilton

Membership: 2,104

❧1924❧
Commander: George W. Morton, Berlin
Senior Vice Commander: C. J. Schottle, Janesville
Junior Vice Commander: W. H. Chesbrough, Beloit
Assistant Adjutant General: E. B. Heimstreet, Lake Mills
Assistant Quartermaster General: E. B. Heimstreet, Lake Mills
Judge Advocate: Charles H. Henry, Eau Claire
Chaplain: George W. Spratt, Sheboygan Falls
Medical Officer: S. S. Hall, Ripon
Inspector: George D. Breed, Chilton

Membership: 1,907

❧1925❧
Commander: Henry Hase, Milwaukee
Senior Vice Commander: Louis Hoberg, Sheboygan
Junior Vice Commander: Robert J. Arthur, Milwaukee
Assistant Adjutant General: E. B. Heimstreet, Lake Mills
Assistant Quartermaster General: E. B. Heimstreet, Lake Mills
Judge Advocate: Charles H. Henry, Eau Claire
Chaplain: Tom L. Johnson, Milwaukee
Medical Officer: A.P. Von Matre, Darlington
Inspector: George D. Breed, Chilton

Membership: 1,669

⚜1926⚜
Commander: Henry Stannard, Greenbush
Senior Vice Commander: Joseph Cooper, Racine
Junior Vice Commander: A. P. Van Matre, Darlington
Assistant Adjutant General: George W. Morton, Berlin
Assistant Quartermaster General: George W. Morton, Berlin
Judge Advocate: Charles H. Henry, Eau Claire
Chaplain: Henry Hase, Milwaukee
Medical Officer: J. H. Hellweg, Hayward
Inspector: George D. Breed, Chilton

Membership: 1,481

⚜1927⚜
Commander: Henry C. Eaton, Fond du Lac
Senior Vice Commander: George H. Pounder, Ft. Atkinson
Junior Vice Commander: J. H. Hellweg, Hayward
Assistant Adjutant General: George W. Morton, Berlin
Assistant Quartermaster General: George W. Morton, Berlin
Judge Advocate: Charles H. Henry, Eau Claire
Chaplain: George Spratt, Sheboygan Falls
Medical Officer: Henry Eichfeld, Milwaukee
Inspector: George D. Breed, Chilton

Membership: 1,222

⚜1928⚜
Commander: George H. Pounder, Ft. Atkinson
Senior Vice Commander: Ed D. Town, Waupun
Junior Vice Commander: Henry Held *, Milwaukee
    C. L. Hooker, Superior
Assistant Adjutant General: E. B. Heimstreet, Lake Mills
Assistant Quartermaster General: E. B. Heimstreet, Lake Mills
Judge Advocate: Robert Law, Neenah
Chaplain: Alfred S. Eaton, Superior
Medical Officer: Henry Eichfeld, Milwaukee
Inspector: George D. Breed, Chilton

Membership: 1,018

⚜1929⚜
Commander: Lloyd D. Sampson, Milwaukee
Senior Vice Commander W. H. Chesbrough, Beloit
Junior Vice Commander: C. L. Hooker, Superior
Assistant Adjutant General: E. B. Heimstreet, Lake Mills
Assistant Quartermaster General: E. B. Heimstreet, Lake Mills
Judge Advocate: Charles H. Henry, Eau Claire
Chaplain: Alfred S. Eaton, Superior
Medical Officer: Henry Eichfeld, Milwaukee
Inspector: George D. Breed, Chilton

Membership: 845

⚜1930⚜
Commander: John H. Hellweg, Hayward
Senior Vice Commander: Joseph D. Vermilyea, Eau Claire
Junior Vice Commander: Milton Selby, La Crosse
Assistant Adjutant General: George L. Thomas, Milwaukee
Assistant Quartermaster General: George L. Thomas, Milwaukee
Judge Advocate: Charles H. Henry, Eau Claire
Chaplain: Alfred S. Eaton, Superior
Medical Officer: Henry Eichfeld, Milwaukee
Inspector: C. D. Hooker, Superior

Membership: Unknown

⚜1931⚜
Commander: William H. Chesbrough, Beloit
Senior Vice Commander: J. A. Bigley, La Crosse
Junior Vice Commander: C. L. Hooker, Superior
Assistant Adjutant General: E. B. Heimstreet, Lake Mills
Assistant Quartermaster General: E. B. Heimstreet, Lake Mills
Judge Advocate: Charles H. Henry, Eau Claire
Chaplain: Alfred S. Eaton, Superior
Medical Officer: Henry Eichfeld, Milwaukee

Membership: 578

⚜1932⚜
Commander: George L. Thomas, Milwaukee
Senior Vice Commander: B. F. Funk, Waukesha
Junior Vice Commander: M. W. Parker , Whitewater
Assistant Adjutant General: E. B. Heimstreet, Lake Mills
Assistant Quartermaster General: E. B. Heimstreet, Lake Mills
Judge Advocate: Charles H. Henry, Eau Claire
Chaplain: J. S. Meyers, Madison
Medical Officer: Henry Eichfeld, Madison
Inspector: William P. Bryant, Sheboygan Falls

Membership: 520

⚜1933⚜
Commander: Henry Held, Milwaukee
Senior Vice Commander: Louis Hoberg, Sheboygan
Junior Vice Commander: William Hopper, Friendship
Assistant Adjutant General: George W. Pounder, Fort Atkinson
Assistant Quartermaster General: George W. Pounder, Fort Atkinson
Judge Advocate: Charles H. Henry, Eau Claire
Chaplain: H. P. Goodman, Whitewater
Medical Officer: Henry Eichfeld, Madison
Inspector: John C. Ellison, Milwaukee

Membership: 363

⚜1934⚜
Commander: Thaddeus Sheerin, Neenah
Senior Vice Commander: John A. Bigley, La Crosse

* Moved up to Senior Vice Commander.

Junior Vice Commander: John C. Ellison, Milwaukee
Assistant Adjutant General: Henry Held, Milwaukee
Assistant Quartermaster General: Henry Held, Milwaukee
Judge Advocate: Charles H. Henry, Eau Claire
Chaplain: Henry Held, Milwaukee

Membership: 319

≈1935≈

Commander: Charles Morris Hambright, Milwaukee
Senior Vice Commander: Charles H. Davis, Oshkosh
Junior Vice Commander: Lloyd Breck, Merrill
Assistant Adjutant General: Henry Held, Milwaukee
Assistant Quartermaster General: Henry Held, Milwaukee
Judge Advocate: Charles Henry, Eau Claire
Chaplain: Harry Held, Milwaukee
Medical Officer: William P. Bryant, Milwaukee
Inspector: John Ellison, Milwaukee

Membership: 248

≈1936≈

Commander: Charles F. Moulton, Madison
Senior Vice Commander: J. H. Bettey, Lone Rock
Junior Vice Commander: C. L. Hooker, Superior
Assistant Adjutant General: George H. Pounder, Whitewater
Assistant Quartermaster General: William P. Bryant, Milwaukee
Judge Advocate: H. P. Goodman, Whitewater
Chaplain: H. P. Goodman, Whitewater
Medical Officer: W. Loomis, Fall River
Inspector: Louis Hoberg, Sheboygan

Membership: 152

≈1937≈

Commander: William P. Bryant, Milwaukee
Senior Vice Commander: John Hart, La Crosse
Junior Vice Commander: Joseph Miller, Richland Center
Assistant Adjutant General: W. H. Chesbrough, Beloit
Judge Advocate: Charles M. Hambright, Milwaukee
Chaplain: Henry Held, West Allis
Medical Officer: Samuel Askew, Madison
Inspector: Alonzo R. Kibbe, New Richmond

Membership: 129

≈1938≈

Commander: John W. Hart, La Crosse
Senior Vice Commander: Joseph Miller, Richland Center
Junior Vice Commander: Alonzo R. Kibbe, New Richmond
Assistant Adjutant General: William P. Bryant, Milwaukee
Judge Advocate: Henry Held, Milwaukee
Chaplain: Henry Held, Milwaukee

Membership: 79

≈1939≈

Commander: Alonzo R. Kibbe, New Richmond
Senior Vice Commander: Joseph Miller, Richland Center
Junior Vice Commander: Balthasar Regli, Eau Claire
Assistant Adjutant General: William P. Bryant, Milwaukee
Chaplain: Henry Alexander, Baraboo

Membership: 62

≈1940≈

Commander: Balthasar Regli, Eau Claire
Senior Vice Commander: Joseph Miller, Richland Center
Junior Vice Commander: James F. Jones, Oconomowoc
Assistant Adjutant General: William P. Bryant, Milwaukee
Chaplain: Henry Alexander, Baraboo

Membership: 27

≈1941≈

Commander: James F. Jones, Oconomowoc
Senior Vice Commander: C. L. Hooker, Superior
Junior Vice Commander: John W. Miller, Osseo
Judge Advocate: Alonzo R. Kibbe, New Richmond
Chaplain: Henry Alexander, Baraboo

Membership: 27

≈1942≈

Commander: John W. Miller, Osseo
Senior Vice Commander: C. L. Hooker, Superior
Junior Vice Commander: Lawrence Snyder, Wonewoc
Assistant Adjutant General: Henry Alexander, Baraboo
Judge Advocate: Alonzo R. Kibbe, New Richmond

Membership: 19

≈1943≈

Commander: Charles L. Hooker, Superior
Senior Vice Commander: Balthasar Regli, Eau Claire
Chaplain: Lansing A. Wilcox, Cadott

Membership: 17

≈1944≈

Commander: Lansing Alphonse Wilcox, Cadott
Senior Vice Commander: Balthasar Regli, Eau Claire
Junior Vice Commander: John W. Miller, Osseo
Assistant Adjutant General: Henry Alexander, Baraboo
Judge Advocate: C. L. Hooker, Superior
Chaplain: Lansing A. Wilcox, Cadott

Membership: 11

≈1945≈

Commander: Lansing Alphonse Wilcox, Cadott
Senior Vice Commander: Ansel Goolsbey, Chetek

Junior Vice Commander: John Hockenbrock, Chippewa Falls
Assistant Adjutant General: Henry Alexander, Baraboo
Judge Advocate: C. L. Hooker, Superior
Chaplain: Lansing A. Wilcox, Cadott

Membership: 5

≈ 1946–1951 ≈
Commander: Lansing Alphonse Wilcox, Cadott

Membership: 1

ANNUAL ENCAMPMENTS

The annual encampment was the Grand Army of the Republic's premier activity, and for most veterans, it was the state encampment rather than the national encampment that claimed their interest.

Most of the G.A.R. experience was lived in the local post meetings. And interspersed with these meetings were social events that made the veterans and their organization an important part of the life of the community.

But once a year the local activities gave way to the annual gathering of all the posts of the department in an encampment of comrades lasting for two or three days somewhere in Wisconsin. There would be business sessions at these encampments, but entertainment as well, with the centerpiece being a huge parade so that veterans would come to participate even if they were not attending the business sessions.

G.A.R. parade passing through the Court of Honor in downtown Ripon during the 1916 state encampment.

Milwaukee was host to the encampments most often—15 times, in fact. Madison was the site of 13. But these numbers are somewhat inflated since both cities were picked almost exclusively in the early years, from 1867 to 1889.

The event reached out throughout the state thereafter, from Beloit to Superior. In all, 25 cities were the site of the encampments.

Oshkosh hosted the veterans six times; Eau Claire, Fond du Lac, and Sheboygan five times each. Janesville, La Crosse, Racine, and Waukesha were encampment sites three times each in the eighty-five years of G.A.R. encampments in Wisconsin. During the peak years of the department, having the veterans come to town was an important event—not only an economic

boon, but a pageant that caught the whole community's fancy. The communities responded with enthusiasm.

That enthusiasm kept on for longer than the old veterans were able to put on a "good show." In the later years, when hosts of "Boys in Blue" could no longer muster and could no longer march, the venerable few still able to attend an encampment basked in the lionizing cheers of the watchers as they rode the appointed route of the heroes.

The business sessions at the encampments were the very heart of the department. They provided a close look at the happenings of the previous year. The outgoing commander gave his estimation of his stewardship, and each department officer gave the status of the matters under his jurisdiction. As routine as it might have seemed, the business of the department, whether choosing the officers for the next year, paying rapt attention to conditions at the G.A.R. home at King, or promoting the erection of monuments around home or at sites of conflict of distant but undimmed memory, was the adhesive that bound the men and their fraternity together.

As the years passed, the days of the encampments were taken up quite as much by the organizations auxiliary to the G.A.R. as by the veterans themselves. The sons', daughters', and wives' organizations—even an organization of secretaries of posts when the men could no longer keep up with the bookwork and hired women to keep everything orderly—participated alongside the G.A.R. men. With five or six separate groups convening, the encampment days were large celebrations that continued for more years than they would have if the encampments had continued to be attended by just the shrinking number of old soldiers themselves.

Yet, the veteran of 1861 to 1865 was the sine qua non. When the last was gone, the encampments could not be prolonged.

The eighty-fourth gathering in Sheboygan in June of 1950 was not, strictly speaking, an annual encampment. It was styled a "Memorial Encampment." It marked conventions of the W.R.C., Ladies of the G.A.R., Daughters of Union Veterans, Sons of Union Veterans, the auxiliary to the Sons, and the Secretaries Association of the G.A.R.

As for the Department of Wisconsin, Grand Army of the Republic, it was by 1950 down to one member, Lansing Wilcox, then a century plus four, who would be spending his final days from the encampment until his death the following year as a resident of King.

ANNUAL ENCAMPMENTS

Encampment	Dates	Place
First	June 19, 1867	Madison
Second	January 8, 1868	Madison
Third	January 26, 1869	Madison
Fourth	January 26, 1870	Madison
Fifth	January 11, 1871	Madison
Sixth	January 17, 1872	Milwaukee
Seventh	January 14, 1873	Berlin
Eighth	January 8, 1874	Milwaukee
Ninth	January 27, 1875	Milwaukee
Tenth	January 12, 1876	Milwaukee
Eleventh	January 25, 1877	Oshkosh
Twelfth	January 24, 1878	Milwaukee
Thirteenth	January 2, 1879	Berlin
Fourteenth	January 21, 1880	Oshkosh
Fifteenth	January 25, 1881	Milwaukee
Sixteenth	January 26, 1882	Milwaukee
Seventeenth	January 23, 1883	Portage
Eighteenth	January 23, 24, 1884	Janesville
Nineteenth	January 22, 23, 1885	Madison
Twentieth	February 3, 4, 1886	Milwaukee
Twenty-first	February 15, 16, 1887	Milwaukee
Twenty-second	February 15, 16, 1888	Milwaukee
Twenty-third	February 20, 21, 1889	Milwaukee
Twenty-fourth	March 18, 19, 1890	Milwaukee
Twenty-fifth	March 10, 11, 1891	Oshkosh
Twenty-sixth	March 9, 10, 1892	Madison
Twenty-seventh	March 8, 9, 1893	La Crosse
Twenty-eighth	April 25, 26, 1894	Janesville
Twenty-ninth	May 22, 23, 1895	Green Bay
Thirtieth	May 20, 21, 1896	Racine
Thirty-first	May 19, 20, 1897	Eau Claire
Thirty-second	May 25, 26, 1898	Appleton
Thirty-third	May 17, 18, 1899	Milwaukee
Thirty-fourth	June 20, 21, 1900	Superior
Thirty-fifth	June 19, 20, 1901	Sheboygan
Thirty-sixth	Jun 11, 12, 1902	Stevens Point
Thirty-seventh	June 9,10, 1903	Chippewa Falls
Thirty-eighth	June 15, 16, 1904	Madison
Thirty-ninth	June 13, 14, 1905	La Crosse
Fortieth	June 12, 13, 1906	Marinette
Forty-first	June 3-6, 1907	Oshkosh
Forty-second	June 16, 17, 1908	Racine
Forty-third	June 15, 16, 1909	Eau Claire

Encampment	Dates	Place
Forty-fourth	June 6-8, 1910	Fond du Lac
Forty-fifth	June 8, 9 1911	Green Bay
Forty-sixth	June 11, 12, 1912	Antigo
Forty-seventh	June 10, 11, 1913	Neenah/Menasha
Forty-eighth	June 10, 11, 1914	Madison
Forty-ninth	June 14-16, 1915	Wausau
Fiftieth	June 15, 16, 1916	Ripon
Fifty-first	June 20, 21, 1917	Kenosha
Fifty-second	June 18, 19, 1918	Ashland
Fifty-third	June 16-18, 1919	Waukesha
Fifty-fourth	June 14-16, 1920	Baraboo
Fifty-fifth	June 8, 9, 1921	Antigo
Fifty-sixth	June 12-14, 1922	Eau Claire
Fifty-seventh	June 11-14, 1923	Oshkosh
Fifty-eighth	June 16-19, 1924	Janesville
Fifty-ninth	June 15-18, 1925	Sheboygan
Sixtieth	June 14-16, 1926	Racine
Sixty-first	June 15-17, 1927	Fond du Lac
Sixty-second	June 12-14, 1928	Madison
Sixty-third	June 24-27, 1929	Beloit
Sixty-fourth	June 9-12, 1930	Eau Claire
Sixty-fifth	June 15-17, 1931	La Crosse
Sixty-sixth	June 13-16, 1932	Waukesha
Sixty-seventh	June 12-14, 1933	Sheboygan
Sixty-eighth	June 11-13, 1934	Appleton
Sixty-ninth	June 9-12, 1935	Oshkosh
Seventieth	June 14-17 1936	Madison
Seventy-first	June 20-23, 1937	Sheboygan
Seventy-second	June 26-29, 1938	Milwaukee
Seventy-third	June 17-21, 1939	Eau Claire
Seventy-fourth	June 9-12, 1940	Baraboo
Seventy-fifth	June 8-11, 1941	Fond du Lac
Seventy-sixth	June 14-17, 1942	Waukesha
Seventy-seventh	June 13-16, 1943	Superior
Seventy-eighth	June 11-14, 1944	Sheboygan
Seventy-ninth	June 10, 11, 1945	Fond du Lac
Eightieth	June 9-12, 1946	Kenosha
Eighty-first	June 1-4, 1947	Madison
Eighty-second	June 6-9, 1948	Fond du Lac
Eighty-third	June 12-15, 1949	Milwaukee
Eighty-fourth	June 11-14, 1950	Sheboygan
Eighty-fifth	June 17-20, 1951	Kenosha

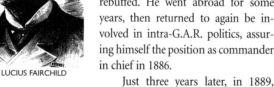

NATIONAL OFFICERS
FROM WISCONSIN

Wisconsin had three men selected to head the Grand Army of the Republic: Lucius Fairchild, Augustus G. Weissert, and Frank A. Walsh.

All three, in addition to being commander in chief, previously served the national body as senior vice commander in chief. There was no tradition of promotion from that office to the top office, so their elections to the separate offices were indications of their stature within the organization; advancement was not automatic nor even an indication of future advancement. Most senior vice commanders, in fact, did not become commander.

Fairchild was the first Wisconsin member to achieve national office, and this was at a time, in 1869 and again in 1870, when the G.A.R. was known for its involvement in politics, with no one more clearly involved than Fairchild.

Nonetheless, when the one-armed Wisconsin veteran coveted returning to the top spot in 1872, he was rebuffed. He went abroad for some years, then returned to again be involved in intra-G.A.R. politics, assuring himself the position as commander in chief in 1886.

LUCIUS FAIRCHILD

Just three years later, in 1889, Wisconsin hosted the national encampment in Milwaukee, and by then there was a tradition that a man from the host department should become senior vice commander.

This was Augustus Weissert, who had been showing the Wisconsin Department some dynamic leadership and gave up the state commander's position (in his second term at that) to move up to the national leadership ranks.

Weissert's talent went rewarded. In 1892 he became the twenty-first man chosen as national commander, and he was only the fourth of those (Fairchild was one of the other three) to have been senior vice commander.

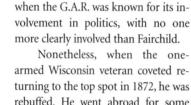
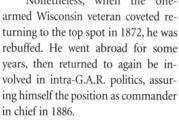
AUGUSTUS G. WEISSERT

Where the stewardship of Fairchild as commander had been a tempestuous one in some respects, with the order striving for a position of power, the term of Weissert came during the years when the order was at the very peak of that power. The pension issue, which dominated the 1880s, had been essentially resolved. Weissert's term came during the G.A.R.'s golden age.

There followed a relatively long period in which Wisconsin was not represented in the top leadership of the G.A.R. The order, indeed, was now on its long decline as membership headed downward through nature's attrition and the decline of fraternal organizations generally. From the heights of nearly 400,000 members in the years Weissert was a national officer, the total had fallen to 76,000 when next a Wisconsin man was chosen to one of the top three offices.

Again it was to the post of senior vice commander. In 1923, Frank A. Walsh, a Milwaukeean like Weissert, was elected at the national encampment at Milwaukee.

Walsh was subsequently elected commander in chief, in 1926. It was still the case that few senior vice commanders had been named to the top post. It was a tribute to Walsh's talent, just as the elevations of Weissert and Fairchild had been.

FRANK A. WALSH

There were two others who held the senior vice commander office in the years that followed, and as usual, they were elected at national encampments held in Wisconsin. In 1937, in Madison, Henry Held was picked for the second spot.

HENRY HELD

Held, like Weissert and Walsh, was from Milwaukee. He was commander of the Department of Wisconsin in 1933.

By now the Department of Wisconsin consisted of just 129 veterans, and the national encampment in 1937 counted just 3,325 members.

Still there would be one more national encampment in Wisconsin and one more senior vice commander from the state. The year was 1943, the place was Milwaukee, and the person was Lansing A. Wilcox of Cadott, chosen for the honor at the encampment. He was one of but 17 members remaining in

LANSING WILCOX

EDWARD FERGUSON

GEORGE POUNDER

the department, and he was the most active. He outlived the other 16 and was the final Department of Wisconsin commander. Wilcox, incidentally, had another distinction. Earlier in the twentieth century, he lived for a number of years in Washington State, and, in 1937, he was the commander of the Department of Washington and Alaska.

Wisconsin's second man to hold one of the three top national offices after Lucius Fairchild was Edward Ferguson of Milwaukee, who was junior vice commander in chief in 1873. It was Ferguson who, as department commander, had cleaned out the Wisconsin roster of languishing and defunct posts in 1871.

Junior vice commanders did occasionally move up to be senior vice commanders when the latter spot became vacant, but few of them, until the ranks were very thin, were subsequently elected as commanders.

One more man from Wisconsin served as junior vice commander. He was George H. Pounder, elected in 1934. Pounder was from Fort Atkinson. He served as department commander in 1928 and later served as assistant adjutant general and as chairman of various committees.

Several other men served the national organization in lesser posts, some appointed by the Wisconsin com-

manders. Historically, the headquarters of the G.A.R. was moved to whatever state the commander was in, and the commander often wanted one of his own men to serve in his top staff person, the adjutant general. Fairchild, in 1886 named Edmund G. Gray of Madison to that position, and six years later Commander-in-Chief Weissert likewise chose Gray as adjutant general. Walsh had three adjutants: Charles H. Henry of Eau Claire, who resigned; Charles Kayser of Milwaukee, who died in office; and finally George W. Morton of Berlin.

Wisconsin also provided one judge advocate general, Benjamin F. Bryant of King, in 1912; a chaplain-in-chief, Reverend Myron W. Reed of Milwaukee, in 1875; two surgeon generals, Dr. J. B. Whiting of Janesville, in 1895, and Dr. Hugo Philler of Waukesha, in 1905. Hosea W. Rood of Madison was national patriotic instructor in 1919.

In all, Wisconsin men were in the top three national offices 11 times. Given that there were 274 such positions during the history of the Grand Army of the Republic, Wisconsin held approximately 4 percent of the top offices. Given the state's record as one of the earliest departments, that may seem to be a somewhat slim slice of the pie.

But any analysis of the departments represented by the holders of those three major offices suggests that size of state population—and interestingly, one may discern here the population shifts in the nation in the years after the Civil War—had the most to do with it, although it might be argued that the office of junior vice commander was accorded to representatives of some of the lesser departments, for example, in the South, as an opportunity to broaden the representation. Only the border state Missouri provided a national commander—twice.

The following table lists the departments by rank according to permanent organization, and the number of officers—commander (Cr.), senior vice commander (Sr.), and junior vice commander (Jr.)—each department contributed to the national leadership:

DEPARTMENTS BY RANK

Department	Cr.	Sr.	Jr.	Total
1. Illinois	13	2	7	22
2. Wisconsin	3	6	2	11
3. Pennsylvania	11	5		16
4. Ohio	7	8	4	19
5. New York	10	8	7	25
6. Connecticut	1		8	9
7. Massachusetts	8	7	3	18
8. New Jersey	1	1	3	5
9. Maine	2	3	1	6
10. California & Nevada	5	11	8	24

Department	Cr.	Sr.	Jr.	Total
11. Rhode Island	2	1	1	4
12. New Hampshire			2	2
13. Vermont	1			1
14. Potomac	1	3	3	7
15. Virginia			2	2
16. Maryland	2	2	2	6
17. Nebraska	3	1	2	6
18. Michigan	2	4	3	9
19. Iowa	3	4		7
20. Indiana	4	5	1	10
21. Colorado & Wyoming	1	2		3

Department	Cr.	Sr.	Jr.	Total
22. Kansas	1	2	2	5
23. Delaware		1	2	3
24. Minnesota	3	4	4	11
25. Missouri	2	2	1	5
26. Oregon	2	3	1	6
27. Kentucky		1	3	4
28. West Virginia				0
29. South Dakota			1	1
30. Washington & Alaska	1		4	5
31. Arkansas			1	1
32. New Mexico				0
33. Utah				0
34. Tennessee		1	2	3

Department	Cr.	Sr.	Jr.	Total
35. Louisiana & Mississippi			2	2
36. Florida			1	1
37. Montana			1	1
38. Texas		2	2	4
39. Idaho			1	1
40. Arizona				0
41. Georgia & South Carolina			3	3
42. Alabama		1	2	3
43. North Dakota			1	1
44. Oklahoma	1	1		2
45. Indian Territory				0

The three tables on the following pages give the complete chronological list of national Grand Army of the Republic officers, with their departments and the date of their death. The date of answering the final roll call was important to the men in the G.A.R.

In a few instances, instead of a date of death, the table lists that he "later withdrew from order," which indicates that the man was stripped of his G.A.R. "honors." No reasons are given for such actions. But providing the date of death was obviously considered one of the "honors" due the men who had faithfully served the Grand Army of the Republic in such responsible capacities.

NATIONAL COMMANDERS

Date	Commander-in-Chief	Department	Died
1866	Benjamin Franklin Stephenson	(Provisional)	August 30, 1871
1866	Stephen Augustus Hurlbut	Illinois	March 27, 1882
1867	Stephen Augustus Hurlbut	Illinois	
1868	John Alexander Logan	Illinois	December 26, 1886
1869	John Alexander Logan	Illinois	
1870	John Alexander Logan	Illinois	
1871	Ambrose Everett Burnside	Rhode Island	September 13, 1881
1872	Ambrose Everett Burnside	Rhode Island	
1873	Charles Devens	Massachusetts	January 7, 1882
1874	Charles Devens	Massachusetts	
1875	John Frederick Hartranft	Pennsylvania	October 17, 1889
1876	John Frederick Hartranft	Pennsylvania	
1877	John Cleveland Robinson	New York	February 18, 1897
1878	John Cleveland Robinson	New York	
1879	William Earnshaw	Ohio	July 17, 1885
1880	Louis Wagner	Pennsylvania	January 15, 1914
1881	George Sargent Merrill	Massachusetts	February 17, 1900
1882	Paul Vandervoot	Maine	July 29, 1902
1883	Robert Burns Beath	Pennsylvania	November 25, 1924
1884	John Stephan Kountz	Ohio	June 14, 1909

Date	Commander-in-Chief	Department	Died
1885	Samuel Swinfin Burdett	District of Columbia	September 24, 1914
1886	**Lucius Fairchild**	**Wisconsin**	**May 22, 1896**
1887	John Patterson Rea	Minnesota	May 28, 1900
1888	William Wagner	Missouri	October 4, 1916
1889	Russell Alexander Alger	Michigan	January 24, 1907
1890	Wheelock Graves Veazey	Vermont	March 22, 1898
1891	John Palmer	New York	April 15, 1905
1892	**Augustus Gordon Weissert**	**Wisconsin**	**April 24, 1923**
1893	John Gregory Bishop Adams	Massachusetts	October 19, 1900
1894	Thomas George Lawlor	Illinois	February 3, 1908
1895	Ivan N. Walker	Indiana	September 22, 1905
1896	Thaddeus Stevens Clarkson	Nebraska	January 16, 1915
1897	John Peter Shindel Gobin	Pennsylvania	May 10, 1910
1898	James Andrew Sexton*	Illinois	February 5, 1899
1899	William Christie Johnson	Ohio	April 27, 1917
1899	Albert Duane Shaw	New York	February 10, 1901
1900	Leo Rassieur	Missouri	June 1, 1929
1901	Eli Torrance	Minnesota	February 18, 1932
1902	Thomas J. Stewart	Pennsylvania	September 11, 1917
1903	John Charles Black	Illinois	August 17, 1915
1904	Wilmon Whilldin Blackmar*	Massachusetts	July 16, 1905
1905	John Rigney King	Maryland	March 3, 1934
1905	James Tanner	New York	October 2, 1927
1906	Robert Burns Brown	Oklahoma	July 30, 1916
1907	Charles Germman Burton	Maryland	February 25, 1926
1908	Henry Martin Nevius	New Jersey	January 28, 1911
1909	Samuel Rogers VanSant	Minnesota	October 3, 1936
1910	John Edward Gilman	Massachusetts	February 20, 1921
1911	Harvey Marion Trimble	Illinois	January 10, 1918
1912	Alfred Bishop Beers	Connecticut	March 31, 1920
1913	Washington Gardner	Michigan	March 31, 1928
1914	David James Palmer	Iowa	November 5, 1928
1915	Elias Riggs Monfort	Ohio	July 29, 1920
1916	William James Patterson	Pennsylvania	November 6, 1926
1917	Orlando Allen Somers	Indiana	July 9, 1921
1918	Clarendon Edwin Adams	Nebraska	February 23, 1924
1919	James David Bell*	New York	November 1, 1919
1919	Daniel Munson Hall	Ohio	October 19, 1925
1920	William Alexander Ketcham	Indiana	December 27, 1921
1921	Lewis Stephen Pilcher	New York	December 24, 1934
1922	James William Willett	Iowa	May 13, 1940
1923	Gaylord Miller Saltzgaber	Ohio	August 25, 1930

* Died in office.

Date	Commander-in-Chief	Department	Died
1924	Louis F. Arensberg	Pennsylvania	September 20, 1934
1925	John Baptist Inman	Illinois	December 15, 1929
1926	**Frank Augustin Walsh**	**Wisconsin**	**March 5, 1932**
1927	Elbridge Lafayette Hawk	California & Nevada	August 13, 1930
1928	John Reese	Nebraska	July 5, 1935
1929	Edwin James Foster	Massachusetts	September 11, 1939
1930	James Esom Jewel	Colorado & Wyoming	November 7, 1939
1931	Samuel P. Town	Pennsylvania	July 9, 1937
1932	William P. Wright,*	Illinois	June 15, 1933
1933	Russell C. Martin	California & Nevada	December 29, 1945
1933	Russell C. Martin	California & Nevada	
1934	Alfred Edwin Stacy	New York	March 9, 1940
1935	Oley Nelson	Iowa	April 15, 1938
1936	Carl Henry William Ruhe	Pennsylvania	May 20, 1941
1937	Overton H. Mennet	California & Nevada	January 25, 1941
1938	Robert McKee Rownd	New York	May 17, 1949
1939	John E. Andrew*	Illinois	June 30, 1940
1939	Alexander T. Anderson	Pennsylvania	September 15, 1944
1940	William W. Nixon	Kansas	March 17, 1944
1941	George Alvin Gay	Massachusetts	December 15, 1944
1942	John Simon Dumser	California & Nevada	December 9, 1949
1943	George Henry Jones	Maine	August 2, 1946
1944	Isaac W. Sharp	Indiana	November 10, 1946
1945	Hiram Randall Gale	Washington & Alaska	March 15, 1951
1946	John Henry Grate	Ohio	June 7, 1949
1947	Robert McKee Rownd	New York	May 17, 1949
1948	Theodore Augustus Penland	Oregon	September 13, 1950
1949	Theodore Augustus Penland	Oregon	

* Died in office.

NATIONAL SENIOR VICE COMMANDERS

Date	Senior Vice Commanders	Department	Died
1866	James Bedell McKean	New York	January 6, 1879
1867	James Bedell McKean	New York	
1868	Joshua Thomas Owen	Pennsylvania	November 7, 1887
1869	Lucius Fairchild	Wisconsin	May 23, 1896
1870	Lucius Fairchild	Wisconsin	
1871	Louis Wagner	Pennsylvania	January 15, 1914
1872	Louis Wagner	Pennsylvania	
1873			
1874	Edward Jardine	New York	March 13, 1896
1875	Joseph Smith Reynolds	California & Nevada	September 18, 1911
1876	Joseph Smith Reynolds	California & Nevada	
1877	Elisha Hunt Rhodes	Rhode Island	January 14, 1917
1878	Paul Van Dervoort	Nebraska	July 29, 1902
1879	John Palmer	New York	April 15, 1905
1880	Edgar Denman Swain	Illinois	April 28, 1904
1881	Charles L. Young	Ohio	September, 1913
1882	William Edward Wyatt Ross	Maryland	November 14, 1907
1883	William Warner	Missouri	October 4, 1916
1884	John Patterson Rea	Minnesota	May 28, 1900
1885	Seldon Connor	Maine	July 9, 1917
1886	Samuel Woolsey Backus	California & Nevada	April 10, 1930
1887	Nelson Cole	Missouri	July 31, 1899
1888	Moses Hoge Neil	Ohio	December 29, 1929
1889	**Augustus Gordon Weissert**	**Wisconsin**	**April 24, 1923**
1890	Richard F. Tobin*	Massachusetts	November 22, 1890
1891	George H. Innis	Massachusetts	January 19, 1907
1891	Henry W. Duffield	Michigan	July 13, 1912
1892	Richard Henry Warfield	California & Nevada	July 19, 1906
1893	Ivan N. Walker	Indiana	September 22, 1905
1894	Albert Pressly Burchfield	Pennsylvania	January 8, 1910
1895	Edward Henry Hobson	Kentucky	September 13, 1901
1896	John H. Mullen	Minnesota	April 3, 1907
1897	Alfred Lyth	New York	December 15, 1924
1898	William Christie Johnson	Ohio	April 27, 1917
1899	Daniel Ross	Delaware	March 26, 1916
1899	Irvin Robbins	Indiana	February 9, 1911
1900	Edwin C. Milliken	Maine	October 21, 1921
1901	John McElroy	Potomac	October 12, 1929
1902	William Miles Olin	Massachusetts	April 18, 1911
1903	Charles Mason Kinne	California & Nevada	December 25, 1913
1904	John Rigney King	Maryland	March 3, 1934

* Died in office.

315

Date	Senior Vice Commanders	Department	Died
1905	George W. Patten	Tennessee	September 19, 1906
1905	George Washington Cook	Colorado & Wyoming	December 17, 1916
1906	William A. Armstrong	Indiana	September 28, 1914
1907	Lewis E. Griffith	New York	October 6, 1912
1908	J. Kent Hamilton	Ohio	December 29, 1918
1909	William M. Bostaph	California & Nevada	April 8, 1935
1910	Charles Burrows	New Jersey	March 17, 1935
1911	Nicholas W. Day	New York	March 6, 1916
1912	Henry Z. Osborne	California & Nevada	March, 1923
1913	Thomas Howard Soward	Oklahoma	August 12, 1918
1914	Joseph Bascom Gristwold*	Michigan	March 9, 1915
1915	William F. Conner	Texas	March 1, 1919
1915	George H. Slaybaugh	Potomac	February 9, 1929
1916	William Haskell Wormstead	Massachusetts	August 16, 1938
1917	John Lincoln Clem	Potomac	May 13, 1937
1918	John G. Chambers	Oregon	later withdrew from order
1919	Charles B. Wilson	California & Nevada	December 1, 1928
1920	George A. Hosley	Massachusetts	May 13, 1930
1921	Robert W. McBride	Indiana	May 15, 1926
1922	Charles S. Brodbent	Texas	April 23, 1931
1923	**Frank Augustin Walsh**	**Wisconsin**	**March 5, 1932**
1924	Wilfred Augustus Wetherbee	Massachusetts	November 13, 1930
1925	Oscar A. Janes	Michigan	April 26, 1933
1926	Alexander G. Beatty	Iowa	November 17, 1928
1927	Calvin A. Brainard	New York	January 12, 1936
1928	James Esom Jewell	Colorado & Wyoming	November 8, 1939
1929	Charles E. Nason	Maine	September 15, 1932
1930	Jacob Secrest	Ohio	November 26, 1935
1931	Oley Nelson	Iowa	April 15, 1938
1932	Russell C. Martin	California & Nevada	December 29, 1945
1933	Charles E. Jones	Alabama	December 26, 1933
1933	Thomas Henry Peacock*	Minnesota	January 23, 1934
1934	Edwin Hale Lincoln	Massachusetts	October 15, 1938
1934	Harding L. Merrill	Kansas	June 22, 1937
1935	Albert C. Estabrook	Michigan	February 12, 1941
1936	Henry F. Russell	Ohio	December 3, 1937
1937	**Henry Held**	**Wisconsin**	**August 6, 1939**
1938	Frank Louis Quade	Iowa	May 9, 1945
1939	Alexander T. Anderson	Pennsylvania	September 15, 1944
1940	William W. Nixon	Kansas	March 17, 1944
1940	Thomas Ambrose	Illinois	November 16, 1949
1941	Thomas Ridenour	Ohio	February 7, 1946
1942	Isaac W. Sharp	Indiana	November 10, 1946

* Died in office.

Date	Senior Vice Commanders	Department	Died
1943	**Lansing Alphonse Wilcox**	**Wisconsin**	**September 23, 1951**
1944	John M. Gudgel	Iowa	March 22, 1947
1945	John Henry Grate	Ohio	June 7, 1949
1946	Theadore Augustus Penland	Oregon	September 13, 1950
1947	Theadore Augustus Penland	Oregon	
1948	Charles L. Chappel	California & Nevada	September 19, 1949
1949	Charles L. Chappel	California & Nevada	
1949	Albert Woolson	Minnesota	August 2, 1956

NATIONAL JUNIOR VICE COMMANDERS

Date	Junior Vice Commanders	Department	Died
1866	Robert G. Foster	Indiana	March 3, 1903
1867	Joseph R. Hawley	Connecticut	March 18, 1905
1868	Joseph R. Hawley	Connecticut	
1869	Joseph R. Hawley	Connecticut	
1870	James Coey	California & Nevada	July 14, 1918
1871	J. Warren Keifer	Ohio	April 22, 1933
1872	J. Warren Keifer	Ohio	
1873	**Edward Ferguson**	**Wisconsin**	**September 18, 1901**
1874	Guy T. Gould	Illinois	March 4, 1919
1875	Charles J. Buckbee	Connecticut	November 5, 1896
1876	Charles J. Buckbee	Connecticut	
1877	William Earnshaw	Ohio	July 17, 1885
1878	Herbert E. Hill	Massachusetts	April 8, 1892
1879	Harrison Dingman	Potomac	September 26, 1925
1880	George Bowers	New Hampshire	February 14, 1884
1881	C. V. R. Pond	Michigan	June 9, 1912
1882	I. S. Bangs	Maine	May 30, 1903
1883	Walter H. Holmes	California & Nevada	March 26, 1889
1884	Ira E. Hicks	Connecticut	March 23, 1919
1885	John R. Lewis	Georgia	February 8, 1900
1886	Edgar Allen	Virginia	October 28, 1904
1887	John C. Linehan	New Hampshire	September 19, 1905
1888	Joseph Hadfield	New York	later withdrew from order
1889	John F. Lovett	New Jersey	March 27, 1926
1890	George B. Creamer	Maryland	September 16, 1896

* Died in office.

Date	Junior Vice Commanders	Department	Died
1891	T. S. Clarkson	Nebraska	January 16, 1915
1892	Peter B. Ayers	Delaware	January 19, 1904
1893	J. C. Bigger	Texas	September 24, 1900
1894	Charles H. Shute	Louisiana	November 26, 1907
1895	S. G. Cosgrove	Washington & Alaska	March 28, 1909
1896	Charles W. Buckley	Alabama	December 4, 1906
1897	Francis B. Allen	Connecticut	July 26, 1921
1898	Daniel Ross	Delaware	March 26, 1916
1899	Michael Minton	Kentucky	October 9, 1911
1900	Frank Seaman	Tennessee	November 20, 1910
1901	James O'Donnell	Illinois	February 15, 1910
1902	James P. Averill	Georgia	October 12, 1904
1903	Harry C. Kessler	Montana	September 10, 1907
1904	George N. Patton	Tennessee	September 19,1906
1905	Ephriam B. Stillings	Massachusetts	December 30, 1917
1905	Silas H. Towler	Minnesota	April 23, 1930
1906	E. B. Fenton	Michigan	November 19, 1927
1907	William M. Scott	Georgia	August 29, 1928
1908	Charles C. Royce	Potomac	February 11, 1923
1909	Alfred B. Beers	Connecticut	March 31, 1920
1910	William James	Florida	December 11, 1923
1911	William A. Ogden	Kansas	October 31, 1914
1912	Americus Whedon	Kentucky	October 18, 1921
1913	A. S. Fowler	Arkansas	October 18, 1922
1914	W. F. Conner	Texas	March 1, 1919
1915	Oscar A. James	Michigan	April 26, 1933
1915	La Vant Dodge	Kentucky	March 6, 1925
1916	E. K. Russ	Louisiana	later withdrew from order
1917	John M. Vernon	Illinois	November 20, 1921
1918	Charles H. Haber	Virginia	November 30, 1927
1919	Isador Isaacs	New York	February 18, 1924
1920	J. E. Gandy	Washington & Alaska	June 5, 1934
1921	Henry A. Johnson	Potomac	December 5, 1935
1922	C. V. Gardner	South Dakota	December 15, 1930
1923	George T. Leech	Maryland	August 4, 1940
1924	John Reese	Nebraska	July 5, 1935
1925	William O. Allen	New Jersey	September 22, 1931
1926	Charles H. Haskins	California & Nevada	October 16, 1933
1927	Samuel E. Mahan	Minnesota	September 20, 1940
1928	Henry J. Kearney	New York	April 30, 1933
1929	James W. Shields	Idaho	December 17, 1933
1930	Charles H. Lewis	Rhode Island	May, 1938
1931	Russell C. Martin	California & Nevada	December 29, 1945

Date	Junior Vice Commanders	Department	Died
1932	Charles E. Jones	Alabama	December 26, 1933
1933	Arthur Dawson	Illinois	April 7, 1940
1933	Edwin H. Lincoln	Massachusetts	October 15, 1938
1934	John E. Andrew	Illinois	June 30, 1940
1934	**George H. Pounder**	**Wisconsin**	**December 10, 1936**
1935	Overton H. Mennett	California & Nevada	January 25, 1941
1936	Thomas Ambrose	Illinois	November 16, 1949
1937	Robert Rownd	New York	May 17, 1949
1938	John W. Carroll	North Dakota	March 3, 1942
1939	William W. Nixon	Kansas	March 17, 1944
1940	William H. McCoy	New Jersey	November 16, 1941
1940	Rustan O. Reed	Washington & Alaska	February 23, 1942
1941	John S. Dumser	California & Nevada	December 9, 1949
1942	Charles H. Perry	Minnesota	
1943	Hiram H. Shumate	Illinois	
1944	Hiram R. Gale	Washington & Alaska	
1945	Theodore A. Penland	Oregon	September 13, 1950
1946	John R. Bennett	Ohio	
1947	William H. Osborne	Missouri	
1947	Robert Rownd	New York	
1948	Robert Rownd	New York	
1948	Charles L. Chappel	California & Nevada	September 19, 1949
1949	Charles L. Chappel	California & Nevada	
1949	Albert Woolson	Minnesota	August 2, 1956
1949	James A. Hard	New York	March 12, 1952

NATIONAL ENCAMPMENTS IN WISCONSIN

The Department of Wisconsin was host to national encampments four times, the first in 1889 during the heady days of the Grand Army's booming successes, and the last in 1943, when only a handful of old comrades were able to attend. Both were held in Milwaukee.

Between those two extremes there were two others. One, in 1923, was also in Milwaukee, and the other, in 1937, was held in Madison when the national G.A.R. wrestled with one of the last major issues in its long life: whether to join with Confederates the next year at a joint reunion at Gettysburg.

The event in 1889 was a triumph for the Department of Wisconsin as the order was approaching the apex of its membership, and the men were in the prime of their lives. It was a celebration of huge proportions, attended by both U. S. Grant and William T. Sherman, as well as by tens of thousands of old soldiers and their kin from across Wisconsin and around the nation. The climax of the civic program to entertain the veterans that week was the staging of a mock naval battle, with "enemy" troops landing on the Lake Michigan shore. The encampment dominated the Milwaukee newspapers throughout the week.

It was 34 years before the national encampment returned to the Cream City, and by then the remaining veterans were more sedate. Sedentary, actually. It was noted that about the time of night that most conventioneers in Milwaukee were going out on the town, the veterans were already turned in for the night. Of course, in 1923, Prohibition was the law, but that

Milwaukee Sentinel *sketch of G.A.R. parade in 1889.*

was less inhibiting than age.

As for celebrities, the most noted at this encampment was Corporal James Tanner, former G.A.R. national commander, former pension commissioner, and a fixture at scores of such encampments. The press made much of the fact that Tanner, who suffered amputations of both legs in the war and then continued in service, had served as stenographer for Secretary of War Edwin Stanton at the bedside of the president as Stanton began taking testimony on the assassination as Lincoln was expiring.

Milwaukee planned something of a replication of the naval engagement that had engaged the attention and received the admiration of the soldiers in 1889. This time they planned to add the element of air power to the show. (This was the hometown of General Billy Mitchell, remember.) As the crowds again gathered at the lakefront, however, dense fog rolled in. The exercise went on as best it could minus air power, but almost nothing of the naval battle and very little of the "repulse" of invading forces could be seen. It was an utter disappointment.

Nor did the encampment dominate the newspapers this time. Concurrent to the gathering was a huge earthquake in Japan that claimed one hundred thousand lives and received coverage for many days.

When next the Grand Army came to Wisconsin for its encampment, the year was 1937. This was in Madison, and the men, now into or pressing into their nineties, were feisty on the major question of the day: whether the G.A.R. should participate as an organization in the 75th anniversary program planned by the State of Pennsylvania for the following July at Gettysburg.

Pennsylvania had invited the former Confederates and told them the hosts were not going to dictate what they were to wear or what they could carry. The latter, presumably, included the Stars and Bars.

That matter was argued for a long time on the floor of the business session and then was referred to a resolutions committee to draft something expressing the sense of the discussion.

"We are willing to attend a reunion of citizens of the United States who at one time were opposed to one another in a civil war and who now wish to join in a reunion at Gettysburg in 1938 for the purpose of showing to the citizens of the United States our reconciliation to the results of that Civil War; and at such reunion to have in view only the flag of the United States of America."

The old soldiers adopted this statement unanimously.

The soldiers were even older—and fewer—the last time the national encampment met in Wisconsin, in Milwaukee in 1943. There were 35 men registered, and the business of the encampment was of almost no consequence other than picking, from among the few, the men who would hold office the ensuing year. As was customary, the encampment picked a man from the host state to be senior vice commander. He was Lansing A. Wilcox, who would eventually be the last Civil War veteran in Wisconsin.

The men, now all in their nineties or above, met in a Council of Administration for an hour or more to iron out a fight between two members of the Department of Minnesota over who was running that department. The issue elicited heated debate for a while. But a compromise was finally reached.

Fraternity in the highest counsels of the Grand Army of the Republic was restored.

NATIONAL ENCAMPMENTS

Date	Location	Commander-in-Chief	Membership
November 20, 1866	Indianapolis	Stephen Augustus Hurlbut, Illinois	
	No encampment held in 1867		
January 15, 1868	Philadelphia	John Alexander Logan, Illinois	
May 12, 13, 1869	Cincinnati	John Alexander. Logan, Illinois	
May 11, 12, 1870	Washington, D.C.	John Alexander Logan, Illinois	
May 10, 11, 1871	Boston	Ambrose E. Burnside, Rhode Island	30,124
May 8, 9, 1872	Cleveland	Ambrose E. Burnside, Rhode Island	28,693
May 14, 15, 1873	New Haven	Charles Devens, Massachusetts	29,851
May 13, 1874	Harrisburg	Charles Devens, Massachusetts	28,323
May 12, 13, 1875	Chicago	John Frederick Hartranft, Pennsylvania	27,966
June 30, 1876	Philadelphia	John Frederick Hartranft, Pennsylvania	26,899
June 26, 27, 1877	Providence	John Cleveland Robinson, New York	27,079
June 4, 1878	Springfield, Mass.	John Cleveland Robinson, New York	31,016
June 17, 18, 1879	Albany	William Earnshaw, Ohio	44,752
June 8, 9, 1880	Dayton	Louis Wagner, Pennsylvania	60,634
June 15, 16, 1881	Indianapolis	George Sargent Merrill, Massachusetts	85,856
June 21-23, 1882	Baltimore	Paul Vandervoot, Maine	134,701
June 25, 26, 1883	Denver	Robert Burns Beath, Pennsylvania	225,446
June 23-25, 1884	Minneapolis	John Stephan Kountz, Ohio	273,168
June 24, 25, 1885	Portland, Maine	Samuel Swimfin Burdett, District of Colombia	294,787
August 4-6, 1886	San Francisco	**Lucius Fairchild, Wisconsin**	323,571
September 28-30, 1887	St. Louis	John Patterson Rea, Minnesota	355,916
September 12-14, 1888	Columbus	William Wagner, Missouri	372,960
August 28-30, 1889	**Milwaukee**	Russell Alexander Alger, Michigan	397,974
August 13, 14, 1890	Boston	Wheelock Graves Veazey, Vermont	409,489
August 5-7, 1891	Detroit	John Palmer, New York	407,781
September 21, 22, 1892	Washington, D.C.	**Augustus Gordon Weissert, Wisconsin**	399,880
September 6, 7, 1893	Ilndianapolis	John Gregory Bishop Adams, Massachusetts	397,223
September 12, 13, 1894	Pittsburgh	Thomas George Lawler, Illinois	369,083
September 11-13, 1895	Louisville	Ivan N. Walker, Indiana	357,639
September 3, 4, 1896	St. Paul	Thaddeus Stevens Clarkson, Nebraska	340,610
August 25-27, 1897	Buffalo	John Peter Shindel Gobin, Pennsylvania	319,465

Date	Location	Commander-in-Chief	Membership
September 5, 6, 1898	Cincinnati	James Andrew Sexton, Illinois*	
		William Christie Johnson, Ohio	305,603
September 6, 7, 1899	Philadelphia	Albert Duane Shaw, New York	287,918
August 29, 30, 1900	Chicago	Leo Rassieur, Missouri	276,612
September 12, 13, 1901	Cleveland	Eli Torrance, Minnesota	269,507
October 9, 10, 1902	Washington, D.C.	Thomas J. Stewart, Pennsylvania	263,745
August 20, 21, 1903	San Francisco	John Charles Black, Illinois	256,510
August 17, 18, 1904	Boston	Wilmon Whilldin Blackmar, Massachusetts*	
		John Rigney King, Maryland	247,340
September 7, 8, 1905	Denver	James Tanner, New York	232,455
August 16, 17, 1906	Minneapolis	Robert Burns Brown, Oklahoma	235,823
September 12, 13, 1907	Saratoga Springs	Charles Germman Burton, Maryland	229,932
September 3, 4, 1908	Toledo	Henry Martin Nevius, New Jersey	225,157
August 12, 13, 1909	Salt Lake City	Samuel Rogers VanSant, Minnesota	220,600
September 22, 23, 1910	Atlantic City	John Edward Gilman, Massachusetts	213,901
August 24, 25, 1911	Rochester, N.Y.	Harvey Marion Trimble, Illinois	203,410
September 9-14,1912	Los Angeles	Albert Bishop Beers, Connecticut	191,346
September 18, 19, 1913	Chattanooga	Washington Gardner, Michigan	180,227
September 3, 4, 1914	Detroit	David James Palmer, Iowa	171,335
Sept. 30, Oct. 1, 1915	Washington, D.C.	Elias Riggs Monfort, Ohio	159,863
Aug. 28, Sept. 2, 1916	Kansas City	William James Patterson, Pennsylvania	149,074
August 20-25, 1917	Boston	Orlando Allen Somers, Indiana	135,931
August 18-24, 1918	Portland, Oregon	Clarendon Edwin Adams, Nebraska	120,916
September 7-13, 1919	Columbus	James David Bell, New York*	
		Daniel Munson Hall, Ohio	110,357
September 19-25, 1920	Indianapolis	William Alexander Ketcham, Indiana	103,258
September 25-29, 1921	Indianapolis	Lewis Stephen Pilcher, New York	93,171
September 24-29, 1922	Des Moines	James William Willett, Iowa	85,621
September 2-8, 1923	**Milwaukee**	Gaylord Miller Saltzgaber, Ohio	76,126
August 10-15, 1924	Boston	Louis F. Arensberg, Pennsylvania	65,382
Aug. 30-Sept. 5, 1925	Grand Rapids	John Baptist Inman, Illinois	55,817
September 19-25, 1926	Des Moines	**Frank Augustin Walsh, Wisconsin**	47,179
September 11-16, 1927	Grand Rapids	Elbridge Lafayette Hawk, California	38,801
September 16-21, 1928	Denver	John Reese, Nebraska	32,614
September 8-13, 1929	Portland, Maine	Edwin James Foster, Massachusetts	26,219
August 24-28, 1930	Cincinnati	James Esom Jewel, Colorado & Wyoming	21,080
September 13-18, 1931	Des Moines	Samuel P. Town, Pennsylvania	16,578
September 18-24, 1932	Springfield,Illinois	William P. Wright,*	
		Russell C. Martin, California	13,066
September 17-22, 1933	St. Paul	Russell C. Martin, California	10,138
August 12-18, 1934	Rochester, N.Y.	Alfred Edwin Stacy, New York	7,807
September 8-14, 1935	Grand Rapids	Oley Nelson, Iowa	6,244

* Died in office.

Date	Location	Commander-in-Chief	Membership
September 20-26, 1936	Washington, D.C.	Carl Henry William Ruhe, Pennsylvania	4,391
September 5-10, 1937	**Madison**	Overton H. Mennet, California & Nevada	3,325
September 4-9, 1938	Des Moines	Robert McKee Rownd, New York	2,443
Aug. 27-Sept. 1, 1939	Pittsburgh	John E. Andrew, Illinois*	
		Alexander T. Anderson, Pennsylvania	1,701
September 8-13, 1940	Springfield Illinois	William W. Nixon, Kansas	1,039
September 14-19, 1941	Columbus	George Alvin Gay, Massachusetts	763
September 13-18, 1942	Indianapolis	John Simon Dumser, California	518
September 19-24, 1943	**Milwaukee**	George Henry Jones, Maine	393
September 10-15, 1944	Des Moines	Isaac W. Sharp, Indiana	249
Sept. 30-Oct. 4, 1945	Columbus	Hiram Randall Gale, Washington & Alaska	163
August 25-30, 1946	Indianapolis	John Henry Grate, Ohio	103
August 10-14, 1947	Cleveland	Robert McKee Rownd, New York	66
September 28-30, 1948	Grand Rapids	Theodore Augustus Penland, Oregon	28
Aug. 28-Sept. 1, 1949	Indianapolis	Theodore Augustus Penland, Oregon	16

* Died in office.

Grand Army of the Republic

SENIORITY OF DEPARTMENTS

T he Department of Wisconsin was not only the first department in the nation, save Illinois, but it was, at the final count at the last national encampment in Indianapolis in 1949, one of only 10 surviving departments.

At its peak, the Grand Army of the Republic had 45 departments. They are listed on the following chart as recorded in the final journal of the Grand Army of the Republic.

The ranking is by dates of "permanent organization," as determined by the national organization. Illinois was accorded first place, although, peculiarly, its ascribed date of organization is that of the organization of the first post. Illinois did not get around to formalizing its department status until its first encampment in the autumn of that year.

Thus the Department of Wisconsin was, technically, the first department organized in the nation, although there was no effort made to dispute the primacy of the Department of Illinois.

The chart from that final G.A.R. journal reveals, possibly unintentionally, the depths to which the organization plummeted in the "Great Falling Away" in the early years.

Eight of the early departments had to be reinstituted in the rebound era of the early 1880s, including Minnesota, Iowa, Michigan, Indiana, Missouri, West Virginia, Maryland, and Kan-

sas. The District of Colombia had a provisional charter in 1867 and was made permanent in 1869.

This early era was difficult for all the departments. All suffered losses of posts and membership in those years, but it was particularly felt in the Middle West. Illinois and Wisconsin were exceptions only in that they managed to survive.

The chart also reveals which departments had succumbed by 1945 (black-shaded) and the reasons for their closure, i.e., surrender, death, or merger.

Among the 45 departments were a number representing states in the South. Membership in these departments was small, of course, since comparatively few residents of these states fought for the Union. G.A.R. members were mostly men who migrated South after the war. They had, in some respects, a difficult time. Membership in the Grand Army of the Republic was usually a detriment to their businesses, in contrast to their comrades in the North. Besides being outsiders, G.A.R. men were perceived—as the G.A.R. was—as part of the radicalism of harsh Reconstruction.

It is easy to understand why, among the 10 surviving departments in 1949, the only border state was Kentucky.

Black boxes denotes Departments which closed for following reasons:
A: Charter surrendered; B: Closed by death of all members; C: Transferred to members at large.

SENIORITY OF DEPARTMENTS: THE FINAL ROSTER

Rank	Department	Permanent Organization	Organized then lapsed	Changed Status	A	Closed B	C
1	Illinois	Apr. 6 1866					
2	Wisconsin	Jun. 7, 1866					
3	Pennsylvania	Jan. 16, 1867					X
4	Ohio	Jan. 30, 1867				X	
5	New York	Apr. 3, 1867					X
6	Connecticut	Apr. 11, 1867					
7	Massachusetts	May 7, 1867				X	
8	New Jersey	Dec. 10. 1867				X	
9	Maine	Jan. 10, 1868				X	
10	California & Nevada	Feb. 21, 1868					
11	Rhode Island	Mar. 24, 1868				X	
12	New Hampshire	Jun. 30, 1868				X	
13	Vermont	Oct. 23, 1868				X	

Rank	Department	Permanent Organization	Organized then lapsed	Changed Status	A	Closed B	C
	Potomac (provisional)		Aug. 7, 1867				
14	Potomac	Feb. 13, 1869			X		
15	Virginia	Jul. 27, 1871					
	Changed to Virginia & North Carolina			May 20, 1892		X	
	Maryland originally organized		Jan. 8, 1868				
16	Maryland reorganized	Jun. 9, 1876				X	
17	Nebraska	Jun. 11, 1877				X	
	Michigan originally organized		May 6, 1868				
18	Michigan reorganized	Jan. 22, 1879				X	
	Iowa originally organized		Sep. 26, 1866				
19	Iowa reorganized	Jan. 23, 1879					
	Indiana originally organized		Aug. 20, 1866				
20	Indiana reorganized	Oct. 3, 1879					
21	Department of the Mountains	Dec. 11, 1879					
	Changed to Colorado			Jul. 31, 1882			
	Changed to Colorado & Wyoming			Aug. 28, 1889			
	Kansas originally organized		Dec. 7, 1867				
22	Kansas reorganized	Mar. 16, 1880				X	
23	Delaware	Jan. 14, 1881				X	
	Minnesota originally organized		Aug. 4, 1867				
24	Minnesota reorganized	Aug. 17, 1881					X
	Missouri originally organized		May 16, 1866				
25	Missouri reorganized	Apr. 22, 1882				X	
26	Oregon	Sep. 28, 1882					
27	Kentucky	Jan.16, 1883					
	West Virginia originally organized		Apr. 9, 1868				
28	West Virginia reorganized	Feb. 20, 1883				X	
29	Dakota	Feb. 27, 1883					
	Changed to South Dakota			Apr. 11, 1890		X	
30	Washington & Alaska	Jun. 20, 1883					
31	Arkansas	Jul. 11, 1883				X	
32	New Mexico	Jul. 14, 1883				X	
33	Utah	Oct. 9, 1883				X	
34	Tennessee	Feb. 26, 1884				X	
35	Department of the Gulf	May 15, 1884					
	Changed to Louisiana & Mississippi			Jun. 13, 1888		X	
36	Florida	Jun. 19, 1884				X	
37	Montana	Mar. 10, 1885				X	
38	Texas	Mar. 25, 1885				X	
39	Idaho	Jan. 11, 1888					X

Rank	Department	Permanent	Organized	Changed		Closed	
		Organization	then lapsed	Status	A	B	C
40	Arizona	Jan. 17, 1888				X	
41	Georgia and South Carolina	Jan. 25, 1889			X		
42	Alabama	Mar. 23, 1890				X	
43	North Dakota	Apr. 23, 1890				X	
44	Oklahoma & Indian Territory	Apr.7, 1890				X	
	Changed to Oklahoma			Jul. 3, 1891			
45	Indian Territory	Jul. 3, 1891					
	Consolidated with Oklahoma			May 19-22, 1908			

WHERE THEY JOINED

I t was the fate of Madison's Camp Randall—where, after all, more than 70 percent of Wisconsin's boys got their first taste of military life in the Civil War—to cause these now-no-longer boys to think about that first taste and wishing against wish that the place (and all the other places) where they ran into the realities of soldiering might be preserved, or at least memorialized.

By the early 1900s, Madison was growing, and its largest single element of growth was the University of Wisconsin. The site of Camp Randall had long since ceased to be the place for the state agricultural fair. More and more, the university was occupying the lands where nearly half a century before these veterans had embarked, most of them, on the greatest adventure of their lives.

Perhaps the impetus came because of the centennial of Abraham Lincoln's birth, hugely commemorated throughout the nation in 1909. At any rate, that year W. J. McKay, at the time patriotic instructor of Lucius Fairchild Post 11 of Madison, thought it might be nice to erect at least a memorial gate and arch at the old Dayton Street entrance to Camp Randall to commemorate forever the site of the camp.

The suggestion was gladly taken up by the Wisconsin Department of the Grand Army of the Republic. State Patriotic Instructor Hosea Rood included in his annual report for 1910 McKay's suggestion and the idea of others that a "piece of ground from 20 to 25 rods square, just inside this gate, be set off by the legislature for a Camp Randall Memorial Park." The land, Rood argued, already belonged to the state as part of the university's property. "It will cost the state nothing to devote a small portion of the old campground to the memory of thousands of boys and young men who took their primary lessons in the service that saved our country from disunion."[1]

The men attending the encampment at Fond du Lac that year voted to petition the legislature for just such a park. "Those grounds are very dear to us in memory and association . . . so dear that we earnestly desire that a small portion of it be set apart as a memorial to those historic days." Establish the park, they asked, and also "provide for the erection at the entrance to said grounds a memorial gate and arch, and . . . make a suitable appropriation therefore."[2]

Rood later noted that the State of Wisconsin was generous toward the old soldiers, granting them everything they reasonably asked for. The Senate voted for the park—and an appropriation to bring it about—23–1, and the Assembly, 68–4. Moreover, a committee was appointed to make plans for the memorial arch

and the appointed comrades had a sketch for such a monument in time to print in the 1911 encampment proceedings.

It was at that encampment at Green Bay that Patriotic Instructor Rood reminded the old soldiers in his annual report that "there were other places of rendezvous than Camp Randall for soldiers during the Civil War. Milwaukee had Camps Scott, Washburn, Sigel, and Holton; Kenosha, Camp Harvey; Racine, Camp Utley; Fond du Lac, Camp Hamilton; Oshkosh, Camp Bragg; Ripon, Camp Fremont; La Crosse, Camp Salomon; and Janesville, Camps Tredway and Barstow. I believe the location of every one of those 12[3] camps should be marked as well as that at Madison."

Rood had no illusions about the status of the sites. "Most of the old camping grounds have been covered with buildings during the last half century since the boys of '61 came together . . . and very few people now living in any of those cities know anything about those old drill grounds. But I think we all agree that they should not thus be forgotten."[4]

---

1. *Forty-Fourth Annual Encampment of the Department of Wisconsin, Grand Army of the Republic, Journal of Proceedings,* (Madison, Wisc.: Democrat Printing, 1910), 105.
2. *Forty-Fourth Annual Encampment,* 133-4.
3. The number of other camps was actually 11. Camp Holton and Camp Sigel proved to be the same camp.
4. *Forty-Fifth Annual Encampment of the Department of Wisconsin, Grand Army of the Republic, Journal of Proceedings,* (Madison, Wisc.: Democrat Printing, 1911), 89-90.

He urged campaigns in those communities where these camps once existed for "appropriate camp markers of bronze or granite"[5] to be financed, he hoped, with five-cent contributions from schoolchildren as an exercise in his favorite topic, patriotic instruction. It may be interesting to notice that neither he, nor the G.A.R., ever suggested that the State of Wisconsin be financially involved in commemorating the sites of the camp other than at Camp Randall.

"I am very much in favor of having the boys and girls in school invited to make their contributions (at a maximum of five cents each). If they do this they will be particularly interested in those historic spots near their own homes. And as they will, almost before we are aware of it, be the men and women of the communities where they live, they will take a patriotic pride in what they once helped erect."[6]

Rood was hoping that the posts and comrades in the communities where those old camps were located would involve themselves and have their individual projects accomplished and dedicated by the time Memorial Day of 1912 rolled around. This did not exactly come to pass, as Rood somewhat ruefully noted the following year. "The comrades and others in those places have not been so prompt as I wish. . . . So far as Ripon, Oshkosh, Fond du Lac and Kenosha are concerned positive active measures have been taken in the matter. . . . But I have not been able . . . to get any response from La Crosse and Janesville."[7]

What did happen in 1912, however, was the fruition of the G.A.R.'s project to have a suitable memorial erected at Camp Randall. On June 18 and 19, 1912, with something close to six hundred old comrades plus several thousand others attending, the commemorative program was held. A campfire comprised of a big pile of burning tar barrels, ringed by the celebrants listening to rousing speeches and singing the old camp songs highlighted the first night.

The next afternoon, with more speeches, and a dedicatory address by Bishop, née Brigadier General, Samuel Fallows of Chicago, late commander of the Forty-ninth Wisconsin, the 36-

foot-high by 36-foot-wide entry arch of Vermont gray granite was formally presented for future generations. A five-and-a-half-foot replica of Old Abe (himself a fledgling soldier at Camp Randall in '61) began its eagle-eyed vigil over the approach from Dayton Street atop the mammoth monument.

The Camp Randall arch was designed to commemorate all

the soldiers of Wisconsin in the War of the Rebellion, whether they rendezvoused there or at one of the nearly dozen additional assembly points across the state. Within the arch, on either side, are bronze tablets celebrating the site and listing each infantry, artillery, and cavalry unit raised in Wisconsin and the camp where its military life began. To the Wisconsin Department of the Grand Army, this was a fulfilling memorial for all.

Still they did not consider that it obviated the need for marking those other sites with appropriate granite and/or bronze markers. In 1912, the same year that Camp Randall's entry arch was dedicated, the veterans of Milwaukee reported to the state encampment that they had painstakingly researched the dimensions of the three camps there—to the extent of going door-to-door in the areas—and presented their findings as a matter of some pride in their original research.

"The department should also provide itself with maps of the boundaries of Camps Tredway and Barstow, Janesville; Camp Utley, Racine; Camp Bragg, Oshkosh; Camp Wood [Hamilton], Fond du Lac; Camp Randall, Madison; Camp Salomon, La Crosse, and Camp Harvey, Kenosha, with a view to designating them for all time," the Milwaukeeans suggested, adding that "brief histories of those camps would also prove valuable additions to the archives of our department."[8]

(1) Confederate Cemetery (2) Camp Randall (3) Arch (4) Capitol

It is interesting that they included Camp Randall in that listing. Although the camp was being well-commemorated by the Memorial Arch, its original dimensions, by 1912, were misty. The arch was built at the Dayton Street entrance, but research in the 1970s suggests that it may be in front of where the actual camp boundary was. The site layout as shown above and at right was given by David Mollenhoff in the *Journal of Historic Madison* in 1978.

Camp Randall, incidentally, in addition to its primary role as a point of rendezvous for Wisconsin troops, also served for a short time as a prisoner-of-war camp. Some of the new Wisconsin soldiers served as guards over the prisoners who had been captured on April 8, 1862, at the surrender of Island No. 10 in the Mississippi River near New Madrid, Missouri. The prisoners were eventually moved to other places before being ex-

---

5. *Forty-Fifth Annual Encampment*, 90.
6. Ibid.
7. *Forty-Sixth Annual Encampment of the Department of Wisconsin, Grand Army of the Republic, Journal of Proceedings*, (Madison, Wisc.: Democrat Printing, 1912), 78.
8. *Forty-Sixth Annual Encampment*, 101.

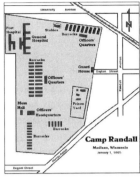

changed, but not before 140 of them died in Madison, mostly from disease, and were buried some distance from Camp Randall. Located within Forest Hill Cemetery, it is the northernmost Confederate cemetery in the country.

The plea of the Milwaukee committee that their research be emulated by comrades in other cities was, sadly, not followed. Except for the three Milwaukee camps and Camp Bragg at Oshkosh, maps on the following pages are simply fair guesses as to what the extent of those camps was, and even more unfortunately, information about the location of Camp Salomon at La Crosse is not available.

(1) Camp Washburn (2) Camp Scott (3) Camp Holton, Camp Sigel, Camp Reno (4) State Historical Marker

The precision of the Milwaukee research is evident. These are the sketches as given in the 1912 encampment journal. But nothing was done to place markers. By then Camps Scott and Sigel/Holton/Reno were completely urbanized, but the committee noted there was still room for a monument in the Camp Washburn area, but this did not happen. Finally, in 1989, the State Historical Society erected a marker at Prospect and Royal, near Camp Sigel.

By the year following the Milwaukeeans' report, 1913, Hosea Rood was able to tell the encampment that only one other marker had been placed at the site of a camp despite his repeated urgings. Nonetheless he was proud to report that a commemoration in granite had been placed at Ripon.

It marked the site where the First Wisconsin Cavalry came together in the early autumn of 1861. This was Camp Fremont, and it occupied, essentially, the entire campus of Ripon College.

The map at right shows the extent of the campus in 1861. The two black squares on the campus represent buildings that

were there at the time and were used by the military. They are still there, the only buildings on any of the camp sites in the state surviving from the Civil War era.

The First Cavalry was moved from Ripon in November 1861, when it was decided that the site was not

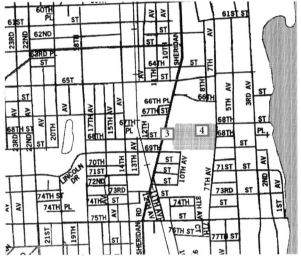

(1) Camp Fremont (2) Camp Marker (3) Camp Harvey (4) Marker

suitable for winter quarters, and Camp Fremont was no longer used. The First Cavalry went to its new camp at Kenosha and arrived there on November 23, 1861.

This was Camp Harvey, located on high ground within sight of Lake Michigan. Its eastern edge was about three blocks from the water. It was near a cemetery, and today all of the camp area is now within the cemetery. Whereas the First Cavalry at Camp Fremont was not yet equipped with horses, the unit became a cavalry regiment at Camp Harvey.

The First remained at Kenosha in drill through the winter months of 1861. On March 17, 1862, the regiment left Camp Harvey and headed south. Camp Harvey, like Fremont, went unused thereafter. Yet Harvey also has a granite memorial, a large irregularly shaped one, near the middle of the cemetery.

After Camp Randall, the most important, or at least the most widely used, camp in Wisconsin was Camp Utley at Racine. It was the rendezvous point for several infantry regiments, but more importantly, it was the place where most of the state's artillery units came together and learned their crafts. It was, in fact, the only other camp to be used throughout the entire Civil War, and was even the site where the Seventh Wisconsin headquartered when that famous Iron Brigade Regiment returned to the state to recruit.

(1) Artillery Range (2) Artillery Range (3) Camp Utley

Wisconsin artillerymen apparently had a fair amount of practice before they went off to war. There were two ranges at Racine. The northernmost, and closest to the town at the time, was in a natural amphitheater where shot and shell had a ready barrier. A large berm was built at the south end of the other, and balls were being extracted from it well into the twentieth century. There are now no signs of that berm, nor any suggestions of the military presence in 1861–65. The precise dimensions of Camp Utley are likewise not known, except for the northern and eastern edges of the camp. And Hosea Rood would be quite disappointed to know that there are no markers to note the one-time presence of Camp Utley and its special artillery role.

The only city other than Milwaukee to have two Civil War camps was Janesville, and both were in operation at approximately the same time.

Camp Tredway was located on the then outskirts of Janesville at the Rock County Fairgrounds. It was the place of gathering for the Thirteenth Infantry Regiment. That unit was mustered in October 17, 1861, and trained at Tredway until it left for Fort Leavenworth, Kansas, on January 18, 1862.

At the same time, the Third Cavalry was being organized and was encamped some distance south of the city at what was called Camp Barstow. It went south just 10 days after the Thirteenth left Janesville, and thereafter neither camp operated.

As at Racine, Janesville lacks any markers to identify the sites of Civil War rendezvous. At least a part of Camp Tredway is still a fairgrounds, and the area that was once Camp Barstow contains a marker identifying the area as the home site of a locally famous circus some time after the war.

The history of the military camp at Fond du Lac is a bit unusual. The excitement that followed Fort Sumter was still at its height when a camp was designated at Fond du Lac to accommodate the newly forming Third Wisconsin. The First Regiment had formed at Camp Scott in Milwaukee, the Second at Camp

Randall. This third camp for the state was named Camp Hamilton, and the troops began arriving at Fond du Lac even as men were filling out the ranks of the Second at Madison during June and July of 1861. They left in the middle of the latter for the Eastern Armies, and, thereafter, Camp Hamilton went unoccupied for five months while other regiments came together in other locations, especially Camp Randall. Then, in November of that year, the Fourteeth Wisconsin was designated to gather at Fond du Lac. This time the largely vacant fields of the place were designated Camp Wood. After the Fourteenth departed, the site was no longer used.

The dimensions of the one-time camp are known, except for the distance it extended north. A marker was placed at the camp, but it has been moved to a park about a block west of the actual camp location.

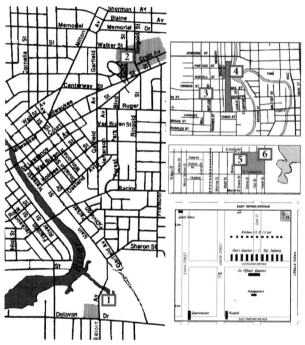

(1) Camp Barstow (2) Camp Tredway (3) Marker
(4) Camp Hamilton (Wood) (5) Marker (6) Camp Bragg

Perhaps one of the reasons for its disuse was that it was not so secure as it might be. When, in 1862 there was a call for extra troops, a new camp was established at Oshkosh, where the fairgrounds had a secure fence.

This was Camp Bragg. It was the place of rendezvous for the Twenty-first Wisconsin beginning in late August 1862. The regiment had no sooner left for the front when the next one came, the Thirty-second Wisconsin, which left the state in late October 1862.

The great crisis of 1862—the invasions of the North by Robert E. Lee and Braxton Bragg—had failed, and recruiting returned to a more normal pace. The camp at Oshkosh was no longer needed.

Camp Bragg is unique in that it is the only Civil War camp in Wisconsin for which the precise dimensions are known. The sketched layout, previous page, is based on a contemporaneous drawing of Camp Bragg in the National Archives. It is presently marked by a memorial having a tablet and four cannons in the northeast corner of the original area.

The memorial lot at Camp Bragg is shown above left. It was probably a result of the Grand Army's efforts to mark all the camps, although Oshkosh's two G.A.R. posts did not have the primary role. It was erected in 1915 largely through the beneficence of Colonel John Hicks, the publisher of the Oshkosh newspaper whose father had been killed in the war. The memorial was dedicated formally in 1917 at a reunion of one of the regiments which gathered there in 1862, the Twenty-first Wisconsin. Bishop Samuel Fallows, who had given the dedicatory address at Camp Randall, delivered this dedicatory address. Although the memorial was moved about a block from its original site, it still is within the Camp Bragg limits.

Camp Hamilton at Fond du Lac was marked but not because of the Grand Army's early campaign. The memorial above right was erected in 1927 by the Ladies of the G.A.R. It originally stood on the site of Camp Hamilton (and Camp Wood) but was later moved to a park about a block from the site of the camp itself.

Amidst the ordered and finely carved stones of Green Ridge Cemetery in Kenosha (shown below) stands a large natural boulder commemorating the fact that a Civil War camp had

been located there. The top has been cut off and polished, and the inscription reads "The First Wisconsin Cavalry Rendezvoused here in 1861. From 1862 to 1865 the regiment fought to preserve the Union. On fame's eternal camping ground their silent tents are spread and glory guards with solemn round the bivouac of the dead. 1917."

The Kenosha G.A.R. had placed a memorial to Civil War soldiers in the cemetery around 1900, so it seems likely that this marker specifically for Camp Harvey (the name of the camp is strangely lacking from the inscription) was probably in response to Hosea Rood's repeated importuning.

At the other camp of the First Cavalry, Camp Fremont at Ripon, a state historical marker commemorates both the formation of the college and its use in 1861 as a military camp. The original granite marker dedicated in 1913 was changed to a level marker in the ground a bit to the left of this one. The building shown was in use as a head-quarters building. It and a nearby building are the only structures remaining from any state Civil War camp.

The state historical marker at right is located half a block from the site of Camp Sigel/Holton/Reno, at Prospect Avenue and Royall Place in Milwaukee. Erected in 1989, it is the newest of the markers commemorating Wisconsin's Civil War camp sites.

Milwaukee's other two camps are now completely urbanized. Camp Scott, for example, was located on what is now the North Side of Wisconsin Avenue in the vicinity of Marquette University.

Even to the old soldiers of the Grand Army of the Republic this march of progress was inexorable and not especially distasteful to them. They lived in an era in which civic progress was highly prized. The bucolic was nice, but when it made way for new and modern conveniences and a fuller lifestyle, that was a result to be embraced.

Still, when the G.A.R. became concerned in the early twentieth century that these camps be not completely forgotten, it certainly was an element of nostalgia to these men who were by now generally in their seventies. There were so few tangible things to remind them of their youthful days.

Here, however, is one, an artist's view of Camp Sigel/

Holton/Reno looking across Prospect Avenue. The headquarters is in right foreground with flagpole nearby. The two buildings  just beyond that are officers quarters. The rest of the buildings around the parade ground are barracks and other buildings such as the quartermaster, commissary, kitchens, and hospital.

Such an accurate rendering of a Wisconsin Civil War camp is rare. The scene above is also from Camp Sigel. It seems to be more fanciful.

There are a few other, more rustic sketches remaining from the era. The one below shows the dining hall at Camp Utley in Racine, apparently drawn at the time. It is the only tangible evidence of Utley, which stood second only to Camp Randall in introducting Wisconsin's more than 90,000 soldiers to their military life.

The comparative dearth of such materials is understandable. Most of the camps were extremely temporary. Even so, it is difficult to explain the absolute lack of any evidence of the existence of Camp Salomon at La Crosse. Camp Salomon had the shortest "lifespan" of any of the Wisconsin camps. Soldiers of the Twenty-fifth Regiment, mostly from western Wisconsin, gathered there in early September 1862. Scarcely two weeks later they were sent to Minnesota to garrison places still worried about the late Indian uprising in the state. They were returned to Wisconsin in January, but went to Camp Randall rather than Camp Salomon. Still, contemporary newspaper reports are lacking. It is assumed that it was on the level areas then south of the town limits rather than amid the hills and hollows where the town was growing up.

This does not explain, however, why the veterans in the western area of Wisconsin did not respond to the efforts of the Department of Wisconsin to commemorate all the sites. There should have been some still alive who began their careers at Camp Salomon. Hosea Rood singled out La Crosse in his reports with some note of discouragement for having ignored his pleas.

The camps of Wisconsin will be further explained on the following pages, giving brief sketches of the man after whom the camp was named and which units began their military life in each. The date given for each is the date, or the span of dates, of their muster into federal service.

CAMP RANDALL, MADISON. Named after Alexander Randall, governor of Wisconsin at the beginning of the war, who proceeded to call for more volunteers after the initial state quota was filled and brought them to the state fairgrounds at Madison. The first regiment to form was the Second Wisconsin, whose colonel, Edgar O'Conner, named the camp in honor of the governor. It was the primary place of rendezvous for Wisconsin troops throughout the war.

GOVERNOR RANDALL

Unit	Date	Unit	Date
2nd Inf	June 11, 1861	46th Inf	February 18 & March 2, 1865
5th Inf	July 13, 1861	47th Inf	February 8 & 23, 1865
6th Inf	July 16, 1861	49th Inf	February 24 & March 3, 1865
7th Inf	August 5 & 13, 1861	50th Inf	March 6 & April 18, 1865
8th Inf	September 5 & 12, 1861	52nd Inf	March 30 & April 18, 1865
11th Inf	September 27 & October 18, 1861	53rd Inf	March 30 & April 12, 1865
12th Inf	November 5, 1861	Light Artillery	
15th Inf	December 1, 1861 & February 12, 1862	11th Arty	February 22, 1862
16th Inf	November 25, 1861 & January 31, 1862	12th Arty	March 3 & April 2, 1862
17th Inf	February 25, 1862	Heavy Artillery	
20th Inf	July 31 & August 23, 1862	A	June 11, 1861
23rd Inf	August 30, 1862	E	October 3, 1864
29th Inf	September 27, 1862	F	October 3, 1864
30th Inf	October 21, 1862	G	November 12, 1864
36th Inf	February 1 & March 22, 1864	H	October 7, 1864
37th Inf	April 9 & June 25, 1864	I	November 12, 1864
38th Inf	April 15 & September 17, 1864	K	October 17, 1864
40th Inf	July 9, 1864	L	September 30, 1864
42nd Inf	August 15 & September 9, 1864	M	September 30, 1864
44th Inf	October 7, 1864 & February 15, 1865	U.S. Sharpshooters	
45th Inf	November 8, 1864 & February 7, 1865		July 1, 1861

EDWARD HOLTON

CAMP HOLTON, MILWAUKEE. Named after Edward Holton, a Milwaukee business leader and prominent abolitionist—he was the Free Soil gubernatorial candidate in 1853, losing to Governor Barstow—which probably indicated a prevailing sentiment in 1861. Camp Holton was located where Camp Sigel was; it may have been a portion of that area since a regiment was in Sigel the same time as a regiment was at Camp Holton. The distinction is unclear.

10th Inf	October 11, 1861		18th Inf	March 15, 1862

GOVERNOR
BARSTOW

CAMP BARSTOW, JANESVILLE. Named after former Governor William Barstow, who raised the Third Cavalry Regiment in 1861. The Democrat Barstow was governor in the 1850s.

3rd Cavalry January 31, 1862

GOVERNOR
WASHBURN

CAMP WASHBURN, MILWAUKEE. Named after C. C. Washburn, colonel of the Second Cavalry who rose to general. After the war he was elected governor of Wisconsin. The camp, at the Milwaukee Fairgrounds, was used sporadically throughout the war and was the only one to have accommodated infantry, cavalry and artillery.

28th Inf	October 14, 1862		51st Inf	March 20 & April 29, 1865
34th Inf	December 2 & 31, 1862		2nd Cav	October 14, 1862
35th Inf	Nov. 27, 1863 & Feb. 27, 1864		13th Art	Nov. 4 & Dec. 29, 1863
39th Inf	June 3, 1864		Heavy Arty:	
41st Inf	June 8 & 15, 1865		B	September 9, 1863
43rd Inf	August 15 & September 30, 1864		C	October 1, 1863
48th Inf	February 20 & April 4, 1865		D	November 17, 1863

GENERAL BRAGG

CAMP BRAGG, OSHKOSH. Named for Edward S. Bragg, a Democratic leader in Fond du Lac who joined the Second Wisconsin when the war began and rose to command of the Iron Brigade by the end. The camp was located at Oshkosh through Republican political pressure, and the name was probably chosen as a political counterbalance.

21st Inf	August 5, 1862		32nd Inf	August 25, 1862

COLONEL UTLEY

CAMP UTLEY, RACINE. Named after Col. William L. Utley, Wisconsin adjutant general at the start of the war. He later commanded the 22nd Wisconsin, which became known as the Abolition Regiment because Utley, with the support of his men, refused to return a runaway slave to a prominent Kentucky judge despite his commander's order. The Racine camp became the primary rendezvous point for Artillery units in Wisconsin.

4th Inf	May 2, 1861		4th Arty	October 1, 1861
22nd Inf	September 2, 1862		5th Arty	October 1, 1861
31st Inf	September 12 & 24, 1862*		6th Arty	October 1, 1861
33rd Inf	October 16, 1862		7th Arty	November 4, 1861
1st Arty	October 10, 1861		8th Arty	January 8, 1862
2nd Arty	October 10, 1861		9th Arty	January 27, 1862
3rd Arty	October 1, 1861		10th Arty	February 10, 1862

*Rendezvoused first at Prairie du Chien

COLONEL
HAMILTON

CAMP HAMILTON, FOND DU LAC. Named for Col. Charles S. Hamilton, a West Pointer (same class as U. S. Grant) and Mexican War officer who was commander of the regiment, the Third, ordered to the camp in June 1861. The camp remained unused after the Third left until later in the year, when it was renamed Camp Wood.

3rd Inf   June 25, 1861

GOVERNOR
HARVEY

CAMP HARVEY, KENOSHA. Named for Louis Powell Harvey, governor of Wisconsin following Governor Randall. Harvey was very popular with the soldiers and was especially mourned when he drowned while visiting Wisconsin troops after Shiloh.

1st Cav   March 10, 1862

GENERAL
FREMONT

CAMP FREMONT, RIPON. Named for Gen. John C. Fremont, a noted prewar figure for his explorations, and at the outset of the war, an early active general in Missouri. He had been a Republican presidential candidate in 1856 and was known as an abolitionist, which was appreciated by Riponites.

1st Cav   Moved to Kenosha

GENERAL RENO

CAMP RENO, MILWAUKEE. Named after Gen. Jessie Reno, killed in the battle of South Mountain in September of 1862. It was originally Camp Sigel. By mid-1862, Sigel's star had lost much of its luster and the camp was renamed, presumably about the time the 27th Infantry Regiment was called there, that is, the month after Reno died.

27th Inf   October 23, 1862 & March 7, 1863

GOVERNOR
SALOMON

CAMP SALOMON, LA CROSSE. Named after the governor of Wisconsin when the camp was designated. Edward Salomon succeeded to the governorship when Governor Louis P. Harvey drowned. The camp was only used for a few weeks when the new 25th Wisconsin Infantry was sent to Minnesota in the aftermath of the Sioux Uprising. When the regiment returned, the soldiers went to Camp Randall instead of to Camp Salomon. The exact location of Camp Salomon has been lost.

25th Inf   September 19, 1862

GENERAL SIGEL

CAMP SIGEL, MILWAUKEE. Named for General Franz Sigel, a German-American who gained recognition early in the war in Missouri and was thus a magnet for enlistments of German immigrants. He was a retired German officer who fled his native land when the revolution of 1848 failed. His early success was not followed by other starring exploits, and his reputation gradually dimmed. The camp was renamed Camp Reno late in 1862.

9th Inf   October 20 & November 26, 1861   26th Inf   September 17, 1862
24th Inf   August 2 & August 15, 1862

GENERAL SCOTT

CAMP SCOTT, MILWAUKEE. Named after Winfield Scott, the War of 1812 and Mexican War hero who was commander of the federal army at the beginning of the Civil War. Camp Scott was actually the first in Wisconsin, accepting the First Wisconsin Infantry three-year regiment to fill the state quota under President Lincoln's initial call for troops.

1st Inf 90-day	May 17, 1861	1st Inf 3-year	October 6, 1861

QUARTERMASTER-
GENERAL
TREDWAY

CAMP TREDWAY, JANESVILLE. Named after William W. Tredway, appointed by Governor Randall a few weeks after Fort Sumter as quartermaster-general for the state of Wisconsin. The state was then ill-positioned to provide for the needs of the flood of new soldiers responding to Lincoln's call. It fell to Tredway, a Madison businessman, to outfit and equip these regiments. As temporary commissary general, also, he was initially responsible for feeding them. Camp Tredway was established at the fairgrounds in Janesville and was home to the 13th Wisconsin at the same time that Camp Barstow in Janesville was receiving the Third Cavalry.

13th Inf   October 7 & November 13, 1862

COLONEL WOOD

CAMP WOOD, FOND DU LAC. The camp was named for Colonel David E. Wood of Fond du Lac. Wood was a lawyer and Fond du Lac County court judge, from 1854 to 1858, who was called to organize another regiment of men of the "northwest" to rendezvous in November 1861, at the site that had been Camp Hamilton earlier in the year. Wood took his regiment south where it was engaged at Shiloh. Not long after, Wood became sick and returned to Fond du Lac to recover, but he did not. He died there on June 17, 1862, at age 37.

14th Inf   January 30, 1862

SURVIVING VETERANS
BY REGIMENTS

For several decades, Wisconsin carried out a statewide census five years after the federal census, and in two of those enumerations, in 1895 and again in 1905, the state broke down its data to show Wisconsin's veterans, and more specifically, what state units they represented.

The two censuses represent an interesting slice of data on the aging veterans and particularly on the shrinking corps of men who were once numbered among the 91,327 who left the Badger State to oppose the Rebellion of 1861 to 1865. These are given for each of the state's 52 infantry regiments, four cavalry regiments, one regiment of heavy artillery, and 13 light artillery batteries. The following table gives the figures for each of those units, both in 1895 and again in 1905.

These totals do not represent the entire number of veterans living in Wisconsin at the time. In 1895, for example, there were 17,292 men in Wisconsin who had served in Wisconsin units. But there were another 7,984 veterans counted in that state census who were then living in Wisconsin but had served with units in other states—generally states in which they were a resident at the time. In addition, the enumeration found 384 former army regulars from Wisconsin and an identical number of navy and marine veterans.

These numbers represent only those still living in Wisconsin who entered Wisconsin units during the war. They are not precise figures on the number of survivors of each unit since those who left Wisconsin after the war are not counted. Most of the regiments, it is safe to assume, had somewhat more surviving veterans than the figures given.

It must be remembered, too, that these census figures do not say anything about the Grand Army of the Republic, Department of Wisconsin, other than that it possibly still had a field from which to recruit. In 1895, when 26,307 veterans were counted, the G.A.R. counted 11,678 members (see Appendix G, Page 357). A decade later the department was down to 7,518 members.

But perhaps it was somewhat successful in recruiting. The department's total was down 36 percent in the decade while the census figures for the surviving members of Wisconsin regiments went down by 45 percent.

Interestingly, this was the era in which unit reunions were popular, so the unit figures do give a rough estimate of the numbers of men who might have been attracted to those reunions.

What the comparisons, unit by unit, do tell vividly and validly, is the attrition going on in the ranks of the men as they passed middle age and began the new century as veterans who were coming to be accorded the respect and veneration due to old soldiers.

SURVIVING VETERANS BY REGIMENTS, 1885 AND 1905

Regiment	1895	1905	Regiment	1895	1905
Infantry			Eleventh	336	182
			Twelfth	478	264
First	290	166	Thirteenth	316	191
Second	209	119	Fourteenth	431	243
Third	459	245	Fifteenth	115	95
Fourth	*See Fourth Cavalry*		Sixteenth	429	236
Fifth	427	235	Seventeenth	424	232
Sixth	459	250	Eighteenth	333	159
Seventh	329	182	Nineteenth	247	126
Eighth	267	146	Twentieth	224	126
Ninth	318	175	Twenty-first	346	195
Tenth	201	125	Twenty-second	326	199

Twenty-third	215	122			
Twenty-fourth	193	99			
Twenty-fifth	339	193			
Twenty-sixth	306	153			
Twenty-seventh	321	175			
Twenty-eighth	247	156			
Twenty-ninth	210	114			
Thirtieth	363	196			
Thirty-first	216	134			
Thirty-second	370	215			
Thirty-third	189	112			
Thirty-fourth	161	74			
Thirty-fifth	222	115			
Thirty-sixth	220	139			
Thirty-seventh	267	167			
Thirty-eighth	243	128			
Thirty-ninth	131	73			
Fortieth	150	88			
Forty-first	123	69			
Forty-second	268	164			
Forty-third	230	114			
Forty-fourth	333	166			
Forty-fifth	307	153			
Forty-sixth	257	146			
Forty-seventh	304	178			
Forty-eighth	271	137			
Forty-ninth	300	165			
Fiftieth	298	161			
Fifty-first	280	140			
Fifty-second	169	89			

Fifty-third	55	41
Totals	**14,521**	**8,067**
Cavalry		
First	454	209
Second	391	176
Third	414	209
Fourth	408	222
Totals	**1670**	**816**
Artillery		
First Heavy Artillery	542	319
First Battery	48	23
Second Battery	44	27
Third Battery	40	23
Fourth Battery	50	28
Fifth Battery	28	16
Sixth Battery	55	43
Seventh Battery	42	20
Eighth Battery	66	35
Ninth Battery	40	27
Tenth Battery	39	19
Eleventh Battery	8	1
Twelfth Battery	51	29
Thirteenth Battery	18	18
Totals	**1071**	**625**
Miscellaneous		
Berdan's Sharpshooters	19	10
Miscellaneous names	11	
Wisconsin totals	**17,292**	**9,521**

POSTS WITH

SECRETARIES

Inevitably, the "boys" were no longer "boys," but old men in need of some degree of assistance to keep their Grand Army posts functioning. They needed the help of someone younger to see that correspondence was maintained and that all the forms and requirements were observed. They needed, and received, the loving help of post secretaries—generally, but not exclusively, women—beginning around the mid-1920s. They were recruited from the allied organizations, most particularly the Women's Relief Corps.

This development had some foundation at the national level in that the national encampment in 1921 ordered that the rules and regulations of the Grand Army of the Republic be changed to authorize posts of the order to hire a secretary or stenographer for their meetings to record and transcribe the proceedings. It has been a firm rule that none but members could be present at post meetings, or state or national encampments for that matter. (In Wisconsin members at the 1926 Encampment took a vote on whether to allow a woman to be present to take stenographic notes of the proceedings. She stayed on a 104–6 vote.)

That national position seems to have been intended to be fairly restricted. Secretaries could be present at meetings and record what happened, but that was about as far as they were authorized to go. In subsequent years, the order specified that these stenographers could in no way be construed to be office-holders and were not to be "installed" into whatever position it was that they were filling. Nonetheless, in Wisconsin, at least, the position of "secretary" became more than just silent note-taking and transcribing.

It was under E. B. Heimstreet, assistant adjutant general for Wisconsin for the years 1922–25, 1928–29, and 1931–32, that the Wisconsin Department began according these helping hands the recognition that had become their due. As the institution apparently evolved, it is not possible to find a precise starting date for the position. But by 1929 it had become firmly entrenched.

Commander George Pounder, in his report of events during his term, said there were 58 posts with secretaries. "These secretaries are furnished badges of which they are proud," he told the delegates. He then went on to praise the assistant adjutant general, noting that the department was "greatly indebted"

to Heimstreet "for his untiring efforts to bring this [post secretaries program] about which I am sure will prolong our patriotic Post life for many years." Commander Pounder added, "I heartily recommend its adoption by other states."[1]

Heimstreet's aggressive program of recruiting secretaries and giving them something of the dignity, albeit, not the title, of an officeholder with the post, was paying off. He and most of the aging men of the Wisconsin G.A.R. were sure the program was making it possible for the men to maintain the post structure and to keep the post viable so long as there was a living member. The badges which the secretaries received and cherished apparently were provided through national channels, although there is no action on record at the national level regarding secretaries' badges and nothing indicating an approved design. At the higher level, there was at least tacit approval of Heimstreet's idea for post secretaries, but there does not seem to have been a great effort to extend the idea to the other departments.

In 1929 the secretaries of the various posts formed a club that met at encampments, exactly as half a dozen allied orders to the G.A.R. did. It was another sign that they were well-advanced from the concept of the quiet note-taker at a post meeting. But their focus was on keeping the posts functioning as long as possible.

In 1932, when Mary Liebmann of Green Bay was president of the Secretaries Club, she wrote a letter to be sent to other states outlining what Wisconsin had done. Through Heimstreet's initiative the state then had 67 secretaries to posts. He said it helped in holding the "Old Boys" together and would improve the longevity of the Wisconsin G.A.R.

She outlined, for the instruction of posts in other states, what the Wisconsin secretaries described as their duties:

"To keep the Wisconsin G.A.R. Posts in existence as long as there is one member left. To act as Secretary to the Adjutant of the Post. To see that all members of the Post have all General Orders read to them. To attend to the correspondence, and reports of the Post. To celebrate the birthday of every member of the Post. And to see that no Grand Army man, or his family, want for living. To see that all members of the G.A.R. are taken and returned from any meeting of any of the auxiliary societies."[2]

Mrs. Liebmann styled the organization The Secretaries Service Club to the Wisconsin G.A.R. Note the words "to the Wisconsin G.A.R." rather than "of the Wisconsin G.A.R." The secretaries were ever mindful of their subordination to the old

1. *Journal of the Sixty-Third Annual Encampment, Grand Army of the Republic,* Beloit, June 24-27, 1929; 28.
2. *Journal of the Sixty-Seventh Annual Encampment, Grand Army of the Republic,* Sheboygan, June 12, 13, 14, 1933; 104.

soldiers. Still, their services to the men only increased with the years. They had gone far beyond just keeping the minutes. They were keeping the life of those old veterans meaningful by making their Grand Army experience more than just a memory.

While the organization remained active for a number of years, its eventual demise was also foreordained. When the secretaries began to be appointed in the mid-1920s, G.A.R. membership was roughly 1,500 men. By 1936, the last year the secretaries' organization met formally, nine out of 10 of the soldiers they had begun to serve had died. Department membership was down to 152 men. The organization ceased to be because its reason for existing had essentially ceased. The remaining men were pretty much on their own by this time. Local posts were few and the life of the Wisconsin Department focused pretty much on the annual encampments.

ALMA CHEESMAN

Ironically, with the departure of the post secretaries, a new but similar position entered at the department level. In 1938, Alma Cheesman of West Allis, the president of the Women's Relief Corps in Wisconsin prior to her appointment, was named department secretary.

It was now beyond caring whether the seretary was held in subordination to the remaining handful of frail old men. Alma Cheesman became the majordomo of the Department of Wisconsin for the remaining years of its existence. She was prominent in the business at the encampment each year, reading the communications to the frail few, reminding them in their forgetfulness of the proper Grand Army formulations and regulations.

In short she kept the Department of Wisconsin functioning efficiently even as the post secretaries had done at the local level in the decade or so previous.

In an era in which the news media had suddenly discovered the Civil War relics at the annual encampments, Alma Cheesman was the spokesperson for the old soldiers and guided the young journalists into their appreciation of what the Grand Army of the Republic was all about.

The secretaries had certainly performed a valuable service to the G.A.R in their day. They were justly proud of their service, and they were proud of the badges they had been given. Here are two forms of such badges:

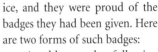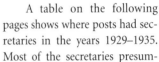

A table on the following pages shows where posts had secretaries in the years 1929–1935.

Most of the secretaries presumably received badges similar to these for their service.

In some cases the secretaries were male. They may have been from the Sons of Union Veterans. Or in some cases—the ubiquitous Hosea Rood in 1929 is an example—one of the veterans themselves may have filled in for a less physically able post adjutant.

POSTS WITH SECRETARIES

No.	Post Name	Town	Secretary	1929	1930	1931	1932	1933	1934	1935
1	E. B. Wolcott	Milwaukee	Lillian Pierce							x
6	George H. Thomas	Delevan	Daisy Wright	x	x	x	x	x	x	
7	J. F. Sawyer	Omro	Mrs. E. C. Bills	x	x	x	x	x	x	x
9	Joe Hooker	Baraboo	Mrs. Oscar Doppler							x
10	Phillip H. Sheridan	Oshkosh	Mrs. G. S. Spink				x		x	x
11	Lucius Fairchild	Madison	Ella Breese	x	x	x	x	x	x	x
12	Jarius Richardson	Sheboygan Falls	Kittie Jones						x	x
13	H. A. Tator	Reedsburg	Alice Collins					x	x	x
14	Lovell H. Rousseau	Portage	Mariam Fox	x	x					
16	Irvin Eckles	Amherst	Mrs. Ruby Peterson		x	x				
17	Gov. Louis P. Harvey	Racine	Edna Christenson							x
18	H. M. Walker	Manitowoc	Emma L. Jaeger		x	x	x	x		
19	William B. Cushing	Waukesha	Edna Blume				x	x	x	x
20	W. H. Sargent	Janesville	Eva Kemmerling				x	x	x	x
21	James A. Garfield	Waupaca	Romelia Gotham		x		x	x	x	x
22	Wood County	Wisconsin Rapids	W. J. Fisher					x	x	x
24	Henry Dillon	Lone Rock	R. A. Hammond					x	x	x
25	George Irwin	Lodi	Sadie Clements					x	x	x

No.	Post Name	Town	Secretary	1929	1930	1931	1932	1933	1934	1935
26	John E. Holmes	Jefferson	Edna Wandschneider	x	x	x				
26	John E. Holmes	Jefferson	Mrs. George Pounder				x	x	x	x
27	James B. McPherson	Lake Geneva	Mrs. Ernest Niles						x	x
29	D. D. Parker	Abrams	Mrs. George Lince		x	x	x	x	x	x
33	W. H. Bennett	Richland Center	Lena Brucker				x	x	x	x
34	Charles E. Curtice	Whitewater	Augusta Scholcher					x		x	x
36	Alex Lowrie	Viroqua	Mrs. Will Best	x	x	x	x	x	x	x
37	Phil W. Plummer	Prairie du Chien	W. R. Graves		x	x				x
38	Wilson Colwell	La Crosse	Carrie Day		x	x	x	x	x	x
39	Thomas J. Hungerford	Spring Green	Helen L. Schwauke	x	x	x		x	x	x
41	Theodore L. Sutphen	Evansville	Cora E. Harris	x	x	x	x	x	x	x
42	Henry W. Cressey	Tomah	Mary Allengham	x	x		x	x	x	x
43	Raymond	Mayville	Mrs. F. McEachron				x	x	x	
44	James P. Shepard	Menasha	Jennie Friedland	x	x	x	x	x		
45	Louis P. Harvey	Darlington	Clara Flood		x	x	x	x	x	x
46	Henry Turner	New London	Anna E. Heath	x	x	x	x	x	x	x
47	Frank Prevy	Elroy	Mrs. Charlotte Morgan	x	x	x	x	x	x	x
48	Charles G. Bacon	Neillsville	Rose Arndt		x	x	x			
50	John Gillespie	Wisconsin Dells	Corrinne E. Marston	x	x	x	x			
52	Eagle	Eau Claire	Mrs.Minnie Fay	X	x					
52	Eagle	Eau Claire	Alice Warner		x					
52	Eagle	Eau Claire	Della Jarvis				x	x	x	x
53	George W. Bell	Wonewoc	Dora E. Tucker		x	x	x	x	x	x
54	Louis H. D. Craine	Beloit	Gladys Miller	x	x	x	x	x	x	
58	William Evans	Menomonie	Edith Edeberg		x	x		x	x	x
59	Angus S. Northrup	Mauston	Lillian Jax					x	x	x
60	A. D. Hamilton	Milton	Hosea Rood	x						
60	A. D. Hamilton	Milton	Mrs. Helen Drew		x					
61	William P. Mitchell	New Lisbon	Grace N. Taylor					x	x	x
65	F. Jackel	Spooner	Mrs. George Petey	x						
66	William T. Sherman	Platteville	J. A. Blakeley							x
68	James Comerford	Chippewa Falls	Agnes Groezinger		x	x		x	x	x
74	Edward A. Ramsey	Oconto	Mrs. John Donlevey	x	x	x	x	x	x	x
76	Rutherford B. Hayes	Elkhorn	Miss Emma Ferguson	x						
76	Rutherford B. Hayes	Elkhorn	Mrs. Emma Milbrath		x					
76	Rutherford B. Hayes	Elkhorn	Lucille French					x	x	x
77	John Flynn	La Crosse	Leona Boardman					x	x	x
78	John A. Kellogg	Antigo	Grace Newbury	x	x	x	x	x	x	x
87	Perrin C. Judkins	Alma Center	Agnes Merrill	x	x					
87	Perrin C. Judkins	Alma Center	Agnes Bopp			x	x	x	x	x
90	Wesley W. Patton	Brodhead	Charlotte Ties		x	x	x	x	x	x
91	Samuel Harrison	Depere	Jennie Haskins	x	x	x	x	x	x	x
92	William Moore	Black River Falls	Sarah Maddocks		x	x	x	x	x	

No.	Post Name	Town	Secretary	1929	1930	1931	1932	1933	1934	1935
94	Oliver D. Pease	Watertown	Mrs. Alice West	x	x	x				
94	Oliver D. Pease	Watertown	May Ceithamer				x	x	x	x
98	John E. Perkins	Augusta	Minnie Lighthuzer		x	x		x		
101	John McDermott	Boscobel	Emma Zilmer	x	x	x		x	x	x
102	Oscar F. Pinney	Monroe	Mr. Brunner						x	x
103	Benjamin I. Humphrey	New Richmond	Mrs. A. R. Kibbe					x	x	x
109	Williamson	Dodgeville	Mrs. Cora Hoskins		x					
110	James G. Blaine	Marshfield	Mrs. George Zimmer		x	x	x	x	x	
112	O. F. Pinney	Colby	Mrs. Eva Fielig	x	x					
114	Hans C. Heg	Waupun	Marion Heath		x	x	x	x		
117	George Hall	Beaver Dam	Ann Schneider		x	x	x	x	x	
121	Joe Morrow	Belleville	Mrs. H. W. Chatterden	x	x					
122	Badgero	Friendship	Frances Hopper		x		x	x	x	
124	Timothy O. Howe	Green Bay	Mary Liebman			x	x	x	x	x
125	George H. Legate	Mineral Point	Edna Holmes					x	x	x
126	F. A. Marden	King	Alice M. Bishop	x	x	x				
126	F. A. Marden	King	Mina Hawes				x	x	x	x
128	Albert Weatherbe	Chetek	Dea C. Wood	x	x	x	x	x	x	x
129	Hiram J. Lewis	Neenah	Mary Sheerin					x	x	x
130	Edwin A. Brown	Fond du Lac	Estelle M. Collins		x	x		x	x	
130	Edwin A. Brown	Fond du Lac	A. Pride							x
131	Lincoln County	Merrill	Rose T. Putnam	x	x	x	x	x	x	x
133	George D. Eggleston	Appleton	A. G. Sykes					x	x	x
135	Edward Saxe	Wautoma	Mrs. M. Ross					x	x	x
137	Henry S. Swift	Edgerton	Olive Wood		x	x	x	x	x	x
140	George A. Custer	Ashland	Katherine Lynch		x	x		x	x	x
141	Henry Didiot	Hillsboro	Mrs. Nellie Baley	x	x	x	x	x		x
142	Emerson Opdike	Clear Lake	Miss M. Harmon	x	x	x				
145	General James Shields	Medford	Ruby Truax	x	x	x	x			
146	Harvey M. Brown	Columbus	Ethel Koblitz		x	x	x	x	x	x
149	Plover	Plover	Vinette Strong	x	x	x		x	x	x
151	Edwin A. Clapp	Hudson	W. B. Webster	x						
151	Edwin A. Clapp	Hudson	Ruth B. Hughes		x	x	x	x	x	x
153	Philo C. Buckman	Stoughton	Mrs. Lynne F. Carr		x		x	x		
154	Allen McVey	LaFarge	Ada Cather			x	x	x	x	x
156	Stevens Point	Stevens Point	Mrs. Nicholas Berens				x	x	x	x
160	Hiram Russell	Fremont	Mary Lovejoy		x					
165	George M. West	Hartford	Anna M. Vetter					x	x	x
166	Martin W. Heller	Rice Lake	Ella George				x	x		
170	Alonzo Palmer	Superior	Anna I. Huot		x	x	x	x	x	x
173	Sam Monteith	Fennimore	Mrs. George Earle	x	x	x	x	x	x	
177	I. N. Nichols	River Falls	Julia M. Baker	x	x	x	x			
181	Allen Jackson	Phillips	A. M. DeBardelebon		x	x				

No.	Post Name	Town	Secretary	1929	1930	1931	1932	1933	1934	1935
181	Allen Jackson	Phillips	Mrs. Victor H. Helms					x	x	x
186	William Payne	Pardeeville	Mrs. B. F. Hall		x	x	x	x	x	
187	Gustave Wintermeyer	Sheboygan	Sidonia Hoberg		x	x	x	x	x	x
191	Lorenzo A. Dixon	Mount Horeb	Esther Gilbertson			x	x	x	x	
191	Lorenzo A. Dixon	Mount Horeb	L. O. Peterson							x
197	Walter Waterman	Plainfield	Blanche Waterman				x	x	x	x
199	H. S. Eggleston	Ripon	Miss Pearle Mowers			x	x	x	x	x
202	Harry Randall	Green Lake	Mrs. F. M. Spencer	x	x					
203	Fred Richter	Lowell	Ada Tanck		x	x	x	x		
205	J. B. Reynolds	Chilton	Mrs. Dodris Dheim	x						
207	Samuel H. Sizer	Marinette	C. H. Showard					x	x	x
209	Plum City	White Creek	Maude Bacon					x	x	x
212	Henry P. Davidson	Greenbush	Henry Stannard					x	x	x
220	John A. Hauff	Horicon	Miss Luella Disher		x	x	x	x	x	x
223	George C. Drake	Milwaukee	Ruby Esser	x		x	x	x	x	x
225	Cumberland	Cumberland	Mrs. Walter Huser					x		x
230	Frederick S. Lovell	Kenosha	Mrs. Gertrude Lewis McNeil		x	x	x	x	x	
234	Cyprian Downer	Bangor	S. C. Fauver					x	x	x
245	W. F. Dawes	Necedah	Elizabeth Demorist	x						
257	Peter Weber	Fountain City	Michael Welsch					x	x	x
258	Charles H. Ford	Galesville	Eva Shappe		x	x				
260	Solomon Meredith	Hayward	Mrs. J. B. Goulette		x	x	x	x	x	x
271	George H. Brayton	Fall River	Mattie M. Hansen			x	x	x	x	x
280	Rusk County	Ladysmith	Mrs. Agnes Goodrich		x	x	x	x	x	x

Grand Army of the Republic
POST BADGES

DELTON PICKET POST 1

CHIVAS POST 2,
MILWAUKEE

CHIVAS POST 2,
MILWAUKEE

WILLIAMS POST 4, BERLIN

POST 5, BUTTERNUT

POST 5, BUTTERNUT

THOMAS POST 6, DELEVAN

SAWYER POST 7, OMRO

VETERANS POST 8,
MILWAUKEE

HOOKER POST 9,
BARABOO

HOOKER POST 9,
BARABOO

OSHKOSH PUBLIC MUSEUM
SHERIDAN POST 10,
OSHKOSH

SHERIDAN POST 10,
OSHKOSH

OSHKOSH PUBLIC MUSEUM
SHERIDAN POST 10,
OSHKOSH

WASHBURN POST 11,
MADISON

WASHBURN POST 11,
MADISON

WASHBURN POST 11,
MADISON

L. FAIRCHILD POST 11,
MADISON

L. FAIRCHILD POST 11,
MADISON

L. FAIRCHILD POST 11,
MADISON

L. FAIRCHILD POST 11,
MADISON

RICHARDSON POST 12,
SHEBOYGAN FALLS

POST BADGES

RICHARDSON POST 12,
SHEBOYGAN FALLS

ROUSSEAU POST 14,
PORTAGE

ROUSSEAU POST 14,
PORTAGE

DROUSSEAU POST 14,
PORTAGE

MCKINLEY POST 15,
LA CROSSE

MCKINLEY POST 15,
LA CROSSE

WISCONSIN VETERANS MUSEUM
HARVEY POST 17, RACINE

CUSHING POST 19,
WAUKESHA

WISCONSIN VETERANS MUSEUM
CUSHING POST 19,
WAUKESHA

SARGENT POST 20,
JANESVILLE

SARGENT POST 20,
JANESVILLE

POST BADGES

SARGENT POST 20,
JANESVILLE

IRWIN POST 25, LODI

IRWIN POST 25, LODI

IRWIN POST 25, LODI

LYNN POST 30, SPARTA

LYNN POST 30, SPARTA

CURTICE POST 34,
WHITEWATER

FROST POST 35,
PRAIRIE DU SAC

SUTPHEN POST 41,
EVANSVILLE

CRESSY POST 42, TOMAH

SHEPARD POST 44,
MENASHA

POST BADGES

WISCONSIN VETERANS MUSEUM
HARVEY POST 45.
DARLINGTON

WISCONSIN VETERANS MUSEUM
HARVEY POST 45.
DARLINGTON

WISCONSIN VETERANS MUSEUM
HARVEY POST 45.
DARLINGTON

TURNER POST 46, NEW
LONDON

TURNER POST 46, NEW
LONDON

WISCONSIN VETERANS MUSEUM
TURNER POST 46,
NEW LONDON

BACON POST 48,
NEILLSVILLE

POST 49, GRANTSBURG

POST 49, GRANTSBURG

NEW LONDON PUBLIC MUSEUM
STARKWEATHER POST 51,
BEAR CREEK

NEW LONDON PUBLIC MUSEUM
STARKWEATHER POST 51,
BEAR CREEK

POST BADGES

WISCONSIN VETERANS MUSEUM
**EAGLE POST 52,
EAU CLAIRE**

CRANE POST 54, BELOIT

CUTLER POST 55, WAUSAU

WISCONSIN VETERANS MUSEUM
POST 60, MILTON

**SHERMAN POST 66,
PLATTEVILLE**

**SHERMAN POST 66,
PLATTEVILLE**

GRANT COUNTY HISTORICAL SOCIETY
**SHERMAN POST 66,
PLATTEVILLE**

WISCONSIN VETERANS MUSEUM
**SHERMAN POST 66,
PLATTEVILLE**

**TALLMAN POST 70,
CLINTON**

WISCONSIN VETERANS MUSEUM
FLYNN POST 77, LA CROSSE

WISCONSIN VETERANS MUSEUM
FLYNN POST 77, LA CROSSE

POST BADGES

WISCONSIN VETERANS MUSEUM
**KELLOGG POST 78,
ANTIGO**

**HAWLEY POST 81,
SHAWANO**

**HAWLEY POST 81,
SHAWANO**

**COLEMAN POST 82,
DURAND**

**FALLEN POST 83,
NORTH FREEDOM**

**FALLEN POST 83,
NORTH FREEDOM**

DEFOREST MUSEUM OF
CIVIL WAR HISTORY
TURNER POST 85, VIOLA

WISCONSIN VETERANS MUSEUM
TURNER POST 85, VIOLA

**JUDKINS POST 87,
ALMA CENTER**

VETERANS MUSEUM
**PATTON POST 90,
BRODHEAD**

**HARRISON POST 91,
DEPERE**

Grand Army of the Republic
POST BADGES

SAUK CO. HISTORICAL SOCIETY
MOORE POST 92, BLACK
RIVER FALLS

VETERANS MUSEUM
PEASE POST 94,
WATERTOWN

VETERANS MUSEUM
PEASE POST 94
WATERTOWN

PEASE POST 94,
WATERTOWN

CHRISTIAN POST 95,
MONDOVI

OATES POST 96,
SHULLSBURG

NELSON POST 97,
FORESTVILLE

PERKINS POST 98, AUGUSTA

VETERANS MUSEUM
STEVENS POST 100,
FOX LAKE

MCDERMOTT POST 101,
BOSCOBEL

MCDERMOTT POST 101,
BOSCOBEL

POST BADGES

MCDERMOTT POST 101,
BOSCOBEL

PINNEY POST 102,
MONROE

VETERANS MUSEUM
PINNEY POST 102,
MONROE

TOWNSEND POST 105,
PEWAUKEE

VETERANS MUSEUM
WILLIAMSON POST 109,
DODGEVILLE

HEG POST 114, WAUPUN

HEG POST 114, WAUPUN

HEG POST 114, WAUPUN

VETERANS MUSEUM
ELLSWORTH POST 118,
ELLSWORTH

VETERANS MUSEUM
STEADMAN POST 120,
MANAWA (LITTLE WOLF)

MOWER POST 121
BELLVILLE

POST BADGES

BADGERO POST 122,
FRIENDSHIP

BADGERO POST 122,
FRIENDSHIP

BADGERO POST 122
FRIENDSHIP

HOWE POST 124,
GREEN BAY

HOWE POST 124,
GREEN BAY

VETERANS MUSEUM
LEGATE POST 125,
MINERAL POINT

LEGATE POST 125,
MINERAL POINT

VETERANS MUSEUM
MARDEN POST 126, KING

BARRON CO. HISTORICAL SOCIETY
WEATHERBE POST 128,
CHETEK

BROWN POST 130,
FOND DU LAC

BROWN POST 130,
FOND DU LAC

POST BADGES

VETERANS MUSEUM
BROWN POST 130,
FOND DU LAC

GRANT CO. HISTORICAL SOCIETY
COX POST 132, LANCASTER

GRANT CO. HISTORICAL SOCIETY
COX POST 132, LANCASTER

EGGLESTON POST 133,
APPLETON

VETERANS MUSEUM
EGGLESTON POST 133,
APPLETON

SAXE POST 135, WAUTOMA

SHELDON POST 136,
BRANDON

GRAVES POST 139, BERLIN

VETERANS MUSEUM
GRAVES POST 139, BERLIN

VETERANS MUSEUM
CUSTER POST 140,
ASHLAND

VETERANS MUSEUM
CUSTER POST 140,
ASHLAND

POST BADGES

BARRON CO. HISTORICAL SOCIETY
DIDIOT POST 141,
HILLSBORO

HASKELL POST 146,
COLUMBUS

PLOVER POST 149, PLOVER

JERRY CARLTON
EUBANK POST 150,
HANCOCK

JERRY CARLTON
EUBANK POST 150,
HANCOCK

CLAPP POST 151, HUDSON

READ POST 155,
KEWAUNEE

READ POST 155,
KEWAUNEE

PALMER POST 170,
SUPERIOR

VETERANS MUSEUM
PALMER POST 170,
SUPERIOR

PALMER POST 170,
SUPERIOR

POST BADGES

CONCKLIN POST 171,
EAST TROY

VETERANS MUSEUM
SANDERS POST 179,
NORWALK

VETERANS MUSEUM
PAYNE POST 186,
PARDEEVILLE

VETERANS MUSEUM
PAYNE POST 186,
PARDEEVILLE

VETERANS MUSEUM
KERSHAW POST 188,
BRIGGSVILLE

LITTLE POST 190, KIEL

ETERANS MUSEUM
DIXON POST 191,
MT. HOREB

ETERANS MUSEUM
DIXON POST 191,
MT. HOREB

WATERMAN POST 197,
PLALINFIELD

WATERMAN POST 197,
PLAINFIELD

EGGLESTON POST 199,
RIPON

POST BADGES

EGGLESTON POST 199,
RIPON

EGGLESTON POST 199,
RIPON

SIZER POST 207,
MARINETTE

SIZER POST 207,
MARINETTE

HAMILTON POST 208,
SUN PRAIRIE

HAMILTON POST 208,
SUN PRAIRIE

VETERANS MUSEUM
GURLEY POST 245,
BLANCHARDVILLE

YOUNG POST 227,
WINNECONNE

VETERANS MUSEUM
POTTER POST 229,
CAMBRIDGE

LOVELL POST 230,
KENOSHA

DOWNER POST 234,
BANGOR

POST BADGES

MONROE CO. HISTORICAL SOCIETY
FISK POST 235, CATARACT

OTIS POST 238, TRIMBELLE

OSHKOSH PUBLIC MUSEUM
SCOTT POST 241,
OSHKOSH

OSHKOSH PUBLIC MUSEUM
SCOTT POST 241,
OSHKOSH

OSHKOSH PUBLIC MUSEUM
SCOTT POST 241,
OSHKOSH

OSHKOSH PUBLIC MUSEUM
SCOTT POST 241,
OSHKOSH

OSHKOSH PUBLIC MUSEUM
SCOTT POST 241,
OSHKOSH

OSHKOSH PUBLIC MUSEUM
SCOTT POST 241,
OSHKOSH

ANDEREGG POST 242,
AHNAPEE

VETERANS MUSEUM
HENDRICKS POST 246,
CAMPBELLSPORT

POST BADGES

VETERANS MUSEUM
BEAULIEU POST 247, KAUKAUNA

VETERANS MUSEUM
BEAULIEU POST 247, KAUKAUNA

VETERANS MUSEUM
BRYANT POST 253, LAKE MILLS

VETERANS MUSEUM
LEDERGERBER POST 261, KESHENA

VETERANS MUSEUM
DAVIS POST 264, PEDEE

VETERANS MUSEUM
BRAYDON POST 271, FALL RIVER

VETERANS MUSEUM
BRAYDON POST 271, FALL RIVER

WATROUS POST 276, SPENCER

BADGES

The comrades were marked men. And the mark was a Grand Army of the Republic lapel pin.

The pin was a familiar and important distinguishing mark for the men of the G.A.R., the wearing of which was a privilege both cherished and jealously guarded. Indeed, the veterans convinced the Wisconsin Legislature to provide by law that none but Grand Army members in good standing could wear the distinctive button. They saw to it, moreover, that the statute was enforced. If someone was seen to be sporting the badge without the authority to do so (most often a veteran who had not maintained his membership), the local post, or perhaps even the department would cite the statute to the offending man.

That emblem, of course, was important to the veterans because it identified themselves to others and others to themselves, as brethren, not only from the late war, but also as veterans worthy of the camaraderie of kindred men, and even more particularly, worthy of patronage by fellow veterans in their postwar endeavors.

Wearing that pin was an everyday thing. It was a quiet way of identifying their affiliation with the Grand Army. The general public was familiar with the emblem for it was a daily reminder of the presence of these veterans in their midst.

But to the veterans themselves, the Grand Army Badge was worn most often at the post meetings and other G.A.R. functions, and became the major symbol of their affiliation. Its use, too, was limited by statute to members. The badge was a specifically prescribed symbol that evolved from the first days of the order.

The original Grand Army Badge, pictured at left, was adopted in 1866, the first year of the Grand Army of the Republic. The design was interesting. Crossed sabers in the bottom half separate the initials G.A.R. Above that is an anchor with bayoneted rifles extending upward. Within that span between bayonets were the number "3" and the letters "B" and "N."

The term that the number and letters represented was apparently "Third Battalion." The order was especially tight-lipped about itself in those days, so the meaning was never recorded. In his history of the order written 22 years later, Robert Beath commented cryptically, "the significance of the symbols will be at once recalled by all who were then members of the Order."[1]

In their book written for the Orders and Medals Society of America, Membership and National Encampment Badges of the Grand Army of the Republic, 1866-1949 Kenneth R. Johnson and Jeffrey B. Floyd note that the meaning of that badge "has all but been lost." However, they construct a hypothesis that is more than plausible.

"During the Civil War, a regiment consisted of two battalions. Once the enlistment of the regiment was over, whether three months or three years, the regiment could be reformed with its original number if sufficient veterans reenlisted. These veterans became a third battalion and were veteran volunteers. In battle, the third battalion stood behind the first two battalions to steady them. After the war, the G.A.R. saw themselves as part of the shield of the Union. The regular army was the first battalion, the militia the second battalion, and the G.A.R. as the third battalion, or the veteran volunteers. Many veterans had taken their weapons home and they were stored in G.A.R. posts ready to return to the field should the South attempt to rise again."[2]

The imagery on and design of that 3BN badge was expanded in 1868. The new badge was topped by an eagle with spread wings, holding a bundle of arrows in its left claw and an olive branch in the right.

Within half a year, by January 1869, variations on that badge were authorized. Officers of the order were permitted to wear a symbol of their military rank on a disc suspended from the 3BN badge. These symbols followed the military designs of the star, eagle, oak leaf, and bar.

This adaptation of the 3BN motif was short-lived, however. By the time a special national encampment convened in New York on October 27, 1869, Inspector General F. A. Starring had designed a completely new badge that received the unanimous approval of the delegates.

Starring's design was based on the Medal of Honor, which had originated during the Civil War. In the center is the figure of the goddess Minerva as an emblem of Loyalty. A soldier and a sailor flank her, clasping hands. These are symbolic of Fraternity. Below the two veterans are figures of two children representing Charity, "receiving benediction and the assurance of protection from these comrades,"[3] in the words of the official circular describing the new badge, sent from national headquarters early in 1870.

1. Robert B. Beath, *History of the Grand Army of the Republic*, (New York: Bryan, Taylor and Co., 1889), 653.
2. Kenneth R. Johnson and Jeffrey B. Floyd, *Membership and National Encampment Badges of the Grand Army of the Republic, 1866-1949*, (Glassboro, NJ: Orders and Medals Society of America, 1997), 3.
3. Beath, *History*, 654.

A circle around the symbolic figures bears the legend: "Grand Army of the Republic, 1861 – Veteran – 1866." The five points of the star which radiate from that central theme bear insignia for the branches of service: bugle, infantry; crossed cannon, artillery; crossed muskets, Marine Corps; crossed sabers, cavalry; and anchor, navy. The reverse of this badge contained the two dozen recognized corps badges.

This badge abandoned the Third Battalion theme, suggesting that by 1869 the G.A.R. felt assured that the South would not rise again. It may not have been one hundred percent assurance, but it was enough to relegate the mystical "3BN" into the mists of the past.

The new star was suspended on a ribbon/flag from an eagle with wings spread wide, talons resting on crossed cannons atop a mound of cannon balls, representing the G.A.R's more self-assured depiction of defense.

Johnson and Floyd point out that this new G.A.R. badge bore striking similarities to the Medal of Honor. "This eagle and cannon suspension is a close facsimile of the eagle suspension of the Army Medal of Honor. The star is also quite similar to the Medal of Honor, so one could be easily confused with the other."[4]

It was the 1869 badge that was made from the bronze of captured Confederate cannon, a practice that the Grand Army of the Republic came to insist upon in the manufacture of such badges, including succeeding versions. But by 1884 there were no captive Confederate cannons available.

This third version of the badge continued in service for a number of years, but its close resemblance to the Congressional Medal of Honor, left, was something of a problem. While the latter's eagle is right atop the star rather than separated by a ribbon, it is still the same pose with upraised wings and clutching a sword hilt with one talon, seemingly resting on the cannon barrels. There was an undercurrent of complaint about the similarities.

So in 1880 the G.A.R. adopted an altered design. The eagle remained on the crossed cannon, but was now clutching the sword with both talons. Its wings, instead of pointing upward, pointed straight out. The new bird might be described as more alert or more warlike than its predecessor. Just the set of its wings seemed to suggest a more aggressive bird.

As a matter of fact, it was not specifically the aggressiveness of the eagle surmounting this fourth design for the membership badge that ended up bringing another change, but it was something akin to that. The points of those wings were a bit too pointed, too prone to poke the unwary wearer.

The 1884 national encampment decreed that the sharp, pointed wings should be slightly rounded. This new feature and some changes to the reverse—the addition of Sheridan's and Wilson's Corps badges as well as Hancock's First Veteran Corps—brought to 27 the corps symbols on the reverse.

It was this fifth style, not too much different from the fourth, that constituted a majority of the badges manufactured.

In 1884, the Grand Army of the Republic adopted the lapel button that marked the Grand Army man to the general public. Its design is essentially the emblem within the center of the star of the regular membership badge.

Very early in its history the Grand Army adopted variations of the membership badge of the time to differentiate national, department, and even post officers. Thus there came into being a fairly wide variety of versions of the basic membership badge.

Perhaps the most important badge to a man in the Grand Army of the Republic, surpassing even the lapel button, was the post badge, showing not only that he was a GAR member, but that he was a member of his particular post.

The post badge can be broadly categorized as either the "memorial" badge or the "parade" badge. But as the illustrations on succeeding pages show, there were a great number of variations in both categories. These were post, rather than department or national badges, purchased by the posts from a variety of suppliers. As tastes differed, so too did the designs the post officers chose for their members.

The "memorial" badge was worn for such occasions as funerals and Memorial Day programs, the men processing in all solemnity to the cemetery, each wearing a badge with a black ribbon bearing a legend such as "In Memoriam" or, occasionally, "Honor Our Fallen Dead."

The "parade" variety was often fairly colorful. Red, white, and blue ribbons were frequently favored, but as the badge upon which the ribbon hung evolved, they included finer artwork in metal or celluloid. The ribbon itself was often only one color: red or blue usually, but occasionally black, or rarely, some other color.

Some of the posts were frugal enough to choose a reversible ribbon. This allowed members to wear the same badge for all occasions. On one side was the somber "In Memoriam" ribbon. Then they could slip the ribbon off, turn it around, and the badge became its more colorful "parade" counterpart.

The "parade" type was probably more often used. They were appropriate for use whenever Grand Army men were outfitted for public display, except, of course, for the somber occasions for which the "memorial" design was appropriate.

Except for those times, the more colorful badge was standard. They were usually worn for post meetings. Some of these might bear devices showing what office, if any, the man was occupying. And naturally, it was essential that they be worn at department or national encampments. They bore the name of the post, its number, and its city. Usually they disclosed the department or the name of the state.

On the inserted pages are color pictures of many post badges used by men of the Department of Wisconsin. They come from a number of collections, and in total, display the great variety of designs and materials in use over many years.

---

4. Johnson and Floyd, *Membership*, 4.

APPENDICES

APPENDIX 'A': Cleaning the Slate

Grand Army of the Republic[1]

> Headquarters Department of Wisconsin, G.A.R
> Milwaukee, Wis. Nov. 20, 1871.

General Orders, No. 6.

I. In accordance with the notice on the 20th day of October, ult., in General orders No. 4, from these Headquarters, the charters of all posts in this Department which are one year in arrears for reports or dues are annulled and cease from and after this date to be of any force or effect, viz.:

Post No. 3, Mazomanie,	Post No. 4, Fond du Lac,
No. 5, Green Bush,	No. 6, Ahnapee,
No. 7, Edgerton,	No. 8, Green Bay,
No. 10, Oshkosh,	No. 11, Racine,
No. 12, Mifflin,	No. 13, Sun Prairie,
No. 14, Menominee,	No. 15, Butte d' Morts,
No. 16, Watertown,	No. 17, Sturgeon Bay,
No. 18, Waterloo,	No. 19, Boscobel,
No. 20, Rome,	No. 21, New London,
No. 23, Black Earth,	No. 24, Richland Center,
No. 25, Mineral Point,	No. 26, Waukau,
No. 27, Martinsville,	No. 28, Jefferson,
No. 29, Lodi,	No. 30, Aztalan,
No. 31, Lake Mills,	No. 32, Stockbridge,
No. 33, Platteville,	No. 34, Hebron,
No. 35, Albion,	No. 36, Eau Claire,
No. 37, Boscobel,	No. 38, Manitowoc,
No. 39, Chilton,	No. 40, Columbus,
No. 41, Dodgeville,	No. 42, Argyle,
No. 43, Princeton,	No. 44, Prescott,
No. 45, Wautoma,	No. 46, Markesan,
No. 47, Durand,	No. 54, River Falls,
No. 57, Sheboygan Falls,	No. 58, Bloomington,
No. 59, Monroe,	No. 60, Prairie du Sac,
No. 61, Mt. Hope,	No. 62, Salem,
No. 63, Lancaster,	No. 66, Cascade,
No. 67, Jamestown,	No. 68, Oregon,
No. 69, Waupaca,	No. 70, Beloit,
No. 71, Black River Falls	No. 72, Patch Grove,
No. 73, Kenosha,	No. 74, Pensaukee,
No. 75, Alma,	No. 79, Waukesha,
No. 77, Geneva,	No. 82, Mukwanago.
No. 88, Wausau	

Charters were never issued for Nos. 49, 50, 51, 52 and 53, and Nos. 55, 56, 65 and 80 were voluntarily surrendered.

II. The following Posts will be designated hereafter by the numbers opposite each:

Cassius Fairchild Post No. 1, Madison	No. 1
Ripon Post No. 2, Ripon	No. 2
Phil. Sheridan Post No. 9, Milwaukee	No. 3
John H. Williams Post No. 22, Berlin	No. 4
Lyon Post No. 48, Cazenovia	No. 5
Beaver Dam Post No. 63, Beaver Dam	No. 6
John Matteson Post No. 78, Embarrass	No. 7
Veteran Post No. 84, National Asylum	No. 8
George H. Thomas Post No. 85, Winneconne	No. 9
[Not named] Post No. 86, Oshkosh	No. 10
[Not named] Post No. 87, Racine	No. 11

The Posts whose charters are hereby annulled will not be recognized as forming any part of the Grand Army of the Republic. But members of such Posts who desire to continue their membership as Comrades may receive transfer papers, in accordance with section 4 of Article 4, Chapter 2d, Revised Rules and Regulations, upon application to these Head Quarters. Provided: such Comrade shall first place himself in good standing by the payment of his dues to date of dissolution of his Post.

The Grand Commander, or any of his Staff, will, as heretofore, take pleasure in rendering the Comrades of Posts whose charters are annulled, any assistance in their power to organize new Posts. Correspondence is invited, and communications addressed to Geo. A. Hannaford, 17 Newhall House, Milwaukee, will receive prompt attention.

The Posts now belonging to the Department are congratulated by the Grand Commander upon their promotion, and he trusts that they will extend to him the same hearty co-operation in the future as they have in the past.

The press in all parts of the State are respectfully requested to publish this order.

> By order of
> E. FERGUSON
> *Grand Commander*
>
> GEO. A. HANNAFORD,
> *Assistant Adjutant General*

---

1. As published in Berlin Courant, December 14, 1871.

APPENDIX 'B': To Go or Not to Go to Gettysburg

The Seventy-first National Encampment of the Grand Army of the Republic was held September 5 through 10, 1937, at the Lorraine Hotel, Madison. It devoted an inordinate amount of time to one subject: Gettysburg.

The discussion was even more specific than that. It was, in fact, whether the G.A.R. ought to agree to a get together with their late protagonists on the field at Gettysburg on the occasion of the seventy-fifth anniversary of that climactic battle, July 1–3, 1938.

What follows are liberal excerpts of the proceedings centered on that issue. Remember that the men taking part in the discussion are all almost 90 years old or more. (Commander C. H. William Ruhe was among the younger ones, at age 88.)

The idea of a Blue and Gray "reunion" at Gettysburg had been broached some two years before and was discussed at earlier national encampments, but any decision whether the G.A.R. would be involved was put off until the gathering at Madison.

The issue came up initially this time at the September 6 meeting of the National Council of Administration. Following are excerpts from the transcripts, first of that meeting, and then of some of the floor discussion before all the delegates later in the week, and finally the action taken by the Grand Army on getting together at Gettysburg:[2]

. . .

Comrade [G. I.] GORDON [Oklahoma]: I don't know that it would be any place even to mention it here at all but nearly a year ago I received a communication from the State of Pennsylvania from some committee stating they were proposing to pay the expenses, the traveling expense and the boarding expense of veterans of the Civil War and their caretakers, and asking whether I would go. They also asked how long a period I was in favor of, mentioning something like two weeks' time. They also asked about having a sort of rehearsal of that final charge there, Pickett's charge, and asked my opinion of that, and so forth.

Now I don't know whether it is any place to bring that matter up at all here or not, but several comrades received the same, just similar invitations. We have answered them, and the answer as given by some of us is to this effect, that we will be glad to go but we think that the time is too long, and so far as I know nearly every one that I have heard from said that he didn't favor any rehearsal or attempt to show us Pickett's charge.

And then there was another suggestion, that we hoped that there would be no placing of the Stars and Bars where any loyal citizen would have to pass under them or appear to be marching behind them, and some such answers as that. I heard it . . . .

I just wondered what the reaction of the comrades with reference to the matter is. . . . It seemed at first as if it was a very fine proposition. I know that my heart responded "Yes, I would like to go." But I don't want to do anything that would seem to cast discredit upon Old Glory.

Comrade [John] SHEARER [Texas]: I live in the South. I have lived there 42 years. When I first went down there it was nothing but Confederate flags, and you never see a Confederate flag now. Those people down there are just as loyal as we are. I received a communication—the same one that we are up against—of the State of Pennsylvania, and that all our expenses are to be paid . . . . Now I will tell you boys, I quit fighting after the battle of Bentonville when Joe Johnston surrendered. I want to tell you it was nothing but a family row, and the only way to get a fair judgment is to place yourself on the other fellow's side and look at it from that side. Now, boys, let's quit fighting. . . .

Comrade [George T.] LEECH [Maryland]: I want to say that I am also from Dixie. I was born in Tennessee, and my mother was a slave owner, so I am pretty well imbued with that kind of material. But I want to tell you this, that there never was the least iota of a drop of rebel blood in my body. It is all right as far as the men are concerned that were in the battle front in the South. I haven't met but one disloyal one since the Civil War. But I tell you I can't say that of the women.

We have got over one thousand women in Maryland that are Daughters of the Confederacy. I want to say that 95 percent of those women are the daughters or granddaughters of men that fought from the Southern States—not from the State of Maryland. There is a big mistake in regard to the interests of the soldiers that went out from Maryland. The record will show in Washington on the books that Maryland sent out over 60,000 men in the Union Army.

Commander-in-chief RUHE: Yes; they were very loyal.

Comrade LEECH: And there wasn't a State in the South but South Carolina that didn't send us a regiment of Union soldiers. That is correct. Very fortunately I came across a man who is a minister in the church that was a member of a regiment in North Carolina that was a Union regiment. He sent me a button. I said, "Where did you get that from?" He said, "I got that where I am a member." He put his hand up and said, "I have got a right to wear that and I am proud of it." And bless your life, it was a Union badge, a Grand Army button. He was as loyal as you could find them.

But you know among the women of Maryland that belong to the Confederate Daughters you will find very little loyalty among them. They have several times paraded on Flag Day—mind you, on Flag Day—and they have flirted that rag they call the flag before our faces. And the first time they started out I was commander of the Department of Maryland, and we had all together about two hundred active women, and children, too, in

---

2. From Journal of the Seventy-First National Encampment of the Grand Army of the Republic, Madison, Wis., September 5 to 10, 1937.

that line. As soon as I heard there was a Confederate body going to march with us I went to the president and said, "Where is your flag?" She pointed to a pole that had something wrapped around it. I went to it and pulled it out and it was a rebel flag. I said; "You are going to march?" She said, "Yes; we are and we are going to carry that." I said, "You carry that and we won't march." I says: "That is not a flag. It has got 16 stars in it. As long as I have lived in Maryland it has never been out of the Union."

I am a Marylander. I am a loyal Marylander, and I am here to say that there never was a time in the State of Maryland that any part of that body voted to go out of the Union. They were loyal from the commencement. Three times they voted as opposed to secession and in favor of the Union. . . .

I want to say that I am opposed to going in a line with any body of men that has a rebel flag with 16 stars or in fact with 11 stars in it.

Commander-in-Chief RUHE: Any further remarks on this question? It is a good place to discuss it.

Comrade [C. H.] KINNEY [Nebraska]: Now, I don't know anything about Maryland and all that, but I got a communication from the South after they had their meeting in Texas, and he said they carried the rebel flag in their organization. And I know from others they had it there, and if they carry a rebel flag they are not in the Union. . . .

As far as the women are concerned, I know that because I have been down South half a dozen or more times since the war. They are more antagonistic than the men.

But I want to say this here, that if they do vote to go to Gettysburg I won't march anywhere near a rebel flag or march alongside of a Southern soldier. I have no antagonism to a southern soldier, it is just the principle that they fought for.

Comrade [Sol] ZARBAUGH [Ohio]: Now I am spending time in southern Florida. I have been down there for 8 years. I have gone all over the State. I have been very much interested in meeting the school boards in cities, and every school in the State of Florida has an American flag and they salute the flag and teach the children to do the same. Georgia just a few days ago passed a bill, if you noticed in the papers, that every school and the teacher in that school has got to see a flag there and salute it by the school, and if they don't do that they cannot draw their pay. I'll tell you, the South has a fine class of people. I like them. And so far as the reunion at Gettysburg is concerned, when I got a long questionnaire to fill out I didn't see that we as a Grand Army had very much to do with it. It is a reunion gotten up by the people paying the expenses, the people of Pennsylvania. If we don't want to go we don't have to go. If we want to go and no effort to go there, and march under the Stars and Stripes, why that is our business. I am going to go if I am living.

Comrade SHEARER: I attended the reunion of the Blue and the Gray at Gettysburg, I think it was in '13, and I never saw a Confederate flag there.

Commander-in-chief RUHE: No. . . .

Comrade [W. H.] BILBEE [New Jersey]: I was down at the one-hundredth anniversary of the surrender of Cornwallis, and as commander of an organization I met Gen. Fitzhugh Lee. He made the remark, "We have buried the hatchet." I had my Grand Army badge on, and in my organization over three-fourths were Grand Army men. He says, "We have buried the hatchet." He said, "Let them leave it to us boys that did the fighting. We will settle it."

Comrade [Ira] STORMES [Utah]: I am from Utah. I am not a Mormon. Two years ago on Memorial Day the women wanted to fly a rebel flag. I said, "Nothing doing." I said, "If they stick it up I am going to tear it down." I went to the head ones of the Legion and told them "if that flag is flown there is going to be a row." It was not flown. It didn't fly and it ain't going to fly, not in Utah, not while I am there.

Comrade LEECH: I want to say that I endorse every word that has been said in regard to the men that was in the front on the rebel side. I have never met but one of those in the last 70 years that had any animosity, and while they are applauding General Lee and saying good things about him I think that he deserves every good word that can be said about him. General Lee has been true to his surrender.

Comrade [M.H.] DAVIDSON [Kentucky]: This question of speaking about the Blue and the Gray, I expect I have had pretty near as much experience among the Gray as among the Blue in Kentucky. I have lived there since the war, and, of course, in Louisville we have more or less Confederate sentiment. But they are like the balance of the Blue, they are dying off, too. . . .

The question that I wish to bring up was this. As I understand it there was put a question to your commander as to whether or not the Grand Army was going to attend the celebration at Gettysburg. I was in Gettysburg during that week of the celebration in July 1913. I spent a week there. I don't remember of seeing a rebel flag, and I know very well I did not march under any. There was none there to march under. I heard many of the Confederates talk, and as they expressed themselves, "our little old flag," "we recognize it as that rag." One of them even went so far as to say, "It is nothing more than a dish rag. Why do we care for that little old rag? We are under the Stars and Stripes today and we are going to stay there, just the same as you fellows will. We are going to support it just the same. . . ."

The question is, Are we going to Gettysburg? That is what I would like to know. I am speaking of the body. Individually I am going—I will say that—if nothing prevents.

Commander-in-Chief RUHE: Any other remarks by any of the comrades?

Comrade GORDON: I believe I am the one that brought this up, or am rather responsible in some way for all of this discussion we have been hearing here. So far as any personal feeling is concerned, the war ended when I was discharged, and, personally, some of my best friends are men who served under the Stars and Bars. . . .

I believe that because of all this thing that we call sentiment the southern women and the southern men saw the Stars and Bars when it represented their aspirations. I think they have a right to cherish it. I allow them that right. I don't believe that the average southern man or woman is disloyal today. I have no reason to think from any conversation that I ever had that southern women really feel toward the North as we would like for them to feel. They may have personal friends, but still there is some feeling of resentment. . . .

Now, I have this to say, that I do not understand for a moment that the Grand Army is invited as an organization to go there to Pennsylvania. My understanding is that it is an individual matter and that we are invited as individuals to come. . . .

But with reference to the rebel flag, I don't see why they should not be allowed to use it in decorations. I see no reason why they should not be allowed to. But I would rather, personally, I would a great deal rather that always the flag that we marched under should be above it. And I am reminded of what Mr. Lincoln said the night that Richmond surrendered when they came to him and serenaded him and asked for a speech. Mr. Lincoln was very careful in those days not to speak without a manuscript because of the misuse of what he might have said. He excused himself from making a speech, and then he said: "We have captured—Richmond—Dixie. We have captured Dixie, and I will ask the band to play 'Dixie.'"

And so Dixie is ours and the rebel flag is ours, and it belongs to us.

It is our capture, and I am willing to march beside a man that was in the Confederacy and march under the Stars and Stripes. And I am willing, if he wants to wear the rebel flag, to let him have the rebel flag. I think he has a right to still have a sentimental feeling toward it, and I will not object to that. . . .

Comrade [Thomas] AMBROSE [Illinois]: May I ask for information? Has this body of the Grand Army of the Republic received officially an invitation to participate in the Gettysburg reunion?

Commander in Chief RUHE: Yes. There was a representative at the encampment in Grand Rapids, and he spoke upon it there at some length. There was a very big controversy over it and it was finally passed on. It was stated that the individual members could go if they wanted to, and those that didn't want to would stay away. But the question of the flag was not raised until the latter end of it and I took part in the discussion. But the matter was referred then to the next encampment. They did not act upon it, but they referred it to this coming encampment.

Now is there any other comrade wishing to speak?

Comrade KINNEY: I just want to say that the Southern Confederacy—Alabama at least—are teaching in their schools that the Southern Confederacy was right in their going from the Union. . . . They are teaching the children of Alabama that the North was in the wrong in the war, and started out and they are teaching then that it is right to hold onto the Southern Confederacy. . . .

Commander-in-Chief RUHE: Any other comrade? If all of the comrades are through, the commander in chief will have a few words to say, but I want to give you all the opportunity first. . . .

We are discussing now the question of the Gettysburg reunion. I was at the 1913 reunion practically the whole time. . . .

The southerners had their rebel flags there, but they were advised they could not unfurl them. They were furled and nobody got to see them. They were advised to that effect.

Now then comes this reunion. It was discussed quite exhaustively at Grand Rapids [1935], and I made there a strong argument against the rebel flag being displayed at any reunion. It was referred to the encampment at Washington [1936], and the encampment at Washington referred it to this one. In the meantime I got in touch and pretty well acquainted with the secretary of that commission, Roy . . .

I saw Mr. Roy a few weeks ago. . . . I told him: "You will have to appear at the encampment at Madison, and you will have to explain to the satisfaction of the members of the Grand Army of the Republic as to whether this reunion you speak of is to be a reunion of rebels and Union men under their respective flags, or whether it is to be a reunion of United States citizens." Said I. "There is only one flag in this country at the present time, and I want everybody to distinctly understand – you and everybody else," and everybody in this room—"that when the surrender took place at Appomattox every rebel soldier was subject to the oath of allegiance that was again taken to support the Constitution and the flag of the United States. . . ."

I will not march under a rebel flag, I will not march in a column where a rebel flag is displayed and I will not take part in any reunion where the different exhibits and everything else is decorated with any flag outside of the Stars and Stripes of the Nation. [Applause.]

The rebel flag represented no principle except that of destruction. They were not injured in any principle. . . .

So we are at the present point at this situation. When the question finally comes up for action in this encampment it will be just simply this. Will we, the northern and southern soldiers, or the Union and Confederate soldiers, as we will call them here, will we in any gathering in which we jointly take part, permit the colors of an institution that represented nothing in God's world except destruction of the United States, will we let that predominate on a par with the Stars and Stripes, the colors of the flag of the United States of America for which we fought? That will be the question that will come up before this encampment when a representative of the commission appears.

I told him he would have to be here and explain this thing. The legislation would be—we cannot compel a Civil War veteran who does not belong to the Grand Army of the Republic to remain away. We can ask him to. But we can say to the Grand Army man: If you want to be true to your country, if you want to be true to your organization made up only of those who took part in that great conflict, you will stay away from a reunion which will permit the exhibition of something that tried to destroy the United States.

The National Council of Administration meeting shortly adjourned.

The matter of the invitation to Gettysburg was an order of business before the full encampment on September 8:

Commander-in-chief RUHE: Comrades, allow me to introduce Mr. Roy, the secretary of the Gettysburg Commission, and we will listen to his statement in reference to this and then the questions that may be propounded will be taken up.

Mr. PAUL L. ROY, of Pennsylvania: Thank you, Mr. Commander, and greetings, members of the G. A. R., it is a happy privilege for me to be the executive secretary of the Pennsylvania State commission, and it is also a double privilege for me to address you this afternoon. . . .

Our commission is established to perfect plans and preparations for the seventy-fifth anniversary of that titanic and historic 3 days' battle at Gettysburg and to prepare plans for the final joint reunion of the Blue and the Gray at Gettysburg, Pa., from June 2 to July 6, 1938—next summer.

In 1913 the fiftieth anniversary of the Battle of Gettysburg was observed. . . . At the fiftieth anniversary—perhaps many of you gentlemen were present—there were 54,000 veterans of the North and the South under canvas at that time. . . .

There will be a tent camp for you and a tent camp for the Gray. They will not be alongside of one another; they will be separate. . . .

Now, the question of a flag, I understand very thoroughly, is a very ticklish proposition. But you gentlemen are not going to be embarrassed in any way or form. I pledge you that, as an adopted son of Pennsylvania. I am a native of Wisconsin, but my home is in Pennsylvania and has been for the last 12 years.

Comrade STREETOR: All right. I want to say this: The crime of Gettysburg is like an unredeemed sinner, the darkness of sin without a cross. . . . The crime of the Southern Confederacy is without a savior, without a redemption. There is not blood enough and never will be, in the Southern United States—never blood enough to wash out the sin, the crime of the Rebellions.

Commander-in-Chief RUHE: There was a comrade here, if he has got anything to say, any question to ask Mr. Roy, he will come to the microphone here and say what he has to say.

Comrade ALBERT GAGE of Illinois: My question is simply this: If I among other participants in the 1913 fiftieth anniversary of the Battle of Gettysburg who took a part in it in such a way that I know from both sides expressing it, therefore I am not

going into any item about the question, but after the Fourth of July at Gettysburg we met in the hotel there, all classes of people, and we decided among ourselves to hold in the year 1938 a peace jubilee as an anniversary of the Battle of Gettysburg, the seventy-fifth anniversary. I corresponded with the secretary of this commission. He wrote me a letter that they would take it up. I have had no answer since. That is the question I want to ask.

Is it possible for this commission and the Grand Army of the Republic and the allied orders, and the whole Nation for that matter, to throw this whole condition into a peace jubilee in 1938. That is what we started in 1913. That is my plea that we do that. All honor to Philadelphia and Pennsylvania for what she has done. If you go you will get what I did, boys, at that battle reunion, you and every one of you here. Let's go anyhow, no matter what they do there. [Applause.] Let's go. Let's go.

If it is possible to make it a national affair, let the committee put their oars in and let us know. If it is not possible, let us know it right here and now and let us confine it locally. That is the question I want to ask him, Commander in Chief, whether this is to be for the Blue and Gray alone, of which I am the commander in chief and have been ever since I was elected. For nearly 30 years I have kept myself under a cloud, for the simple reason that every time that they found out that I had anything to say on the subject some comrade got up and said, "Oh, well, he is a rebel sympathizer." I tell you we are all Americans today, and if you were out associating with Confederates you would find there are men among them just the same as we are.

I want to tell you just what happened here last night. An old lady sat down by the side of me and she said, "What did you do in the Civil War?" "Why," I said, "I shot rebels." "Terrible," she said. "What do you suppose I enlisted for?" I said. "Well," she says, "it is terrible." I said, "We are Union veterans."

Commander in Chief RUHE: Comrade, I don't think Mr. Roy can answer any questions that you and the old woman had up, but he will answer the question about the peace jubilee. Mr. Roy, will you answer the question as to whether the commission can change into a peace jubilee as proposed?

Mr. ROY: Our reunion is for the veterans, but every citizen of the United States is invited. . . . But the whole backbone, the objective of our entire program, is peace, and the biggest feature is the dedication of the peace memorial. That will take place on the anniversary of the 3 days' Battle of Gettysburg, July 3, 1938.

Past Commander-in-chief [James W.] WILLETT [Iowa]: I hold . . . a clipping . . . where they say that the governor of the state of Pennsylvania has authorized and notified the southern boys that they may carry the Stars and Bars. And if they are to carry the Stars and Bars, what sort of compromise is that for Union soldier but hell and damnation? [Applause.] Now that is plains talk, but it is true.

Now then, I feel that this matter should be submitted to a committee to consider this invitation and to specify that in that invitation the infernal Stars and Bars should be kicked out. . . . Under no circumstances should we be called upon, directly or indirectly, to acknowledge and accept the Stars and Bars as a patriotic emblem of peace or of any other institution or period of time. . . .

Commander-in-chief RUHE: Secretary Roy will now answer the statements made and the question involved therein.

Mr. ROY: I appreciate the position of our good comrade, Past Commander Judge Willett, and I am sorry that he feels that way, because it is not the intention of our commission to embarrass . . . and we do not ask you to recognize the southern flag. You are not going to be asked to walk behind it or under it or go anywhere near it. The Stars and Stripes will be, as it has always been since you fellows made it so, the flag of the United States. [Applause.]

A committee was subsequently established in accord with Willett's suggestion. The next day, September 9, the committee submitted one resolution severely chastising the Pennsylvania commission sponsoring the reunion at Gettysburg for referring to the conflict as the "War Between the States" instead of as the "Civil War."

Then the committee, headed by Judge Willett, reported its resolution on the main topic:

Resolved, That the commander-in-chief appoint a committee to notify Paul L. Roy, executive secretary of the Pennsylvania State commission, that we are willing to attend a reunion of citizens of the United States who at one time were opposed to one another in a civil war and who now wish to join in a reunion at Gettysburg in 1938 for the purpose of showing to the citizens of the United States our reconciliation to the results of that Civil War; and at such reunion to have in view only the flag of this United States of America.

Commander-in-chief RUHE: All in favor will give their consent by saying "aye." Contrary. It is unanimous on the floor just as well as in the committee.

APPENDIX 'C': Other Sources

Sources for further study of individual posts of the Grand Army of the Republic, Department of Wisconsin, exist in a variety of places. Some original records may repose in the archives of museums or of other local history organizations. A number of them—a relatively small number, unfortunately—are in the archives of the State of Wisconsin that are kept by the State Historical Society of Wisconsin (SHSW), the official repository for many diverse records. These, in turn, may be housed in Area Research Centers, generally located on University of Wisconsin campuses around the state.

The following list shows what the SHSW has regarding individual posts. It is by no means the only source, even within the state archives, which may have some post records and/or references within collections of papers from individuals.

Given here are those posts for which records are held under title of the post: Records are in Madison unless otherwise noted.

E. B. Wolcott Post 1, Milwaukee: Minutes 1911–30. 3 reels of microfilm (35mm)
Summary: Minutes primarily concerning various patriotic and commemorative events participated in by the post. Information on the Civil War service of various Milwaukee units and the lives of veterans from Milwaukee is scattered throughout the minutes.
Notes: This collection is available only on microfilm
RLIN Number: WIHV88-A382
Location: Archives Main Stacks
Call Number: Micro 1142
Location: Milwaukee Area Research Center
Call Number: Milwaukee Micro 58.

Robert Chivas Post 2, Milwaukee: Minute books, 1875–79, 1907–1916. 0.2 c.f. (1 folder)
Summary: Minutes concerning activities of the post.
RLIN Number: WIHV89-A625
Location: Milwaukee Area Research Center
Call Number: Milwaukee SC 170.

Post 22, Berlin: Charter.
Summary: Charter granted to Post 22, Berlin, District of Green Lake, Wis.
RLIN Number: WIHV96-A130
Location: Archives Main Stacks
Call Number: File 1866 September 8 Oversize

William B. Cushing Post No. 19, (Waukesha): Records [microform] ca. 1904–ca. 1926. n.d. 1 reel of microfilm (35 mm)
Summary: Brief biographies and accounts of Civil War service by post members.
Notes: This collection is available only on microfilm.
RLIN Number: WIHV91-A459
Location: Archives Main Stacks
Call Number: Micro 226

George Irwin Post 25, (Lodi): Records. 1.0 c.f.
Notes: This collection is unprocessed.
RLIN Number: WIHV85-A319.
Location: Z: Unprocessed Accessions
Call Number: unnumbered accession.

P. W. Plummer Post No. 37, Prairie du Chien: Records, 1882–1911. 0.4 c.f. (11 volumes in 1 archives box.)
Summary: Records of Post 37 including minutes; adjutant's

roll and quarterly record, 1886–1908; minute book and register of the Crawford County Veterans Association, 1891–99; and miscellaneous medical and financial records.
RLIN Number: WIHV99-A652.
Location: Platteville Area Research Center
Call Number: Platteville Mss U.

Wilson Colwell Post No. 38, La Crosse: Minutes, 1896–1901. 0.1 x. d. (1 volume)
Summary: Minutes of the post of Civil War Veterans.
RLIN Number: WIHV89-A256.
Location: La Crosse Area Research Center
Call Number: La Crosse SC 75.

Theodore L. Sutphen Post No. 41, Evansville: Records, 1882–1916. 0.43 c.f. (1 archives box)
Summary: Records of the post consisting of descriptive book of members, adjutant's reports (1882–1916), and miscellaneous papers including three 1920 issues of the "National Tribune."
RLIN Number: WIHV93-A994.
Location: Archives Main Stacks
Call Number: Wis Mss 86S/1.

John Gillespie Post No. 50, Kilbourn: Records, 1882–1925. 0.2 c.f.
Summary: Minutes, 1891–94 and 1918–25; a constitution, 1883; and a quartermaster's ledger, 1882–84.
RLIN Number: WIHV85-A1963.
Location: Z: Unprocessed Accessions.
Call Number: M79-249.

William Evans Post No. 58, Menomonie: Records, 1883–1932. 0.4 c.f. (1 archives box and 1 oversize volume.)
Summary: Records including a minute book, 1883–1887 resolution of appreciation for meeting rooms in the Tainter Memorial Building, 1890 dedication of the soldiers monument in Evergreen cemetery, 1901; applications for membership; correspondence; quartermaster's and adjutant's reports; financial records concerning Memorial Day celebrations; and other items. Also includes a partial roster of members indicating each's military entrance and discharge dates, rank, company and regiment, and the date of death and burial place with annotations dated through 1932, and an undated guest register.
RLIN Number: WIHV89-A706.
Location: Stout Area Research Center.
Call Number: Stout Mss 26.

Post No. 66, Platteville: Personal sketches of the members [microform], 1890. 1 reel of microfilm (35mm).

Summary: Brief biographical sketches of members of the post giving their birth and death dates, occupations, and in many cases, details about their military service. Also included are two photographs of post functions.
Note: This collection is available only on microfilm.
RLIN Number: WIHV89-A52
Location: Archives Main Stacks
Call Number: Micro 1153
Location: Platteville Area Research Center
Call Number: Platteville Micro 42.

Joseph Bailey Post No. 138, Palmyra: Records, 1884–1928. 0.2 c.f. (1 archives box)
Summary: Records of Civil War veterans organization in Palmyra, Wis., including a minute book (1916–19), muster roll (1884–1928, adjutant's roll and quarterly record book [muster and finances] (1910–16), burial lists of Palmyra Civil War veterans, and miscellaneous papers.
RLIN Number: WIHV85-A318.
Location: Whitewater Area Research Center
Call Number: Whitewater Mss BS.

J. M. Reed Post 155, Kewaunee: Records, 1884–1910. 0.2 c.f. (1 archives box.)
Summary: Records of a Civil War veterans organization, including a ledger listing receipts and disbursements (1884–85) and dues paid listed by member (1884–90); a cash book also listing receipts and disbursements (1890–1910); and additional dues accounts of members (1890–1907).
RLIN Number: WIHV94-A175.
Location: Green Bay Area Research Center.
Call Number: Green Bay Mss 129.

Post No. 159, Fort Atkinson: Records, 1883–1921. 0.4 c.f. (1 archives box).
Summary: Records of Post 159, a Civil War veterans organization in Fort Atkinson, Wis.; including minute books (1884–1921), muster roll (1883?–1918), membership dues book (1887–1918), and miscellaneous papers (1894–1921).
RLIN Number: WIHV85-A317.
Location: Whitewater Area Research Center.
Call Number: Whitewater Mss BR.

I. N. Nichols Post No. 177, River Falls: Records, 1871–1965. 1.4 c.f. (3 archives boxes, 1 volume); plus 0.7 c.f. of unprocessed additions.
Summary: Records consisting of membership rolls, minutes, financial records, records of the local Woman's Relief Corps and Sons of Veterans groups, and a record of examination by the pension surgeon.
RLIN Number: WIHG1975-A

Location: River Falls Area Research Center
Call Number: River Falls Mss V.
Location: Z:Unprocessed Accessions.
Call Numbers: M83-157; M83-156; M79-309.

William J. Kershaw Post No. 188, Briggsville: Records, 1884–1922.0.2 c.f. (1 archives box).
Summary: Records of the Post, consisting of Adjutant's reports (1884–1922) and order book (1884–85), descriptive book of members, and letter copy book (1884–85).
RLIN Number: WIHV93-A993.
Location: Archives Main Stacks
Call Number: Wis Mss 86S/2.

Walter Waterman Post No. 197, Plainfield: Records 1885–1929. 0.4 c.f. (1 archives box).
Summary: Records of a Civil War veterans organization in Plainfield, Wis., including by-laws (1885), minute book (1894–1919), muster roll (1885–1921), burial record book recording death dates from 1864 to 1913, two financial record books (1866, 1894–1919), and miscellaneous papers.
RLIN Number: WIHV85-A122.
Location: Stevens Point Area Research Center.
Call Number: Stevens Point Mss BB.

Cyprian Downer Post No. 234, Bangor: Records, 1887–1912. 0.2 c.f. (1 archives box).
Summary: Records of a Civil War veterans organization including Adjutant's and Credential Reports (1890–1911), Adjutant's Roll and Quarterly Record (1887–94), by-laws (1888), correspondence (1901–1911), financial record book (1891–1910), membership materials (1890–1901), minutes (1911–12), lists of officers (1891–94), lists of veterans in area cemeteries (n.d.), and orders from state and national headquarters (1901–04). There is also undated material concerning services, songs, and rituals.
RLIN Number: WIHV 87-1076.
Location: La Crosse Area Research Center.
Call Number: La Crosse Mss CM.

APPENDIX 'D': Qualifications for G.A.R. Membership[3]

ARTICLE IV. – CHAPTER I
ELIGIBILITY TO MEMBERSHIP

Soldiers and sailors of the United States Army, Navy or Marine Crops, who served between April 12th, 1861, and April 9th, 1865, in the war for the suppression of the Rebellion, and

those having been honorably discharged therefrom after such service, and of such State regiments as were called into active service and subject to the orders of United States general officers, between the dates mentioned, shall be eligible to membership in the Grand Army of the Republic. No person shall be eligible to membership who has at any time borne arms against the United States.

The original Article IV, Chapter I, (1868) read:
Soldiers and honorably-discharged soldiers of the United States volunteer or Regular Army or Marine Corps, or sailors and honorably discharged sailors of the United States Navy only shall be eligible to membership in the Grand Army of the Republic.

No soldier or sailor who has been convicted by court-martial of desertion or any other infamous crime shall be admitted.

Article IV, Chapter I, was changed in 1869 to read:
Soldiers and sailors of the United States Army, Navy or Marine Crops, who served in the war for the suppression of the Rebellion, and those having been honorably discharged therefrom after such service, shall be eligible to membership in the Grand Army of the Republic. No person shall be eligible to membership who has at any time borne arms against the United States.

The dates of eligibility, i.e., the exact duration of the "Rebellion," were for some years uncertain. In 1875, for instance, Grand Army Judge Advocate-General W. W. Douglas, Rhode Island, held that persons enlisted after Appomattox but before the date on which President Andrew Johnson proclaimed the Rebellion ended in all states—August 20, 1866—and thus that peace had been restored to the United States, were eligible. Federal court cases had used Johnson's proclamation date as the official end of the war. In 1879 the G.A.R. encampment revised the dates and decreed that eligible service had to have been done "between April 12th, 1861, [and] April 9th, 1865."

The same encampment also inserted the words "and of such State regiments as were called into active service and subject to the orders of United States general officers, between the dates mentioned."

It was the 1869 encampment that dropped the stricture against any who had been "convicted by court-martial of desertion or any other infamous crime." It was felt that the requirement that the applicant must have an honorable discharge would be adequate. They did not wish to revisit on an individual basis the matter of desertions which could often be a more technical breach than an overt act, as evidenced by an eventual honorable discharge.

On numerous occasions over the course of years, Judge Advocates-General were called upon to interpret Article IV, Chapter I. One of the more frequent issues involved service early in the war in the "Rebel service" under compulsion, the applicant later having federal service and an honorable discharge.

---

3. From "Rules and Regulations of the Grand Army of the Republic," in *Grand Army Blue Book*, 3d ed., by Robert B. Beath, (Philadelphia: 1886).

Very early, Judge Advocate-General Douglas wrote (1871): "The fact that the service against the Union was involuntary, does not constitute this case an exception to a rule so clearly and unreservedly expressed. There were no persons whom the framers of this rule could have contemplated but this very class who served in the Confederate Army and afterwards in our own. . . . There may be instances . . . where this rule works harshly, but it is of far more importance that the loyalty of every member of our Order should be above reproach than that we should omit from our roll a few good men, who showed weakness, at least, if they escape the suspicion of disloyalty."

The issue arose a number of times in ensuing years, and finally, a proposition to modify the "service in the Rebel army" clause was proposed in 1884 but was rejected by the national encampment of 1885.

An interesting "exception," of sorts, was made a little later in 1885, in an opinion by Judge Advocate-General C. H. Grosvenor of Ohio. A man applied for membership in a post "who, as a slave, was forced to work on rebel fortifications, as servant to a confederate officer for the period of one year, after which time he escaped and enlisted in the Union Navy from which he was honorably discharged. . . ."

Grosvenor found that the man "did not bear arms for the Confederacy in the restricted sense, and yet he, as in this case did 'bear arms' within the meaning of the term in its more enlarged sense." But, he concluded, "he was a thing—a chattel. He had no will. . . . He was without the power to will to do, or the will to refuse to do. That law, that monstrous outrage upon civilization, was our law; that practice was our practice. As a slave he was driven as a dumb beast to work upon rebel fortifications. I hold that for the purposes of this sort of case and this sort of inquiry, the slave must have the benefit of the fact that he was stripped of the power and exercise of volition, and hence is relieved from the consequence of an act which the law on both sides said he must obey. And I hold that emancipation, when it came, related back and made the slave a man from his birth, and tore down the idols of the dark days of his enslavement, and purged him of all the acts, or failures to act, which had grown up under the system under which he had lived. . . . I cannot bring myself to hold otherwise; and if my opinion is not in accord with the law of the Grand Army of the Republic, so much the worse for the law. I hold that the applicant in this case is eligible to become a member of the Grand Army of the Republic."

APPENDIX 'E': G.A.R. Uniforms

ARTICLE IX. – CHAPTER V • UNIFORM – BADGES

Section I. Departments may adopt a uniform for their own members. Where no uniform is prescribed by a Department, each Post may adopt one.

. . .

The Grand Army of the Republic had no specified uniform, leaving the matter to the discretion of each department, or to the local post.

The Department of Wisconsin did not adopt a uniform, and so far as is known, no individual post specified a particular uniform for all its members, either.

Yet the Grand Army man, in parade assembled, anyway, was distinguishable from the general crowd by his attire, and particularly the hat he wore on the occasion.

It was customary in those times for men to don coats and hats at any occasion suggesting wearing something more than work clothes. G.A.R. men usually wore a dark coat, either single or double-breasted, and an appropriate hat. The hat more often than not was a Stetson, basically a civilian model, with the G.A.R. initials on the front. But it was quite usual for the men to wear a kepi or some other military-type cap, again with the order's monogram in the lead.

Of course, it was acceptable for the men on dress occasions to put on their old military uniform. Occasionally pictures of G.A.R. functions show a man outfitted in his old Zouave uniform.

The hallmark of the G.A.R. "uniform," then, was its utter lack of uniformity. Still a Grand Army man at a patriotic function could be pretty easily distinguished by the clothes he was wearing. In that sense, the G.A.R. made use of a "uniform" without having to impose specifics upon the men.

Into this seeming breach strode more than a dozen companies to provide G.A.R. paraphernalia of all sorts to the comrades including coats, hats, hat cords, belts, ribbons, pins, badges, not to mention swords, drums, fifes, and trumpets—in short, all the accouterments of Grand Army membership and accomplishment. Since the order did not mandate specifics, these companies could be somewhat innovative in offering different styles of wear. Thus a member was perfectly attired in either a single or double-breasted coat, a vest as well, if he chose, and on his head either a military-type hat or cap, or for that matter, a latter-day civilian model.

All these were readily obtained through these companies which were primarily catalog order operations.

Catalogs necessarily contain illustrations, and given here are a number gleaned from several of them showing hat styles, coat styles, etc.

The hats below are from the Horstmann Bros. & Co. catalog of 1884.

From the same catalog are the illustrations of two versions of the G.A.R. emblem.

They were worn on the front of the hat.

On the left is a metal pin type, and on the right, an embroidered version.

To go along with the emblem, the veteran could get numbers and/or letters to specify his post or any other pertinent aspect.

Although the different companies might have a variant on some of the design elements, they all were essentially similar. The buttons on the Grand Army man's coat, for instance, didn't disclose whether he got it from Horstmann Bros. or from E. A. Armstrong Co. or any of the others. The button on the left was the coat button and was more distinguishing as to Grand Army membership than the coat itself which, with a different set of buttons, was normally quite useful for any sort of dress up occasion. The button on the right was for vests.

 That monogram with the letters GAR entwined was common to all the buttons.

These sketches of the well-attired Grand Army man are from the 1887 catalog of M. C. Lilley & Co., Columbus, Ohio. The double-breasted coat cost from $9.25 to $15.50. Single-breasted coats went from $7.00 to $14.50. The blouse-type on the right cost from $6.00 to $11.50. The range was based on the quality of material. They were described as "indigo blue." Pants were generally also indigo blue, and they cost from $4.25 to $9.20. Vests, same color, went from $3.50 to $6.10. White duck vests were from $1.00 to $2.00. Lilley also offered light blue pants. Quite possibly the blouses were the most popular; Lilley offered them in quantity lots: $49.50 to $52.50 per dozen.

Incidentally, the hats illustrated previous page, from Horstmann Bros. ranged from $2.50 to $3.50, and for the kepis, $1.00. Horstmann added: "Finer grades made to order if desired."

Of the many styles of hats worn by G.A.R. men, here are three examples: the simple cap, known as the kepi, left; one of the more formal shapes, closer to what was fashionable postwar, center; and a well-worn slouch hat suggestive of the kind the men knew and wore during the war.

Below are three surviving uniforms. Note on the left the high collar and the latter-day civilian-type hat. The center illustrates that vests were a popular part of G.A.R. attire. The relative simplicity of the uniform on the right may show the most common type in use.

APPENDIX 'F': Court Martials

ARTICLE VI. – CHAPTER V • DISCIPLINE[4]

Section I. *Offenses cognizable by the Grand Army of the Republic shall be:*

1 Disloyalty to the United States of America or any other violation of the pledge given at the time of muster.

2. Disobedience of the Rules and Regulations or of lawful orders.

3. The commission of a scandalous offense against the laws of the land.

4. Conduct unbecoming a soldier and a gentleman in his relation to the Grand Army of the Republic.

5. Conduct prejudicial to good order and discipline.

Section II. *Penalties shall be either:*

1. Dishonorable discharge from the Grand Army of the Republic.

4. From "Rules and Regulations of the Grand Army of the Republic," in *Grand Army Blue Book*, 3d ed, by Robert B. Beath (Philadelphia: 1886). The rules for conducting courts martial and the full text of all court martial forms, all quite elaborate, are contained in the Blue Book.

2. Degradation from office.
3. Suspension from, membership for a specified period.
4. Fine; or
5. Reprimand, at the discretion of the court, subject to the review of the proper officer.

. . .

The forms of the court-martial itself were patterned after the "Revised United States Army Regulations" of the time, with modifications suitable to the G.A.R. situation. For instance, if the comrade facing court-martial refuses to attend, the court-martial would proceed as if the accused had pleaded not guilty.

There was also provision for appealing the decision of the court to higher authority.

There was, in other words, consideration given to "due process."

APPENDIX 'G': Membership by County, 1895

Counties	Veterans	G. A. R.	%
Adams	200	67	33.5
Ashland	92	52	56.5
Barron	343	148	43.1
Bayfield	89	33	37
Brown	484	287	59.2
Buffalo	237	143	60.3
Burnett	35	0	0
Calumet	213	132	61.9
Chippewa	354	168	47.4
Clark	401	149	37.1
Columbia	485	340	70.1
Crawford	399	97	24.3
Dane	762	356	46.7
Dodge	410	145	35.3
Door	159	71	44.6
Douglas	186	116	62.3
Dunn	393	127	32.3
Eau Claire	450	168	37.3
Fond du Lac	506	323	63.8
Florence	22	16	72.7
Forest	24	0	0
Grant	841	455	54.1
Green	428	197	46
Green Lake	216	154	71.2
Iowa	281	131	46.6

Counties	Veterans	G. A. R.	%
Iron	20	22	100.1
Jackson	302	140	46.3
Jefferson	381	230	60.3
Juneau	459	198	43.1
Kenosha	176	71	40.3
Kewaunee	130	88	67.6
La Crosse	441	245	56.2
Lafayette	292	170	58.2
Lincoln	75	74	98.6
Langlade	150	84	56
Manitowoc	421	179	42.5
Marathon	200	72	36
Marinette	150	62	41.3
Marquette	197	94	47.7
Milwaukee	3,934	926	23.5
Monroe	533	225	42.2
Oconto	227	48	21.1
Oneida	57	0	0
Outagamie	547	305	55.7
Ozaukee	133	29	21.8
Pepin	123	100	81.3
Pierce	415	203	48.9
Polk	218	86	39.4
Portage	409	144	35.2
Price	63	9	14.2
Racine	447	280	62.6
Richmond	591	235	39.7
Rock	812	385	47.4
Sauk	697	377	54
Sawyer	38	12	31.5
Shawano	170	86	50.5
Sheboygan	524	280	53.4
St. Croix	386	158	40.9
Taylor	76	24	31.5
Trempealeau	215	127	59
Vernon	565	191	33.8
Vilas	20	0	0
Washburn	68	17	25
Washington	216	135	62.6
Walworth	534	258	48.3
Waukesha	409	194	47.4
Waupaca	802	314	39.1
Waushara	468	276	58.9

Counties	Veterans	G. A. R.	%
Winnebago	843	531	62.9
Wood	268	119	44.4
Totals	26,307	11,678	44.3

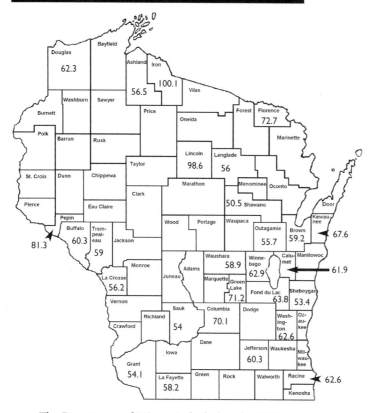

The Department of Wisconsin looked at the 1895 state census and compared where veterans lived and where G.A.R. members lived.

It showed there was room for recruiting. Statewide, members represented 44.3 percent of those eligible. The map above posts the 27 counties where membership was above 50 percent.

Since the census was within the peak years, the figures (except for the low population Northern counties) give an accurate picture of where the G.A.R. was most active. Note Milwaukee County had a dismal 23.5 percent of those eligible.

BIBLIOGRAPHY

BOOKS AND MANUSCRIPTS

Ahlgren, Dorothy Eaton, and Mary Cotter Beeler. *A History of Prescott, Wisconsin.* Prescott, Wis.: Prescott Area Historical Society, 1996.

Anderson-Sannes, Barbara. *Alma on the Mississippi, 1848–1932* Alma, Wis.: Alma Historical Society, 1980.

Bailey, William F., ed. *History of Eau Claire County* Chicago: C. F. Cooper, 1914.

Barland, Lois. *Sawdust City, A History of Eau Claire, Wisconsin, from Earliest Times to 1910.* Stevens Point, Wis.: Worzalla Publishing, 1970.

Beath, Robert B. *History of the Grand Army of the Republic.* New York, Bryan, Taylor, 1889.

Beckwith, Albert Clayton. *History of Walworth County, Wisconsin.* Indianapolis: B. F. Bowen, 1912.

Behnke, Laura, Elliot T. Zander, Robert Van Enkenvoort, Zane Zander, and Noel Zander. *Brillion, Wisconsin, the First 100 Years.* Brillion, Wis.: Zander Press, 1985.

Betz, Maureen, and John Ebert. *Fond du Lac County: The Gathering Place.* Fond du Lac, Wis.: Fond du Lac County Historical Society, 1999.

Bizjak, Charles. *Eaton Center Annals.* Greenwood, Wisc., Clark County, (no pub. Date).

Boatner, Mark M., III. *The Civil War Dictionary.* New York: David McKay, 1962.

Borden, Cliff. "The Early Years", *Veterans Affairs in Wisconsin, King Centennial Issue,* Madison, Wisc.: n.p., 1987.

Brown, H. O., and Mrs. M. A. W. Brown. *Soldiers and Citizens' Album of Biographical Record [of Wisconsin].* Chicago: Grand Army Publishing, 1890.

Brown, William Fiske. *Rock County, Wisconsin.* Chicago: C. F. Cooper, 1903.

Bryant, Edwin E. *History of the Third Regiment of Wisconsin Veteran Volunteer Infantry.* Madison, Wis.: Veterans Association of the Third Wisconsin, 1891.

Burnham, Guy M. *Lake Superior Country in History and Story.* Ashland, Wis.: Ashland Daily Press, 1930.

Campbell, Henry C., ed. *Wisconsin in Three Centuries, 1634–1905.* Vol. 4. New York: Century History, 1906.

Catton, Bruce. *This Hallowed Ground.* Garden City, N.Y.: Doubleday, 1956.

Cauffman, Betty Lou, Gilda A. Finnegan, and Harold Stauffacher. *Fennimore: Then and Now, 1830–1980.* Minneapolis: Josten's, 1980.

Cheek, Philip, and Mair Pointon. *History of the Sauk County Riflemen, Known as Company A, Sixth Wisconsin Veterans Volunteer Infantry.* Madison, Wis.: Democratic Printing, 1909.

Cheever, R. W. *Ancient History of Clinton, Wisconsin.* n.p.: 1898.

Clark, George A. "For Love of County's Sake. In *The Book of Beloit.* Beloit, Wis.: 1936.

Cohen, Stan. *Hands Across the Wall: The 50th and 75th Reunions of the Gettysburg Battle.* Charleston, W.V.: Pictorial Histories Publishing, 1982.

Cole, Harry Ellsworth. *A Standard History of Sauk County, Wisconsin.* Chicago: Lewis Publishing, 1918.

Cravath, Prosper, and Spencer S. Steele. *Early Annals of Whitewater, 1837-1867.* Whitewater, Wis.: Whitewater Federation of Women's Clubs, 1906.

Crawford, Theron Clark. *James G .Blaine: A Study of His Life and Career.* Philadelphia: Edgewood Publishing, 1893.

Cunningham, G. A. *History of Neenah, Illustrated.* Neenah, Wis.: Gazette Printing Establishment, 1878.

Curtis-Wedge, F., and George O. Jones. *History of Dunn County, Wisconsin.* Minneapolis: H. C. Cooper Jr., 1925.

Dawson, George Francis. *Life and Services of Gen. John A. Logan.* Chicago: Belford, Clarke, 1887.

Dearing, Mary. *Veterans in Politics: The Story of the GAR.* Baton Rouge: Louisiana State University Press, 1952.

Densmore, Frances. *Menominee Music.* Washington, D.C.: U.S. Government Printing Office, 1932.

Dessureau, Robert M. *History of Langlade County, Wisconsin.* Antigo, Wis.: Berner Bros. Publishing, 1922.

Diedrich, Nicholas D., and John Britten Gehl. *History of Clintonville, Wisconsin, from Pioneer Days to Present Time.* Clintonville, Wis.: 1937.

Drefcinski, Kyle, Sheri Hagen, Abigail Heller, and Michelle Trudeau, eds. *Out of the Shadows: Memorable People from Portage County's Past.* Amherst, Wis.: Palmer Publications, 1998.

Eberlein, Merton, ed. *Juneau County: The First 100 Years.* Friendship, Wis.: Juneau County Historical Society/ New Past Press, 1988.

Fagg, William. Diaries [microfilm]. Green Bay Area Research Center.

Falge, Louis, ed. *History of Manitowoc County, Wisconsin.* Chicago: Godspeed Historical Association, 1912.

Fallows, Alice H. *Everybody's Bishop: Life and Times of Rt. Rev. Samuel Fallows.* New York: J. H. Sears, 1927.

Faust, Patricia L, ed. *Historical Times Illustrated Encyclopedia of the Civil War.* New York: Harper & Row, 1986.

Flanders, LaVern F. *Look Back and Remember: The First Fifty Years of the Rock Elm Township Area of Pierce County, Wisconsin.* St. Paul, Minn.: Lehman Brothers, 1989.

Freeman, Allie E., and Walter R. Bussewitz. *History of Horicon.* Horicon, Wis.: 1948.

French, Bella. *The American Sketch Book.* Vol. 3. Green Bay, Wis.: The American Sketch Book, 1876.

Gaff, Alan, and Maureen Gaff. *Our Boys: A Civil War Photograph Album.* Lancaster, Wis.: Grant County Historical Society, 1996.

Gallagher, Gary W., and Alan T. Nolan, eds. *The Myth of the Lost Cause and Civil War History.* Bloomington: Indiana University Press, 2000.

Glaatthaar, Joseph T. *The March to the Sea and Beyond.* New York: New York University Press, 1985.

Glaze, A.T. *Incidents and Anecdotes of Early Days and History of Business the City and County of Fond du Lac.* Fond du Lac, Wis.: P.B. Haber Printing, 1905.

Goc, Michael J. *Many a Fine Harvest: Sauk County 1840-1990.* Friendship, Wis.: New Past Press, 1990.

———. *From Past to Present: The History of Adams County.* Friendship, Wis.: Adams County Historical Society/New Past Press, 1999.

Goff, Charles D. "Torchlight Soldiers: A Wisconsin View of the Torchlight Parades of the Republican Party 'Tanners' and the Democratic Party 'White Boys in Blue' in the Presidential Election of U.S. Grant in 1868." Paper prepared for reading before the Wisconsin Academy of Sciences, Arts and Letters, May 7, 1977.

Gordon, Newton S., ed. *History of Barron County, Wisconsin.* Minneapolis: H. C. Cooper Jr., 1922.

Gregory, John G., ed. *A History of Old Crawford County.* Chicago: S. J. Clarke Publishing, 1932.

Griswold, Ada. *Catalogue of Newspaper Files in the Library of the State Historical Society of Wisconsin.* Madison, Wis.: 1911.

Groves, R. H. *Captain Owen Griffith.* n.p., privately published, 1990.

Guyant, Wayne A. *History and Memories: Portage County, Belmont Township.* Vol. 2. Amherst, Wis.: Palmer Publications, 1986.

Hartwig, D. Scott. 'The Most Notable Event at Gettysburg Since the War:' The Reunion of the Philadelphia Brigade and Pickett's Division, July, 1887. Vol. 6, No. 3, Civil War Regiments. Mason City, Iowa: Savas Publishing, 1999.

Hauptman, Laurence M. *The Iroquois in the Civil War* Syracuse, N.Y.: Syracuse University Press, 1993.

Heck, Frank H. *The Civil War Veteran.* Oxford, Ohio: Mississippi Valley Press, 1941.

Heiple, Robert W., and Emma B. Heiple. *A Heritage History of Beautiful Green Lake County Wisconsin.* Green Lake, Wis.: Heritage Edition, 1976.

Hieb, Jane. *Eau Claire Heartland of the Chippewa Valley: An Illustrated History.* Northridge, Calif.: Windsor Publications, 1988.

Hildebrand, Janice. *Sheboygan County: 150 Years of Progress.* Northridge, Calif.: Windsor Publications, 1988.

Hinckley, Julian W. *Narrative of Service with the Third Wisconsin Infantry.* Madison, Wis.: Wisconsin History Commission, 1912.

Hodge, William H. *The First Americans: Then and Now.* New York: Holt, Rinehart and Winston, 1981.

Holand, Hjalmar R. *History of Door County, Wisconsin: The County Beautiful.* Ellison Bay, Wis.: Wm. Caxton, 1993.

Holberton, William B. *Homeward Bound: The Demobilization of the Union and Confederate Armies, 1865–1866,* Mechanicsburg, Pa.: Stackpole Books, 2001.

Holford, Castello N. *History of Grant County, Wisconsin.* Lancaster, Wis.: The Teller Print, 1900.

Holmes, Fred L., ed. *Wisconsin: Stability, Progress, Beauty.* Vol. 2. Chicago: Lewis Publishing, 1946.

Horner, Charles F. *Life of James Redpath.* New York: 1926.

Hubbell, Homer Bishop. *Dodge County Wisconsin Past and Present.* Chicago: S. J. Clark Publishing, 1913.

Jenkins, Richard: *Columbia County, Wisconsin in 1880.* Oklahoma City, Okla.: Gateway Press, 1996.

Johnson, Kenneth R., and Jeffrey B. Floyd. *Membership and National Encampment Badges of the Grand Army of the Republic, 1866–1949.* Glassboro, N.J.: Orders and Medals Society of America, 1997.

Jones, George O., Norman S. McVean, et al. *History of Lincoln, Oneida and Vilas Counties, Wisconsin.* Minneapolis: H. C. Cooper Jr., 1924.

———. *History of Wood County, Wisconsin.* Minneapolis: H. C. Cooper Jr., 1923.

Jones, J. E. *A History of Portage County Wisconsin.* Chicago: Lewis Publishing, 1914.

Kelly, June, ed. *Waupun, Wisconsin: The First 150 Years, 1839–1989.* Waupun, Wis.: James Laird/Richard T. Peters, 1989.

Keyes, Elisha W. *History of Dane County.* Madison, Wis.: Western Historical Association, 1906.

Kittle, William. *The History of the Township and Village of Mazomanie.* Mazomanie, Wis.: 1985.

Klement, Frank L. *Wisconsin in the Civil War.* Madison: State Historical Society of Wisconsin, 1997.

Koehler, Lyle. *History of Cataract, Wisconsin.* La Crosse: University of Wisconsin–La Crosse, 1967.

Kronenwetter, Michael. *The Story of Wausau and Marathon County.* Midland, Mich.: Pendell Publishing, 1984.

Langkau, David A. *Civil War Veterans of Winnebago County Wisconsin.* Vol. 1. Bowie, Md.: Heritage Books, 1993.

———. *Civil War Veterans of Winnebago County Wisconsin.* Vol. 2. Bowie, Md.: Heritage Books, 1993.

Larson, Trixie. 977.575 R531, in *Richland County Wisconsin.* Richland Center, Wisc.: Richland County Historical Society, 1986.

Leach, Eugene Walter. *Racine County Militant: An Illustrated Narrative of War Times, and a Soldiers' Roster; a Pioneer Publication Undertaken in the Interest of Patriotic Americans in Racine County, Wisconsin. A Home-made Book, about Home People, for Home People.* Racine, Wis.: 1915.

Letter of Lucius Fairchild to his sister. May 30–31, 1868. RLIN# WIHV85-A105. Wisconsin State Historical Society, Fairchild Manuscript Collection.

Lynch, Larry, and John M. Russell, eds. *Where the Wild Rice Grows: A Sesquicentennial Portrait of Menomonie,1846–1996.* Menomonie, Wisc.: Menomonie Sesquicentennial Commission, 1996.

Long, E. B., with Barbara Long. *The Civil War Day by Day: An Almanac, 1861–1865.* Garden City, N.Y., 1971.

Logan, John A. *The Volunteer Soldier of America,* n.p.: 1887.

Lord, Francis A. *They Fought for the Union.* New York: Bonanza Books, 1960.

Love, William D. *Wisconsin in the War of the Rebellion.* Chicago: 1866.

Madaus, Howard Michael, and Richard H. Zeitlin: *The Flags of the Iron Brigade.* Madison: Wisconsin Veterans Museum, 1997.

Magdeburg, F. H. *Wisconsin at Shiloh* Madison: Wisconsin Shiloh Monument Commission, 1909.

Majkrzak, Edwin. *History of Kiel.* Chilton, Wis.: The Printing Express, 2000.

Marchetti, Louis. *History of Marathon County.* Chicago: Richmond-Arnold Publishing Co., 1913.

Marsh, Lillian Groetzinger. "I Remember When," *Tales of Old Chilton.* Lil Smith, ed. Chilton, Wis.: Chilton Women's Club, 1977.

Martin, Deborah B. *History of Brown County, Wisconsin: Past and Present* Chicago: S. J. Clark Publishing, 1913.

McConnell, Stuart. *Glorious Contentment: The Grand Army of the Republic, 1865–1900.* Chapel Hill: University of North Carolina Press, 1992.

McDevitt, Robert, ed. *The History of Marion.* Marion, Wis.: Marion High School/Marion Advertiser, 1988.

McGlachlin, Ed. *History of Portage County.* Chicago: Lewis Publishing, 1919.

McKenna, Maurice, ed. *Fond du Lac County, Wisconsin: Past and Present.* Chicago: S. J. Clarke Publishing, 1912.

McLenegan, Annie S. *Centennial History of the Town of Turtle, Rock County, Wisconsin.* n.p.: 1936.

Metz, James I. *When Oshkosh Went to War.* Oshkosh, Wis.: Polemics Press, 1997.

Miller, Louise. *Just People of the Friendly Valley.* St. Paul, Minn.: Library of Wall Street, 1988.

Miller, Willis H. *Hudson Tales Retold.* Hudson, Wis.: Star-Observer Publishing, 1992.

Mollenhoff, David. "Rowdies in Blue: Madison as a Civil War Camp Town." *The Journal of Historic Madison* 4 (1978).

Montgomery, Ruth Ann. *Evansville Glimpses of the Grove.* Evansville, Wis.: Star Printing, 1990.

Nesbit, Robert C. *History of Wisconsin.* Vol. 3. Edited by William Fletcher Thompson. Madison: State Historical Society of Wisconsin, 1985.

Ourada, Patricia K. *The Menominee Indians: A History.* Norman, Okla.: University of Oklahoma Press, n.d.

Polleys, A. D. *Stories of Pioneer Days in the Black River Valley.* Black River Falls, Wis.: Banner-Journal, 1948.

Quad, M. *Field, Fort and Fleet: An Outline History of the Grand Army of the Republic, Together with a History of Henry Bertram Post 194 and Wm. B. Cushing Post 19.* Detroit, Mich.: Detroit Free Press Publishing, 1886.

Quiner, E.B. *Military History of Wisconsin.* Chicago: Clark and Company, 1866.

Raab, Steven S., ed. *With the Third Wisconsin Badgers: The Living Experience of the Civil War Through the Journals of Van R. Willard.* Mechanicsburg, Pa.: Stackpole Books, 1999.

Rappel, Joseph C., ed. *Manitowoc County Historical Markers and Monuments.* Manitowoc, Wis.: Manitowoc County Historical Society, 1964.

Richards, Randolph A. *History of Monroe County.* Chicago: C. F. Cooper, 1912.

Rogers, Daisy E. *Winneconne, 1849–1949.* Winneconne, Wis.: Larson Publishing, 1949.

Rood, Hosea W. "The Grand Army of the Republic and the Wisconsin Department." In *Wisconsin: Its History and Its People,* by Milo Quaife. Chicago: 1924.

———. *History of Wisconsin Veterans' Home, 1886–1926,* Madison, Wisc.: Democrat Printing, 1926.

Rosholt, Malcolm. *Our County Our Story, Portage County, Wisconsin.* Stevens Point, Wis.: Portage County Board of Supervisors, 1959.

Ross, Sam. *The Empty Sleeve: A Biography of Lucius Fairchild.* Madison: State Historical Society of Wisconsin, 1964.

Roster of Lucius Fairchild Post No. 11, Department of Wisconsin, Grand Army of the Republic. Madison: January 1, 1922.

Ryan, Thomas H., ed. *History of Outagamie County.* Chicago: Goodspeed Historical Association, 1911.

Sackett, F. W. *History of Price County.* Unpublished manuscript. n.p.: 1906.

Sandburg, Carl. *Abraham Lincoln: The Prairie Years.* New York: Harcourt, Brace, 1926.

Scheier, Kathy, Joy Waterbury, Ruth Plautz, and Judy Bender. *Common Threads: A History of Four Wisconsin Communities in Green Lake County.* Kingston, Wis.: Mill Pond Library, 1998.

Schultz, Jeffrey D., John G. West Jr., Iain Maclean, eds. *Encyclopedia of Religion in American Politics.* Phoenix, Ariz.: Orynx Press, 1999.

Smith, Paige. *Trial by Fire.* New York: McGraw-Hill, 1982.

Stare, F. A. "The Story of Columbus." Columbus Public Library.

Statement and Proofs in Reference to John H. Williams Post No. 4 of Berlin, Wis. to the Right of Seniority of Posts in the Department of Wisconsin. Berlin, Wis: 1892.

Stemler, Joyce Bennett. *They Went South: Biographical Sketches of the Civil War Veterans from Berlin, Wisconsin.* Berlin, Wis.: Berlin Historical Society, 1966.

Stephenson, Mary Harriet. *Dr. B. F. Stephenson, Founder of the Grand Army of the Republic: A Memoir.* Springfield, Illinois.: H. W. Rokker Printing House, 1894.

Swart, Hannah. *Koshkonong Country Revisited.* Fort Atkinson, Wis.: Fort Atkinson Historical Society/Marek Lithographic, 1981.

Trudeau, Noah Andre. *Out of the Storm: The End of the Civil War, April–June 1865* Baton Rouge: Louisiana State University Press, 1994.

Wakefield, J. *History of Waupaca County.* Waupaca, Wis.: D. L. Stinchfield, 1890.

Ware, John M., ed. *A Standard History of Waupaca County Wisconsin.* Chicago: Lewis Publishing, 1917.

Watrous, Jerome, ed. *Memoirs of Milwaukee County.* Madison, Wis.: Western Historical Association, 1909.

Wells, Robert W. *Wisconsin in the Civil War.* Milwaukee: Milwaukee Journal, 1961.

Willis, Bessie, Gertie Fuller, Dennis Fuller, and Dorothy Berg. *Inscriptions from Greenwood Cemetery, Formerly Known as Pine Creek or O'Flanagan Cemetery, Town of Dallas, Barron County, Wisconsin.* Barron County: 1958.

Wilson, Mary M. *A History of Lake Mills: Creating a Society.* Lake Mills, Wis.: M. M. Wilson, 1983.

World Book Encyclopedia. Chicago: World Books, 1887.

Worthing, Ruth Shaw. *The History of Fond du Lac County as Told by its Place-Names.* Oshkosh, Wis.: Globe Printing, 1976.

Zeitlin, Richard H. *In Peace and War: Union Veterans and Cultural Symbols; The Flags of the Iron Brigade. In Giants in their Tall Black Hats: Essays on the Iron Brigade,* eds. Alan T. Nolan and Sharon Eggleston Vipond. Bloomington: Indiana University Press, 1998.

———. "Charles King," *Veterans Affairs in Wisconsin, King Centennial Issue,* (Madison, Wisc.: Wisconsin Department of Veterans Affairs, 1987), 31-32.

———. "The Debt of Gratitude: The Wisconsin G.A.R.", in *Veterans Affairs in Wisconsin; King Centennial Issue,* 1987, Madison: Wisconsin Department of Veterans Affairs, 5-6.

———. *Old Abe the War Eagle.* Madison, Wis.: State Historical Society of Wisconsin, 1986.

The Bicentennial History of Milton. Milton, Wis.: Milton Bicentennial Committee, 1976.

Biographical History of La Crosse, Trempealeau and Buffalo Counties, Wisconsin. Chicago: Lewis Publishing, 1892.

Celebrating Our Heritage: Kendall, Wis., 1894–1994. Kendall, Wis.: Kendall Centennial Committee, 1994.

Chippewa County Wisconsin: Past and Present. Chicago: S. J. Clarke Publishing, 1913.

A Civic Century: 1855–1955. Clintonville, Wis.: Clintonville Harvest Festival, 1955.

Colombian Biographical Descriptions and Portraits Gallery of the Representative Men of the United States. Wisconsin Vol. Chicago: Lewis Publishing, 1895.

Commemorative Biographical Record of the Fox River Valley. Chicago: J. H. Beers, 1895.

Commemorative Biographical Record of the Upper Lake Region. Chicago: J. H. Beers, 1905.

The Eagle Regiment: Eighth Wisconsin Infantry Volunteers. Belleville, Wis.: Recorder Printers, 1890.

The Edgerton Story: A History of Edgerton, Wisconsin, from Oxen to Jets. Edgerton, Wis.: 1953.

Evansville's Century of Progress. Evansville, Wis.: 1939.

For the Good of the Order: A History of Wesley W. Patton Post 90. Brodhead, Wis.: Wesley H. Patton Women's Relief Corps #19, 1985.

Fox Lake, Wisconsin: 150 Years, 1838–1988. Fox Lake, Wis.: Fox Lake Sesquicentennial Committee, 1988.

Grand Army Blue Book. Philadelphia: J. B. Lippincott, 1891.

Greenwood: Hub of Clark County Wisconsin Greenwood, Wis.: Neuenfeldt and O'Connell, 1934.

Harvard, Nebraska: 100 Years Plus 2. Harvard, Neb.: Harvard History Book Committee, 1973.

Historical Album, 1848-1973. Lodi, Wis.: 1973.

History of Crawford and Richland Counties, Wisconsin. Springfield, Ill.: Union Publishing, 1884.

History of Dane County, Wisconsin. Chicago: Western Historical, 1880.

History of Green County Wisconsin. Springfield, Ill.: Union Publishing, 1884.

History of La Crosse County, Wisconsin. Chicago: Western Historical 1881.

History of Milwaukee, Wisconsin. Chicago: Western Historical, 1881.

History of Sauk County Wisconsin. Chicago: Western Historical, 1880.

History of Racine and Kenosha Counties, Wisconsin. Chicago: Western Historical, 1879.

History of Rock County, Wisconsin. Chicago: Western Historical, 1879.

History of Vernon County Wisconsin. Evansville, Ind.: Unigraphic, 1975.

History of Walworth County. Chicago: Western Historical, 1882.

Memorial Addresses on the Life and Character of Joseph Rankin. Washington, D.C.: U.S. Government Printing Office, 1886.

Osseo Centennial, June 28, 29, 39, 1957. Osseo, Wis.: 1957.

Portrait and Biographical Album of Fond du Lac County. Chicago: Acme Publishing, 1889.

Portrait and Biographical Album of Green Lake, Marquette and Waushara Counties. Chicago: Acme Publishing, 1890.

Report and Collections of the State Historical Society of Wisconsin for the Years 1880, 1881 and 1882. Madison, Wis.: 1882.

Report of the Wisconsin Monument Commission Appointed to Erect a Monument at Andersonville, Georgia: Madison, Wis.: Democrat Printing, 1911.

Roll of Honor, Vol. XVIII Washington, D.C.: U.S. Government Printing Office, 1868.

Soldiers' and Citizens' Album of Biographical Record Containing Personal Sketches of Army Men and Citizens Prominent in Loyalty to the Union. Chicago: Grand Army Publishing, 1888.

A Stroll Through the Village: Fall River, WI, 1846–1996. Fall River, Wis.: 1996.

United States Biographical Dictionary and Portrait Gallery of Eminent and Self-made Men. Wisconsin Edition. Chicago: American Biographical Publishing, 1877.

Waupaca Centennial Book, 1857–1957. Waupaca, Wis.: 1957.

Wisconsin at Shiloh: Report of Wisconsin Shiloh Monument Commission. Madison, Wis.: Democrat Printing, 1909.

Wisconsin Blue Book. Madison, Wis.: 1905.

Wisconsin Blue Book. Madison, Wis.: 1909.

Wisconsin Census Enumeration 1895. Madison, Wis.: Democrat Printing, 1896.

Wisconsin Census Enumeration 1905. Madison, Wis.: Democrat Printing, 1906.

Wisconsin Soldiers and Sailors Reunion Roster, 1880. Fond du Lac, Wis.: Star Steam Job and Book Printers, 1880.

NEWSPAPERS

Adams County Press, 1895.

Ahnapee Record, January 19, 1888.

Algoma Record-Herald, March 14, 1941.

Algoma Record-Herald, December 26, 1941.

Amery Echo, October 31, 1889.

Appleton Crescent, September 12, 1885.

Appleton Post Crescent, October 1, 1951.

Arena Star, September 1, 1883.

Arena Star, September 14, 1883.

Ashland Daily Press, August 23, 1903

Ashland Daily Press, January 19, 1974.

Black River Falls Badger State Banner, June 15, 1883.

Black River Falls Badger State Banner, June 22, 1883.

Black River Falls Badger State Banner, May 5, 1884.

Baraboo Republic, May 20, 1895.

Baraboo News Republic, June 9–12, 1940.

Barron County Shield, February 22, 1884.

Barron County Shield, April 4, 1884.

Barron County Shield, May 23, 1884.

Barron County Shield, July 18, 1884.

Bayfield County Press, March 30, 1889.

Berlin Courant, November 2, 1867.

Berlin Courant, November 17, 1870.

Berlin Courant, January 5, 1871.

Berlin Courant, August 17, 1871.

Berlin Courant, "Department of Wisconsin General Order No. 6, November 20, 1871," December 14, 1871.

Berlin Courant, January 4, 1879.

Berlin Courant, January 4, 1879.

Berlin Courant, October 31, 1907.

Berlin Journal, September 3, 1872.

Berlin Journal, November 27, 1878.

Berlin Journal, January 8, 1879.

Berlin Evening Journal, December 7, 1894.

Berlin Evening Journal, December 10, 1894.

Berlin Evening Journal, December 11, 1894.

Berlin Evening Journal, January 4, 1895.

Berlin Evening Journal, January 24, 1895.

Berlin Evening Journal, February 11, 1895.

Berlin Evening Journal, September 10, 1931.

Berlin Evening Journal, April 19, 1937.

Berlin Evening Journal, April 22, 1937.

Berlin Weekly Journal, August 7, 1890.

Boscobel Dial, August 15, 1873.

Boscobel Dial, February 18, 1942.

Cadott Sentinel, October 6, 1951.

Cedarburg Weekly News, January 23, 1889.

Chilton Times, September 5, 1885.

Columbus Republican, March 22, 1884.

Darlington Republican, July 20, 1883.

De Pere Journal Democrat, June 24, 1883.

Dodgeville Chronicle, September 2, 1883.

Dunn County News, January 13, 1883.

Dunn County News, May 12, 1883.

Dunn County News, April 12, 1884.

Eau Claire Daily Free Press, September 24, 1883.

Eau Claire Leader, June 19–21, 1939.

Eau Claire News, April 2, 1939.

Elroy Tribune, October 13, 1882.

Florence Mining News, July 4, 1891.

Fond du Lac Daily Commonwealth, August 28, 1894.

Fond du Lac Commonwealth-Reporter, June 8–11, 1941

Fond du Lac Commonwealth-Reporter, June 10–11, 1945.

Grand Army Sentinel, September 1874.

Grand Army Sentinel, October 1874.

Grand Army Sentinel, February 1875.

Grand Army Sentinel, June 1875.

Grand Army Sentinel, September 1875.

Grant County Witness, March 29, 1883.

Grant County Herald, June 21, 1886.

Grant County Herald, June 27, 1942.

Green Bay Advocate, September 1, 1899.

Hartford Press, June 6, 1884.

Hayward North Wisconsin News, November 6, 1886.

Hayward North Wisconsin News, August 20, 1889.

Hudson Star Observer, September 19, 1884.

Hurley Gogebic Iron News August 3, 1889.

Jackson County Journal, March 13, 1901.

Jefferson Banner, April 20, 1882.

Juneau County Argus, January 25, 1883.

Juneau Telephone, June 2, 1882.

Kewaunee Enterprise, May 9, 1884.

La Crosse Republican and Leader, August 18, 1882.

La Crosse Republican and Leader, May 12, 1883.

Ladysmith Gates County Journal, January 11, 1902.

Lake Mills Leader, May 30, 1889.

Madison Capital Times, June 14–17, 1936.

Madison Capital Times, September 5–10, 1937

Madison Capital Times, June 1–4, 1947.

Madison Soldier's Record, November 14, 1868.

Madison Soldier's Record, May 1869.

Marinette Weekly Eagle, February 23, 1889.

Milwaukee Sentinel, June 1–12, 1880.

Milwaukee Sentinel, August 25–30, 1889

Milwaukee Sentinel, September 2–8, 1923.

Milwaukee Sentinel, June 26–29, 1938.

Monroe Sentinel, October 10, 1883.

Montello Express, March 3, 183.

Neillsville Republican and Press, November 30, 1882.

New York Soldier's Friend, January 1868.

New York Times, September 9, 1937.

New York Times, September 10, 1937.

New York Times, September 14, 1937.

Oshkosh City Times, September 29, 1868.

Oshkosh Daily Northwestern, "G.A.R.: Annual Encampment of the State Department." January 26, 1877.

Oshkosh Northwestern, November 5, 1868.

Oshkosh Northwestern, August 25–29, 1889.

Oshkosh Northwestern, February 27, 1904.

Oshkosh Northwestern, June 9–12, 1923.

Oshkosh Northwestern, September 16, 1966.

Oshkosh Weekly Northwestern, February 1, 1876.

Palmyra Enterprise, February 22, 1884.

Pepin County Courier, May 25, 1883.

Pepin County Courier, July 13, 1884.

Phillips Times, October 11, 1884.

Pierce County Herald, November 28, 1883.

Pierce County Herald, August 12, 1885.

Platteville Witness, September 15, 1937.

Plymouth Reporter, November 12, 1885.

Portage County Gazette, March 26, 1884.

Portage Daily Register, May 27, 1891.

Port Washington Star, June 30, 1889.

Rice Lake Chronotype, January 3, 1884.

Ripon Commonwealth, June 22, 1866.

Ripon Free Press, June 23, 1870.

River Falls Journal, August 28, 1884.

St. Croix Republican, September 19, 1883.

Shawano County Advocate, May 7, 1883.

Sheboygan County News, March 4, 1885.

Sheboygan Press, June 11–14, 1944.

Spencer Tribune, August 24, 1883.

Spring Green News, August 10, 1882.

Superior Inter Ocean, August 14, 1884.

Superior Evening Telegraph, June 13–16, 1943.

Superior Times, May 28, 1887.

Superior Times, April 11, 1891.

Superior Times, January 21, 1893.

Superior Times, August 16, 1894.

Taylor County Star and News, March 25, 1884.

Trempealeau County Republican Leader, July 1, 1889.

Vernon County Censor, July 19, 1882.

Vernon County Censor, March 19, 1884.

Waterloo Democrat, February 23, 1906.

Watertown Gazette, July 13, 1883.

Waukesha Daily Freeman, June 14–17, 1942.

Waushara Argus, July 30, 1874.

West Bend Times, March 25, 1885.

Westfield Central Union, November 1, 1884.

Whitehall Times, September 6, 1883.

Whitehall Times, July 18, 1889.

Wisconsin State Journal, May 11–16, 1861.

Wisconsin State Journal, February 27, 1904.

Wisconsin State Journal, June 18 and 19, 1912.

Wisconsin State Journal, November 27, 1933.

UNPUBLISHED, MISCELLANEOUS
Encampment Journals, Proceedings

Encampment Journal of United Spanish War Veterans, Held in Manitowoc, 1907.

Fiftieth Annual Encampment of the Department of Wisconsin, Grand Army of the Republic, Held at Ripon June 15 and 16, 1916, Journal of Proceedings. Madison, Wis.: Cantwell Printing, 1916.

Fifty-fifth Annual Encampment of the Department of Wisconsin, Grand Army of the Republic, Held at Antigo June 6-9, 1921, Journal of Proceedings. Madison: 1921. : Oshkosh, Wisc.: Castle Pierce Printing Company, 1921.

Fifty-first Annual Encampment of the Department of Wisconsin, Grand Army of the Republic, Held at Kenosha June 20 and 21, 1917, Journal of Proceedings. Madison, Wis.: Democrat Printing, 1917.

Fifty-fourth Annual Encampment of the Department of Wisconsin, Grand Army of the Republic, Held at Baraboo June 14-16, 1920, Journal of Proceedings. Madison, Wis.: Democrat Printing, 1920.

Fifty-second Annual Encampment of the Department of Wisconsin, Grand Army of the Republic, Held at Ashland June 18 and 19, 1918, Journal of Proceedings. Madison, Wis.: Democrat Printing, 1918.

Fifty-sixth Annual Encampment of the Department of Wisconsin, Grand Army of the Republic, Held at Eau Claire June 12-14, 1922, Journal of the Proceedings. Madison: 1922.

Fifty-third Annual Encampment of the Department of Wisconsin, Grand Army of the Republic, Held at Waukesha June 16-18, 1919, Journal of Proceedings. Madison, Wis.: Democrat Printing, 1919.

Fortieth Annual Encampment of the Department of Wisconsin, Grand Army of the Republic, Held at Marinette June 12 and 13, 1906, Journal of Proceedings. Madison, Wis.: Democrat Printing, 1906.

Forty-eighth Annual Encampment of the Department of Wisconsin, Grand Army of the Republic, Held at Madison June 10 and 11, 1914, Journal of Proceedings. Madison, Wis.: Democrat Printing, 1914.

Forty-fifth Annual Encampment of the Department of Wisconsin, Grand Army of the Republic, Held at Green Bay June 8 and 9 1911, Journal of Proceedings. Madison, Wis.: Democrat Printing, 1911.

Forty-first Annual Encampment of the Department of Wisconsin, Grand Army of the Republic, Held at Oshkosh June 3 to 6, 1907, Journal of Proceedings. Madison, Wis.: Democrat Printing, 1907.

Forty-fourth Annual Encampment of the Department of Wisconsin, Grand Army of the Republic, Held at Fond du Lac June 6 to 8, 1910, Journal of Proceedings. Madison, Wis.: Democrat Printing, 1910.

Forty-ninth Annual Encampment of the Department of Wisconsin, Grand Army of the Republic, Held at Wausau June 15 and 16, 1915, Journal of Proceedings. Madison, Wis.: Cantwell Printing, 1915.

Forty-second Annual Encampment of the Department of Wisconsin, Grand Army of the Republic, Held at Racine June 16 and 17, 1908, Journal of Proceedings. Madison, Wis.: Democrat Printing, 1908.

Forty-seventh Annual Encampment of the Department of Wisconsin, Grand Army of the Republic, Held at Menasha-Neenah June 10 and 11, 1913, Journal of Proceedings. Madison, Wis.: Democrat Printing, 1913.

Forty-sixth Annual Encampment of the Department of Wisconsin, Grand Army of the Republic, Held at Antigo June 11 and 12, 1912, Journal of Proceedings. Madison, Wis.: Democrat Printing, 1912.

Forty-third Annual Encampment of the Department of Wisconsin, Grand Army of the Republic, Held at Eau Claire June 15 and 16, 1909, Journal of Proceedings. Madison, Wis.: Democrat Printing, 1909.

Journal of the Fifty-eighth Annual Encampment of the Department of Wisconsin, Grand Army of the Republic, Janesville, June 16 to 19, 1924.

Journal of the Fifty-ninth Annual Encampment of the Department of Wisconsin, Grand Army of the Republic, Sheboygan, June 15 to 18, 1925.

Journal of the Fifty-seventh Annual Encampment of the Department of Wisconsin, Grand Army of the Republic, Oshkosh, June 11 to 14, 1923.

Journal of the Fifty-seventh National Encampment, Grand Army of the Republic, September 2 to 8, 1923, Milwaukee. Washington, D.C.: U.S. Government Printing Office, 1924.

Journal of the Seventy-first National Encampment, Grand Army of the Republic, September 5 to 10, 1937, Madison. Washington, D.C.: U.S. Government Printing Office, 1938.

Journal, Seventy-second Annual Encampment, Grand Army of the Republic, Department of Wisconsin, Milwaukee, June 26, 27, 28, 29, 1938.

Journal of the Seventh-seventh National Encampment, Grand Army of the Republic, September 19 to 24, 1943, Milwaukee. Washington, D.C.: U.S. Government Printing Office, 1945.

Journal of the Seventh-third Annual Encampment, Grand Army of the Republic, Department of Wisconsin, Eau Claire, June 18, 19, 20, 21, 1939.

Journal of the Sixtieth Annual Encampment of the Department of Wisconsin, Grand Army of the Republic, Racine, June 14-15-16, 1926.

Journal of the Sixty-eighth Annual Encampment of the Department of Wisconsin, Grand Army of the Republic, Appleton, June 11, 12, 13, 1934.

Journal of the Sixty-fifth Annual Encampment of the Department of Wisconsin, Grand Army of the Republic, La Crosse, June 15-16-17, 1931.

Journal of the Sixty-first Annual Encampment of the Department of Wisconsin, Grand Army of the Republic, Fond du Lac, June 15-16-17, 1927.

Journal of the Sixty-second Annual Encampment of the Department of Wisconsin, Grand Army of the Republic, Madison, June 12-13-14, 1928. Berlin.

Journal of the Sixty-seventh Annual Encampment, Grand Army of the Republic, Sheboygan, June 12, 13, 14, 1933.

Journal of the Sixty-sixth Annual Encampment of the Department of Wisconsin, Grand Army of the Republic, Waukesha, June 13, 14, 15, 16, 1932.

Journal of the Sixty-third Annual Encampment of the Department of Wisconsin, Grand Army of the Republic, Beloit, June 24-27, 1929.

Journal of the Twenty-fourth Annual Session of the National Encampment, Grand Army of the Republic, August 13 and 14, 1890, Boston. Detroit: Richard Backus, 1890.

Journal of the Twenty-third Annual Session of the National Encampment, Grand Army of the Republic, August 28, 29, 30, 1889, Milwaukee. St. Louis: A. Wipple, 1889.

Journal of the Twenty-Sixth National Encampment, Grand Army of the Republic, September 21 and 22, 1892, Washington D.C. Albany, New York: S. H. Wentworth, 1892.

1930 Journal of the Sixty-fourth Annual Encampment of the Department of Wisconsin, Grand Army of the Republic, Eau Claire, June 9-12, 1930.

1933 Journal of the Sixty-seventh Annual Encampment of the Department of Wisconsin, Grand Army of the Republic, Sheboygan, June 12 to 14, 1933.

Official program of the Seventieth Annual Encampment of the Department of Wisconsin, Grand Army of the Republic, Madison, June 14, 15, 16, 17, 1936.

Proceedings of the Department Encampment of the State of Wisconsin Seventeenth Annual Session, Held at Portage, January 23, 1883. Waukesha, Wis.: Freeman Book and Job Printing, 1883.

Proceedings of the Eighteenth Annual Encampment of the Department of Wisconsin, Grand Army of the Republic, Held at Janesville January 23 and 24, 1884. Baraboo, Wis.: Republic Print, 1884.

Proceedings of the Nineteenth Annual Encampment of the Department of Wisconsin, Grand Army of the Republic, Held at Madison January 22 and 23, 1885. Baraboo, Wis.: Republic Print, 1885.

Proceedings of the Thirtieth Annual Encampment of the Department of Wisconsin, Grand Army of the Republic, Held at Racine May 20 and 21, 1896. Milwaukee: Ed. Keogh Printer, 1896.

Proceedings of the Thirty-first Annual Encampment of the Department of Wisconsin, Grand Army of the Republic, Held at Eau Claire May 19 and 20, 1897. Milwaukee, Wisc.: The Evening Wisconsin Co., 1897.

Proceedings of the Twentieth Annual Encampment of the Department of Wisconsin, Grand Army of the Republic, Held at Milwaukee February 3 and 4, 1886. Baraboo, Republic Print, 1886.

Proceedings of the Twenty-eighth Annual Encampment of the Department of Wisconsin, Grand Army of the Republic, Held at Janesville April 25 and 26, 1894. Ashland, Wis.: A.W. Bowron, Printer, 1894.

Proceedings of the Twenty-fifth Annual Encampment of the Department of Wisconsin, Grand Army of the Republic, Held at Oshkosh March 10 and 11, 1891. Milwaukee: Ed. Keogh, Printer, 1891.

Proceedings of the Twenty-first Annual Encampment of the Department of Wisconsin, Grand Army of the Republic, Held at Milwaukee February 15 and 16, 1887. Baraboo, Wis.: Republic Print, 1887.

Proceedings of the Twenty-fourth Annual Encampment of the Department of Wisconsin, Grand Army of the Republic, Held at Milwaukee March 18 and 19, 1890. Milwaukee: Ed. Keogh, Printer, 1890.

Proceedings of the Twenty-ninth Annual Encampment of the Department of Wisconsin, Grand Army of the Republic, Held at Green Bay May 22 and 23, 1895. Milwaukee: Swain and Tate Printers, 1895.

Proceedings of the Twenty-second Annual Encampment of the Department of Wisconsin, Grand Army of the Republic, Held at Milwaukee February 15 and 16, 1888. Eau Claire, Wis.: Daily Free Press, 1888.

Proceedings of the Twenty-seventh Annual Encampment of the Department of Wisconsin, Grand Army of the Republic, Held at La Crosse March 8 and 9, 1893. Madison, Wis.: M.J. Cantwell, Printer, 1893.

Proceedings of the Twenty-sixth Annual Encampment of the Department of Wisconsin, Grand Army of the Republic, Held at Madison March 9 and 10, 1892. Milwaukee, Ed. Keogh, Printer, 1892.

Proceedings of the Twenty-third Annual Encampment of the Department of Wisconsin, Grand Army of the Republic, Held at Milwaukee February 20 and 21, 1889. Milwaukee: Ed. Keogh, Printer, 1889.

Program, Memorial Encampment, Department of Wisconsin, Grand Army of the Republic, Sheboygan, June 11-14, 1950.

Proceedings of the Twenty-fourth Annual Encampment of the Department of Wisconsin, Grand Army of the Republic, Held at Milwaukee March 18 and 19, 1890. Milwaukee: Ed. Keogh, Printer, 1890.

Seventh Annual Meeting of the National Encampment, Grand Army of the Republic, New Haven, Conn., May 15, 16, 1873. Boston, Mass.: Grand Army of the Republic Adjutant General's Office, 1873.

Thirty-eighth Annual Encampment of the Department of Wisconsin, Grand Army of the Republic, Held at Madison June 15 and 16, 1904, Journal of Proceedings. Madison, Wis.: Democrat Printing, 1904

Thirty-fifth Annual Encampment of the Department of Wisconsin, Grand Army of the Republic, Held at Sheboygan June 19 and 20, 1901, Journal of Proceedings. Madison, Wis.: Democrat Printing, 1901.

Thirty-fourth Annual Encampment of the Department of Wisconsin, Grand Army of the Republic, Held at West Superior June 21 and 22, 1900, Journal of Proceedings. (n.p.)

Thirty-ninth Annual Encampment of the Department of Wisconsin, Grand Army of the Republic, Held at La Crosse June 13 and 14, 1905, Journal of Proceedings. Madison, Wis.: Democrat Printing, 1905.

Thirty-second Annual Encampment of the Department of Wisconsin, Grand Army of the Republic, Held at Appleton May 25 and 26, 1898, Journal of Proceedings. (n.p.)

Thirty-seventh Annual Encampment of the Department of Wisconsin, Grand Army of the Republic, Held at Chippewa Falls June 9 and 10, 1903, Journal of Proceedings. Madison, Wis.: Democrat Printing, 1903.

Thirty-sixth Annual Encampment of the Department of Wisconsin, Grand Army of the Republic, Held at Stevens Point June 11 and 12, 1908, Journal of Proceedings. Madison, Wis.: Democrat Printing, 1902.

Thirty-third Annual Encampment of the Department of Wisconsin, Grand Army of the Republic, Held at Milwaukee May 17 and 18, 1899, Journal of Proceedings. (n.p.)

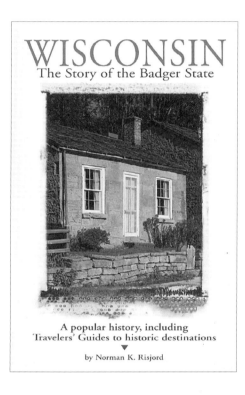